Date Due

FOLKLORE IN AMERICAN LITERATURE

FOLKLORE IN AMERICAN LITERATURE

Edited by

JOHN T. FLANAGAN
University of Illinois

and

ARTHUR PALMER HUDSON
University of North Carolina

GREENWOOD PRESS, PUBLISHERS
WESTPORT, CONNECTICUT

Headings and old-style cuts furnished by

RAY H. ABRAMS
University of
Pennsylvania

810.8
F583f

CONTENTS

Section IX. Yankees

Section X. Negro Tales

Section XI. Folk Songs and Ballads

Section XII. Folk Wisdom

Biographical Notes

Bibliography

Index of Authors and Titles

INTRODUCTION

INTRODUCTION

Professional interest in folklore in the United States dates back at least as far as 1888, in which year the American Folklore Society was organized and the *Journal of American Folklore* inaugurated. Specialists in anthropology, philology, and literary history subsequently turned their attention to the subject, and collectors, field workers, and archivists have multiplied. State and local folklore societies have been organized, in which amateur and professional can find common ground and a common interest. Today at least four regional folklore journals are flourishing: *New York Folklore Quarterly, Southern Folklore Quarterly, Western Folklore,* and *Midwest Folklore.* These periodicals not only furnish a needed stimulus for folklore activity but provide a medium for the publication of transcriptions and interpretations. Literary critics too have begun to evaluate the employment of folklore characters and motifs by major American authors, from Cotton Mather and Benjamin Franklin to Vachel Lindsay and William Faulkner. Moreover, a whole school of publicists and interpreters has arisen, including figures as disparate in background and training as Burl Ives, Woodie Guthrie, John Jacob Niles, Josh White, Richard Dyer-Bennet, Andrew Rowan Summers, Jean Ritchie, and Leadbelly. The great collection of American ballads and folk songs in the Library of Congress has proved a stimulating resource for scholars and singers. Indeed it might be argued that one of the most exciting developments in the study of American literature and culture during the twentieth century has been the accelerating interest in folklore.

Enthusiasm and sympathy led collectors into the field of American folklore, however, long before the age of specialization. And even if they were untrained or failed to labor with maximum objectivity, they performed yeoman service in recovering materials which otherwise might well have disappeared. We owe a considerable debt to Henry Rowe Schoolcraft for his services in preserving the tales and legends of the Ojibwa Indians despite the fact that, in his desire to achieve superior literary art, he reshaped some of his raw material. Certainly his *Algic Researches,* published in 1839, is one of our most valuable early collections of Indian lore. It was not until after the Civil War that an effort was made to compile and record some of the Negro slave songs and spirituals, but the work thus initiated opened up one of the most fascinating areas of American culture. In 1881 Joel Chandler Harris published the first of his Uncle Remus books and introduced not only plantation legends and superstitions but a central character who has become today an American myth. Together the Indian and the Negro have supplied a very large and significant part of the corpus of American folklore.

For a long time it was supposed that the most isolated and most provincial regions of the United States were necessarily the richest in folk traditions and customs. The geographical barriers which confined the mountaineers of the Cumberlands and the Ozarks preserved without substantial change many of the ballads and tales first imported to those areas, whereas in a more heterogeneous society such survivals would have been unlikely. The Pennsylvania Dutch had no such physical wall around them but preserved social and psychological barriers which enabled them to hold tenaciously to their own traditions. In Louisiana a Creole society separated linguistically from its immediate neighbors likewise retained characteristic tales, superstitions, and practices. The Spanish Southwest is still another example of a homogeneous area in which a characteristic folk culture survived. These regions have long been the focus of attention by the folklore specialists, and they have yielded rich and varied material. More recently, however, students have agreed that occupations, with or without a single geographical center, are even more rewarding than physical regions; and the folklore of the cowboy, the miner, the lumberjack, the sailor, the farmer has been studied with diligence and profit.

Reader and specialist remember today with gratitude the pioneer work of John A. Lomax (later joined by his son, Alan Lomax) in collecting the ballads of the cowboy at a time when such field work seemed not only undignified but futile. Franz Rickaby's early compilation of lumberjack ballads has been supplemented by many similar volumes of songs and tales from the pineries of the northern border. A small library of books attests to Vance Randolph's indefatigable labor in collecting the folklore of the Ozarks in Missouri and Arkansas. Richard Dorson, after producing a superb compilation of Yankee tall tales and anecdotes in *Jonathan Draws the Long Bow*, has turned his attention to the mixed inhabitants of Michigan. Richard Chase has brought together the Jack tales of North Carolina, and Carl Carmer and Harold Thompson have demonstrated the wealth of folk material in the state of New York. The folklore of Texas and the Southwest has found an intelligent and sympathetic chronicler in J. Frank Dobie, whose interests range from wild mustangs and coyotes to fabulous silver treasures lost since Spanish days. Indeed, the annual volumes of the Texas Folklore Society extending back to 1916 provide a rich treasure of popular song, legend, and superstition. Probably the most industrious collector of American folklore, to use the term in its most catholic sense, has been Benjamin A. Botkin, who has supplemented his original *A Treasury of American Folklore* (1944) with regional collections of New England, southern, and western folklore, with volumes of Negro and railroad folklore, with a compilation of the folklore of urban America, and with an anthology of Mississippi River material.

In recent years folklore has also reached the dignity of academic attention. More than fifty American colleges and universities now offer courses in folklore, sometimes taught under the auspices of departments of history and English, sometimes offered independently. These courses represent a considerable variation in method, approach, and substance; indeed they are almost as miscellaneous as the definition of folklore itself. But collectively they indicate a serious approach to the subject, and they train students in collecting and classifying folk material, in recognizing cognate forms, and in utilizing such tools of the folklore specialist as the Aarne-Thompson index of motifs. Various institutions—Franklin and Marshall College, Wayne University, Michigan State University, Murray State College in Kentucky, the University of North Carolina, to mention no others—have also organized folklore archives, to which the students make substantial yearly contributions. Indiana University has even established a graduate curriculum in folklore where it is possible for a student to work toward the Ph.D. degree through a program intelligently divided among such areas as linguistics, history, sociology, and anthropology. Such a curriculum is the best tribute possible to the foresight and organizational ability of its founder, Stith Thompson. Almost simultaneously a similar curriculum was established at the University of North Carolina by R. S. Boggs and A. P. Hudson.

Many of the books which include folk material today are collections of *raw folklore* (possibly *pure folklore* to the specialist), recorded or transcribed at the sources, unpolished and often rough but authentic and untampered with. The delight of the professional folklorist is an informant who is intelligent but somewhat unsophisticated and is gifted with a retentive memory and with storytelling or singing ability. From such a person, particularly if he has lived for some time in a relatively inaccessible region, a spate of tales, anecdotes, legends, superstitions, ballads, and songs may pour, but their appeal to the general reader will often be largely sociological. Because such material lacks artistry and often subtlety it is less important as literature than as the revelation of popular mores at an untutored level. On the other hand, this very material in the hands of dramatists, musicians, painters, poets, and writers of fiction has provided a significant amount of the artistic wealth of the Western world. One thinks of the Faust legend, of the quest for the Holy Grail, of the Knights of the Round Table stories, of the Grimm brothers' *Märchen,* of Peer Gynt and Don Quixote, of Thomas Hardy's Wessex novels and Melville's *The Confidence Man,* of Wagner's music drama, of the songs of Stephen Foster, of the regional paintings by Grant Wood and John Steuart Curry or the regional music by Aaron Copland and Ferde Grofé, of *Hiawatha* and *John Brown's Body,* of *Moby-Dick* and *Huckleberry Finn* and *The House of the Seven Gables.* In all these cases folklore has been utilized creatively and imaginatively, and at the same time particular folk themes and characters have been universalized.

The purpose of this book is to illustrate by representative selections of prose and verse the artistic use of folklore by American authors. Not all American writers have been equally conscious of folklore or equally adept and comprehensive in their use of it. Folklore has contributed little to the work of Henry James or Henry Adams, but it is vitally important in Irving, Melville, Hawthorne, and Mark Twain. From Colonial times, as Richard Dorson has convincingly demonstrated, to the days of Stephen Vincent Benét, Julia Peterkin, Elizabeth Madox Roberts, and John Steinbeck, American authors have levied on the rich accretion of native folklore with significant artistic success.

The divisions of this book were designed to exemplify the basic kinds of folklore appearing in American literature. The need to choose the best examples has required the republication of some familiar material, but no folklore enthusiast would condone the omission of "The Legend of Sleepy Hollow" or "The Gold-Bug." The strong element of superstition in popular thought is represented by three categories: tales of ghosts, of witchcraft, and of devils. Incidentally, the three tales by Irving, Hawthorne, and Benét represent strikingly different treatments of the old notions of the compact between man and the devil, just as they reveal curious dissimilarities in the devil's appearance, clothes, and manners. One observes also in comparing these stories a striking difference in tone, which varies from mild disbelief and sophisticated amusement to a profound and disturbing conviction of diabolical interference in the affairs of daily life. Another interesting facet is the success of Hawthorne and MacKaye—novelist and dramatist—in using the same material for different literary purposes.

Since the days of Sir Henry Morgan and Captain Kidd nothing has been dearer to the American imagination than tales of buried treasure. If caches of pirate loot apparently exist mostly along the Atlantic seaboard, such a book as J. Frank Dobie's *Coronado's Children* demonstrates clearly the persistent popular acceptance of the notion of hidden mines or concealed treasure in the Southwest. Not all seekers after mineral wealth are as successful as Legrand in Poe's tale, but the motive, circumstances, and methods are familiar. In the Middle West bundles of greenbacks substitute for secreted doubloons, and the original hoarder is more likely to be Jesse James than Jean Lafitte; yet men rise to stories of hidden wealth like trout to a fly and search for it in caves, crumbling dwellings, or sunken hulks rotting in fresh-water lakes.

Although Baron von Münchhausen and Cyrano de Bergerac belong to other lands and the American mind has no corner on exaggeration, the tall tale seems peculiarly indigenous to the United States and to the frontier in particular. Just as no other country has quite approximated the conditions of the American frontier, so the tall tale has assumed unusual color and flavor in the New World ever since Benjamin Franklin described the marvelous leap of the whale up the falls of Niagara. The best American tall tales exemplify the frame or box technique, in which one narrator repeats the story of another narrator who may also be the protagonist of the main tale. This concentric structure permits the reader to find as much interest in the contrast of narrative styles and idioms as in the stories themselves and also provides sharp differences in characterization. The tall tale's width and variety are admirably illustrated here by Twain's story of a bet and by Thorpe's hunting fantasy.

One of the oldest types of folk literature is the ballad, the traditional story told in song. A great many of the English and Scottish popular ballads collected by Francis J. Child and published in his memorable edition (1882–98) have made their way to the United States—notably "Lord Randal" and the ubiquitous "Barbara Allen"—where they exist in variant forms. Nineteenth-century poets produced many literary ballads, often less vigorous and fresh than the popular ballads but superior in euphony and polish. One of the best known of all is of course Walter Scott's "Lochinvar." But Longfellow and Whittier wrote excellent ballads, and the more recent work of Stephen Vincent Benét is proof that in our own time the art has not disappeared. "The Ballad of William Sycamore" is not only a striking representative of its literary type; it also epitomizes in sharp detail a frontier existence and a frontier destiny.

It has been convenient to group some selections around the figures who dominate them: Yankee, Indian, Negro. Yankee tales hinge chiefly on rustic manners, customs, idioms, and superstitions, with rural shrewdness and bargaining ability usually coming out superior to the sophistication of urbanites. Indian tales tend to introduce the supernatural and frequently involve the transformation of gods into men or of men into gods; the genesis of plants and animals; creation myths; animal mates; trickster tales, with the coyote or raven being the successful protagonist; and combats between men and deities. The Negro, occupying a subordinate position in the American social scale, had to depend on cunning rather than on strength. Hence his imagination employed animals as characters and usually endowed the rabbit—the softest and most inoffensive of four-legged creatures—with superior intelligence. Thus Br'er Rabbit (transformed at a later date into Peter Cottontail or possibly Harvey) could outwit the other animals if he could not overpower them. In the same way the Negro occasionally got the best of his master and habitual adversary, the plantation white man or "buckra," or slyly satirized and mocked him.

If occupational groups like the cowboys have not stimulated literary artists of greater stature than Owen Wister and Alfred Henry Lewis, the epic heroes who dot the American horizon have appealed to dramatists, poets, and novelists. Genuine leaders like Davy Crockett, Andrew Jackson, and Lincoln himself have, since their deaths, become focal points for vast accretions of legend; and invented geniuses like Paul Bunyan or John Henry are, through imaginative projection, familiar to millions. To some extent Crockett was his own biographer and publicist; John Henry owes much of his celebrity to the literary skill of Roark Bradford; and Paul Bunyan, to whose saga a whole generation of fabulists has contributed, has provided themes for both Robert Frost and Carl Sandburg. John G. Neihardt was attracted to the story of Mike Fink and made the final days of this last of the boatmen into a successful poetic narrative. Johnny Appleseed has stimulated both Vachel Lindsay and Edgar Lee Masters to write dramatic appreciations. Moreover, the annual spate of books about Abraham Lincoln suggests that the Lincoln myth is still in the process of formation.

The final section of the book illustrates the proverbial wisdom of the folk in many shades and forms. Thousands of readers have been amused and interested by Franklin's celebrated "The Way to Wealth," even though some of the master's best maxims were not prudential. Possibly fewer readers know the plantation proverbs of Joel Chandler Harris or the heterogeneous but inspired collection of Carl Sandburg. The homely sense of Abe Martin of Brown County, which was reprinted in metropolitan newspapers long after the death of Kin Hubbard, belongs to the crackerbox tradition of pungent comment which includes Jack Downing, Mr. Dooley, and Will Rogers. Proverbs and saws and pithy observations, like ballads and tales, are of the folk. In their homely parlance, their compression, their capsule wisdom, they are in particular the voice of the people, of *homo Americanus.*

The difficulty of any anthologist, particularly the anthologist working in a field so rich and diversified as folklore, is that of selection. Here one man's meat is certainly another man's poison. But at least the material presented in this volume is clear proof of the rich contribution made by folklore to American literature. Surely our national legacy would be vastly the poorer without it. In the words of Walt Whitman, "a bard is to be commensurate with a people."

It is a pleasure to acknowledge here the suggestions of several workers in the same field. We are indebted to Professor Ernest E. Leisy of Southern Methodist University, to Director Robert B. Downs of the University of Illinois Library, and to Professor Richard Dorson of Michigan State University. Without their advice and encouragement the book would have suffered indeed. But the final decision as to content and plan was of course the responsibility of the editors.

JOHN T. FLANAGAN

ARTHUR PALMER HUDSON

March, 1958

THE INDIAN

The extent of the Indian's contribution to North American folklore has been understood only in recent times. One might add that only in our own century has there been a really serious effort to study and record the imaginative life of the Indian. To the original settlers of the Atlantic seaboard the aborigines were mere savages, to be exterminated or at least driven into the remote forests as soon as possible. An occasional Puritan like John Eliot strove to bring the Bible to the Indian, but few indeed were those who attempted to gather the tribal lore and traditions in wigwam or camp. In the early decades of the nineteenth century collectors of folk tales like James Athearn Jones and Henry Rowe Schoolcraft published their compilations, some of which became the source and stimulus of popular literary interpretations. Longfellow's *Song of Hiawatha* would not have existed without Schoolcraft's pioneer collection of Ojibwa folk material, *Algic Researches,* published in 1839, even though both the poet and the ethnologist misinterpreted the character of their folk hero. Subsequently much research has been done, so that today we have a wealth of data not only about the eastern woodland tribes but about the plains Indians and, particularly, about the advanced tribes of the Southwest, the Navahos, Zuñis, and Pueblos. Frances Densmore's studies of Indian music, Stith Thompson's analysis of Indian folk tales, and Franz Boas' anthropological inquiries have helped to fill in the picture which the early centuries of American settlement left blank. Most of the recent writing about the Indian, however, is limited to scientific recording and interpretation. As a result, despite the obvious tendency of the author to sentimentalize and romanticize, Longfellow's poem about Hiawatha remains one of the most successful attempts by an American writer to use Indian material imaginatively.

INDIAN NAMES

by Lydia H. Sigourney

Mrs. Sigourney was a popular poet in the first half of the nineteenth century and was generally admired for her facile and sentimental verse. She was especially interested in the Indian heritage and wrote several long poems with aboriginal themes. The lyric "Indian Names," which appeared in Poems *(1834), suggests her sensitivity to Indian nomenclature and reveals the pleasant effect of juxtaposing musical place names. Later versions of the poem omit the last two stanzas, probably because of their moralistic import.*

Ye say they all have passed away,
  That noble race and brave,
That their light canoes have vanished
  From off the crested wave;
That 'mid the forests where they roamed
  There rings no hunter's shout,
But their name is on your waters,
  Ye may not wash it out.

'Tis where Ontario's billow
  Like Ocean's surge is curled,
Where strong Niagara's thunders wake
  The echo of the world.
Where red Missouri bringeth
  Rich tribute from the west,
And Rappahannock sweetly sleeps
  On green Virginia's breast.

Ye say their cone-like cabins,
  That clustered o'er the vale,
Have fled away like withered leaves
  Before the autumn gale,
But their memory liveth on your hills,
  Their baptism on your shore,
Your everlasting rivers speak
  Their dialect of yore.

Old Massachusetts wears it
  Within her lordly crown,
And broad Ohio bears it,
  Amid his young renown;
Connecticut hath wreathed it
  Where her quiet foliage waves,
And bold Kentucky breathed it hoarse
  Through all her ancient caves.

Wachuset hides its lingering voice
   Within his rocky heart,
And Alleghany graves its tone
   Throughout his lofty chart;
Monadnock on his forehead hoar
   Doth seal the sacred trust,
Your mountains build their monument,
   Though ye destroy their dust.

Ye call these red-browed brethren
   The insects of an hour,
Crushed like the noteless worm amid
   The regions of their power;

Ye drive them from their father's lands,
   Ye break of faith the seal,
But can ye from the court of Heaven
   Exclude their last appeal?

Ye see their unresisting tribes,
   With toilsome step and slow,
On through the trackless desert pass,
   A caravan of woe;
Think ye the Eternal's ear is deaf?
   His sleepless vision dim?
Think ye the *soul's blood* may not cry
   From that far land to him?

THE WHITE STONE CANOE

by Henry Rowe Schoolcraft

   Henry Rowe Schoolcraft was one of the earliest observers to become sincerely interested in the intellectual life of the American Indian. His position as government agent to the Ojibwas and his marriage to the granddaughter of an Ojibwa chief gave him an unusual opportunity to study the legends and tales of at least one northern tribe. In a number of books he recorded the stories he heard. Despite his tendency to tamper with his material according to his own aesthetic standards, his work, as Stith Thompson accurately points out, "serves as a landmark in the history of the recording of American Indian tales."[1] The stories that follow utilize several motifs that are familiar to primitive people. Men have always been fascinated by the idea of a journey to another world and the report of conditions that are usually foreign to human existence. The white stone canoe is just one of many details borrowed from authentic Indian life. The other tales are concerned with the origin of phenomena in the natural world. The storyteller gives a dramatic explanation of the appearance of the corn plant and the color of the robin in a way that would appeal to an audience convinced that the universe is full of manitos. The Indian acceptance of an animistic world makes these stories seem like gospel.

There was once a very beautiful young girl, who died suddenly on the day she was to have been married to a handsome young man. He was also brave, but his heart was not proof against this loss. From the hour she was buried, there was no more joy or peace for him. He went often to visit the spot where the women had buried her, and sat musing there, when, it was thought, by some of his friends, he would have done better to try to amuse himself in the chase, or by diverting his thoughts in the war-path. But war and hunting had both lost their charms for him. His heart was already dead within him. He pushed aside both his war-club and his bow and arrows.

He had heard the old people say, that there was a path that led to the land of souls, and he determined to follow it. He accordingly set out, one morning, after having completed his preparations for the journey. At first he hardly knew which way to go. He was only guided by the tradition that he must go south. For a while he could see no change in the face of the country. Forests, and hills, and valleys, and streams had the same looks which they wore in his native place. There was snow on the ground, when he set out, and it was sometimes seen to be piled and matted on the thick trees and bushes. At length it began to diminish, and finally disappeared. The forest assumed a more cheerful appearance, and the leaves put forth their buds, and before he was aware of the completeness of the change, he found himself surrounded by spring. He had left behind him the land of snow and ice. The air became mild; the dark clouds of winter had rolled away from the sky; a pure field of

blue was above him, and as he went he saw flowers beside his path, and heard the songs of birds. By these signs he knew that he was going the right way, for they agreed with the traditions of his tribe. At length he spied a path. It led him through a grove, then up a long and elevated ridge, on the very top of which he came to a lodge. At the door stood an old man, with white hair, whose eyes, though deeply sunk, had a fiery brilliancy. He had a long robe of skins thrown loosely around his shoulders, and a staff in his hands. It was Chebiabos.

The young Chippewa began to tell his story; but the venerable chief arrested him, before he had proceeded to speak ten words. "I have expected you," he replied, "and had just risen to bid you welcome to my abode. She whom you seek, passed here but a few days since, and being fatigued with her journey, rested herself here. Enter my lodge and be seated, and I will then satisfy your inquiries, and give you directions for your journey from this point." Having done this, they both issued forth to the lodge door. "You see yonder gulf," said he, "and the wide stretching blue plains beyond. It is the land of souls. You stand upon its borders, and my lodge is the gate of entrance. But you cannot take your body along. Leave it here with your bow and arrows, your bundle, and your dog. You will find them safe on your return." So saying, he re-entered the lodge, and the freed traveller bounded forward, as if his feet had suddenly been endowed with the power of wings. But all things retained their natural colors and shapes. The woods and leaves, and streams and lakes, were only more bright and comely than he had

1. Stith Thompson, *Tales of the North American Indians* (Cambridge, Mass.: Harvard University Press, 1929), p. xv.

ever witnessed. Animals bounded across his path, with a freedom and a confidence which seemed to tell him, there was no blood shed here. Birds of beautiful plumage inhabited the groves, and sported in the waters. There was but one thing, in which he saw a very unusual effect. He noticed that his passage was not stopped by trees or other objects. He appeared to walk directly through them. They were, in fact, but the souls or shadows of material trees. He became sensible that he was in a land of shadows. When he had travelled half a day's journey, through a country which was continually becoming more attractive, he came to the banks of a broad lake, in the centre of which was a large and beautiful island. He found a canoe of shining white stone, tied to the shore. He was now sure that he had come the right path, for the aged man had told him of this. There were also shining paddles. He immediately entered the canoe, and took the paddles in his hands, when to his joy and surprise, on turning round, he beheld the object of his search in another canoe, exactly its counterpart in everything. She had exactly imitated his motions, and they were side by side. They at once pushed out from shore and began to cross the lake. Its waves seemed to be rising, and at a distance looked ready to swallow them up; but just as they entered the whitened edge of them they seemed to melt away, as if they were but the images of waves. But no sooner was one wreath of foam passed, than another, more threatening still, rose up. Thus they were in perpetual fear; and what added to it, was the clearness of the water, through which they could see heaps of beings who had perished before, and whose bones lay strewed on the bottom of the lake. The Master of Life had, however, decreed to let them pass, for the actions of neither of them had been bad. But they saw many others struggling and sinking in the waves. Old men and young men, males and fe-

males of all ages and ranks, were there; some passed, and some sank. It was only the little children whose canoes seemed to meet no waves. At length, every difficulty was gone, as in a moment, and they both leaped out on the happy island. They felt that the very air was food. It strengthened and nourished them. They wandered together over the blissful fields, where everything was formed to please the eye and the ear. There were no tempests—there was no ice, no chilly winds—no one shivered for the want of warm clothes: no one suffered for hunger—no one mourned the dead. They saw no graves. They heard of no wars. There was no hunting of animals; for the air itself was their food. Gladly would the young warrior have remained there forever, but he was obliged to go back for his body. He did not see the Master of Life, but he heard his voice in a soft breeze. "Go back," said this voice, "to the land from whence you come. Your time has not yet come. The duties for which I made you, and which you are to perform, are not yet finished. Return to your people and accomplish the duties of a good man. You will be the ruler of your tribe for many days. The rules you must observe will be told you by my messenger, who keeps the gate. When he surrenders back your body, he will tell you what to do. Listen to him, and you shall afterwards rejoin the spirit, which you must now leave behind. She is accepted, and will be ever here, as young and as happy as she was when I first called her from the land of snows." When this voice ceased, the narrator awoke. It was the fancy work of a dream, and he was still in the bitter land of snows, and hunger, and tears.

MON-DAW-MIN; OR, THE ORIGIN OF INDIAN CORN

by Henry Rowe Schoolcraft

In times past, a poor Indian was living with his wife and children in a beautiful part of the country. He was not only poor, but inexpert in procuring food for his family, and his children were all too young to give him assistance. Although poor, he was a man of a kind and contented disposition. He was always thankful to the Great Spirit for everything he received. The same disposition was inherited by his eldest son, who had now arrived at the proper age to undertake the ceremony of the Ke-ig-uish-im-o-win, or fast, to see what kind of a spirit would be his guide and guardian through life. Wunzh, for this was his name, had been an obedient boy from his infancy, and was of a pensive, thoughtful, and mild disposition, so that he was beloved by the whole family. As soon as the first indications of spring appeared, they built him the customary little lodge at a retired spot, some distance from their own, where he would not be disturbed during this solemn rite. In the mean time he prepared himself, and immediately went into it, and commenced his fast. The first few days, he amused himself, in the morning, by walking in the woods and over the mountains, examining the early plants and flowers, and in this way prepared himself to enjoy his sleep, and, at the same time, stored his mind with pleasant ideas for his dreams. While he rambled through the woods, he felt a strong desire to know how the plants, herbs, and berries grew, without any aid from man, and why it was that some species were good to eat, and others possessed medicinal or poisonous juices. He recalled these thoughts to mind after he became too languid to walk about, and had

confined himself strictly to the lodge; he wished he could dream of something that would prove a benefit to his father and family, and to all others. "True!" he thought, "the Great Spirit made all things, and it is to him that we owe our lives. But could he not make it easier for us to get our food, than by hunting animals and taking fish? I must try to find out this in my visions."

On the third day he became weak and faint, and kept his bed. He fancied, while thus lying, that he saw a handsome young man coming down from the sky and advancing towards him. He was richly and gayly dressed, having on a great many garments of green and yellow colors, but differing in their deeper or lighter shades. He had a plume of waving feathers on his head, and all his motions were graceful.

"I am sent to you, my friend," said the celestial visitor, "by that Great Spirit who made all things in the sky and on the earth. He has seen and knows your motives in fasting. He sees that it is from a kind and benevolent wish to do good to your people, and to procure a benefit for them, and that you do not seek for strength in war or the praise of warriors. I am sent to instruct you, and show you how you can do your kindred good." He then told the young man to arise, and prepare to wrestle with him, as it was only by this means that he could hope to succeed in his wishes. Wunzh knew he was weak from fasting, but he felt his courage rising in his heart, and immediately got up, determined to die rather than fail. He commenced the trial, and after a protracted effort, was almost exhausted, when the beautiful stranger

7

said, "My friend, it is enough for once; I will come again to try you"; and, smiling on him, he ascended in the air in the same direction from which he came. The next day the celestial visitor reappeared at the same hour and renewed the trial. Wunzh felt that his strength was even less than the day before, but the courage of his mind seemed to increase in proportion as his body became weaker. Seeing this, the stranger again spoke to him in the same words he used before, adding, "Tomorrow will be your last trial. Be strong, my friend, for this is the only way you can overcome me, and obtain the boon you seek." On the third day he again appeared at the same time and renewed the struggle. The poor youth was very faint in body, but grew stronger in mind at every contest, and was determined to prevail or perish in the attempt. He exerted his utmost powers, and after the contest had been continued the usual time, the stranger ceased his efforts and declared himself conquered. For the first time he entered the lodge, and sitting down beside the youth, he began to deliver his instructions to him, telling him in what manner he should proceed to take advantage of his victory.

"You have won your desires of the Great Spirit," said the stranger. "You have wrestled manfully. To-morrow will be the seventh day of your fasting. Your father will give you food to strengthen you, and as it is the last day of trial, you will prevail. I know this, and now tell you what you must do to benefit your family and your tribe. To-morrow," he repeated, "I shall meet you and wrestle with you for the last time; and, as soon as you have prevailed against me, you will strip off my garments and throw me down, clean the earth of roots and weeds, make it soft, and bury me in the spot. When you have done this, leave my body in the earth, and do not disturb it, but come occasionally to visit the place, to see whether I have come

to life, and be careful never to let the grass or weeds grow on my grave. Once a month cover me with fresh earth. If you follow my instructions, you will accomplish your object of doing good to your fellow-creatures by teaching them the knowledge I now teach you." He then shook him by the hand and disappeared.

In the morning the youth's father came with some slight refreshments, saying, "My son, you have fasted long enough. If the Great Spirit will favor you, he will do it now. It is seven days since you have tasted food, and you must not sacrifice your life. The Master of Life does not require that." "My father," replied the youth, "wait till the sun goes down. I have a particular reason for extending my fast to that hour." "Very well," said the old man, "I shall wait till the hour arrives, and you feel inclined to eat."

At the usual hour of the day the sky-visitor returned, and the trial of strength was renewed. Although the youth had not availed himself of his father's offer of food, he felt that new strength had been given to him, and that exertion had renewed his strength and fortified his courage. He grasped his angelic antagonist with supernatural strength, threw him down, took from him his beautiful garments and plume, and finding him dead, immediately buried him on the spot, taking all the precautions he had been told of, and being very confident, at the same time, that his friend would again come to life. He then returned to his father's lodge, and partook sparingly of the meal that had been prepared for him. But he never for a moment forgot the grave of his friend. He carefully visited it throughout the spring, and weeded out the grass, and kept the ground in a soft and pliant state. Very soon he saw the tops of the green plumes coming through the ground; and the more careful he was to obey his instructions in keeping the ground in order, the faster they grew.

He was, however, careful to conceal the exploit from his father. Days and weeks had passed in this way. The summer was now drawing towards a close, when one day, after a long absence in hunting, Wunzh invited his father to follow him to the quiet and lonesome spot of his former fast. The lodge had been removed, and the weeds kept from growing on the circle where it stood, but in its place stood a tall and graceful plant, with bright-colored silken hair, surmounted with nodding plumes and stately leaves, and golden clusters on each side. "It is my friend," shouted the lad; "it is the friend of all mankind. It is Mondawmin. We need no longer rely on hunting alone; for, as long as this gift is cherished and taken care of, the ground itself will give us a living." He then pulled an ear. "See, my father," said he, "this is what I fasted for. The Great Spirit has listened to my voice, and sent us something new, and henceforth our people will not alone depend upon the chase or upon the waters."

He then communicated to his father the instructions given him by the stranger. He told him that the broad husks must be torn away, as he had pulled off the garments in his wrestling; and having done this, directed him how the ear must be held before the fire till the outer skin became brown, while all the milk was retained in the grain. The whole family then united in a feast on the newly-grown ears, expressing gratitude to the Merciful Spirit who gave it. So corn came into the world.

OPEECHEE; OR, THE ORIGIN OF THE ROBIN

by Henry Rowe Schoolcraft

An old man had an only son named Opeechee, who had come to that age which is thought to be most proper to make the long and final fast, that is to secure through life a guardian genius or spirit. In the influence of this choice, it is well known, our people have relied for their prosperity in after life; it was, therefore, an event of deep importance.

The old man was ambitious that his son should surpass all others in whatever was deemed most wise and great among his tribe; and, to fulfil his wishes, he thought it necessary that he should fast a much longer time than any of those persons, renowned for their prowess or wisdom, whose fame he coveted. He therefore directed his son to prepare, with great ceremony, for the important event. After he had been in the sweating lodge and bath several times, he ordered him to lie down upon a clean mat, in a little lodge expressly prepared for him; telling him, at the same time, to endure his fast like a man, and that, at the expiration of *twelve* days, he should receive food and the blessing of his father.

The lad carefully observed this injunction, lying with perfect composure, with his face covered, awaiting those mystic visitations which were to seal his good or evil fortune. His father visited him regularly every morning, to encourage him to perseverance, expatiating at length on the honor and renown that would attend him through life if he accomplished the full term prescribed. To these admonitions and encouragements the boy never replied, but lay, without the least sign of discontent or murmuring, until the ninth day, when he addressed his father as follows:—

"My father, my dreams forebode evil. May I break my fast now, and at a more propitious time make a new fast?" The father answered—

"My son, you know not what you ask. If you get up now, all your glory will depart. Wait patiently a little longer. You have but three days yet to accomplish your desire. You know it is for your own good, and I encourage you to persevere."

The son assented; and covering himself closer, he lay till the eleventh day, when he repeated his request. Very nearly the same answer was given him by his father, who added that the next day he would himself prepare his first meal, and bring it to him. The boy remained silent, but lay as motionless as a corpse. No one would have known he was living but by the gentle heaving of his breast.

The next morning, the father, elated at having gained his end, prepared a repast for his son, and hastened to set it before him. On coming to the door, he was surprised to hear his son talking to himself. He stopped to listen; and, looking through a small aperture, was more astonished when he beheld his son painted with ver-

milion over all his breast, and in the act of finishing his work by laying on the paint as far back on his shoulders as he could reach with his hands, saying, at the same time, to himself, "My father has destroyed my fortune as a man. He would not listen to my requests. He will be the loser. I shall be forever happy in my new state, for I have been obedient to my parent; he alone will be the sufferer, for my guardian spirit is a just one; though not propitious to me in the manner I desired, he has shown me pity in another way; he has given me another shape, and now I must go."

At this moment the old man broke in, exclaiming, "My son! my son! I pray you leave me not." But the young man, with the quickness of a bird, had flown to the top of the lodge, and perched himself on the highest pole, having been changed into a beautiful robin redbreast.

He looked down upon his father with pity beaming in his eyes, and addressed him as follows: "Regret not, my father, the change you behold. I shall be happier in my present state than I could have been as a man. I shall always be the friend of men, and keep near their dwellings. I shall ever be happy and contented; and although I could not gratify your wishes as a warrior, it will be my daily aim to make you amends for it as a harbinger of peace and joy. I will cheer you by my songs, and strive to inspire in others the joy and lightsomeness I feel in my present state. This will be some compensation to you for the loss of the glory you expected. I am now free from the cares and pains of human life. My food is spontaneously furnished by the mountains and fields, and my pathway of life is in the bright air." Then stretching himself on his toes, as if delighted with the gift of wings, he carolled one of his sweetest songs, and flew away into a neighboring grove.

HIAWATHA AND MUDJEKEEWIS

by Henry Wadsworth Longfellow

Although Longfellow successfully used American themes in much of his longer verse, his sources were books rather than life. Thus his widely read Song of Hiawatha was based on the legends and tales collected by Henry R. Schoolcraft. Longfellow even preserved Schoolcraft's error of confusing the quasi-historical Iroquois chieftain Hiawatha with the Chippewa deity Manabozho. The exploits of Hiawatha take place in unhistoric time, before the advent of the white men, and show the Indian usually in conflict with birds, beasts, and external nature. Hiawatha is not concerned with tribal feuds but is a kind of culture hero who strives to improve the life of his people and who is not afraid to face such enemies as the king of the sturgeons and the great magician, the Pearl-Feather. In the fourth canto of the poem, Hiawatha, celebrated for his swiftness and the possessor of magic mittens and moccasins, faces his father Mudjekeewis. The fight lasts three days and results in black rock and bulrushes being strewn over the visible world; but, as Mudjekeewis is immortal, there can be no final victory. At the end of the poem, Hiawatha, who can suffer and grieve but who also possesses eternal life, leaves his people, like King Arthur, to a new dispensation and goes westward to his own particular Elysium.[1]

Out of childhood into manhood
Now had grown my Hiawatha,
Skilled in all the craft of hunters,
Learned in all the lore of old men,
In all youthful sports and pastimes,
In all manly arts and labors.

Swift of foot was Hiawatha;
He could shoot an arrow from him,
And run forward with such fleetness,
That the arrow fell behind him!
Strong of arm was Hiawatha;
He could shoot ten arrows upward,

• Canto IV of *The Song of Hiawatha.*
1. Cf. Rose M. Davis, "How Indian Is Hiawatha?" *Midwest Folklore* (Spring, 1957), **7**: 5–25.

Shoot them with such strength and swift-
    ness,
That the tenth had left the bow-string
Ere the first to earth had fallen!
    He had mittens, Minjekahwun,
Magic mittens made of deer-skin;
When upon his hands he wore them,
He could smite the rocks asunder,
He could grind them into powder.
He had moccasins enchanted,
Magic moccasins of deerskin;
When he bound them round his ankles,
When upon his feet he tied them,
At each stride a mile he measured!
    Much he questioned old Nokomis
Of his father Mudjekeewis;
Learned from her the fatal secret
Of the beauty of his mother,
Of the falsehood of his father;
And his heart was hot within him,
Like a living coal his heart was.
    Then he said to old Nokomis,
"I will go to Mudjekeewis,
See how fares it with my father,
At the doorways of the West-Wind,
At the portals of the Sunset!"
    From his lodge went Hiawatha,
Dressed for travel, armed for hunting;
Dressed in deerskin shirt and leggins,
Richly wrought with quills and wam-
    pum;
On his head his eagle-feathers,
Round his waist his belt of wampum,
In his hand his bow of ash-wood,
Strung with sinews of the reindeer;
In his quiver oaken arrows,
Tipped with jasper, winged with feathers;
With his mittens, Minjekahwun,
With his moccasins enchanted.
    Warning said the old Nokomis,
"Go not forth, O Hiawatha!
To the kingdom of the West-Wind,
To the realms of Mudjekeewis,
Lest he harm you with his magic,
Lest he kill you with his cunning!"
    But the fearless Hiawatha
Heeded not her woman's warning;

Forth he strode into the forest,
At each stride a mile he measured;
Lurid seemed the sky above him,
Lurid seemed the earth beneath him,
Hot and close the air around him,
Filled with smoke and fiery vapors,
As of burning woods and prairies,
For his heart was hot within him,
Like a living coal his heart was.
    So he journeyed westward, westward,
Left the fleetest deer behind him,
Left the antelope and bison;
Crossed the rushing Esconaba,
Crossed the mighty Mississippi,
Passed the Mountains of the Prairie,
Passed the land of Crows and Foxes,
Passed the dwellings of the Blackfeet,
Came unto the Rocky Mountains,
To the kingdom of the West-Wind,
Where upon the gusty summits
Sat the ancient Mudjekeewis,
Ruler of the winds of heaven.
    Filled with awe was Hiawatha
At the aspect of his father.
On the air about him wildly
Tossed and streamed his cloudy tresses,
Gleamed like drifting snow his tresses,
Glared like Ishkoodah, the comet,
Like the star with fiery tresses.
    Filled with joy was Mudjekeewis
When he looked on Hiawatha,
Saw his youth rise up before him
In the face of Hiawatha,
Saw the beauty of Wenonah
From the grave rise up before him.
    "Welcome!" said he, "Hiawatha,
To the kingdom of the West-Wind!
Long have I been waiting for you!
Youth is lovely, age is lonely,
Youth is fiery, age is frosty;
You bring back the days departed,
You bring back my youth of passion,
And the beautiful Wenonah!"
    Many days they talked together,
Questioned, listened, waited, answered;
Much the mighty Mudjekeewis
Boasted of his ancient prowess.

Of his perilous adventures,
His indomitable courage,
His invulnerable body.

Patiently sat Hiawatha,
Listening to his father's boasting;
With a smile he sat and listened,
Uttered neither threat nor menace,
Neither word nor look betrayed him,
But his heart was hot within him,
Like a living coal his heart was.

Then he said, "O Mudjekeewis,
Is there nothing that can harm you?
Nothing that you are afraid of?"
And the mighty Mudjekeewis,
Grand and gracious in his boasting,
Answered, saying, "There is nothing,
Nothing but the black rock yonder,
Nothing but the fatal Wawbeek!"

And he looked at Hiawatha
With a wise look and benignant,
With a countenance paternal,
Looked with pride upon the beauty
Of his tall and graceful figure,
Saying, "O my Hiawatha!
Is there anything can harm you?
Anything you are afraid of?"

But the wary Hiawatha
Paused awhile, as if uncertain,
Held his peace, as if resolving,
And then answered, "There is nothing,
Nothing but the bulrush yonder,
Nothing but the great Apukwa!"

And as Mudjekeewis, rising,
Stretched his hand to pluck the bulrush,
Hiawatha cried in terror,
Cried in well-dissembled terror,
"Kago! kago! do not touch it!"
"Ah, kaween!" said Mudjekeewis,
"No indeed, I will not touch it!"

Then they talked of other matters;
First of Hiawatha's brothers,
First of Wabun, of the East-Wind,
Of the South-Wind, Shawondasee,
Of the North, Kabibonokka;
Then of Hiawatha's mother,
Of the beautiful Wenonah,
Of her birth upon the meadow,

Of her death, as old Nokomis
Had remembered and related.

And he cried, "O Mudjekeewis,
It was you who killed Wenonah,
Took her young life and her beauty,
Broke the Lily of the Prairie,
Trampled it beneath your footsteps;
You confess it! you confess it!"
And the mighty Mudjekeewis
Tossed upon the wind his tresses,
Bowed his hoary head in anguish,
With a silent nod assented.

Then up started Hiawatha,
And with threatening look and gesture
Laid his hand upon the black rock,
On the fatal Wawbeek laid it,
With his mittens, Minjekahwun,
Rent the jutting crag asunder,
Smote and crushed it into fragments,
Hurled them madly at his father,
The remorseful Mudjekeewis,
For his heart was hot within him,
Like a living coal his heart was.

But the ruler of the West-Wind
Blew the fragments backward from him,
With the breathing of his nostrils,
With the tempest of his anger,
Blew them back at his assailant;
Seized the bulrush, the Apukwa,
Dragged it with its roots and fibres
From the margin of the meadow,
From its ooze the giant bulrush;
Long and loud laughed Hiawatha!

Then began the deadly conflict,
Hand to hand among the mountains;
From his eyry screamed the eagle,
The Keneu, the great war-eagle,
Sat upon the crags around them,
Wheeling flapped his wings above them.

Like a tall tree in the tempest
Bent and lashed the giant bulrush;
And in masses huge and heavy
Crashing fell the fatal Wawbeek;
Till the earth shook with the tumult
And confusion of the battle,
And the air was full of shoutings,
And the thunder of the mountains,

Starting, answered, "Baim-wawa!"
    Back retreated Mudjekeewis,
Rushing westward o'er the mountains,
Stumbling westward down the mountains,
Three whole days retreated fighting,
Still pursued by Hiawatha
To the doorways of the West-Wind,
To the portals of the Sunset,
To the earth's remotest border,
Where into the empty spaces
Sinks the sun, as a flamingo
Drops into her nest at nightfall
In the melancholy marshes.
    "Hold!" at length cried Mudjekeewis,
"Hold, my son, my Hiawatha!
'Tis impossible to kill me,
For you cannot kill the immortal.
I have put you to this trial,
But to know and prove your courage;
Now receive the prize of valor!
    "Go back to your home and people,
Live among them, toil among them,
Cleanse the earth from all that harms it,
Clear the fishing-grounds and rivers,
Slay all monsters and magicians,
All the Wendigoes, the giants,
All the serpents, the Kenabeeks,
As I slew the Mishe-Mokwa,
Slew the Great Bear of the mountains.
    "And at last when Death draws near
        you,
When the awful eyes of Pauguk
Glare upon you in the darkness,
I will share my kingdom with you,
Ruler shall you be thenceforward
Of the Northwest-Wind, Keewaydin,
Of the home-wind, the Keewaydin."
    Thus was fought that famous battle
In the dreadful days of Shah-shah,
In the days long since departed,
In the kingdom of the West-Wind.
Still the hunter sees its traces
Scattered far o'er hill and valley;
Sees the giant bulrush growing
By the ponds and water-courses,
Sees the masses of the Wawbeek
Lying still in every valley.

    Homeward now went Hiawatha;
Pleasant was the landscape round him,
Pleasant was the air above him,
For the bitterness of anger
Had departed wholly from him,
From his brain the thought of vengeance,
From his heart the burning fever.
    Only once his pace he slackened,
Only once he paused or halted,
Paused to purchase heads of arrows
Of the ancient Arrow-maker,
In the land of the Dacotahs,
Where the Falls of Minnehaha
Flash and gleam among the oak-trees,
Laugh and leap into the valley.
    There the ancient Arrow-maker
Made his arrow-heads of sandstone,
Arrow-heads of chalcedony,
Arrow-heads of flint and jasper,
Smoothed and sharpened at the edges,
Hard and polished, keen and costly.
    With him dwelt his dark-eyed daughter,
Wayward as the Minnehaha,
With her moods of shade and sunshine,
Eyes that smiled and frowned alternate,
Feet as rapid as the river,
Tresses flowing like the water,
And as musical a laughter:
And he named her from the river,
From the water-fall he named her,
Minnehaha, Laughing Water.
    Was it then for heads of arrows,
Arrow-heads of chalcedony,
Arrow-heads of flint and jasper,
That my Hiawatha halted
In the land of the Dacotahs?
    Was it not to see the maiden,
See the face of Laughing Water
Peeping from behind the curtain,
Hear the rustling of her garments
From behind the waving curtain,
As one sees the Minnehaha
Gleaming, glancing through the branches,
As one hears the Laughing Water
From behind its screen of branches?
    Who shall say what thoughts and
        visions

Fill the fiery brains of young men?
Who shall say what dreams of beauty
Filled the heart of Hiawatha?
All he told to old Nokomis,
When he reached the lodge at sunset,

Was the meeting with his father,
Was his fight with Mudjekeewis;
Not a word he said of arrows,
Not a word of Laughing Water.

OECHE-MONESAH; THE WANDERER

by Mary Eastman

The northern plains tribes may not have had so rich a mythology as the Ojibwas, or it may be that they simply lacked a gifted observer like Henry Rowe Schoolcraft to study and record it. But Mrs. Mary Eastman demonstrated that the Sioux or Dakotas, at least, were not deficient in a store of legends and myths. Chaskè's journey to another world, the transformation of human beings into birds or beasts, and the taking of animal mates by men are not unfamiliar themes to students of the North American Indian. Mrs. Eastman worked these ideas deftly into a leisurely told story, but she could not resist the impulse to contrast Indian religion unfavorably with Christianity toward the end. The final paragraphs introduce a common aboriginal conception, that of thunder as a gigantic bird with lightning streaks on its wings. This tale was published in Dahcotah *(1849).*

Chaskè was tired of living in the village, where the young men, finding plenty of small game to support life, and yielding to the languor and indolence produced by a summer's sun, played at checker's, or drank, or slept, from morn till night, and seemed to forget that they were the greatest warriors and hunters in the world. This did very well for a time; but, as I said, Chaskè got tired of it. So he determined to go on a long journey, where he might meet with some adventures.

Early one morning he shouldered his quiver of arrows, and drawing out one arrow from the quiver, he shot it in the direction he intended to go.

"Now," said he, "I will follow my arrow." But it seemed as if he were destined never to find it, for morning and noon had passed away, and the setting sun warned him, not only of the approach of night, but of musquitoes too. He thought he would build a fire to drive the musquitoes away; besides, he was both hungry and tired, though he had not yet found his arrow, and had nothing to eat.

When he was hesitating as to what he should do, he saw in the bushes a dead elk, and behold! his arrow was sticking in its side. He drew the arrow out, then cut out the tongue, and after making a fire, he put the tongue upon a stick to roast. But while the tongue was roasting, Chaskè fell asleep and slept many hours.

At day-break a woman came up to him and shook him, as if to awaken him. Chaskè started and rubbed his eyes, and the woman pointed to the path which led across the prairies. Was he dreaming? No, he felt sure he was awake. So he got up and followed the woman.

He thought it very strange that the woman did not speak to him. "I will ask her who she is," said he; but as he turned to address her she raised her arms in the air, and changing her form to that of a beautiful bird, blue as the sky that hangs over the morning's mist, she flew away. Chaskè was surprised and delighted too. He loved adventures; had he not left home to seek them? so he pursued his journey, quite forgetting his supper, which was cooking when he fell asleep.

He shot his arrow off again and followed it. It was late in the evening when he found it, and then it was in the heart of a moose. "I will not be cheated out of my supper to-night," said he; so he cut the tongue out of the moose and placed it before the fire to roast. Hardly had he seated himself to smoke, when sleep overcame him, and he knew nothing until morning, when a woman approached him and shook him as before, pointing to the path.

He arose quickly and followed her; and as he touched her arm, determined to find out who she was, she, turning upon him a brow black as night, was suddenly changed into a crow.

The Dahcotah was completely puzzled. He had never cared for women; on the contrary, had avoided them. He never wasted his time telling them they were beautiful, or playing on the flute to charm their senses. He thought he had left all such things behind him, but already had he been twice baffled by a woman. Still he continued his journey. He had this consolation, the Dahcotah girls did not turn into birds and fly away. At least there was the charm of novelty in the incidents. The next day he killed a bear, but as usual he fell asleep while the tongue was roasting, and this time was waked by a porcupine. The fourth day he found his arrow in a buffalo. "Now," said he, "I will eat at last, and I will find out, too, who and what it is that wakes me."

But he fell asleep as usual, and was waked in the morning by a female who touched him lightly and pointed to the path. Her back was turned towards him, and instead of rising to follow her, he caught her in his arms, determined to see and talk with her.

Finding herself a prisoner, the girl turned her face to him, and Chaskè had never seen anything so beautiful.

Her skin was white as the fairest flower that droops its head over the banks of the "Lac qui parle." Her hair was not plaited, neither was it black like the Dahcotah maidens', but it was hung in golden ringlets about her face and neck. The warm blood tinted her cheeks as she met the ardent gaze of the Dahcotah, and Chaskè could not ask her who she was. How could he speak when his heart was throbbing, and every pulse beating wildly?

"Let me go," said the girl; "why do you seek to detain me? I am a beaver-woman,* and you are a Dahcotah warrior. Turn from me and find a wife among the dark-faced maidens of your tribe."

"I have always despised them," said the Dahcotah, "but you are more beautiful than the Spirits of the water. I love you, and will make you my wife."

"Then you must give up your people," replied the girl, "for I cannot live as the Dahcotah women. Come with me to my white lodge, and we will be happy; for see the bright water as it falls on the rocks. We will sit by its banks during the heat of the day, and when we are tired, the music of its waves will lull us to sleep."

So she took Chaskè by the hand, and they walked on till they came to an empty white lodge, and there they lived and were very happy. They were still happier when their little boy began to play about the lodge; for although they loved each other very much, still it was lonely where they lived, and the child was company for them both.

There was one thing, however, that troubled the Dahcotah; he could not turn his mind from it, and day after day passed without relieving him from his perplexity.

His beautiful wife never ate with him. When he returned in the evening from hunting, she was always glad to see him, and while he rested himself and smoked, she would cook his meat for him, and seem anxious to make him comfortable. But he had never seen her eat; and when he would tell her that he did not like to eat alone, and beg her to sit down and eat with him, she would say she was not hungry; and

then employ herself about her wigwam, as if she did not wish him to say any more about it.

Chaskè made up his mind that he would find out what his wife lived upon. So the next morning he took his bow and arrows, as if he were going out on a day's hunt. After going a short distance from the lodge, he hid himself in the trees, where he could watch the motions of his wife.

She left the lodge after a while, and with an axe in her hand she approached a grove of poplar trees. After carefully looking round to satisfy herself that there was no one near, she cut down a number of the small and tender poplars, and, carrying them home, ate them as if she enjoyed them very much. Chaskè was infinitely relieved when he saw that his wife did eat; for it frightened him to think that she lived on nothing but air. But it was so droll to think she should eat young trees! surely venison was a great deal better.

But, like a good husband, he thought it was his duty to humor his wife's fancies. And then he loved her tenderly—he had given up country and home for her. She was so good and kind, and her beautiful hair! Chaskè called her "The Moccasin Flower," for her golden ringlets reminded him of that beautiful flower. "She shall not have to cut the trees down herself," said Chaskè, "I will bring her food while she prepares mine." So he went out to hunt, and returned in the evening; and while his wife was cooking his supper, he went to the poplar grove and cut a number of young trees; he then brought them to the lodge, and, laying them down, he said to his wife, "I have found out at last what you like."

No one would suppose but that the beaver-woman would have been grateful to her husband for thinking of her. Instead of that, she was very angry; and, taking her child in her arms, she left the lodge. Chaskè was astonished to see his gentle

---

* According to the wise men of the Dahcotahs, beavers and bears have souls. They have many traditions about bear and beaver-women.

wife angry, but he concluded he would eat his supper, and then follow her, hoping that in the meantime she would recover her good temper.

When he went out, she was nowhere to be seen. He called her—he thought at first that she had hid herself. But, as night came on, and neither she nor the child returned, the deserted husband grew desperate; he could not stay in his lodge, and the only thing that he could do was to start in search of her.

He walked all night, but saw no trace of her. About sunrise he came to a stream, and following it up a little way he came to a beaver dam, and on it sat his wife with her child in her arms. And beautiful she looked, with her long tresses falling into the water.

Chaskè was delighted to find her. "Why did you leave me?" called he. "I should have died of grief if I had not found you."

"Did I not tell you that I could not live like the Dahcotah women?" replied Moccasin Flower. "You need not have watched me to find out what I eat. Return to your own people; you will find there women enough who eat venison."

The little boy clapped his hands with delight when he saw his father, and wanted to go to him; but his mother would not let him. She tied a string to his leg and told him to go, and the child would plunge into the water, and when he had nearly reached the shore where his father sat, then would the beaver-woman draw him back.

In the meantime the Dahcotah had been trying to persuade his wife to come to him, and return to the lodge; but she refused to do so, and sat combing her long hair. The child had cried itself to sleep; and the Dahcotah, worn out with fatigue and grief, thought he would go to sleep too.

After a while a woman came and touched him on the shoulder, and awaked him as of old. He started and looked at her, and perceiving it was not his wife, felt inclined to take little notice of her.

"What," said she, "does a Dahcotah warrior still love a woman who hates him?"

"Moccasin Flower loves me well," replied the Dahcotah; "she has been a good wife."

"Yes," replied the woman, "she was for a time; but she sighs to return home—her heart yearns towards the lover of her youth."

Chaskè was very angry. "Can this be true?" he said; and he looked towards the beaver dam where his wife still sat. In the meantime the woman who had waked him, brought him some food in bark dishes worked with porcupine.

"Eat," she said to the Dahcotah; "you are hungry."

But who can tell the fury that Moccasin Flower was in when she saw that strange woman bringing her husband food. "Who are you?" she cried, "that you are troubling yourself about my husband? I know you well; you are the 'Bear-Woman.'"

"And if I am," said the Bear woman, "do not the souls of the bears enjoy forever the heaven of the Dahcotah?"

Poor Chaskè! he could not prevent their quarrelling, so, being very hungry, he soon disposed of what the Bear woman had brought him. When he had done eating, she took the bark dishes. "Come with me," she said; "you cannot live in the water, and I will take you to a beautiful lodge, and we will be happy."

The Dahcotah turned to his wife, but she gave him no encouragement to remain. "Well," said he, "I always loved adventures, and I will go and seek some more."

The new wife was not half so pretty as the old one. Then she was so wilful, and ordered him about—as if women were anything but dogs in comparison with a Dahcotah warrior. Yes, he who had scorned the Dahcotah girls, as they smiled upon him, was now the slave of a bear-woman; but there was one comfort—there were no warriors to laugh at him.

For a while they got on well enough. His wife had twin children—one was a fine young Dahcotah, and the other was a smart active little bear, and it was very amusing to see them play together. But in all their fights the young Dahcotah had the advantage; though the little bear would roll and tumble, and stick his claws into the Dahcotah, yet it always ended by the little bear's capering off and roaring after his mother. Perhaps this was the reason, but for some reason or other the mother did not seem contented and happy. One morning she woke up very early, and while telling her husband that she had a bad dream, the dog commenced barking outside the lodge.

"What can be the matter?" said Chaskè.

"Oh!" said the woman, "I know; there is a hunter out there who wants to kill me, but I am not afraid."

So saying, she put her head out of the door, which the hunter seeing, shot his arrow; but instead of hurting her, the arrow fell to the ground, and the bear-woman catching up her little child, ran away and was soon out of sight.

"Ha!" said Chaskè, "I had better have married a Dahcotah girl, for they do not run away from their husbands except when another wife comes to take their place. But I have been twice deserted." So saying, he took the little Dahcotah in his arms, and followed his wife. Towards evening he came up with her, but she did not seem glad to see him. He asked her why she left him; she replied, "I want to live with my own people." "Well," said the Dahcotah, "I will go with you." The woman consented, though it was plain she did not want him; for she hated her Dahcotah child, and would not look at him.

After travelling a few days, they approached a grove of trees, which grew in a large circle. "Do you see that nest of trees?" said the woman. "There is a great village of the bears. There are many young men

there that loved me, and they will hate you because I preferred you to them. Take your boy, then, and return to your people." But the Dahcotah feared not, and they approached the village of the bears.

There was a great commotion among the bears as they discovered them. They were glad to see the young bear-woman back again, but they hated the Dahcotah, and determined on his death. However, they received him hospitably, conducted him and his wife to a large lodge, gave them food, and the tired travellers were soon asleep.

But the Dahcotah soon perceived he was among enemies, and he kept a careful look out upon them. The little Dahcotah was always quarrelling with the young bears; and on one occasion, being pretty hungry, a cub annoying him at the time very much, he deliberately shot the cub with his bow and arrow, and ate him up. This aroused the vengeance of the bears; they had a consultation among themselves, and swore they would kill both father and son.

It would be impossible to tell of the troubles of Chaskè. His wife, he could see, loved one of the bears, and was anxious for his own death; but whenever he contended with the bears he came off victor. Whether in running a foot race, or shooting with a bow and arrow, or whatever it might be, he always won the prize, and this made his enemies still more venomous.

Four years had now passed since Chaskè left his native village, and nothing had ever been heard of him. But at length the wanderer returned.

But who would have recognized, in the crest-fallen, melancholy-looking Indian, the gay warrior that had left home but a few years before? The little boy that held his hand was cheerful enough, and seemed to recognize acquaintances, instead of looking for the first time on the faces of his father's friends.

How did the young girls laugh when he told of the desertion of his first wife; but when he continued his story, and told them of the faithlessness of the bear woman also, you heard nothing but shouts of derision. Was it not a triumph for the Dahcotah women? How had he scorned them before he went away! Did he not say that women were only dogs, or worse than dogs?

But there was one among his old acquaintances who would not join in the laughter. As she looked on the care-worn countenance of the warrior, she would fain have offered to put new moccasins upon his feet, and bring him food. But she dared not subject herself to the ridicule of her companions—though as night came on, she sought him when there was no one to heed her.

"Chaskè," she called—and the Dahcotah turned hastily towards her, attracted by the kindness of her voice—"there are no women who love as the Dahcotah women. I would have gone to the ends of the earth with you, but you despised me. You have come back, and are laughed at. Care has broken your spirit, or you would not submit to the sneers of your old friends, and the contempt of those who once feared you. I will be your wife, and, mingling again in the feasts and customs of your race, you will soon be the bold and fearless warrior that you were when you left us."

And her words were true; for the Indians soon learned that they were not at liberty to talk to Chaskè of his wanderings. He never spoke of his former wives, except to compare them with his present, who was as faithful and obedient as they were false and troublesome. "And he found," says Chequered Cloud, "that there was no land like the Dahcotah's, no river like the Father of waters, and no happiness like that of following the deer across the open prairies, or of listening, in the long summer days, to the wisdom of the medicine men."

And she who had loved him in his youth, and wept for him in his absence, now lies by his side—for Chaskè has taken another long journey. Death has touched him, but not lightly, and pointed to the path which leads to the Land of Spirits—and he did not go alone; for her life closed with his, and together their spirits watch over the mortal frames that they once tenanted.

"Look at the white woman's life," said Chequered Cloud, as she concluded the story of Chaskè, "and then at the Dahcotah's. You sleep on a soft bed, while the Dahcotah woman lays her head upon the ground, with only her blanket for a covering; when you are hungry you eat, but for days has the Dahcotah woman wanted for food, and there was none to give it. Your children are happy, and fear nothing; ours have crouched in the earth at night, when the whoop and yell of the Chippeways sent terror to their young hearts, and trembling to their tender limbs.

"And when the fire-water of the white man has maddened the senses of the Dahcotah, so that the blow of his war club falls upon his wife instead of his enemy, even then the Dahcotah woman must live and suffer on." "But, Chequered Cloud, the spirit of the Dahcotah watches over the body which remains on earth. Did you not say the soul went to the house of spirits?"

"The Dahcotah has four souls," replied the old woman; "one wanders about the earth, and requires food; another protects the body; the third goes to the Land of Spirits, while the fourth forever hovers around his native village."

"I wish," said I, "that you would believe in the God of the white people. You would then learn that there is but one soul, and that that soul will be rewarded for the good it has done in this life, or punished for the evil."

"The Great Spirit," she replied, "is the God of the Dahcotahs. He made all things but thunder and wild rice. When we do wrong we are punished in this world. If we do not live up to the laws of our forefathers, the spirits of the dead will punish us. We must keep up the customs of our tribe. If we are afraid that the thunder will strike us, we dance in honor of it, and destroy its power. Our great medicine feasts are given in honor of our sacred medicine, which will not only heal the sick, but will preserve us in danger; and we make feasts for the dead.

"Our children are taught to do right. They are not to injure one who has not harmed them; but where is the Dahcotah who will not rejoice as he takes the life of his enemy?"

"But," said I, "you honor the thunder, and yet it strikes you. What is the thunder, and where does it come from?"

"Thunder is a large bird, flying through the air; its bright tracks are seen in the heavens, before you hear the clapping of its wings. But it is the young ones who do the mischief. The parent bird would not hurt a Dahcotah. Long ago a thunder bird fell dead from the heavens; and our fathers saw it as it lay not far from Little Crow's village.

"It had a face like a Dahcotah warrior, with a nose like an eagle's bill. Its body was long and slender, its wings were large, and on them was painted the lightning. Our warriors were once out hunting in the winter, when a terrible storm came on, and a large thunder bird descended to the earth, wearing snow-shoes; he took but a few steps and then rose up, leaving his tracks in the snow. That winter our hunters killed many bears."

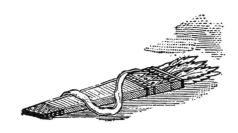

II

DEVIL TALES

Perhaps no figure has such a ubiquitous existence in religion, mythology, or folklore as the devil. Whether as the Prince of Darkness, the Arch-Fiend, the great adversary of God, or simply the incarnation of evil, he has always impinged strongly on the mind and imagination of man. But he has seldom had the regal dignity of Milton's Satan. More often, at least in recent times, he is given such names as "Old Harry," "Old Nick," "Clootie," and "Scratch," appellatives suggesting an uneasy familiarity with the person designated, perhaps even a relationship which cannot be denied. People today disavow belief in the devil as a person, yet the prevalence of the old proverb "Speak of the devil and the devil appears" suggests that some of this skepticism is lip service. The great diabolical figures of literature, such as Mephistopheles, do not depend on their appearance for their effect; but in many stories the devil-character is emphasized by details of shape, color, and smell. A smell of brimstone commonly suggests something of the preternatural to the victim or spectator. The devil is frequently a black man, handsome in a sinister sort of way, with clothes which disguise but never quite conceal certain physical peculiarities: pointed ears, a cloven hoof in place of a foot, a tail, and possibly the suggestion of bat's wings on the shoulders and horns on the forehead. Before the compact, which is a standard part of most stories in which a devil-character is involved, is entered into, the villain is sleek and suave and amiable. Thereafter he is hard and ruthless until he captures his victim completely or is himself bested by the superior power of, say, a Daniel Webster. The reduction of the statute of the devil in modern times, in religion and folklore alike, perhaps explains why today stories in which the devil is triumphant are rarely found. But in a world which still finds it difficult to explain the existence of evil, it is convenient to use the devil as a universal scapegoat.

The Devil and Tom Walker

by Washington Irving

Although it is less famous than his tales of Ichabod Crane and Rip Van Winkle, Irving's story of Tom Walker and his meeting with the devil is a skillful and interesting mélange of folk beliefs. Irving first sets the scene carefully. The darkness during much of the action, the swamp, the gloomy forest with its reminiscences of savage warfare—all emphasize the lurid atmosphere. Personal details—such as his great red eyes and sooty face— then establish the devil's physical appearance, while his true identity is suggested by the various appellations given him. The basic theme of the tale— the bargain between Tom and the devil—forcibly reminds us of the famous compact between Faust and Mephistopheles. But Irving also employs other folk notions: the belief in treasure buried long years before by pirates, the prevalence of witchcraft, the conviction that usury is a diabolical occupation, and the tradition that a female scold is a match even for Satan. Despite Irving's attempts to introduce realistic details, he protects himself by citing old legends or rumors as his sources, and he tells the story in a half-ironic tone which is not the least of its charms. His final admission that the story is really little more than an animated proverb illustrates both his own consummate art in presenting the tale and the strength of the folk tradition which generated it.

A few miles from Boston in Massachusetts, there is a deep inlet, winding several miles into the interior of the country from Charles Bay, and terminating in a thickly-wooded swamp or morass. On one side of this inlet is a beautiful dark grove; on the opposite side the land rises abruptly from the water's edge into a high ridge, on which grow a few scattered oaks of great age and immense size. Under one of these gigantic trees, according to old stories, there was a great amount of treasure buried by Kidd the pirate. The inlet allowed a facility to bring the money in a boat secretly and at night to the very foot of the hill; the elevation of the place permitted a good look-out to be kept that no one was at hand; while the remarkable trees formed good landmarks by which the place might easily be found again. The old stories add, moreover, that the devil presided at the hiding of the money, and took it under his guardianship; but this it is well known he always does with buried treasure, particularly when it has been ill-gotten. Be that as it may, Kidd never returned to recover his wealth; being shortly after seized at Boston, sent out to England, and there hanged for a pirate.

About the year 1727, just at the time that earthquakes were prevalent in New-England, and shook many tall sinners down upon their knees, there lived near this place a meagre, miserly fellow, of the name of Tom Walker. He had a wife as miserly as himself: they were so miserly that they even conspired to cheat each other. Whatever the woman could lay hands on, she hid away; a hen could not cackle but she was on the alert to secure the new-laid egg. Her husband was continually prying about to detect her secret hoards, and many and fierce were the conflicts that took place about what ought to have been common property. They lived in a forlorn-looking house that stood alone, and had an air of starvation. A few straggling savin-trees, emblems of sterility, grew near it; no smoke ever curled from its chimney; no traveller stopped at its door. A miserable horse, whose ribs were as articulate as the bars of a gridiron, stalked about a field, where a thin carpet of moss, scarcely covering the ragged beds of pudding-stone, tantalized and balked his hunger; and sometimes he would lean his head over the fence, look piteously at the passer-by, and seem to petition deliverance from this land of famine.

The house and its inmates had altogether a bad name. Tom's wife was a tall termagant, fierce of temper, loud of tongue, and strong of arm. Her voice was often heard in wordy warfare with her husband; and his face sometimes showed signs that their conflicts were not confined to words. No one ventured, however, to interfere between them. The lonely wayfarer shrunk within himself at the horrid clamor and clapper-clawing; eyed the den of discord askance; and hurried on his way, rejoicing, if a bachelor, in his celibacy.

One day that Tom Walker had been to a distant part of the neighborhood, he took what he considered a short cut homeward, through the swamp. Like most short cuts, it was an ill-chosen route. The swamp was thickly grown with great gloomy pines and hemlocks, some of them ninety feet high, which made it dark at noonday, and a retreat for all the owls of the neighborhood. It was full of pits and quagmires, partly covered with weeds and mosses, where the green surface often betrayed the traveller into a gulf of black, smothering mud: there were also dark and stagnant pools, the abodes of the tadpole, the bullfrog, and the water-snake; where the trunks of pines and hemlocks lay half-drowned, half-rotting, looking like alligators sleeping in the mire.

Tom had long been picking his way cautiously through this treacherous forest; stepping from tuft to tuft of rushes and roots, which afforded precarious footholds among deep sloughs; or pacing carefully, like a cat, along the prostrate trunks of trees; startled now and then by the sudden screaming of the bittern, or the quacking of a wild duck rising on the wing from some solitary pool. At length he arrived at a firm piece of ground, which ran out like a peninsula into the deep bosom of the swamp. It had been one of the strongholds of the Indians during their wars with the first colonists. Here they had thrown up a kind of fort, which they had looked upon as almost impregnable, and had used as a place of refuge for their squaws and children. Nothing remained of the old Indian fort but a few embankments, gradually sinking to the level of the surrounding earth, and already overgrown in part by oaks and other forest trees, the foliage of which formed a contrast to the dark pines and hemlocks of the swamp.

It was late in the dusk of evening when Tom Walker reached the old fort, and he paused there awhile to rest himself. Any one but he would have felt unwilling to linger in this lonely, melancholy place, for the common people had a bad opinion of it, from the stories handed down from the time of the Indian wars; when it was asserted that the savages held incantations here, and made sacrifices to the evil spirit.

Tom Walker, however, was not a man to be troubled with any fears of the kind. He reposed himself for some time on the trunk of a fallen hemlock, listening to the boding cry of the tree-toad, and delving with his walking-staff into a mound of black mould at his feet. As he turned up the soil unconsciously, his staff struck against something hard. He raked it out of the vegetable mould, and lo! a cloven skull, with an Indian tomahawk buried deep in it, lay before him. The rust on the weapon showed the time that had elapsed since this deathblow had been given. It was a dreary memento of the fierce struggle that had taken place in this last foothold of the Indian warriors.

"Humph!" said Tom Walker, as he gave it a kick to shake the dirt from it.

"Let that skull alone!" said a gruff voice. Tom lifted up his eyes, and beheld a great black man seated directly opposite him, on the stump of a tree. He was exceedingly surprised, having neither heard nor seen any one approach; and he was still more perplexed on observing, as well as the gathering gloom would permit, that the stranger was neither negro nor Indian. It is true he was dressed in a rude half-Indian garb, and had a red belt or sash swathed round his body; but his face was neither black nor copper-color, but swarthy and dingy, and begrimed with soot, as if he had been accustomed to toil among fires and forges. He had a shock of coarse black hair, that stood out from his head in all directions, and bore an axe on his shoulder.

He scowled for a moment at Tom with a pair of great red eyes.

"What are you doing on my grounds?" said the black man, with a hoarse growling voice.

"Your grounds!" said Tom, with a sneer, "no more your grounds than mine; they belong to Deacon Peabody."

"Deacon Peabody be d——d," said the stranger, "as I flatter myself he will be, if he does not look more to his own sins and less to those of his neighbors. Look yonder, and see how Deacon Peabody is faring."

Tom looked in the direction that the stranger pointed, and beheld one of the great trees, fair and flourishing without, but rotten at the core, and saw that it had been nearly hewn through, so that the first high wind was likely to blow it down. On the bark of the tree was scored the name of Deacon Peabody, an eminent man, who had waxed wealthy by driving shrewd bargains with the Indians. He now looked around, and found most of the tall trees marked with the name of some great man of the colony, and all more or less scored by the axe. The one on which he had been seated, and which had evidently just been hewn down, bore the name of Crowninshield; and he recollected a mighty rich man of that name, who made a vulgar display of wealth, which it was whispered he had acquired by buccaneering.

"He's just ready for burning!" said the black man, with a growl of triumph. "You see I am likely to have a good stock of firewood for winter."

"But what right have you," said Tom, "to cut down Deacon Peabody's timber?"

"The right of a prior claim," said the

other. "This woodland belonged to me long before one of your white-faced race put foot upon the soil."

"And pray, who are you, if I may be so bold?" said Tom.

"Oh, I go by various names. I am the wild huntsman in some countries; the black miner in others. In this neighborhood I am known by the name of the black woodsman. I am he to whom the red men consecrated this spot, and in honor of whom they now and then roasted a white man, by way of sweet-smelling sacrifice. Since the red men have been exterminated by you white savages, I amuse myself by presiding at the persecutions of Quakers and Anabaptists; I am the great patron and prompter of slave-dealers, and the grandmaster of the Salem witches."

"The upshot of all which is, that, if I mistake not," said Tom, sturdily, "you are he commonly called Old Scratch."

"The same, at your service!" replied the black man, with a half-civil nod.

Such was the opening of this interview, according to the old story; though it has almost too familiar an air to be credited. One would think that to meet with such a singular personage, in this wild, lonely place, would have shaken any man's nerves; but Tom was a hard-minded fellow, not easily daunted, and he had lived so long with a termagant wife, that he did not even fear the devil.

It is said that after this commencement they had a long and earnest conversation together, as Tom returned homeward. The black man told him of great sums of money buried by Kidd the pirate, under the oak-trees on the high ridge, not far from the morass. All these were under his command, and protected by his power, so that none could find them but such as propitiated his favor. These he offered to place within Tom Walker's reach, having conceived an especial kindness for him; but they were to be had only on certain conditions. What

these conditions were may easily be surmised, though Tom never disclosed them publicly. They must have been very hard, for he required time to think of them, and he was not a man to stick at trifles where money was in view. When they had reached the edge of the swamp, the stranger paused —"What proof have I that all you have been telling me is true?" said Tom. "There is my signature," said the black man, pressing his finger on Tom's forehead. So saying, he turned off among the thickets of the swamp, and seemed, as Tom said, to go down, down, down, into the earth, until nothing but his head and shoulders could be seen, and so on, until he totally disappeared.

When Tom reached home, he found the black print of a finger, burnt, as it were, into his forehead, which nothing could obliterate.

The first news his wife had to tell him was the sudden death of Absalom Crowninshield, the rich buccaneer. It was announced in the papers with the usual flourish, that "A great man had fallen in Israel."

Tom recollected the tree which his black friend had just hewn down, and which was ready for burning. "Let the freebooter roast," said Tom, "who cares!" He now felt convinced that all he had heard and seen was no illusion.

He was not prone to let his wife into his confidence; but as this was an uneasy secret, he willingly shared it with her. All her avarice was awakened at the mention of hidden gold, and she urged her husband to comply with the black man's terms, and secure what would make them wealthy for life. However Tom might have felt disposed to sell himself to the Devil, he was determined not to do so to oblige his wife; so he flatly refused, out of the mere spirit of contradiction. Many and bitter were the quarrels they had on the subject, but the more she talked, the more resolute was Tom not to be damned to please her.

At length she determined to drive the bargain on her own account, and if she succeeded, to keep all the gain to herself. Being of the same fearless temper as her husband, she set off for the old Indian fort towards the close of a summer's day. She was many hours absent. When she came back, she was reserved and sullen in her replies. She spoke something of a black man, whom she had met about twilight, hewing at the root of a tall tree. He was sulky, however, and would not come to terms: she was to go again with a propitiatory offering, but what it was she forbore to say.

The next evening she set off again for the swamp, with her apron heavily laden. Tom waited and waited for her, but in vain; midnight came, but she did not make her appearance: morning, noon, night returned, but still she did not come. Tom now grew uneasy for her safety, especially as he found she had carried off in her apron the silver teapot and spoons, and every portable article of value. Another night elapsed, another morning came; but no wife. In a word, she was never heard of more.

What was her real fate nobody knows, in consequence of so many pretending to know. It is one of those facts which have become confounded by a variety of historians. Some asserted that she lost her way among the tangled mazes of the swamp, and sank into some pit or slough; others, more uncharitable, hinted that she had eloped with the household booty, and made off to some other province; while others surmised that the tempter had decoyed her into a dismal quagmire, on the top of which her hat was found lying. In confirmation of this, it was said a great black man, with an axe on his shoulder, was seen late that very evening coming out of the swamp, carrying a bundle tied in a check apron, with an air of surly triumph.

The most current and probable story, however, observes, that Tom Walker grew so anxious about the fate of his wife and his property, that he set out at length to seek them both at the Indian fort. During a long summer's afternoon he searched about the gloomy place, but no wife was to be seen. He called her name repeatedly, but she was nowhere to be heard. The bittern alone responded to his voice, as he flew screaming by; or the bull-frog croaked dolefully from a neighborhood pool. At length, it is said, just in the brown hour of twilight, when the owls began to hoot, and the bats to flit about, his attention was attracted by the clamor of carrion crows hovering about a cypress-tree. He looked up, and beheld a bundle tied in a check apron, and hanging in the branches of the tree, with a great vulture perched hard by, as if keeping watch upon it. He leaped with joy; for he recognized his wife's apron, and supposed it to contain the household valuables.

"Let us get hold of the property," said he, consolingly to himself, "and we will endeavor to do without the woman."

As he scrambled up the tree, the vulture spread its wide wings, and sailed off screaming into the deep shadows of the forest. Tom seized the check apron, but woful sight! found nothing but a heart and liver tied up in it!

Such, according to the most authentic old story, was all that was to be found of Tom's wife. She had probably attempted to deal with the black man as she had been accustomed to deal with her husband; but though a female scold is generally considered a match for the devil, yet in this instance she appears to have had the worst of it. She must have died game, however; for it is said Tom noticed many prints of cloven feet deeply stamped about the tree, and found handfuls of hair, that looked as if they had been plucked from the coarse black shock of the woodman. Tom knew his wife's prowess by experience. He shrugged his shoulders, as he looked at the signs of a fierce clapper-clawing. "Egad," said he to himself, "Old Scratch must have had a tough time of it!"

Tom consoled himself for the loss of his property, with the loss of his wife, for he was a man of fortitude. He even felt something like gratitude towards the black woodman, who, he considered, had done him a kindness. He sought, therefore, to cultivate a further acquaintance with him, but for some time without success; the old black-legs played shy, for whatever people may think, he is not always to be had for calling for: he knows how to play his cards when pretty sure of his game.

At length, it is said, when delay had whetted Tom's eagerness to the quick, and prepared him to agree to any thing rather than not gain the promised treasure, he met the black man one evening in his usual woodman's dress, with his axe on his shoulder, sauntering along the swamp, and humming a tune. He affected to receive Tom's advances with great indifference, made brief replies, and went on humming his tune.

By degrees, however, Tom brought him to business, and they began to haggle about the terms on which the former was to have the pirate's treasure. There was one condition which need not be mentioned, being generally understood in all cases where the devil grants favors; but there were others about which, though of less importance, he was inflexibly obstinate. He insisted that the money found through his means should be employed in his service. He proposed, therefore, that Tom should employ it in the black traffic; that is to say, that he should fit out a slave-ship. This, however, Tom resolutely refused: he was bad enough in all conscience; but the devil himself could not tempt him to turn slave-trader.

Finding Tom so squeamish on this

point, he did not insist upon it, but proposed, instead, that he should turn usurer; the devil being extremely anxious for the increase of usurers, looking upon them as his peculiar people.

To this no objections were made, for it was just to Tom's taste.

"You shall open a broker's shop in Boston next month," said the black man.

"I'll do it to-morrow, if you wish," said Tom Walker.

"You shall lend money at two per cent a month."

"Egad, I'll charge four!" replied Tom Walker.

"You shall extort bonds, foreclose mortgages, drive the merchants to bankruptcy"——

"I'll drive them to the d——," cried Tom Walker.

"You are the usurer for my money!" said black-legs with delight. "When will you want the rhino?"

"This very night."

"Done!" said the devil.

"Done!" said Tom Walker.—So they shook hands and struck a bargain.

A few days' time saw Tom Walker seated behind his desk in a counting-house in Boston.

His reputation for a ready-moneyed man, who would lend money out for a good consideration, soon spread abroad. Everybody remembers the time of Governor Belcher, when money was particularly scarce. It was a time of paper credit. The country had been deluged with government bills; the famous Land Bank had been established; there had been a rage for speculating; the people had run mad with schemes for new settlements; for building cities in the wilderness; land-jobbers went about with maps of grants, and townships, and Eldorados, lying nobody knew where, but which everybody was ready to purchase. In a word, the great speculating fever which breaks out every now and then in the country, had raged to an alarming degree, and everybody was dreaming of making sudden fortunes from nothing. As usual the fever had subsided; the dream had gone off, and the imaginary fortunes with it; the patients were left in doleful plight, and the whole country resounded with the consequent cry of "hard times."

At this propitious time of public distress did Tom Walker set up as usurer in Boston. His door was soon thronged by customers. The needy and adventurous; the gambling speculator; the dreaming land-jobber; the thriftless tradesman; the merchant with cracked credit; in short, everyone driven to raise money by desperate means and desperate sacrifices, hurried to Tom Walker.

Thus Tom was the universal friend of the needy, and acted like a "friend in need"; that is to say, he always exacted good pay and good security. In proportion to the distress of the applicant was the highness of his terms. He accumulated bonds and mortgages; gradually squeezed his customers closer and closer; and sent them at length, dry as a sponge, from his door.

In this way he made money hand over hand; became a rich and mighty man, and exalted his cocked hat upon 'Change. He built himself, as usual, a vast house, out of ostentation; but left the greater part of it unfinished and unfurnished, out of parsimony. He even set up a carriage in the fulness of his vainglory, though he nearly starved the horses which drew it; and as the ungreased wheels groaned and screeched on the axle-trees, you would have thought you heard the souls of the poor debtors he was squeezing.

As Tom waxed old, however, he grew thoughtful. Having secured the good things of this world, he began to feel anxious about those of the next. He thought with regret on the bargain he had made with his black friend, and set his wits to work

to cheat him out of the conditions. He became, therefore, all of a sudden, a violent church-goer. He prayed loudly and strenuously, as if heaven were to be taken by force of lungs. Indeed, one might always tell when he had sinned most during the week, by the clamor of his Sunday devotion. The quiet Christians who had been modestly and steadfastly travelling Zionward, were struck with self-reproach at seeing themselves so suddenly outstripped in their career by this new-made convert. Tom was as rigid in religious as in money matters; he was a stern supervisor and censurer of his neighbors, and seemed to think every sin entered up to their account became a credit on his own side of the page. He even talked of the expediency of reviving the persecution of Quakers and Anabaptists. In a word, Tom's zeal became as notorious as his riches.

Still, in spite of all this strenuous attention to forms, Tom had a lurking dread that the devil, after all, would have his due. That he might not be taken unawares, therefore, it is said he always carried a small Bible in his coat-pocket. He had also a great folio Bible on his countinghouse desk, and would frequently be found reading it when people called on business; on such occasions he would lay his green spectacles in the book, to mark the place, while he turned round to drive some usurious bargain.

Some say that Tom grew a little crack-brained in his old days, and that, fancying his end approaching, he had his horse new shod, saddled and bridled, and buried with his feet uppermost; because he supposed that at the last day the world would be turned upside down; in which case he should find his horse standing ready for mounting, and he was determined at the worst to give his old friend a run for it. This, however, is probably a mere old wives' fable. If he really did take such a precaution, it was totally superfluous; at least so says the authentic old legend; which closes his story in the following manner.

One hot summer afternoon in the dog-days, just as a terrible black thunder-gust was coming up, Tom sat in his counting-house, in his white linen cap and India silk morning-gown. He was on the point of foreclosing a mortgage, by which he would complete the ruin of an unlucky land-speculator for whom he had professed the greatest friendship. The poor land-jobber begged him to grant a few months' indulgence. Tom had grown testy and ir-ritated, and refused another day.

"My family will be ruined, and brought upon the parish," said the land-jobber.

"Charity begins at home," replied Tom; "I must take care of myself in these hard times."

"You have made so much money out of me," said the speculator.

Tom lost his patience and his piety. "The devil take me," said he, "if I have made a farthing!"

Just then there were three loud knocks at the street-door. He stepped out to see who was there. A black man was holding a black horse, which neighed and stamped with impatience.

"Tom, you're come for," said the black fellow, gruffly. Tom shrank back, but too late. He had left his little Bible at the bottom of his coat-pocket, and his big Bible on the desk buried under the mort-gage he was about to foreclose: never was sinner taken more unawares. The black man whisked him like a child into the saddle, gave the horse the lash, and away he galloped, with Tom on his back, in the midst of the thunder-storm. The clerks stuck their pens behind their ears, and stared after him from the windows. Away went Tom Walker, dashing down the streets; his white cap bobbing up and down; his morning-gown fluttering in the wind, and his steed striking fire out of the pavement at every bound. When the clerks turned to look for the black man, he had disappeared.

Tom Walker never returned to foreclose the mortgage. A countryman, who lived on the border of the swamp, reported that in the height of the thunder-gust he had heard a great clattering of hoofs and a howling along the road, and running to the window caught sight of a figure, such as I have de-scribed, on a horse that galloped like mad across the fields, over the hills and down into the black hemlock swamp towards the old Indian fort; and that shortly after a thunderbolt falling in that direction seemed to set the whole forest in a blaze.

The good people of Boston shook their heads and shrugged their shoulders, but had been so much accustomed to witches and goblins and tricks of the devil, in all kind of shapes from the first settlement of the colony, that they were not so much horror-struck as might have been expected. Trustees were appointed to take charge of Tom's effects. There was nothing, how-ever, to administer upon. On searching his coffers all his bonds and mortgages were found reduced to cinders. In place of gold and silver his iron chest was filled with chips and shavings; two skeletons lay in his stable instead of his half-starved horses, and the very next day his great house took fire and was burnt to the ground.

Such was the end of Tom Walker and his ill-gotten wealth. Let all griping money-brokers lay this story to heart. The truth of it is not to be doubted. The very hole under the oak-trees, whence he dug Kidd's money, is to be seen to this day; and the neighboring swamp and old Indian fort are often haunted in stormy nights by a figure on horseback, in morning-gown and white cap, which is doubtless the troubled spirit of the usurer. In fact, the story has resolved itself into a proverb, and is the origin of that popular saying, so prevalent throughout New England, of "The Devil and Tom Walker."

Young Goodman Brown

by Nathaniel Hawthorne

Although Hawthorne liked to think of himself as a writer of romances, he was actually extremely conversant with New England history and drew much of the material for his tales from that source. One of his ancestors was a judge at the Salem witch trials, and Hawthorne himself was familiar, through close reading, with the old Massachusetts theocracy. "Young Goodman Brown," like the novel The Scarlet Letter, *is historical fiction only by stretching the definition, yet few stories are richer in the atmosphere of the Puritan past. An earnest young citizen leaves his recently wedded wife for a midnight walk in the forest, and he returns with a vivid sense of sin in the universe which burdens him for the rest of his life. Did the young man actually see the devil, the witches, the sinister Indians, the deacons and ministers all hurrying to a diabolic Sabbath in the blackest of woods, or did he simply imagine these marvels? Hawthorne always was ambiguous in his use of the supernatural and allowed the reader to choose his own explanation. But his tale is nevertheless rich in what Cotton Mather liked to call the wonders of the invisible world. "Young Goodman Brown" is one of the stories in* Mosses from an Old Manse *(1846).*

Young Goodman Brown came forth at sunset into the street at Salem village; but put his head back, after crossing the threshold, to exchange a parting kiss with his young wife. And Faith, as the wife was aptly named, thrust her own pretty head into the street, letting the wind play with the pink ribbons of her cap while she called to Goodman Brown.

"Dearest heart," whispered she, softly and rather sadly, when her lips were close to his ear, "prithee put off your journey until sunrise and sleep in your own bed to-night. A lone woman is troubled with such dreams and such thoughts that she's afeard of herself sometimes. Pray tarry with me this night, dear husband, of all nights in the year."

"My love and my Faith," replied young Goodman Brown, "of all nights in the year, this one night must I tarry away from thee. My journey, as thou callest it, forth and back again, must needs be done 'twixt now and sunrise. What, my sweet, pretty wife, dost thou doubt me already, and we but three months married?"

"Then God bless you!" said Faith, with the pink ribbons; "and may you find all well when you come back."

"Amen!" cried Goodman Brown. "Say thy prayers, dear Faith, and go to bed at dusk, and no harm will come to thee."

So they parted; and the young man pursued his way until, being about to turn the corner by the meetinghouse, he looked back and saw the head of Faith still peeping after him with a melancholy air, in spite of her pink ribbons.

"Poor little Faith!" thought he, for his heart smote him. "What a wretch am I to leave her on such an errand! She talks of dreams, too. Methought as she spoke there was trouble in her face, as if a dream had warned her what work is to be done tonight. But no, no; 'twould kill her to think it. Well, she's a blessed angel on earth; and after this one night I'll cling to her skirts and follow her to heaven."

With this excellent resolve for the future, Goodman Brown felt himself justified in making more haste on his present evil purpose. He had taken a dreary road, darkened by all the gloomiest trees of the forest, which barely stood aside to let the narrow path creep through, and closed immediately behind. It was all as lonely as could be; and there is this peculiarity in such a solitude, that the traveller knows not who may be concealed by the innumerable trunks and the thick boughs overhead; so that with lonely footsteps he may yet be passing through an unseen multitude.

"There may be a devilish Indian behind every tree," said Goodman Brown to himself; and he glanced fearfully behind him as he added, "What if the devil himself should be at my very elbow!"

His head being turned back, he passed a crook of the road, and, looking forward again, beheld the figure of a man, in grave and decent attire, seated at the foot of an old tree. He arose at Goodman Brown's approach and walked onward side by side with him.

"You are late, Goodman Brown," said he. "The clock of the Old South was striking as I came through Boston, and that is full fifteen minutes agone."

"Faith kept me back a while," replied the young man, with a tremor in his voice, caused by the sudden appearance of his companion, though not wholly unexpected.

It was now deep dusk in the forest, and deepest in that part of it where these two were journeying. As nearly as could be discerned, the second traveller was about fifty years old, apparently in the same rank of life as Goodman Brown, and bearing a considerable resemblance to him, though perhaps more in expression than features. Still they might have been taken for father and son. And yet, though the elder person was as simply clad as the younger, and as simple in manner too, he had an indescribable air of one who knew the world, and who would not have felt abashed at the governor's dinner table or in King William's court, were it possible that his affairs should call him thither. But the only thing about him that could be fixed upon as remarkable was his staff, which bore the likeness of a great black snake, so curiously wrought that it might almost be seen to twist and wriggle itself like a living serpent. This, of course, must have been an ocular deception, assisted by the uncertain light.

"Come, Goodman Brown," cried his fellow-traveller, "this is a dull pace for the beginning of a journey. Take my staff, if you are so soon weary."

"Friend," said the other, exchanging his slow pace for a full stop, "having kept covenant by meeting thee here, it is my purpose now to return whence I came. I have scruples touching the matter thou wot'st of."

"Sayest thou so?" replied he of the serpent, smiling apart. "Let us walk on, nevertheless, reasoning as we go; and if I convince thee not thou shalt turn back. We are but a little way in the forest yet."

"Too far! too far!" exclaimed the goodman, unconsciously resuming his walk. "My father never went into the woods on such an errand, nor his father before him. We have been a race of honest men and good Christians since the days of the martyrs; and shall I be the first of the name of Brown that ever took this path and kept"—

"Such company, thou wouldst say," observed the elder person, interpreting his pause. "Well said, Goodman Brown! I have been as well acquainted with your family as with ever a one among the Puritans; and that's no trifle to say. I helped your grandfather, the constable, when he lashed the Quaker woman so smartly through the streets of Salem; and it was I that brought your father a pitch-pine knot, kindled at my own hearth, to set fire to an Indian village, in King Philip's war. They were my good friends, both; and many a pleasant walk have we had along this path, and returned merrily after midnight. I would fain be friends with you for their sake."

"If it be as thou sayest," replied Goodman Brown, "I marvel they never spoke of these matters; or, verily, I marvel not, seeing that the least rumor of the sort would have driven them from New England. We are a people of prayer, and good works to boot, and abide no such wickedness."

"Wickedness or not," said the traveller with the twisted staff, "I have a very general acquaintance here in New England. The deacons of many a church have drunk the communion wine with me; the selectmen of divers towns make me their chairman; and a majority of the Great and General Court are firm supporters of my interest. The governor and I, too— But these are state secrets."

"Can this be so?" cried Goodman Brown, with a stare of amazement at his undisturbed companion. "Howbeit, I have nothing to do with the governor and council; they have their own ways, and are no rule for a simple husbandman like me. But, were I to go on with thee, how should I meet the eye of that good old man, our minister, at Salem village? Oh, his voice would make me tremble both Sabbath day and lecture day."

Thus far the elder traveller had listened with due gravity; but now burst into a fit of irrepressible mirth, shaking himself so violently that his snake-like staff actually seemed to wriggle in sympathy.

"Ha! ha! ha!" shouted he again and again; then composing himself, "Well, go on, Goodman Brown, go on; but, prithee, don't kill me with laughing."

"Well, then, to end the matter at once," said Goodman Brown, considerably nettled, "there is my wife, Faith. It would break her dear little heart; and I'd rather break my own."

"Nay, if that be the case," answered the other, "e'en go thy ways, Goodman Brown. I would not for twenty old women like the one hobbling before us that Faith should come to any harm."

As he spoke he pointed his staff at a female figure on the path, in whom Goodman Brown recognized a very pious and exemplary dame, who had taught him his catechism in youth, and was still his moral and spiritual adviser, jointly with the minister and Deacon Gookin.

"A marvel, truly, that Goody Cloyse should be so far in the wilderness at nightfall," said he. "But with your leave, friend, I shall take a cut through the woods until we have left this Christian woman behind. Being a stranger to you, she might ask whom I was consorting with and whither I was going."

"Be it so," said his fellow-traveller. "Betake you the woods, and let me keep the path."

Accordingly the young man turned aside, but took care to watch his companion, who advanced softly along the road until he had come within a staff's length of the old dame. She, meanwhile, was making the best of her way, with singular speed for so aged a woman, and mumbling some indistinct words—a prayer, doubtless—as she went. The traveller put forth his staff and touched her withered neck with what seemed the serpent's tail.

"The devil!" screamed the pious old lady.

"Then Goody Cloyse knows her old friend?" observed the traveller, confronting her and leaning on his writhing stick.

"Ah, forsooth, and is it your worship indeed?" cried the good dame. "Yea, truly is it, and in the very image of my old gossip, Goodman Brown, the grandfather of the silly fellow that now is. But—would your worship believe it?—my broomstick hath strangely disappeared, stolen, as I suspect, by that unhanged witch, Goody Cory, and that, too, when I was all anointed with the juice of smallage, and cinquefoil, and wolf's bane"—

"Mingled with fine wheat and the fat of a new-born babe," said the shape of old Goodman Brown.

"Ah, your worship knows the recipe," cried the old lady, cackling aloud. "So, as I was saying, being all ready for the meeting, and no horse to ride on, I made up my mind to foot it; for they tell me there is a nice young man to be taken into communion to-night. But now your good worship will lend me your arm, and we shall be there in a twinkling."

"That can hardly be," answered her friend. "I may not spare you my arm, Goody Cloyse; but here is my staff, if you will."

So saying, he threw it down at her feet, where, perhaps, it assumed life, being one of the rods which its owner had formerly lent to the Egyptian magi. Of this fact, however, Goodman Brown could not take cognizance. He had cast up his eyes in astonishment, and, looking down again, beheld neither Goody Cloyse nor the serpentine staff, but his fellow-traveller alone, who waited for him as calmly as if nothing had happened.

"That old woman taught me my catechism," said the young man; and there was a world of meaning in this simple comment.

They continued to walk onward, while the elder traveller exhorted his companion to make good speed and persevere in the path, discoursing so aptly that his arguments seemed rather to spring up in the bosom of his auditor than to be suggested by himself. As they went, he plucked a branch of maple to serve for a walking stick, and began to strip it of the twigs and little boughs, which were wet with evening dew. The moment his fingers touched them they became strangely withered and dried up as with a week's sunshine. Thus the pair proceeded, at a good free pace, until suddenly, in a gloomy hollow of the road, Goodman Brown sat himself down on the stump of a tree and refused to go any farther.

"Friend," said he, stubbornly, "my mind is made up. Not another step will I budge on this errand. What if a wretched old woman do choose to go to the devil when I thought she was going to heaven: is that any reason why I should quit my dear Faith and go after her?"

"You will think better of this by and by," said his acquaintance, composedly. "Sit here and rest yourself a while; and when you feel like moving again, there is my staff to help you along."

Without more words, he threw his companion the maple stick, and was as speedily out of sight as if he had vanished into the deepening gloom. The young man sat a few moments by the roadside, applauding himself greatly, and thinking with how clear a conscience he should meet the minister in his morning walk, nor shrink from the eye of good old Deacon Gookin. And what calm sleep would be his that very night, which was to have been spent so wickedly, but so purely and sweetly now, in the arms of Faith! Amidst these pleasant and praiseworthy meditations, Goodman Brown heard the tramp of horses along the road, and deemed it advisable to conceal himself within the verge of the forest, conscious of the guilty purpose that had brought him thither, though now so happily turned from it.

On came the hoof tramps and the voices of the riders, two grave old voices, conversing soberly as they drew near. These mingled sounds appeared to pass along the road, within a few yards of the young man's hiding-place; but, owing doubtless to the depth of the gloom at that particular spot, neither the travellers nor their steeds were visible. Though their figures brushed the small boughs by the wayside, it could not be seen that they intercepted, even for a moment, the faint gleam from the strip of bright sky athwart which they must have passed. Goodman Brown alternately crouched and stood on tiptoe, pulling aside the branches and thrusting forth his head as far as he durst without discerning so much as a shadow. It vexed him the more, because he could have sworn, were such a thing possible, that he recognized the voices of the minister and Deacon Gookin, jogging along quietly, as they were wont to do, when bound to some ordination or ecclesiastical council. While yet within hearing, one of the riders stopped to pluck a switch.

"Of the two, reverend sir," said the voice like the deacon's, "I had rather miss an ordination dinner than to-night's meeting. They tell me that some of our community are to be here from Falmouth and beyond, and others from Connecticut and Rhode Island, besides several of the Indian powwows, who, after their fashion, know almost as much deviltry as the best of us. Moreover, there is a goodly young woman to be taken into communion."

"Mighty well, Deacon Gookin!" replied the solemn old tones of the minister. "Spur up, or we shall be late. Nothing can be done, you know, until I get on the ground."

The hoofs clattered again; and the voices, talking so strangely in the empty air, passed on through the forest, where no church had ever been gathered or solitary Christian prayed. Whither, then, could these holy men be journeying so deep into the heathen wilderness? Young Goodman Brown caught hold of a tree for support, being ready to sink down on the ground, faint and overburdened with the heavy sickness of his heart. He looked up to the sky, doubting whether there really was a heaven above him. Yet there was the blue arch, and the stars brightening in it.

"With heaven above and Faith below, I will yet stand firm against the devil!" cried Goodman Brown.

While he still gazed upward into the deep arch of the firmament and had lifted his hands to pray, a cloud, though no wind was stirring, hurried across the zenith and hid the brightening stars. The blue sky was still visible, except directly overhead, where this black mass of cloud was sweeping swiftly northward. Aloft in the air, as if from the depths of the cloud, came a confused and doubtful sound of voices. Once the listener fancied that he could distinguish the accents of townspeople of his own, men and women, both pious and ungodly, many of whom he had met at the communion table, and had seen others rioting at the tavern. The next moment, so indistinct were the sounds, he doubted whether he had heard aught but the murmur of the old forest, whispering without a wind. Then came a stronger swell of those familiar tones, heard daily in the sunshine at Salem village, but never until now from a cloud of night. There was one voice, of a young woman, uttering lamentations, yet with an uncertain sorrow, and entreating for some favor, which, perhaps, it would grieve her to obtain; and all the unseen multitude, both saints and sinners, seemed to encourage her onward.

"Faith!" shouted Goodman Brown, in a voice of agony and desperation; and the echoes of the forest mocked him, crying, "Faith! Faith!" as if bewildered wretches were seeking her all through the wilderness.

The cry of grief, rage, and terror was yet piercing the night, when the unhappy husband held his breath for a response. There was a scream, drowned immediately in a louder murmur of voices, fading into far-off laughter, as the dark cloud swept away, leaving the clear and silent sky above Goodman Brown. But something fluttered lightly down through the air and caught on the branch of a tree. The young man seized it, and beheld a pink ribbon.

"My Faith is gone!" cried he, after one stupefied moment. "There is no good on earth; and sin is but a name. Come, devil; for to thee is this world given."

And, maddened with despair, so that he laughed loud and long, did Goodman Brown grasp his staff and set forth again, at such a rate that he seemed to fly along the forest path rather than to walk or run. The road grew wilder and drearier and more faintly traced, and vanished at length, leaving him in the heart of the dark wilderness, still rushing onward with the instinct that guides mortal man to evil. The whole forest was peopled with frightful sounds—the creaking of the trees, the howling of wild beasts, and the yell of Indians; while sometimes the wind tolled like a distant church bell, and sometimes gave a broad roar around the traveller, as if all Nature were laughing him to scorn. But he was himself the chief horror of the scene, and shrank not from its other horrors.

"Ha! ha! ha!" roared Goodman Brown when the wind laughed at him. "Let us

hear which will laugh loudest. Think not to frighten me with your deviltry. Come witch, come wizard, come Indian powwow, come devil himself, and here comes Goodman Brown. You may as well fear him as he fear you."

In truth, all through the haunted forest there could be nothing more frightful than the figure of Goodman Brown. On he flew among the black pines, brandishing his staff with frenzied gestures, now giving vent to an inspiration of horrid blasphemy, and now shouting forth such laughter as set all the echoes of the forest laughing like demons around him. The fiend in his own shape is less hideous than when he rages in the breast of man. Thus sped the demoniac on his course, until, quivering among the trees, he saw a red light before him, as when the felled trunks and branches of a clearing have been set on fire, and throw up their lurid blaze against the sky, at the hour of midnight. He paused, in a lull of the tempest that had driven him onward, and heard the swell of what seemed a hymn, rolling solemnly from a distance with the weight of many voices. He knew the tune; it was a familiar one in the choir of the village meetinghouse. The verse died heavily away, and was lengthened by a chorus, not of human voices, but of all the sounds of the benighted wilderness pealing in awful harmony together. Goodman Brown cried out, and his cry was lost to his own ear by its unison with the cry of the desert.

In the interval of silence he stole forward until the light glared full upon his eyes. At one extremity of an open space, hemmed in by the dark wall of the forest, arose a rock, bearing some rude, natural resemblance either to an altar or a pulpit, and surrounded by four blazing pines, their tops aflame, their stems untouched, like candles at an evening meeting. The mass of foliage that had overgrown the summit of the rock was all on fire, blazing high into the night and fitfully illuminating the whole field. Each pendent twig and leafy festoon was in a blaze. As the red light arose and fell, a numerous congregation alternately shone forth, then disappeared in shadow, and again grew, as it were, out of the darkness, peopling the heart of the solitary woods at once.

"A grave and dark-clad company," quoth Goodman Brown.

In truth they were such. Among them, quivering to and fro between gloom and splendor, appeared faces that would be seen next day at the council board of the province, and others which, Sabbath after Sabbath, looked devoutly heavenward, and benignantly over the crowded pews, from the holiest pulpits in the land. Some affirm that the lady of the governor was there. At least there were high dames well known to her, and wives of honored husbands, and widows, a great multitude, and ancient maidens, all of excellent repute, and fair young girls, who trembled lest their mothers should espy them. Either the sudden gleams of light flashing over the obscure field bedazzled Goodman Brown, or he recognized a score of the church members of Salem village famous for their especial sanctity. Good old Deacon Gookin had arrived, and waited at the skirts of that venerable saint, his revered pastor. But, irreverently consorting with these grave, reputable, and pious people, these elders of the church, these chaste dames and dewy virgins, there were men of dissolute lives and women of spotted fame, wretches given over to all mean and filthy vice, and suspected even of horrid crimes. It was strange to see that the good shrank not from the wicked, nor were the sinners abashed by the saints. Scattered also among their pale-faced enemies were the Indian priests, or powwows, who had often scared their native forest with more hideous incantations than any known to English witchcraft.

"But where is Faith?" thought Goodman Brown; and, as hope came into his heart, he trembled.

Another verse of the hymn arose, a slow and mournful strain, such as the pious love, but joined to words which expressed all that our nature can conceive of sin, and darkly hinted at far more. Unfathomable to mere mortals is the lore of fiends. Verse after verse was sung; and still the chorus of the desert swelled between like the deepest tone of a mighty organ; and with the final peal of that dreadful anthem there came a sound, as if the roaring wind, the rushing streams, the howling beasts, and every other voice of the unconcerted wilderness were mingling and according with the voice of guilty man in homage to the prince of all. The four blazing pines threw up a loftier flame, and obscurely discovered shapes and visages of horror on the smoke wreaths above the impious assembly. At the same moment the fire on the rock shot redly forth and formed a glowing arch above its base, where now appeared a figure. With reverence be it spoken, the figure bore no slight similitude, both in garb and manner, to some grave divine of the New England churches.

"Bring forth the converts!" cried a voice that echoed through the field and rolled into the forest.

At the word, Goodman Brown stepped forth from the shadow of the trees and approached the congregation, with whom he felt a loathful brotherhood by the sympathy of all that was wicked in his heart. He could have well-nigh sworn that the shape of his own dead father beckoned him to advance, looking downward from a smoke wreath, while a woman, with dim features of despair, threw out her hand to warn him back. Was it his mother? But he had no power to retreat one step, nor to resist, even in thought, when the minister and good old Deacon Gookin seized his arms and led him to the blazing rock. Thither came also the slender form of a veiled female, led between Goody Cloyse, that pious teacher of the catechism, and Martha Carrier, who had received the devil's promise to be queen of hell. A rampant hag was she. And there stood the proselytes beneath the canopy of fire.

"Welcome, my children," said the dark figure, "to the communion of your race. Ye have found thus young your nature and your destiny. My children, look behind you!"

They turned; and flashing forth, as it were, in a sheet of flame, the fiend worshippers were seen; the smile of welcome gleamed darkly on every visage.

"There," resumed the sable form, "are all whom ye have reverenced from youth. Ye deemed them holier than yourselves, and shrank from your own sin, contrasting it with their lives of righteousness and prayerful aspirations heavenward. Yet here are they all in my worshipping assembly. This night it shall be granted you to know their secret deeds: how hoary-bearded elders of the church have whispered wanton words to the young maids of their households; how many a woman, eager for widows' weeds, has given her husband a drink at bedtime and let him sleep his last sleep in her bosom; how beardless youths have made haste to inherit their fathers' wealth; and how fair damsels—blush not, sweet ones—have dug little graves in the garden, and bidden me, the sole guest, to an infant's funeral. By the sympathy of your human hearts for sin ye shall scent out all the places—whether in church, bedchamber, street, field, or forest—where crime has been committed, and shall exult to behold the whole earth one stain of guilt, one mighty blood spot. Far more than this. It shall be yours to penetrate, in every bosom, the deep mystery of sin, the fountain of all wicked arts, and which inexhaustibly supplies more evil impulses than human power—than my power at its

utmost—can make manifest in deeds. And now, my children, look upon each other."

They did so; and, by the blaze of the hell-kindled torches, the wretched man beheld his Faith, and the wife her husband, trembling before that unhallowed altar.

"Lo, there ye stand, my children," said the figure, in a deep and solemn tone, almost sad with its despairing awfulness, as if his once angelic nature could yet mourn for our miserable race. "Depending upon one another's hearts, ye had still hoped that virtue were not all a dream. Now are ye undeceived. Evil is the nature of mankind. Evil must be your only happiness. Welcome again, my children, to the communion of your race."

"Welcome," repeated the fiend worshippers, in one cry of despair and triumph.

And there they stood, the only pair, as it seemed, who were yet hesitating on the verge of wickedness in this dark world. A basin was hollowed, naturally, in the rock. Did it contain water, reddened by the lurid light? or was it blood? or, perchance, a liquid flame? Herein did the shape of evil dip his hand and prepare to lay the mark of baptism upon their foreheads, that they might be partakers of the mystery of sin, more conscious of the secret guilt of others, both in deed and thought, than they could now be of their own. The husband cast one look at his pale wife, and Faith at him. What polluted wretches would the next glance show them to each other, shuddering alike at what they disclosed and what they saw!

"Faith! Faith!" cried the husband, "look up to heaven, and resist the wicked one."

Whether Faith obeyed he knew not. Hardly had he spoken when he found himself amid calm night and solitude, listening to a roar of the wind which died heavily away through the forest. He staggered against the rock, and felt it chill and damp; while a hanging twig, that had been all on fire, besprinkled his cheek with the coldest dew.

The next morning young Goodman Brown came slowly into the street of Salem village, staring around him like a bewildered man. The good old minister was taking a walk along the graveyard to get an appetite for breakfast and meditate his sermon, and bestowed a blessing, as he passed, on Goodman Brown. He shrank from the venerable saint as if to avoid an anathema. Old Deacon Gookin was at domestic worship, and the holy words of his prayer were heard through the open window. "What God doth the wizard pray to?" quoth Goodman Brown. Goody Cloyse, that excellent old Christian, stood in the early sunshine at her own lattice, catechizing a little girl who had brought her a pint of morning's milk. Goodman Brown snatched away the child as from the grasp of the fiend himself. Turning the corner by the meetinghouse, he spied the head of Faith, with the pink ribbons, gazing anxiously forth, and bursting into such joy at sight of him that she skipped along the street and almost kissed her husband before the whole village. But Goodman Brown looked sternly and sadly into her face, and passed on without a greeting.

Had Goodman Brown fallen asleep in the forest and only dreamed a wild dream of a witch-meeting?

Be it so if you will; but, alas! it was a dream of evil omen for young Goodman Brown. A stern, a sad, a darkly meditative, a distrustful, if not a desperate man did he become from the night of that fearful dream. On the Sabbath day, when the congregation were singing a holy psalm, he could not listen because an anthem of sin rushed loudly upon his ear and drowned all the blessed strain. When the minister spoke from the pulpit with power and fervid eloquence, and, with his hand on the open Bible, of the sacred truths of our religion, and of saint-like lives and triumphant deaths, and of future bliss or misery unutterable, then did Goodman Brown turn pale, dreading lest the roof should thunder down upon the gray blasphemer and his hearers. Often, awaking suddenly at midnight, he shrank from the bosom of Faith; and at morning or eventide, when the family knelt down at prayer, he scowled and muttered to himself, and gazed sternly at his wife, and turned away. And when he had lived long, and was borne to his grave a hoary corpse, followed by Faith, an aged woman, and children and grandchildren, a goodly procession, besides neighbors not a few, they carved no hopeful verse upon his tombstone, for his dying hour was gloom.

The Devil and Daniel Webster

by Stephen Vincent Benét

Few American short stories of the twentieth century are better known than "The Devil and Daniel Webster." Partly because it deals with one of the most celebrated figures in American history, partly because it is written with wit and brilliance, it has won wide acclaim. Although the story supposedly concerns a New Hampshire farmer who has entered into a seven-year compact with Satan, the two real antagonists are Daniel Webster and the devil. Benét has given his villain modern dress but has deftly retained many traditional bits. Thus Scratch is supposed to have pointed ears and filed teeth; he imprisons human souls in his pocketbook like moths; and at his midnight appearance the lights burn blue. Moreover, although his true nature is unremarked by most adults, he cannot impose on a dog. Webster himself enjoys heroic dimensions as fisherman, farmer, and orator. One of the most original touches is the jury assembled to try the unrecorded case of the devil vs. Jabez Stone, a jury which disappears when a cock's cry announces the dawn. The climax to this most unusual suit is a tribute to American democracy and the sterling qualities of its advocate.

It's a story they tell in the border country, where Massachusetts joins Vermont and New Hampshire.

Yes, Dan'l Webster's dead—or, at least, they buried him. But every time there's a thunderstorm around Marshfield, they say you can hear his rolling voice in the hollows of the sky. And they say that if you go to his grave and speak loud and clear, "Dan'l Webster—Dan'l Webster!" the ground'll begin to shiver and the trees begin to shake. And after a while you'll hear a deep voice saying, "Neighbor, how stands the Union?" Then you better answer the Union stands as she stood, rock-bottomed and copper-sheathed, one and indivisible, or he's liable to rear right out of the ground. At least, that's what I was told when I was a youngster.

You see, for a while, he was the biggest man in the country. He never got to be President, but he was the biggest man.

There were thousands that trusted in him right next to God Almighty, and they told stories about him and all the things that belonged to him that were like the stories of patriarchs and such. They said, when he stood up to speak, stars and stripes came right out in the sky, and once he spoke against a river and made it sink into the ground. They said, when he walked the woods with his fishing rod, Killall, the trout would jump out of the streams right into his pockets, for they knew it was no use putting up a fight against him; and when he argued a case, he could turn on the harps of the blessed and the shaking of the earth underground. That was the kind of man he was, and his big farm up at Marshfield was suitable to him. The chickens he raised were all white meat down through the drumsticks, the cows were tended like children, and the big ram he called Goliath had horns with a curl like a morning-glory vine and could butt through an iron door. But Dan'l wasn't one of your gentlemen farmers; he knew all the ways of the land, and he'd be up by candlelight to see that the chores got done. A man with a mouth like a mastiff, a brow like a mountain, and eyes like burning anthracite—that was Dan'l Webster in his prime. And the biggest case he argued never got written down in the books, for he argued it against the devil, nip and tuck and no holds barred. And this is the way I used to hear it told.

There was a man named Jabez Stone, lived at Cross Corners, New Hampshire. He wasn't a bad man to start with, but he was an unlucky man. If he planted corn, he got borers; if he planted potatoes, he got blight. He had good-enough land, but it didn't prosper him; he had a decent wife and children, but the more children he had, the less there was to feed them. If stones cropped up in his neighbor's field, boulders boiled up in his; if he had a horse with the spavins, he'd trade it for one with the staggers and give something extra. There's some folks bound to be like that, apparently. But one day Jabez Stone got sick of the whole business.

He'd been plowing that morning and he'd just broke the plowshare on a rock that he could have sworn hadn't been there yesterday. And as he stood at the plowshare, the off horse began to cough—that ropy kind of cough that means sickness and horse doctors. There were two children down with the measles, his wife was ailing, and he had a whitlow on his thumb. It was about the last straw for Jabez Stone. "I vow," he said, and he looked around him kind of desperate, "I vow it's enough to make a man want to sell his soul to the devil! And I would, too, for two cents!"

Then he felt a kind of queerness come over him at having said what he'd said; though, naturally, being a New Hampshireman, he wouldn't take it back. But all the same, when it got to be evening and, as far as he could see, no notice had been taken, he felt relieved in his mind, for he was a religious man. But notice is always taken, sooner or later, just like the Good Book says. And, sure enough, next day, about suppertime, a soft-spoken, dark-dressed stranger drove up in a handsome buggy and asked for Jabez Stone.

Well, Jabez told his family it was a lawyer, come to see him about a legacy. But he knew who it was. He didn't like the looks of the stranger, nor the way he smiled with his teeth. They were white teeth, and plentiful—some say they were filed to a point, but I wouldn't vouch for that. And he didn't like it when the dog took one look at the stranger and ran away howling, with his tail between his legs. But having passed the word, more or less, he stuck to it, and they went out behind the barn and made their bargain. Jabez Stone had to prick his finger to sign, and the stranger lent him a silver pin. The wound healed clean, but it left a little white scar.

After that, all of a sudden, things began to pick up and prosper for Jabez Stone. His cows got fat and his horses sleek, his crops were the envy of the neighborhood, and lightning might strike all over the valley, but it wouldn't strike his barn. Pretty soon he was one of the prosperous people of the county; they asked him to stand for selectman, and he stood for it; there began to be talk of running him for state senate. All in all, you might say the Stone family was as happy and contented as cats in a dairy. And so they were, except for Jabez Stone.

He'd been contented enough the first few years. It's a great thing when bad luck turns; it drives most other things out of your head. True, every now and then, especially in rainy weather, the little white scar on his finger would give him a twinge. And once a year, punctual as clockwork, the stranger with the handsome buggy would come driving by. But the sixth year the stranger lighted, and, after that, his peace was over for Jabez Stone.

The stranger came up through the lower field, switching his boots with a cane—they were handsome black boots, but Jabez Stone never liked the look of them, particularly the toes. And, after he'd passed the time of day, he said, "Well, Mr. Stone, you're a hummer! It's a very pretty property you've got here, Mr. Stone."

"Well, some might favor it and others might not," said Jabez Stone, for he was a New Hampshireman.

"Oh, no need to decry your industry!" said the stranger, very easy, showing his teeth in a smile. "After all, we know what's been done, and it's been according to contract and specifications. So when—ahem—the mortgage falls due next year, you shouldn't have any regrets."

"Speaking of that mortgage, mister," said Jabez Stone, and he looked around for help to the earth and the sky, "I'm beginning to have one or two doubts about it."

"Doubts?" said the stranger not quite so pleasantly.

"Why, yes," said Jabez Stone. "This being the U.S.A. and me always having been a religious man." He cleared his throat and got bolder. "Yes sir," he said, "I'm beginning to have considerable doubts as to that mortgage holding in court."

"There's courts and courts," said the stranger, clicking his teeth. "Still, we might as well have a look at the original document." And he hauled out a big black pocketbook, full of papers. "Sherwin, Slater, Stevens, Stone," he muttered. " 'I, Jabez Stone, for a term of seven years—' Oh, it's quite in order, I think."

But Jabez Stone wasn't listening, for he saw something else flutter out of the black pocketbook. It was something that looked like a moth, but it wasn't a moth. And as Jabez Stone stared at it, it seemed to speak to him in a small sort of piping voice, terrible small and thin, but terrible human. "Neighbor Stone!" it squeaked. "Neighbor Stone! Help me! For God's sake, help me!"

But before Jabez Stone could stir hand or foot, the stranger whipped out a big bandanna handkerchief, caught the creature up in it, just like a butterfly, and started tying up the ends of the bandanna.

"Sorry for the interruption," he said. "As I was saying—"

But Jabez Stone was shaking all over like a scared horse.

"That's Miser Stevens' voice!" he said, in a croak. "And you've got him in your handkerchief!"

The stranger looked a little embarrassed.

"Yes, I really should have transferred him to the collecting box," he said with a simper, "but there were some rather unusual specimens there and I didn't want them crowded. Well, well, these little con-tretemps will occur."

"I don't know what you mean by con-tertan," said Jabez Stone, "but that was Miser Stevens' voice! And he ain't dead! You can't tell me he is! He was just as spry and mean as a woodchuck, Tuesday!"

"In the midst of life—" said the stranger, kind of pious. "Listen!" Then a bell began to toll in the valley and Jabez Stone listened, with the sweat running down his face. For he knew it was tolled for Miser Stevens and that he was dead.

"These long-standing accounts," said the stranger with a sigh; "one really hates to close them. But business is business."

He still had the bandanna in his hand, and Jabez Stone felt sick as he saw the cloth struggle and flutter.

"Are they all as small as that?" he asked hoarsely.

"Small?" said the stranger. "Oh, I see what you mean. Why, they vary." He measured Jabez Stone with his eyes, and his teeth showed. "Don't worry, Mr. Stone," he said. "You'll go with a very good grade. I wouldn't trust you outside the collecting box. Now, a man like Dan'l Webster, of course—well, we'd have to build a special box for him, and even at that, I imagine the wing spread would astonish you. But, in your case, as I was saying—"

"Put that handkerchief away!" said Jabez Stone, and he began to beg and pray. But the best he could get at the end was a three years' extension, with con-ditions.

But till you make a bargain like that, you've got no idea of how fast four years can run. By the last months of those years, Jabez Stone's known all over the state and there's talk of running him for governor—and it's dust and ashes in his mouth. For every day, when he gets up, he thinks, "There's one more night gone," and every night when he lies down, he thinks of the black pocketbook and the soul of Miser Stevens, and it makes him sick at heart. Till, finally, he can't bear it any longer, and, in the last days of the last year, he hitches up his horse and drives off to seek Dan'l Webster. For Dan'l was born in New Hampshire, only a few miles from Cross Corners, and it's well known that he has a particular soft spot for old neigh-bors.

It was early in the morning when he got to Marshfield, but Dan'l was up already, talking Latin to the farm hands and wres-tling with the ram, Goliath, and trying out a new trotter and working up speeches to make against John C. Calhoun. But when he heard a New Hampshireman had come to see him, he dropped everything else he was doing, for that was Dan'l's way. He gave Jabez Stone a breakfast that five men couldn't eat, went into the living history of every man and woman in Cross Corners, and finally asked him how he could serve him.

Jabez Stone allowed that it was a kind of mortgage case.

"Well, I haven't pleaded a mortgage case in a long time, and I don't generally plead now, except before the Supreme Court," said Dan'l, "but if I can, I'll help you."

"Then I've got hope for the first time in ten years," said Jabez Stone, and told him the details.

Dan'l walked up and down as he lis-tened, hands behind his back, now and then asking a question, now and then plunging his eyes at the floor, as if they'd bore through it like gimlets. When Jabez Stone had finished, Dan'l puffed out his cheeks and blew. Then he turned to Jabez Stone and a smile broke over his face like the sunrise over Monadnock.

"You've certainly given yourself the devil's own row to hoe, Neighbor Stone," he said, "but I'll take your case."

"You'll take it?" said Jabez Stone, hardly daring to believe.

"Yes," said Dan'l Webster. "I've got seventy-five other things to do and the Missouri Compromise to straighten out, but I'll take your case. For if two New Hampshiremen aren't a match for the devil, we might as well give the country back to the Indians."

Then he shook Jabez Stone by the hand and said, "Did you come down here in a hurry?"

"Well, I admit I made time," said Jabez Stone.

"You'll go back faster," said Dan'l Webster, and he told 'em to hitch up Constitution and Constellation to the carriage. They were matched grays with one white forefoot, and they stepped like greased lightning.

Well, I won't describe how excited and pleased the whole Stone family was to have the great Dan'l Webster for a guest, when they finally got there. Jabez Stone had lost his hat on the way, blown off when they overtook a wind, but he didn't take much account of that. But after supper he sent the family off to bed, for he had most particular business with Mr. Webster. Mrs. Stone wanted them to sit in the front parlor, but Dan'l Webster knew front parlors and said he preferred the kitchen. So it was there they sat, waiting for the stranger, with a jug on the table between them and a bright fire on the hearth—the stranger being scheduled to show up on the stroke of midnight, according to specifications.

Well, most men wouldn't have asked for better company than Dan'l Webster and a jug. But with every tick of the clock Jabez Stone got sadder and sadder. His eyes roved round, and though he sampled the jug you could see he couldn't taste it. Finally, on the stroke of 11:30 he reached over and grabbed Dan'l Webster by the arm.

"Mr. Webster, Mr. Webster!" he said,

and his voice was shaking with fear and a desperate courage. "For God's sake, Mr. Webster, harness your horses and get away from this place while you can!"

"You've brought me a long way, neighbor, to tell me you don't like my company," said Dan'l Webster, quite peaceable, pulling at the jug.

"Miserable wretch that I am!" groaned Jabez Stone. "I've brought you a devilish way, and now I see my folly. Let him take me if he wills. I don't hanker after it, I must say, but I can stand it. But you're the Union's stay and New Hampshire's pride! He mustn't get you, Mr. Webster! He mustn't get you!"

Dan'l Webster looked at the distracted man, all gray and shaking in the firelight, and laid a hand on his shoulder.

"I'm obliged to you, Neighbor Stone," he said gently. "It's kindly thought of. But there's a jug on the table and a case in hand. And I never left a jug or a case half finished in my life."

And just at that moment there was a sharp rap on the door.

"Ah," said Dan'l Webster very coolly, "I thought your clock was a trifle slow, Neighbor Stone." He stepped to the door and opened it. "Come in!" he said.

The stranger came in—very dark and tall he looked in the firelight. He was carrying a box under his arm—a black japanned box with little air holes in the lid. At the sight of the box Jabez Stone gave a low cry and shrank into a corner of the room.

"Mr. Webster, I presume," said the stranger, very polite, but with his eyes glowing like a fox's deep in the woods.

"Attorney of record for Jabez Stone," said Dan'l Webster, but his eyes were glowing too. "Might I ask your name?"

"I've gone by a good many," said the stranger carelessly. "Perhaps Scratch will do for the evening. I'm often called that in these regions."

Then he sat down at the table and poured himself a drink from the jug. The liquor was cold in the jug, but it came steaming into the glass.

"And now," said the stranger, smiling and showing his teeth, "I shall call upon you, as a law-abiding citizen, to assist me in taking possession of my property."

Well, with that the argument began—and it went hot and heavy. At first Jabez Stone had a flicker of hope, but when he saw Dan'l Webster being forced back at point after point, he just sat scrunched in his corner, with his eyes on that japanned box. For there wasn't any doubt as to the deed or the signature—that was the worst of it. Dan'l Webster twisted and turned and thumped his fist on the table, but he couldn't get away from that. He offered to compromise the case; the stranger wouldn't hear of it. He pointed out the property had increased in value, and state senators ought to be worth more; the stranger stuck to the letter of the law. He was a great lawyer, Dan'l Webster, but we know who's the King of Lawyers, as the Good Book tells us, and it seemed as if, for the first time, Dan'l Webster had met his match.

Finally, the stranger yawned a little. "Your spirited efforts on behalf of your client do you credit, Mr. Webster," he said, "but if you have no more arguments to adduce, I'm rather pressed for time . . ." and Jabez Stone shuddered.

Dan'l Webster's brow looked dark as a thundercloud.

"Pressed or not, you shall not have this man!" he thundered. "Mr. Stone is an American citizen, and no American citizen may be forced into the service of a foreign prince. We fought England for that in '12 and we'll fight all hell for it again!"

"Foreign?" said the stranger. "And who calls me a foreigner?"

"Well, I never yet heard of the dev—of your claiming American citizenship," said Dan'l Webster with surprise.

"And who with better right?" said the stranger with one of his terrible smiles. "When the first wrong was done to the first Indian, I was there. When the first slaver put out for the Congo, I stood on her deck. Am I not in your books and stories and beliefs, from the first settlements on? Am I not spoken of still in every church in New England? 'Tis true the North claims me for a Southerner and the South for a Northerner, but I am neither. I am merely an honest American like yourself—and of the best descent—for, to tell the truth, Mr. Webster, though I don't like to boast of it, my name is older in this country than yours."

"Aha!" said Dan'l Webster with the veins standing out in his forehead. "Then I stand on the Constitution! I demand a trial for my client!"

"The case is hardly one for an ordinary court," said the stranger, his eyes flickering. "And, indeed, the lateness of the hour—"

"Let it be any court you choose, so it is an American judge and an American jury!" said Dan'l Webster in his pride. "Let it be the quick or the dead; I'll abide the issue!"

"You have said it," said the stranger, and pointed his finger at the door. And with that, and all of a sudden, there was a rushing of wind outside and a noise of footsteps. They came, clear and distinct, through the night. And yet they were not like the footsteps of living men.

"In God's name, who comes by so late?" cried Jabez Stone in an ague of fear.

"The jury Mr. Webster demands," said the stranger, sipping at his boiling glass. "You must pardon the rough appearance of one or two; they will have come a long way."

And with that the fire burned blue and the door blew open and twelve men entered, one by one.

If Jabez Stone had been sick with terror

before, he was blind with terror now. For there was Walter Butler, the loyalist, who spread fire and horror through the Mohawk Valley in the times of the Revolution; and there was Simon Girty, the renegade, who saw white men burned at the stake and whooped with the Indians to see them burn. His eyes were green, like a catamount's, and the stains on his hunting shirt did not come from the blood of the deer. King Philip was there, wild and proud as he had been in life, with the great gash in his head that gave him his death wound, and cruel Governor Dale, who broke men on the wheel. There was Morton of Merry Mount, who so vexed the Plymouth Colony, with his flushed, loose, handsome face and his hate of the godly. There was Teach, the bloody pirate, with his black beard curling on his breast. The Reverend John Smeet, with his strangler's hands and his Geneva gown, walked as daintily as he had to the gallows. The red print of the rope was still around his neck, but he carried a perfumed handkerchief in one hand. One and all, they came into the room with the fires of hell still upon them, and the stranger named their names and their deeds as they came, till the tale of twelve was told. Yet the stranger had told the truth—they had all played a part in America.

"Are you satisfied with the jury, Mr. Webster?" said the stranger mockingly, when they had taken their places.

The sweat stood upon Dan'l Webster's brow, but his voice was clear.

"Quite satisfied," he said. "Though I miss General Arnold from the company."

"Benedict Arnold is engaged upon other business," said the stranger, with a glower. "Ah, you asked for a justice, I believe."

He pointed his finger once more, and a tall man, soberly clad in Puritan garb, with the burning gaze of the fanatic, stalked into the room and took his judge's place.

"Justice Hathorne is a jurist of experience," said the stranger. "He presided at certain witch trials once held in Salem. There were others who repented of the business later, but not he."

"Repent of such notable wonders and undertakings?" said the stern old justice. "Nay, hang them—hang them all!" And he muttered to himself in a way that struck ice into the soul of Jabez Stone.

Then the trial began, and, as you might expect, it didn't look anyways good for the defense. And Jabez Stone didn't make much of a witness in his own behalf. He took one look at Simon Girty and screeched, and they had to put him back in his corner in a kind of swoon.

It didn't halt the trial, though; the trial went on, as trials do. Dan'l Webster had faced some hard juries and hanging judges in his time, but this was the hardest he'd ever faced, and he knew it. They sat there with a kind of glitter in their eyes, and the stranger's smooth voice went on and on. Every time he'd raise an objection, it'd be "Objection sustained," but whenever Dan'l objected, it'd be "Objection denied." Well, you couldn't expect fair play from a fellow like this Mr. Scratch.

It got to Dan'l in the end, and he began to heat, like iron in the forge. When he got up to speak he was going to flay that stranger with every trick known to the law, and the judge and jury too. He didn't care if it was contempt of court or what would happen to him for it. He didn't care any more what happened to Jabez Stone. He just got madder and madder, thinking of what he'd say. And yet, curiously enough, the more he thought about it, the less he was able to arrange his speech in his mind.

Till, finally, it was time for him to get up on his feet, and he did so, all ready to bust out with lightnings and denunciations. But before he started he looked over the judge and jury for a moment, such being his custom. And he noticed the glitter in their eyes was twice as strong as before, and they all leaned forward. Like hounds just before they get the fox, they looked, and the blue mist of evil in the room thickened as he watched them. Then he saw what he'd been about to do, and he wiped his forehead, as a man might who's just escaped falling into a pit in the dark.

For it was him they'd come for, not only Jabez Stone. He read it in the glitter of their eyes and in the way the stranger hid his mouth with one hand. And if he fought them with their own weapons, he'd fall into their power; he knew that, though he couldn't have told you how. It was his own anger and horror that burned in their eyes; and he'd have to wipe that out or the case was lost. He stood there for a moment, his black eyes burning like anthracite. And then he began to speak.

He started off in a low voice, though you could hear every word. They say he could call on the harps of the blessed when he chose. And this was just as simple and easy as a man could talk. But he didn't start out by condemning or reviling. He was talking about the things that make a country a country, and a man a man.

And he began with the simple things that everybody's known and felt—the freshness of a fine morning when you're young, and the taste of food when you're hungry, and the new day that's every day when you're a child. He took them up and he turned them in his hands. They were good things for any man. But without freedom, they sickened. And when he talked of those enslaved, and the sorrows of slavery, his voice got like a big bell. He talked of the early days of America and the men who had made those days. It wasn't a spread-eagle speech, but he made you see it. He admitted all the wrong that had ever been done. But he showed how,

out of the wrong and the right; the suffering and the starvations, something new had come. And everybody had played a part in it, even the traitors.

Then he turned to Jabez Stone and showed him as he was—an ordinary man who'd had hard luck and wanted to change it. And, because he'd wanted to change it, now he was going to be punished for all eternity. And yet there was good in Jabez Stone, and he showed that good. He was hard and mean, in some ways, but he was a man. There was sadness in being a man, but it was a proud thing too. And he showed what the pride of it was till you couldn't help feeling it. Yes, even in hell, if a man was a man, you'd know it. And he wasn't pleading for any one person any more, though his voice rang like an organ. He was telling the story and the failures and the endless journey of mankind. They got tricked and trapped and bamboozled, but it was a great journey. And no demon that was ever foaled could know the inwardness of it—it took a man to do that.

The fire began to die on the hearth and the wind before morning to blow. The light was getting gray in the room when Dan'l Webster finished. And his words came back at the end to New Hampshire ground, and the one spot of land that each man loves and clings to. He painted a picture of that, and to each one of that jury he spoke of things long forgotten. For his voice could search the heart, and that was his gift and his strength. And to one, his voice was like the forest and its secrecy, and to another like the sea and the storms of the sea; and one heard the cry of his lost nation in it, and another saw a little harmless scene he hadn't remembered for years. But each saw something. And when Dan'l Webster finished he didn't know whether or not he'd saved Jabez Stone. But he knew he'd done a miracle. For the glitter was gone from the eyes of judge and jury, and, for the moment, they were men again, and knew they were men.

"The defense rests," said Dan'l Webster and stood there like a mountain. His ears were still ringing with his speech, and he didn't hear anything else till he heard Judge Hathorne say, "The jury will retire to consider its verdict."

Walter Butler rose in his place and his face had a dark, gay pride on it.

"The jury has considered its verdict," he said and looked the stranger full in the eye. "We find for the defendant, Jabez Stone."

With that, the smile left the stranger's face, but Walter Butler did not flinch.

"Perhaps 'tis not strictly in accordance with the evidence," he said, "but even the damned may salute the eloquence of Mr. Webster."

With that, the long crow of a rooster split the gray morning sky, and judge and jury were gone from the room like a puff of smoke and as if they had never been there. The stranger returned to Dan'l Webster, smiling wryly.

"Major Butler was always a bold man," he said. "I had not thought him quite so bold. Nevertheless, my congratulations, as between two gentlemen."

"I'll have that paper first, if you please," said Dan'l Webster, and he took it and tore it into four pieces. It was queerly warm to the touch. "And now," he said, "I'll have you!" and his hand came down like a bear trap on the stranger's arm. For he knew that once you bested anybody like Mr. Scratch in fair fight, his power on you was gone. And he could see that Mr. Scratch knew it too.

The stranger twisted and wriggled, but he couldn't get out of that grip. "Come, come, Mr. Webster," he said, smiling palely. "This sort of thing is ridic—ouch! —is ridiculous. If you're worried about the costs of the case, naturally, I'd be glad to pay—"

"And so you shall!" said Dan'l Web-

ster, shaking him till his teeth rattled. "For you'll sit right down at that table and draw up a document, promising never to bother Jabez Stone nor his heirs or assigns nor any other New Hampshireman till doomsday! For any hades we want to raise in this state, we can raise ourselves, without assistance from strangers."

"Ouch!" said the stranger. "Ouch! Well, they never did run very big to the barrel, but—ouch!—I agree!"

So he sat down and drew up the document. But Dan'l Webster kept his hand on his coat collar all the time.

"And now may I go?" said the stranger, quite humble, when Dan'l'd seen the document was in proper and legal form.

"Go?" said Dan'l, giving him another shake. "I'm still trying to figure out what I'll do with you. For you've settled the costs of the case, but you haven't settled with me. I think I'll take you back to Marshfield," he said, kind of reflective. "I've got a ram there named Goliath that can butt through an iron door. I'd kind of like to turn you loose in his field and see what he'd do."

Well, with that the stranger began to beg and to plead. And he begged and he pled so humble that finally Dan'l, who was naturally kindhearted, agreed to let him go. The stranger seemed terrible grateful for that and said, just to show they were friends, he'd tell Dan'l's fortune before leaving. So Dan'l agreed to that, though he didn't take much stock in fortunetellers ordinarily. But, naturally, the stranger was a little different.

Well, he pried and he peered at the lines in Dan'l's hands. And he told him one thing and another that was quite remarkable. But they were all in the past.

"Yes, all that's true, and it happened," said Dan'l Webster. "But what's to come in the future?"

The stranger grinned, kind of happily, and shook his head.

"The future's not as you think it," he said. "It's dark. You have a great ambition, Mr. Webster."

"I have," said Dan'l firmly, for everybody knew he wanted to be President.

"It seems almost within your grasp," said the stranger, "but you will not attain it. Lesser men will be made President and you will be passed over."

"And, if I am, I'll still be Daniel Webster," said Dan'l. "Say on."

"You have two strong sons," said the stranger, shaking his head. "You look to found a line. But each will die in war and neither reach greatness."

"Live or die, they are still my sons," said Dan'l Webster. "Say on."

"You have made great speeches," said the stranger. "You will make more."

"Ah," said Dan'l Webster.

"But the last great speech you make will turn many of your own against you," said the stranger. "They will call you Ichabod; they will call you by other names. Even in New England some will say you have turned your coat and sold your country, and their voices will be loud against you till you die."

"So it is an honest speech, it does not matter what men say," said Dan'l Webster. Then he looked at the stranger and their glances locked.

"One question," he said. "I have fought for the Union all my life. Will I see that fight won against those who would tear it apart?"

"Not while you live," said the stranger grimly, "but it will be won. And after you are dead, there are thousands who will fight for your cause, because of words that you spoke."

"Why, then, you long-barreled, slab-sided, lantern-jawed, fortune-telling note shaver," said Dan'l Webster with a great roar of laughter, "be off with you to your own place before I put my mark on you! For, by the thirteen original colonies, I'd go to the Pit itself to save the Union!"

And with that he drew back his foot for a kick that would have stunned a horse. It was only the tip of his shoe that caught the stranger, but he went flying out of the door with his collecting box under his arm.

"And now," said Dan'l Webster, seeing Jabez Stone beginning to rouse from his swoon, "let's see what's left in the jug, for it's dry work talking all night. I hope there's pie for breakfast, Neighbor Stone."

But they say that whenever the devil comes near Marshfield, even now, he gives it a wide berth. And he hasn't been seen in the state of New Hampshire from that day to this. I'm not talking about Massachusetts or Vermont.

How Jack O'Lanterns Came To Be

by Zora Neale Hurston

Miss Hurston became interested in Negro folklore for two main reasons: she remembered tales and characters from her youth, and she was trained in anthropology by Franz Boas. The remarkable collection of folklore which she published in Mules and Men *(1935) is the result of extensive field work which she did in Florida and Louisiana. The herculean exploits of Big Sixteen and the ease with which he eventually triumphs over the devil himself are reminiscent of the deeds of other mythical champions, but the denouement, with its explanation of the real genesis of the ignis fatuus or will-o'-the-wisp, seems peculiarly regional.*

It was slavery time . . . when Big Sixteen was a man. They called 'im Sixteen 'cause dat was de number of de shoe he wore. He was big and strong and Ole Massa looked to him to do everything.

One day Ole Massa said, "Big Sixteen, Ah b'lieve Ah want you to move dem sills Ah had hewed out down in he swamp."

"I yassuh, Massa."

Big Sixteen went down in de swamp and picked up dem 12 × 12's and brought 'em on up to de house and stack 'em. No one man ain't never toted a 12 × 12 befo' nor since.

So Ole Massa said one day, "Go fetch in de mules. Ah want to look 'em over."

Big Sixteen went on down to de pasture and caught dem mules by de bridle but they was contrary and balky and he tore de bridles to pieces pullin' on 'em, so he picked one of 'em up under each arm and brought 'em up to Old Massa.

He says, "Big Sixteen, if you kin tote a pair of balky mules, you kin do anything. You kin ketch de Devil."

"Yassuh, Ah kin, if you git me a nine-pound hammer and a pick and shovel!"

Ole Massa got Sixteen de things he ast for and tole 'im to go ahead and bring him de Devil.

Big Sixteen went out in front of de house and went to diggin'. He was diggin' nearly a month befo' he got where he wanted. Then he took his hammer and went and knocked on de Devil's door. Devil answered de door hisself.

"Who dat out dere?"

"It's Big Sixteen."

"What you want?"

"Wanta have a word wid you for a minute."

Soon as de Devil poked his head out de door, Sixteen lammed him over de head wid dat hammer and picked 'im up and carried 'im back to Old Massa.

Ole Massa looked at de dead Devil and hollered, "Take dat ugly thing 'way from here, quick! Ah didn't think you'd ketch de Devil sho 'nuff."

So Sixteen picked up de Devil and throwed 'im back down de hole.

Way after while, Big Sixteen died and went up to Heben. But Peter looked at him and tole 'im to g'wan 'way from dere. He was too powerful. He might git outa order and there wouldn't be nobody to handle 'im. But he had to go somewhere so he went on to hell.

Soon as he got to de gate de Devil's children was playin' in de yard and they seen 'im and run to de house, says, "Mama, mama! Dat man's out dere dat kilt papa!"

So she called 'im in de house and shet de door. When Sixteen got dere she handed 'im a li'l piece of fire and said, "You ain't comin' in here. Here, take dis hot coal and g'wan off and start you a hell uh yo' own."

So when you see a Jack O'Lantern in de woods at night you know it's Big Sixteen wid his piece of fire lookin' for a place to go.

● From *Mules and Men,* by Zora Neale Hurston. Copyright, 1935, by Zora Neale Hurston. Published by J. B. Lippincott Company.

The Devil's Pretty Daughter

by Vance Randolph

Vance Randolph has been for many years a sedulous collector of Ozark traditions and tales. His versions derive from a number of informants and are transcribed with a minimum of editorial revision. Often, too, the tales that he records are Arkansas or Missouri variants of tales that appear in many other parts of the world. In "The Devil's Pretty Daughter" a talking rooster and magical obstacles to the hero's flight are combined with realistic details of hill-country life. Two ancient folklore beliefs are also introduced —the devil's inability to cross running water and his helplessness when confronted with Holy Scripture. The living-happily-ever-after denouement is in the best tradition of folk narrative.

One time there was a man lived in a fine house, and he owned a big scope of land. Some folks thought he was the Devil, and they used to call him that behind his back. But all the young fellows for miles around wanted to get a job on his place, because he had a pretty daughter named Ruthie-ma-Toothy. The old Devil hired everybody that come along and worked 'em till they was nothing but skin and bones. But nary one of them boys ever got next to Ruthie. She just laughed and never paid no mind to what they said at all.

There was one fellow named Alf Knight worked there seven years, and he bantered Ruthie-ma-Toothy to run off with him. She says he better shut up, because the big black rooster can talk and tell the Devil everything that is going on. So Alf kept out of the rooster's way after that. But he went right on a-bantering her to run off with him. Finally Ruthie saddled two horses, and then she give the big black rooster a bushel of corn. "Let's hit the

mountain right now," she says. "Soon as the rooster eats all the corn, he'll tell Pop we're gone."

Alf and Ruthie rode fast as they could, but pretty soon they looked back, and there come the old Devil on his big black horse. He was smelling their track just like a tree-dog follers possums. It looked like the old Devil was going to catch them sure, but Ruthie-ma-Toothy pulled some bramble-briars out of her pocket. "Throw them down in the road behind us," she says, and Alf done it. The bramble-briars took root and growed a mile a minute; they kept on growing till the valley was plumb full, and it looked like a high level prairie. The old Devil had to ride a thousand miles out of his way to get around that briar-patch.

Alf and Ruthie kept on a-riding, and after while they looked back, and there come the old Devil still follering the trail. It looked like he was going to catch them sure, but Ruthie-ma-Toothy pulled three little gravels out of her pocket. "Throw them down in the road behind us," she says, and Alf done it. The little gravels took root and growed a mile a minute; the whole country was covered with loose gravels and quicksand fifty foot deep. There was long chat-piles everywhere, like what they got up around Joplin, only bigger. The old Devil had to ride two thousand miles out of his way to get around that gravel-bar.

Alf figured they had the old Devil beat this time, but Ruthie knowed better. So they kept on a-riding, and after while they looked back, and sure enough there come the old Devil. It looked like he was going to catch them after all, but Ruthie-ma-Toothy pulled out a bottle of water. "Pour it down in the road behind us," she says, and Alf done it. The water took root and growed a mile a minute; the creek busted out of its banks and run all over the country. There was big barns a-floating off down stream, and haystacks with chickens a-riding on 'em. The old Devil cain't cross running water, and he had to ride three thousand miles out of his way to get around that flood.

Alf and Ruthie kept on a-riding, but along the next evening they looked back, and there come the old Devil. He was a-moving pretty slow now, but he was still follering the trail. It looked like he was going to catch 'em soon or late, no matter what happened. Ruthie-ma-Toothy pulled a little Bible out of her pocket. "Throw it down on the road behind us," she says, and Alf done it. The little Bible took root and growed a mile a minute; the whole country was full of paper with holy words on it, and everybody knows the old Devil cain't stand Bibles. He couldn't get through and he couldn't go round, so finally he just give up and went back home.

Alf and Ruthie kept on a-riding, and pretty soon they come to the place where his folks lived. So they went in for dinner, and everybody liked Ruthie-ma-Toothy fine. Next day there was a preacher come along, so her and Alf got married without no more foolishness. She took up piecing quilts and making soap and having babies, and never mixed in no devilment. Everybody for miles around thought Ruthie was wonderful. Alf he thought so too, and him and her lived happy ever after.

III

GHOST TALES

Under whatever name they appear—specters, wraiths, phantoms, apparitions, revenants—ghosts are a familiar part of folklore. The spirits of the departed, restless because of some unsatisfied commitment or lured back to earth because of curiosity or friendship, play a universal role and are honored alike by Christians (All Souls' Day) and Buddhists (Feast of the Lanterns). Ghosts are tangible or intangible: sometimes, like Hamlet's father, they appear only to a chosen few; sometimes they are disembodied voices or merely shadows; and sometimes they participate in the normal activities of mankind, such as eating, drinking, and talking. To the narrator of ghost stories the revenant is versatile and protean. Ghosts can laugh, shriek, cough, wail, yell, moan, and holler, and at least in European stories they can clank chains in deserted castles. Traditionally a ghost could not cross water, was obliged to return to his domicile before cockcrow, and could be exorcized by a cleric using proper rituals. In the United States, despite the prevalence in various locales of the tale about the ghostly hitchhiker, ghost stories are given less credence than other forms of folklore and are usually told for their humorous effect. As B. A. Botkin has observed, "To have fun with ghosts, as with witches, the story-teller must not take them too seriously." But at least from the time of Daniel Defoe the ghost story has had a place in literature, and the Headless Horseman and Peter Rugg are valuable American contributions to the gallery of revenants. More than most tales which utilize folklore materials, the success of ghost stories depends on the narrator's ability to create a mood built on suspension of disbelief. Washington Irving's "Legend of Sleepy Hollow" is a classic example of this mood, for here is a tale in which style, tone, and substance all contribute substantially to the totality of the story.

THE GHOST IN THE MILL

by Harriet Beecher Stowe

Mrs. Stowe is commonly identified as the author of the most successful propagandist novel in American literature, but she was also adept at presenting New England character and manners. Depending partly on her own observation and partly on the reminiscences of her husband, Calvin Stowe, she wrote many stories of Yankee life which revealed her mastery of place and idiom. She created Sam Lawson as a narrator for such tales—a blacksmith and handy man who loved to talk, who had a fund of anecdotes to retail, and who inserted homely analogies, proverbs, and bits of sly moralizing into his stories. Sam often sat in the kitchen as he yarned away, and two boys and their family provided the audience. "The Ghost in the Mill" is the initial story in the collection called Sam Lawson's Oldtown Fireside Stories *(1872), and is, of course, told by Sam Lawson.*

Come, Sam, tell us a story," said I, as Harry and I crept to his knees, in the glow of the bright evening firelight, while Aunt Lois was busily rattling the tea-things, and grandmamma was quietly setting the heel of a blue-mixed yarn stocking at the other end of the fireplace.

In those days we had no magazines and daily papers, each reeling off a serial story. Once a week, the *Columbian Sentinel* came from Boston with its slender stock of news and editorial; but all the multiform devices, pictorial, narrative, and poetical, which keep the mind of the present generation ablaze with excitement, had not then even an existence. There was no theater, no opera; there were in Oldtown no parties or balls, except, perhaps, the annual election or Thanksgiving festival; and when winter came, and the sun went down at half past four o'clock and left the long dark hours of evening to be provided for, the necessity of amusement became urgent. Hence in those days chimney-corner story-telling became an art and an accomplishment. Society then was full of traditions and narratives which had all the uncertain

glow and shifting mystery of the firelit hearth upon them. They were told to sympathetic audiences, by the rising and falling light of the solemn embers, with the hearth crickets filling up every pause. Then the aged told their stories to the young,— tales of early life, tales of war and adventure, of forest-days, of Indian captivities and escapes, of bears and wild-cats and panthers, of rattlesnakes, of witches and wizards, and strange and wonderful dreams and appearances and providences.

In those days of early Massachusetts, faith and credence were in the very air. Two-thirds of New England was then dark, unbroken forest, through whose tangled paths the mysterious winter wind groaned and shrieked and howled with weird noises and unaccountable clamors. Along the iron-bound shore the stormful Atlantic raved and thundered, and dashed its moaning waters, as if to deaden and deafen any voice that might tell of the settled life of the old civilized world, and shut us forever into the wilderness. A good story-teller, in those days, was always sure of a warm seat at the hearth-stone, and the delighted homage of children; and in all Oldtown there was no better story-teller than Sam Lawson.

"Do, do, tell us a story," said Harry, pressing upon him and opening very wide blue eyes, in which undoubting faith shone as in a mirror; "and let it be something strange, and different from common."

"Wal, I know lots o' strange things," said Sam, looking mysteriously into the fire. "Why, I know things, that ef I should tell, why, people might say they wa'n't so; but then they *is* so, for all that."

"Oh, *do, do,* tell us."

"Why, I should scare ye to death, mebbe," said Sam, doubtingly.

"Oh, pooh! no, you wouldn't," we both burst out at once.

But Sam was possessed by a reticent spirit, and loved dearly to be wooed and importuned; and so he only took up the great kitchen tongs and smote on the hick-ory forestick, when it flew apart in the middle and scattered a shower of clear, bright coals all over the hearth.

"Mercy on us, Sam Lawson!" said Aunt Lois, in an indignant voice, spinning round from her dish-washing.

"Don't you worry a grain, Miss Lois," said Sam, composedly. "I see that are stick was e'en a'most in two, and I thought I'd jest settle it. I'll sweep up the coals now," he added, vigorously applying a turkey-wing to the purpose, as he knelt on the hearth, his spare, lean figure glowing in the blaze of the firelight, and getting quite flushed with exertion.

"There, now," he said, when he had brushed over and under and between the fire-irons, and pursued the retreating ashes so far into the red, fiery citadel, that his finger-ends were burning and tingling, "that are's done now as well as Hepsy herself could 'a' done it. I allers sweeps up the haarth: I think it's part o' the man's bisness when he makes the fire. But Hepsy's so used to seein' me a-doin on't that she

don't see no kind o' merit in't. It's just as Parson Lothrop said in his sermon,—folks allers overlook their common marcies—"

"But come, Sam, that story," said Harry and I, coaxingly, pressing upon him, and pulling him down into his seat in the corner.

"Lordy massy, these 'ere young uns!" said Sam, "there's never no contentin' on 'em; ye tell 'em one story, and they jest swallows it as a dog does a gob o' meat, and they're all ready for another. What do ye want to hear now?"

Now the fact was that Sam's stories had been told us so often that they were all arranged and ticketed in our minds. We knew every word in them, and could set him right if he varied a hair from the usual track, and still the interest in them was unabated. Still we shivered, and clung to his knee at the mysterious parts, and felt gentle, cold chills run down our spines at appropriate places. We were always in the most receptive and sympathetic condi-tion. To-night, in particular, was one of those thundering stormy ones when the winds appeared to be holding a perfect mad carnival over my grandfather's house. They yelled and squealed round the cor-ners. They collected in troops and came tumbling and roaring down the chimney. They shook and rattled the buttery-door and the sink-room door and the cellar-door and the chamber-door, with a con-stant undertone of squeak and clatter, as if at every door were a cold, discontented spirit, tired of the chill outside, and long-ing for the warmth and comfort within.

"Wal, boys," said Sam, confidentially, "what'll ye have?"

"Tell us, 'Come down, come down,' " we both shouted with one voice. This was in our mind an A. No. 1 among Sam's stories.

"Ye mus'n't be frightened, now," said Sam, paternally.

"Oh, no! we ar'n't frightened *ever*," said we both in one breath.

"Not when ye go down the cellar arter cider?" said Sam, with severe scrutiny. "Ef ye should be down cellar, and the candle should go out, now?"

"I ain't," said I: "I ain't afraid of any thing. I never knew what it was to be afraid in my life."

"Wal, then," said Sam, "I'll tell ye. This 'ere's what Cap'n Eb Sawin told me when I was a boy about your bigness, I reckon.

"Cap'n Eb Sawin was a most respectable man; your gran'ther knew him very well, and he was a deacon in the church in Dedham afore he died. He was at Lexington when the fust gun was fired agin the British. He was a dreffle smart man, Cap'n Eb was, and driv team a good many years atween here and Boston. He married Lois Peabody, that was cousin to your gran'ther then. Lois was a rael sensible woman, and I've heard her tell the story as he told her, and it was jest as he told it to me, jest exactly; and I shall never forget it if I live to be nine hundred years old, like Mathusaleh.

"Ye see, along back in them times, there used to be a fellow come round these 'ere parts, spring and fall, a peddlin' goods, with his pack on his back; and his name was Jehiel Lommedieu. Nobody rightly knew where he come from. He wasn't much of a talker, but the women rather liked him, and kind o' liked to have him round; women will like some fellows, when men can't see no sort o' reason why they should, and they liked this 'ere Lommedieu, though he was kind o' mournful and thin and shad-bellied, and hadn't nothin' to say for himself. But it got to be so that the women would count and calculate, so many weeks afore 'twas time for Lommedieu to be along, and they'd make up ginger-snaps and preserves and pies, and make him stay to tea at their houses, and

feed him up on the best there was: and the story went round that he was acourtin' Phebe Ann Parker, or Phebe Ann was acourtin' him,—folks didn't rightly know which. Wal, all of a sudden Lommedieu stopped comin' round, and nobody knew why, only jest he didn't come. It turned out that Phebe Ann Parker had got a letter from him, sayin' he'd be along afore Thanksgiving, but he didn't come, neither afore nor at Thanksgiving time, nor arter, nor next spring; and finally the women they gin up lookin' for him. Some said he was dead, some said he was gone to Canada, and some said he hed gone over to the old country. Wal, as to Phebe Ann, she acted like a gal o' sense, and married 'Bijah Moss and thought no more 'bout it. She said she was sartin that all things was ordered out for the best; and it was jest as well folks couldn't always have their own way; and so in time Lommedieu was gone out o' folks' minds, much as a last year's apple-blossom. It's relly affectin' to think how little these 'ere folks is missed that's so much sot by! There ain't nobody, ef they's ever so important, but what the world gets to goin' on without 'em pretty much as it did with 'em, though there's some little flurry at fust. Wal, the last thing that was in anybody's mind was that they ever should hear from Lommedieu ag'in. But there ain't nothin' but what has its time o' turnin' up, and it seems his turn was to come.

"Wal, ye see, 'twas the nineteenth o' March, when Cap'n Eb Sawin started with a team for Boston. That day there come on about the biggest snow-storm that there'd been in them parts sence the oldest man could remember. 'Twas this 'ere fine, siftin' snow, that drives in your face like needles, with a wind to cut your nose off: it made teamin' pretty tedious work. Cap'n Eb was about the toughest man in them parts. He'd spent days in the woods aloggin', and he'd been up to the deestrict o'

Maine a lumberin', and was about up to any sort o' thing a man gen'ally could be up to; but these 'ere March winds sometimes does set on a fellow so that neither natur' nor grace can stan' 'em. The Cap'n used to say he could stan' any wind that blew one way't time for five minutes, but come to winds that blew all four p'ints at the same minit, why, they flustered him.

"Wal, that was the sort o' weather it was all day, and by sundown Cap'n Eb he got clean bewildered, so that he lost his road; and when night came on he didn't know nothin' where he was. Ye see the country was all under drift, and the air so thick with snow that he couldn't see a foot afore him, and the fact was he got off the Boston road without knowin' it and come out at a pair o' bars nigh upon Sherburn, where old Cack Sparrock's mill is. Your gran'ther used to know old Cack, boys. He was a drefful drinkin' old crittur that lived there all alone in the woods by himself, a tendin' saw and grist mill. He wa'n't allers jest what he was then. Time was that Cack was a pretty consid'rably likely young man, and his wife was a very respectable woman,—Deacon Amos Petengalls's dater, from Sherburn.

"But ye see, the year arter his wife died, Cack he gin up goin' to meetin' Sundays, and all the tithingmen and selectmen could do they couldn't get him out to meetin'; and when a man neglects means o' grace and sanctuary privileges there ain't no sayin' *what* he'll do next. Why, boys, jist think on't! an immortal crittur lyin' round loose all day Sunday, and not puttin' on so much as a clean shirt, when all 'spectable folks has on their best close, and is to meetin' worshippin' the Lord! What can you spect to come of it, when he lies idlin' round in his old week-day close, fishing, or some sich, but what the Devil should be arter him at last, as he was arter old Cack?"

Here Sam winked impressively to my grandfather in the opposite corner, to call his attention to the moral which he was interweaving with his narrative.

"Wal, ye see, Cap'n Eb he told me, that when he come to them bars and looked up, and saw the dark a-comin' down and the storm a-thickenin' up, he felt that things was gettin' pretty consid'able serious. There was a dark piece o' woods on ahead of him inside the bars, and he knew come to get in there the light would give out clean. So he jest thought he'd take the hoss out o' the team, and go ahead a little, and see where he was. So he driv his oxen up ag'in the fence, and took out the hoss, and got on him, and pushed along through the woods, not rightly knowin' where he was goin'.

"Wal, afore long he see a light through the trees, and sure enough he come out to Cack Sparrock's old mill.

"It was a pretty consid'able gloomy sort of a place, that are old mill was. There was a great fall of water that come rushin' down the rocks and fell in a deep pool, and it sounded sort o' wild and lonesome, but Cap'n Eb he knocked on the door with his whiphandle and got in.

"There, to be sure, sot old Cack beside a great blazin' fire, with his rum-jug at his elbow. He was a drefful fellow to drink, Cack was. For all that, there was some good in him, for he was pleasant-spoken and 'bliging, and he made the Cap'n welcome.

"'Ye see, Cack,' said Cap'n Eb, 'I'm off my road, and got snowed up down by your bars,' says he.

"'Want ter know!' says Cack. 'Calculate you'll jest have to camp down here till mornin',' says he.

"Wal, so old Cack he got out his tin lantern, and went with Cap'n Eb back to the bars to help him fetch along his critturs; he told him he could put 'em under the mill-shed. So they got the critturs up to the shed and got the cart under; and by that time the storm was awful.

"But Cack he made a great roarin' fire, 'cause ye see Cack allers had slab-wood a plenty from his mill, and a roarin' fire is jest so much company. It sort o' keeps a fellow's spirits up, a good fire does. So Cack he sot on his old teakettle and made a swingeing lot o' toddy, and he and Cap'n Eb were havin' a tol'able comfortable time there. Cack was a pretty good hand to tell stories, and Cap'n Eb warn't no ways backward in that line, and kep' up his end pretty well, and pretty soon they was a roarin' and haw-hawin' inside about as loud as the storm outside; when all of a sudden, 'bout midnight, there came a loud rap on the door.

" 'Lordy massy! what's that?' says Cack. Folks is rather startled allers to be checked up sudden when they are a carryin' on and laughin', and it was such an awful blowy night, it was a little scary to have a rap on the door.

"Wal, they waited a minit, and didn't hear nothin' but the wind a screechin' round the chimbley; and old Cack was jest goin' on with his story, when the rap come ag'in, harder'n ever, as if it'd shook the door open.

" 'Wal,' says old Cack, 'if 'tis the Devil, we'd jest as good's open, and have it out with him to onst,' says he; and so he got up and opened the door, and, sure enough, there was old Ketury there. Expect you've heard your grandma tell about old Ketury. She used to come to meetin's sometimes, and her husband was one o' the prayin' Indians; but Ketury was one of the rael wild sort, and you couldn't no more convert *her* than you could convert a wild-cat or a painter (panther). Lordy massy! Ketury used to come to meetin', and sit there on them Indian benches, and when the second bell was a-tollin', and when Parson Lothrop and his wife was comin' up the broad aisle, and everybody in the house ris' up and stood, Ketury would sit there and look at 'em out o' the corner o'

her eyes, and folks used to say she rattled them necklaces o' rattlesnakes' tails and wild-cat teeth and sich like heathen trumpery, and looked for all the world as if the spirit of the old Sarpent himself was in her. I've seen her sit and look at Lady Lothrop out of the corner o' her eyes, and her old brown baggy neck would kind o' twist and work; and her eyes they looked so, that 'twas enough to scare a body. For all the world she looked jest as if she was aworkin' up to spring at her. Lady Lothrop was jest as kind to Ketury as she always was to every poor crittur. She'd bow and smile as gracious to her when meetin' was over, and she come down the aisle, passin' out o' meetin'; but Ketury never took no notice. Ye see, Ketury's father was one o' those great powwows of Martha's Vineyard, and people used to say she was set apart when she was a child to the service o' the Devil; any way, she never could be made nothin' of in a Christian way. She come down to Parson Lothrop's study once or twice to be catechised, but he couldn't get a word out o' her, and she kind o' seemed to sit scornful while he was atalkin'. Folks said, if it was in old times, Ketury wouldn't have been allowed to go on so, but Parson Lothrop's so sort o' mild, he let her take pretty much her own way. Everybody thought that Ketury was a witch; at least she knew consid'able more'n she ought to know, and so they was kind o' 'fraid on her. Cap'n Eb says he never see a fellow seem scareder than Cack did when he see Ketury astandin' there.

"Why, ye see, boys, she was as withered and wrinkled and brown as an old frosted punkin-vine, and her little snaky eyes sparkled and snapped, and it made yer head kind o' dizzy to look at 'em, and folks used to say that anybody that Ketury got mad at was sure to get the worst of it, fust or last; and so, no matter what day or hour Ketury had a mind to rap at anybody's door, folks gen'lly thought it was best to let her in; but then, they never thought her coming was for any good, for she was just like the wind,—she came when the fit was on her, she staid jest so long as it pleased her, and went when she got ready, and not before. Ketury understood English, and could talk it well enough, but always seemed to scorn it, and was allers mowin' and mutterin' to herself in Indian, and winkin' and blinkin' as if she saw more folks round than you did, so that she wa'n't no ways pleasant company; and yet everybody took good care to be polite to her.

"So old Cack asked her to come in, and didn't make no question where she come from, or what she come on; but he knew it was twelve good miles from where she lived to his hut, and the snow was drifted above her middle, and Cap'n Eb declared that there wa'n't no track nor sign o' a track, of anybody's coming through that snow next morning."

"How did she get there, then?" said I.

" 'Didn't ye never see brown leaves a ridin' on the wind? Well,' Cap'n Eb, he says, 'she came on the wind,' and I'm sure it was strong enough to fetch her. But Cack he got her down into the warm corner, and he poured her out a mug o' hot toddy, and give her; but ye see her bein' there sort o' stopped the conversation, for she sot there a rockin' back'ards and for'ards, a-sippin' her toddy, and a-mutterin' and lookin' up chimbley.

"Cap'n Eb says in all his born days he never hearn such screeches and yells as the wind give over that chimbley; and old Cack got so frightened you could fairly hear his teeth chatter.

"But Cap'n Eb he was a putty brave man, and he wa'n't goin' to have conversation stopped by no woman, witch or no witch; and so, when he see her mutterin', and lookin' up chimbley, he spoke up, and says he, 'Well, Ketury, what do you see?'

says he. 'Come, out with it; don't keep it to yourself.' Ye see Cap'n Eb was a hearty fellow, and then he was a leetle warmed up with the toddy.

"Then he said he see an evil kind o' smile on Ketury's face, and she rattled her necklace o' bones and snakes' tails; and her eyes seem to snap, and she looked up the chimbley and called out, 'Come down, come down. Let's see who ye be.'

"Then there was a scratchin' and a rumblin' and a groan; and a pair of feet come down the chimbley, and stood right in the middle of the haarth, the toes pi'ntin' out'rds, with shoes and silver buckles a-shinin' in the firelight. Cap'n Eb says he never comé so near bein' scared in his life, and as to old Cack he jest wilted right down in his chair.

"Then old Ketury got up, and reached her stick up chimbley, and called out louder, 'Come down, come down! let's see who ye be'; and sure enough down came a pair o' legs, and j'ined right on to the feet; good fair legs they was, with ribbed stockings and leather breeches.

" 'Wal, we're in for it now,' says Cap'n Eb; 'go it, Ketury, and let's have the rest on him.'

"Ketury didn't seem to mind him; she stood there as stiff as a stake and kep' callin' out, 'Come down, come down! let's see who ye be,' and then come down the body of a man with a brown coat and yellow vest, and j'ined right on to the legs; but there wa'n't no arms to it. Then Ketury shook her stick up chimbley, and called, 'Come down, come down!' And there came down a pair o' arms, and went on each side o' the body; and there stood a man all finished, only there wa'n't no head on him.

" 'Wal, Ketury,' says Cap'n Eb, 'this 'ere's getting serious. I 'spec you must finish him up, and let's see what he wants of us.'

"Then Ketury called out once more, louder'n ever, 'Come down, come down!

let's see who ye be'; and sure enough, down comes a man's head and settled on the shoulders straight enough, and Cap'n Eb, the minit he sot eyes on him knew he was Jehiel Lommedieu.

"Old Cack knew him too, and he fell flat on his face, and prayed the Lord to have mercy on his soul; but Cap'n Eb he was for gettin' to the bottom of matters, and not have his scare for nothin', so he says to him, 'What do you want, now you have come?'

"The man he didn't speak, he only sort o' moaned and p'inted to the chimbley; he seemed to try to speak but couldn't, for ye see it isn't often that his sort o' folks is permitted to speak; but just then there came a screechin' blast o' wind, and blowed the door open, and blowed the smoke and fire all out into the room, and there seemed to be a whirlwind and darkness and moans and screeches; and when it all cleared up, Ketury and the man was both gone, and only old Cack lay on the ground rolling and moaning as if he'd die.

"Wal, Cap'n Eb he picked him up, and built up the fire, and sort o' comforted him up, 'cause the crittur was in distress o' mind that was drefful. The awful Providence ye see had awakened him, and his sin had been set home to his soul, and he was under such conviction that it all had to come out,—how old Cack's father had murdered poor Lommedieu for his money, and Cack had been privy to it, and helped his father build the body up in that very chimbley; and he said that he hadn't had neither peace nor rest since then, and that was what had driv' him away from ordinances, for ye know sinnin' will always make a man leave prayin'. Wal, Cack didn't live but a day or two. Cap'n Eb he got the minister o' Sherburn and one o' the selectmen down to see him; and they took his deposition. He seemed railly quite penitent; and Parson Carryl he prayed with him, and was faithful in settin' home

the providence to his soul, and so at the eleventh hour poor old Cack might have got in,—at least it looks a leetle like it. He was distressed to think he couldn't live to be hung. He sort o' seemed to think, that if he was fairly tried, and hung, it would make it all square. He made Parson Carryl promise to have the old mill pulled down and bury the body, and after he was dead they did it.

"Cap'n Eb he was one of a party o' eight that pulled down the chimbley, and there sure enough was the skeleton of poor Lommedieu.

"So there you see, boys, there can't be no iniquity so hid but what it'll come out. The wild Indians of the forest and the stormy winds and tempests j'ined together to bring out this 'ere."

"For my part," said Aunt Lois sharply, "I never believed that story."

"Why, Lois," said my grandmother, "Cap'n Eb Sawin was a regular church-member, and a most respectable man."

"Law, mother, I don't doubt he thought so. I suppose he and Cack got drinking toddy together, till he got asleep, and dreamed it. I wouldn't believe such a thing if it did happen right before my face and eyes. I should only think I was crazy, that's all."

"Come, Lois, if I was you I wouldn't talk so like a Sadducee," said my grandmother. "What would become of all the accounts in Dr. Cotton Mather's 'Magnilly' if folks were like you?"

"Wal," said Sam Lawson, drooping contemplatively over the coals, and gazing into the fire, "there's a putty consid'able sight o' things in this world that's true; and then ag'in there's a sight o' things that ain't true. Now, my old gran'ther used to say, 'Boys,' says he, 'if ye want to lead a pleasant and prosperous life, ye must contrive allers to keep jest the *happy medium* between truth and falsehood.' Now, that are's my doctrine."

THE LEGEND OF SLEEPY HOLLOW

FOUND AMONG THE PAPERS OF THE LATE DIEDRICH KNICKERBOCKER

by Washington Irving

No American writer has been more successful in the artistic use of folklore than Irving. Although scholarship has established that few of his themes were original and that, on the contrary, he borrowed freely from European folklore, there can be no doubt about his skill in adapting foreign tales and characters to his beloved Hudson Valley setting. In the famous account of Ichabod Crane he carefully established the mood and tone of the narrative by emphasizing the appetite of the neighborhood for the marvelous and by alluding to the traditions that were generally current. He also disavowed responsibility for the final truth of the narrative and instead, in the best tradition of the taleteller, invoked gossip and rumor as his authorities. The ambiguity which results adds to the dreamlike quality and charm of the story. Daniel Hoffman has pointed out that, in addition to other legendary aspects of the tale, it is possible to identify Ichabod Crane as the rustic Yankee, literate and sophisticated but also credulous and timid, and Brom Bones as the typical backwoodsman, uncouth, uneducated, but spoiling for a fight. In the historic encounters between these two American folk heroes, the backwoodsman usually emerged triumphant.[1]

> *A pleasing land of drowsy head it was,*
> *Of dreams that wave before the half-shut eye,*
> *And of gay castles in the clouds that pass,*
> *Forever flushing round a summer sky.*
> Castle of Indolence

In the bosom of one of those spacious coves which indent the eastern shore of the Hudson, at that broad expansion of the river denominated by the ancient Dutch navigators the Tappan Zee, and where they always prudently shortened sail and implored the protection of St. Nicholas when they crossed, there lies a small market town or rural port, which by some is called Greensburgh, but which is more generally and properly known by the name of Tarry Town. This name was given, we are told, in former days, by the good housewives of the adjacent country, from the inveterate propensity of their husbands to linger about the village tavern on mar-

1. See Daniel G. Hoffman, "Irving's Use of American Folklore in 'The Legend of Sleepy Hollow,' " *Publications of the Modern Language Association of America* (June, 1953), LXVIII, 425–35.

ket days. Be that as it may, I do not vouch for the fact, but merely advert to it, for the sake of being precise and authentic. Not far from this village, perhaps about two miles, there is a little valley or rather lap of land among high hills, which is one of the quietest places in the whole world. A small brook glides through it, with just murmur enough to lull one to repose; and the occasional whistle of a quail or tapping of a woodpecker is almost the only sound that ever breaks in upon the uniform tranquillity.

I recollect that, when a stripling, my first exploit in squirrel-shooting was in a grove of tall walnut-trees that shades one side of the valley. I had wandered into it at noontime, when all nature is peculiarly quiet, and was startled by the roar of my own gun, as it broke the Sabbath stillness around and was prolonged and reverberated by the angry echoes. If ever I should wish for a retreat whither I might steal from the world and its distractions, and dream quietly away the remnant of a troubled life, I know of none more promising than this little valley.

From the listless repose of the place, and the peculiar character of its inhabitants, who are descendants from the original Dutch settlers, this sequestered glen has long been known by the name of SLEEPY HOLLOW, and its rustic lads are called the Sleepy Hollow Boys throughout all the neighboring country. A drowsy, dreamy influence seems to hang over the land, and to pervade the very atmosphere. Some say that the place was bewitched by a High German doctor, during the early days of the settlement; others, that an old Indian chief, the prophet or wizard of his tribe, held his powwows there before the country was discovered by Master Hendrick Hudson. Certain it is, the place still continues under the sway of some witching power, that holds a spell over the minds of the good people, causing them to walk in a continual reverie. They are given to all kinds of marvellous beliefs; are subject to trances and visions, and frequently see strange sights, and hear music and voices in the air. The whole neighborhood abounds with local tales, haunted spots, and twilight superstitions, stars shoot and meteors glare oftener across the valley than in any other part of the country, and the nightmare, with her whole ninefold, seems to make it the favorite scene of her gambols.

The dominant spirit, however, that haunts this enchanted region, and seems to be commander-in-chief of all the powers of the air, is the apparition of a figure on horseback, without a head. It is said by some to be the ghost of a Hessian trooper, whose head had been carried away by a cannon-ball, in some nameless battle during the Revolutionary War, and who is ever and anon seen by the country folk hurrying along in the gloom of night, as if on the wings of the wind. His haunts are not confined to the valley, but extend at times to the adjacent roads, and especially to the vicinity of a church at no great distance. Indeed, certain of the most authentic historians of those parts, who have been careful in collecting and collating the floating facts concerning this spectre, allege that the body of the trooper, having been buried in the church-yard, the ghost rides forth to the scene of battle in nightly quest of his head; and that the rushing speed with which he sometimes passes along the Hollow, like a midnight blast, is owing to his being belated, and in a hurry to get back to the church-yard before daybreak.

Such is the general purport of this legendary superstition, which has furnished materials for many a wild story in that region of shadows; and the spectre is known, at all the country firesides, by the name of the Headless Horseman of Sleepy Hollow.

It is remarkable that the visionary propensity I have mentioned is not confined to the native inhabitants of the valley, but is unconsciously imbibed by every one who resides there for a time. However wide awake they may have been before they entered that sleepy region, they are sure, in a little time, to inhale the witching influence of the air, and begin to grow imaginative —to dream dreams, and see apparitions.

I mention this peaceful spot with all possible laud; for it is in such little retired Dutch valleys, found here and there embosomed in the great State of New-York, that population, manners, and customs, remain fixed; while the great torrent of migration and improvement, which is making such incessant changes in other parts of this restless country, sweeps by them unobserved. They are like those little nooks of still water which border a rapid stream; where we may see the straw and bubble riding quietly at anchor, or slowly revolving in their mimic harbor, undisturbed by the rush of the passing current. Though many years have elapsed since I trod the drowsy shades of Sleepy Hollow, yet I question whether I should not still find the same trees and the same families vegetating in its sheltered bosom.

In this by-place of nature, there abode, in a remote period of American history, that is to say, some thirty years since, a worthy wight of the name of Ichabod Crane; who sojourned, or, as he expressed it, "tarried," in Sleepy Hollow, for the purpose of instructing the children of the vicinity. He was a native of Connecticut; a State which supplies the Union with pioneers for the mind as well as for the forest, and sends forth yearly its legions of frontier woodsmen and country schoolmasters. The cognomen of Crane was not inapplicable to his person. He was tall, but exceedingly lank, with narrow shoulders, long arms and legs, hands that dangled a mile out of his sleeves, feet that might have served for shovels, and his whole frame most loosely hung together.

His head was small, and flat at top, with huge ears, large green glassy eyes, and a long snipe nose, so that it looked like a weather-cock, perched upon his spindle neck, to tell which way the wind blew. To see him striding along the profile of a hill on a windy day, with his clothes bagging and fluttering about him, one might have mistaken him for the genius of famine descending upon the earth, or some scarecrow eloped from a cornfield.

His school-house was a low building of one large room, rudely constructed of logs; the windows partly glazed, and partly patched with leaves of old copy-books. It was most ingeniously secured at vacant hours, by a withe twisted in the handle of the door, and stakes set against the window shutters; so that, though a thief might get in with perfect ease, he would find some embarrassment in getting out; an idea most probably borrowed by the architect, Yost Van Houten, from the mystery of an eel-pot. The school-house stood in a rather lonely but pleasant situation, just at the foot of a woody hill, with a brook running close by, and a formidable birch tree growing at one end of it. From hence the low murmur of his pupils' voices, conning over their lessons, might be heard in a drowsy summer's day, like the hum of a bee-hive; interrupted now and then by the authoritative voice of the master, in the tone of menace or command; or, peradventure, by the appalling sound of the birch, as he urged some tardy loiterer along the flowery path of knowledge. Truth to say, he was a conscientious man, and ever bore in mind the golden maxim, "Spare the rod and spoil the child." Ichabod Crane's scholars certainly were not spoiled.

I would not have it imagined, however, that he was one of those cruel potentates of the school who joy in the smart of their subjects; on the contrary, he administered justice with discrimination rather than severity; taking the burden off the backs of the weak, and laying it on those of the strong. Your mere puny stripling, that winced at the least flourish of the rod, was passed by with indulgence; but the claims of justice were satisfied by inflicting a double portion on some little tough, wrong-headed, broad-skirted Dutch urchin, who sulked and swelled and grew dogged and sullen beneath the birch. All this he called "doing his duty by their parents"; and he never inflicted a chastisement without following it by the assurance, so consolatory to the smarting urchin, that "he would remember it and thank him for it the longest day he had to live."

When school hours were over, he was even the companion and playmate of the larger boys; and on holiday afternoons would convoy some of the smaller ones home, who happened to have pretty sisters, or good housewives for mothers, noted for the comforts of the cupboard. Indeed, it behooved him to keep on good terms with his pupils. The revenue arising from his school was small, and would have been scarcely sufficient to furnish him with daily bread, for he was a huge feeder, and, though lank, had the dilating powers of an anaconda; but to help out his maintenance, he was, according to country custom in those parts, boarded and lodged at the houses of the farmers whose children he instructed. With these he lived successively a week at a time, thus going the rounds of the neighborhood, with all his worldly effects tied up in a cotton handkerchief.

That all this might not be too onerous on the purses of his rustic patrons, who are apt to consider the costs of schooling a grievous burden, and school-masters as mere drones, he had various ways of rendering himself both useful and agreeable. He assisted the farmers occasionally in the lighter labors of their farms, helped to make hay, mended the fences, took the horses to water, drove the cows from pasture, and cut wood for the winter fire. He laid aside, too, all the dominant dignity and absolute sway with which he lorded it in his little empire, the school, and became wonderfully gentle and ingratiating. He found favor in the eyes of the mothers by petting the children, particularly the youngest; and like the lion bold, which whilom so magnanimously the lamb did hold, he would sit with a child on one knee, and rock a cradle with his foot for whole hours together.

In addition to his other vocations, he was the singing-master of the neighborhood, and picked up many bright shillings by instructing the young folks in psalmody. It was a matter of no little vanity to him on Sundays, to take his station in front of the church gallery, with a band of chosen singers; where, in his own mind, he completely carried away the palm from the parson. Certain it is, his voice resounded far above all the rest of the congregation; and there are peculiar quavers still to be heard in that church, and which may even be heard half a mile off, quite to the opposite side of the mill-pond, on a still Sunday morning, which are said to be legitimately descended from the nose of Ichabod Crane. Thus, by divers little makeshifts, in that ingenious way which is commonly denominated "by hook and by crook," the worthy pedagogue got on tolerably enough, and was thought, by all who understood nothing of the labor of head-work, to have a wonderful easy life of it.

The school-master is generally a man of some importance in the female circle of a rural neighborhood; being considered a kind of idle gentleman-like personage, of vastly superior taste and accomplishments to the rough country swains, and indeed, inferior in learning only to the parson. His appearance, therefore, is apt to occasion some little stir at the tea-table of a farm-house, and the addition of a supernumerary dish of cakes or sweetmeats, or per-adventure, the parade of a silver tea-pot. Our man of letters, therefore, was pecul-iarly happy in the smiles of all the coun-try damsels. How he would figure among them in the church-yard, between services on Sundays! gather grapes for them from the wild vines that overrun the surround-ing trees; reciting for their amusement all the epitaphs on the tombstones; or saunter-ing, with a whole bevy of them, along the banks of the adjacent mill-pond; while the more bashful country bumpkins hung sheepishly back, envying his superior ele-gance and address.

From his half itinerant life, also, he was a kind of travelling gazette, carrying the whole budget of local gossip from house to house; so that his appearance was al-ways greeted with satisfaction. He was, moreover, esteemed by the women as a man of great erudition, for he had read several books quite through, and was a perfect master of Cotton Mather's history of New England witchcraft, in which, by the way, he most firmly and potently be-lieved.

He was, in fact, an odd mixture of small shrewdness and simple credulity. His appe-tite for the marvellous, and his powers of digesting it, were equally extraordinary; and both had been increased by his resi-dence in this spellbound region. No tale was too gross or monstrous for his capa-cious swallow. It was often his delight, after his school was dismissed in the after-noon, to stretch himself on the rich bed of clover, bordering the little brook that whimpered by his school-house, and there con over old Mather's direful tales, until the gathering dusk of the evening made the printed page a mere mist before his eyes. Then, as he wended his way, by swamp and stream and awful woodland, to the farmhouse where he happened to be quar-tered, every sound of nature, at that witch-ing hour, fluttered his excited imagination;

the moan of the whip-poor-will from the hill-side; the boding cry of the tree-toad, that harbinger of storm; the dreary hoot-ing of the screech-owl, or the sudden rus-tling in the thicket of birds frightened from their roost. The fire-flies, too, which sparkled most vividly in the darkest places, now and then startled him, as one of un-common brightness would stream across his path; and if, by chance, a huge blockhead of a beetle came winging his blundering flight against him, the poor varlet was ready to give up the ghost, with the idea that he was struck with a witch's token. His only resource on such occasions, either to drown thought, or drive away evil spir-its, was to sing psalm tunes;—and the good people of Sleepy Hollow, as they sat by their doors of an evening, were often filled with awe, at hearing his nasal melody, "in linked sweetness long drawn out," floating from the distant hill, or along the dusky road.

Another of his sources of fearful pleas-ure was, to pass long winter evenings with the old Dutch wives, as they sat spinning by the fire, with a row of apples roasting and spluttering along the hearth, and listen to their marvellous tales of ghosts and goblins, and haunted fields, and haunted brooks, and haunted bridges, and haunted houses, and particularly of the headless horseman, or galloping Hessian of the Hollow, as they sometimes called him. He would delight them equally by his anec-dotes of witchcraft, and of the direful omens and portentous sights and sounds in the air, which prevailed in the earlier times of Connecticut; and would frighten them wofully with speculations upon comets and shooting stars; and with the alarming fact that the world did absolutely turn round, and that they were half the time topsy-turvy!

But if there was a pleasure in all this, while snugly cuddling in the chimney cor-ner of a chamber that was all of a ruddy glow from the crackli.ig wood fire, and where, of course, no spectre dared to show his face, it was dearly purchased by the terrors of his subsequent walk homewards. What fearful shapes and shadows beset his path amidst the dim and ghastly glare of a snowy night!—With what wistful look did he eye every trembling ray of light streaming across the waste fields from some distant window!—How often was he appalled by some shrub covered with snow, which, like a sheeted spectre, beset his very path!—How often did he shrink with curdling awe at the sound of his own steps on the frosty crust beneath his feet; and dread to look over his shoulder, lest he should behold some uncouth being tramping close behind him!—and how often was he thrown into complete dismay by some rushing blast, howling among the trees, in the idea that it was the Galloping Hessian on one of his nightly scourings!

All these, however, were mere terrors of the night, phantoms of the mind that walk in darkness; and though he had seen many spectres in his time, and been more than once beset by Satan in divers shapes, in his lonely perambulations, yet daylight put an end to all these evils; and he would have passed a pleasant life of it, in spite of the Devil and all his works, if his path had not been crossed by a being that causes more perplexity to mortal man than ghosts, goblins, and the whole race of witches put together, and that was—a woman.

Among the musical disciples who assembled, one evening in each week, to receive his instructions in psalmody, was Katrina Van Tassel, the daughter and only child of a substantial Dutch farmer. She was a blooming lass of fresh eighteen; plump as a partridge; ripe and melting and rosy-cheeked as one of her father's peaches, and universally famed, not merely for her beauty, but her vast expectations. She was withal a little of a coquette, as might be perceived even in her dress, which was a mixture of ancient and modern fashions, as most suited to set off her charms. She wore the ornaments of pure yellow gold, which her great-great-grandmother had brought over from Saardam; the tempting stomacher of the olden time, and withal a provokingly short petticoat, to display the prettiest foot and ankle in the country round.

Ichabod Crane had a soft and foolish heart towards the sex; and it is not to be wondered at, that so tempting a morsel soon found favor in his eyes, more especially after he had visited her in her paternal mansion. Old Baltus Van Tassel was a perfect picture of a thriving, contented, liberal-hearted farmer. He seldom, it is true, sent either his eyes or his thoughts beyond the boundaries of his own farm; but within those everything was snug, happy and well-conditioned. He was satisfied with his wealth, but not proud of it; and piqued himself upon the hearty abundance, rather than the style in which he lived. His stronghold was situated on the banks of the Hudson, in one of those green, sheltered, fertile nooks in which the Dutch farmers are so fond of nestling. A great elm tree spread its broad branches over it, at the foot of which bubbled up a spring of the softest and sweetest water, in a little well formed of a barrel; and then stole sparkling away through the grass, to a neighboring brook, that babbled along among alders and dwarf willows. Hard by the farmhouse was a vast barn, that might have served for a church: every window and crevice of which seemed bursting forth with the treasures of the farm; the flail was busily resounding within it from morning to night; swallows and martins skimmed twittering about the eaves; and rows of pigeons, some with one eye turned up, as if watching the weather, some with their heads under their wings or buried in their bosoms, and others swelling, and cooing, and bowing about their dames, were enjoying the sunshine on the roof. Sleek un-wieldy porkers were grunting in the re-pose and abundance of their pens, from whence sallied forth, now and then, troops of sucking pigs, as if to snuff the air. A stately squadron of snowy geese were rid-ing in an adjoining pond, convoying whole fleets of ducks; regiments of turkeys were gobbling through the farmyard, and Guinea fowls fretting about it, like ill-tempered housewives, with their peevish, discontented cry. Before the barn door strutted the gallant cock, that pattern of a husband, a warrior and a fine gentleman, clapping his burnished wings and crowing in the pride and gladness of his heart,— sometimes tearing up the earth with his feet, and then generously calling his ever-hungry family of wives and children to enjoy the rich morsel which he had dis-covered.

The pedagogue's mouth watered as he looked upon this sumptuous promise of luxurious winter fare. In his devouring mind's eye, he pictured to himself every roasting-pig running about with a pud-ding in his belly, and an apple in his mouth; the pigeons were snugly put to bed in a comfortable pie, and tucked in with a coverlet of crust; the geese were swim-ming in their own gravy; and the ducks pairing cosily in dishes, like snug married couples, with a decent competency of onion sauce. In the porkers he saw carved out the future sleek side of bacon, and juicy relishing ham; not a turkey but he beheld daintily trussed up, with its gizzard under its wing, and, peradventure, a necklace of savory sausages; and even bright chanti-cleer himself lay sprawling on his back, in a side dish, with uplifted claws, as if craving that quarter which his chivalrous spirit disdained to ask while living.

As the enraptured Ichabod fancied all this, and as he rolled his great green eyes over the fat meadow lands, the rich fields of wheat, of rye, of buckwheat, and Indian corn, and the orchards burdened with ruddy fruit, which surrounded the warm tenement of Van Tassel, his heart yearned after the damsel who was to inherit these domains, and his imagination expanded with the idea, how they might be readily turned into cash, and the money invested in immense tracts of wild land, and shingle palaces in the wilderness. Nay, his busy fancy already realized his hopes, and pre-sented to him the blooming Katrina, with a whole family of children, mounted on the top of a wagon loaded with house-hold trumpery, with pots and kettles dangling beneath; and he beheld himself, bestriding a pacing mare, with a colt at her heels, setting out for Kentucky, Ten-nessee,—or the Lord knows where!

When he entered the house the conquest of his heart was complete. It was one of those spacious farm-houses, with high-ridged, but lowly-sloping roofs, built in the style handed down from the first Dutch settlers; the low projecting eaves forming a piazza along the front, capable of being closed up in bad weather. Under this were hung flails, harness, various utensils of hus-bandry, and nets for fishing in the neigh-boring river. Benches were built along the sides for summer use; and a great spinning-wheel at one end, and a churn at the other, showed the various uses to which this important porch might be devoted. From this piazza the wondering Ichabod en-tered the hall, which formed the centre of the mansion and the place of usual resi-dence. Here, rows of resplendent pewter, ranged on a long dresser, dazzled his eyes. In one corner stood a huge bag of wool ready to be spun; in another a quantity of linsey-woolsey just from the loom; ears of Indian corn, and strings of dried apples and peaches, hung in gay festoons along the walls, mingled with the gaud of red peppers; and a door left ajar gave him a peep into the best parlor, where the claw-footed chairs, and dark mahogany tables, shone like mirrors; andirons, with their accompanying shovel and tongs, glistened from their covert of asparagus tops; mock-oranges and conch-shells decorated the mantel-piece; strings of various colored birds' eggs were suspended above it: a great ostrich egg was hung from the centre of the room, and a corner cupboard, knowingly left open, displayed immense treasures of old silver and well-mended china.

From the moment Ichabod laid his eyes upon these regions of delight, the peace of his mind was at an end, and his only study was how to gain the affections of the peerless daughter of Van Tassel. In this enterprise, however, he had more real difficulties than generally fell to the lot of a knight-errant of yore, who seldom had any thing but giants, enchanters, fiery dragons, and such like easily-conquered adversaries, to contend with; and had to make his way merely through gates of iron and brass, and walls of adamant, to the castle keep, where the lady of his heart was confined; all which he achieved as easily as a man would carve his way to the centre of a Christmas pie; and then the lady gave him her hand as a matter of course. Ichabod, on the contrary, had to win his way to the heart of a country coquette, beset with a labyrinth of whims and caprices, which were for ever presenting new difficulties and impediments; and he had to encounter a host of fearful adversaries of real flesh and blood, the numerous rustic admirers, who beset every portal to her heart; keeping a watchful and angry eye upon each other, but ready to fly out in the common cause against any new competitor.

Among these the most formidable was a burly, roaring, roystering blade, of the name of Abraham, or, according to the Dutch abbreviation, Brom Van Brunt, the hero of the country round, which rang with his feats of strength and hardihood. He was broad-shouldered and double-jointed, with short curly black hair, and a bluff, but not unpleasant countenance, having a mingled air of fun and arrogance. From his Herculean frame and great powers of limb, he had received the nickname of BROM BONES, by which he was universally known. He was famed for great knowledge and skill in horsemanship, being as dexterous on horseback as a Tartar. He was foremost at all races and cock-fights; and, with the ascendency which bodily strength acquires in rustic life, was the umpire in all disputes, setting his hat on one side, and giving his decisions with an air and tone that admitted of no gainsay or appeal. He was always ready for either a fight or a frolic; but had more mischief than ill-will in his composition; and with all his overbearing roughness, there was a strong dash of waggish good humor at bottom. He had three or four boon companions, who regarded him as their model, and at the head of whom he scoured the country, attending every scene of feud or merriment for miles round. In cold weather he was distinguished by a fur cap, surmounted with a flaunting fox's tail; and when the folks at a country gathering descried this well-known crest at a distance, whisking about among a squad of hard riders, they always stood by for a squall. Sometimes his crew would be heard dashing along past the farm-houses at midnight, with whoop and halloo, like a troop of Don Cossacks; and the old dames, startled out of their sleep, would listen for a moment till the hurry-scurry had clattered by, and then exclaim, "Ay, there goes Brom Bones and his gang!" The neighbors looked upon him with a mixture of awe, admiration, and good-will; and, when any madcap prank or rustic brawl occurred in the vicinity, always shook their heads, and warranted Brom Bones was at the bottom of it.

This rantipole hero had for some time singled out the blooming Katrina for the object of his uncouth gallantries, and though his amorous toyings were something like the gentle caresses and endearments of a bear, yet it was whispered that she did not altogether discourage his hopes. Certain it is, his advances were signals for rival candidates to retire, who felt no inclination to cross a lion in his amours; insomuch, that when his horse was seen tied to Van Tassel's paling, on a Sunday night, a sure sign that his master was courting, or, as it is termed, "sparking," within, all other suitors passed by in despair, and carried the war into other quarters.

Such was the formidable rival with whom Ichabod Crane had to contend, and, considering all things, a stouter man than he would have shrunk from the competition, and a wiser man would have despaired. He had, however, a happy mixture of pliability and perseverance in his nature; he was in form and spirit like a supple-jack—yielding, but tough; though he bent, he never broke; and though he bowed beneath the slightest pressure, yet, the moment it was away—jerk!—he was as erect, and carried his head as high as ever.

To have taken the field openly against his rival would have been madness; for he was not a man to be thwarted in his amours, any more than that stormy lover, Achilles. Ichabod, therefore, made his advances in a quiet and gently insinuating manner. Under cover of his character of singing-master, he made frequent visits at the farm-house; not that he had anything to apprehend from the meddlesome interference of parents, which is so often a stumbling-block in the path of lovers. Balt Van Tassel was an easy, indulgent soul; he loved his daughter better even than his pipe, and, like a reasonable man and an excellent father, let her have her way in everything. His notable little wife, too, had enough to do to attend to her housekeeping and manage her poultry; for, as she sagely observed, ducks and geese are foolish things, and must be looked after, but girls can take care of themselves. Thus, while the busy dame bustled about the house, or plied her spinning-wheel at one end of the piazza, honest Balt would sit smoking his evening pipe at the other, watching the achievements of a little wooden warrior, who, armed with a sword in each hand, was most valiantly fighting the wind on the pinnacle of the barn. In the mean time, Ichabod would carry on his suit with the daughter by the side of the spring under the great elm, or sauntering along in the twilight, that hour so favorable to the lover's eloquence.

I profess not to know how women's hearts are wooed and won. To me they have always been matters of riddle and admiration. Some seem to have but one vulnerable point, or door of access; while others have a thousand avenues, and may be captured in a thousand different ways. It is a great triumph of skill to gain the former, but a still greater proof of generalship to maintain possession of the latter, for a man must battle for his fortress at every door and window. He that wins a thousand common hearts, is therefore entitled to some renown; but he who keeps undisputed sway over the heart of a coquette, is indeed a hero. Certain it is, this was not the case with the redoubtable Brom Bones; and from the moment Ichabod Crane made his advances, the interests of the former evidently declined; his horse was no longer seen tied at the palings on Sunday nights, and a deadly feud gradually arose between him and the preceptor of Sleepy Hollow.

Brom, who had a degree of rough chivalry in his nature, would fain have carried matters to open warfare, and have settled their pretensions to the lady, according to the mode of those most concise and simple reasoners, the knights-errant of yore—by single combat; but Ichabod was too conscious of the superior might of his adversary to enter the lists against him: he had overheard a boast of Bones, that he would "double the school-master up, and lay him on a shelf of his own school-house"; and he was too wary to give him an opportunity. There was something extremely provoking in this obstinately pacific system; it left Brom no alternative but to draw upon the funds of rustic waggery in his disposition, and to play off boorish practical jokes upon his rival. Ichabod became the object of whimsical persecution to Bones and his gang of rough riders. They harried his hitherto peaceful domains; smoked out his singing school, by stopping up the chimney; broke into the school-house at night, in spite of its formidable fastenings of withe and window stakes, and turned every thing topsy-turvy: so that the poor school-master began to think all the witches in the country held their meetings there. But what was still more annoying, Brom took all opportunities of turning him into ridicule in presence of his mistress, and had a scoundrel dog whom he taught to whine in the most ludicrous manner, and introduced as a rival of Ichabod's to instruct her in psalmody.

In this way matters went on for some time, without producing any material effect on the relative situation of the contending powers. On a fine autumnal afternoon, Ichabod, in pensive mood, sat enthroned on the lofty stool whence he usually watched all the concerns of his little literary realm. In his hand he swayed a ferule, that sceptre of despotic power; the birch of justice reposed on three nails, behind the throne, a constant terror to evil doers; while on the desk before him might be seen sundry contraband articles and prohibited weapons, detected upon the persons of idle urchins; such as half-munched apples, popguns, whirligigs, fly-cages, and whole legions of rampant little paper game-cocks. Apparently there had been some appalling act of justice recently inflicted, for his scholars were all busily intent upon their books, or slyly whispering behind them with one eye kept upon the master; and a kind of buzzing stillness reigned throughout the school-room. It was suddenly interrupted by the appearance of a negro, in tow-cloth jacket and trowsers, a round-crowned fragment of a hat, like the cap of Mercury, and mounted on the back of a ragged, wild, half-broken colt, which he managed with a rope by way of halter. He came clattering up to the school door with an invitation to Ichabod to attend a merry-making or "quilting frolic," to be held that evening at Mynheer Van Tassel's; and having delivered his message with that air of importance, and effort at fine language, which a negro is apt to display on petty embassies of the kind, he dashed over the brook, and was seen scampering away up the hollow, full of the importance and hurry of his mission.

All was now bustle and hubbub in the late quiet school-room. The scholars were hurried through their lessons, without stopping at trifles; those who were nimble skipped over half with impunity, and those who were tardy, had a smart application now and then in the rear, to quicken their speed, or help them over a tall word. Books were flung aside without being put away on the shelves, inkstands were overturned, benches thrown down, and the whole school was turned loose an hour before the usual time, bursting forth like a legion of young imps, yelping and racketing about the green, in joy at their early emancipation.

The gallant Ichabod now spent at least an extra half hour at his toilet, brushing and furbishing up his best, and indeed only suit of rusty black, and arranging his looks by a bit of broken looking-glass, that hung up in the school-house. That he might make his appearance before his mistress in the true style of a cavalier, he borrowed a horse from the farmer with whom he was domiciliated, a choleric old Dutchman by the name of Hans Van Ripper, and, thus gallantly mounted, issued forth like a knight-errant in quest of adventures. But it is meet I should, in the true spirit of romantic story, give some account of the looks and equipments of my hero and his steed. The animal he bestrode was a broken-down plow-horse, that had outlived almost everything but its viciousness. He was gaunt and shagged, with a ewe neck, and a head like a hammer; his rusty mane and tail were tangled and knotted with burs; one eye had lost its pupil, and was glaring and spectral, but the other had a gleam of a genuine devil in it. Still he must have had fire and mettle in his day, if we may judge from the name he bore of Gunpowder. He had, in fact, been a favorite steed of his master's, the choleric Van Ripper, who was a furious rider, and had infused, very probably, some of his own spirit into the animal; for, old and broken-down as he looked, there was more of the lurking devil in him than in any young filly in the country.

Ichabod was a suitable figure for such a steed. He rode with short stirrups, which brought his knees nearly up to the pommel of the saddle; his sharp elbows stuck out like grasshoppers'; he carried his whip perpendicularly in his hand, like a sceptre, and as his horse jogged on, the motion of his arms was not unlike the flapping of a pair of wings. A small wool hat rested on the top of his nose, for so his scanty strip of forehead might be called, and the skirts of his black coat fluttered out almost to the horse's tail. Such was the appearance of Ichabod and his steed as they shambled out of the gate of Hans Van Ripper, and it was altogether such an apparition as is seldom to be met with in broad daylight.

It was, as I have said, a fine autumnal day; the sky was clear and serene, and nature wore that rich and golden livery which we always associate with the idea of abundance. The forests had put on their sober brown and yellow, while some trees of the tenderer kind had been nipped by the frosts into brilliant dyes of orange, purple, and scarlet. Streaming files of wild ducks began to make their appearance high in the air; the bark of the squirrel might be heard from the groves of beech and hickory-nuts, and the pensive whistle of the quail at intervals from the neighboring stubble field.

The small birds were taking their farewell banquets. In the fullness of their revelry, they fluttered, chirping and frolicking from bush to bush, and tree to tree, capricious from the very profusion and variety around them. There was the honest cockrobin, the favorite game of stripling sportsmen, with its loud querulous note; and the twittering blackbirds flying in sable clouds; and the golden-winged woodpecker, with his crimson crest, his broad black gorget, and splendid plumage; and the cedar-bird, with its red-tipt wings and yellow-tipt tail and its little monteiro cap of feathers; and the blue jay, that noisy coxcomb in his gay light blue coat and white underclothes, screaming and chattering, nodding and bobbing and bowing, and pretending to be on good terms with every songster of the grove.

As Ichabod jogged slowly on his way, his eye, ever open to every symptom of culinary abundance, ranged with delight over the treasures of jolly autumn. On all sides he beheld vast store of apples: some hanging in oppressive opulence on the trees; some gathered into baskets and barrels for the market; others heaped up in rich piles for the cider-press. Farther on he beheld great fields of Indian corn, with its golden ears peeping from their leafy coverts, and holding out the promise of cakes and hasty-pudding; and the yellow pumpkins lying beneath them, turning up their fair round bellies to the sun, and giving ample prospects of the most luxurious of pies; and anon he passed the fragrant buckwheat fields breathing the odor of the beehive; and as he beheld them, soft anticipations stole over his mind of dainty slapjacks, well-buttered, and garnished with honey or treacle, by the delicate little dimpled hand of Katrina Van Tassel.

Thus feeding his mind with many sweet thoughts and "sugared suppositions," he journeyed along the sides of a range of hills which look out upon some of the goodliest scenes of the mighty Hudson. The sun gradually wheeled his broad disk down in the west. The wide bosom of the Tappan Zee lay motionless and glassy, excepting that here and there a gentle undulation waved and prolonged the blue shadow of the distant mountain. A few amber clouds floated in the sky, without a breath of air to move them. The horizon was of a fine golden tint, changing gradually into a pure apple green, and from that into the deep blue of the mid-heaven. A slanting ray lingered on the woody crests of the precipices that overhung some parts of the river, giving greater depth to the dark-gray and purple of their rocky sides. A sloop was loitering in the distance, dropping slowly down with the tide, her sail hanging uselessly against the mast; and as the reflection of the sky gleamed along the still water, it seemed as if the vessel was suspended in the air.

It was toward evening that Ichabod arrived at the castle of the Heer Van Tassel, which he found thronged with the pride and flower of the adjacent country. Old farmers, a spare leathern-faced race, in homespun coats and breeches, blue stockings, huge shoes, and magnificent pewter buckles. Their brisk withered little dames, in close crimped caps, long-waisted short-gowns, homespun petticoats, with scissors and pincushions, and gay calico pockets hanging on the outside. Buxom lasses, almost as antiquated as their mothers, ex-

cepting where a straw hat, a fine ribbon, or perhaps a white frock, gave symptoms of city innovation. The sons, in short squareskirted coats with rows of stupendous brass buttons, and their hair generally queued in the fashion of the times, especially if they could procure an eel-skin for the purpose, it being esteemed, throughout the country, as a potent nourisher and strengthener of the hair.

Brom Bones, however, was the hero of the scene, having come to the gathering on his favorite steed Dare-devil, a creature, like himself, full of mettle and mischief, and which no one but himself could manage. He was, in fact, noted for preferring vicious animals, given to all kinds of tricks, which kept the rider in constant risk of his neck, for he held a tractable well-broken horse as unworthy of a lad of spirit.

Fain would I pause to dwell upon the world of charms that burst upon the enraptured gaze of my hero, as he entered the state parlor of Van Tassel's mansion. Not those of the bevy of buxom lasses, with their luxurious display of red and white; but the ample charms of a genuine Dutch country tea-table, in the sumptuous time of autumn. Such heaped-up platters of cakes of various and almost indescribable kinds, known only to experienced Dutch housewives! There was the doughty doughnut, the tenderer "oly koek," and the crisp and crumbling cruller; sweet cakes and short cakes, ginger cakes and honey cakes, and the whole family of cakes. And then there were apple pies and peach pies and pumpkin pies; besides slices of ham and smoked beef; and moreover delectable dishes of preserved plums, and peaches, and pears, and quinces; not to mention broiled shad and roasted chickens; together with bowls of milk and cream, all mingled higgledy-piggledy, pretty much as I have enumerated them, with the motherly teapot sending up its clouds of vapor from the midst—Heaven bless the mark! I want breath and time to discuss this banquet as it deserves, and am too eager to get on with my story. Happily, Ichabod Crane was not in so great a hurry as his historian, but did ample justice to every dainty.

He was a kind and thankful creature, whose heart dilated in proportion as his skin was filled with good cheer; and whose spirits rose with eating as some men's do with drink. He could not help, too, rolling his large eyes round him as he ate, and chuckling with the possibility that he might one day be lord of all this scene of almost unimaginable luxury and splendor. Then, he thought, how soon he'd turn his back upon the old school-house; snap his fingers in the face of Hans Van Ripper, and every other niggardly patron, and kick any itinerant pedagogue out of doors that should dare to call him comrade!

Old Baltus Van Tassel moved about among his guests with a face dilated with content and good humor, round and jolly as the harvest moon. His hospitable attentions were brief, but expressive, being confined to a shake of the hand, a slap on the shoulder, a loud laugh, and a pressing invitation to "fall to, and help themselves."

And now the sound of the music from the common room, or hall, summoned to the dance. The musician was an old gray-headed negro, who had been the itinerant orchestra of the neighborhood for more than half a century. His instrument was as old and battered as himself. The greater part of the time he scraped on two or three strings, accompanying every movement of the bow with a motion of the head; bowing almost to the ground, and stamping with his foot whenever a fresh couple were to start.

Ichabod prided himself upon his dancing as much as upon his vocal powers. Not a limb, not a fibre about him was idle; and to have seen his loosely hung frame in full motion, and clattering about the room,

you would have thought St. Vitus himself, that blessed patron of the dance, was figuring before you in person. He was the admiration of all the negroes; who, having gathered, of all ages and sizes, from the farm and the neighborhood, stood forming a pyramid of shining black faces at every door and window; gazing with delight at the scene; rolling their white eyeballs, and showing grinning rows of ivory from ear to ear. How could the flogger of urchins be otherwise than animated and joyous? the lady of his heart was his partner in the dance, and smiling graciously in reply to all his amorous oglings; while Brom Bones, sorely smitten with love and jealousy, sat brooding by himself in one corner.

When the dance was at an end, Ichabod was attracted to a knot of the sager folks, who, with Old Van Tassel, sat smoking at one end of the piazza, gossiping over former times, and drawing out long stories about the war.

This neighborhood, at the time of which I am speaking, was one of those highly favored places which abound with chronicle and great men. The British and American line had run near it during the war; it had, therefore, been the scene of marauding, and infested with refugees, cow-boys, and all kinds of border chivalry. Just sufficient time had elapsed to enable each story-teller to dress up his tale with a little becoming fiction, and, in the indistinctness of his recollection, to make himself the hero of every exploit.

There was the story of Doffue Martling, a large blue-bearded Dutchman, who had nearly taken a British frigate with an old iron nine-pounder from a mud breastwork, only that his gun burst at the sixth discharge. And there was an old gentleman who shall be nameless, being too rich a mynheer to be lightly mentioned, who, in the battle of White Plains, being an excellent master of defence, parried a musket-ball with a small-sword, insomuch that he absolutely felt it whiz round the blade, and glance off at the hilt; in proof of which he was ready at any time to show the sword, with the hilt a little bent. There were several more that had been equally great in the field, not one of whom but was persuaded that he had a considerable hand in bringing the war to a happy termination.

But all these were nothing to the tales of ghosts and apparitions that succeeded. The neighborhood is rich in legendary treasures of the kind. Local tales and superstitions thrive best in these sheltered, long-settled retreats; but are trampled under foot by the shifting throng that forms the population of most of our country places. Besides, there is no encouragement for ghosts in most of our villages, for they have scarcely had time to finish their first nap and turn themselves in their graves, before their surviving friends have travelled away from the neighborhood; so that when they turn out at night to walk their rounds, they have no acquaintance left to call upon. This is perhaps the reason why we so seldom hear of ghosts except in our long-established Dutch communities.

The immediate cause, however, of the prevalence of supernatural stories in these parts, was doubtless owing to the vicinity of Sleepy Hollow. There was a contagion in the very air that blew from that haunted region; it breathed forth an atmosphere of dreams and fancies infecting all the land. Several of the Sleepy Hollow people were present at Van Tassel's, and, as usual, were doling out their wild and wonderful legends. Many dismal tales were told about funeral trains, and mourning cries and wailings heard and seen about the great tree where the unfortunate Major André was taken, and which stood in the neighborhood. Some mention was made also of the woman in white, that haunted the dark glen at Raven Rock, and was often heard to shriek on winter nights before a storm, having perished there in the snow. The chief part of the stories, however, turned upon the favorite spectre of Sleepy Hollow, the Headless Horseman, who had been heard several times of late, patrolling the country; and, it was said, tethered his horse nightly among the graves in the church-yard.

The sequestered situation of this church seems always to have made it a favorite haunt of troubled spirits. It stands on a knoll, surrounded by locust-trees, and lofty elms, from among which its decent whitewashed walls shine modestly forth, like Christian purity beaming through the shades of retirement. A gentle slope descends from it to a silver sheet of water, bordered by high trees, between which, peeps may be caught at the blue hills of the Hudson. To look upon its grass-grown yard, where the sunbeams seem to sleep so quietly, one would think that there at least the dead might rest in peace. On one side of the church extends a wide woody dell, along which raves a large brook among broken rocks and trunks of fallen trees. Over a deep black part of the stream, not far from the church, was formerly thrown a wooden bridge; the road that led to it, and the bridge itself, were thickly shaded by overhanging trees, which cast a gloom about it, even in the daytime; but occasioned a fearful darkness at night. Such was one of the favorite haunts of the Headless Horseman, and the place where he was most frequently encountered. The tale was told of old Brouwer, a most heretical disbeliever in ghosts, how he met the Horseman returning from his foray into Sleepy Hollow, and was obliged to get up behind him; how they galloped over bush and brake, over hill and swamp, until they reached the bridge; when the Horseman suddenly turned into a skeleton, threw old Brouwer into the brook, and sprang away over the tree-tops with a clap of thunder.

This story was immediately matched by a thrice marvellous adventure of Brom Bones, who made light of the Galloping Hessian as an arrant jockey. He affirmed that on returning one night from the neighboring village of Sing Sing, he had been overtaken by this midnight trooper; that he had offered to race with him for a bowl of punch, and should have won it too, for Dare-devil beat the goblin horse all hollow, but, just as they came to the church bridge, the Hessian bolted, and vanished in a flash of fire.

All these tales, told in that drowsy undertone with which men talk in the dark, the countenances of the listeners only now and then receiving a casual gleam from the glare of a pipe, sank deep in the mind of Ichabod. He repaid them in kind with large extracts from his invaluable author, Cotton Mather, and added many marvellous events that had taken place in his native State of Connecticut, and fearful sights which he had seen in his nightly walks about Sleepy Hollow.

The revel now gradually broke up. The old farmers gathered together their families in their wagons, and were heard for some time rattling along the hollow roads, and over the distant hills. Some of the damsels mounted on pillions behind their favorite swains, and their lighthearted laughter, mingling with the clatter of hoofs, echoed along the silent woodlands, sounding fainter and fainter until they gradually died away—and the late scene of noise and frolic was all silent and deserted. Ichabod only lingered behind, according to the custom of country lovers, to have a tête-à-tête with the heiress, fully convinced that he was now on the high road to success. What passed at this interview I will not pretend to say, for in fact I do not know. Something, however, I fear me, must have gone wrong, for he certainly sallied forth, after no very great interval, with an air quite desolate and chop-fallen.—Oh these women! these women! Could that girl have been playing off any of her coquettish tricks?—Was her encouragement of the poor pedagogue all a mere sham to secure her conquest of his rival?—Heaven only knows, not I!—Let it suffice to say, Ichabod stole forth with the air of one who had been sacking a hen-roost, rather than a fair lady's heart. Without looking to the right or left to notice the scene of rural wealth, on which he had so often gloated, he went straight to the stable, and with several hearty cuffs and kicks, roused his steed most uncourteously from the comfortable quarters in which he was soundly sleeping, dreaming of mountains of corn and oats, and whole valleys of timothy and clover.

It was the very witching time of night that Ichabod, heavy-hearted, and crestfallen, pursued his travel homewards, along the sides of the lofty hills which rise above Tarry Town, and which he had traversed so cheerily in the afternoon. The hour was as dismal as himself. Far below him the Tappan Zee spread its dusky and indistinct waste of waters, with here and there the tall mast of a sloop, riding quietly at anchor under the land. In the dead hush of midnight, he could even hear the barking of the watch-dog from the opposite shore of the Hudson; but it was so vague and faint as only to give an idea of his distance from this faithful companion of man. Now and then, too, the long-drawn crowing of a cock, accidentally awakened, would sound far, far off, from some farm-house away among the hills—but it was like a dreaming sound in his ear. No sign of life occurred near him, but occasionally the melancholy chirp of a cricket, or perhaps the guttural twang of a bull-frog from a neighboring marsh, as if sleeping uncomfortably and turning suddenly in his bed.

All the stories of ghosts and goblins that he had heard in the afternoon now came crowding upon his recollection. The night grew darker and darker; the stars seemed to sink deeper in the sky, and driving clouds occasionally hid them from his sight. He had never felt so lonely and dismal. He was, moreover, approaching the very place where many of the scenes of the ghost stories had been laid. In the centre of the road stood an enormous tulip-tree, which towered like a giant above all the other trees of the neighborhood, and formed a kind of landmark. Its limbs were gnarled and fantastic, large enough to form trunks for ordinary trees, twisting down almost to the earth, and rising again into the air. It was connected with the tragical story of the unfortunate André, who had been taken prisoner hard by; and was universally known by the name of Major André's tree. The common people regarded it with a mixture of respect and superstition, partly out of sympathy for the fate of its ill-starred namesake, and partly from the tales of strange sights, and doleful lamentations, told concerning it.

As Ichabod approached this fearful tree, he began to whistle; he thought his whistle was answered; it was but a blast sweeping sharply through the dry branches. As he approached a little nearer, he thought he saw something white, hanging in the midst of the tree: he paused, and ceased whistling; but, on looking more narrowly, perceived that it was a place where the tree had been scathed by lightning, and the white wood laid bare. Suddenly he heard a groan—his teeth chattered, and his knees smote against the saddle: it was but the rubbing of one huge bough upon another, as they were swayed about by the breeze. He passed the tree in safety, but new perils lay before him.

About two hundred yards from the tree, a small brook crossed the road, and ran into a marshy and thickly-wooded glen, known by the name of Wiley's Swamp. A few rough logs, laid side by side, served for a bridge over this stream. On that side of the road where the brook entered the wood, a group of oaks and chestnuts, matted thick with wild grapevines, threw a cavernous gloom over it. To pass this bridge was the severest trial. It was at this identical spot that the unfortunate André was captured, and under the covert of those chestnuts and vines were the sturdy yeomen concealed who surprised him. This has ever since been considered a haunted stream, and fearful are the feelings of the school-boy who has to pass it alone after dark.

As he approached the stream his heart began to thump; he summoned up, however, all his resolution, gave his horse half a score of kicks in the ribs, and attempted to dash briskly across the bridge; but instead of starting forward, the perverse old animal made a lateral movement, and ran broadside against the fence. Ichabod, whose fears increased with the delay, jerked the reins on the other side, and kicked lustily with the contrary foot: it was all in vain; his steed started, it is true, but it was only to plunge to the opposite side of the road into a thicket of brambles and alder-bushes. The school-master now bestowed both whip and heel upon the starveling ribs of old Gunpowder, who dashed forward, snuffling and snorting, but came to a stand just by the bridge, with a suddenness that had nearly sent his rider sprawling over his head. Just at this moment a splashy tramp by the side of the bridge caught the sensitive ear of Ichabod. In the dark shadow of the grove, on the margin of the brook, he beheld something huge, misshapen, black and towering. It stirred not, but seemed gathered up in the gloom, like some gigantic monster ready to spring upon the traveller.

The hair of the affrighted pedagogue rose upon his head with terror. What was to be done? To turn and fly was now too late; and besides, what chance was there of escaping ghost or goblin, if such it was, which could ride upon the wings of the wind? Summoning up, therefore, a show of courage, he demanded in stammering accents—"Who are you?" He received no reply. He repeated his demand in a still more agitated voice. Still there was no answer. Once more he cudgelled the sides of the inflexible Gunpowder, and, shutting his eyes, broke forth with involuntary fervor into a psalm tune. Just then the shadowy object of alarm put itself in motion, and, with a scramble and a bound, stood at once in the middle of the road. Though the night was dark and dismal, yet the form of the unknown might now in some degree be ascertained. He appeared to be a horseman of large dimensions, and mounted on a black horse of powerful frame. He made no offer of molestation or sociability, but kept aloof on one side of the road, jogging along on the blind side of old Gunpowder, who had now got over his fright and waywardness.

Ichabod, who had no relish for this strange midnight companion, and bethought himself of the adventure of Brom Bones with the Galloping Hessian, now quickened his steed, in hopes of leaving him behind. The stranger, however, quickened his horse to an equal pace. Ichabod pulled up, and fell into a walk, thinking to lag behind—the other did the same. His heart began to sink within him; he endeavored to resume his psalm tune, but his parched tongue clove to the roof of his mouth, and he could not utter a stave. There was something in the moody and dogged silence of this pertinacious companion, that was mysterious and appalling. It was soon fearfully accounted for. On mounting a rising ground, which brought the figure of his fellow-traveller in relief against the sky, gigantic in height, and muffled in a cloak, Ichabod was horror-struck, on perceiving that he was headless!

—but his horror was still more increased, on observing that the head, which should have rested on his shoulders, was carried before him on the pommel of the saddle: his terror rose to desperation; he rained a shower of kicks and blows upon Gunpowder, hoping, by a sudden movement, to give his companion the slip—but the spectre started full jump with him. Away then they dashed, through thick and thin; stones flying, and sparks flashing at every bound. Ichabod's flimsy garments fluttered in the air, as he stretched his long lank body away over his horse's head, in the eagerness of his flight.

They had now reached the road which turns off to Sleepy Hollow; but Gunpowder, who seemed possessed with a demon, instead of keeping up it, made an opposite turn, and plunged headlong down hill to the left. This road leads through a sandy hollow, shaded by trees for about a quarter of a mile, where it crosses the bridge famous in goblin story, and just beyond swells the green knoll on which stands the whitewashed church.

As yet the panic of the steed had given his unskilful rider an apparent advantage in the chase; but just as he had got half way through the hollow, the girths of the saddle gave way, and he felt it slipping from under him. He seized it by the pommel, and endeavored to hold it firm, but in vain; and had just time to save himself by clasping old Gunpowder round the neck, when the saddle fell to the earth, and he heard it trampled under foot by his pursuer. For a moment the terror of Hans Van Ripper's wrath passed across his mind—for it was his Sunday saddle; but this was no time for petty fears; the goblin was hard on his haunches; and (unskilful rider that he was!) he had much ado to maintain his seat; sometimes slipping on one side, sometimes on another, and sometimes jolted on the high ridge of his horse's backbone, with a violence that he verily feared would cleave him asunder.

An opening in the trees now cheered him with the hopes that the church bridge was at hand. The wavering reflection of a silver star in the bosom of the brook told him that he was not mistaken. He saw the walls of the church dimly glaring under the trees beyond. He recollected the place where Brom Bones's ghostly competitor had disappeared. "If I can but reach that bridge," thought Ichabod, "I am safe." Just then he heard the black steed panting and blowing close behind him; he even fancied that he felt his hot breath. Another convulsive kick in the ribs, and old Gunpowder sprang upon the bridge; he thundered over the resounding planks; he gained the opposite side; and now Ichabod cast a look behind to see if his pursuer should vanish, according to rule, in a flash of fire and brimstone. Just then he saw the goblin rising in his stirrups, and in the very act of hurling his head at him. Ichabod endeavored to dodge the horrible missile, but too late. It encountered his cranium with a tremendous crash,—he was tumbled headlong into the dust, and Gunpowder, the black steed, and the goblin rider, passed by like a whirlwind.

The next morning the old horse was found without his saddle, and with the bridle under his feet, soberly cropping the grass at his master's gate. Ichabod did not make his appearance at breakfast; dinner-hour came, but no Ichabod. The boys assembled at the school-house, and strolled idly about the banks of the brook; but no school-master. Hans Van Ripper now began to feel some uneasiness about the fate of poor Ichabod, and his saddle. An inquiry was set on foot, and after diligent investigation they came upon his traces. In one part of the road leading to the church was found the saddle trampled in the dirt; the tracks of horses' hoofs deeply dented in the road, and evidently at furious speed, were traced to the bridge, beyond which, on the bank of a broad part of the brook, where the water ran deep and black, was found the hat of the unfortunate Ichabod, and close beside it a shattered pumpkin.

The brook was searched, but the body of the school-master was not to be discovered. Hans Van Ripper, as executor of his estate, examined the bundle which contained all his worldly effects. They consisted of two shirts and a half; two stocks for the neck; a pair or two of worsted stockings; an old pair of corduroy smallclothes; a rusty razor; a book of psalm tunes full of dog's-ears; and a broken pitchpipe. As to the books and furniture of the school-house, they belonged to the community, excepting Cotton Mather's History of Witchcraft, a New England Almanac, and a book of dreams and fortune-telling; in which last was a sheet of foolscap much scribbled and blotted in several fruitless attempts to make a copy of verses in honor of the heiress of Van Tassel. These magic books and the poetic scrawl were forthwith consigned to the flames by Hans Van Ripper; who, from that time forward, determined to send his children no more to school; observing that he never knew any good come of this same reading and writing. Whatever money the school-master possessed, and he had received his quarter's pay but a day or two before, he must have had about his person at the time of his disappearance.

The mysterious event caused much speculation at the church on the following Sunday. Knots of gazers and gossips were collected in the church-yard, at the bridge, and at the spot where the hat and pumpkin had been found. The stories of Brouwer, of Bones, and a whole budget of others were called to mind; and when they had diligently considered them all, and compared them with the symptoms of the present case, they shook their heads, and came to the conclusion, that Ichabod had been carried off by the galloping Hessian. As he was a bachelor, and in nobody's debt, nobody troubled his head any more about him; the school was removed to a different quarter of the Hollow, and another pedagogue reigned in his stead.

It is true, an old farmer, who had been down to New York on a visit several years after, and from whom this account of the ghostly adventure was received, brought home the intelligence that Ichabod Crane was still alive; that he had left the neighborhood partly through fear of the goblin and Hans Van Ripper, and partly in mortification at having been suddenly dismissed by the heiress; that he had changed his quarters to a distant part of the country; had kept school and studied law at the same time; had been admitted to the bar; turned politician; electioneered; written for the newspapers; and finally, had been made a Justice of the Ten Pound Court. Brom Bones, too, who, shortly after his rival's disappearance, conducted the blooming Katrina in triumph to the altar, was observed to look exceedingly knowing whenever the story of Ichabod was related, and always burst into a hearty laugh at the mention of the pumpkin; which led some to suspect that he knew more about the matter than he chose to tell.

The old country wives, however, who are the best judges of these matters, maintain to this day that Ichabod was spirited away by supernatural means; and it is a favorite story often told about the neighborhood round the winter evening fire. The bridge became more than ever an object of superstitious awe, and that may be the reason why the road has been altered of late years, so as to approach the church by the border of the mill-pond. The school-house, being deserted, soon fell to decay, and was reported to be haunted by the ghost of the unfortunate pedagogue;

and the ploughboy, loitering homeward of a still summer evening, has often fancied his voice at a distance, chanting a melancholy psalm tune among the tranquil solitudes of Sleepy Hollow.

POSTSCRIPT

FOUND IN THE HANDWRITING OF MR. KNICKERBOCKER

The preceding tale is given almost in the precise words in which I heard it related at a Corporation meeting of the ancient city of the Manhattoes, at which were present many of its sagest and most illustrious burghers. The narrator was a pleasant, shabby, gentlemanly old fellow in pepper-and-salt clothes, with a sadly humorous face; and one whom I strongly suspected of being poor,—he made such efforts to be entertaining. When his story was concluded there was much laughter and approbation, particularly from two or three deputy aldermen, who had been asleep the greater part of the time. There was, however, one tall, dry-looking old gentleman, with beetling eyebrows, who maintained a grave and rather severe face throughout; now and then folding his arms, inclining his head, and looking down upon the floor, as if turning a doubt over in his mind. He was one of your wary men, who never laugh but upon good grounds —when they have reason and the law on their side. When the mirth of the rest of the company had subsided, and silence was restored, he leaned one arm on the elbow of his chair, and sticking the other akimbo, demanded, with a slight but exceedingly sage motion of the head, and contraction of the brow, what was the moral of the story, and what it went to prove.

The story-teller, who was just putting a glass of wine to his lips, as a refreshment after his toils, paused for a moment, looked at his inquirer with an air of infinite deference, and, lowering the glass slowly to the table, observed that the story was intended most logically to prove:

"That there is no situation in life but has its advantages and pleasures, provided we will but take a joke as we find it;

"That, therefore, he that runs races with goblin troopers is likely to have rough riding of it;

"Ergo, for a country school-master to be refused the hand of a Dutch heiress is a certain step to high preferment in the state."

The cautious old gentleman knit his brows tenfold closer after this explanation, being sorely puzzled by the ratiocination of the syllogism; while, methought, the one in pepper-and-salt eyed him with something of a triumphant leer. At length he observed that all this was very well, but still he thought the story a little on the extravagant; there were one or two points on which he had his doubts.

"Faith, sir," replied the story-teller, "as to that matter, I don't believe one half of it myself."

D. K.

PETER RUGG, THE MISSING MAN

by William Austin

William Austin's story of "Peter Rugg, the Missing Man," is probably the most successful adaptation of the Wandering Jew theme to American soil. Like the Ahasuerus of biblical tradition, Peter Rugg cannot die and must spend his years in constant wandering. Despite the passage of time, he does not age, and his horse and buggy are generally seen on New England roads not too far from Boston. By citing supposed eyewitnesses the author skillfully builds up the credibility of the tale; yet the most careful investigation by the narrator never quite solves the mystery. Perhaps, as is the case with folk tales, the impact of the story of Peter Rugg will be felt most by those who have a strong will to believe. Austin's tale was originally published in the New England Galaxy *(1824).*

Sir,—Agreeably to my promise, I now relate to you all the particulars of the lost man and child which I have been able to collect. It is entirely owing to the humane interest you seemed to take in the report that I have pursued the inquiry to the following result.

You may remember that business called me to Boston in the summer of 1820. I sailed in the packet to Providence; and when I arrived there, I learned that every seat in the stage was engaged. I was thus obliged either to wait a few hours, or accept a seat with the driver, who civilly offered me that accommodation. Accordingly I took my seat by his side, and soon found him intelligent and communicative. When we had travelled about ten miles, the horses suddenly threw their ears on their necks as flat as a hare's. Said the driver, "Have you a surtout with you?"

"No," said I; "why do you ask?"

"You will want one soon," said he. "Do you observe the ears of all the horses?"

"Yes"; and was just about to ask the reason.

"They see the storm-breeder, and we shall see him soon."

At this moment there was not a cloud visible in the firmament; soon after a small speck appeared in the road.

"There," said my companion, "comes the storm-breeder; he always leaves a Scotch mist behind him. By many a wet jacket do I remember him. I suppose the poor fellow suffers much himself—much more than is known to the world."

Presently a man with a child beside him, with a large black horse and a weather-beaten chair, once built for a chaise-body, passed in great haste, apparently at the rate of twelve miles an hour. He seemed to grasp the reins of his horse with firmness, and appeared to anticipate his speed. He seemed dejected, and looked anxiously at the passengers, particularly at the stage-driver and myself. In a moment after he passed us, the horses' ears were up, and bent themselves forward so that they nearly met.

"Who is that man?" said I; "he seems in great trouble."

"Nobody knows who he is; but his person and the child are familiar to me. I have met him more than a hundred times, and have been so often asked the way to Boston by that man, even when he was travelling directly from that town, that of late I have refused any communication with him; and that is the reason he gave me such a fixed look."

"But does he never stop anywhere?"

"I have never known him to stop anywhere longer than to inquire the way to Boston. And let him be where he may, he will tell you he cannot stay a moment, for he must reach Boston that night."

We were now ascending a high hill in Walpole; and as we had a fair view of the heavens, I was rather disposed to jeer the driver for thinking of his surtout, as not a cloud as big as a marble could be discerned.

"Do you look," said he, "in the direction whence the man came; that is the place to look. The storm never meets him, it follows him."

We presently approached another hill; and when at the height the driver pointed out in an eastern direction a little black speck about as big as a hat,—"There," said he, "is the seed storm; we may possibly reach Polley's before it reaches us, but the wanderer and his child will go to Providence through rain, thunder, and lightning."

And now the horses, as though taught by instinct, hastened with increased speed. The little black cloud came on rolling over the turnpike, and doubled and trebled itself in all directions. The appearance of this cloud attracted the notice of all the passengers; for after it had spread itself to a great bulk, it suddenly became more limited in circumference, grew more compact, dark, and consolidated. And now the successive flashes of chain lightning caused the whole cloud to appear like a sort of irregular network, and displayed a thousand fantastic images. The driver bespoke my attention to a remarkable configuration in the cloud; he said every flash of lightning near its centre discovered to him distinctly the form of a man sitting in an open carriage drawn by a black horse. But in truth I saw no such thing. The man's fancy was doubtless at fault. It is a very common thing for the imagination to paint for the senses, both in the visible and invisible world.

In the mean time the distant thunder gave notice of a shower at hand; and just as we reached Polley's tavern the rain poured down in torrents. It was soon over, the cloud passing in the direction of the turnpike toward Providence. In a few moments after, a respectable-looking man in a chaise stopped at the door. The man and child in the chair having excited some little sympathy among the passengers, the gentleman was asked if he had observed them. He said he had met them; that the man seemed bewildered, and inquired the way to Boston; that he was driving at great speed, as though he expected to outstrip the tempest; that the moment he had passed him, a thunder-clap broke directly over the man's head, and seemed to envelop both man and child, horse and carriage. "I stopped," said the gentleman, "supposing the lightning had struck him, but the horse only seemed to loom up and increase his speed; and as well as I could judge, he travelled just as fast as the thunder-cloud."

While this man was speaking, a pedlar with a cart of tin merchandise came up all dripping; and on being questioned, he said he had met that man and carriage, within a fortnight, in four different States; that at each time he had inquired the way to Boston, and that a thunder-shower, like the present, had each time deluged his wagon and his wares, setting his tinpots, etc., afloat, so that he had determined to get marine insurance done for the future. But that which excited his surprise most was the strange conduct of his horse; for that long before he could distinguish the man in the chair, his own horse stood still in the road, and flung back his ears. "In short," said the pedlar, "I wish never to see that man and horse again; they do not look to me as though they belonged to this world."

This was all I could learn at that time; and the occurrence soon after would have become with me "like one of those things which had never happened," had I not, as I stood recently on the doorstep of Bennett's Hotel in Hartford, heard a man say, "There goes Peter Rugg and his child! He looks wet and weary, and farther from Boston than ever." I was satisfied it was the same man I had seen more than three years before; for whoever has once seen Peter Rugg can never after be deceived as to his identity.

"Peter Rugg!" said I; "and who is Peter Rugg?"

"That," said the stranger, "is more than any one can tell exactly. He is a famous traveller, held in light esteem by all inn-holders, for he never stops to eat, drink, or sleep. I wonder why the Government does not employ him to carry the mail."

"Ay," said a bystander; "that is a thought bright only on one side. How long would it take in that case to send a letter to Boston?—for Peter has already, to my knowledge, been more than twenty years travelling to that place."

"But," said I, "does the man never stop anywhere? Does he never converse with any one? I saw the same man more than three years since near Providence, and I heard a strange story about him. Pray, sir, give me some account of this man."

"Sir," said the stranger, "those who know the most respecting that man say the least. I have heard it asserted that Heaven sometimes sets a mark on a man either for judgment or a trial. Under which Peter Rugg now labors, I cannot say; therefore I am rather inclined to pity than to judge."

"You speak like a humane man," said I; "and if you have known him so long, I pray you will give me some account of him. Has his appearance much altered in that time?"

"Why, yes; he looks as though he never ate, drank, or slept; and his child looks older than himself; and he looks like time broken off from eternity, and anxious to gain a resting-place."

"And how does his horse look?" said I.

"As for his horse, he looks fatter and gayer, and shows more animation and courage, than he did twenty years ago. The last time Rugg spoke to me he inquired how far it was to Boston. I told him just one hundred miles.

" 'Why,' said he, 'how can you deceive me so? It is cruel to mislead a traveller. I have lost my way; pray direct me the nearest way to Boston.'

"I repeated, it was one hundred miles.

" 'How can you say so?' said he; 'I was told last evening it was but fifty, and I have travelled all night.'

" 'But,' said I, 'you are now travelling from Boston. You must turn back.'

" 'Alas!' said he, 'it is all turn back! Boston shifts with the wind, and plays all around the compass. One man tells me it is to the east, another to the west; and the guide-posts, too, they all point the wrong way.'

" 'But will you not stop and rest?' said I; 'you seem wet and weary.'

" 'Yes,' said he; 'it has been foul weather since I left home.'

" 'Stop, then, and refresh yourself.'

" 'I must not stop; I must reach home to-night, if possible; though I think you must be mistaken in the distance to Boston.'

"He then gave the reins to his horse, which he restrained with difficulty, and disappeared in a moment. A few days afterward I met the man a little this side of Claremont, winding around the hills in Unity, at the rate, I believe, of twelve miles an hour."

"Is Peter Rugg his real name, or has he accidentally gained that name?"

"I know not, but presume he will not deny his name; you can ask him—for see, he has turned his horse, and is passing this way."

In a moment a dark-colored, high-spirited horse approached, and would have passed without stopping; but I had resolved to speak to Peter Rugg, or whoever the man might be. Accordingly I stepped into the street, and as the horse approached, I made a feint of stopping him. The man immediately reined in his horse. "Sir," said I, "may I be so bold as to inquire if you are not Mr. Rugg?—for I think I have seen you before."

"My name is Peter Rugg," said he; "I have unfortunately lost my way. I am wet and weary, and will take it kindly of you to direct me to Boston."

"You live in Boston, do you?—and in what street?"

"In Middle Street."

"When did you leave Boston?"

"I cannot tell precisely; it seems a considerable time."

"But how did you and your child become so wet? It has not rained here to-day."

"It has just rained a heavy shower up the river. But I shall not reach Boston to-night if I tarry. Would you advise me to take the old road, or the turnpike?"

"Why, the old road is one hundred and seventeen miles, and the turnpike is ninety-seven."

"How can you say so? You impose on me! It is wrong to trifle with a traveller. You know it is but forty miles from Newburyport to Boston."

"But this is not Newburyport; this is Hartford."

"Do not deceive me, sir. Is not this town Newburyport, and the river that I have been following the Merrimac?"

"No, sir; this is Hartford, and the river the Connecticut."

He wrung his hands and looked incredulous.

"Have the rivers, too, changed their courses, as the cities have changed places? But see! the clouds are gathering in the south, and we shall have a rainy night. Ah, that fatal oath!"

He would tarry no longer. His impatient horse leaped off, his hind flanks rising like wings; he seemed to devour all before him, and to scorn all behind.

I had now, as I thought, discovered a clew to the history of Peter Rugg, and I determined, the next time my business called me to Boston, to make a further inquiry. Soon after, I was enabled to collect the following particulars from Mrs. Croft, an aged lady in Middle Street, who has resided in Boston during the last twenty years. Her narration is this:

The last summer, a person, just at twilight, stopped at the door of the late Mrs. Rugg. Mrs. Croft, on coming to the door, perceived a stranger, with a child by his side, in an old weather-beaten carriage, with a black horse. The stranger asked for Mrs. Rugg, and was informed that Mrs. Rugg had died in a good old age more than twenty years before that time.

The stranger replied, "How can you deceive me so? Do ask Mrs. Rugg to step to the door."

"Sir, I assure you Mrs. Rugg has not lived here these nineteen years; no one lives here but myself, and my name is Betsy Croft."

The stranger paused, and looked up and down the street, and said: "Though the painting is rather faded, this looks like my house."

"Yes," said the child; "that is the stone before the door that I used to sit on to eat my bread and milk."

"But," said the stranger, "it seems to be on the wrong side of the street. Indeed everything here seems to be misplaced. The streets are all changed, the people are all changed, the town seems changed; and, what is strangest of all, Catherine Rugg has deserted her husband and child. Pray," continued the stranger, "has John Foy come home from sea? He went a long voyage; he is my kinsman. If I could see him, he could give me some account of Mrs. Rugg."

"Sir," said Mrs. Croft, "I never heard of John Foy. Where did he live?"

"Just above here, in Orange Tree Lane."

"There is no such place in this neighborhood."

"What do you tell me? Are the streets gone? Orange Tree Lane is at the head of Hanover Street, near Pemberton's Hill."

"There is no such lane now."

"Madam! you cannot be serious. But you doubtless know my brother, William Rugg. He lives in Royal Exchange Lane, near King Street."

"I know of no such lane, and I am sure there is no such street as King Street in this town."

"No such street as King Street! Why, woman, you mock me! You may as well tell me there is no King George! However, madam, you see I am wet and weary; I must find a resting-place. I will go to Hart's tavern, near the market."

"Which market, sir?—for you seem perplexed; we have several markets."

"You know there is but one market,— near the Town dock."

"Oh, the old market; but no such person has kept there these twenty years."

Here the stranger seemed disconcerted, and uttered to himself quite audibly: "Strange mistake! How much this looks like the town of Boston! It certainly has a great resemblance to it; but I perceive my mistake now. Some other Mrs. Rugg, some other Middle Street."

"Then," said he, "madam, can you direct me to Boston?"

"Why, this is Boston, the city of Boston. I know of no other Boston."

"City of Boston it may be; but it is not the Boston where I live. I recollect now, I came over a bridge instead of a ferry.

Pray what Bridge is that I just came over?"

"It is Charles River Bridge."

"I perceive my mistake; there is a ferry between Boston and Charlestown; there is no bridge. Ah, I perceive my mistake. If I were in Boston my horse would carry me directly to my own door. But my horse shows by his impatience that he is in a strange place. Absurd, that I should have mistaken this place for the old town of Boston! It is a much finer city than the town of Boston. It has been built long since Boston. I fancy it must lie at a distance from this city, as the good woman seems ignorant of it."

At these words his horse began to chafe and strike the pavement with his fore-feet. The stranger seemed a little bewildered, and said, "No home to-night"; and giving the reins to his horse, passed up the street, and I saw no more of him.

It was evident that the generation to which Peter Rugg belonged had passed away.

This was all the account of Peter Rugg I could obtain from Mrs. Croft; but she directed me to an elderly man, Mr. James Felt, who lived near her, and who had kept a record of the principal occurrences for the last fifty years. At my request she sent for him; and after I had related to him the object of my inquiry, Mr. Felt told me he had known Rugg in his youth; that his disappearance had caused some surprise; but as it sometimes happens that men run away, sometimes to be rid of others, and sometimes to be rid of themselves; and Rugg took his child with him, and his own horse and chair; and as it did not appear that any creditors made a stir, —the occurrence soon mingled itself in the stream of oblivion, and Rugg and his child, horse and chair, were soon forgotten.

"It is true," said Mr. Felt, "sundry stories grew out of Rugg's affair,—whether true or false I cannot tell; but stranger things have happened in my day, without even a newspaper notice."

"Sir," said I, "Peter Rugg is now living; I have lately seen Peter Rugg and his child, horse, and chair. Therefore I pray to relate to me all you know or ever heard of him."

"Why, my friend," said James Felt, "that Peter Rugg is now a living man, I will not deny; but that you have seen Peter Rugg and his child is impossible, if you mean a small child; for Jenny Rugg, if living, must be at least—let me see—Boston Massacre, 1770—Jenny Rugg was about ten years old. Why, sir, Jenny Rugg, if living, must be more than sixty years of age. That Peter Rugg is living, is highly probable, as he was only ten years older than myself, and I was only eighty last March; and I am as likely to live twenty years longer as any man."

Here I perceived that Mr. Felt was in his dotage; and I despaired of gaining any intelligence from him on which I could depend.

I took my leave of Mrs. Croft, and I proceeded to my lodgings at the Marlborough Hotel.

If Peter Rugg, thought I, has been travelling since the Boston Massacre, there is no reason why he should not travel to the end of time. If the present generation know little of him, the next will know less; and Peter and his child will have no hold on this world.

In the course of the evening I related my adventure in Middle Street.

"Ha!" said one of the company, smiling, "do you really think you have seen Peter Rugg? I have heard my grandfather speak of him as though he seriously believed his own story."

"Sir," said I, "pray let us compare your grandfather's story of Mr. Rugg with my own."

"Peter Rugg, sir, if my grandfather was worthy of credit, once lived in Middle Street, in this city. He was a man in comfortable circumstances, had a wife and one daughter, and was generally esteemed for his sober life and manners. But, unhappily, his temper at times was altogether ungovernable; and then his language was terrible. In these fits of passion, if a door stood in his way, he would never do less than kick a panel through. He would sometimes throw his heels over his head and come down on his feet, uttering oaths in a circle; and thus in a rage he was the first who performed a somerset, and did what others have since learned to do for merriment and money. Once Rugg was seen to bite a tenpenny nail in halves. In those days everybody, both men and boys, wore wigs; and Peter, at these moments of violent passion, would become so profane that his wig would rise up from his head. Some said it was on account of his terrible language; others accounted for it in a more philosophical way, and said it was caused by the expansion of his scalp,—as violent passion, we know, will swell the veins and expand the head. While these fits were on him Rugg had no respect for heaven or earth. Except this infirmity, all agreed that Rugg was a good sort of man; for when his fits were over, nobody was so ready to commend a placid temper as Peter.

"It was late in autumn, one morning, that Rugg, in his own chair, with a fine large bay horse, took his daughter and proceeded to Concord. On his return a violent storm overtook him. At dark he stopped in Menotomy, now West Cambridge, at the door of a Mr. Cutter, a friend of his, who urged him to tarry the night. On Rugg's declining to stop, Mr. Cutter urged him vehemently. 'Why, Mr. Rugg,' said Cutter, 'the storm is overwhelming you: the night is exceeding dark: your little daughter will perish: you are in an open chair, and the tempest is increasing.' 'Let the storm increase,' said Rugg, with a fearful oath; 'I will see home to-night, in spite of the last tempest, or *may I never see home!'* At these words he gave his whip to his high-spirited horse, and disappeared in a moment. But Peter Rugg did not reach home that night, or the next; nor, when he became a missing man, could he ever be traced beyond Mr. Cutter's in Menotomy.

"For a long time after, on every dark and stormy night, the wife of Peter Rugg would fancy she heard the crack of a whip, and the fleet tread of a horse, and the rattling of a carriage passing her door. The neighbors, too, heard the same noises; and some said they knew it was Rugg's horse, the tread on the pavement was perfectly familiar to them. This occurred so repeatedly, that at length the neighbors watched with lanterns, and saw the real Peter Rugg, with his own horse and chair, and child sitting beside him, pass directly before his own door, his head turned toward his house, and himself making every effort to stop his horse, but in vain.

"The next day the friends of Mrs. Rugg exerted themselves to find her husband and child. They inquired at every public-house and stable in town; but it did not appear that Rugg made any stay in Boston. No one, after Rugg had passed his own door, could give any account of him; though it was asserted by some that the clatter of Rugg's horse and carriage over the pavements shook the houses on both sides of the streets. And this is credible, if indeed Rugg's horse and carriage did pass on that night. For at this day, in many of the streets, a loaded truck or team in passing will shake the houses like an earthquake. However, Rugg's neighbors never afterward watched; some of them treated it all as a delusion, and thought no more of it. Others, of a different opinion, shook their heads and said nothing.

"Thus Rugg and his child, horse, and chair, were soon forgotten, and probably many in the neighborhood never heard a word on the subject.

"There was, indeed, a rumor that Rugg afterward was seen in Connecticut, between Suffield and Hartford, passing through the country with head-long speed. This gave occasion to Rugg's friends to make further inquiry. But the more they inquired, the more they were baffled. If they heard of Rugg one day in Connecticut, the next day they heard of him winding round the hills in New Hampshire; and soon after, a man in a chair with a small child, exactly answering the description of Peter Rugg, would be seen in Rhode Island inquiring the way to Boston.

"But that which chiefly gave a color of mystery to the story of Peter Rugg was the affair at Charleston Bridge. The toll-gatherer asserted that sometimes on the darkest and most stormy nights, when no object could be discerned, about the time Rugg was missing, a horse and wheel carriage, with a noise equal to a troop, would at midnight, in utter contempt of the rates of toll, pass over the bridge. This occurred so frequently, that the toll-gatherer resolved to attempt a discovery. Soon after, at the usual time, apparently the same horse and carriage approached the bridge from Charleston Square. The toll-gatherer, prepared, took his stand as near the middle of the bridge as he dared, with a large three-legged stool in his hand. As the appearance passed, he threw the stool at the horse, but heard nothing, except the noise of the stool skipping across the bridge. The toll-gatherer, on the next day, asserted that the stool went directly through the body of the horse; and he persisted in that belief ever after. Whether Rugg, or whoever the person was, ever passed the bridge again, the toll-gatherer would never tell; and when questioned, seemed anxious to waive the subject. And thus Peter Rugg and his child, horse, and carriage, remain a mystery to this day."

This, sir, is all that I could learn of Peter Rugg in Boston.

THE WITCH OF COÖS

by Robert Frost

For many years Robert Frost has been celebrated for his interpretations of New England rural life. He has presented the Yankee farmers with sympathy and insight, and he has faithfully revealed their reticences, their angularities, their rarely expressed emotions, and their pawky humor. The New England countryman, despite his veneer of sanity and practicality, still retains a little of the interest in the supernatural which motivated some of his ancestors many decades ago to do violent deeds at Salem. In "The Witch of Coös" Frost has a wayfarer stop for a night's lodging at a mountain farm. The family ghost tale has been preserved so long by the mother and son that eventually they must confess it, and the solitary guest provides the necessary audience. It is interesting to note that he neither accepts nor rejects the tale as true; he simply listens to the old-believers in the supernatural, and "they did all the talking."

I stayed the night for shelter at a farm
Behind the mountain, with a mother and son,
Two old-believers. They did all the talking.

MOTHER. Folks think a witch who has familiar spirits
She could call up to pass a winter evening,
But won't, should be burned at the stake or something.
Summoning spirits isn't 'Button, button,
Who's got the button,' I would have them know.

SON. Mother can make a common table rear
And kick with two legs like an army mule.

MOTHER. And when I've done it, what good have I done?
Rather than tip a table for you, let me

Tell you what Ralle the Sioux Control once told me.
He said the dead had souls, but when I asked him
How could that be—I thought the dead were souls,
He broke my trance. Don't that make you suspicious
That there's something the dead are keeping back?
Yes, there's something the dead are keeping back.

SON. You wouldn't want to tell him what we have
Up attic, mother?

MOTHER. Bones—a skeleton.

SON. But the headboard of mother's bed is pushed
Against the attic door: the door is nailed.
It's harmless. Mother hears it in the night
Halting perplexed behind the barrier
Of door and headboard. Where it wants to get
Is back into the cellar where it came from.

MOTHER. We'll never let them, will we, son! We'll never!

SON. It left the cellar forty years ago
And carried itself like a pile of dishes
Up one flight from the cellar to the kitchen,
Another from the kitchen to the bedroom,
Another from the bedroom to the attic,
Right past both father and mother, and neither stopped it.
Father had gone upstairs; mother was downstairs.
I was a baby: I don't know where I was.

MOTHER The only fault my husband found with me—
I went to sleep before I went to bed,
Especially in winter when the bed
Might just as well be ice and the clothes snow.
The night the bones came up the cellar-stairs
Toffile had gone to bed alone and left me,
But left an open door to cool the room off
So as to sort of turn me out of it.
I was just coming to myself enough

To wonder where the cold was coming from,
When I heard Toffile upstairs in the bedroom
And thought I heard him downstairs in the cellar.
The board we had laid down to walk dry-shod on
When there was water in the cellar in spring
Struck the hard cellar bottom. And then someone
Began the stairs, two footsteps for each step,
The way a man with one leg and a crutch,
Or a little child, comes up. It wasn't Toffile:
It wasn't anyone who could be there.
The bulkhead double-doors were double-locked
And swollen tight and buried under snow.
The cellar windows were banked up with sawdust
And swollen tight and buried under snow.
It was the bones. I knew them—and good reason.
My first impulse was to get to the knob
And hold the door. But the bones didn't try
The door; they halted helpless on the landing,
Waiting for things to happen in their favor.
The faintest restless rustling ran all through them.
I never could have done the thing I did
If the wish hadn't been too strong in me
To see how they were mounted for this walk.
I had a vision of them put together
Not like a man, but like a chandelier.
So suddenly I flung the door wide on him.
A moment he stood balancing with emotion,
And all but lost himself. (A tongue of fire
Flashed out and licked along his upper teeth.
Smoke rolled inside the sockets of his eyes.)

Then he came at me with one hand outstretched,
The way he did in life once; but this time
I struck the hand off brittle on the floor,
And fell back from him on the floor myself.
The finger-pieces slid in all directions.
(Where did I see one of those pieces lately?
Hand me my button-box—it must be there.)
I sat up on the floor and shouted, 'Toffile,
It's coming up to you.' It had its choice
Of the door to the cellar or the hall.
It took the hall door for the novelty,
And set off briskly for so slow a thing,
Still going every which way in the joints, though,
So that it looked like lightning or a scribble,
From the slap I had just now given its hand.
I listened till it almost climbed the stairs
From the hall to the only finished bedroom,
Before I got up to do anything;
Then ran and shouted, 'Shut the bedroom door,
Toffile, for my sake!' 'Company?' he said,
'Don't make me get up; I'm too warm in bed.'
So lying forward weakly on the handrail
I pushed myself upstairs, and in the light
(The kitchen had been dark) I had to own
I could see nothing. 'Toffile, I don't see it.
It's with us in the room though. It's the bones.'
'What bones?' 'The cellar bones—out of the grave.'
That made him throw his bare legs out of bed
And sit up by me and take hold of me.
I wanted to put out the light and see
If I could see it, or else mow the room,
With our arms at the level of our knees,
And bring the chalk-pile down. 'I'll tell you what—
It's looking for another door to try.
The uncommonly deep snow has made him think
Of his old song, *The Wild Colonial Boy*,
He always used to sing along the tote-road.
He's after an open door to get out-doors.
Let's trap him with an open door up attic.'
Toffile agreed to that, and sure enough,
Almost the moment he was given an opening,
The steps began to climb the attic stairs.
I heard them. Toffile didn't seem to hear them.

'Quick!' I slammed to the door and held the knob.
'Toffile, get nails.' I made him nail the door shut
And push the headboard of the bed against it.
Then we asked was there anything
Up attic that we'd ever want again.
The attic was less to us than the cellar.
If the bones liked the attic, let them have it.
Let them stay in the attic. When they sometimes
Come down the stairs at night and stand perplexed
Behind the door and headboard of the bed,
Brushing their chalky skull with chalky fingers,
With sounds like the dry rattling of a shutter,
That's what I sit up in the dark to say—
To no one any more since Toffile died.
Let them stay in the attic since they went there.
I promised Toffile to be cruel to them
For helping them be cruel once to him.

SON. We think they had a grave down in the cellar.

MOTHER. We know they had a grave down in the cellar.

SON. We never could find out whose bones they were.

MOTHER. Yes, we could too, son. Tell the truth for once.
They were a man's his father killed for me.
I mean a man he killed instead of me.
The least I could do was to help dig their grave.
We were about it one night in the cellar.
Son knows the story: but 'twas not for him
To tell the truth, suppose the time had come.
Son looks surprised to see me end a lie
We'd kept all these years between ourselves
So as to have it ready for outsiders.
But tonight I don't care enough to lie—
I don't remember why I ever cared.
Toffile, if he were here, I don't believe
Could tell you why he ever cared himself. . . .

She hadn't found the finger-bone she wanted
Among the buttons poured out in her lap.
I verified the name next morning: Toffile.
The rural letter-box said Toffile Lajway.

THE GHOSTS
OF THE BUFFALOES

by Vachel Lindsay

Vachel Lindsay liked to think of his native city of Springfield, Illinois, as a future capital of the world and frequently concerned himself with the history of his prairie state. He had no difficulty in imagining the hordes of buffalo which once lived on the grasslands in the valley of the Mississippi River, and he pictured them as so many stampeding demons. The poem is enriched by many of the strident acoustic effects which made his so-called "jazz verse" memorable.

Last night at black midnight I woke with a cry,
The windows were shaking, there was thunder on high,
The floor was a-tremble, the door was a-jar,
White fires, crimson fires, shone from afar.
I rushed to the door yard. The city was gone.
My home was a hut without orchard or lawn.
It was mud-smear and logs near a whispering stream,
Nothing else built by man could I see in my dream . . .
Then . . .
Ghost-kings came headlong, row upon row,
Gods of the Indians, torches aglow.

They mounted the bear and the elk and the deer,
And eagles gigantic, aged and sere,
They rode long-horn cattle, they cried "A-la-la."
They lifted the knife, the bow, and the spear,
They lifted ghost-torches from dead fires below,
The midnight made grand with the cry "A-la-la."

The midnight made grand with a red-god charge,
A red-god show,
A red-god show,
"A-la-la, a-la-la, a-la-la, a-la-la."

With bodies like bronze, and terrible eyes
Came the rank and the file, with catamount cries,
Gibbering, yipping, with hollow-skull clacks,
Riding white bronchos with skeleton backs,
Scalp-hunters, beaded and spangled and bad,
Naked and lustful and foaming and mad,
Flashing primeval demoniac scorn,
Blood-thirst and pomp amid darkness reborn,
Power and glory that sleep in the grass
While the winds and the snows and the great rains pass.
They crossed the gray river, thousands abreast,
They rode in infinite lines to the west,
Tide upon tide of strange fury and foam,
Spirits and wraiths, the blue was their home,
The sky was their goal where the star-flags were furled,
And on past those far golden splendors they whirled.
They burned to dim meteors, lost in the deep.
And I turned in dazed wonder, thinking of sleep.

And the wind crept by
Alone, unkempt, unsatisfied,
The wind cried and cried—
Muttered of massacres long past,
Buffaloes in shambles vast . . .
An owl said: "Hark, what is a-wing?"
I heard a cricket carolling,
I heard a cricket carolling,
I heard a cricket carolling.

Then . . .
Snuffing the lightning that crashed from on high
Rose royal old buffaloes, row upon row.
The lords of the prairie came galloping by.
And I cried in my heart "A-la-la, a-la-la,
A red-god show,
A red-god show,
A-la-la, a-la-la, a-la-la, a-la-la."

Buffaloes, buffaloes, thousands abreast,
A scourge and amazement, they swept to the west.
With black bobbing noses, with red rolling tongues,
Coughing forth steam from their leather-wrapped lungs,

Cows with their calves, bulls big and vain,
Goring the laggards, shaking the mane,
Stamping flint feet, flashing moon eyes,
Pompous and owlish, shaggy and wise.
Like sea-cliffs and caves resounded their ranks
With shoulders like waves, and undulant flanks.
Tide upon tide of strange fury and foam,
Spirits and wraiths, the blue was their home,
The sky was their goal where the star-flags are furled,
And on past those far golden splendors they whirled.
They burned to dim meteors, lost in the deep,
And I turned in dazed wonder, thinking of sleep.

I heard a cricket's cymbals play,
A scarecrow lightly flapped his rags,
And a pan that hung by his shoulder rang,
Rattled and thumped in a listless way,
And now the wind in the chimney sang,
The wind in the chimney,
The wind in the chimney,
The wind in the chimney,
Seemed to say:—
"Dream, boy, dream,
If you anywise can.
To dream is the work
Of beast or man.
Life is the west-going dream-storms' breath,
Life is a dream, the sigh of the skies,
The breath of the stars, that nod on their pillows
With their golden hair mussed over their eyes."
The locust played on his musical wing,
Sang to his mate of love's delight.
I heard the whippoorwill's soft fret,
I heard a cricket carolling,
I heard a cricket carolling,
I heard a cricket carolling,
I heard a cricket say: "Good-night, good-night,
Good-night, good-night, . . . good-night."

THE LAVENDER EVENING DRESS

by Carl Carmer

A ghost story having wide currency and many variations throughout the United States concerns a person who seems quite normal and healthy but who suddenly disappears; upon inquiry, the people who have been in his company learn that he has been dead for some time. In older forms of the story the person may perhaps be identified with the restless ghost who can wander during the night but must return to his supernatural bourn before cockcrow; contemporary versions often describe the solitary figure as a hitchhiker. Alexander Woollcott once introduced such a tale into a memorable radio broadcast. In the following version of the story, as recorded by Carl Carmer, a factual incident is first reported, and then an anecdote of the kind that floats in the popular memory is told. The juxtaposition of the two narratives makes a peculiarly interesting ghost story. "The Lavender Evening Dress" appeared in Dark Trees to the Wind *(1949).*

A few years ago the postmaster in a village that lies beside the lonely waters of the Ramapo River, dappled by light and leaf shadow in the morning and darkened by hill shadows in the afternoon, talked often about a lithe tawny girl with hyacinth eyes and wheat-yellow hair. He was a sophisticated gentleman, traveled and urbane, a member of a distinguished family in those parts. To atone for his sins, he said, he taught a boys' class in a Sunday school that was in session on the first day of each week after the preaching in a tiny, weathered church back in the Ramapo hills.

From the summits of those hills, on a clear day washed by recent rain, the slim gray towers on Manhattan Island seem to advance into sight and hang, like figures long ago worked into the tapestry on the old blue sky wall. None of the boys in the Sunday school had ever entered the city on the horizon and only a few of them had been to Hillburn or Sloatsburg in York State or any of the New Jersey towns to the west. They were a shy lot but wild as woods animals are wild, and they found the simple lessons in Christian ethics the postmaster was trying to teach difficult at best and impossible at those times when that girl was around.

She went through his class, the postmaster said, like a slow pestilence. A boy would be gone for a month, sometimes two months, and then he would come back on a Sunday, glowering and sheepish, and one of his schoolmates would be absent for a while. The Sunday-school teacher would sometimes see him and the girl picking wild blackberries on a hillside or, on a Saturday night, walking the road shoes in hand to a country dance.

There was much talk about the girl among the hill-folk gossips; and the postmaster, whose job gave him speaking acquaintance with most of these, gathered

99

from what they said that she was gay and hot tempered and amoral—feeling that the general admiration gave her the privilege of disobeying the somewhat eccentric conventions of her own community. The only time he had a good look at her was during a Wednesday night prayer meeting at which, according to an announcement the previous Sunday, the contents of three barrels of old clothes from the members of a New York City church would be distributed. The girl came in after the service and just as the preacher beat in the head of the first barrel. She was barefoot and it was obvious that she wore only a stained and patched calico-check dress much too small for her. She sat in the back pew and paid no attention as the usual pathetic garments that are contained in such shipments were displayed and granted to those who could argue the greatest need.

There was a gasp when the preacher pulled from the middle of the second barrel a lavender evening dress covered with sequins that glinted like tiny amethysts. It was cut low off the shoulders and as soon as the preacher saw that he rolled it up into a shapeless bundle holding it helpless and waiting for someone to speak for it. No one did but the girl stood up and padded swiftly down the aisle. Without saying a word she grabbed the dress from the good man's hands and raced out of the church.

From that time on, the postmaster said, no one ever saw the girl in other costume. Rain or shine, day or night, she was a brush stroke of lavender against the brown of dirt roads, the green of hill slopes, the khaki-colored shirts and pants of whatever boy strode beside her.

Frost came early that year and leaves dropped. The air was clear and the New York towers came nearer and stayed longer. The hill people were all talking about a letter that had come to the girl from cousins in Jersey City. The postmaster had told one of his Sunday-school boys that the letter had come and the next day she had stood before his window and quietly asked for it, the sequins glinting purple in the shadowy room. People who dropped in the next day said her cousins had invited her to visit them and they had sent the money for her bus fare. A week later, a witness regaled the postmaster with a description of the expressions on the faces of the bus passengers down on the asphalt highway twelve miles away when the girl climbed aboard, holding her long skirt about her waist.

In mid-December came a cold snap and the thermometer outside showed eighteen degrees below zero when the postmaster opened his window for business. The people in the line of waiters-for-mail were more eager to give him the news than to receive their letters. The body of the girl in the lavender dress had been found frozen and stiff on the road a few miles above the bus stop. Returning from Jersey City, she had left the bus and begun the long walk home, but the evening dress proved too flimsy wear for such a night.

The postmaster said that after this tragedy all the students in his class came regularly to Sunday school, and that was the end of the story of the girl.

The girl froze to death about 1939 and for a decade nothing reflected doubt on the postmaster's conclusion. But now a growing number of people feel that his narrative, the truth of which is easily provable by many witnesses, has had an inexplicable consequence, overtones that have transcended his matter-of-fact realism. For a strange report recently began its rounds of upstate towns and, particularly, colleges. It had many variants, as such tales do, but in none of them was it in any way connected with the account of the girl, her dress, and her death, a factual record known only in the vicinity of her Ramapo home, and the suggestion of such a connection is made here possibly for the first time.

As I heard it, two Hamilton College juniors motoring to a dance at Tuxedo Park after sunset of a warm Indian summer Saturday on the road that runs through the valley of the little Ramapo River saw a girl waiting. She was wearing a party dress the color of the mist rising above the dark water of the stream and her hair was the color of ripe wheat. The boys stopped their car and asked the girl if they could take her in the direction she was going. She eagerly seated herself between them and asked if they were going to the square dance at Sterling Furnace. The thin, tanned face with high cheekbones, the yellow hair, the flashing smile, the quicksilver quality of her gestures, enchanted the boys and it was soon a matter of amused debate whether they would go along with her to Sterling Furnace or she would accompany them to the dance at Tuxedo. The majority won and the boys were soon presenting their new friend to the young couple who were their hosts at the Park. "Call me 'Lavender,'" she said to them. "It's my nickname because I always wear that color."

After an evening in which the girl, quiet and smiling, made a most favorable impression by her dancing, drifting dreamily through the waltzes in a sparkling cloud of lavender sequins, stepping more adeptly than any of the other dancers through the complications of revived square dances —Money Musk—Hull's Victory—Nellie Gray—the boys took her out to their car for the ride home. She said that she was cold and one of them doffed his tweed topcoat and helped her into it. They were both shocked into clichés of courtesy when, after gaily directing the driver through dusty woodland roads she finally bade him stop before a shack so dilapidated that it would have seemed deserted had it not been for a ragged lace curtain over the small window in the door. After promising to see them again soon, she waved good night, standing beside the road until they had turned around and rolled away. They were almost in Tuxedo before the chill air made the coatless one realize that he had forgotten to reclaim his property and they decided to return for it on their way back to college the next day.

The afternoon was clear and sunny when, after considerable difficulty in finding the shack, the boys knocked on the door with the ragged lace curtain over its window. A decrepit white-haired woman answered the door and peered at them out of piercing blue eyes when they asked for Lavender.

"Old friends of hers?" she asked, and the boys, fearing to get the girl into the bad graces of her family by telling the truth about their adventure of the day before, said yes they were old friends.

"Then ye couldn't a-heerd she's dead," said the woman. "Been in the graveyard down the road fer near ten years."

Horrified the boys protested that this was not the girl they meant—that they were trying to find someone they had seen the previous evening.

"Nobody else o' that name ever lived round here," said the woman. "'Twan't her real name anyway. Her paw named her Lily when she was born. Some folks used to call her Lavender on account o' the pretty dress she wore all the time. She was buried in it."

The boys once more turned about and started for the paved highway. A hundred yards down the road the driver jammed on the brakes.

"There's the graveyard," he said, pointing to a few weathered stones standing in bright sunlight in an open field overgrown with weeds, "and just for the hell of it I'm going over there."

They found the stone—a little one marked "Lily"—and on the curving mound in front of it, neatly folded, the tweed topcoat.

IV

WITCHCRAFT
and
SUPERSTITION

Witchcraft has a long and dishonorable history. All lands and all ages reveal its existence, even down to the present; and magicians, sorcerers, medicine men, witches, and conjurers have been all but ubiquitous. In the fifteenth and sixteenth centuries the pursuit of witches and demons reached its frenzied peak, and the American culmination of the craze occurred with the execution of nineteen accused persons at Salem in 1692. Small wonder, then, that writers have, with various degrees of success, utilized popular superstitions for specific purposes. In the hands of a moralist and allegorist like Nathaniel Hawthorne, witchcraft served as a convenient narrative medium which, at the same time, gave point to his tales. A good deal of a skeptic himself, he always relied on ambiguity to provide a reasonable explanation for untoward events. To the primitive Negro, however, the chants and spells of the conjure man were horribly real and had an important place in daily life: The Negress tricked by love went to a trusted practitioner of the black art for solace and aid, and to her mind the mystery and grotesqueness of the rites only increased their efficacy. Charles Chesnutt and Julia Peterkin both show the important role of witchcraft in Negro life. But, to sophisticated minds, witchcraft assumes a comic aspect, and shamanism or necromancy survives largely as evidence of the provincialism of our ancestors. The werewolf, the windigo, the vampire of old have been superseded by the Halloween witch and the jack-o'-lantern. It is somewhat in this spirit that James Hall told the tale of the puzzled frontier hunter who owed his troubles to a befuddled mind. Perhaps the modern attitude toward witchcraft might be expressed in the words of Mr. Dooley: "Th' Apostles' Creed niver was as con-vincin' to me afther I larned to r-read it as it was whin I cudden't read it, but believed it."

FEATHERTOP

A MORALIZED LEGEND

by Nathaniel Hawthorne

Hawthorne, as his notebooks reveal, often proceeded not from a character or an event but from an idea or a moral to a story. In other words, he came upon an allegorical theme first and then determined to give it a narrative dress. The frequent result was that his story, although finely literary in style and craftsmanship, wanted vitality. "Feathertop," one of the tales in Mosses from an Old Manse *(1846), is adroit and humorous but lacking in emotional appeal. On the other hand, the scarecrow suddenly become human is an excellent means of satirizing the vanity and pretension of men until the reflection of his true image in a mirror reveals his real self. Then there is a flash of pity for Feathertop; but the witch calmly reduces him to the original sticks and straw and sends him off to his traditional duty in a cornfield. It is interesting to note that there is no real foil for Mother Rigby and that Dickon, the servant with remarkable powers, never appears or speaks. Yet the story seems constantly on the fringe of the marvelous.*

Dickon," cried Mother Rigby, "a coal for my pipe!"

The pipe was in the old dame's mouth when she said these words. She had thrust it there after filling it with tobacco, but without stooping to light it at the hearth, where indeed there was no appearance of a fire having been kindled that morning. Forthwith, however, as soon as the order was given, there was an intense red glow out of the bowl of the pipe, and a whiff of smoke from Mother Rigby's lips. Whence the coal came, and how brought thither by an invisible hand, I have never been able to discover.

"Good!" quoth Mother Rigby, with a nod of her head. "Thank ye, Dickon! And now for making this scarecrow. Be within call, Dickon, in case I need you again."

The good woman had risen thus early (for as yet it was scarcely sunrise) in order to set about making a scarecrow, which she intended to put in the middle of her corn-patch. It was now the latter week of May, and the crows and blackbirds had already discovered the little, green, rolled-up leaf of the Indian corn just peeping out of the soil. She was determined, therefore, to contrive as lifelike a scarecrow as ever was seen, and to finish it immediately, from top to toe, so that it should begin its sentinel's duty that very morning. Now Mother Rigby (as everybody must have heard) was one of the most cunning and potent witches in New England, and might, with very little trouble, have made a scarecrow ugly enough to frighten the minister himself. But on this occasion, as she had awakened in an uncommonly pleasant humor, and was further dulcified by her pipe of tobacco, she resolved to produce something fine, beautiful, and splendid, rather than hideous and horrible.

"I don't want to set up a hobgoblin in my own corn-patch, and almost at my own doorstep," said Mother Rigby to herself, puffing out a whiff of smoke; "I could do it if I pleased, but I'm tired of doing marvellous things, and so I'll keep within the bounds of every-day business just for variety's sake. Besides, there is no use in scaring the little children for a mile roundabout, though 't is true I'm a witch."

It was settled, therefore, in her own mind, that the scarecrow should represent a fine gentleman of the period, so far as the materials at hand would allow. Perhaps it may be as well to enumerate the chief of the articles that went to the composition of this figure.

The most important item of all, probably, although it made so little show, was a certain broomstick, on which Mother Rigby had taken many an airy gallop at midnight, and which now served the scarecrow by way of a spinal column, or, as the unlearned phrase it, a backbone. One of its arms was a disabled flail which used to be wielded by Goodman Rigby, before his spouse worried him out of this troublesome world; the other, if I mistake not, was composed of the pudding stick and a broken rung of a chair, tied loosely together at the elbow. As for its legs, the right was a hoe handle, and the left an undistinguished and miscellaneous stick from the

woodpile. Its lungs, stomach, and other affairs of that kind were nothing better than a meal bag stuffed with straw. Thus we have made out the skeleton and entire corporosity of the scarecrow, with the exception of its head; and this was admirably supplied by a somewhat withered and shrivelled pumpkin, in which Mother Rigby cut two holes for the eyes, and a slit for the mouth, leaving a bluish-colored knob in the middle to pass for a nose. It was really quite a respectable face.

"I've seen worse ones on human shoulders, at any rate," said Mother Rigby. "And many a fine gentleman has a pumpkin head, as well as my scarecrow."

But the clothes, in this case, were to be the making of the man. So the good old woman took down from a peg an ancient plum-colored coat of London make, and with relics of embroidery on its seams, cuffs, pocket-flaps, and button-holes, but lamentably worn and faded, patched at the elbows, tattered at the skirts, and threadbare all over. On the left breast was a round hole, whence either a star of nobility had been rent away, or else the hot heart of some former wearer had scorched it through and through. The neighbors said that this rich garment belonged to the Black Man's wardrobe, and that he kept it at Mother Rigby's cottage for the convenience of slipping it on whenever he wished to make a grand appearance at the governor's table. To match the coat there was a velvet waistcoat of very ample size, and formerly embroidered with foliage that had been as brightly golden as the maple leaves in October, but which had now quite vanished out of the substance of the velvet. Next came a pair of scarlet breeches, once worn by the French governor of Louisbourg, and the knees of which had touched the lower step of the throne of Louis le Grand. The Frenchman had given these smallclothes to an Indian powwow, who parted with them to the old witch for a gill of strong waters, at one of their dances in the forest. Furthermore, Mother Rigby produced a pair of silk stockings and put them on the figure's legs, where they showed as unsubstantial as a dream, with the wooden reality of the two sticks making itself miserably apparent through the holes. Lastly, she put her dead husband's wig on the bare scalp of the pumpkin, and surmounted the whole with a dusty three-cornered hat, in which was stuck the longest tail feather of a rooster.

Then the old dame stood the figure up in a corner of her cottage and chuckled to behold its yellow semblance of a visage, with its nobby little nose thrust into the air. It had a strangely self-satisfied aspect, and seemed to say, "Come look at me!"

"And you are well worth looking at, that's a fact!" quoth Mother Rigby, in admiration at her own handiwork. "I've made many a puppet since I've been a witch, but methinks this is the finest of them all. 'T is almost too good for a scarecrow. And, by the by, I'll just fill a fresh pipe of tobacco and then take him out to the corn-patch."

While filling her pipe the old woman continued to gaze with almost motherly affection at the figure in the corner. To say the truth, whether it were chance, or skill, or downright witchcraft, there was something wonderfully human in this ridiculous shape, bedizened with its tattered finery; and as for the countenance, it appeared to shrivel its yellow surface into a grin—a funny kind of expression betwixt scorn and merriment, as if it understood itself to be a jest at mankind. The more Mother Rigby looked the better she was pleased.

"Dickon," cried she sharply, "another coal for my pipe!"

Hardly had she spoken, than, just as before, there was a red-glowing coal on the top of the tobacco. She drew in a long whiff and puffed it forth again into the bar of morning sunshine which struggled through the one dusty pane of her cottage window. Mother Rigby always liked to flavor her pipe with a coal of fire from the particular chimney corner whence this had been brought. But where that chimney corner might be, or who brought the coal from it,—further than that the invisible messenger seemed to respond to the name of Dickon,—I cannot tell.

"That puppet yonder," thought Mother Rigby, still with her eyes fixed on the scarecrow, "is too good a piece of work to stand all summer in a corn-patch, frightening away the crows and blackbirds. He's capable of better things. Why, I've danced with a worse one, when partners happened to be scarce, at our witch meetings in the forest! What if I should let him take his chance among the other men of straw and empty fellows who go bustling about the world?"

The old witch took three or four more whiffs of her pipe and smiled.

"He'll meet plenty of his brethren at every street corner!" continued she. "Well; I didn't mean to dabble in witchcraft today, further than the lighting of my pipe, but a witch I am, and a witch I'm likely to be, and there's no use trying to shirk it. I'll make a man of my scarecrow, were it only for the joke's sake!"

While muttering these words, Mother Rigby took the pipe from her own mouth and thrust it into the crevice which represented the same feature in the pumpkin visage of the scarecrow.

"Puff, darling, puff!" said she. "Puff away, my fine fellow! your life depends on it!"

This was a strange exhortation, undoubtedly, to be addressed to a mere thing of sticks, straw, and old clothes, with nothing better than a shrivelled pumpkin for a head,—as we know to have been the scarecrow's case. Nevertheless, as we must carefully hold in remembrance,

Mother Rigby was a witch of singular power and dexterity; and, keeping this fact duly before our minds, we shall see nothing beyond credibility in the remarkable incidents of our story. Indeed, the great difficulty will be at once got over, if we can only bring ourselves to believe that, as soon as the old dame bade him puff, there came a whiff of smoke from the scarecrow's mouth. It was the very feeblest of whiffs, to be sure; but it was followed by another and another, each more decided than the preceding one.

"Puff away, my pet! puff away, my pretty one!" Mother Rigby kept repeating, with her pleasantest smile. "It is the breath of life to ye; and that you may take my word for."

Beyond all question the pipe was bewitched. There must have been a spell either in the tobacco or in the fiercely-glowing coal that so mysteriously burned on top of it, or in the pungently-aromatic smoke which exhaled from the kindled weed. The figure, after a few doubtful attempts, at length blew forth a volley of smoke extending all the way from the obscure corner into the bar of sunshine. There it eddied and melted away among the motes of dust. It seemed a convulsive effort; for the two or three next whiffs were fainter, although the coal still glowed and threw a gleam over the scarecrow's visage. The old witch clapped her skinny hands together, and smiled encouragingly upon her handiwork. She saw that the charm worked well. The shrivelled, yellow face, which heretofore had been no face at all, had already a thin, fantastic haze, as it were of human likeness, shifting to and fro across it; sometimes vanishing entirely, but growing more perceptible than ever with the next whiff from the pipe. The whole figure, in like manner, assumed a show of life, such as we impart to ill-defined shapes among the clouds, and half

deceive ourselves with the pastime of our own fancy.

If we must needs pry closely into the matter, it may be doubted whether there was any real change, after all, in the sordid, worn-out, worthless, and ill-jointed substance of the scarecrow; but merely a spectral illusion, and a cunning effect of light and shade so colored and contrived as to delude the eyes of most men. The miracles of witchcraft seem always to have had a very shallow subtlety; and, at least, if the above explanation do not hit the truth of the process, I can suggest no better.

"Well puffed, my pretty lad!" still cried old Mother Rigby. "Come, another good stout whiff, and let it be with might and main. Puff for thy life, I tell thee! Puff out of the very bottom of thy heart, if any heart thou hast, or any bottom to it! Well done, again! Thou didst suck in that mouthful as if for the pure love of it."

And then the witch beckoned to the scarecrow, throwing so much magnetic potency into her gesture that it seemed as if it must inevitably be obeyed, like the mystic call of the loadstone when it summons the iron.

"Why lurkest thou in the corner, lazy one?" said she. "Step forth! Thou hast the world before thee!"

Upon my word, if the legend were not one which I heard on my grandmother's knee, and which had established its place among things credible before my childish judgment could analyze its probability, I question whether I should have the face to tell it now.

In obedience to Mother Rigby's word, and extending its arm as if to reach her outstretched hand, the figure made a step forward—a kind of hitch and jerk, however, rather than a step—then tottered and almost lost its balance. What could the witch expect? It was nothing, after all, but a scarecrow stuck upon two sticks. But the strong-willed old beldam scowled, and beckoned, and flung the energy of her purpose so forcibly at this poor combination of rotten wood, and musty straw, and ragged garments, that it was compelled to show itself a man, in spite of the reality of things. So it stepped into the bar of sunshine. There it stood—poor devil of a contrivance that it was!—with only the thinnest vesture of human similitude about it, through which was evident the stiff, rickety, incongruous, faded, tattered, good-for-nothing patchwork of its substance, ready to sink in a heap upon the floor, as conscious of its own unworthiness to be erect. Shall I confess the truth? At its present point of vivification, the scarecrow reminds me of some of the lukewarm and abortive characters, composed of heterogeneous materials, used for the thousandth time, and never worth using, with which romance writers (and myself, no doubt, among the rest) have so over-peopled the world of fiction.

But the fierce old hag began to get angry and show a glimpse of her diabolic nature (like a snake's head, peeping with a hiss out of her bosom), at this pusillanimous behavior of the thing which she had taken the trouble to put together.

"Puff away, wretch!" cried she, wrathfully. "Puff, puff, puff, thou thing of straw and emptiness! thou rag or two! thou meal bag! thou pumpkin head! thou nothing! Where shall I find a name vile enough to call thee by? Puff, I say, and suck in thy fantastic life along with the smoke! else I snatch the pipe from thy mouth and hurl thee where that red coal came from."

Thus threatened, the unhappy scarecrow had nothing for it but to puff away for dear life. As need was, therefore, it applied itself lustily to the pipe, and sent forth such abundant volleys of tobacco smoke that the small cottage kitchen became all vaporous. The one sunbeam struggled mistily through, and could but imperfectly define the image of the cracked and dusty window pane on the opposite wall. Mother Rigby, meanwhile, with one brown arm akimbo and the other stretched towards the figure, loomed grimly amid the obscurity with such port and expression as when she was wont to heave a ponderous nightmare on her victims and stand at the bedside to enjoy their agony. In fear and trembling did this poor scarecrow puff. But its efforts, it must be acknowledged, served an excellent purpose; for, with each successive whiff, the figure lost more and more of its dizzy and perplexing tenuity and seemed to take denser substance. Its very garments, moreover, partook of the magical change, and shone with the gloss of novelty and glistened with the skilfully embroidered gold that had long ago been rent away. And, half revealed among the smoke, a yellow visage bent its lustreless eyes on Mother Rigby.

At last the old witch clinched her fist and shook it at the figure. Not that she was positively angry, but merely acting on the principle—perhaps untrue, or not the only truth, though as high a one as Mother Rigby could be expected to attain—that feeble and torpid natures, being incapable of better inspiration, must be stirred up by fear. But here was the crisis. Should she fail in what she now sought to effect, it was her ruthless purpose to scatter the miserable simulacre into its original elements.

"Thou hast a man's aspect," said she, sternly. "Have also the echo and mockery of a voice! I bid thee speak!"

The scarecrow gasped, struggled, and at length emitted a murmur, which was so incorporated with its smoky breath that you could scarcely tell whether it were indeed a voice or only a whiff of tobacco. Some narrators of this legend hold the opinion that Mother Rigby's conjurations and the fierceness of her will had compelled a familiar spirit into the figure, and that the voice was his.

"Mother," mumbled the poor stifled voice, "be not so awful with me! I would fain speak; but being without wits, what can I say?"

"Thou canst speak, darling, canst thou?" cried Mother Rigby, relaxing her grim countenance into a smile. "And what shalt thou say, quotha! Say, indeed! Art thou of the brotherhood of the empty skull, and demandest of me what thou shalt say? Thou shalt say a thousand things, and saying them a thousand times over, thou shalt still have said nothing! Be not afraid, I tell thee! When thou comest into the world (whither I purpose sending thee forthwith) thou shalt not lack the wherewithal to talk. Talk! Why, thou shalt babble like a mill-stream, if thou wilt. Thou hast brains enough for that, I trow!"

"At your service, mother," responded the figure.

"And that was well said, my pretty one," answered Mother Rigby. "Then thou spakest like thyself, and meant nothing. Thou shalt have a hundred such set phrases, and five hundred to the boot of them. And now, darling, I have taken so much pains with thee and thou art so beautiful, that, by my troth, I love thee better than any witch's puppet in the world; and I've made them of all sorts—clay, wax, straw, sticks, night fog, morning mist, sea foam, and chimney smoke. But thou art the very best. So give heed to what I say."

"Yes, kind mother," said the figure, "with all my heart!"

"With all thy heart!" cried the old witch, setting her hands to her sides and laughing loudly. "Thou hast such a pretty way of speaking. With all thy heart! And thou didst put thy hand to the left side of thy waistcoat as if thou really hadst one!"

So now, in high good humor with this fantastic contrivance of hers, Mother Rigby told the scarecrow that it must go and play its part in the great world, where not one man in a hundred, she affirmed, was gifted with more real substance than itself. And, that he might hold up his head with the best of them, she endowed him, on the spot, with an unreckonable amount of wealth. It consisted partly of a gold mine in Eldorado, and of ten thousand shares in a broken bubble, and of half a million acres of vineyard at the North Pole, and of a castle in the air, and a chateau in Spain, together with all the rents and income therefrom accruing. She further made over to him the cargo of a certain ship, laden with salt of Cadiz, which she herself, by her necromantic arts, had caused to founder, ten years before, in the deepest part of mid-ocean. If the salt were not dissolved, and could be brought to market, it would fetch a pretty penny among the fishermen. That he might not lack ready money, she gave him a copper farthing of Birmingham manufacture, being all the coin she had about her, and likewise a great deal of brass, which she applied to his forehead, thus making it yellower than ever.

"With that brass alone," quoth Mother Rigby, "thou canst pay thy way all over the earth. Kiss me, pretty darling! I have done my best for thee."

Furthermore, that the adventurer might lack no possible advantage towards a fair start in life, this excellent old dame gave him a token by which he was to introduce himself to a certain magistrate, member of the council, merchant, and elder of the church (the four capacities constituting but one man), who stood at the head of society in the neighboring metropolis. The token was neither more nor less than a single word, which Mother Rigby whispered to the scarecrow, and which the scarecrow was to whisper to the merchant.

"Gouty as the old fellow is, he'll run

thy errands for thee, when once thou hast given him that word in his ear," said the old witch. "Mother Rigby knows the worshipful Justice Gookin, and the worshipful Justice knows Mother Rigby!"

Here the witch thrust her wrinkled face close to the puppet's, chuckling irrepressibly, and fidgeting all through her system, with delight at the idea which she meant to communicate.

"The worshipful Master Gookin," whispered she, "hath a comely maiden to his daughter. And hark ye, my pet! Thou hast a fair outside, and a pretty wit enough of thine own. Yea, a pretty wit enough! Thou wilt think better of it when thou hast seen more of other people's wits. Now, with thy outside and thy inside, thou art the very man to win a young girl's heart. Never doubt it! I tell thee it shall be so. Put but a bold face on the matter, sigh, smile, flourish thy hat, thrust forth thy leg like a dancing-master, put thy right hand to the left side of thy waistcoat, and pretty Polly Gookin is thine own!"

All this while the new creature had been sucking in and exhaling the vapory fragrance of his pipe, and seemed now to continue this occupation as much for the enjoyment it afforded as because it was an essential condition of his existence. It was wonderful to see how exceedingly like a human being it behaved. Its eyes (for it appeared to possess a pair) were bent on Mother Rigby, and at suitable junctures it nodded or shook its head. Neither did it lack words proper for the occasion: "Really! Indeed! Pray tell me! Is it possible! Upon my word! By no means! Oh! Ah! Hem!" and other such weighty utterances as imply attention, inquiry, acquiescence, or dissent on the part of the auditor. Even had you stood by and seen the scarecrow made, you could scarcely have resisted the conviction that it perfectly understood the cunning counsels which the old witch poured into its counterfeit of an ear. The more earnestly it applied its lips to the pipe, the more distinctly was its human likeness stamped among visible realities, the more sagacious grew its expression, the more lifelike its gestures and movements, and the more intelligibly audible its voice. Its garments, too, glistened so much the brighter with an illusory magnificence. The very pipe, in which burned the spell of all this wonderwork, ceased to appear as a smoke-blackened earthen stump, and became a meerschaum, with painted bowl and amber mouthpiece.

It might be apprehended, however, that as the life of the illusion seemed identical with the vapor of the pipe, it would terminate simultaneously with the reduction of the tobacco to ashes. But the beldam foresaw the difficulty.

"Hold thou the pipe, my precious one," said she, "while I fill it for thee again."

It was sorrowful to behold how the fine gentleman began to fade back into a scarecrow while Mother Rigby shook the ashes out of the pipe and proceeded to replenish it from her tobacco-box.

"Dickon," cried she, in her high, sharp tone, "another coal for this pipe!"

No sooner said than the intensely red speck of fire was glowing within the pipe-bowl; and the scarecrow, without waiting for the witch's bidding, applied the tube to his lips and drew in a few short, convulsive whiffs, which soon, however, became regular and equable.

"Now, mine own heart's darling," quoth Mother Rigby, "whatever may happen to thee, thou must stick to thy pipe. Thy life is in it; and that, at least, thou knowest well, if thou knowest nought besides. Stick to thy pipe, I say! Smoke, puff, blow thy cloud; and tell the people, if any question be made, that it is for thy health, and that so the physician orders thee to do. And, sweet one, when thou shalt find thy pipe getting low, go apart into some corner, and (first filling thyself with smoke) cry sharply, 'Dickon, a fresh pipe of tobacco!' and, 'Dickon, another coal for my pipe!' and have it into thy pretty mouth as speedily as may be. Else, instead of a gallant gentleman in a gold-laced coat, thou wilt be but a jumble of sticks and tattered clothes, and a bag of straw, and a withered pumpkin! Now depart, my treasure, and good luck go with thee!"

"Never fear, mother!" said the figure, in a stout voice, and sending forth a courageous whiff of smoke, "I will thrive, if an honest man and a gentleman may!"

"Oh, thou wilt be the death of me!" cried the old witch, convulsed with laughter. "That was well said. If an honest man and a gentleman may! Thou playest thy part to perfection. Get along with thee for a smart fellow; and I will wager on thy head, as a man of pith and substance, with a brain and what they call a heart, and all else that a man should have, against any other thing on two legs. I hold myself a better witch than yesterday, for thy sake. Did not I make thee? And I defy any witch in New England to make such another! Here; take my staff along with thee!"

The staff, though it was but a plain oaken stick, immediately took the aspect of a gold-headed cane.

"That gold head has as much sense in it as thine own," said Mother Rigby, "and it will guide thee straight to worshipful Master Gookin's door. Get thee gone, my pretty pet, my darling, my precious one, my treasure; and if any ask thy name, it is Feathertop. For thou hast a feather in thy hat, and I have thrust a handful of feathers into the hollow of thy head, and thy wig, too, is of the fashion they call Feathertop,—so be Feathertop thy name!"

And, issuing from the cottage, Feathertop strode manfully towards town. Mother Rigby stood at the threshold, well pleased to see how the sunbeams glistened on him, as if all his magnificence were real, and how diligently and lovingly he smoked his pipe, and how handsomely he walked, in spite of a little stiffness of his legs. She watched him until out of sight, and threw a witch benediction after her darling, when a turn of the road snatched him from her view.

Betimes in the forenoon, when the principal street of the neighboring town was just at its acme of life and bustle, a stranger of very distinguished figure was seen on the sidewalk. His port as well as his garments betokened nothing short of nobility. He wore a richly-embroidered plum-colored coat, a waistcoat of costly velvet, magnificently adorned with golden foliage, a pair of splendid scarlet breeches, and the finest and glossiest of white silk stockings. His head was covered with a peruke, so daintily powdered and adjusted that it would have been sacrilege to disorder it with a hat; which, therefore (and it was a gold-laced hat, set off with a snowy feather), he carried beneath his arm. On the breast of his coat glistened a star. He managed his gold-headed cane with an airy grace, peculiar to the fine gentlemen of the period; and, to give the highest possible finish to his equipment, he had lace ruffles at his wrist, of a most ethereal delicacy, sufficiently avouching how idle and aristocratic must be the hands which they half concealed.

It was a remarkable point in the accoutrement of this brilliant personage that he held in his left hand a fantastic kind of a pipe, with an exquisitely painted bowl and an amber mouthpiece. This he applied to his lips as often as every five or six paces, and inhaled a deep whiff of smoke, which, after being retained a moment in his lungs, might be seen to eddy gracefully from his mouth and nostrils.

As may well be supposed, the street was all astir to find out the stranger's name.

"It is some great nobleman, beyond question," said one of the towns-people.

"Do you see the star at his breast?"

"Nay; it is too bright to be seen," said another. "Yes; he must needs be a nobleman, as you say. But by what conveyance, think you, can his lordship have voyaged or travelled hither? There has been no vessel from the old country for a month past; and if he have arrived overland from the southward, pray where are his attendants and equipage?"

"He needs no equipage to set off his rank," remarked a third. "If he came among us in rags, nobility would shine through a hole in his elbow. I never saw such dignity of aspect. He has the old Norman blood in his veins, I warrant him."

"I rather take him to be a Dutchman, or one of your high Germans," said another citizen. "The men of those countries have always the pipe at their mouths."

"And so has a Turk," answered his companion. "But, in my judgment, this stranger hath been bred at the French court, and hath there learned politeness and grace of manner, which none understand so well as the nobility of France. That gait, now! A vulgar spectator might deem it stiff— he might call it a hitch and jerk—but, to my eye, it hath an unspeakable majesty, and must have been acquired by constant observation of the deportment of the Grand Monarque. The stranger's character and office are evident enough. He is a French ambassador, come to treat with our rulers about the cession of Canada."

"More probably a Spaniard," said another, "and hence his yellow complexion; or, most likely, he is from the Havana, or from some port on the Spanish main, and comes to make investigation about the piracies which our government is thought to connive at. Those settlers in Peru and Mexico have skins as yellow as the gold which they dig out of their mines."

"Yellow or not," cried a lady, "he is a beautiful man!—so tall, so slender! such a fine, noble face, with so well-shaped a nose, and all that delicacy of expression about the mouth! And, bless me, how bright his star is! It positively shoots out flames!"

"So do your eyes, fair lady," said the stranger, with a bow and a flourish of his pipe; for he was just passing at the instant. "Upon my honor, they have quite dazzled me."

"Was ever so original and exquisite a compliment?" murmured the lady, in an ecstasy of delight.

Amid the general admiration excited by the stranger's appearance, there were only two dissenting voices. One was that of an impertinent cur, which, after snuffing at the heels of the glistening figure, put its tail between its legs and skulked into its master's back yard, vociferating an execrable howl. The other dissentient was a young child, who squalled at the fullest stretch of his lungs, and babbled some unintelligible nonsense about a pumpkin.

Feathertop meanwhile pursued his way along the street. Except for the few complimentary words to the lady, and now and then a slight inclination of the head in requital of the profound reverences of the bystanders, he seemed wholly absorbed in his pipe. There needed no other proof of his rank and consequence than the perfect equanimity with which he comported himself, while the curiosity and admiration of the town swelled almost into clamor around him. With a crowd gathering behind his footsteps, he finally reached the mansion-house of the worshipful Justice Gookin, entered the gate, ascended the steps of the front door, and knocked. In the interim, before his summons was answered, the stranger was observed to shake the ashes out of his pipe.

"What did he say in that sharp voice?" inquired one of the spectators.

"Nay, I know not," answered his friend. "But the sun dazzles my eyes strangely. How dim and faded his lordship looks all of a sudden! Bless my wits, what is the matter with me?"

"The wonder is," said the other, "that his pipe, which was out only an instant ago, should be all alight again, and with the reddest coal I ever saw. There is something mysterious about this stranger. What a whiff of smoke was that! Dim and faded did you call him? Why, as he turns about the star on his breast is all ablaze."

"It is, indeed," said his companion; "and it will go near to dazzle pretty Polly Gookin, whom I see peeping at it out of the chamber window."

The door being now opened, Feathertop turned to the crowd, made a stately bend of his body like a great man acknowledging the reverence of the meaner sort, and vanished into the house. There was a mysterious kind of a smile, if it might not better be called a grin or grimace, upon his visage; but, of all the throng that beheld him, not an individual appears to have possessed insight enough to detect the illusive character of the stranger except a little child and a cur dog.

Our legend here loses somewhat of its continuity, and, passing over the preliminary explanation between Feathertop and the merchant, goes in quest of the pretty Polly Gookin. She was a damsel of a soft, round figure, with light hair and blue eyes, and a fair, rosy face, which seemed neither very shrewd nor very simple. This young lady had caught a glimpse of the glistening stranger while standing at the threshold, and had forthwith put on a laced cap, a string of beads, her finest kerchief, and her stiffest damask petticoat in preparation for the interview. Hurrying from her chamber to the parlor, she had ever since been viewing herself in the large looking-glass and practising pretty airs— now a smile, now a ceremonious dignity of aspect, and now a softer smile than the former, kissing her hand likewise, tossing her head, and managing her fan; while

within the mirror an unsubstantial little maid repeated every gesture and did all the foolish things that Polly did, but without making her ashamed of them. In short, it was the fault of pretty Polly's ability rather than her will if she failed to be as complete an artifice as the illustrious Feathertop himself; and, when she thus tampered with her own simplicity, the witch's phantom might well hope to win her.

No sooner did Polly hear her father's gouty footsteps approaching the parlor door, accompanied with the stiff clatter of Feathertop's high-heeled shoes, than she seated herself bolt upright and innocently began warbling a song.

"Polly! daughter Polly!" cried the old merchant. "Come hither, child."

Master Gookin's aspect, as he opened the door, was doubtful and troubled.

"This gentleman," continued he, presenting the stranger, "is the Chevalier Feathertop,—nay, I beg his pardon, my Lord Feathertop,—who hath brought me a token of remembrance from an ancient friend of mine. Pay your duty to his lordship, child, and honor him as his quality deserves."

After these few words of introduction, the worshipful magistrate immediately quitted the room. But, even in that brief moment, had the fair Polly glanced aside at her father instead of devoting herself wholly to the brilliant guest, she might have taken warning of some mischief nigh at hand. The old man was nervous, fidgety, and very pale. Purposing a smile of courtesy, he had deformed his face with a sort of galvanic grin, which, when Feathertop's back was turned, he exchanged for a scowl, at the same time shaking his fist and stamping his gouty foot—an incivility which brought its retribution along with it. The truth appears to have been that Mother Rigby's word of introduction, whatever it might be, had operated far more on the rich merchant's fears than on his good will. Moreover, being a man of wonderfully acute observation, he had noticed that these painted figures on the bowl of Feathertop's pipe were in motion. Looking more closely, he became convinced that these figures were a party of little demons, each duly provided with horns and a tail, and dancing hand in hand, with gestures of diabolical merriment, round the circumference of the pipe bowl. As if to confirm his suspicions, while Master Gookin ushered his guest along a dusky passage from his private room to the parlor, the star on Feathertop's breast had scintillated actual flames, and threw a flickering gleam upon the wall, the ceiling, and the floor.

With such sinister prognostics manifesting themselves on all hands, it is not to be marvelled at that the merchant should have felt that he was committing his daughter to a very questionable acquaintance. He cursed, in his secret soul, the insinuating elegance of Feathertop's manners, as this brilliant personage bowed, smiled, put his hand on his heart, inhaled a long whiff from his pipe, and enriched the atmosphere with the smoky vapor of a fragrant and visible sigh. Gladly would poor Master Gookin have thrust his dangerous guest into the street; but there was a constraint and terror within him. This respectable old gentleman, we fear, at an earlier period of life, had given some pledge or other to the evil principle, and perhaps was now to redeem it by the sacrifice of his daughter.

It so happened that the parlor door was partly of glass, shaded by a silken curtain, the folds of which hung a little awry. So strong was the merchant's interest in witnessing what was to ensue between the fair Polly and the gallant Feathertop that, after quitting the room, he could by no means refrain from peeping through the crevice of the curtain.

But there was nothing very miraculous to be seen; nothing—except the trifles previously noticed—to confirm the idea of a supernatural peril environing the pretty Polly. The stranger it is true was evidently a thorough and practised man of the world, systematic and self-possessed, and therefore the sort of a person to whom a parent ought not to confide a simple, young girl without due watchfulness for the result. The worthy magistrate, who had been conversant with all degrees and qualities of mankind, could not but perceive every motion and gesture of the distinguished Feathertop came in its proper place; nothing had been left rude or native in him; a well-digested conventionalism had incorporated itself thoroughly with his substance and transformed him into a work of art. Perhaps it was this peculiarity that invested him with a species of ghastliness and awe. It is the effect of anything completely and consummately artificial, in human shape, that the person impresses us as an unreality and as having hardly pith enough to cast a shadow upon the floor. As regarded Feathertop, all this resulted in a wild, extravagant, and fantastical impression, as if his life and being were akin to the smoke that curled upward from his pipe.

But pretty Polly Gookin felt not thus. The pair were now promenading the room: Feathertop with his dainty stride and no less dainty grimace; the girl with a native maidenly grace, just touched, not spoiled, by a slightly affected manner, which seemed caught from the perfect artifice of her companion. The longer the interview continued, the more charmed was pretty Polly, until, within the first quarter of an hour (as the old magistrate noted by his watch), she was evidently beginning to be in love. Nor need it have been witchcraft that subdued her in such a hurry; the poor child's heart, it may be, was so very fervent that it melted her with its own warmth as reflected from the hollow semblance of a lover. No matter what

Feathertop said, his words found depth and reverberation in her ear; no matter what he did, his action was heroic to her eye. And by this time it is to be supposed there was a blush on Polly's cheek, a tender smile about her mouth, and a liquid softness in her glance; while the star kept coruscating on Feathertop's breast, and the little demons careered with more frantic merriment than ever about the circumference of his pipe bowl. O pretty Polly Gookin, why should these imps rejoice so madly that a silly maiden's heart was about to be given to a shadow! Is it so unusual a misfortune, so rare a triumph?

By and by Feathertop paused, and throwing himself into an imposing attitude, seemed to summon the fair girl to survey his figure and resist him longer if she could. His star, his embroidery, his buckles glowed at that instant with unutterable splendor; the picturesque hues of his attire took a richer depth of coloring; there was a gleam and polish over his whole presence betokening the perfect witchery of well-ordered manners. The maiden raised her eyes and suffered them to linger upon her companion with a bashful and admiring gaze. Then, as if desirous of judging what value her own simple comeliness might have side by side with so much brilliancy, she cast a glance towards the full-length looking-glass in front of which they happened to be standing. It was one of the truest plates in the world and incapable of flattery. No sooner did the images therein reflected meet Polly's eye than she shrieked, shrank from the stranger's side, gazed at him for a moment in the wildest dismay, and sank insensible upon the floor. Feathertop likewise had looked towards the mirror, and there beheld, not the glittering mockery of his outside show, but a picture of the sordid patchwork of his real composition, stripped of all witchcraft.

The wretched simulacrum! We almost pity him. He threw up his arms with an expression of despair that went further than any of his previous manifestations towards vindicating his claims to be reckoned human; for, perchance the only time since this so often empty and deceptive life of mortals began its course, an illusion had seen and fully recognized itself.

Mother Rigby was seated by her kitchen hearth in the twilight of this eventful day, and had just shaken the ashes out of a new pipe, when she heard a hurried tramp along the road. Yet it did not seem so much the tramp of human footsteps as the clatter of sticks or the rattling of dry bones.

"Ha!" thought the old witch, "what step is that? Whose skeleton is out of its grave now, I wonder?"

A figure burst headlong into the cottage door. It was Feathertop! His pipe was still alight; the star still flamed upon his breast; the embroidery still glowed upon his garments; nor had he lost, in any degree or manner that could be estimated, the aspect that assimilated him with our mortal brotherhood. But yet, in some indescribable way (as is the case with all that has deluded us when once found out), the poor reality was felt beneath the cunning artifice.

"What has gone wrong?" demanded the witch. "Did yonder sniffling hypocrite thrust my darling from his door? The villain! I'll set twenty fiends to torment him till he offer thee his daughter on his bended knees!"

"No, mother," said Feathertop despondingly; "it was not that."

"Did the girl scorn my precious one?" asked Mother Rigby, her fierce eyes glowing like two coals of Tophet. "I'll cover her face with pimples! Her nose shall be as red as the coal in thy pipe! Her front teeth shall drop out! In a week hence she shall not be worth thy having!"

"Let her alone, mother," answered poor

Feathertop; "the girl was half won; and methinks a kiss from her sweet lips might have made me altogether human. But," he added, after a brief pause and then a howl of self-contempt, "I've seen myself, mother! I've seen myself for the wretched, ragged, empty thing I am! I'll exist no longer!"

Snatching the pipe from his mouth, he flung it with all his might against the chimney, and at the same instant sank upon the floor, a medley of straw and tattered garments, with some sticks protruding from the heap, and a shrivelled pumpkin in the midst. The eyeholes were now lustreless; but the rudely-carved gap, that just before had been a mouth, still seemed to twist itself into a despairing grin, and was so far human.

"Poor fellow!" quoth Mother Rigby, with a rueful glance at the relics of her ill-fated contrivance. "My poor, dear, pretty Feathertop! There are thousands upon thousands of coxcombs and charlatans in the world, made up of just such a jumble of worn-out, forgotten, and good-for-nothing trash as he was! Yet they live in fair repute, and never see themselves for what they are. And why should my poor puppet be the only one to know himself and perish for it?"

While thus muttering, the witch had filled a fresh pipe of tobacco, and held the stem between her fingers, as doubtful whether to thrust it into her own mouth or Feathertop's.

"Poor Feathertop!" she continued. "I could easily give him another chance and send him forth again to-morrow. But no; his feelings are too tender, his sensibilities too deep. He seems to have too much heart to bustle for his own advantage in such an empty and heartless world. Well! well! I'll make a scarecrow of him after all. 'T is an innocent and useful vocation, and will suit my darling well; and, if each of his human brethren had as fit a one, 't would be the better for mankind; and as for this pipe of tobacco, I need it more than he."

So saying, Mother Rigby put the stem between her lips. "Dickon!" cried she, in her high, sharp tone, "another coal for my pipe!"

THE SCARECROW
by Percy MacKaye

Percy MacKaye, the author of dramas, verse, and fiction, customarily drew his inspiration from books. Thus, "The Scarecrow" is a dramatic adaptation of Nathaniel Hawthorne's short story "Feathertop." A comparison of the two literary treatments of the same material is both interesting and profitable. MacKaye, writing a play, had to supply almost all the dialogue and had to fill in the characters sufficiently to hold audience attention. In particular, he changed the figure of Dickon, who, in addition to

*being the collaborator and servant of the old witch, has many of the quali-
ties commonly associated with the devil. In Hawthorne's hands the story
is a kind of apologue, in which the characters seldom transcend abstractions.
In MacKaye's hands the dialogue is more colloquial than literary, the action
is clarified, and the story is less the revenge of the witch than the attempt of
Lord Ravensbane to become a human being. MacKaye also introduced several subordinate incidents which contribute indirectly to the main action.
The idea of transforming inanimate elements into a living human being is
familiar in folklore and myth. One of the best examples is the story of
Pygmalion and Galatea. The recent transposition of George Bernard Shaw's*
Pygmalion *to the musical stage as* My Fair Lady *suggests the perennial
appeal of the idea.*

CAST OF CHARACTERS

At the First Professional Performance

Middlesex Theatre,
Middletown, Connecticut,
December 30, 1910

JUSTICE GILEAD MERTON . . . . Mr. Brigham Royce
GOODY RICKBY ("Blacksmith Bess") . . . . . Miss Alice Fischer
LORD RAVENSBANE ("Marquis of Oxford, Baron
    of Wittenberg, Elector of Worms, and Count
    of Cordova"), their hypothetical son   . . .   Mr. Frank Reicher
DICKON, a Yankee improvisation of the Prince of
    Darkness . . . . Mr. Edmund Breese
RACHEL MERTON, niece of the Justice . . . . Miss Beatrice Irwin
MISTRESS CYNTHIA MERTON, sister of the Justice . . Mrs. Felix Morris
RICHARD TALBOT, ESQUIRE, betrothed to RACHEL . Mr. Earle Browne
SIR CHARLES REDDINGTON, Lieutenant-Governor . . Mr. H. J. Carvill
MISTRESS REDDINGTON ⎫   ⎧ . Miss Zenaidee Williams
                     ⎬ his daughters, ⎨
AMELIA REDDINGTON ⎭   ⎩ . . Miss Georgia Dvorak
CAPTAIN BUGBY, the Governor's Secretary . . . Mr. Regan Hughston
MINISTER DODGE . . . . Mr. Clifford Leigh
MISTRESS DODGE, his wife . . . . Miss Eleanor Sheldon
REV. MASTER RAND, of Harvard College . . . . Mr. William Lewis
REV. MASTER TODD, of Harvard College . . . . Mr. Harry Lillford
MICAH, a servant of the Justice . . . . . Mr. Harold N. Cheshir

Time—Late seventeenth century.
Place—A town in Massachusetts.

● *The Scarecrow; or, The Glass of Truth; a Tragedy of the Ludicrous,* by Percy MacKaye. Copyright,
1908 and 1929, by The Macmillan Company. Reprinted by permission of Henry Barnes, Executor of the
Estate of Percy Wallace MacKaye.

ACT FIRST.

The interior of a blacksmith shop. On the right of the stage toward the center there is a forge. On the left stands a loft, from which are hanging dried corn-stalks, hay, and the yellow ears of cattle-corn. Toward the rear is a wide double door, closed when the curtain rises. Through this door—when later it is opened—is visible a New England land-scape in the late springtime: a distant wood; stone walls, high elms, a well-sweep; and, in the near foreground, a ploughed field, from which the green shoots of early corn are just appearing. The blackened walls of the shop are cov-ered with a miscellaneous collection of old iron, horseshoes, and cart-wheels, the usual appurtenances of a smithy. In the right-hand corner, however, is an array of things quite out of keeping with the shop proper: musical instru-ments, puppets, tall clocks, and fantas-tical junk. Conspicuous amongst these articles is a large standing mirror, framed grotesquely in old gold and cur-tained by a dull stuff, embroidered with peaked caps and crescent moons.

Just before the scene opens, a hammer is heard ringing briskly upon steel. As the curtain rises there is discovered, standing at the anvil in the flickering light of a bright flame from the forge, a woman—powerful, ruddy, proud with a certain masterful beauty, white-haired (as though prematurely), bare-armed to the elbows, clad in a dark skirt (above her ankles), a loose blouse, open at the throat; a leathern apron and a work-man's cap. The woman is GOODY RICKBY. *On the anvil she is shaping a piece of iron. Beside her stands a frame-work of iron formed like the ribs and backbone of a man. For a few moments she continues to ply her hammer, amid a shower of sparks, till suddenly the flame on the forge dies down.*

GOODY RICKBY. Dickon! More flame.

A VOICE. (*Above her.*) Yea, Goody.

(*The flame in the forge spurts up high and suddenly.*)

GOODY RICKBY. Nay, not so fierce.

THE VOICE. (*At her side.*) *Votre par-don, madame.* (*The flame subsides.*) Is that better?

GOODY RICKBY. That will do. (*With her tongs, she thrusts the iron into the flame; it turns white-hot.*) Quick work; nothing like brimstone for the smithy trade. (*At the anvil, she begins to weld the iron rib onto the framework.*) There, my beauty! We'll make a stout set of ribs for you. I'll see to it this year that I have a scarecrow can outstand all the nor'easters that blow. I've no notion to lose my corn-crop this sum-mer. (*Outside, the faint cawings of crows are heard. Putting down her tongs and hammer,* GOODY RICKBY *strides to the double door, and flinging it wide open, lets in the gray light of dawn. She looks out over the fields and shakes her fist.*) So ye're up before me and the sun, are ye? (*Squinting against the light.*) There's one! Nay, two. Aha!

> One for sorrow,
> Two for mirth——

Good! This time we'll have the laugh on our side. (*She returns to the forge, where again the fire has died out.*) Dickon! Fire! Come, come, where be thy wits?

THE VOICE. (*Sleepily from the forge.*) 'Tis early, dame.

GOODY RICKBY. The more need—

(*Takes up her tongs.*)

THE VOICE. (*Screams.*) Ow!

GOODY RICKBY. Ha! Have I got thee? (*From the blackness of the forge she pulls out with her tongs, by the right ear, the figure of a devil, horned and tailed. In general aspect, though he re-sembles a mediaeval familiar demon, yet*

the suggestions of a goatish beard, a shrewdly humorous smile, and (when he speaks) the slightest of nasal drawls, remotely simulate a species of Yankee rustic. GOODY RICKBY *substitutes her fingers for the tongs.)* Now, Dickon!

DICKON. *Deus!* I haven't been nabbed like that since St. Dunstan tweaked my nose. Well, sweet Goody?

GOODY RICKBY. The bellows!

DICKON. *(Going slowly to the forge.)* Why, 'tis hardly dawn yet. Honest folks are still abed. It makes a long day.

GOODY RICKBY. *(Working while* DICKON *plies the bellows.)* Aye, for your black pets, the crows, to work in. That's why we must be at it early. You heard 'em. We must have this scarecrow of ours out in the field at his post before sunrise. Here, I've made the frame strong, so as to stand the weather; *you* must make the body lifelike so as to fool the crows. This year, we must make 'em think it's a real human crittur.

DICKON. To fool the philosophers is my specialty, but the crows—hm!

GOODY RICKBY. Pooh! That staggers thee!

DICKON. Madame Rickby, prod not the quick of my genius. I am Phidias, I am Raphael, I am the Lord God!—You shall see—*(Demands with a gesture.)* Yonder broomstick.

GOODY RICKBY. *(Fetching him a broom from the corner.)* Good boy!

DICKON. *(Straddling the handle.)* Ha, ha! gee up! my Salem mare. *(Then, pseudo-*

philosophically.) A broomstick—that's for imagination! *(He begins to construct the scarecrow, while* GOODY RICKBY, *assisting, brings the constructive parts from various nooks and corners.)* We are all pretty artists, to be sure, Bessie. Phidias, he sculptures the gods; Raphael, he paints the angels; the Lord God, he creates Adam; and Dickon —fetch me the poker—aha! Dickon! What doth Dickon? He nullifies 'em all; he endows the Scarecrow! A poker: here's his conscience. There's two fine legs to walk on,—imagination and conscience. Yonder flails now! The ideal— the *beau idéal,* dame—that's what we artists seek. The apotheosis of scarecrows! And pray, what's a scarecrow? Why, the antithesis of Adam.—"Let there be candles!" quoth the Lord God, sitting in the dark. "Let there be candle-extinguishers," saith Dickon. "I am made in the image of my maker," quoth Adam. "Look at yourself in the glass," saith Goodman Scarecrow. *(Taking two implements from* GOODY RICKBY.) Fine! fine! here are flails—one for wit, t'other for satire. *Sapristi!* with two such arms, my lad, how thou wilt work thy way in the world!

GOODY RICKBY. You talk as if you were making a real mortal, Dickon.

DICKON. To fool a crow, Goody, I must fashion a crittur that will first deceive a man.

GOODY RICKBY. He'll scarce do that without a head. *(Pointing to the loft.)* What think ye of yonder Jack-o'-lantern? 'Twas made last Hallowe'en.

DICKON. Rare, my Psyche! We shall collaborate. Here! *(Running up the ladder, he tosses down a yellow hollowed pumpkin to* GOODY RICKBY, *who catches it. Then rummaging forth an armful of cornstalks, ears, tassels, dried squashes, gourds, beets, etc., he descends and throws them in a heap on the* floor.) Whist! (*As he drops them.*) Gourd, carrot, turnip, beet:—the anatomy.

GOODY RICKBY. (*Placing the pumpkin on the shoulders.*) Look!

DICKON. *O Johannes Baptista!* What wouldst thou have given for such a head! I helped Salome to cut his off, dame, and it looked not half so appetizing on her charger. Tut! Copernicus wore once such a pumpkin, but it is rotten. Look at his golden smile! Hail, Phœbus Apollo!

GOODY RICKBY. 'Tis the finest scarecrow in town.

DICKON. Nay, poor soul, 'tis but a skeleton yet. He must have a man's heart in him. (*Picking a big red beet from among the cornstalks, he places it under the left side of the ribs.*) Hush! Dost thou hear it *beat*?

GOODY RICKBY. Thou merry rogue!

DICKON. Now for the lungs of him. (*Snatching a small pair of bellows from a peg on the wall.*) That's for eloquence! He'll preach the black knaves a sermon on theft. And now—(*Here, with* GOODY RICKBY'S *help, he stuffs the framework with the gourds, corn, etc., from the loft, weaving the husks about the legs and arms.*) Here goes for digestion and inherited instincts! More corn, Goody. Now he'll fight for his own flesh and blood!

GOODY RICKBY. (*Laughing.*) Dickon, I am proud of thee.

DICKON. Wait till you see his peruke. (*Seizing a feather duster made of crow's feathers.*) *Voici!* Scalps of the enemy! (*Pulling them apart, he arranges the feathers on the pumpkin, like a gentleman's wig.*) A rare conqueror!

GOODY RICKBY. Oh, you beauty!

DICKON. And now a bit of comfort for dark days and stormy nights. (*Taking a piece of corn-cob with the kernels on it,* DICKON *makes a pipe, which he puts into the scarecrow's mouth.*) So! There, Goody! I tell thee, with yonder brand-new coat and breeches of mine—those there in my cupboard!—we'll make him a lad to be proud of. (*Taking the clothes, which* GOODY RICKBY *brings—a pair of fine scarlet breeches and a gold-embroidered coat with ruffles of lace—he puts them upon the scarecrow. Then, eying it like a connoisseur, makes a few finishing touches.*) Why, dame, he'll be a son to thee.

GOODY RICKBY. A son? Aye, if I had but a son!

DICKON. Why, here you have him. (*To the scarecrow.*) Thou wilt scare the crows off thy mother's cornfield—won't my pretty? And send 'em all over t'other side the wall to her dear neighbor's, the Justice Gilead Merton's.

GOODY RICKBY. Justice Merton! Nay, if they'd only peck his eyes out, instead of his corn.

DICKON. (*Grinning.*) Yet the Justice was a dear friend of "Blacksmith Bess."

GOODY RICKBY. Aye, "Blacksmith Bess"! If I hadn't had a good stout arm when he cast me off with the babe, I might have starved for all his worship cared.

DICKON. True, Bessie; 'twas a scurvy trick he played on thee—and on me, that took such pains to bring you together—to steal a young maid's heart—

GOODY RICKBY. And then toss it away like a bad penny to the gutter! And the child—to die! (*Lifting her hammer in rage.*) Ha! If I could get the worshipful Justice Gilead into my power again—(*She drops the hammer sullenly on the anvil.*) But no! I shall beat my life away on this anvil, whilst my justice clinks his gold, and drinks his port to a fat old age. Justice! Ha—justice of God!

DICKON. Whist, dame! Talk of angels and hear the rustle of their relatives.

GOODY RICKBY. (*Turning, watches out-*

side a girl's figure approaching.) His niece—Rachel Merton! What can she want so early? Nay, I mind me; 'tis the mirror. She's a maid after our own hearts, boy,—no Sabbath-go-to-meeting airs about *her!* She hath read the books of the *magi* from cover to cover, and paid me good guineas for 'em, though her uncle knows naught on't. Besides, she's in love, Dickon.

DICKON. (*Indicating the scarecrow.*) Ah? With *him?* Is it a rendezvous?

GOODY RICKBY. (*With a laugh.*) Pff! Begone!

DICKON. (*Shakes his finger at the scarecrow.*) Thou naughty rogue!

> (*Then, still smiling slyly, with his head placed confidentially next to the scarecrow's ear, as if whispering, and with his hand pointing to the maiden outside,* DICKON *fades away into air.* RACHEL *enters, nervous and hesitant.* GOODY RICKBY *makes her a curtsy, which she acknowledges by a nod, half absent-minded.*)

GOODY RICKBY. Mistress Rachel Merton— so early! I hope your uncle, our worshipful Justice, is not ill?

RACHEL. No, my uncle is quite well. The early morning suits me best for a walk. You are—quite alone?

GOODY RICKBY. Quite alone, mistress. (*Bitterly.*) Oh, folks don't call on Goody Rickby—except on business.

RACHEL. (*Absently, looking round in the dim shop.*) Yes—you must be busy. Is it—is it here?

GOODY RICKBY. You mean the—

RACHEL. (*Starting back, with a cry.*) Ah! who's that?

GOODY RICKBY. (*Chuckling.*) Fear not, mistress; 'tis nothing but a scarecrow. I'm going to put him in my cornfield yonder. The crows are so pesky this year.

RACHEL. (*Draws her skirts away with a shiver.*) How loathsome!

GOODY RICKBY. (*Vastly pleased.*) He'll do.

RACHEL. Ah, here!—This is *the* mirror?

GOODY RICKBY. Yea, mistress, and a wonderful glass it is, as I told you. I wouldn't sell it to most comers, but seeing how you and Master Talbot—

RACHEL. Yes; that will do.

GOODY RICKBY. You see, if the town folks guessed what it was, well— You've heard tell of the gibbets on Salem Hill? There's not many in New England like you, Mistress Rachel. You know enough to approve some miracles—outside the Scriptures.

RACHEL. You are quite sure the glass will do all you say? It—never fails?

GOODY RICKBY. Ah, now, mistress, how could it? 'Tis the glass of truth—(*insinuatingly*)—the glass of true lovers. It shows folks just as they are; no shams, no varnish. If a wolf should dress himself in a white sheep's wool, this glass would reflect the black beast inside it.

RACHEL. (*With awe.*) The black beast! But what of the sins of the soul, Goody? Vanity, hypocrisy, and—and inconstancy? Will it surely reveal them?

GOODY RICKBY. I have told you, my young lady. If it doth not as I say, bring it back and get your money again. Oh, trust me, sweeting, an old dame hath eyes in her heart yet. If your lover be false, this glass shall pluck his fine feathers!

RACHEL. (*With aloofness.*) 'Tis no question of that. I wish the glass to—to amuse me.

GOODY RICKBY. (*Laughing.*) Why, then, try it on some of your neighbors.

RACHEL. You ask a large price for it.

GOODY RICKBY. (*Shrugs.*) I run risks. Besides, where will you get another?

RACHEL. That is true. Here, I will buy

it. That is the sum you mentioned, I believe?

(*She hands a purse to* GOODY RICKBY, *who opens it and counts over some coin.*)

GOODY RICKBY. Let see; let see.

RACHEL. Well?

GOODY RICKBY. Good: 'tis good. Folks call me a witch, mistress. Well—harkee —a witch's word is as good as a justice's gold. The glass is yours—with my blessing.

RACHEL. Spare yourself that, dame. But the glass: how am I to get it? How will you send it to me—quietly?

GOODY RICKBY. Trust me for that. I've a willing lad that helps me with such errands; a neighbor o' mine. (*Calls.*) Ebenezer!

RACHEL. (*Startled.*) What! is he here?

GOODY RICKBY. In the hayloft. The boy's an orphan; he sleeps there o' times. Ebenezer!

(*A raw, disheveled country boy appears in the loft, slides down the ladder, and shuffles up sleepily.*)

THE BOY. Evenin'.

RACHEL. (*Drawing* GOODY RICKBY *aside.*) You understand; I desire no comment about this purchase.

GOODY RICKBY. Nor I, mistress, be sure.

RACHEL. Is he—?

GOODY RICKBY. (*Tapping her forehead significantly.*) Trust his wits who hath no wit; he's mum.

RACHEL. Oh!

THE BOY. (*Gaping.*) Job?

GOODY RICKBY. Yea, rumple-head! His job this morning is to bear yonder glass to the house of Justice Merton—the big one on the hill; to the side door. Mind, no gabbing. Doth he catch?

THE BOY. (*Nodding and grinning.*) 'E swallows.

RACHEL. But is the boy strong enough?

GOODY RICKBY. Him? (*Pointing to the anvil.*) Ebenezer!

(*The boy spits on his palms, takes hold of the anvil, lifts it, drops it again, sits on it, and grins at the door, just as* RICHARD TALBOT *appears there, from outside.*)

RACHEL. Gracious!

GOODY RICKBY. Trust him. He'll carry the glass for you.

RACHEL. I will return home at once, then. Let him go quietly to the side door, and wait for me. Good-morning.

(*Turning, she confronts* RICHARD.)

RICHARD. Good-morning.

RACHEL. Richard!—Squire Talbot, you —you are abroad early.

RICHARD. As early as Mistress Rachel. Is it pardonable? I caught sight of you walking in this direction, so I thought it wise to follow, lest—

(*Looks hard at* GOODY RICKBY.)

RACHEL. Very kind. Thanks. We can return together. (*To* GOODY RICKBY.) You will make sure that I receive the— the article.

GOODY RICKBY. Trust me, mistress.

(*She curtsies to* RICHARD.)

RICHARD. (*Bluntly, looking from one to the other.*) What article?

(RACHEL *ignores the question and starts to pass out.* RICHARD *frowns at* GOODY RICKBY, *who stammers.*)

GOODY RICKBY. Begging your pardon, sir?

RICHARD. What article? I said. (*After a short, embarrassed pause, more sternly.*) Well?

GOODY RICKBY. Oh, the article! Yonder old glass, to be sure, sir. A quaint piece, your honor.

RICHARD. Rachel, you haven't come here at sunrise to buy—that thing?

RACHEL. Verily, "that thing," and at sunrise. A pretty time for a pretty purchase. Are you coming?

RICHARD. (*In a low tone.*) More witchcraft nonsense? Do you realize this is serious?

RACHEL. Oh, of course. You know I am desperately mystical, so pray let us not discuss it. Good-bye.

RICHARD. Rachel, just a moment. If you want a mirror, you shall have the prettiest one in New England. Or I will import you one from London. Only—I beg of you—don't buy stolen goods.

GOODY RICKBY. Stolen goods?

RACHEL. (*Aside to* RICHARD.) Don't! don't!

RICHARD. (*To* GOODY RICKBY.) Can you account for this mirror—how you came by it?

GOODY RICKBY. I'll show ye! I'll show ye! Stolen—ha!

RICHARD. Come, old swindler, keep your mirror, and give this lady back her money.

GOODY RICKBY. I'll damn ye both, I will! —Stolen!

RACHEL. (*Imploringly.*) Will you come?

RICHARD. Look you, old Rickby; this is not the first time. Charm all the broomsticks in town, if you like; bewitch all the tables and saucepans and mirrors you please; but gull no more money out of young girls. Mind you! We're not so enterprising in this town as at Salem; but—*it may come to it!* So look sharp! I'm not blind to what's going on here.

GOODY RICKBY. Not blind, Master Puritan? Oho! You can see through all my counterfeits, can ye? So! you would scrape all the wonder out'n the world, as I've scraped all the meat out'n my punkin-head yonder! Aha! wait and see! Afore sundown, I'll send ye a nut to crack, shall make your orthodox jaws ache. Your servant, Master Deuteronomy!

RICHARD. (*To* RACHEL, *who has seized his arm.*) We'll go.

(*Exeunt* RICHARD *and* RACHEL.)

GOODY RICKBY. (*Calls shrilly after them.*) Trot away, pretty team; toss your heads. I'll unhitch ye and take off your blinders.

THE SLOUCHING BOY. (*Capering and grimacing in front of the mirror, shrieks with laughter.*) Ohoho!

GOODY RICKBY. (*Returning, she mutters savagely.*) "Stolen goods!" (*Screams.*) Dickon! Stop laughing.

THE BOY. O Lord! O Lord!

GOODY RICKBY. What tickles thy mirth now?

THE BOY. For to think that the soul of an orphan innocent, what lives in a hayloft, should wear horns.

(*On looking into the mirror, the spectator perceives therein that the reflection of the slouching boy is the horned demon figure of* DICKON, *who performs the same antics in pantomime within the glass as the boy does without.*)

GOODY RICKBY. Yea; 'tis a wise devil that knows his own face in the glass. But hark now! thou must find me a rival for this cock-squire,—dost hear? A rival, that shall steal away the heart of his Mistress Rachel.

DICKON. And take her to church?

GOODY RICKBY. To church or to hell. All's one.

DICKON. A rival! (*Pointing at the glass.*) How would *he* serve—in there? Dear Ebenezer! Fancy the deacons in the vestry, Goody, and her uncle, the Justice, when they saw him escorting the bride to the altar, with his tail round her waist!

GOODY RICKBY. Tut, tut! Think it over in earnest, and meantime take her the glass. Wait, we'd best fold it up small, so as not to attract notice on the road. (DICKON, *who has already drawn the curtains over the glass, grasps one side of the large frame,* GOODY RICKBY *the other.*) Now! (*Pushing their shoulders against the two sides, the frame disappears and* DICKON *holds in his hand a mirror about a foot square, of the same design.*) So! Be off! And mind, a rival for Richard!

DICKON.

> For Richard a rival,
> Dear Goody Rickby
> Wants Dickon's connival:
> Lord! What can the trick be?

(*To the scarecrow.*) By-by, Sonny; take care of thy mother.

> (DICKON *slouches out with the glass, whistling.*)

GOODY RICKBY. Mother! Yea, if only I had a son—the Justice Merton's and mine! If the brat had but lived now to remind him of those merry days, which he has forgotten. Zooks, wouldn't I put a spoke in his wheel! But no such luck for me! No such luck!

> (*As she goes to the forge, the stout figure of a man appears in the doorway behind her. Under one arm he carries a large book, in the other hand a gold-headed cane. He hesitates, embarrassed.*)

THE MAN. Permit me, madam.

GOODY RICKBY. (*Turning.*) Ah, him— Justice Merton!

JUSTICE MERTON. (*Removing his hat, steps over the sill, and lays his great book on the table; then with a supercilious look, he puts his hat firmly on again.*) Permit me, dame.

GOODY RICKBY. You!

> (*With confused, affected hauteur, the JUSTICE shifts from foot to foot, flourishing his cane. As he speaks, GOODY RICKBY, with a shrewd, painful expression, draws slowly backward toward the door, left, which opens into an inner room. Reaching it, she opens it part way, stands facing him, and listens.*)

JUSTICE MERTON. I have had the honor— permit me—to entertain suspicions; to rise early, to follow my niece, to meet just now Squire Talbot; to hear his re-

marks concerning—hem!—you, dame! to call here—permit me—to express myself and inquire—

GOODY RICKBY. Concerning your waistcoat?

> (*Turning quickly, she snatches an article of apparel which hangs on the inner side of the door, and holds it up.*)

JUSTICE MERTON. (*Starting, crimson.*) Woman!

GOODY RICKBY. You left it behind—the last time.

JUSTICE MERTON. I have not the honor to remember—

GOODY RICKBY. The one I embroidered?

JUSTICE MERTON. 'Tis a matter of—

GOODY RICKBY. Of some two-and-twenty years. (*Stretching out the narrow width of the waistcoat.*) Will you try it on now, dearie?

JUSTICE MERTON. Unconscionable! Un-un-unconscionable witch!

GOODY RICKBY. Witchling—thou used to say.

JUSTICE MERTON. Pah! pah! I forget myself. Pride, permit me, goeth before a fall. As a magistrate, Rickby, I have already borne with you long! The last straw, however, breaks the camel's back.

GOODY RICKBY. Poor camel!

JUSTICE MERTON. You have soiled, you have smirched, the virgin reputation of my niece. You have inveigled her into notions of witchcraft; already the neighbors are beginning to talk. 'Tis a long lane which hath no turning, saith the Lord. Permit me—as a witch, thou art judged. Thou shalt hang.

A VOICE. (*Behind him.*) And me, too?

JUSTICE MERTON. (*Turns about and stares.*) I beg pardon.

THE VOICE. (*In front of him.*) Not at all.

JUSTICE MERTON. Did—did somebody speak?

THE VOICE. Don't you recognize my

voice? *Still and small,* you know. If you will kindly let me out, we can chat.

JUSTICE MERTON. (*Turning fiercely on* GOODY RICKBY.) These are thy sorceries. But I fear them not. The righteous man walketh with God. (*Going to the book which lies on the table.*) Satan, I ban thee! I will read from the Holy Scriptures!

> (*Unclasping the Bible, he flings open the ponderous covers.*—DICKON *steps forth in smoke.*)

DICKON. Thanks; it was stuffy in there.

JUSTICE MERTON. (*Clasping his hands.*) Dickon!

DICKON. (*Moving a step nearer on the table.*) Hullo, Gilly! Hullo, Bess!

JUSTICE MERTON. Dickon! No! No!

DICKON. Do ye mind Auld Lang Syne—the chorus that night, Gilly? (*Sings.*)

> Gil-ead, Gil-ead, Gil-ead Merton,
> He was a silly head, silly head, Certain,
> When he forgot to steal a bed-Curtain.

Encore, now!

JUSTICE MERTON. No, no, be merciful! I will not harm her; she shall not hang; I swear it, I swear it! (DICKON *disappears.*) I swear—ah! Is he gone? Witchcraft! Witchcraft! I have witnessed it. 'Tis proved on thee, slut. I swear it: thou shalt hang.

> (*Exit wildly.*)

GOODY RICKBY. Ay, Gilead! I shall hang on! Ahaha! Dickon, thou angel! Ah, Satan! Satan! For a son now!

DICKON. (*Reappearing.*) *Videlicet,* in law—a bastard. *N'est ce pas?*

GOODY RICKBY. Yea, in law and in justice, I should 'a' had one now. Worse luck that he died.

DICKON. One-and-twenty years ago? (GOODY RICKBY *nods.*) Good; he should be of age now. One-and-twenty—a pretty age, too, for a rival. Haha!—For arrival?—Marry, he shall arrive, then; arrive and marry and inherit his patrimony—all on his birthday! Come, to work!

GOODY RICKBY. What rant is this?

DICKON. Yet, Dickon, it pains me to perform such an anachronism. All this mediævalism in Massachusetts!—These old-fashioned flames and alchemic accompaniments, when I've tried so hard to be a native American product; it jars. But *che vuole!* I'm naturally middle-aged. I haven't been really myself, let me think,—since 1492!

GOODY RICKBY. What art thou mooning about?

DICKON. (*Still impenetrable.*) There was my old friend in Germany, Dr. Johann Faustus; he was nigh such a bag of old rubbish when I made him over. Ain't it trite! No, you can't teach an old dog like me new tricks. Still, a scarecrow! that's decidedly local color. Come, then; a Yankee masterpiece! (*Seizing* GOODY RICKBY *by the arm, and placing her before the scarecrow, he makes a bow and wave of introduction.*) Behold, madam, your son—illegitimate; the future affianced of Mistress Rachel Merton, the heir-elect, through matrimony, of Merton House,—Gilead Merton second: Lord Ravensbane! Your lordship—your mother.

GOODY RICKBY. Dickon! Can you do it?

DICKON. I can—try.

GOODY RICKBY. You will create him for me?—(*wickedly*)—and for Gilead!

DICKON. I will—for a kiss.

GOODY RICKBY. (*About to embrace him.*) Dickon!

DICKON. (*Dodging her.*) Later. Now, the waistcoat.

GOODY RICKBY. (*Handing it.*) Rare! Rare! He shall go wooing in't—like his father.

DICKON. (*Shifting the scarecrow's gold-trimmed coat, slips on the embroidered waistcoat and replaces the coat.*) Stand still, Jack! So, my macaroni. *Perfecto!* Stay—a walking-stick!

GOODY RICKBY. (*Wrenching a spoke out of an old rickety wheel.*) Here: the spoke for Gilead. He used to take me to drive in the chaise it came out of.

DICKON. (*Placing the spoke as a cane, in the scarecrow's sleeve, views him with satisfaction.*) *Sic!* There, Jacky! *Filius fit non nascitur.*—Sam Hill! My Latin is stale. "In the beginning, was the—gourd!" Of these thy modest ingredients may thy spirit smack!

(*Making various mystic passes with his hands,* DICKON *intones, now deep and solemn, now with fanciful shrill rapidity, this incantation.*)

> Flail, flip;
> Broom, sweep;
>   *Sic itur!*
> Cornstalk
> And turnip, talk!
>   Turn crittur!
>
> Pulse, beet;
> Gourd, eat;
>   *Ave* Hellas!
> Poker and punkin,
> Stir the old junk in;
>   Breathe, bellows!
>
> Corn-cob,
> And crow's feather,
> End the job;
> Jumble the rest o' the
>   rubbish together;
> Dovetail and tune 'em.
> *E pluribus unum!*

(*The scarecrow remains stock still.*) The devil! Have I lost the hang of it? Ah! Hullo! He's dropped his pipe. What's a dandy without his 'baccy! (*Picking up the pipe, he shows it to* GOODY RICKBY, *pointing into the pipe-bowl.*) 'Tis my own brand, Goody: brimstone. Without it he'd be naught but a scarecrow. (*Restoring the corn-cob pipe to the scarecrow's mouth.*) 'Tis the life and breath of him. So; hand me yon hazel switch, Goody. (*Waving it.*) Presto!

> Brighten, coal,
> I' the dusk between us!
> Whiten, soul!
> *Propinquat Venus!*

(*A whiff of smoke puffs from the scarecrow's pipe.*)

Sic! Sic! Jacobus! (*Another whiff.*) Bravo!

(*The whiffs grow more rapid and the thing trembles.*)

GOODY RICKBY. Puff! puff, manny, for thy life!

DICKON. *Fiat, foetus!*—Huzza! *Noch einmal!* Go it!

(*Clouds of smoke issue from the pipe, half fill the shop, and envelop the creature, who staggers.**)

GOODY RICKBY. See! See his eyes!

DICKON. (*Beckoning with one finger.*) *Veni fili! Veni!* Take 'ee first step, bambino!—Toddle!

(*The* SCARECROW *makes a stiff lurch forward and falls sidewise against the anvil, propped half-reclining against which he leans rigid, emitting fainter puffs of smoke in gasps.*)

GOODY RICKBY. (*Screams.*) Have a care! He's fallen.

DICKON. Well done, Punkin Jack! Thou shalt be knighted for that! (*Striking him on the shoulder with the hazel rod.*) Rise, Lord Ravensbane!

(*The* SCARECROW *totters to his feet, and makes a forlorn rectilinear salutation.*)

GOODY RICKBY. Look! He bows.—He flaps his flails at thee. He smiles like a tik-doo-loo-roo!

DICKON. (*With a profound reverence, backing away.*) Will his lordship deign to follow his tutor?

(*With hitches and jerks, the* SCARECROW *follows* DICKON.)

GOODY RICKBY. O Lord! Lord! the style o' the broomstick!

DICKON. (*Holding ready a high-backed*

---

* At Dickon's words, "Come, to work!" on p. 126 the living actor, concealed by the smoke, and disguised, has substituted himself for the elegantly clad effigy. His make-up, of course, approximates to the latter, but the grotesque contours of his expression gradually, throughout the remainder of the act, become refined and sublimated till, at the *finale*, they are of a lordly and distinguished cast.

chair.) Will his lordship be seated and rest himself? (*Awkwardly the* SCARE-CROW *half falls into the chair; his head sinks sideways, and his pipe falls out.* DICKON *snatches it up instantly and restores it to his mouth.*) Puff! Puff, *puer;* 'tis thy life. (*The* SCARECROW *puffs again.*) Is his lordship's tobacco refreshing?

GOODY RICKBY. Look now! The red color in his cheeks. The beet-juice is pumping, oho!

DICKON. (*Offering his arm.*) Your lordship will deign to receive an audience? (*The* SCARECROW *takes his arm and rises.*) The Marchioness of Rickby, your lady mother, entreats leave to present herself.

GOODY RICKBY. (*Curtsying low.*) My son!

DICKON. (*Holding the pipe, and waving the hazel rod.*) *Dicite!* Speak! (*The* SCARECROW, *blowing out his last mouthful of smoke, opens his mouth, gasps, gurgles, and is silent.*) *In principio erat verbum!* Accost thy mother! (*The* SCARECROW, *clutching at his side in a struggle for coherence, fixes a pathetic look of pain on* GOODY RICKBY.)

THE SCARECROW. Mother!

GOODY RICKBY. (*With a scream of hysterical laughter, seizes both* DICKON'S *hands and dances him about the forge.*) O, Beelzebub! I shall die!

DICKON. Thou hast thy son.
(DICKON *whispers in the* SCARE-CROW'S *ear, shakes his finger, and exit.*)

GOODY RICKBY. He called me "mother." Again, boy, again.

THE SCARECROW. From the bottom of my heart—mother.

GOODY RICKBY. "The bottom of his heart"!—Nay, thou killest me.

THE SCARECROW. Permit me, madam!

GOODY RICKBY. Gilead! Gilead himself!

Waistcoat, "permit me," and all: thy father over again, I tell thee.

THE SCARECROW. (*With a slight stammer.*) It gives me—I assure you—lady —the deepest happiness.

GOODY RICKBY. Just so the old hypocrite spoke when I said I'd have him. But thou hast a sweeter deference, my son.

(*Reënter* DICKON; *he is dressed all in black, save for a white stock—a suit of plain elegance.*)

DICKON. Now, my lord, your tutor is ready.

THE SCARECROW. (*To* GOODY RICKBY.) I have the honor—permit me—to wish you—good-morning.
(*Bows and takes a step after* DICKON, *who, taking a three-cornered cocked hat from a peg, goes toward the door.*)

GOODY RICKBY. Whoa! Whoa, Jack! Whither away?

DICKON. (*Presenting the hat.*) Deign to reply, sir.

THE SCARECROW. I go—with my tutor— Master Dickonson—to pay my respects —to his worship—the Justice—Merton —to solicit—the hand—of his daughter—the fair Mistress—Rachel. (*With another bow.*) Permit me.

GOODY RICKBY. Permit ye? God speed ye! Thou must teach him his tricks, Dickon.

DICKON. Trust me, Goody. Between here and Justice Merton's, I will play the mother-hen, and I promise thee, our bantling shall be as stuffed with compliments as a callow chick with caterpillars. (*As he throws open the big doors, the cawing of crows is heard again.*) Hark! your lordship's retainers acclaim you on your birthday. They bid you welcome to your majority. Listen! "Long live Lord Ravensbane! Caw!"

GOODY RICKBY. Look! Count 'em, Dickon.

One for sorrow,
Two for mirth,
Three for a wedding,
Four for a birth—

Four on 'em! So! Good luck on thy birthday! And see! There's three on 'em flying into the Justice's field.

—Flight o' the crows
Tells how the wind blows!—

A wedding! Get thee gone. Wed the girl, and sting the Justice. Bless ye, my son!

THE SCARECROW. (*With a profound reverence.*) Mother—believe me—to be—your ladyship's—most devoted—and obedient—son.

DICKON. (*Prompting him aloud.*) Ravensbane.

THE SCARECROW. (*Donning his hat, lifts his head in hauteur, shakes his lace ruffle over his hand, turns his shoulder, nods slightly, and speaks for the first time with complete mastery of his voice.*) Hm! Ravensbane!

(*With one hand in the arm of* DICKON, *the other twirling his cane* (*the converted chaise-spoke*), *wreathed in halos of smoke from his pipe, the fantastical figure hitches elegantly forth into the daylight, amid louder acclamations of the crows.*)

ACT SECOND.

The same morning. JUSTICE MERTON'S *parlor, furnished and designed in the style of the early colonial period. On the right wall hangs a portrait of the* JUSTICE *as a young man; on the left wall, an old-fashioned looking-glass. At the right of the room stands the Glass of Truth, draped—as in the blacksmith shop—with the strange, embroidered curtain. In front of it are discovered* RACHEL *and* RICHARD; RACHEL *is about to draw the curtain.*

RACHEL. Now! Are you willing?

RICHARD. So you suspect me of dark, villainous practices?

RACHEL. No, no, foolish Dick.

RICHARD. Still, I am to be tested; is that it?

RACHEL. That's it.

RICHARD. As your true lover.

RACHEL. Well, yes.

RICHARD. Why, of course, then, I consent. A true lover always consents to. the follies of his lady-love.

RACHEL. Thank you, Dick; I trust the glass will sustain your character. Now; when I draw the curtain—

RICHARD. (*Staying her hand.*) What if I be false?

RACHEL. Then, sir, the glass will reflect you as the subtle fox that you are.

RICHARD. And you—as the goose?

RACHEL. Very likely. Ah! but, Richard, dear, we mustn't laugh. It may prove very serious. You do not guess—you do not dream all the mysteries—

RICHARD. (*Shaking his head, with a grave smile.*) You pluck at too many mysteries. Remember our first mother Eve!

RACHEL. But this is the glass of truth; and Goody Rickby told me—

RICHARD. Rickby, forsooth!

RACHEL. Nay, come; let's have it over. (*She draws the curtain, covers her eyes, steps back by* RICHARD'S *side, looks at the glass, and gives a joyous cry.*) Ah! there you are, dear! There we are, both of us—just as we have always seemed to each other, true. 'Tis proved. Isn't it wonderful?

RICHARD. Miraculous! That a mirror bought in a blacksmith shop, before sunrise, for twenty pounds, should prove to be actually—a mirror!

RACHEL. Richard, I'm so happy.

(*Enter* JUSTICE MERTON *and* MISTRESS MERTON.)

RICHARD. (*Embracing her.*) Happy, art

thou, sweet goose? Why, then, God bless Goody Rickby.

JUSTICE MERTON. Strange words from you, Squire Talbot.

(RACHEL and RICHARD part quickly; RACHEL draws the curtain over the mirror; RICHARD stands stiffly.)

RICHARD. Justice Merton! Why, sir, the old witch is more innocent, perhaps, than I represented her.

JUSTICE MERTON. A witch, believe me, is never innocent. (Taking their hands, he brings them together and kisses RACHEL on the forehead.) Permit me, young lovers. I was once young myself, young and amorous.

MISTRESS MERTON. (In a low voice.) Verily!

JUSTICE MERTON. My fair niece, my worthy young man, beware of witchcraft.

MISTRESS MERTON. And Goody Rickby, too, brother?

JUSTICE MERTON. That woman shall answer for her deeds. She is proscribed.

RACHEL. Proscribed? What is that?

MISTRESS MERTON. (Examining the mirror.) What is this?

JUSTICE MERTON. She shall hang.

RACHEL. Uncle, no! Not merely because of my purchase this morning?

JUSTICE MERTON. Your purchase?

MISTRESS MERTON. (Pointing to the mirror.) That, I suppose.

JUSTICE MERTON. What! you purchased that mirror of her? You brought it here?

RACHEL. No, the boy brought it; I found it here when I returned.

JUSTICE MERTON. What! From her shop? From her infamous den, into my parlor! (To MISTRESS MERTON.) Call the servant. (Himself calling.) Micah! Away with it! Micah!

RACHEL. Uncle Gilead, I bought—

JUSTICE MERTON. Micah, I say! Where is the man?

RACHEL. Listen, uncle. I bought it with my own money.

JUSTICE MERTON. Thine own money! Wilt have the neighbors gossip? Wilt have me, thyself, my house, suspected of complicity with witches?

(Enter MICAH.)

Micah, take this away.

MICAH. Yes, sir; but, sir—

JUSTICE MERTON. Out of my house!

MICAH. There be visitors.

JUSTICE MERTON. Away with—

MISTRESS MERTON. (Touching his arm.) Gilead!

MICAH. Visitors, sir; gentry.

JUSTICE MERTON. Ah!

MICAH. Shall I show them in, sir?

JUSTICE MERTON. Visitors! In the morning? Who are they?

MICAH. Strangers, sir. I should judge they be very high gentry; lords, sir.

ALL. Lords!

MICAH. At least, one on 'em, sir. The other—the dark gentleman—told me they left their horses at the inn, sir.

MISTRESS MERTON. Hark! (The faces of all wear suddenly a startled expression.) Where is that unearthly sound?

JUSTICE MERTON. (Listening.) Is it in the cellar?

MICAH. 'Tis just the dog howling, madam. When he spied the gentry he turned tail and run below.

MISTRESS MERTON. Oh, the dog!

JUSTICE MERTON. Show the gentlemen here, Micah. Don't keep them waiting. A lord! (To RACHEL.) We shall talk of this matter later.—A lord!

(Turning to the small glass on the wall, he arranges his peruke and attire.)

RACHEL. (To RICHARD.) What a fortunate interruption! But, dear Dick! I wish we needn't meet these strangers now.

RICHARD. Would you really rather we were alone together?
>   (*They chat aside, absorbed in each other.*)

JUSTICE MERTON. Think of it, Cynthia, a lord!

MISTRESS MERTON. (*Dusting the furniture hastily with her handkerchief.*) And such dust!

RACHEL. (*To* RICHARD.) You know, dear, we need only be introduced, and then we can steal away together.

>   (*Reënter* MICAH.)

MICAH. (*Announcing.*) Lord Ravensbane: Marquis of Oxford, Baron of Wittenberg, Elector of Worms, and Count of Cordova; Master Dickonson.

>   (*Enter* RAVENSBANE *and* DICKON.)

JUSTICE MERTON. Gentlemen, permit me, you are excessively welcome. I am deeply gratified to meet—

DICKON. Lord Ravensbane, of the Rookeries, Somersetshire.

JUSTICE MERTON. Lord Ravensbane—his lordship's most truly honored.

RAVENSBANE. Truly honored.

JUSTICE MERTON. (*Turning to* DICKON.) His lordship's—?

DICKON. Tutor.

JUSTICE MERTON. (*Checking his effusiveness.*) Ah, so!

DICKON. Justice Merton, I believe.

JUSTICE MERTON. Of Merton House.— May I present—permit me, your lordship—my sister, Mistress Merton.

RAVENSBANE. Mistress Merton.

JUSTICE MERTON. And my—and my— (*under his breath*)—Rachel! (RACHEL *remains with a bored expression behind* RICHARD.)—My young neighbor, Squire Talbot, Squire Richard Talbot of—of—

RICHARD. Of nowhere, sir.

RAVENSBANE. (*Nods.*) Nowhere.

JUSTICE MERTON. And permit me, Lord Ravensbane, my niece—Mistress Rachel Merton.

RAVENSBANE. (*Bows low.*) Mistress Rachel Merton.

RACHEL. (*Curtsies.*) Lord Ravensbane.
>   (*As they raise their heads, their eyes meet and are fascinated.* DICKON *just then takes* RAVENSBANE'S *pipe and fills it.*)

RAVENSBANE. Mistress Rachel!

RACHEL. Your lordship!
>   (DICKON *returns the pipe.*)

MISTRESS MERTON. A pipe! Gilead!—in the parlor!
>   (JUSTICE MERTON *frowns silence.*)

JUSTICE MERTON. Your lordship—ahem! —has just arrived in town?

DICKON. From London, via New Amsterdam.

RICHARD. (*Aside.*) Is he staring at *you*? Are you ill, Rachel?

RACHEL. (*Indifferently.*) What?

JUSTICE MERTON. Lord Ravensbane honors my humble roof.

DICKON. (*Touches* RAVENSBANE'S *arm.*) Your lordship—"roof."

RAVENSBANE. (*Starting, turns to* MERTON.) Nay, sir, the roof of my father's oldest friend bestows generous hospitality upon his only son.

JUSTICE MERTON. Only son—ah, yes! Your father—

RAVENSBANE. My father, I trust, sir, has never forgotten the intimate companionship, the touching devotion, the unceasing solicitude for his happiness which you, sir, manifested to him in the days of his youth.

JUSTICE MERTON. Really, your lordship, the—the slight favors which—hem! some years ago, I was privileged to show your illustrious father—

RAVENSBANE. Permit me!—Because, however, of his present infirmities—for I regret to say that my father is suffering a temporary aberration of mind—

JUSTICE MERTON. You distress me!

RAVENSBANE. My lady mother has charged me with a double mission here in New England. On my quitting my home, sir, to explore the wideness and the mystery of this world, my mother bade me be sure to call upon his worship, the Justice Merton; and deliver to him, first, my father's remembrances; and secondly, my mother's epistle.

DICKON. (*Handing to* JUSTICE MERTON *a sealed document.*) Her ladyship's letter, sir.

JUSTICE MERTON. (*Examining the seal with awe, speaks aside to* MISTRESS MERTON.) Cynthia!—a crested seal!

DICKON. His lordship's crest, sir: rooks rampant.

JUSTICE MERTON. (*Embarrassed, breaks the seal.*) Permit me.

RACHEL. (*Looking at* RAVENSBANE.) Have you noticed his bearing, Richard: what personal distinction! what inbred nobility! Every inch a true lord!

RICHARD. He may be a lord, my dear, but he walks like a broomstick.

RACHEL. How dare you!
    (*Turns abruptly away; as she does so, a fold of her gown catches in a chair.*)

RAVENSBANE. Mistress Rachel—permit me.
    (*Stooping, he extricates the fold of her gown.*)

RACHEL. Oh, thank you.
            (*They go aside together.*)

JUSTICE MERTON. (*To* DICKON, *glancing up from the letter.*) I am astonished—overpowered!

RICHARD. (*To* MISTRESS MERTON.) So Lord Ravensbane and his family are old friends of yours?

MISTRESS MERTON. (*Monosyllabically.*) I never heard the name before, Richard.

RAVENSBANE. (*To* RACHEL, *taking her hand after a whisper from* DICKON.) Believe me, sweet lady, it will give me the deepest pleasure.

RACHEL. Can you really tell fortunes?

RAVENSBANE. More than that; I can bestow them.
    (RAVENSBANE *leads* RACHEL *off, left, into an adjoining room, the door of which remains open.* RICHARD *follows them.* MISTRESS MERTON *follows him, murmuring,* "Richard!" DICKON *stands where he can watch them in the room off scene, while he speaks to the* JUSTICE.)

JUSTICE MERTON. (*To* DICKON, *glancing up from the letter.*) I am astonished—overpowered! But is her ladyship really serious? An offer of marriage!

DICKON. Pray read it again, sir.

JUSTICE MERTON. (*Reads.*) "To the Worshipful, the Justice Gilead Merton, Merton House.
"My Honorable Friend and Benefactor:
    "With these brief lines I commend to you our son"—*our son!*

DICKON. She speaks likewise for his young lordship's father, sir.

JUSTICE MERTON. Ah! of course. (*Reads.*) "In a strange land, I entrust him to you as to a father." Honored, believe me! "I have only to add my earnest hope that the natural gifts, graces, and inherited fortune"—ah—!

DICKON. Twenty thousand pounds—on his father's demise.

JUSTICE MERTON. Ah!—"fortune of this young scion of nobility will so propitiate the heart of your niece, Mistress Rachel Merton, as to cause her to accept his proffered hand in matrimony";—but—but—but Squire Talbot is betrothed to—well, well, we shall see;—"in matrimony, and thus cement the early bonds of interest and affection between your honored self and his lordship's father; not to mention, dear sir, your worship's ever grateful and obedient admirer,

                    "ELIZABETH,
                    "Marchioness of R."

Of R.! of R.! Will you believe me, my dear sir, so long is it since my travels in England—I visited at so many—hem! noble estates—permit me, it is so awkward, but—

DICKON. (*With his peculiar intonation of Act First.*) Not at all.

RAVENSBANE. (*Calls from the adjoining room.*) Dickon, my pipe!

(DICKON *glides away.*)

JUSTICE MERTON. (*Starting in perturbation. To* DICKON.) Permit me, one moment; I did not catch your name.

DICKON. My name? Dickonson.

JUSTICE MERTON. (*With a gasp of relief.*) Ah, Dickonson! Thank you, I mistook the word.

DICKON. A compound, your worship. (*With a malignant smile.*) Dickon-(*then, jerking his thumb toward the next room*) son! (*Bowing.*) Both at your service.

JUSTICE MERTON. Is he—he there?

DICKON. Bessie's brat; yes; it didn't die, after all, poor suckling! Dickon weaned it. Saved it for balm of Gilead. Raised it for joyful home-coming. Prodigal's return! Twenty-first birthday! Happy son! Happy father!

JUSTICE MERTON. My—son!

DICKON. Felicitations!

JUSTICE MERTON. (*Faintly.*) What—what do you want?

DICKON. Only the happiness of your dear ones—the union of these young hearts and hands.

JUSTICE MERTON. What! he will dare—an illegitimate—

DICKON. Fie, fie, Gilly! Why, the brat is a lord now.

JUSTICE MERTON. Oh, the disgrace! Spare me that, Dickon. And she is innocent; she is already betrothed.

DICKON. Twiddle-twaddle! 'Tis a brilliant match; besides, her ladyship's heart is set upon it.

JUSTICE MERTON. Her ladyship—?

DICKON. The Marchioness of Rickby.

JUSTICE MERTON. (*Glowering.*) Rickby! —I had forgotten.

DICKON. Her ladyship has never forgotten. So, you see, your worship's alternatives are most simple. Alternative one: advance his lordship's suit with your niece as speedily as possible, and save all scandal. Alternative two: impede his lordship's suit, and—

JUSTICE MERTON. Don't, Dickon! don't reveal the truth; not disgrace now!

DICKON. Good; we are agreed, then?

JUSTICE MERTON. I have no choice.

DICKON. (*Cheerfully.*) Why, true; we ignored that, didn't we?

MISTRESS MERTON. (*Reëntering.*) This young lord—Why, Gilead, are you ill?

JUSTICE MERTON. (*With a great effort, commands himself.*) Not in the least.

MISTRESS MERTON. Rachel's deportment, my dear brother—I tell you, they are fortune-telling!

JUSTICE MERTON. Tush! Tush!

MISTRESS MERTON. Tush? "Tush" to me? Tush! (*She goes out right.*)

(RAVENSBANE *and* RACHEL *reënter from the adjoining room, followed shortly by* RICHARD.)

RACHEL. I am really at a loss. Your lordship's hand is so very peculiar.

RAVENSBANE. Ah! Peculiar.

RACHEL. This, now, is the line of life.

RAVENSBANE. Of life, yes?

RACHEL. But it begins so abruptly, and see! it breaks off and ends nowhere. And just so here with this line—the line of—of love.

RAVENSBANE. Of love. So; it breaks?

RACHEL. Yes.

RAVENSBANE. Ah, then, that must be the *heart* line.

RACHEL. Why, Lord Ravensbane, your pulse. Really, if I am cruel, you are quite heartless. I declare I can't feel your heart beat at all.

RAVENSBANE. Ah, mistress, that is because I have just lost it.

RACHEL. (*Archly.*) Where?

RAVENSBANE. (*Faintly.*) Dickon, my pipe!

RACHEL. Alas! my lord, are you ill?

DICKON. (*Restoring the lighted pipe to* RAVENSBANE, *speaks aside.*) Pardon me, sweet young lady, I must confide to you that his lordship's heart is peculiarly responsive to his emotions. When he feels very ardently, it quite stops. Hence the use of his pipe.

RACHEL. Oh! Is smoking, then, necessary for his heart?

DICKON. Absolutely—to equilibrate the valvular palpitations. Without his pipe —should his lordship experience, for instance, the emotion of love—he might die.

RACHEL. You alarm me!

DICKON. But this is for you only, Mistress Rachel. We may confide in you?

RACHEL. Oh, utterly, sir.

DICKON. His lordship, you know, is so sensitive.

RAVENSBANE. (*To* RACHEL.) You have given it back to me. Why did not you keep it?

RACHEL. What, my lord?

RAVENSBANE. My heart.

RICHARD. Intolerable! Do you approve of *this*, sir? Are Lord Ravensbane's credentials satisfactory?

JUSTICE MERTON. Eminently, eminently.

RICHARD. Ah! So her ladyship's letter is—

JUSTICE MERTON. Charming; charming. (*To* RAVENSBANE.) Your lordship will, I trust, make my house your home.

RAVENSBANE. My home, sir.

RACHEL. (*To* DICKON, *who has spoken to her.*) Really? (*To* JUSTICE MERTON.) Why, uncle, what is this Master Dickonson tells us?

JUSTICE MERTON. What! What! he has revealed—

RACHEL. Yes, indeed.

JUSTICE MERTON. Rachel! Rachel!

RACHEL. (*Laughingly to* RAVENSBANE.) My uncle is doubtless astonished to find you so grown.

RAVENSBANE. (*Laughingly to* JUSTICE MERTON.) I am doubtless astonished, sir, to be so grown.

JUSTICE MERTON. (*To* DICKON.) You have—

DICKON. Merely remarked, sir, that your worship had often dandled his lordship —as an infant.

JUSTICE MERTON. (*Smiling lugubriously.*) Quite so—as an infant merely.

RACHEL. How interesting! Then you must have seen his lordship's home in England.

JUSTICE MERTON. As you say.

RACHEL. (*To* RAVENSBANE.) Do describe it to us. We are so isolated here from the grand world. Do you know, I always imagine England to be an enchanted isle, like one of the old Hesperides, teeming with fruits of solid gold.

RAVENSBANE. Ah, yes! my mother raises them.

RACHEL. Fruits of gold?

RAVENSBANE. Round like the rising sun. She calls them—ah! punkins.

MISTRESS MERTON. "Punkins"!

JUSTICE MERTON. (*Aside, grinding his teeth.*) Scoundrel! Scoundrel!

RACHEL. (*Laughing.*) Your lordship pokes fun at us.

DICKON. His lordship is an artist in words, mistress. I have noticed that in whatever country he is traveling, he tinges his vocabulary with the local idiom. His lordship means, of course, not pumpkins, but pomegranates.

RACHEL. We forgive him. But, your lordship, please be serious and describe to us your hall.

RAVENSBANE. Quite serious: the hall. Yes,

yes; in the middle burns a great fire—on a black—ah! black altar.

DICKON. A Druidical heirloom. His lordship's mother collects antiques.

RACHEL. How fascinating!

RAVENSBANE. Fascinating! On the walls hang pieces of iron.

DICKON. Trophies of Saxon warfare.

RAVENSBANE. And rusty horseshoes.

GENERAL MURMURS. Horseshoes!

DICKON. Presents from the German Emperor. They were worn by the steeds of Charlemagne.

RAVENSBANE. Quite so; and broken cartwheels.

DICKON. Relics of British chariots.

RACHEL. How mediæval it must be! (*To* JUSTICE MERTON.) And to think you never described it to us!

MISTRESS MERTON. True, brother; you have been singularly reticent.

JUSTICE MERTON. Permit me; it is impossible to report all one sees on one's travels.

MISTRESS MERTON. Evidently.

RACHEL. But surely your lordship's mother has other diversions besides collecting antiques. I have heard that in England ladies followed the hounds; and sometimes—(*looking at her aunt and lowering her voice*)—they even dance.

RAVENSBANE. Dance—ah, yes; my lady mother dances about the—the altar; she swings high a hammer.

DICKON. Your lordship, your lordship! Pray, sir, check this vein of poetry. Lord Ravensbane symbolizes as a hammer and altar a golf-stick and tee—a Scottish game, which her ladyship plays on her Highland estates.

RICHARD. (*To* MISTRESS MERTON.) What do you think of this?

MISTRESS MERTON. (*With a scandalized look toward her brother.*) He said to me "tush."

RICHARD. (*To* JUSTICE MERTON, *indicating* DICKON.) Who is this magpie?

JUSTICE MERTON. (*Hisses in fury.*) Satan!

RICHARD. I beg pardon!

JUSTICE MERTON. Satan, sir,—makes you jealous.

RICHARD. (*Bows stiffly.*) Good-morning. (*Walking up to* RAVENSBANE.) Lord Ravensbane, I have a rustic colonial question to ask. Is it the latest fashion to smoke incessantly in ladies' parlors, or is it—mediæval?

DICKON. His lordship's health, sir, necessitates—

RICHARD. I addressed his lordship.

RAVENSBANE. In the matter of fashions, sir— (*Hands his pipe to be refilled.*) My pipe, Dickon!

> (*While* DICKON *holds his pipe— somewhat longer than usual—* RAVENSBANE, *with his mouth open as if about to speak, relapses into a vacant stare.*)

RICHARD. Well?

DICKON. (*As he lights the pipe for* RAVENSBANE, *speaks suavely and low as if not to be overheard by him.*) Pardon me. The fact is, my young pupil is sensitive; the wound from his latest duel is not quite healed; you observe a slight lameness, an occasional—absence of mind.

RACHEL. A wound—in a real duel?

DICKON. (*Aside.*) You, mistress, know the *true* reason—his lordship's heart.

RICHARD. (*To* RAVENSBANE, *who is still staring vacantly into space.*) Well, well, your lordship. (RAVENSBANE *pays no attention.*) You were saying—? (DICKON *returns the pipe*)—in the matter of fashions, sir—?

RAVENSBANE. (*Regaining slowly a look of intelligence, draws himself up with affronted hauteur.*) Permit me! (*Puffs several wreaths of smoke into the air.*) I *am* the fashions.

RICHARD. (*Going.*) Insufferable!
> (*He pauses at the door.*)

MISTRESS MERTON. (*To* JUSTICE MERTON.) Well—what do you think of that?

JUSTICE MERTON. Spoken like King Charles himself.

MISTRESS MERTON. Brother! brother! is there nothing wrong here?
> (*Going out, she passes* DICKON, *starts at a look which he gives her, and goes out, right, flustered. Following her,* JUSTICE MERTON *is stopped by* DICKON, *and led off left by him.*)

RACHEL. (*To* RAVENSBANE.) I—object to the smoke? Why, I think it is charming.

RICHARD. (*Who has returned from the door, speaks in a low, constrained voice.*) Rachel!

RACHEL. Oh!—you?

RICHARD. You take quickly to European fashions.

RACHEL. Yes? To what one in particular?

RICHARD. Two; smoking and flirtation.

RACHEL. Jealous?

RICHARD. Of an idiot? I hope not. Manners differ, however. Your confidences to his lordship have evidently not included—your relation to me.

RACHEL. Oh, our relations!

RICHARD. Of course, since you wish him to continue in ignorance—

RACHEL. Not at all. He shall know at once. Lord Ravensbane!

RAVENSBANE. Fair mistress!

RICHARD. Rachel, stop! I did not mean—

RACHEL. (*To* RAVENSBANE.) My uncle did not introduce to you with sufficient elaboration this gentleman. Will you allow me to do so now?

RAVENSBANE. I adore Mistress Rachel's elaborations.

RACHEL. Lord Ravensbane, I beg to present Squire Talbot, *my betrothed.*

RAVENSBANE. Betrothed! Is it—(*noticing* RICHARD'S *frown*)—is it pleasant?

RACHEL. (*To* RICHARD.) Are you satisfied?

RICHARD. (*Trembling with feeling.*) *More* than satisfied. (*Exit.*)

RAVENSBANE. (*Looking after him.*) Ah! Betrothed is *not* pleasant.

RACHEL. Not always.

RAVENSBANE. (*Anxiously.*) Mistress Rachel is not pleased?

RACHEL. (*Biting her lip, looks after* RICHARD.) With him.

RAVENSBANE. Mistress Rachel will smile again?

RACHEL. Soon.

RAVENSBANE. (*Ardent.*) Ah! What can Lord Ravensbane do to make her smile? See! will you puff my pipe? It is very pleasant. (*Offering the pipe.*)

RACHEL. (*Smiling.*) Shall I try?
> (*Takes hold of it mischievously.*)

(*Enter* JUSTICE MERTON *and* DICKON, *left.*)

JUSTICE MERTON. (*In a great voice.*) Rachel!

RACHEL. Why, uncle!

JUSTICE MERTON. (*Speaks suavely to* RAVENSBANE.) Permit me, your lordship—Rachel, you will kindly withdraw for a few moments; I desire to confer with Lord Ravensbane concerning his mother's—her ladyship's letter—(*obsequiously to* DICKON)—that is, if you think, sir, that your noble pupil is not too fatigued.

DICKON. Not at all; I think his lordship will listen to you with much pleasure.

RAVENSBANE. (*Bowing to* JUSTICE MERTON, *but looking at* RACHEL.) With much pleasure.

DICKON. And in the mean time, if Mistress Rachel will allow me, I will assist her in writing those invitations which your worship desires to send in her name.

JUSTICE MERTON. Invitations—from my niece?

DICKON. To his Excellency, the Lieutenant-Governor; to your friends, the Reverend Masters at Harvard College, etc., etc.; in brief, to all your worship's select social acquaintance in the vicinity —to meet his lordship. It was so thoughtful in you to suggest it, sir, and believe me, his lordship appreciates your courtesy in arranging the reception in his honor for this afternoon.

RACHEL. (*To* JUSTICE MERTON.) This afternoon! Are we really to give his lordship a reception? And will it be here, uncle?

DICKON. (*Looking at him narrowly.*) Your worship said here, I believe?

JUSTICE MERTON. Quite so, sir; quite so, quite so.

DICKON. Permit me to act as your scribe, Mistress Rachel.

RACHEL. With pleasure. (*With a curtsy to* RAVENSBANE.) Till we meet again!
(*Exit, right.*)

DICKON. (*Aside to* JUSTICE MERTON.) I advise nothing rash, Gilly; the brat has a weak heart. (*Aside, as he passes* RAVENSBANE.) Remember, Jack! Puff! Puff!

RAVENSBANE. (*Staring at the door.*) She is gone.

JUSTICE MERTON. Impostor! You, at least, shall not play the lord and master to my face.

RAVENSBANE. Quite—gone!

JUSTICE MERTON. I know with whom I have to deal. If I be any judge of my own flesh and blood—permit me—you shall quail before me.

RAVENSBANE. (*Dejectedly.*) She did not smile— (*Joyously.*) She smiled!

JUSTICE MERTON. Affected rogue! I know thee. I know thy feigned pauses, thy assumed vagaries. Speak; how much do you want?

RAVENSBANE. (*Ecstatically.*) Ah! Mistress Rachel!

JUSTICE MERTON. Her! Scoundrel, if thou dost name her again, my innocent —my sweet maid! If thou dost—thou godless spawn of temptation—mark you, I will put an end—
(*Reaching for a pistol that rests in a rack on the wall,—the intervening form of* DICKON *suddenly appears, pockets the pistol, and exit.*)

DICKON. I beg pardon; I forgot something.

JUSTICE MERTON. (*Sinking into a chair.*) God, Thou art just!
(*He holds his head in his hands and weeps.*)

RAVENSBANE. (*For the first time, since* RACHEL'S *departure, observing* MERTON.) Permit me, sir, are you ill?

JUSTICE MERTON. (*Recoiling.*) What art thou!

RAVENSBANE. (*Monotonously.*) I am Lord Ravensbane: Marquis of Oxford, Baron of Wittenberg, Elector of Worms, and— (*As* JUSTICE MERTON *covers his face again.*) Shall I call Dickon? (*Walking quickly toward the door, calls.*) Dickon!

JUSTICE MERTON (*Starting up.*) No, do not call him. Tell me: I hate thee not; thou wast innocent. Tell me!—I thought thou hadst died as a babe.— Where has Dickon, our tyrant, kept thee these twenty years?

RAVENSBANE. (*With gentle courtesy.*) Master Dickonson is my tutor.

JUSTICE MERTON. And why has thy mother—Ah, I know well; I deserve all. But yet, it must not be published now! I am a justice now, an honored citizen —and my young niece—Thy mother will not demand so much.

RAVENSBANE. My mother is the Marchioness of Rickby.

JUSTICE MERTON. Yes, yes; 'twas well planned, a clever trick. 'Twas skillful of her. But surely thy mother gave thee commands to—

RAVENSBANE. My mother gave me her blessing.

JUSTICE MERTON. Ah, 'tis well, then. Young man, my son, I too will give thee my blessing, if thou wilt but go—go instantly—go with half my fortune—but leave me my honor—and my Rachel?

RAVENSBANE. Rachel? Rachel is yours? No, no, Mistress Rachel is mine. We are ours.

JUSTICE MERTON. (*Pleadingly.*) Consider the disgrace—you, an illegitimate—and she—oh, think what thou art!

RAVENSBANE. (*Monotonously, puffing smoke at the end.*) I am Lord Ravensbane: Marquis of Oxford, Baron of Wittenberg, Elector of Worms, and Count—

JUSTICE MERTON. (*Wrenching the pipe from* RAVENSBANE'S *hand and lips.*) Devil's child! Boor! Buffoon! (*Flinging the pipe away.*) I will stand thy insults no longer. If thou hast no heart—

RAVENSBANE. (*Putting his hand to his side, staggers.*) Ah! my heart!

JUSTICE MERTON. Hypocrite! Thou canst not fool me. I am thy father.

RAVENSBANE. (*Faintly, stretches out his hand to him for support.*) Father!

JUSTICE MERTON. Stand away. Thou mayst break thy heart and mine and the devil's, but thou shalt not break Rachel's.

RAVENSBANE. (*Faintly.*) Mistress Rachel is mine— (*He staggers again, and falls, half reclining, upon a chair. More faintly he speaks, beginning to change expression.*) Her eyes are mine; her smiles are mine.

(*His eyes close.*)

JUSTICE MERTON. Good God! Can it be —his heart? (*With agitated swiftness, he feels and listens at* RAVENSBANE'S *side.*) Not a motion; not a sound! Yea, God, Thou art good! 'Tis his heart. He is—ah! he is my son. Judge Almighty, if he should die now; may I not be still

a moment more and make sure? No, no, my son—he is changing. (*Calls.*) Help! Help! Rachel! Master Dickonson! Help! Richard! Cynthia! Come hither!

(*Enter* DICKON *and* RACHEL.)

RACHEL. Uncle!

JUSTICE MERTON. Bring wine. Lord Ravensbane has fainted.

RACHEL. Oh! (*Turning swiftly to go.*) Micah, wine.

DICKON. (*Detaining her.*) Stay! His pipe! Where is his lordship's pipe?

RACHEL. Oh, terrible!

(*Enter, at different doors,* MISTRESS MERTON *and* RICHARD.)

MISTRESS MERTON. What's the matter?

JUSTICE MERTON. (*To* RACHEL.) He threw it away. He is worse. Bring the wine.

MISTRESS MERTON. Look! How strange he appears!

RACHEL. (*Searching distractedly.*) The pipe! His lordship's pipe! It is lost, Master Dickonson.

DICKON. (*Stooping, as if searching, with his back turned, having picked up the pipe, is filling and lighting it.*) It must be found. This is a heart attack, my friends; his lordship's life depends on the nicotine.

(*Deftly he places the pipe in* RA-CHEL'S *way.*)

RACHEL. Thank God! Here it is. (*Carrying it to the prostrate form of* RAVENS-BANE, *she lifts his head and is about to put the pipe in his mouth.*) Shall I—shall I put it in?

RICHARD. No! not you.

RACHEL. Sir!

RICHARD. Let his tutor perform that office.

RACHEL. (*Lifting* LORD RAVENSBANE'S *head again.*) My lord!

RICHARD *and* JUSTICE MERTON. (*Together.*) Rachel!

DICKON. Pardon me, Mistress Rachel; give the pipe at once. Only a token of true affection can revive his lordship now.

RICHARD. (As RACHEL puts the pipe to RAVENSBANE'S lips.) I forbid it, Rachel.

RACHEL. (Watching only RAVENSBANE.) My lord—my lord!

MISTRESS MERTON. Give him air; unbutton his coat. (RACHEL unbuttons RAVENSBANE'S coat, revealing the embroidered waistcoat.) Ah, Heavens! What do I see?

JUSTICE MERTON. (Looks, blanches, and signs silence to MISTRESS MERTON.) Cynthia!

MISTRESS MERTON. (Aside to JUSTICE MERTON, with deep tensity.) That waistcoat! that waistcoat! Brother, hast thou never seen it before?

JUSTICE MERTON. Never, my sister.

DICKON. See! He puffs—he revives. He is coming to himself.

RACHEL. (As RAVENSBANE rises to his feet.) At last!

DICKON. Look! he is restored.

RACHEL. God be thanked!

DICKON. My lord, Mistress Rachel has saved your life.

RAVENSBANE. (Taking RACHEL'S hand.) Mistress Rachel is mine; we are ours.

RICHARD. Dare to repeat that.

RAVENSBANE. (Looking at RACHEL.) Her eyes are mine.

RICHARD. (Flinging his glove in his face.) And that, sir, is yours.

RACHEL. Richard!

RICHARD. I believe such is the proper fashion in England. If your lordship's last dueling wound is sufficiently healed, perhaps you will deign a reply.

RACHEL. Richard! Your lordship!

RAVENSBANE. (Stoops, picks up the glove, pockets it, bows to RACHEL, and steps close to RICHARD.) Permit me!
(He blows a puff of smoke full in RICHARD'S face.)

ACT THIRD.

The same day. Late afternoon. The same scene as in Act Second.

RAVENSBANE and DICKON are seated at the table, on which are lying two flails. RAVENSBANE is dressed in a costume which, composed of silk and jewels, subtly approximates in design to that of his original grosser composition. So artfully, however, is this contrived that, to one ignorant of his origin, his dress would appear to be merely an odd personal whimsy; whereas, to one initiated, it would stamp him grotesquely as the apotheosis of scarecrows.

DICKON is sitting in a pedagogical attitude; RAVENSBANE stands near him, making a profound bow in the opposite direction.

RAVENSBANE. Believe me, ladies, with the true sincerity of the heart.

DICKON. Inflection a little more lachrymose, please: "The true sincerity of the heart."

RAVENSBANE. Believe me, ladies, with the true sincerity of the heart.

DICKON. Prettily, prettily! Next!

RAVENSBANE. (Changing his mien, as if addressing another person.) Verily, sir, as that prince of poets, the immortal Virgil, has remarked:—

Adeo in teneris consuescere multum est.

DICKON. Basta! The next.

RAVENSBANE. (With another change to courtly manner.) Trust me, your Excellency, I will inform his Majesty of your courtesy.

DICKON. "His Majesty" more emphatic. Remember! You must impress all of the guests this afternoon. But continue, Cobby, dear; the retort now to the challenge!

RAVENSBANE. (With a superb air.) The second, I believe.

DICKON. Quite so, my lord.

RAVENSBANE. Sir! the local person whom you represent has done himself the honor of submitting to me a challenge to mortal combat. Sir! Since the remotest times of my feudal ancestors, in such affairs of honor, choice of weapons has ever been the—

DICKON. Prerogative!

RAVENSBANE. Prerogative of the challenged. Sir! This right of etiquette must be observed. Nevertheless, believe me, I have no selfish desire that my superior—

DICKON. Attainments!

RAVENSBANE. Attainments in this art should assume advantage over my challenger's ignorance. I have, therefore, chosen those combative utensils most appropriate both to his own humble origin and to local tradition. Permit me, sir, to reveal my choice. (*Pointing grandly to the table.*) There are my weapons!

DICKON. Delicious! O thou exquisite flower of love! How thy natal composites have burst in bloom!—The pumpkin in thee to a golden collarette; thy mop of crow's wings to these raven locks; thy broomstick to a lordly limp; thy corn-silk to these pale-tinted tassels. Verily in the gallery of scarecrows, thou art the Apollo Belvedere!

RAVENSBANE. Mistress Rachel—I may see her now?

DICKON. Romeo! Romeo! Was ever such an amorous puppet show!

RAVENSBANE. Mistress Rachel!

DICKON. Wait; let me think! Thou art wound up now, my pretty apparatus, for at least six-and-thirty hours. The wooden angel Gabriel that trumpets the hours on the big clock in Venice is not a more punctual manikin than thou with my speeches. Thou shouldst run, therefore,—

RAVENSBANE. (*Frowning darkly at DICKON.*) Stop talking; permit me! A tutor should know his place.

DICKON. (*Rubbing his hands.*) Nay, your lordship is beyond comparison.

RAVENSBANE. (*In a terrible voice.*) She will come? I shall see her?

(*Enter* MICAH.)

MICAH. Pardon, my lord.

RAVENSBANE. (*Turning joyfully to* MICAH.) Is it she?

MICAH. Captain Bugby, my lord, the Governor's secretary.

DICKON. Good. Squire Talbot's second. Show him in.

RAVENSBANE. (*Flinging despairingly into a chair.*) Ah! ah!

MICAH. (*Lifting the flails from the table.*) Beg pardon, sir; shall I remove—

DICKON. Drop them; go.

MICAH. But, sir—

DICKON. Go, thou slave! (*Exit* MICAH. DICKON *hands* RAVENSBANE *a book.*) Here, my lord; read. You must be found reading.

RAVENSBANE. (*In childlike despair.*) She will not come! I shall not see her! (*Throwing the book into the fireplace.*) She does not come!

DICKON. Fie, fie, Jack; thou must not be breaking thy Dickon's apron-strings with a will of thine own. Come!

RAVENSBANE. Mistress Rachel—

DICKON. Be good, boy, and thou shalt see her soon.

(*Enter* CAPTAIN BUGBY.)

Your lordship was saying—Oh! Captain Bugby?

CAPTAIN BUGBY. (*Nervous and awed.*) Captain Bugby, sir, ah! at Lord Ravensbane's service—ah!

DICKON. I am Master Dickonson, his lordship's tutor.

CAPTAIN BUGBY. Happy, sir.

DICKON. (*To* RAVENSBANE.) My lord, this gentleman waits upon you from Squire Talbot. (*To* CAPTAIN BUGBY.)

In regard to the challenge this morning, I presume?

CAPTAIN BUGBY. The affair, ah! the affair of this morning, sir.

RAVENSBANE. (*With his former superb air—to* CAPTAIN BUGBY.) The second, I believe?

CAPTAIN BUGBY. Quite so, my lord.

RAVENSBANE. Sir! the local person whom you represent has done himself the honor of submitting to me a challenge to mortal combat. Sir! Since the remotest times of my feudal ancestors, in such affairs of honor, choice of weapons has ever been the pre-pre- (DICKON *looks at him intensely.*) prerogative of the challenged. Sir! this right of etiquette must be observed.

CAPTAIN BUGBY. Indeed, yes, my lord.

DICKON. Pray do not interrupt. (*To* RAVENSBANE.) Your lordship: "observed."

RAVENSBANE. —observed. Nevertheless, believe me, I have no selfish desire that my superior a-a-at-attainments in this art should assume advantage over my challenger's ignorance. I have, therefore, chosen those combative utensils most appropriate both to his own humble origin and to local tradition. Permit me, sir, to reveal my choice. (*Pointing to the table.*) There are my weapons!

CAPTAIN BUGBY. (*Looking bewildered.*) These, my lord?

RAVENSBANE. Those.

CAPTAIN BUGBY. But these are—are flails.

RAVENSBANE. Flails.

CAPTAIN BUGBY. Flails, my lord?—Do I understand that your lordship and Squire Talbot—

RAVENSBANE. Exactly.

CAPTAIN BUGBY. But your lordship— flails!

(DICKON'S *intense glance focusses on* RAVENSBANE'S *face with the faintest of smiles.*)

RAVENSBANE. My adversary should be deft in their use. He has doubtless wielded them frequently on his barn floor.

CAPTAIN BUGBY. Ahaha! I understand now. Your lordship—ah! is a wit. Haha! Flails!

DICKON. His lordship's satire is poignant.

CAPTAIN BUGBY. Indeed, sir, so keen that I must apologize for laughing at my principal's expense. But— (*soberly to* RAVENSBANE)—my lord, if you will deign to speak one moment seriously—

RAVENSBANE. Seriously?

CAPTAIN BUGBY. I will take pleasure in informing Squire Talbot—ah! as to your *real* preference for—

RAVENSBANE. For flails, sir. I have, permit me, nothing further to say. Flails are final. (*Turns away haughtily.*)

CAPTAIN BUGBY. Eh! What! Must I really report—?

DICKON. Lord Ravensbane's will is inflexible.

CAPTAIN BUGBY. And his wit, sir, incomparable. I am sorry for the Squire, but 'twill be the greatest joke in years. Ah! will you tell me—is it— (*indicating* RAVENSBANE'S *smoking*) —is it the latest fashion?

DICKON. Lord Ravensbane is always the latest.

CAPTAIN BUGBY. Obliged servant, sir. Aha! Such a joke as—O Lord! flails.

(*Exit.*)

DICKON. (*Gayly to* RAVENSBANE.) Bravo, my pumpky dear! That squelches the jealous betrothed. Now nothing remains but for you to continue to dazzle the enamored Rachel, and so present yourself to the Justice as a pseudo-son-nephew-in-law.

RAVENSBANE. I may go to Mistress Rachel?

DICKON. She will come to you. She is reading now a poem from you, which I left on her dressing-table.

RAVENSBANE. She is reading a poem from me?

DICKON. With your pardon, my lord, I penned it for you. I am something of a poetaster. Indeed, I flatter myself that I have dictated some of the finest lines in literature.

RAVENSBANE. Dickon! She will come?

DICKON. She comes!

(*Enter* RACHEL, *reading from a piece of paper.*)

(DICKON *draws* RAVENSBANE *back.*)

RACHEL. (*Reads.*) "To Mistress R———, enchantress:—

> If faith in witchcraft be a sin,
> Alas! what peril he is in
> Who plights his faith and love in thee,
> Sweetest maid of sorcery.

> If witchcraft be a whirling brain,
> A roving eye, a heart of pain,
> Whose wound no thread of fate can stitch,
> How hast thou conjured, cruel witch,—

With the brain, eye, heart, and total mortal residue of thine enamored.
JACK LANTHORNE,
[LORD R———.]"

(DICKON *goes out.*)

RACHEL. "To Mistress R———, enchantress:" R! It *must* be. R——— must mean—

RAVENSBANE. (*With passionate deference.*) Rachel!

RACHEL. Ah! How you surprised me, my lord!

RAVENSBANE. You are come again; you are come again.

RACHEL. Has anything happened? Oh, my lord, I have been in such terror. Promise me that there shall be—no—duel!

RAVENSBANE. No duel.

RACHEL. Oh, I am so gratefully happy!

RAVENSBANE. I know I am only a thing to make Mistress Rachel happy. Ah! look at me once more. When you look at me, I live.

RACHEL. It is strange, indeed, my lord, how the familiar world, the daylight, the heavens themselves have changed since your arrival.

RAVENSBANE. This is the world; this is the light; this is the heavens themselves. Mistress Rachel is looking at me.

RACHEL. For me, it is less strange, perhaps. I never saw a real lord before. But you, my lord, must have seen so many, many girls in the great world.

RAVENSBANE. No, no; never.

RACHEL. No other girls before to-day, my lord!

RAVENSBANE. Before to-day? I do not know; I do not care. I was not—here. To-day I was born—in your eyes. Ah! my brain whirls!

RACHEL. (*Smiling.*)

> If witchcraft be a whirling brain,
> A roving eye, a heart of pain,—

(*In a whisper.*) My lord, do you really believe in witchcraft?

RAVENSBANE. With all my heart.

RACHEL. And approve of it?

RAVENSBANE. With all my soul.

RACHEL. So do I—that is, innocent witchcraft; not to harm anybody, you know, but just to feel all the dark mystery and the trembling excitement—the way you feel when you blow out your candle all alone in your bedroom and watch the little smoke fade away in the moonshine.

RAVENSBANE. Fade away in the moonshine!

RACHEL. Oh, but we mustn't speak of it. In a town like this, all such mysticism is considered damnable. But your lordship understands and approves? I am so glad! Have you read the *Philosophical Considerations* of Glanville, the *Saducismus Triumphatus,* and the *Presignifications of Dreams?* What kind of witchcraft, my lord, do you believe in?

RAVENSBANE. In all yours.

RACHEL. Nay, your lordship must not take me for a real witch. I can only tell fortunes, you know—like this morning.

RAVENSBANE. I know; you told how my heart would break.

RACHEL. Oh, that's palmistry, and that isn't always certain. But the surest way to prophesy—do you know what it is?

RAVENSBANE. Tell me.

RACHEL. To count the crows. Do you know how?

One for sorrow—

RAVENSBANE. Ha, yes!—

Two for mirth!

RACHEL.

Three for a wedding—

RAVENSBANE.

Four for a birth—

RACHEL.

And five for the happiest thing on earth!

RAVENSBANE. Mistress Rachel, come! Let us go and count five crows.

RACHEL. (*Delightedly.*) Why, my lord, how did *you* ever learn it? I got it from an old goody here in town—a real witch-wife. If you will promise not to tell a secret, I will show you—But you must promise!

RAVENSBANE. I promise.

RACHEL. Come, then. I will show you a real piece of witchcraft that I bought from her this morning—the glass of truth. There! Behind that curtain. If you look in, you will see— But come; I will show you. (*They put their hands on the cords of the curtain.*) Just pull that string, and—ah!

DICKON. (*Stepping out through the curtain.*) My lord, your pipe.

RACHEL. Master Dickonson, how you frightened me!

DICKON. So excessively sorry!

RACHEL. But how did you—?

DICKON. I believe you were showing his lordship—

RACHEL. (*Turning hurriedly away.*) Oh, nothing; nothing at all.

RAVENSBANE. (*Sternly to* DICKON.) Why do you come?

DICKON. (*Handing back* RAVENSBANE'S *pipe, filled.*) Allow me. (*Aside.*) 'Tis high time you came to the point, Jack; 'tis near your lordship's reception. Woo and win, boy; woo and win.

RAVENSBANE. (*Haughtily.*) Leave me.

DICKON. Your lordship's humble, very humble. (*Exit.*)

RACHEL. (*Shivering.*) My dear lord, why do you keep this man?

RAVENSBANE. I—keep this man?

RACHEL. Pardon my rudeness—I cannot endure him.

RAVENSBANE. You do not like him? Ah, then, I do not like him also. We will send him away—you and I.

RACHEL. You, my lord, of course; but I—

RAVENSBANE. You will be Dickon! You will be with me always and light my pipe. And I will live for you, and fight for you, and kill your betrothed!

RACHEL. (*Drawing away.*) No, no!

RAVENSBANE. Ah! but your eyes say "yes." Mistress Rachel leaves me; but Rachel in her eyes remains. Is it not so?

RACHEL. What can I say, my lord! It is true that since my eyes met yours, a new passion has entered into my soul. I have felt—but 'tis so impertinent, my lord, so absurd in me, a mere girl, and you a nobleman of power—yet I have felt it irresistibly, my dear lord,—a longing to help you. I am so sorry for you—so sorry for you! I pity you deeply.— Forgive me; forgive me, my lord!

RAVENSBANE. It is enough.

RACHEL. Indeed, indeed, 'tis so rude of me,—'tis so unreasonable.

RAVENSBANE. It is enough. I grow—I grow—I grow! I am a plant; you give it rain and sun. I am a flower; you give it light and dew. I am a soul, you give it love and speech. I grow. Toward you —toward you I grow!

RACHEL. My lord, I do not understand it, how so poor and mere a girl as I can have helped you. Yet I do believe it is so; for I feel it so. What can I do for you?

RAVENSBANE. Be mine. Let me be yours.

RACHEL. But, my lord—do I love you?

RAVENSBANE. What is "I love you"? Is it a kiss, a sigh, an embrace? Ah! then, you do not love me.—"I love you": is it to nourish, to nestle, to lift up, to smile upon, to make greater—a worm? Ah! then, you love me.

(*Enter* RICHARD *at left back, unobserved.*)

RACHEL. Do not speak so of yourself, my lord; nor exalt me so falsely.

RAVENSBANE. Be mine.

RACHEL. A great glory has descended upon this day.

RAVENSBANE. Be mine.

RACHEL. Could I but be sure that this glory is love—Oh, *then!*
(*Turns toward* RAVENSBANE.)

RICHARD. (*Stepping between them.*) It is *not* love; it is witchcraft.

RACHEL. Who are you?—Richard?

RICHARD. You have, indeed, forgotten me? Would to God, Rachel, I could forget you.

RAVENSBANE. Ah, permit me, sir—

RICHARD. Silence! (*To* RACHEL.) Against my will, I am a convert to your own mysticism; for nothing less than damnable illusion could so instantly wean your heart from me to—this. I do not pretend to understand it; but that it is witchcraft I am convinced; and I will save you from it.

RACHEL. Go; please go.

RAVENSBANE. Permit me, sir; you have not replied yet to flails!

RICHARD. Permit *me*, sir. (*Taking something from his coat.*) My answer is— bare cob! (*Holding out a shelled corn-cob.*) Thresh this, sir, for your antago-nist. T'is the only one worthy your lordship.
(*Tosses it contemptuously toward him.*)

RAVENSBANE. Upon my honor, as a man—

RICHARD. As a *man*, forsooth! Were you, indeed, a man, Lord Ravensbane, I would have accepted your weapons, and flailed you out of New England. But it is not my custom to chastise runagates from asylums, or to banter further words with a natural and a ninny.

RACHEL. Squire Talbot! Will you leave my uncle's house?

RAVENSBANE. One moment, mistress:—I did not wholly catch the import of this gentleman's speech, but I fancy I have insulted him by my reply to his challenge. One insult may perhaps be remedied by another. Sir, permit me to call *you* a ninny, and to offer you— (*drawing his sword and offering it*)—swords.

RICHARD. Thanks; I reject the offer.

RAVENSBANE. (*Turning away despondently.*) He rejects it. Well!

RACHEL. (*To* RICHARD.) And *now* will you leave?

RICHARD. At once. But one word more. Rachel—Rachel, have you forgotten this morning and the Glass of Truth?

RACHEL. (*Coldly.*) No.

RICHARD. Call it a fancy now if you will. I scoffed at it; yes. Yet *you* believed it. I loved you truly, you said. Well, have I changed?

RACHEL. Yes.

RICHARD. Will you test me again—in the glass?

RACHEL. No. Go; leave us.

RICHARD. I will go. I have still a word with your aunt.

RAVENSBANE. (*To* RICHARD.) I beg your pardon, sir. You said just now that had I been a man—

RICHARD. I say, Lord Ravensbane, that the straight fiber of a true man never warps the love of a woman. As for yourself, you have my contempt and pity. Pray to God, sir, pray to God to make you a man. (*Exit.*)

RACHEL. Oh! it is intolerable! (*To RA-VENSBANE.*) My dear lord, I do believe in my heart that I love you, and if so, I will with gratitude be your wife. But, my lord, strange glamors, strange dark-nesses reel, and bewilder my mind. I must be alone; I must think and decide. Will you give me this tassel?

RAVENSBANE. (*Unfastening a silk tassel from his coat and giving it to her.*) Oh, take it.

RACHEL. If I decide that I love you, that I will be your wife—I will wear it this afternoon at the reception. Good-bye.
(*Exit, right.*)

RAVENSBANE. Mistress Rachel!— (*He is left alone. As he looks about gropingly, and raises his arms in vague prayer, DICKON appears from the right and watches him, with a smile.*) God, are you here? Dear God, I pray to you— make me to be a man! (*Exit, left.*)

DICKON. Poor Jacky! Thou shouldst 'a' prayed to t'other one.

(*Enter, right, JUSTICE MERTON.*)

JUSTICE MERTON. (*To DICKON.*) Will you not listen? Will you not listen!

DICKON. Such a delightful room!

JUSTICE MERTON. Are you merciless?

DICKON. And such a living portrait of your worship! The waistcoat is so beau-tifully executed.

JUSTICE MERTON. If I pay him ten thou-sand pounds—

(*Enter, right, MISTRESS MERTON, who goes toward the table. Enter, left, MICAH.*)

MISTRESS MERTON. Flails! Flails in the parlor!

MICAH. The minister and his wife have turned into the gate, madam.

MISTRESS MERTON. The guests! Is it so late?

MICAH. Four o'clock, madam.

MISTRESS MERTON. Remove these things at once.

MICAH. Yes, madam. (*He lifts them, and starts for the door where he pauses to look back and speak.*) Madam, in all my past years of service at Merton House, I never waited upon a lord till to-day. Madam, in all my future years of service at Merton House, I trust I may never wait upon a lord again.

MISTRESS MERTON. Micah, mind the knocker.

MICAH. Yes, madam.
(*Exit at left back. Sounds of a brass knocker outside.*)

MISTRESS MERTON. Rachel! Rachel!
(*Exit, left.*)

JUSTICE MERTON. (*To DICKON.*) So you are contented with nothing less than the sacrifice of my niece!

(*Enter MICAH.*)

MICAH. Minister Dodge, your Worship; and Mistress Dodge. (*Exit.*)

(*Enter the MINISTER and his WIFE.*)

JUSTICE MERTON. (*Stepping forward to receive them.*) Believe me, this is a great privilege.—Madam! (*Bowing.*)

MINISTER DODGE. (*Taking his hand.*) The privilege is ours, Justice; to enter a righteous man's house is to stand, as it were, on God's threshold.

JUSTICE MERTON. (*Nervously.*) Amen, amen. Permit me—ah! Lord Ravens-bane, my young guest of honor, will be here directly—permit me to present his lordship's tutor, Master Dickonson; the Reverend Master Dodge, Mistress Dodge.

MINISTER DODGE. (*Offering his hand.*) Master Dickonson, sir—

DICKON. (*Barely touching the minister's fingers, bows charmingly to his wife.*) Madam, of all professions in the world, your husband's most allures me.

MISTRESS DODGE. 'Tis a worthy one, sir.

DICKON. Ah! Mistress Dodge, and so arduous—especially for a minister's wife. (*He leads her to a chair.*)

MISTRESS DODGE. (*Accepting the chair.*) Thank you.

MINISTER DODGE. Lord Ravensbane comes from abroad?

JUSTICE MERTON. From London.

MINISTER DODGE. An old friend of yours, I understand.

JUSTICE MERTON. From London, yes. Did I say from London? Quite so; from London.

(*Enter* MICAH.)

MICAH. Captain Bugby, the Governor's secretary. (*Exit.*)

(*Enter* CAPTAIN BUGBY. *He walks with a slight lameness, and holds daintily in his hand a pipe, from which he puffs with dandy deliberation.*)

CAPTAIN BUGBY. Justice Merton, your very humble servant.

JUSTICE MERTON. Believe me, Captain Bugby.

CAPTAIN BUGBY. (*Profusely.*) Ah, Master Dickonson! my dear friend Master Dickonson—this is, indeed—ah! How is his lordship since—aha! but discretion! Mistress Dodge—her servant! Ah! yes—(*indicating his pipe with a smile of satisfaction*)—the latest, I assure you; the very latest from London. Ask Master Dickonson.

MINISTER DODGE. (*Looking at* CAPTAIN BUGBY.) These will hatch out in the springtime.

CAPTAIN BUGBY. (*Confidentially to* DICKON.) But really, my good friend, may not I venture to inquire how his lordship—ah! has been in health since the—ah! since—

DICKON. (*Impressively.*) Oh! quite, quite!

(*Enter* MISTRESS MERTON; *she joins* JUSTICE MERTON *and* MINISTER DODGE.)

CAPTAIN BUGBY. You know, I informed Squire Talbot of his lordship's epigrammatic retort—his retort of—shh! ha, haha! Oh, that reply was a stiletto; 'twas sharper than a sword-thrust, I assure you. To have conceived it—'twas inspiration; but to have expressed it—oh! 'twas genius. Hush! "Flails"! Oh! It sticks me now in the ribs. I shall die with concealing it.

MINISTER DODGE. (*To* MISTRESS MERTON.) 'Tis true, mistress; but if there were more like your brother in the parish, the conscience of the community would be clearer.

(*Enter* MICAH.)

MICAH. The Reverend Master Rand of Harvard College; the Reverend Master Todd of Harvard College. (*Exit.*)

(*Enter two elderly, straight-backed divines.*)

JUSTICE MERTON. (*Greeting them.*) Permit me, gentlemen; this is fortunate—before your return to Cambridge.

(*He conducts them to* MISTRESS MERTON *and* MINISTER DODGE. DICKON *is ingratiating himself with* MISTRESS DODGE; CAPTAIN BUGBY, *laughed at by both parties, is received by neither.*)

CAPTAIN BUGBY. (*Puffing smoke toward the ceiling.*) Really, I cannot understand what keeps his Excellency, the Lieutenant-Governor, so long. He has two such charming daughters, Master Dickonson—

DICKON. (*To* MISTRESS DODGE.) Yes, yes; such suspicious women with their charms are an insult to the virtuous ladies of the parish.

CAPTAIN BUGBY. How, sir!

MISTRESS DODGE. And to think that she should actually shoe horses herself!

CAPTAIN BUGBY. (*Piqued, walks another way.*) Well!

REV. MASTER RAND. (*To* JUSTICE MERTON.) It would not be countenanced in the college yard, sir.

REV. MASTER TODD. A pipe! Nay, *mores inhibitae!*

JUSTICE MERTON. 'Tis most unfortunate, gentlemen; but I understand 'tis the new vogue in London.

(*Enter* MICAH.)

MICAH. His Excellency, Sir Charles Reddington, Lieutenant-Governor; the Mistress Reddingtons.

CAPTAIN BUGBY. At last!

MISTRESS MERTON. (*Aside.*) Micah.

(MICAH *goes to her.*)

(*Enter* SIR CHARLES, MISTRESS REDDINGTON, *and* AMELIA REDDINGTON.)

JUSTICE MERTON. Your Excellency, this is, indeed, a distinguished honor.

SIR CHARLES. (*Shaking hands.*) Fine weather, Merton. Where's your young lord?

THE TWO GIRLS. (*Curtsying.*) Justice Merton, Mistress Merton.

(MICAH *goes out.*)

CAPTAIN BUGBY. Oh, my dear Mistress Reddington! Charming Mistress Amelia! You are so very late, but you shall hear —hush!

MISTRESS REDDINGTON. (*Noticing his pipe.*) Why, what is this, Captain?

CAPTAIN BUGBY. Oh, the latest, I assure you, the very latest. Wait till you see his lordship.

AMELIA. What! isn't he here? (*Laughing.*) La, Captain! Do look at the man!

CAPTAIN BUGBY. Oh, he's coming directly. Quite the mode—what?

(*He talks to them aside, where they titter.*)

SIR CHARLES. (*To* DICKON.) What say? Traveling for his health?

DICKON. Partially, your Excellency; but my young pupil and master is a singularly affectionate nature.

THE TWO GIRLS. (*To* CAPTAIN BUGBY.) What! flails—really!

(*They burst into laughter among themselves.*)

DICKON. He has journeyed here to Massachusetts peculiarly to pay this visit to Justice Merton—his father's dearest friend.

SIR CHARLES. Ah! knew him abroad, eh?

DICKON. In Rome, your Excellency.

MISTRESS DODGE. (*To* JUSTICE MERTON.) Why, I thought it was in London.

JUSTICE MERTON. London, true, quite so; we made a trip together to Lisbon—ah! Rome.

DICKON. Paris, was it not, sir?

JUSTICE MERTON. (*In great distress.*) Paris, Paris, very true; I am—I am— sometimes I am—

(*Enter* MICAH, *right.*)

MICAH. (*Announces.*) Lord Ravensbane.

(*Enter right,* RAVENSBANE *with* RACHEL.)

JUSTICE MERTON. (*With a gasp of relief.*) Ah! his lordship is arrived.

(*Murmurs of "his lordship" and a flutter among the girls and* CAPTAIN BUGBY.)

CAPTAIN BUGBY. Look!—Now!

JUSTICE MERTON. Welcome, my lord! (*To* SIR CHARLES.) Your Excellency, let me introduce—permit me—

RAVENSBANE. Permit *me;* (*addressing her*) Mistress Rachel!—Mistress Rachel will introduce—

RACHEL. (*Curtsying.*) Sir Charles, allow me to present my friend, Lord Ravensbane.

MISTRESS REDDINGTON. (*Aside to* AMELIA.) Her *friend*—did you hear?

SIR CHARLES. Mistress Rachel, I see you are as pretty as ever. Lord Ravensbane, your hand, sir.

RAVENSBANE. Trust me, your Excellency,

I will inform his Majesty of your courtesy.

CAPTAIN BUGBY. (*Watching* RAVENS-BANE *with chagrin.*) On my life! he's lost his limp.

RAVENSBANE. (*Apart to* RACHEL.) You said: "A great glory has descended upon this day."

RACHEL. (*Shyly.*) My lord!

RAVENSBANE. Be sure—O mistress, be sure—that this glory is love.

SIR CHARLES. My daughters, Fanny and Amelia—Lord Ravensbane.

THE TWO GIRLS. (*Curtsying.*) Your lordship!

SIR CHARLES. Good girls, but silly.

THE TWO GIRLS. Papa!

RAVENSBANE. Believe me, ladies, with the *true* sincerity of the *heart*.

MISTRESS REDDINGTON. Isn't he perfection!

CAPTAIN BUGBY. What said I?

AMELIA. (*Giggling.*) I can't help thinking of flails.

SIR CHARLES. (*In a loud whisper aside to* JUSTICE MERTON.) Is it congratulations for your niece?

JUSTICE MERTON. Not—not precisely.

DICKON. (*To* JUSTICE MERTON.) Your worship—a word. (*Leads him aside.*)

RAVENSBANE. (*Whom* RACHEL *continues to introduce to the guests, speaks to* MASTER RAND.) Verily, sir, as that prince of poets, the immortal Virgil, has remarked:

Adeo in teneris consuescere multum est.

REV. MASTER TODD. His lordship is evidently a university man.

REV. MASTER RAND. Evidently most accomplished.

JUSTICE MERTON. (*Aside to* DICKON.) A song! Why, it is beyond all bounds of custom and decorum.

DICKON. Believe me, there is no such flatterer to win the maiden heart as music.

JUSTICE MERTON. And here; in this presence! Never!

DICKON. Nevertheless, it will amuse me vastly, and you will announce it.

JUSTICE MERTON. (*With hesitant embarrassment, which he seeks to conceal.*) Your Excellency and friends, I have great pleasure in announcing his lordship's condescension in consenting to regale our present company—with a song.

SEVERAL VOICES. (*In various degrees of amazement and curiosity.*) A song!

MISTRESS MERTON. Gilead! What is this?

JUSTICE MERTON. The selection is a German ballad—a particular favorite at the court of Prussia, where his lordship last rendered it. His tutor has made a translation which is entitled—

DICKON. "The Prognostication of the Crows."

ALL. Crows!

JUSTICE MERTON. And I am requested to remind you that in the ancient heathen mythology of Germany, the crow or raven was the fateful bird of the god Woden.

CAPTAIN BUGBY. How prodigiously novel!

MINISTER DODGE. (*Frowning.*) Unparalleled!

SIR CHARLES. A ballad! Come now, that sounds like old England again. Let's have it. Will his lordship sing without music?

JUSTICE MERTON. Master Dickonson, hem! has been—persuaded—to accompany his lordship on the spinet.

AMELIA. How delightful!

REV. MASTER RAND. (*Aside to* TODD.) Shall we remain?

REV. MASTER TODD. We must.

RAVENSBANE. (*To* RACHEL.) My tassel, dear mistress; you do not wear it?

RACHEL. My heart still wavers, my lord. But whilst you sing, I will decide.

RAVENSBANE. Whilst I sing? My fate, then, is waiting at the end of a song?

RACHEL. At the end of a song.

DICKON. (*Calling to* RAVENSBANE.) Your lordship!

RAVENSBANE. (*Starting, turns to the company.*) Permit me.

(DICKON *sits at the spinet. At first, his fingers in playing give sound only to the soft tinkling notes of that ancient instrument; but gradually, strange notes and harmonies of an aërial orchestra mingle with, and at length drown, the spinet. The final chorus is produced solely by fantastic symphonic cawings, as of countless crows, in harsh but musical accord. During the song* RICHARD *enters.* DICKON'S *music, however, does not cease but fills the intervals between the verses. To his accompaniment, amid the whispered and gradually increasing wonder, resentment, and dismay of the assembled guests,* RAVENSBANE, *with his eyes fixed upon* RACHEL, *sings.*)

Baron von Rabentod arose;
  (The golden sun was rising)
Before him flew a flock of crows:
  Sing heigh! Sing heigh! Sing heigh! Sing—

Ill speed, ill speed thee, baron-wight;
  Ill speed thy palfrey pawing!
Blithe is the morn but black the night
  That hears a raven's cawing.
        (*Chorus.*)
      Caw! Caw! Caw!

MISTRESS DODGE. (*Whispers to her husband.*) Did you hear them?

MINISTER DODGE. Hush!

AMELIA. (*Sotto voce.*) What *can* it be?

CAPTAIN BUGBY. Oh, the latest, be sure.

DICKON. You note, my friends, the accompanying harmonics; they are an intrinsic part of the ballad, and may not be omitted.

RAVENSBANE. (*Sings.*)

The baron reckèd not a pin;
  (For the golden sun was rising)
He rode to woo, he rode to win;
  Sing heigh! Sing heigh! Sing heigh! Sing—

He rode into his prince's hall
  Through knights and damsels flow'ry:
'Thy daughter, prince, I bid thee call;
  I claim her hand and dowry.'

(*Enter* RICHARD. MISTRESS MERTON *seizes his arm nervously.*)

SIR CHARLES. (*To* CAPTAIN BUGBY.) This gentleman's playing is rather ventriloquistical.

CAPTAIN BUGBY. Quite, as it were.

REV. MASTER TODD. This smells unholy.

REV. MASTER RAND. (*To* TODD.) Shall we leave?

RAVENSBANE. (*Sings.*)

'What cock is this, with crest so high,
  That crows with such a pother?'
'Baron von Rabentod am I;
  Methinks we know each other.'
'Now welcome, welcome, dear guest of mine,
  So long why didst thou tarry?
Now, for the sake of auld lang syne,
  My daughter thou shalt marry.'

AMELIA. (*To* BUGBY.) And he kept right on smoking!

MINISTER DODGE. (*Who, with* RAND *and* TODD, *has risen uneasily.*) This smacks of witchcraft.

RAVENSBANE. (*Sings.*)

The bride is brought, the priest as well;
  (The golden sun was passing)
They stood beside the altar rail;
  Sing ah! Sing ah! Sing ah! Sing—
'Woman, with this ring I thee wed.'
  What makes his voice so awing?
The baron by the bride is dead:
  Outside the crows were cawing.

(*Chorus, which grows tumultuous, seeming to fill the room with the invisible birds.*)

      Caw! Caw! Caw!

(*The guests rise in confusion.* DICKON *still plays delightedly, and the strange music continues.*)

MINISTER DODGE. This is no longer godly. —Justice Merton! Justice Merton, sir!—

RAVENSBANE. (*To* RACHEL, *who holds his tassel in her hand.*) Ah! and you have my tassel!

RACHEL. See! I will wear it now. You yourself shall fasten it.

RAVENSBANE. Rachel! Mistress!

RACHEL. My dear lord!

(*As* RAVENSBANE *is placing the silken tassel on* RACHEL'S *breast to fasten it there,* RICHARD, *by the mirror, takes hold of the curtain strings.*)

RICHARD. I told you—witchcraft, like murder will out! Lovers! Behold yourselves! (*He pulls the curtain back.*)

RACHEL. (*Looking into the glass, screams and turns her gaze fearfully upon* RAVENSBANE.) Ah! Do not look!

DICKON. (*Who, having turned round from the spinet, has leaped forward, now turns back again, biting his finger.*) Too late!

(*In the glass are reflected the figures of* RACHEL *and* RAVENSBANE— RACHEL *just as she herself appears, but* RAVENSBANE *in his essential form of a scarecrow, in every movement reflecting* RAVENSBANE'S *motions. The thing in the glass is about to pin a wisp of corn-silk on the mirrored breast of the maiden.*)

RAVENSBANE. What is there?

RACHEL. (*Looking again, starts away from* RAVENSBANE.) Leave me! Leave me!—Richard!

(*She faints in* RICHARD'S *arms.*)

RAVENSBANE. Fear not, mistress, I will kill the thing. (*Drawing his sword, he rushes at the glass. Within, the scarecrow, with a drawn wheel-spoke, approaches him at equal speed. They come face to face and recoil.*) Ah! ah! Fear'st thou me? What art thou? Why, 'tis a glass. Thou mockest me? Look, look, mistress, it mocks me! O God, no! no! Take it away. Dear God, do not look!—It is I!

ALL. (*Rushing to the doors.*) Witchcraft! Witchcraft!

(*As* RAVENSBANE *stands frantically*

confronting his abject reflection, struck in a like posture of despair, the curtain falls.)

ACT FOURTH.

The scene is the same, but it is night. The moon, shining in broadly at the window, discovers RAVENSBANE *alone, prostrate before the mirror. Raised on one arm to a half-sitting posture, he gazes fixedly at the vaguely seen image of the scarecrow prostrate in the glass.*

RAVENSBANE. All have left me—but not thou. Rachel has left me; her eyes have turned away from me; she is gone. All that I loved, all that loved me, have left me. A thousand ages—a thousand ages ago, they went away; and thou and I have gazed upon each other's desertedness. Speak! and be pitiful! If thou art I, inscrutable image, if thou dost feel these pangs thine own, show then self-mercy; speak! What art thou? What am I? Why are we here? How comes it that we feel and guess and suffer? Nay, though thou answer not these doubts, yet mock them, mock them aloud, even as there, monstrous, thou counterfeitest mine actions. Speak, abject enigma!— Speak, poor shadow, thou— (*Recoiling wildly.*) Stand back, inanity! Thrust not thy mawkish face in pity toward me. Ape and idiot! Scarecrow!—to console me! Haha!—A flail and broom-stick! a cob, a gourd and pumpkin, to fuse and sublimate themselves into a mage-philosopher, who discourseth metaphysics to itself—itself, God! Dost Thou hear? Itself! For even such am I—I whom Thou madest to love Rachel. Why, God—haha! dost Thou dwell in this thing? Is it Thou that peerest forth at me—*from* me? Why, hark then; Thou shalt listen, and answer—if Thou canst. Between the rise and setting of a sun, I have walked in this world of Thine. I have been thrilled with wonder; I have been calmed with knowledge; I have trembled with joy and passion. Power, beauty, love have ravished me. Infinity itself, like a dream, has blazed before me with the certitude of prophecy; and I have cried, "This world, the heavens, time itself, are mine to conquer," and I have thrust forth mine arm to wear Thy shield forever— and lo! for my shield Thou reachest me—a mirror, and whisperest: "Know thyself! Thou art—a scarecrow: a tinkling clod, a rigmarole of dust, a lump of ordure, contemptible, superfluous, inane!" Haha! Hahaha! And with such scarecrows Thou dost people a planet! O ludicrous! Monstrous! Ludicrous! At least, I thank Thee, God! at least this breathing bathos can laugh at itself. Thou hast vouchsafed to me, Spirit,— hahaha!—to know myself. Mine, mine is the consummation of man—even self-contempt! (*Pointing in the glass with an agony of derision.*) Scarecrow! Scarecrow! Scarecrow!

THE IMAGE IN THE GLASS. (*More and more faintly.*) Scarecrow! Scarecrow! Scarecrow!

(RAVENSBANE *throws himself prone upon the floor, beneath the window, sobbing. There is a pause of silence, and the moon shines brighter.—Slowly then* RAVENSBANE, *getting to his knees, looks out into the night.*)

RAVENSBANE. What face are you, high up through the twinkling leaves? Do you not, like all the rest, turn, aghast, your eyes away from me—me, abject enormity, groveling at your feet? Gracious being, do you not fear—despise me? O white peace of the world, beneath your gaze the clouds glow silver, and the herded cattle, slumbering far afield, crouch—beautiful. The slough shines

lustrous as a bridal veil. Beautiful face, you are Rachel's, and you have changed the world. Nothing is mean, but you have made it miraculous; nothing is loathsome, nothing ludicrous, but you have converted it to loveliness, that even this shadow of a mockery myself, cast by your light, gives me the dear assurance I am a man. Rachel, mistress, mother, out of my suffering you have brought forth my soul. I am saved!

THE IMAGE IN THE GLASS. A very pretty sophistry.

(*The moonlight grows dimmer, as at the passing of a cloud.*)

RAVENSBANE. Ah! what voice has snatched you from me?

THE IMAGE. A most poetified pumpkin!

RAVENSBANE. Thing! dost thou speak at last? My soul abhors thee.

THE IMAGE. I *am* thy soul.

RAVENSBANE. Thou liest.

THE IMAGE. Our daddy Dickon and our mother Rickby begot and conceived us at sunrise, in a Jack-o'-lantern.

RAVENSBANE. Thou liest, torturing illusion. Thou art but a phantom in a glass.

THE IMAGE. Why, very true. So art thou. *We* are a pretty phantom in a glass.

RAVENSBANE. It is a lie. I am no longer thou. I feel it; I am a man.

THE IMAGE.

And prithee, what's a man? Man's but a mirror,
Wherein the imps and angels play charades,
Make faces, mope, and pull each other's hair—
Till crack! the sly urchin Death shivers the glass.
And the bare coffin boards show underneath.

RAVENSBANE. Yea! if it be so, thou coggery! if both of us be indeed but illusions, why, now let us end together. But if it be not so, then let *me* for evermore be free of thee. Now is the test— the glass! (*Springing to the fireplace, he seizes an iron crosspiece from the andirons.*) I'll play your urchin Death and shatter it. Let see what shall survive!

(*He rushes to strike the glass with the iron.* DICKON *steps out of the mirror, closing the curtain.*)

DICKON. I wouldn't, really!

RAVENSBANE. Dickon! dear Dickon! is it you?

DICKON. Yes, Jacky! it's dear Dickon, and I really wouldn't.

RAVENSBANE. Wouldn't what, Dickon?

DICKON. Sweep the cobwebs off the sky with thine aspiring broomstick. When a man questions fate, 'tis bad digestion. When a scarecrow does it, 'tis bad taste.

RAVENSBANE. At last, *you* will tell me the truth, Dickon! Am I, then—that thing?

DICKON. You mustn't be so skeptical. Of course you're that thing.

RAVENSBANE. Ah me despicable! Rachel, why didst thou ever look upon me?

DICKON. I fear, cobby, thou hast never studied woman's heart and hero-worship. Take thyself now. I remarked to Goody Bess, thy mother, this morning, as I was chucking her thy pate from the hayloft, that thou wouldst make a Mark Antony or an Alexander before night.

RAVENSBANE. Cease! cease! in pity's name. You do not know the agony of being ridiculous.

DICKON. Nay, Jacky, all mortals are ridiculous. Like you, they were rummaged out of the muck; and like you, they shall return to the dunghill. I advise 'em, like you, to enjoy the interim, and smoke.

RAVENSBANE. This pipe, this ludicrous pipe that I forever set to my lips and puff! Why must I, Dickon? Why?

DICKON. To avoid extinction—merely. You see, 'tis just as your fellow in there (*pointing to the glass*) explained. You yourself are the subtlest of mirrors, polished out of pumpkin and pipe-smoke. Into this mirror the fair Mistress Rachel has projected her lovely image, and thus provided you with what men call a soul.

RAVENSBANE. Ah! then, I have a soul—the truth of me? Mistress Rachel has indeed made me a man?

DICKON. Don't flatter thyself, cobby. Break thy pipe, and whiff—soul, Mistress Rachel, man, truth, and this pretty world itself, go up in the last smoke.

RAVENSBANE. No, no! not Mistress Rachel.

DICKON. Mistress Rachel exists for your lordship merely in your lordship's pipe-bowl.

RAVENSBANE. Wretched, niggling caricature that I am! All is lost to me—lost!

DICKON. "Paradise Lost" again! Always blaming it on me. There's that gaunt fellow in England has lately wrote a parody on me when I was in the apple business.

RAVENSBANE. (*Falling on his knees and bowing his head.*) O God! I am so contemptible!

(*Enter, at door back,* GOODY RICKBY; *her blacksmith garb is hidden under a dingy black mantle with a peaked hood.*)

DICKON. Good verse, too, for a parody! (*Ruminating, raises one arm rhetorically above* RAVENSBANE.)

—Farewell, happy fields
Where joy forever dwells! Hail, horrors; hail,
Infernal world! and thou, profoundest hell,
Receive thy new possessor.

GOODY RICKBY. (*Seizing his arm.*) Dickon!

DICKON. Hullo! You, Bess!

GOODY RICKBY. There's not a minute to lose. Justice Merton and the neighbors have ended their conference at Minister Dodge's, and are returning here.

DICKON. Well, let 'em come. We're ready.

GOODY RICKBY. But thou toldst me they had discovered—

DICKON. A scarecrow in a mirror. Well? The glass is bewitched; that's all.

GOODY RICKBY. All? Witchcraft is hanging—that's all! And the mirror was bought of me—of me, the witch. Wilt thou be my hangman, Dickon?

DICKON. Wilt thou give me a kiss, Goody? When did ever thy Dickon desert thee?

GOODY RICKBY. But how, boy, wilt thou—

DICKON. Trust me, and thy son. When the Justice's niece is thy daughter-in-law, all will be safe. For the Justice will cherish his niece's family.

GOODY RICKBY. But when he knows—

DICKON. But he shall not know. How can he? When the glass is denounced as a fraud, how will he, or any person, ever know that we made this fellow out of rubbish? Who, forsooth, but a poet —or a devil—would believe it? You mustn't credit men with our imaginations, my dear.

GOODY RICKBY. Then thou wilt pull me through this safe?

DICKON. As I adore thee—and my own reputation.

GOODY RICKBY. (At the window.) I see their lanterns down the road.

DICKON. Stay, marchioness—his lordship! My lord—your lady mother.

GOODY RICKBY. (Curtsying, laughs shrilly.) Your servant—my son!
(About to depart.)

RAVENSBANE. Ye lie! both of you!—I was born of Rachel.

DICKON. Tut, tut, Jacky; you mustn't mix up mothers and prospective wives at your age. It's fatal.

GOODY RICKBY. (Excitedly.) They're coming!   (Exit.)

DICKON. (Calling after her.) Fear not; I'll overtake thee.

RAVENSBANE. She is coming; Rachel is coming, and I may not look upon her!

DICKON. Eh? Why not?

RAVENSBANE. I am a monster.

DICKON. Fie! fie! Thou shalt have her.

RAVENSBANE. Have her, Dickon?

DICKON. For lover and wife.

RAVENSBANE. For wife?

DICKON. For wife and all. Thou hast but to obey.

RAVENSBANE. Ah! who will do this for me?

DICKON. I!

RAVENSBANE. Dickon! Wilt make me a man—a man and worthy of her?

DICKON. Fiddlededee! I make over no masterpieces. Thy mistress shall be Cinderella, and drive to her palace with her gilded pumpkin.

RAVENSBANE. It is the end.

DICKON. What! You'll not?

RAVENSBANE. Never.

DICKON. Harkee, manikin. Hast thou learned to suffer?

RAVENSBANE. (Wringing his hands.) O God!

DICKON. I taught thee. Shall I teach thee further?

RAVENSBANE. Thou canst not.

DICKON. Cannot—ha! What if I should teach Rachel, too?

RAVENSBANE. Rachel!—Ah! now I know thee.

DICKON. (Bowing.) Flattered.

RAVENSBANE. Devil! Thou wouldst not torment Rachel?

DICKON. Not if my lord—

RAVENSBANE. Speak! What must I do?

DICKON. Not speak. Be silent, my lord, and acquiesce in all I say.

RAVENSBANE. I will be silent.

DICKON. And acquiesce?

RAVENSBANE. I will be silent.

(Enter MINISTER DODGE, accompanied by SIR CHARLES REDDINGTON, CAPTAIN BUGBY, the REVEREND MASTERS RAND and TODD, and followed by JUSTICE MERTON, RICHARD, MISTRESS MERTON, and RACHEL. RICHARD and RACHEL stand somewhat apart, RACHEL drawing close to RICHARD and hiding her face. All wear their outer wraps, and two or three hold lanterns, which, save the moon, throw the only *light upon the scene. All enter solemn and silent.)*

MINISTER DODGE. Lord, be Thou present with us, in this unholy spot!

SEVERAL MEN'S VOICES. Amen.

DICKON. Friends! Have you seized her?

MINISTER DODGE. Stand from us.

DICKON. Sir, the witch! Surely you did not let her escape?

ALL. The witch?

DICKON. A dame in a peaked hood. She has but now fled the house. She called herself—Goody Rickby.

ALL. Goody Rickby!

MISTRESS MERTON. She here!

DICKON. Yea, mistress, and hath confessed all the damnable art, by which all of us have lately been so terrorized.

JUSTICE MERTON. What confessed she?

MINISTER DODGE. What said she?

DICKON. This: It appeareth that, for some time past, she hath cherished revengeful thoughts against our honored host, Justice Merton.

MINISTER DODGE. Yea, he hath often righteously condemned her!

DICKON. Precisely! So, in revenge, she bewitched yonder mirror, and this very morning unlawfully inveigled this sweet young lady into purchasing it.

SIR CHARLES. Mistress Rachel!

MINISTER DODGE. (*To* RACHEL.) Didst thou purchase that glass?

RACHEL. (*In a low voice.*) Yes.

MINISTER DODGE. From Goody Rickby?

RACHEL. Yes. (*Clinging to* RICHARD.) O, Richard!

MINISTER DODGE. But the image; what was the damnable image in the glass?

DICKON. A familiar devil of hers—a sly imp, who wears to mortal eyes the shape of a scarecrow. It seems she commanded this devil to reveal himself in the glass as my lord's own image, that thus she might wreck Justice Merton's family felicity.

MINISTER DODGE. Infamous!

DICKON. Indeed, sir, it was this very devil whom but now she stole here to consult withal, when she encountered me, attendant here upon my poor prostrate lord, and—held by the wrath in my eye —confessed it all.

SIR CHARLES. Thunder and brimstone! Where is this accursed hag?

DICKON. Alas—gone, gone! If you had but stopped her.

MINISTER DODGE. I know her den—the blacksmith shop. Let us seize her there!

SIR CHARLES. (*Starting.*) Which way?

MINISTER DODGE. To the left.

SIR CHARLES. Go on, there.

MINISTER DODGE. My honored friends, come with us. Heaven shield, with her guilt, the innocent!

(*Exeunt all but* RICHARD, RACHEL, DICKON, *and* RAVENSBANE.)

DICKON. So, then, dear friends, this strange incident is happily elucidated. Bygones, therefore, be bygones. The future brightens—with orange-blossoms. Hymen and Felicity stand with us here ready to unite two amorous and bashful lovers. His lordship is reticent; yet to you alone, of all beautiful ladies, Mistress Rachel—

RAVENSBANE. (*In a mighty voice.*) Silence!

DICKON. My lord would—

RAVENSBANE. Silence! Dare not to speak to her!

DICKON. (*Biting his lip.*) My babe is weaned.

(*He steps back, and disappears, left, in the dimness.*)

RACHEL. (*Still at* RICHARD'S *side.*) Oh, my lord, if I have made you suffer—

RICHARD. (*Appealingly.*) Rachel!

RAVENSBANE. (*Approaching her, raises one arm to screen his face.*) Gracious lady! let fall your eyes; look not upon me. If I dare now speak once more to

you, 'tis because I would have you know
—Oh, forgive me!—that I love you.

RICHARD. Sir! This lady has renewed her
promise to be my wife.

RAVENSBANE. Your wife, or not, I love
her.

RICHARD. Zounds!

RAVENSBANE. Forbear, and hear me! For
one wonderful day I have gazed upon
this, your world. A million forms—of
trees, of stones, of stars, of men, of common things—have swum like motes before my eyes; but one alone was wholly
beautiful. That form was Rachel: to
her alone I was not ludicrous; to her I
also was beautiful. Therefore, I love
her.

RICHARD. Sir!

RAVENSBANE. You talk to me of mothers,
mistresses, lovers, and wives and sisters,
and you say men love these. What is
love? The night and day of the world
—the *all* of life, the all which must include both you and me and God, of
whom you dream. Well, then, I love
you, Rachel. What shall prevent me?
Mistress, mother, wife—thou art all to
me!

RICHARD. My lord, I can only reply for
Mistress Rachel, that you speak like one
who does not understand this world.

RAVENSBANE. O, God! sir, and do you?
If so, tell me—tell me before it be too
late—why, in this world, such a thing
as *I* can love and talk of love. Why, in
this world, a true man and woman, like
you and your betrothed, can look upon
this counterfeit and be deceived.

RACHEL and RICHARD. Counterfeit?

RAVENSBANE. Me—on me—the ignominy
of the earth, the laughing-stock of the
angels!

RACHEL. Are you not Lord Ravensbane?

RAVENSBANE. No, I am *not* Lord Ravensbane. I am a nobleman of husks, bewitched from a pumpkin. I am Lord
Scarecrow!

RACHEL. Ah me, the image in the glass
was true?

RAVENSBANE. Yes, true. It is the glass
of truth—Thank God for you, dear.

DICKON. (*His face only reappearing in
the mirror, speaks low.*) Remember! if
you dare—Rachel shall suffer for it.

RAVENSBANE. You lie. She is above your
power.

DICKON. Still, thou darest not—

RAVENSBANE. Fool, I dare. (RAVENS-
BANE *turns to* RACHEL. *While he speaks,*
DICKON'S *face slowly fades and disappears.*) Mistress, this pipe is I. This
intermittent smoke holds, in its nebula,
Venus, Mars, the world. If I should
break it—chaos and the dark! And this
of me that now stands up will sink jum-
bled upon the floor—a scarecrow. See!
I break it. (*He breaks the pipe in his
hands, and flings the pieces to the
ground; then turns, agonized, to*
RACHEL.) Oh, Rachel, could I have
been a man—!

(*He sways, staggering.*)

RACHEL. Richard! Richard! support him.
(*She draws the curtain of the mirror,
just opposite which* RAVENSBANE *has
sunk upon the floor. At her cry, he
starts up faintly and gazes at his reflection, which is seen to be a normal image
of himself.*) Look, look: the glass!

RAVENSBANE. Who is it?

RACHEL. Yourself, my lord—'tis the glass
of truth.

RAVENSBANE. (*His face lighting with an
exalted joy, starts to his feet, erect, before the glass.*) A man! (*He falls back
into the arms of the two lovers.*)
Rachel!

RICHARD. (*Bending over him.*) Dead!

RACHEL. (*With an exalted look.*) But a
man!

NEW ORLEANS SUPERSTITIONS

by Lafcadio Hearn

Lafcadio Hearn was interested in and knew intimately the folklore of three continents: Europe, North America, and Asia. Although not primarily a field collector, he heard tales in New Orleans, Martinique, and Japan which he later transcribed, and he widened his acquaintance with legend and ballad by wide reading in many literatures. The essay on the superstitions of New Orleans, which appeared first in Harper's Weekly *for December 25, 1886, is an excellent example of how Hearn synthesized reading and personal experience. As a reporter for New Orleans newspapers, he observed many incidents and bits of behavior which he utilized in his daily journalism. But he was rarely content with simply reporting, and he liked to speculate on the origin or the transformation of the beliefs and practices which fascinated him. The essay also illustrates his desire to classify his examples on a racial basis and shows how, on the principle of association, one bit of folklore suggests another. Hearn was at his best in short pieces where his brilliant style and acute sense of color could compensate for his lack of a sustained narrative. Later reports on the folk life of New Orleans would seem to suggest that Hearn's comments are not as dated as he implied.*

The question "What is Voudooism?" could scarcely be answered to-day by any resident of New Orleans unfamiliar with the life of the African west coast, or the superstitions of Hayti, either through study or personal observation. The old generation of planters in whose day Voudooism had a recognized existence—so dangerous as a motive power for black insurrection that severe measures were adopted against it—has passed away; and the only person I ever met who had, as a child in his colored nurse's care, the rare experience of witnessing a Voudoo ceremonial, died some three years ago, at the advanced age of seventy-six. As a religion—an imported faith—Voudooism in Louisiana is really dead; the rites of its serpent worship are forgotten; the meaning of its strange and frenzied chants, whereof some fragments linger as refrains in Negro song, is not now known even to those who remember the words; and the story of its former existence is only revealed to the folklorists by the multitudinous debris of African superstition which it has left behind it. These only I propose to consider now; for what is to-day called Voudooism in New Orleans means, not an African cultus, but a curious class of Negro practices, some possibly derived from it, and others which bear resemblance to the magic of the Middle Ages. What could be more medi-aeval, for instance, than molding a waxen heart, and sticking pins in it, or melting it slowly before a fire, while charms are being repeated with the hope that as the waxen heart melts or breaks, the life of some enemy will depart? What, again, could remind us more of thirteenth-century superstition than the burning of a certain number of tapers to compel some absent person's return, with the idea that before the last taper is consumed a mysterious mesmerism will force the wanderer to cross rivers and mountains if necessary on his or her way back?

The fear of what are styled "Voudoo charms" is much more widely spread in Louisiana than any one who had con-versed only with educated residents might suppose; and the most familiar supersti-tion of this class is the belief in what I might call *pillow magic,* which is the sup-posed art of causing wasting sickness or even death by putting certain objects into the pillow of the bed in which the hated person sleeps. Feather pillows are supposed to be particularly well-adapted to this kind of witchcraft. It is believed that by secret spells a "Voudoo" can cause some mon-strous kind of bird or nondescript animal to shape itself into being out of the pillow feathers—like the *tupilek* of the Esquimau *iliseenek* (witchcraft). It grows very slowly, and by night only; but when com-pletely formed, the person who has been using the pillow dies. Another practice of pillow witchcraft consists in tearing a liv-ing bird asunder—usually a cock—and putting portions of the wings into the pillow. A third form of the black-art is confined to putting certain charms or fetiches—consisting of bones, hair, feathers, rags, strings, or some fantastic combination of these and other trifling objects—into any sort of a pillow used by the party whom

it is desired to injure. The pure Africanism of this practice needs no comment. Any exact idea concerning the use of each par-ticular kind of charm I have not been able to discover; and I doubt whether those who practice such fetichism know the origi-nal African beliefs connected with it. Some say that putting grains of corn into a child's pillow "prevents it from growing any more"; others declare that a bit of cloth in a grown person's pillow will cause wasting sickness; but different parties ques-tioned by me gave each a different significa-tion to the use of similar charms. Putting an open pair of scissors under the pillow before going to bed is supposed to insure a pleasant sleep in spite of fetiches; but the surest way to provide against being "hoo-dooed," as American residents call it, is to open one's pillow from time to time. If any charms are found, they must be first sprinkled with salt, then burned. A Spanish resident told me that their eldest daughter had been unable to sleep for weeks, owing to a fetich that had been put into her pillow by a spiteful colored do-mestic. After the object had been duly exorcised and burned, all the young lady's restlessness departed. A friend of mine liv-ing in one of the country parishes once found a tow string in his pillow, into the fibers of which a great number of feather stems had either been introduced or had introduced themselves. He wished to retain it as a curiosity, but no sooner did he ex-hibit it to some acquaintance than it was denounced as a Voudoo "trick," and my friend was actually compelled to burn it in the presence of witnesses. Everybody knows or ought to know that feathers in pillows have a natural tendency to cling and form clots or lumps of more or less curious form, but the discovery of these in some New Orleans households is enough to create a panic. They are viewed as in-cipient Voudoo tupileks. The sign of the cross is made over them by Catholics, and they are promptly committed to the flames.

Pillow magic alone, however, is far from being the only recognized form of maleficent Negro witchcraft. Placing charms before the entrance of a house or room, or throwing them over a wall into a yard, is believed to be a deadly practice. When a charm is laid before a room door or hall door, oil is often poured on the floor or pavement in front of the threshold. It is supposed that whoever *crosses an oil line* falls into the power of the Voudoos. To break the oil charm, sand or salt should be strewn upon it. Only a few days before writing this article a very intelligent Spaniard told me that shortly after having discharged a dishonest colored servant he found before his bedroom door one evening a pool of oil with a charm lying in the middle of it, and a candle burning near it. The charm contained some bones, feathers, hairs, and rags—all wrapped together with a string—and a dime. No superstitious person would have dared to use that dime; but my friend, not being superstitious, forthwith put it into his pocket.

The presence of that coin I can only attempt to explain by calling attention to another very interesting superstition connected with New Orleans fetichism. The Negroes believe that in order to make an evil charm operate it is necessary *to sacrifice something*. Wine and cake are left occasionally in dark rooms, or candies are scattered over the sidewalk, by those who want to make their fetich hurt somebody. If food or sweetmeats are thus thrown away, they must be abandoned without a parting glance; the witch or wizard must not look back while engaged in the sacrifice.

Scattering dirt before a door, or making certain figures on the wall of a house with chalk, or crumbling dry leaves with the fingers and scattering the fragments before a residence, are also forms of a maleficent conjuring which sometimes cause serious annoyance. Happily the conjurers are almost as afraid of the counter-charms as the most superstitious persons are of the conjuring. An incident which occurred recently in one of the streets of the old quarter known as "Spanish Town" afforded me ocular proof of the fact. Through malice or thoughtlessness, or possibly in obedience to secret orders, a young Negro girl had been tearing up some leaves and scattering them on the sidewalk in front of a cottage occupied by a French family. Just as she had dropped the last leaf the irate French woman rushed out with a broom and a handful of salt, and began to sweep away the leaves, after having flung salt both upon them and upon the little Negress. The latter actually screamed with fright, and cried out, "*Oh, pas jeté plis disel après moin, madame! pas bisoin jeté disel après moin; mo pas pé vini icite encore.*" (Oh, madam, don't throw any more salt after me; you needn't throw any more salt after me; I won't come here any more.)

Another strange belief connected with these practices was well illustrated by a gift made to my friend Professor William Henry by a Negro servant for whom he had done some trifling favor. The gift consisted of a "frizzly hen"—one of those funny little fowls whose feathers all seem to curl. "Mars'r Henry, you keep dat frizzly hen, an' ef eny niggers frow eny *conjure* in your yard, *dat frizzly hen will eat de conjure.*" Some say, however, that one is not safe unless he keeps two frizzly hens.

The naughty little Negress at whom the salt was thrown seemed to fear the salt more than the broom pointed at her. But she was not yet fully educated, I suspect, in regard to superstitions. The Negro's terror of a broom is of very ancient date—it may have an African origin. It was commented upon by Moreau de Saint-Méry in his work on San Domingo, published in 1796. "What especially irritates the Negro," he wrote, "is to have a broom passed over any part of his body. He asks at once whether the person imagined that he was dead, and remains convinced that the act shortens his life." Very similar ideas concerning the broom linger in New Orleans. To point either end of a broom at a person is deemed bad luck; and many an ignorant man would instantly knock down or violently use the party who should point a broom at him. Moreover, the broom is supposed to have mysterious power as a means of getting rid of people. "If you are pestered by visitors whom you would wish never to see again, sprinkle salt on the floor after they go, and sweep it out by the same door through which they have gone, and they will never come back." To use a broom in the evening is bad luck: *balayer le soir, on balaye sa fortune* (to sweep in the evening is to sweep your good luck away), remains a well-quoted proverb.

I do not know of a more mysterious disease than muscular atrophy in certain forms, yet it is by no means uncommon either in New Orleans or in the other leading cities of the United States. But in New Orleans, among the colored people, and among many of the uneducated of other races, the victim of muscular atrophy is believed to be the victim of Voudooism. A notion is prevalent that Negro witches possess knowledge of a secret poison which may terminate life instantly or cause a slow "withering away," according as the dose is administered. A Frenchman under treatment for paralysis informed me that his misfortune was certainly the work of Voudoos, and that his wife and children had died through the secret agency of Negro wizards. Mental aberration is also said to be caused by the administration of poisons whereof some few Negroes are alleged to possess the secret. In short, some very superstitious persons of both races live in perpetual dread of imaginary Voudoos, and fancy that the least ailment from which they suffer is the work of sorcery. It is very doubtful whether any knowledge of those animal or vegetable poisons which leave no trace of their presence in the blood, and which may have been known to some slaves of African birth, still lingers in Louisiana, wide-spread as is the belief to the contrary. During the last decade there have been a few convictions of blacks for the crime of poisoning, but there was nothing at all mysterious or peculiar about these cases, and the toxic agent was invariably the most vulgar of all—arsenic, or some arsenious preparation in the shape of rat poison.

II

The story of the frizzly hen brings me to the subject of superstitions regarding animals. Something of the African, or at least of the San Domingan, worship of the cock seems to have been transplanted hither by the blacks, and to linger in New Orleans under various metamorphoses. A Negro charm to retain the affections of a lover consists in tying up the legs of the bird to the head, and plunging the creature alive into a vessel of gin or other spirits. Tearing the live bird asunder is another cruel charm, by which some Negroes believe that a sweetheart may become magically fettered to the man who performs the quartering. Here, as in other parts of the world, the crowing hen is killed, the hooting of the owl presages death or bad luck, and the crowing of the cock by day presages the arrival of company. The wren (*roitelet*) must not be killed: *c'est zozeau bon Dié* (it is the good God's bird)—a belief, I think, of European origin.

It is dangerous to throw hair-combings away instead of burning them, because birds may weave them into their nests, and while the nest remains the person to whom the hair belonged will have a continual headache. It is bad luck to move a cat from one house to another; seven years' bad luck to kill a cat; and the girl who steps, accidentally or otherwise, on a cat's tail need not expect to be married the same year. The apparition of a white butterfly means good news. The neighing of a horse before one's door is bad luck. When a fly bothers one very persistently, one may expect to meet an acquaintance who has been absent many years.

There are many superstitions about marriage, which seem to have a European origin, but are not less interesting on that account. "Twice a bridesmaid, never a bride," is a proverb which needs no comment. The bride must not keep the pins which fastened her wedding dress. The husband must never take off his wedding ring: to take it off will insure him bad luck of some kind. If a girl who is engaged accidentally lets a knife fall, it is a sign that her lover is coming. Fair or foul weather upon her marriage day augurs a happy or unhappy married life.

The superstitions connected with death may be all imported, but I have never been able to find a foreign origin for some of them. It is bad luck to whistle or hum the air that a band plays at a funeral. If a funeral stops before your house, it means that the dead wants company. It is bad luck to cross a funeral procession, or to count the number of carriages in it; if you do count them, you may expect to die after the expiration of as many weeks as there were carriages at the funeral. If at the cemetery there be any unusual delay in burying the dead, caused by any unlooked-for circumstances, such as the tomb proving too small to admit the coffin, it is a sign that the deceased is selecting a companion from among those present, and one of the mourners must soon die. It is bad luck to carry a spade through a house. A bed should never be placed with its foot pointing toward the street door, for corpses leave the house feet foremost. It is bad luck to travel with a priest; this idea seems to me of Spanish

importation; and I am inclined to attribute a similar origin to the strange tropical superstition about the banana, which I obtained, nevertheless, from an Italian. You must not *cut* a banana, but simply break it with the fingers, because in cutting it you *cut the cross*. It does not require a very powerful imagination to discern in a severed section of the fruit the ghostly suggestion of a crucifix.

Some other Creole superstitions are equally characterized by naïve beauty. Never put out with your finger the little red spark that tries to linger on the wick of a blown-out candle: just so long as it burns, some soul in purgatory enjoys rest from torment. Shooting-stars are souls escaping from purgatory: if you can make a good wish three times before the star disappears, the wish will be granted. When there is sunshine and rain together, a colored nurse will tell the children, *"Gadé! djabe apé batte so femme."* (Look! the devil's beating his wife!)

I will conclude this little paper with selections from a list of superstitions which I find widely spread, not citing them as of indubitable Creole origin, but simply calling attention to their prevalence in New Orleans, and leaving the comparative study of them to folklorists.

Turning the foot suddenly in walking means bad or good luck. If the right foot turns, it is bad luck; if the left, good. This superstition seems African according to a statement made by Moreau de Saint-Méry. Some reverse the conditions, making the turning of the left foot bad luck. It is also bad luck to walk about the house with one shoe on and one shoe off, or, as a Creole acquaintance explained it to me, *"c'est appeler sa mère ou son père dans le tombeau."* (It is calling one's mother or one's father into the grave.) An itching in the right palm means coming gain; in the left, coming loss.

Never leave a house by a different door

from that by which you entered it; it is "carrying away the good luck of the place." Never live in a house you build before it has been rented for at least a year. When an aged person repairs his or her house, he or she is soon to die. Never pass a child through a window; it stops his growth. Stepping over a child does the same; therefore, whoever takes such a step inadvertently must step back again to break the evil spell. Never tilt a rocking-chair when it is empty. Never tell a bad dream before breakfast, unless you want it "to come true"; and never pare the nails on Monday morning before taking a cup of coffee. A funny superstition about windows is given me in this note by a friend: "Il ne faut pas faire passer un enfant par la fenêtre, car avant un an il y en aura un autre" (A child must not be passed through a window, for if so passed you will have another child before the lapse of a year.) This proverb, of course, interests only those who desire small families, and as a general rule Creoles are proud of large families, and show extraordinary affection toward their children.

If two marriages are celebrated simultaneously, one of the husbands will die. Marry at the time of the moon's waning and your good luck will wane also. If two persons think and express the same thought at the same time, one of them will die before the year passes. To chop up food in a pot with a knife means a dispute in the house. If you have a ringing in your ears, some person is speaking badly of you; call out the names of all whom you suspect, and when the ringing stops at the utterance of a certain name, you know who the party is. If two young girls are combing the hair of a third at the same time, it may be taken for granted that the youngest of the three will soon die. If you want to make it stop raining, plant a cross in the middle of the yard and sprinkle it with salt. The red-fish has the print of St. Peter's fingers

on its tail. If water won't boil in the kettle, there may be a toad or a toad's egg in it. Never kill a spider in the afternoon or evening, but always kill the spider unlucky enough to show himself early in the morning, for the old French proverb says:

Araignée du matin—chagrin;
Araignée du midi—plaisir;
Araignée du soir—espoir

(A spider seen in the morning is a sign of grief; a spider seen at noon, of joy; a spider seen in the evening, of hope).

Even from this very brief sketch of New Orleans superstitions the reader may perceive that the subject is peculiar enough to merit the attention of experienced folklorists. It might be divided by a competent classifier under three heads: I. Negro superstitions confined to the black and colored population; II. Negro superstitions which have proved contagious, and have spread among the uneducated classes of whites; III. Superstitions of Latin origin imported from France, Spain, and Italy. I have not touched much upon superstitions inherited from English, Irish, or Scotch sources, inasmuch as they have nothing especially local in their character here. It must be remembered that the refined classes have no share in these beliefs, and that, with a few really rational exceptions, the practices of Creole medicine are ignored by educated persons. The study of Creole superstitions has only an ethnological value, and that of Creole medicine only a botanical one, in so far as it is related to empiricism.

All this represents an under side of New Orleans life; and if anything of it manages to push up to the surface, the curious growth makes itself visible only by some really pretty blossoms of feminine superstition in regard to weddings or betrothal rings, or by some dainty sprigs of child-lore, cultivated by those colored nurses who tell us that the little chickens throw up their heads while they drink to thank the good God for giving them water.

PO' SANDY

by Charles W. Chesnutt

The narrative of a slave who was turned into a tree in order to evade his duties sounds like a plantation variant of an ancient Greek myth. But genuine local color is supplied by the emphasis on the slave-master relationship and by the use of "goopher" tactics. Charles Chesnutt utilized a frame technique very successfully. The story is told primarily from the point of view of a northern white man who has recently acquired property in rural North Carolina. But the real narrator is the uneducated Negro coachman who has a fund of local legends and superstitions. Julius McAdoo may or may not have believed his yarn of a tragic conjuring—the white man is obviously skeptical—but there is no doubt that he had an ulterior motive in telling it. "Po' Sandy" was published in The Conjure Woman *(1899).*

On the northeast corner of my vineyard in central North Carolina, and fronting on the Lumberton plank-road, there stood a small frame house, of the simplest construction. It was built of pine lumber, and contained but one room, to which one window gave light and one door admission. Its weather-beaten sides revealed a virgin innocence of paint. Against one end of the house, and occupying half its width, there stood a huge brick chimney: the crumbling mortar had left large cracks between the bricks; the bricks themselves had begun to scale off in large flakes, leaving the chim-

ney sprinkled with unsightly blotches. These evidences of a decay were but partially concealed by a creeping vine, which extended its slender branches hither and thither in an ambitious but futile attempt to cover the whole chimney. The wooden shutter, which had once protected the unglazed window, had fallen from its hinges, and lay rotting in the rank grass and jimson weeds beneath. This building, I learned when I bought the place, had been used as a schoolhouse for several years prior to the breaking out of the war, since which time it had remained unoccupied, save when some stray cow or vagrant hog had sought shelter within its walls from the chill rains and nipping winds of winter.

One day my wife requested me to build her a new kitchen. The house erected by us, when we first came to live upon the vineyard, contained a very conveniently arranged kitchen; but for some occult reason my wife wanted a kitchen in the back yard, apart from the dwelling-house, after the usual Southern fashion. Of course I had to build it.

To save expense, I decided to tear down the old schoolhouse, and use the lumber, which was in a good state of preservation, in the construction of the new kitchen. Before demolishing the old house, however, I made an estimate of the amount of material contained in it, and found that I would have to buy several hundred feet of lumber additional, in order to build the new kitchen according to my wife's plan.

One morning old Julius McAdoo, our colored coachman, harnessed the gray mare to the rockaway, and drove my wife and me over to the sawmill from which I meant to order the new lumber. We drove down the long lane which led from our house to the plank-road; following the plank-road for about a mile, we turned into a road running through the forest and across the swamp to the sawmill beyond. Our carriage jolted over the half-rotted corduroy road which traversed the swamp, and then climbed the long hill leading to the sawmill. When we reached the mill, the foreman had gone over to a neighboring farmhouse, probably to smoke or gossip, and we were compelled to await his return before we could transact our business. We remained seated in the carriage, a few rods from the mill, and watched the leisurely movements of the mill-hands. We had not waited long before a huge pine log was placed in position, the machinery of the mill was set in motion, and the circular saw began to eat its way through the log, with a loud whir which resounded

throughout the vicinity of the mill. The sound rose and fell in a sort of rhythmic cadence, which, heard from where we sat, was not unpleasing, and not loud enough to prevent conversation. When the saw started on its second journey through the log, Julius observed, in a lugubrious tone, and with a perceptible shudder: —

"Ugh! but dat des do cuddle my blood!"

"What's the matter, Uncle Julius?" inquired my wife, who is of a very sympathetic turn of mind. "Does the noise affect your nerves?"

"No, Mis' Annie," replied the old man, with emotion, "I ain' narvous; but dat saw, a-cuttin' en grindin' thoo dat stick er timber, en moanin', en groanin', en sweekin', kyars my 'memb'ance back ter ole times, en 'min's me er po' Sandy." The pathetic intonation with which he lengthened out the "po' Sandy" touched a responsive chord in our own hearts.

"And who was poor Sandy?" asked my wife, who takes a deep interest in the stories of plantation life which she hears from the lips of the older colored people. Some of these stories are quaintly humorous; others wildly extravagant, revealing the Oriental cast of the negro's imagination; while others, poured freely into the sympathetic ear of a Northern-bred woman, disclose many a tragic incident of the darker side of slavery.

"Sandy," said Julius, in reply to my wife's question, "was a nigger w'at useter b'long ter ole Mars Marrabo McSwayne. Mars Marrabo's place wuz on de yuther side'n de swamp, right nex'ter yo' place. Sandy wuz a monst'us good nigger, en could do so many things erbout a plantation, en alluz 'ten' ter his wuk so well, dat w'en Mars Marrabo's chilluns growed up en married off, dey all un 'em wanted dey daddy fer ter gin 'em Sandy fer a weddin' present. But Mars Marrabo knowed de res' wouldn' be satisfied ef he gin Sandy ter a'er one un 'em; so w'en dey wuz all done married, he fix it by 'lowin' one er his chilluns ter take Sandy fer a mont' er so, en den ernudder fer a mont' er so, en so on dat erway tel dey had all had 'im de same lenk er time; en den dey would all take him roun' ag'in, 'cep'n' oncet in a w'ile w'en Mars Marrabo would len' 'im ter some er his yuther kinfolks 'roun' de country, w'en dey wuz short er han's; tel bimeby it got so Sandy did n' hardly knowed whar he wuz gwine ter stay fum one week's een' ter de yuther.

"One time w'en Sandy wuz lent out ez yushal, a spekilater come erlong wid a lot er niggers, en Mars Marrabo swap' Sandy's wife off fer a noo 'oman. W'en Sandy come back, Mars Marrabo gin 'im a dollar, en 'lowed he wuz monst'us sorry fer ter break up de fambly, but de spekilater had gin 'im big boot, en times wuz hard en money skase, en so he wuz bleedst ter make de trade. Sandy tuk on some 'bout losin' his wife, but he soon seed dey want no use cryin' ober spilt merlasses; en bein' ez he lacked de looks er de noo 'oman, he tuk up wid her atter she'd be'n on de plantation a mont' er so.

"Sandy en his noo wife got on mighty well tergedder, en de niggers all 'mence' ter talk about how lovin' dey wuz. W'en Tenie wuz tuk sick oncet, Sandy useter set up all night wid 'er, en den go ter wuk in de mawnin' des lack he had his reg'lar sleep; en Tenie would 'a' done anythin' in de worl' fer her Sandy.

"Sandy en Tenie had n' be'n libbin' tergedder fer mo' d'n two mont's befo' Mars Marrabo's old uncle, w'at libbed down in Robeson County, sent up ter fin' out ef Mars Marrabo could n' len' 'im er hire 'im a good han' fer a mont' er so. Sandy's marster wuz one er dese yer easy-gwine folks w'at wanter please eve'ybody, en he says yas, he could len' 'im Sandy. En Mars Marrabo tol' Sandy fer ter git ready ter go down ter Robeson nex' day, fer ter stay a mont' er so.

"It wuz monst'us hard on Sandy fer ter

take 'im 'way fum Tenie. It wuz so fur down ter Robeson dat he did n' hab no chance er comin' back ter see her tel de time wuz up; he would n' 'a' mine comin' ten er fifteen mile at night ter see Tenie, but Mars Marrabo's uncle's plantation wuz mo' d'n forty mile off. Sandy wuz mighty sad en cas' down atter w'at Mars Marrabo tol' 'im, en he says ter Tenie, sezee:—

" 'I'm gittin' monst'us ti'ed er dish yer gwine roun' so much. Here I is lent ter Mars Jemms dis mont', en I got ter do so-en-so; en ter Mars Archie de nex' mont', en I got ter do so-en-so; den I got ter go ter Miss Minnie's; en hit's Sandy dis en Sandy dat, en Sandy yer en Sandy dere, tel it 'pears ter me I ain' got no home, ner no master, ner no mistiss, ner no nuffin. I can't eben keep a wife: my yuther ole 'oman wuz sol' away widout my gittin' a chance fer ter tell her good-by; en now I got ter go off en leab you, Tenie, en I dunno whe'r I'm eber gwine ter see you ag'in er no. I wisht I wuz a tree, er a stump, er a rock, er sump'n w'at could stay on de plantation fer a w'ile.'

"Atter Sandy got thoo talkin', Tenie did n' say naer word, but des sot dere by de fier, studyin' en studyin'. Bimeby she up'n' says:—

" 'Sandy, is I eber tol' you I wuz a cunjuh 'oman?'

"Co'se Sandy had n' nebber dremp' er nuffin lack dat, en he made a great 'miration w'en he hear w'at Tenie say. Bimeby Tenie went on:—

" 'I ain' goophered nobody, ner done no conjuh wuk, fer fifteen year er mo'; en w'en I got religion I made up my mine I would n' wuk no mo' goopher. But dey is some things I doan b'lieve it's no sin fer ter do; en ef you doan wanter be sent roun' fum pillar ter pos', en ef you doan wanter go down ter Robeson, I kin fix things so you won't haf ter. Ef you'll des say de word, I kin turn you ter w'ateber you wanter be, en you kin stay right whar you wanter, ez long ez you mineter.'

"Sandy say he doan keer; he's willin' fer ter do anythin' fer ter stay close ter Tenie. Den Tenie ax 'im ef he doan wanter be turnt inter a rabbit.

"Sandy say, 'No, de dogs mought git atter me.'

" 'Shill I turn you ter a wolf?' sez Tenie.

" 'No, eve'ybody's skeered er a wolf, en I doan want nobody ter be skeered er me.'

" 'Shill I turn you ter a mawkin'-bird?'

" 'No, a hawk mought ketch me. I wanter be turnt inter sump'n w'at 'll stay in one place.'

" 'I kin turn you ter a tree,' sez Tenie. 'You won't hab no mouf ner years, but I kin turn you back oncet in a w'ile, so you kin git sump'n ter eat, en hear w'at's gwine on.'

"Well, Sandy say dat 'll do. En so Tenie tuk 'im down by de aidge er de swamp, not fur fum de quarters, en turnt 'im inter a big pine-tree, en sot 'im out 'mongs' some yuther trees. En de nex' mawnin', ez some er de fiel' han's wuz gwine long dere, dey seed a tree w'at dey did n' 'member er habbin' seed befo'; it wuz monst'us quare, en dey wuz bleedst ter 'low dat dey had n' 'membered right, er e'se one er de saplin's had be'n growin' monst'us fas'.

"W'en Mars Marrabo 'skiver' dat Sandy wuz gone, he 'lowed Sandy had runned away. He got de dogs out, but de las' place dey could track Sandy ter wuz de foot er dat pine-tree. En dere de dogs stood en barked, en bayed, en pawed at de tree, en tried ter climb up on it; en w'en dey wuz tuk roun' thoo de swamp ter look fer de scent, dey broke loose en made fer dat tree ag'in. It wuz de beatenis' thing de w'ite folks eber hearn of, en Mars Marrabo 'lowed dat Sandy must 'a' clim' up on de tree en jump' off on a mule er

sump'n, en rid fur ernuff fer ter spile de scent. Mars Marrabo wanted ter 'cuse some er de yuther niggers er heppin' Sandy off, but dey all 'nied it ter de las'; en eve'ybody knowed Tenie sot too much sto' by Sandy fer ter he'p 'im run away whar she could n' nebber see 'im no mo'.

"W'en Sandy had be'n gone long ernuff fer folks ter think he done got clean away, Tenie useter go down ter de woods at night en turn 'im back, en den dey'd slip up ter de cabin en set by de fire en talk. But dey ha' ter be monst'us keerful, er e'se somebody would 'a' seed 'em, en dat would 'a' spile' de whole thing; so Tenie alluz turnt Sandy back in de mawnin' early, befo' anybody wuz a-stirrin'.

"But Sandy did n' git erlong widout his trials en tribberlations. One day a woodpecker come erlong en 'mence' ter peck at de tree; en de nex' time Sandy wuz turnt back he had a little roun' hole in his arm, des lack a sharp stick be'n stuck in it. Atter dat Tenie sot a sparrer-hawk fer ter watch de tree; en w'en de woodpecker come erlong nex' mawnin' fer ter finish his nes', he got gobble' up mos' 'fo' he stuck his bill in de bark.

"Nudder time, Mars Marrabo sent a nigger out in de woods fer ter chop tuppentime boxes. De man chop a box in dish yer tree, en hack' de bark up two or th'ee feet, fer ter let de tuppentime run. De nex' time Sandy wuz turnt back he had a big skyar on his lef' leg, des lack it be'n skunt; en it tuk Tenie nigh 'bout all night fer ter fix a mixtry ter kyo it up. Atter dat, Tenie sot a hawnet fer ter watch de tree; en w'en de nigger come back ag'in fer ter cut ernudder box on de yuther side'n de tree, de hawnet stung 'im so hard dat de ax slip en cut his foot nigh 'bout off.

"W'en Tenie see so many things happenin' ter de tree, she 'cluded she'd ha' ter turn Sandy ter sump'n e'se; en atter studyin' de matter ober, en talkin' wid Sandy one ebenin', she made up her mine fer ter fix up a goopher mixtry w'at would turn herse'f en Sandy ter foxes, er sump'n, so dey could run away en go some'rs whar dey could be free en lib lack w'ite folks.

"But dey ain' no tellin' w'at 's gwine ter happen in dis worl'. Tenie had got de night sot fer her en Sandy ter run away, w'en dat ve'y day one er Mars Marrabo's sons rid up ter de big house in his buggy, en say his wife wuz monst'us sick, en he want his mammy ter len' 'im a 'oman fer ter nuss his wife. Tenie's mistiss say sen' Tenie; she wuz a good nuss. Young mars wuz in a tarrible hurry fer ter git back home. Tenie wuz washin' at de big house dat day, en her mistiss say she should go right 'long wid her young marster. Tenie tried ter make some 'scuse fer ter git away en hide 'tel night, w'en she would have eve'ything fix' up fer her en Sandy; she say she wanter go ter her cabin fer ter git her bonnet. Her mistiss say it doan matter 'bout de bonnet; her head-hankcher wuz good ernuff. Den Tenie say she wanter git her bes' frock; her mistiss say no, she doan need no mo' frock, en w'en dat one got dirty she could git a clean one whar she wuz gwine. So Tenie had ter git in de buggy en go 'long wid young Mars Dunkin ter his plantation, w'ich wuz mo' d'n twenty mile away; en dey wa'n't no chance er her seein' Sandy no mo' 'tel she come back home. De po' gal felt monst'us bad 'bout de way things wuz gwine on, en she knowed Sandy mus' be a wond'rin' why she did n' come en turn 'im back no mo'.

"W'iles Tenie wuz away nussin' young Mars Dunkin's wife, Mars Marrabo tuk a notion fer ter buil' 'im a noo kitchen; en bein' ez he had lots er timber on his place, he begun ter look 'roun' fer a tree ter hab de lumber sawed out'n. En I dunno how it come to be so, but he happen fer ter hit on de ve'y tree w'at Sandy wuz turnt inter. Tenie wuz gone, en dey wa'n't nobody ner nuffin fer ter watch de tree.

"De two men w'at cut de tree down say dey nebber had sech a time wid a tree befo': dey axes would glansh off, en did n' 'pear ter make no progress thoo de wood; en of all de creakin', en shakin', en wobblin' you eber see, dat tree done it w'en it commence' ter fall. It wuz de beatenis' thing!

"W'en dey got de tree all trim' up, dey chain it up ter a timber waggin, en start fer de sawmill. But dey had a hard time gittin' de log dere: fus' dey got stuck in de mud w'en dey wuz gwine crosst de swamp, en it wuz two or th'ee hours befo' dey could git out. W'en dey start' on ag'in, de chain kep' a-comin' loose, en dey had ter keep a-stoppin' en a-stoppin' fer ter hitch de log up ag'in. W'en dey commence' ter climb de hill ter de sawmill, de log broke loose, en roll down de hill en in 'mongs' de trees, en hit tuk nigh 'bout half a day mo' ter git it haul' up ter de sawmill.

"De nex' mawnin' atter de day de tree wuz haul' ter de sawmill, Tenie come home. W'en she got back ter her cabin, de fus' thing she done wuz ter run down ter de woods en see how Sandy wuz gittin' on. W'en she seed de stump standin' dere, wid de sap runnin' out'n it, en de limbs layin' scattered roun', she nigh 'bout went out'n her min'. She run ter her cabin, en got her goopher mixtry, en den follered de track er de timber waggin ter de sawmill. She knowed Sandy could n' lib mo' d'n a minute er so ef she turnt him back, fer he wuz all chop' up so he 'd 'a' be'n bleedst ter die. But she wanted ter turn 'im back long ernuff fer ter 'splain ter 'im dat she had n' went off a-purpose, en lef' 'im ter be chop' down en sawed up. She did n' want Sandy ter die wid no hard feelin's to'ds her.

"De han's at de sawmill had des got de big log on de kerridge, en wuz startin' up de saw, w'en dey seed a 'oman runnin' up de hill, all out er bref, cryin' en gwine on des lack she wuz plumb 'stracted. It wuz Tenie; she come right inter de mill, en th'owed herse'f on de log, right in front er de saw, a-hollerin' en cryin' ter her Sandy ter fergib her, en not ter think hard er her, fer it wa'n't no fault er hern. Den Tenie 'membered de tree did n' hab no years, en she wuz gittin' ready fer ter wuk her goopher mixtry so ez ter turn Sandy back, w'en de mill-hands kotch holt er her en tied her arms wid a rope, en fasten' her to one er de posts in de sawmill; en den dey started de saw up ag'in, en cut de log up into bo'ds en scantlin's right befo' her eyes. But it wuz mighty hard wuk; fer of all de sweekin', en moanin', en groanin', dat log done it w'iles de saw wuz a-cuttin' thoo it. De saw wuz one er dese yer ole-timey, up-en-down saws, en hit tuk longer dem days ter saw a log 'en it do now. Dey greased de saw, but dat did n' stop de fuss; hit kep' right on, tel fin'ly dey got de log all sawed up.

"W'en de oberseah w'at run de sawmill come fum breakfas', de han's up en tell him 'bout de crazy 'oman—ez dey s'posed she wuz—w'at had come runnin' in de sawmill, a-hollerin' en gwine on, en tried ter th'ow herse'f befo' de saw. En de oberseah sent two or th'ee er de han's fer ter take Tenie back ter her marster's plantation.

"Tenie 'peared ter be out'n her min' fer a long time, en her marster ha' ter lock her up in de smoke-'ouse 'tel she got ober her spells. Mars Marrabo wuz monst'us mad, en hit would 'a' made yo' flesh crawl fer ter hear him cuss, 'caze he say de spekilater w'at he got Tenie fum had fooled 'im by wukkin' a crazy 'oman off on him. W'iles Tenie wuz lock up in de smoke-'ouse, Mars Marrabo tuk 'n' haul de lumber fum de sawmill, en put up his noo kitchen.

"W'en Tenie got quiet' down, so she could be 'lowed ter go 'roun' de plantation, she up 'n' tole her marster all erbout Sandy en de pine-tree; en w'en Mars Marrabo hearn it, he 'lowed she wuz de wuss 'stracted nigger he eber hearn of. He did

n' know w'at ter do wid Tenie: fus' he thought he'd put her in de po'-house; but fin'ly, seein' ez she did n' do no harm ter nobody ner nuffin, but des went 'roun' moanin', en groanin', en shakin' her head, he 'cluded ter let her stay on de plantation en nuss de little nigger chilluns w'en dey mammies wuz ter wuk in de cotton-fiel'.

"De noo kitchen Mars Marrabo buil' wuz n' much use, fer it had n' be'n put up long befo' de niggers 'mence' ter notice quare things erbout it. Dey could hear sump'n moanin' en groanin' 'bout de kitchen in de night-time, en w'en de win' would blow dey could hear sump'n a-hollerin' en sweekin' lack it wuz in great pain en sufferin'. En it got so atter a w'ile dat it wuz all Mars Marrabo's wife could do ter git a 'oman ter stay in de kitchen in de daytime long ernuff ter do de cookin'; en dey wa'n't naer nigger on de plantation w'at would n' rudder take forty dan ter go 'bout dat kitchen atter dark,—dat is, 'cep'n' Tenie; she did n' 'pear ter min' de ha'nts. She useter slip 'roun' at night, en set on de kitchen steps, en lean up agin de do'-jamb, en run on ter herse'f wid some kine er foolishness w'at nobody could n' make out; fer Mars Marrabo had th'eaten' ter sen' her off'n de plantation ef she say anything ter any er de yuther niggers 'bout de pine-tree. But somehow er 'nudder de niggers foun' out all erbout it, en dey all knowed de kitchen wuz ha'nted by Sandy's sperrit. En bimeby hit got so Mars Marrabo's wife herse'f wuz skeered ter go out in de yard atter dark.

"W'en it come ter dat, Mars Marrabo tuk en to' de kitchen down, en use' de lumber fer ter buil' dat ole school'ouse w'at you er talkin' 'bout pullin' down. De school'ouse wuz n' use' 'cep'n' in de daytime, en on dark nights folks gwine 'long de road would hear quare soun's en see quare things. Po' ole Tenie useter go down dere at night, en wander 'roun' de school-'ouse; en de niggers all 'lowed she went fer ter talk wid Sandy's sperrit. En one winter mawnin', w'en one er de boys went ter school early fer ter start de fire, w'at should he fin' but po' ole Tenie, layin' on de flo', stiff, en col', en dead. Dere did n' 'pear ter be nuffin pertickler de matter wid her,—she had des grieve' herse'f ter def fer her Sandy. Mars Marrabo did n' shed no tears. He thought Tenie wuz crazy, en dey wa'n't no tellin' w'at she mought do nex'; en day ain' much room in dis worl' fer crazy w'ite folks, let 'lone a crazy nigger.

"Hit wa'n't long atter dat befo' Mars Marrabo sol' a piece er his track er lan' ter Mars Dugal' McAdoo,—*my* ole marster, —en dat's how de ole school'ouse happen to be on yo' place. W'en de wah broke out, de school stop', en de ole school'ouse be'n stannin' empty ever sence,—dat is, 'cep'n' fer de ha'nts. En folks sez dat de ole school'ouse, er any yuther house w'at got any er dat lumber in it w'at wuz sawed out'n de tree w'at Sandy wuz turnt inter, is gwine ter be ha'nted tel de las' piece er plank is rotted en crumble' inter dus'."

Annie had listened to this gruesome narrative with strained attention.

"What a system it was," she exclaimed, when Julius had finished, "under which such things were possible!"

"What things?" I asked, in amazement. "Are you seriously considering the possibility of a man's being turned into a tree?"

"Oh, no," she replied quickly, "not that"; and then she murmured absently, and with a dim look in her fine eyes, "Poor Tenie!"

We ordered the lumber, and returned home. That night, after we had gone to bed, and my wife had to all appearances been sound asleep for half an hour, she startled me out of an incipient doze by exclaiming suddenly,—

"John, I don't believe I want my new kitchen built out of the lumber in that old schoolhouse."

"You wouldn't for a moment allow yourself," I replied, with some asperity, "to be influenced by that absurdly impossible yarn which Julius was spinning today?"

"I know the story is absurd," she replied dreamily, "and I am not so silly as to believe it. But I don't think I should ever be able to take any pleasure in that kitchen if it were built out of that lumber. Besides, I think the kitchen would look better and last longer if the lumber were all new."

Of course she had her way. I bought the new lumber, though not without grumbling. A week or two later I was called away from home on business. On my return, after an absence of several days, my wife remarked to me,—

"John, there has been a split in the Sandy Run Colored Baptist Church, on the temperance question. About half the members have come out from the main body, and set up for themselves. Uncle Julius is one of the seceders, and he came to me yesterday and asked if they might not hold their meetings in the old schoolhouse for the present."

"I hope you didn't let the old rascal have it," I returned, with some warmth. I had just received a bill for the new lumber I had bought.

"Well," she replied, "I couldn't refuse him the use of the house for so good a purpose."

"And I'll venture to say," I continued, "that you subscribed something toward the support of the new church?"

She did not attempt to deny it.

"What are they going to do about the ghost?" I asked, somewhat curious to know how Julius would get around this obstacle.

"Oh," replied Annie, "Uncle Julius says that ghosts never disturb religious worship, but that if Sandy's spirit *should* happen to stray into meeting by mistake, no doubt the preaching would do it good."

PETE FEATHERTON

by James Hall

Much of the early fiction about the frontier sentimentalized the settlers and pictured the Indians as unmitigated savages. Yet the hunters and pioneers who gradually moved westward were not immune to the force of legend or superstition and preserved many a tale familiar to them since childhood. Moreover, the frontier spawned its own folklore, which intertwined the myths of white men and red men. In his long expository beginning to his account of a backwoods nimrod, James Hall called attention to the supposed lack of the usual material of supernaturalism. He then proceeded to introduce deftly three familiar folklore motifs: the appearance of the devil in disguise, the spell cast on a weapon which only another touch of magic can remove, and the reliance on a silver bullet. The interest of the story is enhanced by the author's pretense to authenticity and by the hint that part of Pete Featherton's trouble is due to his addiction to liquid refreshment. The intervention of the Indian doctor, who enabled the hunter to fight magic with magic, and the suggestion of a formula which Pete was enjoined to follow strictly are further examples of the author's reliance on folk practices.[1] The tale first appeared in Hall's literary miscellany, The Western Souvenir *(1828). A revised text, which is used here, was published in* The Wilderness and the War Path *(1846).*

Every country has its superstitions, and will continue to have them, so long as men are blessed with lively imaginations, and while any portion of mankind remain ignorant of the causes of natural phenomena. That which cannot be reconciled with experience, will always be attributed to supernatural influence; and those who know little, will imagine much more to exist than has ever been witnessed by their own senses. I am not displeased with this state of things, for the journey of life would be dull indeed, if those who travel it were confined for ever to the beaten highway, worn smooth by the sober feet of experience. To turnpikes, for our beasts of burden, I have no objection; but I cannot consent to the erection of railways for the mind, even though the architect be "wisdom, whose ways are pleasant, and whose paths are peace." It is sometimes agreeable to stray off into the wilderness which fancy creates, to recline in fairy bowers, and to listen to the murmurs of imaginary fountains. When the beaten road becomes tiresome, there are many sunny spots where the pilgrim may loiter with advantage— many shady paths, whose labyrinths may be traced with delight. The mountain, and the vale, on whose scenery we gaze enchanted, derive new charms, when their deep caverns and gloomy recesses are peopled with imaginary beings.

But above all, the enlivening influence

---

1. For a discussion of James Hall's general indebtedness to folklore in his fiction see John T. Flanagan, "Folklore in the Stories of James Hall," *Midwest Folklore* (Fall, 1955), V, 159–68.

of fancy is felt, when it illumines our fire-sides, giving to the wings of time, when they grow heavy, a brighter plumage, and a more sprightly motion. There are seasons, when the spark of life within us seems to burn with less than its wonted vigour; the blood crawls heavily through the veins; the contagious dullness seizes on our companions, and the sluggish hours roll painfully along. Something more than a common impulse is then required to awaken the indolent mind, and give a new tone to the flagging spirits. If necromancy draws her magic circle, we cheerfully enter the ring; if folly shakes her cap and bells, we are amused; a witch becomes an interesting personage, and we are even agreeably surprised by the companionable qualities of a ghost.

We, who live on the frontier, have little acquaintance with imaginary beings. These gentry never emigrate; they seem to have strong local attachments, which not even the charms of a new country can overcome. A few witches, indeed, were imported into New England by the Puritans; but were so badly used, that the whole race seems to have been disgusted with new settlements. With them, the spirit of adventure expired, and the weird women of the present day wisely cling to the soil of the old countries. That we have but few ghosts will not be deemed a matter of surprise by those who have observed how miserably destitute we are of accommodations for such inhabitants. We have no baronial castles, nor ruined mansions; no turrets crowned with ivy, nor ancient abbeys crumbling into decay; and it would be a paltry spirit, who would be content to wander in the forest, by silent rivers and solitary swamps.

It is even imputed to us as a reproach by enlightened foreigners, that our land is altogether populated with the living descendants of Adam—creatures with thews and sinews, who eat when they are hungry, laugh when they are tickled, and die when they are done living. The creatures of romance, say they, exist not in our territory. A witch, a ghost, or a brownie, perishes in America, as a serpent is said to die the instant it touches the uncongenial soil of Ireland. This is true, only in part. If we have no ghosts, we are not without miracles. Wonders have happened in these United States. Mysteries have occurred in the valley of the Mississippi. Supernatural events have transpired on the borders of "the beautiful stream"; and in order to rescue my country from undeserved reproach, I shall proceed to narrate an authentic history, which I received from the lips of the party principally concerned.

A clear morning had succeeded a stormy night in December; the snow laid ankle-deep upon the ground, and glittered on the boughs, while the bracing air, and the cheerful sunbeams, invigorated the animal creation, and called forth the tenants of the forest from their warm lairs and hidden lurking-places.

The inmates of a small cabin on the margin of the Ohio were commencing with the sun the business of the day. A stout, raw-boned forester plied his keen axe, and, lugging log after log, erected a pile on the ample hearth, sufficiently large to have rendered the last honours to the stateliest ox. A female was paying her morning visit to the cow-yard, where a numerous herd of cattle claimed her attention. The plentiful breakfast followed; corn-bread, milk, and venison, crowned the oaken board, while a tin coffee-pot of ample dimensions supplied the beverage which is seldom wanting at the morning repast of the substantial American farmer.

The breakfast over, Mr. Featherton reached down a long rifle from the rafters, and commenced certain preparations, fraught with danger to the brute inhabitants of the forest. The lock was carefully examined, the screws tightened, the pan wiped, the flint renewed, and the springs oiled; and the keen eye of the backwoodsman glittered with an ominous lustre, as its glance rested on the destructive engine. His blue-eyed partner, leaning fondly on her husband's shoulder, essayed those coaxing and captivating blandishments, which every young wife so well understands, to detain her husband from the contemplated sport. Every pretext was urged with affectionate pertinacity, which female ingenuity could supply:—the wind whistled bleakly over the hills, the snow lay deep in the valleys, the deer would surely not venture abroad in such bitter cold weather, the adventurous hunter might get his toes frostbitten, and her own hours would be sadly lonesome in his absence. He smiled in silence at the arguments of his bride, for such she was, and continued his preparations, with the cool, but good-natured determination of one who is not to be turned from his purpose.

He was indeed a person with whom such arguments, except the last, would not be very likely to prevail. Mr. Peter Featherton, or as he was familiarly called by all who knew him, Pete Featherton, was a bold, rattling Kentuckian, of twenty-five, who possessed the characteristic peculiarities of his countrymen—good and evil—in a striking degree. His red hair and sanguine complexion, announced an ardent temperament; his tall form, and bony limbs, indicated an active frame inured to hardships; his piercing eye and high cheek bones, evinced the keenness and resolution of his mind. He was adventurous, frank, and social—boastful, credulous, illiterate, and at times wonderfully addicted to the marvellous. His imagination was a warm and fruitful soil, in which "tall oaks from little acorns grew," and his vocabulary was overstocked with superlatives. He loved his wife—no mistake about that—but next to her his affections entwined themselves about his gun, and expanded over his horse; he was true to his friends, never missed an election day, turned his back upon a frolic, nor affected to dislike a social glass.

He believed that the best qualities of all countries were combined in Kentucky; and had the most whimsical manner of expressing his national attachments. He was firmly convinced that the battle of the Thames was the most sanguinary conflict of the age—"a raal reg'lar skrimmage,"—and extolled Colonel Dick Johnson as a "severe old colt." He would admit freely that Napoleon was a great genius—Metternich, Castlereagh, "and them fellows" knew "a thing or two," but then they "were no part of a priming to Henry Clay."

When entirely "at himself"—to use his own language—that is to say, when duly sober, Pete was friendly and rational, courteous and considerate, and a better tempered fellow never shouldered a rifle. But he was a social man, who was liable to be "overtaken," and let him get a glass too much, and there was no end to his extravagance. Then it was that his genius bloomed and brought forth strange boasts, and strong oaths, his loyalty to old Kentuck waxed warm, and his faith in his horse, his gun, and his own manhood grew into idolatry. Always bold and self-satisfied, and habitually energetic in the expression of his predilections, he now became invested with the agreeable properties of the snapping-turtle, the alligator, and the steamboat, and gifted with the most affable and affectionate spirit of auto-biography. It was now that he would dwell upon his own bodily powers and prowess, with the enthusiasm of a devotee, and as the climax of this rhetorical display, would slap his hands together, spring perpendicularly into the air, and after uttering a yell worthy of the stoutest Winnebago, swear that he was "the best man in the country," and "could whip his weight in wild cats," "no two ways about it"—he was "not afraid of no man, no way you could fix it"; and finally, after many other extravagancies, he would urge, with no gentle asseveration, his ability to "ride through a crab-apple orchard on a streak of lightning."

In addition to all this, which one would think was enough for any reasonable man, Pete would sometimes brag that he had the best gun, the prettiest wife, the best-looking sister, and the fastest nag, in all Kentuck; and that no man dare say to the contrary. It is but justice to remark, that there was more truth in this last boast, than is usually found on such occasions, and that Pete had good reason to be proud of his horse, his gun, and his lady love.

These, however, were the happy moments, which are few and far between; they were the brilliant inspirations, playing like the lightning in an overheated atmosphere,—gleaming over the turbid stream of existence, as the meteor flashes through the gloom of the night. When the fit was off, Pete was a quiet, good-natured, listless soul, as one would see on a summer's day—strolling about with a grave aspect, a drawling, and a deliberate gait, a stoop of the shoulders, and a kind of general relaxation of the whole outward and inward man—in a state of entire freedom from restraint, reflection, and want, and without any impulse strong enough to call forth his latent manhood—as the panther, with whom he often compared himself, when his appetite for food is sated, sleeps calmly in his lair, or wanders harmlessly through his native thickets.

Our hero was a farmer, or, as the very appropriate phrase is, "made a *crap*" on his own land—for besides making a crop he performed but few of the labours of the husbandman. While planting his corn, tending it, and gathering in the harvest, he worked with a good will; but these, thanks to a prolific soil, and a free country, were

all his toils, and they occupied not half of the year, the remainder of which was spent in the more manly and gentlemanly employments of hunting, attending elections, and officiating at horse races. He was a rare hand at a "shucking," a house raising, or a log rolling; merry and strong, he worked like a young giant, and it was worth while to hear the gladsome tones of his clear voice, and the inspiring sound of his loud laugh; while the way he handled the ax, the beauty and keenness of the implement, the weight and precision of the blows, and the gracefulness of the action, were such as are not seen except in the "wilderness," where chopping is an accomplishment as well as the most useful of labours.

It will readily be perceived, that our hunter was not one who could be turned from his purpose by the prospect of danger or fatigue; and a few minutes sufficed to complete his preparations. His feet were cased in moccasins, and his legs in wrappers of dressed deer-skin; and he was soon accoutred with a powder horn, quaintly carved all over with curious devices,—an ample pouch with flints, patches, balls, and other "fixens"—and a hunter's knife,—and throwing "Brown Bess," for so he called his rifle, over his shoulder, he sallied forth.

But in passing a store hard by, which supplied the country with gunpowder, whiskey, and other necessaries, as well as with the luxuries of tea, sugar, coffee, calico, calomel, and chandlery, he was hailed by one of the neighbours, who invited him to "light off and take something." Pete said he had "no occasion," but "rather than be nice," he dismounted, and joined a festive circle, among whom the cup was circulating freely. Here he was soon challenged to swap rifles, and being one of those who could not "stand a banter," he bantered back again, without the least intention of parting with his favourite weapon. Making offers, like a skilful diplomatist, which he knew would not be accepted, and feigning great eagerness to accede to any reasonable proposition, while inwardly resolved to reject all, he magnified the perfections of Brown Bess.

"She can do any thing but talk," said he. "If she had legs she could hunt by herself. It is a pleasure to *tote* her—I naturally believe there is not a rifle south of Green river, that can throw a ball so far, or so true. I can put a bullet in that tree, down the road, a mile off."

"You can't do it, Pete—I'll bet a treat for the whole company."

"No"—said the hunter. "I could do it —but I don't want to strain my gun."

These discussions consumed much time and much whiskey—for the rule on such occasions is, that he who rejects an offer to trade, must treat the company, and thus every point in the negociation costs a pint of spirits.

At length, bidding adieu to his companions, Pete struck into the forest—it was getting late, and he "must look about pretty peart," he said, to get a venison before night. Lightly crushing the snow beneath his active feet, he beat up the coverts, and traversed all the accustomed haunts of the deer. He mounted every hill, and descended into every valley—not a thicket escaped the penetrating glance of his practised eye. Fruitless labour! not a deer was to be seen. Pete marvelled at this unusual circumstance, as the deer were very abundant in this neighbourhood, and no one knew better where to look for them than himself.

But what surprised him still more, was, that the woods were less familiar to him than formerly. He knew them "like a book." He thought he was acquainted with every tree within ten miles of his cabin; but now, although he certainly had not wandered so far, some of the objects around him seemed strange, while others

again were faintly recognized; and there was, altogether, a singular confusion in the character of the scenery, which was partly familiar, and partly new; or rather, in which many of the component parts were separately well known, but were so mixed up and changed in relation to each other, as to baffle even the knowledge of an expert woodsman.

The more he looked, the more he was bewildered. Had such a thing been possible, he would have thought himself a lost man. He came to a stream which had heretofore rolled to the west, but now its course pointed to the east; and the shadows of the tall trees, which, according to Pete's experience and philosophy, ought at noon to fall towards the north, all pointed to the south. He looked at his right and his left hands, somewhat puzzled to know which was which; then scratched his head—but scratching his head, though a good thing in its way, will not always get a man out of a scrape. He cast his eye upon his own shadow, which had never deceived him— when lo! a still more extraordinary phenomenon presented itself. It was travelling round him like the shade on a dial—only a great deal faster, as it veered round to all the points of the compass in the course of a single minute. Mr. Peter Featherton was "in a bad fix."

It was very evident too, from the dryness of the snow, and the brittleness of the twigs, which snapped off as he brushed his way through the thickets, that the weather was intensely cold; yet the perspiration was rolling in large drops from his brow. He stopped at a clear spring, and thrusting his hands into the cold water, attempted to carry a portion of it to his lips; but the element recoiled and hissed, as if his hands and lips had been composed of red hot iron. Pete felt quite puzzled when he reflected on all these contradictions in the aspect of nature; and began to consider what act of wickedness he had been guilty of, which could have rendered him so hateful, that the deer fled at his approach, the streams turned back, and the shadows fell the wrong way, or danced round their centre.

He began to grow alarmed, and would have liked to turn back; but was ashamed to betray such weakness, even to himself; and being naturally bold, he resolutely kept on his way. At last, to his great joy he espied the tracks of deer imprinted on the snow; they were fresh signs—and, dashing upon the trail, with the alacrity of a well-trained hound, he pursued, in hopes of soon overtaking the game. Presently he discovered the tracks of a man, who had struck the same trail in advance of him, and supposing it to be one of his neighbours, he quickened his pace, as well to gain a companion, which in the present state of his feelings he so much needed, as to share the spoil with his fellow hunter. Indeed, in his present situation and condition of mind, Pete thought he would be willing to give half of what he was worth, for the sight of a human face.

"I don't like the signs, no how," said he, casting a rapid glance around him; and then throwing his eyes downwards at his own shadow, which had ceased its rotatory motion, and was now swinging backward and forward like a pendulum—"I don't like the signs, no way they can be fixed."

"You are not scared, are you, Pete?" he continued, smiling at the oddity of such a question.

"Oh no, bless your heart, Mr. Featherton, I'm not scared—I'm not of that breed of dogs—there's no back out in me—but then I must say—to speak sentimentally —that I feel sort o' jubus—I do so. But I'll soon see whether other people's shadows act the fool like mine."

Upon futher observation, there appeared to be something peculiar in the human tracks before him, which were evidently made by a pair of feet which were not fellows—or were *odd fellows*—for one of them was larger than the other. As there was no person in the settlement who was thus deformed, Pete began to doubt whether it might not be the devil, who in borrowing shoes to conceal his cloven hoofs might have got those that did not match. He stopped, and scratched his head, as many a learned philosopher has done, when placed between the horns of a dilemma less perplexing than that which now vexed the spirit of our hunter. It was said long ago, that there is a tide in the affairs of men; and although our good friend Pete had never seen this sentiment in black and white, yet it is one of those truths, which are written in the heart of every reasonable being, and was only copied by the poet, from the great book of nature, a source from which he was a great borrower. It readily occurred to Pete on this occasion; and as he had enjoyed through life an uninterrupted tide of success, he reflected whether the stream of fortune might not have changed its course, like the brooks he had crossed, whose waters, for some sinister reason, seemed to be crawling up-hill.

He stopped, drew out his handkerchief, and wiped the perspiration from his brow. "This thing of being scared," said he, "makes a man feel mighty queer—the way it brings the sweat out is curious!" And again it occurred to him, that it was incumbent on him to see the end of the adventure, as otherwise he would show a want of that courage, which he had been taught to consider as the chief of the cardinal virtues.

"I can't back out," said he, "I never was raised to it, no how; and if the devil's a mind to hunt in this range, he shan't have all the game."

Then falling into the sentimental vein, as one naturally does from the heroic: "Here's this hankercher, that my Polly hemmed for me, and marked the two first letters of my name on it—P. for Pete and F. for Featherton—would she do the like of that for a coward? Could I ever look in her pretty face again, if I was mean enough to be scared? No—I'll go ahead—let what will come."

He soon overtook the person in advance of him, who, as he had suspected, was a perfect stranger. He had halted and was quietly seated on a log, gazing at the sun, when our hunter approached, and saluted him with the usual hearty, "How are you, stranger?" The person addressed made no reply, but continued to gaze at the sun, as if totally unconscious that any other individual was present. He was a small, thin, old man, with a grey beard of about a month's growth, and a long sallow melancholy visage, while a tarnished suit of snuff-coloured clothes, cut after the quaint fashion of some religious sect, hung loosely about his shrivelled person.

Our bold backwoodsman, somewhat awed, now coughed, threw the butt end of his gun heavily upon the frozen ground, and, still failing to elicit any attention, quietly seated himself on the other end of the log occupied by the stranger. Both remained silent for some minutes—Pete with open mouth, and glaring eyeballs, observing his companion with mute astonishment, and the latter looking at the sun.

"It's a warm day, this," said Pete, at length, passing his hand across his brow, as he spoke, and sweeping off the heavy drops of perspiration that hung there. But receiving no answer, he began to get nettled. He thought himself not civilly treated. His native assurance, which had been damped by the mysterious deportment of the person who sat before him, revived. "One man's as good as another"—thought he; and screwing up his courage to the sticking point, he arose, approached the silent man, and slapping him on the back, exclaimed—

"Well, stranger! don't the sun look mighty droll away out there in the north?"

As the heavy hand fell on his shoulder, the stranger slowly turned his face towards Pete, who recoiled several paces,—then rising without paying the abashed hunter any further attention, he began to pursue the trail of the deer. Pete prepared to follow, when the other turning upon him with a stern glance, enquired:

"Who are you tracking?"

"Not you," replied the hunter, whose alarm had subsided when the enemy began to retreat; and whose pride, piqued by the abruptness with which he had been treated, enabled him to assume his usual boldness of manner.

"Why do you follow this trail, then?"

"I trail deer."

"You must not pursue them further, they are mine!"

The sound of the stranger's voice broke the spell, which had hung over Peter's natural impudence, and he now shouted—

"*Your* deer! that's droll too! who ever heard of a man claiming the deer in the woods!"

"Provoke me not,—I tell you they are mine."

"Well, now—you're a comical chap! Why stranger,—the deer are wild! They're jist nateral to the woods here, the same the timber. You might as well say the wolves and the painters are yours, and all the rest of the wild varments."

"The tracks you behold here, are those of wild deer, undoubtedly—but they are mine. I routed them from their bed, and am driving them home."

"Home—where is your home?" inquired Pete, at the same time casting an inquisitive glance at the stranger's feet.

To this home question no reply was given, and Pete, fancying that he had got the best of the altercation, pushed his advantage,—adding sneeringly—

"Couldn't you take a pack or two of

wolves along? We can spare you a small gang. It is mighty wolfy about here.''

"If you follow any further it is at your peril,'' said the stranger.

"You don't reckon I'm to be skeered, do you? If you do, you are barking up the wrong tree. There's no back out in none of my breed, no how. You mustn't come over them words agin, stranger.''

"I repeat—''

"You had best not repeat—I allow no man to do that to me,—'' interrupted the irritated woodsman, "You must not imitate the like of that. I'm Virginy born, and Kentucky raised, and drot my skin, if I take the like of that from any man—no, Sir!''

"Desist, rash man, from altercation—I despise your threats!''

"The same to you, Sir!''

"I tell you what, stranger!'' continued Pete, endeavouring to imitate the coolness of the other, "as to the vally of a deer or two—I don't vally them to the tantamount of this here cud of tobacco; but I'm not to be backed out of my tracks. So keep off, stranger—don't come fooling about me. I might hurt you. I feel mighty wolfy about the head and shoulders. Keep off, I say, or you might run agin a snag.''

With this the hunter "squared himself, and sot his triggers,'' fully determined either to hunt the disputed game, or be vanquished in combat. To his surprise, the stranger, without appearing to notice his preparations, advanced and blew with his breath upon his rifle.

"Your gun is charmed!'' said he. "From this day forward you will kill no deer.''

So saying, that mysterious old man, with the most provoking coolness, resumed his way; while Pete remained bewildered; and fancied that he smelt brimstone.

Pete Featherton remained a moment or two lost in confusion. He then thought he would pursue the stranger, and punish him as well for his threats, as for the insult intended to his gun; but a little reflection induced him to change his decision. The confident manner in which that singular being had spoken, together with a kind of vague assurance in his own mind, that the spell had really taken effect, so unmanned and stupefied him, that he quietly, "took the back track,'' and strode homewards. He had not gone far, when he saw a fine buck, half concealed among the hazel bushes which beset his path, and resolved to know at once how matters stood between Brown Bess and the pretended conjurer, he took a deliberate aim, fired,—and away bounded the buck unharmed!

With a heavy heart, our mortified forester re-entered his own dwelling, and replaced his degraded weapon in its accustomed berth under the rafters.

"You have been long gone,'' said his wife, "but where is the venison you promised me?''

Pete was constrained to confess that he had shot nothing.

"That is strange!'' said the lady, "I never knew you fail before.''

Pete framed twenty excuses. He had felt unwell—his gun was out of fix—it was a bad day for hunting—the moon was not in the right place—and there were no deer stirring.

Had not Pete been a very young husband, he would have known that the vigilant eye of a wife is not to be deceived by feigned apologies. Female curiosity never sleeps; and the love of a devoted wife is the most sincere and the most absorbing of human passions. Pretty Mrs. Featherton saw, at a glance, that something had happened to her helpmate, more than he was willing to confess; and being quite as tenacious as himself, in her reluctance against being "backed out of her tracks,'' she determined to bring her inferior moiety to auricular confession, and advanced firmly to her object, until Pete was compelled to own, "That he believed Brown Bess was, somehow—sort o'—charmed."

"Now, Mr. Featherton!" remonstrated his sprightly bride, leaning fondly on his shoulder, and parting the long red locks on his forehead—"are you not ashamed to tell me such a tale as that? Charmed indeed! Ah well, I know how it is. You have been down at the store, shooting for half pints!"

"No, indeed—" replied the husband emphatically, "I wish I may be kissed to death, if I've pulled a trigger for a drop of liquor this day."

Ah, Peter—what a sad evasion was that! Surely the adversary when he blew his breath—sadly sulphureous of smell—upon thy favourite gun, breathed into thee the spirit of lying, of which he is the father. Mrs. Featherton saw farther into a millstone than he was aware of—but she kept her own counsel.

"I believe you, Peter,—you did not *shoot* for it—but do now—that's a dear good soul!—tell me where you have been, and what has happened? You are not well—or something is wrong—for never did Pete Featherton and Brown Bess fail to get a venison any day in the year."

Soothed by this well-timed compliment, and not unwilling to have the aid of counsel in this trying emergency, and to apply to his excited spirit the balm of conjugal sympathy, Pete narrated minutely to his wife all the particulars of his meeting with the mysterious stranger. The lady was all attention; but was as much wonder-struck as Pete himself. She had heard of spells being cast upon guns, and so had Peter—often—but then neither of them had ever known such a case, in their own experience; and although she had recipes for pickling fruit, and preserving life, and preventing various maladies, she knew of no remedy which would remove the spell from a rifle. As she could give no sage advice, she prescribed sage tea, bathing the

feet, and going to bed, and Pete submitted passively to all this—not perceiving, however, how it could possibly affect his gun.

When Pete awoke the next morning, the events which we have described appeared to him as a dream; indeed, he had been dreaming of them all night, and it was somewhat difficult to unravel the tangled thread of recollection, so as to separate the realities of the day from the illusions of the pillow. But resolving to know the truth, he seized his gun, and hastened to the woods. Alas! every experiment produced the same vexatious result. The gun was charmed! "No two ways about that!" It was too true to make a joke of, and the hunter stalked harmlessly through the forest.

Day after day he went forth, and returned with no better success. The very deer became sensible of his inoffensiveness, and would raise their heads, and gaze mildly at him as he passed; or throw back their antlers, and bound carelessly across his path. Day after day, and week after week, passed without bringing any change; and Pete began to feel very ridiculously. A harmless man—a fellow with a gun, that could not shoot! he could imagine no situation more miserable than his own. To walk through the woods, to see the game, to come within gun-shot of it, and yet to be unable to kill a deer, seemed to be the height of human wretchedness. He felt as if he was "the meanest kind of a white man." There was a littleness, an insignificance, attached to the idea of not being able to kill a deer, which, to Pete's mind, was downright disgrace. More than once, he was tempted to throw the gun into the river; but the excellence of the weapon, and the recollection of former exploits, restrained him; and he continued to stroll through the woods, firing now and then at a fat buck, under the hope that the charm would expire some time or other, by its own limitation; but the fat bucks continued to treat him with a familiarity amounting to contempt, and to frisk fearlessly in his path.

At length Pete bethought him of a celebrated Indian doctor, who lived at no great distance. We do not care to say much of doctors, as they are a touchy race—and shall therefore touch upon this one briefly. An Indian doctor is not necessarily a descendant of the Aborigines. The title, it is true, originates from the confidence which many of our countrymen repose in the medical skill of the Indian tribes. But to make an Indian doctor a red skin is by no means indispensable. To have been taught by a savage, to have seen one, or, at all events, to have heard of one, is all that is necessary, to enable any individual to practise this lucrative and popular branch of the healing art. Neither is any great proficiency in literature requisite; it is important only to be expert in spell-ing. Your Indian doctor is one who practises without a diploma—the only degree he exhibits, is a high degree of confidence. He neither nauseates the stomach with odious drugs, nor mars the fair proportions of nature with the sanguinary lancet. He believes in the sympathy which is supposed to exist between the body and the mind, which, like the two arms of a syphon, always preserve a corresponding relation to each other; and the difference between him and the regular physician—called in the vernacular of the frontier, the marcury doctor —is that they operate at different points of the same figure—the one practising on the immaterial spirit, while the other grapples with the bones and muscles. I cannot determine which is right; but must award to the Indian doctor at least this advantage, that his art is the most widely beneficial; for while your doctor of medicine restores a lost appetite, his rival can, in addition, recover a strayed or stolen horse. If the former can bring back the faded lustre to a fair maiden's cheeks, the latter

remove the spell from a churn or a rifle. The dyspeptic and the dropsical may hie to the disciples of Rush and Wistar, but the crossed-in-love, and lack-a-daysical, find a charm in the practitioner who professes to follow nature.

To a sage of this order, did Pete disclose his misfortune, and apply for relief. The doctor examined the gun, and looked wise; and having measured the calibre of the bore, with a solemnity which was as imposing as it was unquestionably proper on so serious an occasion, directed the applicant to come again.

At the appointed time, the hunter returned, and received from the wise man two balls, one of pink, the other of a silver hue. The doctor instructed him to load his piece with one of these bullets, which he pointed out, and proceed through the woods to a certain secluded hollow, at the head of which was a spring. Here he would see a white fawn, at which he was to shoot. It would be wounded, but would escape, and he was to pursue its trail, until he found a buck, which he was to kill with the other ball. If he accomplished all this accurately, the charm would be broken; but success would depend upon his having faith, keeping up his courage, and firing with precision.

Pete, who was well acquainted with all the localities, carefully pursued the route which had been indicated, treading lightly along, sometimes elated with the prospect of speedily breaking the spell, and restoring his beloved gun to usefulness and respectability—sometimes doubting the skill of the doctor—admiring the occult knowledge of men who could charm and uncharm deadly weapons—and ashamed alternatively of his doubts and his belief. At length he reached the lonely glen; and his heart bounded with delight, as he beheld the white fawn quietly grazing by the fountain. The ground was open, and he was unable to get within his usual distance, before the fawn raised her delicate head, looked timidly around, and snuffed the breeze, as if conscious of the approach of danger. Pete trembled with excitement —his heart palpitated. It was a long shot and a bad chance—but he could not advance a step further, without danger of starting the game—and Brown Bess could carry a ball farther than that, with fatal effect.

"Luck's a lord," said he, as he drew the gun up to his face, took a deliberate aim, and pulled the trigger. The fawn bounded aloft at the report, and then darted away through the brush, while the hunter hastened to examine the signs. To his great joy he found the blood profusely scattered; and now flushed with the confidence of success, he stoutly rammed down the other ball, and pursued the trail of the wounded fawn. Long did he trace the crimson drops upon the snow, without beholding the promised victim. Hill after hill he climbed, vale after vale he passed— searching every thicket with penetrating eyes; and he was about to renounce the chase, the wizard, and the gun, when lo! —directly in his path, stood a noble buck, with numerous antlers branching over his fine head!

"Aha! my jolly fellow! I've found you at last!" exclaimed the delighted hunter, "you are the very chap I've been looking after. Your blood shall wipe off the disgrace from my charming Bess, that never hung fire, burned priming, nor missed the mark in her born days, till that vile abominable varment blowed his brimstone breath on her! Here goes—"

He shot the buck. The spell was broken —Brown Bess was restored to favour, and Pete Featherton never again wanted venison.

UNTO SUCH GLORY

A COMEDY IN ONE ACT

by Paul Green

Perhaps the best-known dramatic work of Paul Green is concerned with the Negro sharecroppers of his native North Carolina. Certainly he has presented their superstitions, prejudices, and visions with admirable insight. But he is equally adept at interpreting the life of the white farmers of his state. His plays often depend for their impact upon a combination of earthy simplicity and fundamentalist religion. Interesting use is made in "Unto Such Glory" of the literal acceptance of biblical imagery, and the influence of the preacher is marked until it is discovered that he is motivated by sexual desire more than by genuine religious ecstasy. Green developed a similar theme in greater detail in the full-length drama entitled "The Field God." "Unto Such Glory" was collected with other plays in the volume In the Valley and Other Carolina Plays *(1928).*

CHARACTERS

BROTHER SIMPKINS, *an itinerant revivalist preacher*
WALT ENNIS, *a young farmer*
LANIE ENNIS, *his wife*
JODIE MAYNARD, *her brother*
SUT MAYNARD, *her father*

TIME

The latter part of the nineteenth century

PLACE

The southern part of the United States

In the rural sections of the South the people begin to think about the Lord when late July and August come. Crops are laid by—corn hilled and cotton ploughed for the last time, even tobacco-curing held in abeyance—and every little church from Bethel to Shiloh is rocked for a week by the fighting paradox of God and the Devil. Then it is that the way of the transgressor grows hard. Little children are herded terrified into the fold, the drunkard denies his dram, the profane man softens his speech, and shy, tough-knotted old fellows with land lawsuits greet each other gently as "Brother." Then too the way of the chicken grows hard. He is slaughtered by the thousands and his plucked feathers blow heavenward by the impersonal winds. The smoke-house suffers its onslaughts, the bin is visited and revisited, the pig is snatched and barbecued, the watermelon and "mushmelon" patches are devastated. The tired housewife sings "Blessed be the name," sweats and grows sick before a red-hot stove, and the farmer's last dollar is pleaded forth from its hiding place. For now it is that the preachers are abroad in the land. And now too the city cousins and their kin come down like Assyrian kings to eat and talk of the pleasures of farming and the open air—and to attend "big-meeting." Through it all the providing farmer moves quiet and subdued, comforted by the presence of the men of God and vaguely hoping to profit somehow thereby. He listens to the blarney of the city-bred, his impassive face concealing the superiority he knows is his. To the preachers he is all respect and gentleness. And bless God, even when he suspects their thievery and quackery, he comforts himself that the True Message can never be contaminated by scurvy containers—a metaphysic St. Thomas himself could not surpass. And accordingly under all pomp and circumstance his faith remains. There are exceptions, of course—for instance one of the farmers depicted in this piece. But all glory

---

sional, amateur, motion pictures, recitations, public reading, radio and television broadcasting and the rights of translation into foreign languages are strictly reserved. Amateurs may produce this play upon payment of a royalty of Five Dollars for each performance one week before the play is to be given to Samuel French, Inc., at 25 W. 45th St., New York 36, N.Y., or 7623 Sunset Blvd., Hollywood 46, Calif., or if in Canada to Samuel French (Canada) Ltd., 27 Grenville St., Toronto, Ont., Canada. Reprinted by permission of the author and of Samuel French.

to the general type, for I doubt that even in the time of *Piers the Plowman* when the land was likewise overrun by heavenly grafters was the burden borne more dutifully and stoically. But wonderful cures were wrought then and wonderful cures are wrought now, and the response now as then remains a general and irrational "hallelujah." And these gentlemen go their rounds and will go. Let them. They saved me and they may save others.—*Preachers thin and wan and holy; preachers fat, oily and unctuous; preachers dashing and handsome crying out with pleasurable anguish the story of their red-light days—God wot;—preachers Hebraic, awful and thundering. They will go their way in the service of imagination and the Lord. Thanks be. . . . Where is he who used to leave his photograph to delight the daughters?—it meets me now from many a country mantelpiece.—He is still doing the Lord's work and passing the plate to pay the photographers. And he who was wont in the old days to leave more real and distressing images of himself behind? He too pursues his labors to the glory and profit of God. All honor to them and their brethering. Let us continue to feed and clothe them and leave the subtlety of an ethic to furnish them forth to action. For fairies and fierce convictions are salty savor to a land.*

So it is as the curtain rises on Lanie Ennis sweating up supper on a hot August evening for a carnivorous man of God. She is a rather pretty young country woman, neatly and plainly dressed, with large babyish blue eyes and a quick bird-like step. From behind a door on the left come desultory sounds of a booming voice lifted in exclamations, snatches of song and hallelujahing. Lanie stands listening a moment with a steaming dish of food in her hands. She places the food on the table and waits, abstractedly fingering the chain of a locket around her throat.

Voice [*Within*]. Hallelujah, hallelujah.
Lanie [*Softly*]. Hallelujah! [*The sound of her own voice seems to wake her from her abstraction and she moves swiftly through an open door at the right onto the porch and calls out through the darkness.*] Come on to supper, Walt!
A Voice [*Near at hand, outside*]. I'm coming.
[LANIE *turns back into the room and goes into the kitchen at the rear.* WALT *enters at the right, carrying a bucket. He is a hot sunburned young farmer below medium height, slender and wiry and with a steel-like hardness about him.*]
Walt. Got any slops for the pigs, Lanie?
Lanie. There's some pot liquor there by the stove. [*He disappears into the kitchen. The voice at the left is quiet and* LANIE *goes to the door and calls.*] Supper's about ready, Brother Simpkins.
Voice. Thankee, sister, thankee. . . .
Walt [*Reappearing with his bucket*]. How long till you're ready to eat?
Lanie. Soon as the coffee boils.
Walt. I'll be back in a minute then. [*He starts out at the right and then stops.*] Won't your Brother Simpkins be too late for service?
Lanie [*Working rapidly about the table*]. Brother Jackson preaches first tonight.
Walt. Ah! [*He goes out, but immediately returns and sits down in a chair near the door.*]
Lanie. Ain't you going to feed the pigs?
Walt. Are you going to the church tonight?
Lanie [*Defensively*]. I can't miss the last meeting, Walt.
Brother Simpkins [*Within*]. Hallelujah, hallelujah, glory! [*He is heard singing and clapping his hands.*]
Walt. Makes more racket than usual.
Lanie [*Quickly*]. He's thinking of certain sinners that'll not be saved when the

meeting ends. [*With a catch in her voice.*] Might be singing with you in his mind, Walt.

Walt. Better change his tune then.

Lanie. Oh, Walt!

Walt. Yeh and he had.

Lanie. All of them preachers and prayers ain't made any impression on you.

Walt. Made an impression on my smokehouse all right. Been feeding Brother Simpkins for the last week. That's an eating white man, I'm here to tell you.

Lanie. We'd ought to count it a privilege to feed him, a chosen disciple of God. [WALT *sits looking at the floor, pondering.*] Ain't you going tonight?

Walt. No.

[BROTHER SIMPKINS *is heard washing himself in a basin, splashing and blowing through his hands.*]

Lanie. All the evening I been thinking about that song—"Why not tonight?" [*Chanting in a childlike voice.*]

> Tomorrow's sun may never rise,
> To bless thy long deluded sight

Walt. Don't worry about me.

Lanie. I can't help it.

Walt. And I'm worried about a heap of other folks myself. [*He gives* LANIE *a sharp look.*]

Lanie. You're about the only sinner in the neighborhood not saved.

Walt. No, your daddy'll keep me company.

Lanie. He got saved this evening, and went home shouting.

Walt. Good gracious!

Lanie. He did, Walt. And he stood up in the church and testified to every single mean thing he'd ever done.

Walt. He couldn't a-done that.

Lanie. Oh, Walt, tonight's the last night and won't you go?

Walt [*A bit sharply*]. You've been going enough lately for both of us.

Lanie. And two weeks ago I was lost to

God and the world and now— [*She raises her face to heaven.*]

Walt. Ah! [*He sits looking at her mournfully and then picks up his bucket and goes quickly out and down the steps.* BROTHER SIMPKINS *comes through the door at the left carrying a Bible in his hand. He is a dark bearded man of middle age, heavy-set, with a bloated ignorant face, but somewhat kindly withal. He is dressed in a thin black seersucker suit and a celluloid collar with an enormous white tie.*]

Brother Simpkins [*In a deep throaty voice, hoarse from thundering in the pulpit*]. Ah, sister, he's unworthy. Yes, I fear he is.

Lanie. I don't know—I—

Brother Simpkins [*Coming close to her*]. I've told you— [*Suddenly opening the Bible and pointing to a verse.*] Read there—it's the message again, coming another way—plain—plain. [*Reading in a low vehement voice.*] "For both he that sanctifieth and they who are sanctified are of one." [*His eyes bore into hers and he lays his hand on her shoulder.*]

Lanie. Yes, yes.

Brother Simpkins. Ah, you are sanctified—the seal is on your forehead—pure and holy. [*He bends quickly and kisses her.*]

Lanie. Oh—I—

Brother Simpkins. It is written in Corinthians, one, one and two, "They that are sanctified are called the saints." And the saints are those saved forever, sealed for the rapture, and they can do no harm.

Lanie. I know it, I feel it—

Brother Simpkins. Amen!

[WALT *comes abruptly in again with his bucket.*]

Walt. I forgot to put any meal in these slops.

[*He brings a dipper of meal from the kitchen, pours it into the bucket and stirs it.*]

Brother Simpkins. How ye tonight, Brother Ennis?

Walt. Tired—How're you?

Brother Simpkins. Bless God, I'm carrying on happy towards the Glory Land. [LANIE *moves around the table arranging supper, now and then looking at* WALT *with a puzzled expression.*]

Walt [*With sudden admiration in his voice*]. You *are* a big strong man, ain't you?

Brother Simpkins. Nothing but sinful clay. [LANIE *looks at him with undisguised admiration.* WALT'S *eyes narrow a bit.*] God gave me a big voice and a big body to use in his vineyard and I've brung him big harvest for twenty year.

Walt. He's proud of you, I bet.

Brother Simpkins [*Softly*]. Hanh— And the biggest harvest of all has been gathered here in this neighborhood these two weeks. . . .

Walt. Can you shoulder a sack of guano?

Brother Simpkins. Well, I don't know —I've never—

Walt. They don't have guano 'way off yonder where you come from, do they?

Brother Simpkins. I don't know—My work has been in the church.

Walt. You were talking about a vineyard.

Brother Simpkins [*Perplexed*]. The Lord's Vineyard.

Walt. Brother Simpkins, let me tell you something.

Brother Simpkins. Yes.

Walt. I can shoulder a sack of guano.

Lanie. Yes, he can.

Brother Simpkins. Yes.

Walt. Two hundred pounds.

Brother Simpkins. That's a right smart weight.

Walt. Yeh, it is, and that ain't all. I can shoulder it standing in a half bushel peck-measure.

Brother Simpkins [*Looking around him uncertainly.*] Yes, yes.

Walt [*Pleasantly*]. I weigh a hundred and fifteen pounds. How much do you weigh, Brother Simpkins?

Brother Simpkins. Two hundred and twenty.

Walt. A right smart weight. Hum— well, Lanie, you and Brother Simpkins better go ahead with your supper. I hear the folks starting their music over at the church. [*He gets up and goes out again with his bucket.*]

Brother Simpkins. Seemed like your husband was making fun.

Lanie. No, he wan't thinking of that.

Brother Simpkins. I fear he'll never turn from his ways. Ah, I mis-doubt it.

Lanie. We must do all we can this last night.

Brother Simpkins [*After a moment, sternly*]. No. He's refused again and again, and there's nothing to be done.

Lanie [*Nervously*]. I don't know—I've tried to get him to the meeting tonight.

Brother Simpkins. It's better for him not to be there.

Lanie. Yes—

Brother Simpkins. We'll go straight on from the church.

Lanie [*Sitting down in her chair by the table*]. Oh, I don't see how I can do it.

Brother Simpkins. It's the hand of God behind it. He's sending us forth to labor together for bringing souls to the anxious seat, and set them forth in the morning light.

Lanie [*Standing up, as he puts his arm around her*]. Yes, yes. . . .

Brother Simpkins. Like a lily of the valley, a sister of mercy. . . . [*He kisses her and strokes her hair.*] Unto such glory thou wilt go.

Lanie [*Her face shining*]. Wonderful, wonderful! It is fine there where we're going?

Brother Simpkins. Fine, fine, but sinful. The wastefulness of the rich, the pride of the haughty, the sweating and groaning of the poor and oppressed, injustice and crime, sin—sin—sin. The houses lift themselves up high to heaven, their chimneys spit dust and ashes in God's face, silk and finery, lights and crowds and moving, moving, moving down the devil's sinful road. I've stood on the streets there and cried: "Repent, repent, remember Sodom and Gomorrah!" Like them sunken cities they pay no heed—but you and me'll go back there, go back there and keep crying: "Repent!"

Lanie. Keep crying repent, and they will repent. [*Slipping out of his arms.*] Oh, but people will think hard of me, I'm afraid.

Brother Simpkins. They hadn't ought to.

Lanie. No, they can't, they won't, and me going with you, will they? [*Looking up at him suddenly.*] But I ain't told him yet—Walt, I mean.

Brother Simpkins. You mustn't tell him . . . maybe.

Lanie. But you've preached about deceiving.

Brother Simpkins. I don't know. I been thinking . . . while ago he talked funny, like he already knew something.

Lanie. You will explain everything, I know you will. There they go singing at the church.

[*Far off across the fields comes the pulsating rhythm of the meeting's song.* BROTHER SIMPKINS *raises his face in a ragged smile.*]

Brother Simpkins. Hear Brother Jackson's voice—hallelujah, amen!

Lanie [*Softly*]. Amen.

Brother Simpkins [*Moving up and down the room*]. That great old song, how they sing it! [*Listening.*] There's Sister Eason's alto, and Sister Jernigan's soprano rising to heaven in the night. Amen, amen, give 'em power, hold up Brother Jackson's arms, touch his tongue with fire, amen, amen. Let him prepare the way, for tonight I come with the power.

Lanie [*Watching him in loving terror*]. Hallelujah!

Brother Simpkins [*Joining in the faraway song with a roar*].

As I journey thro' the land, singing as I go,
Pointing souls to Calvary—to the crimson flow,
Many arrows pierce my soul—from without, within—

[*He suddenly flings out his arms, turning upon* LANIE.] Yes, tell your husband everything. He can't stand out against me, nothing can. I'll sweep on, move everything before me with you at my side.

Lanie [*Her gestures hypnotically beginning to resemble his*]. Yes, yes.

Brother Simpkins [*Singing*].

On the streets of Glory let me lift my voice,
Cares all past,
Home at last,
Ever to rejoice.

Lanie [*Joining in with a high piping voice*]. "When in valleys low I look towards the mountain height."

Brother Simpkins. Yea, yea, sealed for the rapture! [*Brokenly.*] Lanie, Lanie! [*Speaking into the air.*] Hurt not the earth, neither the sea nor the trees, till we have sealed the servants of God in their foreheads.

Lanie [*Chanting and staring at him wide-eyed*]. Sealed and set unto the day of redemption.

Brother Simpkins. Glory!

Lanie [*With a sharp hysterical giggle*]. Hallelujah.

Brother Simpkins [*Shouting*]. The power, the blessing coming down!

Lanie [*Moaning*]. I can't stand it no more. I can't stand it—

Brother Simpkins. Pour out, pour it out on us, God. Let it come down like buckets of water, let it come down, let it come down drenching us, flooding us.

Lanie [*Springing up and down in the room, her face set in a sort of mask*]. Let it come down, let it come down—give it to me, give it to me—give—give—give—

Brother Simpkins [*Prancing back and forth as he throws his hands above his head*]. Glory—glory—glory—glory. Give it to us—gloryglorygloryglory-rrry. [*His words pass into a frenzy of senseless sounds.*] Meeny-meeny-meeny-eeny-eeny—yari-yari-yari-hi-hi-hi-ee-ee-ee-ee— [*He shudders, closes his eyes, swings his head from side to side, his lips fluttering in a flood of sound.*] Hic-y-hic-y-hic-hree-hree—whizzem-whizzem—loki-loki—

Lanie [*Fluttering towards him and stretching out her arms before her*]. Manny-yan-manny-yan—kari-kari—manny-yan-yan-manny-yan-yan. [*She dances into his arms, and wrapped in each other's embrace they dance up and down, skip back and forth, all the while with their faces lifted towards the sky as if peering directly at a blinding light.*]

Brother Simpkins. Hah-hah-hah.

Lanie [*Laughing in oblivion*]. Hee-hee-hee.

[BROTHER SIMPKINS *closes his eyes, a smile spreads over his face, and he falls to whistling a thumping barbaric tune to which their heels click rhythmically against the floor. LANIE closes her eyes and abandons herself to him. They whirl up and down the floor faster and faster. Now and then the whistled tune is punctuated by a shout or scream.*]

Brother Simpkins [*With a blood-curdling yell*]. Yee-ee-ee-h!

Lanie. Glory—glory—glorrrryyyrryy-rryy!

[*Presently* WALT *rushes in at the right and stops thunderstruck.*]

Walt [*Shouting*]. Heigh, you! Lord have mercy! Stop that!

Brother Simpkins. Give it—give it—give it—

Walt. Great God A'mighty!

Brother Simpkins. The blessing—the blessing—it's come—it's here—here—

Lanie. Hallelujah—hallelujah!

Brother Simpkins. Hallelujah—glory—hoofey-beigh—hoofey-beigh—loki-loki—

Walt [*Running up and snatching* LANIE *from him.*] Stop it, stop it! [*He spins* LANIE *around and shakes her like a rag.*]

Brother Simpkins [*Slapping himself as if trying to beat off a spell*]. Brother Ennis, Brother Ennis!

Walt. Don't "Brother Ennis" me. [*He flings* LANIE *down in a chair by the table.*] I thought you'd done enough of that unknown tongue business at the church without doing it here.

Lanie. Everything looks so purty. Walt, Walt, I love everybody. Your face is so purty. [*She springs up and throws her arms around his neck. He fights her away from him.*] Oh, I wisht you could see how purty this room is!

Walt. Have you gone plumb crazy?

[LANIE *drops into her chair and begins to cry softly, her body quivering and jerking.*]

Brother Simpkins [*Twisting and looking around him*]. I must get on to the church—we must get on.

Walt. Yeh, and I reckon so. From the sound of it there's a big outpouring over there and you'd do better to spill yours in the pulpit. [BROTHER SIMPKINS *rushes into the room at the left and reappears with a worn derby hat. He crams it on his head and stands looking down at* LANIE.]

Brother Simpkins. Sister, let's be going on.

Walt. She ain't fitten to go nowheres till she's had some supper.

Lanie [*Quavering*]. Le's all sit down and eat.

[WALT *furtively sits down, the preacher hesitates a moment and then sits to the table without removing his derby.*]

Brother Simpkins [*Regretfully*]. And this is my last supper here.

Walt. Ah!

Lanie. I'll get the coffee. [*She rises to her feet and then falls weakly back in her chair.*]

Walt. I will for you. [*He goes into the kitchen.*]

Lanie. I'm so h-happy-happy. [*Her hands writhe and twist uncontrollably in her lap.* BROTHER SIMPKINS *bends over and strokes her head, and she suddenly grasps his hand and covers it with crazy, hysterical kisses.*]

Brother Simpkins. Let your tears be joyful at your deliverance.

Lanie [*Shivering*]. Yes, yes.

Brother Simpkins. Now you can tell him— [*Turning from the table.*] Listen, listen, a second day of Pentecost—but wait —wait, when I get there— [*Lifting up his eyes.*] And when the day of Pentecost was fully come, they were all with one accord in one place. And suddenly there came a sound from heaven as of a rushing mighty wind, and it filled all the house where they were sitting. And there appeared unto them cloven tongues like as of fire and it sat upon each of them. [*Raising his voice.*] Yea, yea, hear my prayer! [WALT *comes in with the coffee.*] Let me bring the wind to them and fetch tongues of fire for them when I do come. Go on, go on, Brother Jackson,—make ready— make ready! [*Looking through the door at the right.*] I can almost see the fire now.

Walt [*Looking out*]. What's that— where?

Brother Simpkins. The fire from heaven!

Walt [*Pouring out the coffee*]. Let's eat something.

Brother Simpkins [*Bowing his head*]. Now may— [*He remembers his hat and snatches it off*].

Walt [*His face suddenly hard*]. Lemme ask the blessing.

Brother Simpkins. You! . . . Hallelujah

. . . amen! He's beginning to yield, Sister Lanie, he's—

Walt. Bow your heads.

Brother Simpkins. Him, Sister Lanie! It's him bowing his head.

Walt [*With sudden roughness*].

> Bless the bread and damn the meat,
> Great God, let's eat!

[*He falls to eating.*]

Brother Simpkins [*Starting back*]. Blasphemy! [WALT *goes on eating, watching the two of them now with a hard face.*]

Walt. Have some bread, Brother Simpkins.

Brother Simpkins. Ah! [*He bows his head in inaudible prayer a moment and then begins to eat.*]

Walt. Help yourself, Lanie.

Lanie. I can't eat a thing. [*She drops her head weeping on the table.*]

Brother Simpkins. A man blessed with such a wife as yours, and such blasphemy!

Walt. Yeh, two weeks ago there wan't no better wife nowhere.

Brother Simpkins. Two weeks ago!

Lanie. No, I was lost then, Walt.

Brother Simpkins. Yes, lost. Now look into her face and see the hand of God. Today she was consecrated and sanctified.

Walt. Was! Didn't look like it while ago. You two cutting up.

Lanie. Oh, Walt, everything is specially peaceful and happy now. Used to I'd sit here and be so lonesome, the house all so quiet and you off in the field. There was a great emptiness in here around my heart. Now I'm full, full. I feel like crying all the time, I'm so happy.

Brother Simpkins. Bless God! You hear her, Brother.

Lanie. I feel like I'll never be lonesome any more, never any more. [WALT *bends his head over his plate eating heavily and saying nothing. There is a step on the porch at the right and* JODIE, *a country boy about sixteen years old, comes in carrying a rope in his hand.*]

Jodie. You all seen Pa?

Walt. No. Ain't he at the church?

Jodie. He ain't.

Brother Simpkins. Is that Brother Sut Maynard's boy?

Jodie. Yessir. [*He eyes the preacher rather boldly.*]

Brother Simpkins. In all my twenty years of toiling in the vineyard I ain't seen a happier man than your Pa was today when the power come on him.

Jodie. Wish you'd tell me where he is now. Muh's just about crazy.

Brother Simpkins. No doubt he's in some quiet place offering up prayers on bended knee.

Jodie. Reckon his knees are bended, but I'm misdoubtful about the prayers.

Walt. When'd you see him last?

Jodie. About sunset. [*Bursting out.*] He's been like a wild man ever since he got home this evening from the church. I started off to get the cow in the pasture a while ago, and Muh run out and said Pa was gone. We couldn't find him nowhere. I been all down in the swamp but I can't find him.

Walt. I spect he's at the church then. And who would a-thought it?

Jodie. He come home from church talking them old unknown tongues, and then he took off near-about all his clothes and got down on his all-fours and run about the house like a dog.

Brother Simpkins. He's humbling himself. Tomorrow he'll come out clothed in his right mind and praising God.

Jodie [*Almost whimpering*]. He's run mad or something.

Walt. You know how your Pa is, Jodie. When he gets a thing he gets it good.

Lanie [*Sharply*]. It's what'll keep Pa's soul out of the clutches of the old Bad Boy.

Brother Simpkins [*With a fond look*]. Ah, Sister. [*To* JODIE.] Go home,—no, go to the church and pray for your father.

Jodie. Something bad has happened to him?

Brother Simpkins. Can't nothing happen to him. He's one of the consecrated now. I told him what to do to test his faith. Romans eight, twenty-eight.

Jodie. Pa's been talking about that man in the Bible that went around on his all-fours.

Brother Simpkins [*His mouth full of food*]. Nebuchadnezzar. But afterwards he returned to the fold a wiser and a better man. Likewise your father.

Jodie. Ma says she bets he's off eating grass like a cow somewhere, and he out in the damp without his shoes.

Brother Simpkins. He needs no shoes to protect him.

Jodie [*Pleadingly*]. Walt, come help me ketch him.

Walt [*Jumping up from the table*]. Yeh, I'll go. [*He starts out through the door, looks back at Lanie and the preacher and hesitates.*]

Jodie. Come on, he'll mind you if we find him.

Walt [*Coming back to the table*]. No, I can't go now, Jodie. I'm needed here.

Jodie. Can't you come, Walt?

Walt. Not tonight. If you ain't found him in the morning, I'll help you. I just can't leave here tonight.

Jodie. If your folks was in such a fix I'd help you. [JODIE *suddenly goes off in a huff.*]

Lanie. I'm glad you didn't go, Walt.

Walt. Yah.

Lanie. Now tell him, Brother Simpkins, please do.

Brother Simpkins. No, you'd better tell it like the message come to you. [LANIE *looks down and says nothing.*]

Walt. Well, go ahead. [*He waits and they are silent.*] But I already know what you're gonna tell.

Lanie. Then I won't have to tell it?

Walt. Brother Simpkins spoke about it while ago. And I reckon I got eyes to see what I saw when I come in.

Brother Simpkins [*Hurriedly*]. I don't remember it.

Lanie. Are you willing to it, Walt?

Walt. I ain't willing, but I don't see what I can do about it.

Brother Simpkins. No, no, there's nothing you can do about it. We can't go against the will of the almighty.

Lanie. It'll be hard, I know, but it's all come so clear to me. And Brother Simpkins has had a vision from above.

Walt. I know it. No, I ain't willing, but the whole country's turned upside down from Rocky Mount to Fayetteville, and I can't blame you entirely. [*Nodding his head at* BROTHER SIMPKINS.] He's the one to be blamed most.

Lanie. Both of us have received the command.

Walt. I thought you had more sense, Lanie, than to get all wropped up in such stuff.

Lanie. I don't know how you'll get along at first; I suppose after while you'll get used to it.

Walt. I betcha Sut Maynard'll be back cussing and chewing tobacco as bad as ever in a month. And you'll soon forget it all too, Lanie.

Lanie. No, I won't, no I won't. I'd rather die.

Brother Simpkins. Never. She's stamped and sealed, and the mark will never pass away.

Lanie. Reckon you'll mind after a month or two, Walt?

Walt. It'll all be passed out of my mind. [BROTHER SIMPKINS *smiles broadly and looks at* LANIE *happily.*]

Brother Simpkins. Hallelujah.

Lanie. Brother Simpkins said at first you might try to get the law on him.

Walt [*Staring at her*]. Law on him— not me. I got more sense than that.

Brother Simpkins. Amen!

Lanie [*Piteously*]. I got everything fixed where you can find it.

Walt. Hanh?

Lanie. And be sure to feed the chickens regular. And don't you let the flowers dry up. [*Suddenly wringing her hands.*] Oh, I don't see how you can get along without me.

Walt. Get along without you?

Lanie. I know it'll be lonesome for you.

Walt. I ain't going to be here by myself.

Lanie. Would you get somebody else to come and stay with you? No, no, I couldn't let you do that.

Walt [*Bounding out of his chair*]. You mean you're thinking of going away?

Lanie. Yes, yes, I got to go off and leave you.

Walt. Lanie!

Lanie [*Wretchedly*]. I can't help it. It's got to be done.

Walt [*Sitting down with a gasp*]. Where you going?

Lanie [*Beginning to sob*]. Oh, way off somewheres.

Walt [*To* BROTHER SIMPKINS]. Are you mixed up in her wild ideas about leaving?

Brother Simpkins. It's a power beyond either of us.

Walt. What power?

Brother Simpkins [*Gesturing*]. Up there.

Walt. And what does the power up there say?

Brother Simpkins. That she shall go out and labor in the vineyard with me.

Walt [*Springing out of his chair again*]. Great God! I thought she was talking about all that getting sanctified and filled with tongues. [*He moves towards the preacher who pushes himself behind his chair.*] You old goat, I'll—

Brother Simpkins. Ask her, ask her about it.

Walt. Lanie, what'n the world you mean by all this?

Lanie. I can't help it, I can't help it. Don't blame me.

Walt. I ain't blaming you completely.

Lanie. I been feeling the call all the week to do something, to go out and work and help spread the message. It's got stronger all the time. Oh, I've just got to go.

Walt. Has he been talking to you about it?

Lanie. He's sympathized with me all the time.

Walt [*Gripping his chair*]. 'Y God, I reckon so.

Lanie. Don't think he's the fault, I am. I've been having dreams about it, and several times a voice has come to me telling me I had to give up home and everything— Yes, it said I'd have to give up you—and go forth.

Walt. Did that voice say for you to go with him?

Lanie [*Weeping*]. Yes, It said, "Lanie Ennis, go with Brother Simpkins."

Walt [*Looking helplessly around him a moment and then sitting down in his chair*]. What else did it say?

Lanie. That's about all it said to me. But I might have still stayed with you if it hadn't a-been for the vision.

Walt. What did the vision say?

Lanie. He's the one had it; he'll tell you. It was so beautiful. He'll tell you.

Walt. I ain't interested in what he had, nor how beautiful. If you didn't have no vision, why you want to put dependence in his?

Brother Simpkins. What you do is done at the call of your own sinful self, the movement of man. What I do is in obedience to a higher power. Without him I am nothing; with him I am everything.

Walt. Then why you want her if he's everything to you?

Brother Simpkins. He will work with me through her.

Walt. Will he?

Brother Simpkins. He will—glory!

Walt [*Suddenly turning upon* LANIE]. What's that you got around your neck?

Lanie [*Covering her throat with her hands*]. A little chain.

Walt. I been watching that. Who give it to you?

Lanie. He did.

Walt. Did God tell you to give that locket to her, Brother?

Lanie. It was so purty I thought I'd wear it.

Brother Simpkins. I asked you not to.

Walt [*Sharply*]. Thought you'd wait till you toled her off with it, did you?

Brother Simpkins [*With childish sullenness*]. You never give her nothing.

Lanie [*Plaintively*]. He don't make a lot of money the way you do, Brother Simpkins.

Walt. No, 'y God, I don't. I don't go around preaching and begging the folks and taking up collections in dishpans. By God, I ain't got that low yet. I work for my living.

Brother Simpkins [*Breaking out*]. I had the vision and I'll heed the vision. If she's willing we will go.

Walt. Are you willing, Lanie?

Lanie. There's nothing else to do. [*She buries her face in her arms weeping.*]

Brother Simpkins. Come, come, and we'll go forth to new fields, to new labors.

Walt [*Imploringly*]. Lanie, you can't go off thataway. [*Helplessly.*] You ain't got your clothes fixed.

Lanie. They're all packed in the suitcase. Brother Simpkins will take 'em up the road. We're gonna leave from the church. Oh, I can't go off and leave all this. [*She begins smoothing a pattern in the tablecloth affectionately.*] Aunt Rachel gave me that tablecloth. [*She bursts into sobs again.* WALT *looks at her in consternation,*

*beating his hands together. Presently he
stands up.*]

Walt [*Threateningly*]. Brother Simpkins, you'd better go on by yourself, and
you better go mighty quick.

Brother Simpkins [*Staring ahead of
him and booming*]. It come to me in the
night clear as the broad daytime, an angel,
the angel Gabriel. He brung a message to
me like the message of old to the prophets.
I was in that room there, he come in
through that door [*Gesturing to the left
and the right.*]—and stood with a flood
of glory around him. He spoke to me in
a loud voice and said he'd choosed one
of the fairest daughters of men to be an
aid to me on my way. [LANIE *looks at
him with shining face.*] And no sooner
had he said she was fair than I knowed it
was Sister Lanie, for they's none fairer
than her, like a pearl, like a dewdrop on
the mountain, like a diamond lost among
swine. He said stoop down and lift her up,
and she will hold up your arms in times
of trouble. Your powers will be multiplied, your labors will be fruitful under
the sun. Then to make sure I bowed my
head and asked who the chosen one was,
and he said it was her, Sister Lanie. It
was a message. And then I slept and behold she appeared to me in a dream and
said that whither thou goest I will go and
whither thou lodgest I will lodge. Then I
awoke and praised God, hallelujah! Next
morning she told me she'd had a dream
telling her to go with me. [*Glaring at*
WALT, *who sits hunched in his chair,
taken aback.*] Before the angel Gabriel
left, he told me to let no man put his
message astray. And no man can. [LANIE
*moves towards him now and takes his out-
stretched hand.*]

Walt. Lanie!

Lanie. I wish it could be different, but
it can't. I could never stay here any more.
The lonesomeness would eat my heart out.
There's something calling me off—calling

me on towards it. I don't know what it is,
but I know it's wonderful and great.

Walt [*In a low voice*]. Suppose the
vision hadn't come, Brother Simpkins,
would you a' wanted her anyhow?

Brother Simpkins. But it did come, and
that settles it for me.

Walt [*Softly*]. Does it?

Brother Simpkins. I am nothing but a
weak and empty vessel. As I am filled I am
powerful and give forth the waters of salvation in his name—hallelujah!

Lanie [*Weeping*]. Hallelujah!

Brother Simpkins [*Looking down at*
LANIE]. The gift of tongues will come
upon the multitude, the sick will be healed,
and such an outpouring of the blessing
this night as these old fields and woods
have never seen. [*He leads her towards the
door at the right.*] Listen there, listen there
at the children of the Lord.

[*The singing and shouting from the
church rise clear and strong, punctuated by high screams.*]

Lanie. Goodby, Walt, goodby. [*She
runs up to him and throws her arms
around him, weeping over him.*]

Walt [*Suddenly convulsed as if with an
electric shock*]. What's that, what's that,
what's got hold of me? [*Springing from
his chair and whirling around the room,
his eyes set like one seized with a fit.*] Turn
me loose, turn me loose!

Lanie [*Aghast*]. There's something happened to him.

Walt. [*Staring before him and beginning to talk as if to some person immediately before him.*] Who's that? Is that
you? Who? [*He answers himself in a
strange far-away voice.*] It's me, the angel
Michael.

Brother Simpkins. The power's coming
on him—hallelujah.

Lanie. Glory, glory!

Walt [*Beginning to jabber*]. Yimmy-
yam-yimmy-yam. [*He skips up and down
the floor.*] Yee-yee-yee. Yamm-yamm-

yamm. [*His voice lowers itself into a growl, like an animal mouthing something.*] Hanh—hanh-hanh-we-we-we-we—whee-ee-h!

Brother Simpkins. It's come on him like a flood. Glory, glory to God!

Lanie [*Clapping her hands*]. Glory-glory-glory!

Walt [*Stopping and speaking as if to an unseen person*]. Yes, yes, yes, I hear you. [*His voice coming out faint and funereally.*] Go towards him, come to him. [*He moves like a blind man towards the preacher.*]

Brother Simpkins. He's seeing a vision.

Walt. I see an angel with a rod and staff in his hand.

Brother Simpkins. Glory!

Lanie. He's saved.

Walt [*Speaking in the voice of the angel*]. He's a liar, he's a dirty low-down suck-egg dog. [*In his own voice.*] No, he's a servant of God. I'm willing for her to go with him. Let her go. [*With the angel's voice.*] Step up to him, choke his liver out, crucify him. [*He draws nearer the preacher.*] Oh, I see the angel Michael killing a man with a stick!

Brother Simpkins. What is it, Brother, what is it?

Walt [*In the angel's voice*]. He's a dirty scoundrel trying to ruin your wife. Scratch his eyes out. [*Shuddering and speaking in his own voice.*] No, no, I can't hurt him, don't make me hurt him. [*In the voice of the angel.*] He's led women off before, don't let him do it again. [*With the fury of a wildcat he suddenly flies on the preacher, clawing and biting him.*]

Brother Simpkins [*Screaming*]. Help! Help! Keep him off'n me, sister!

Lanie. Walt, Walt, don't you know what you're doing? [*She throws up her hands and drops in a chair. The preacher is helpless before the attack of* WALT, *who is all over him, around him and under him.*]

Walt [*On top of* BROTHER SIMPKINS *and tearing him in the face*]. I hate to do it! I hate to do it!

Brother Simpkins [*Roaring*]. Mercy! Mercy!

Walt [*Astride of the preacher as he crawls about the room squealing in pain*]. Tear him all to pieces! [*He rips the preacher's coat and shirt from him, leaving him almost bare above the waist.*]

Brother Simpkins [*Falling exhausted on the floor*]. So was the prophets persecuted before me. [*He lays himself out on the floor whimpering.*]

Walt [*Standing up presently and shaking himself as if coming out of a dream*]. Lord'a mercy, what I been doing! [*He stares at the prone figure amazed.*]

Lanie. You done beat him near-about to death.

Walt. Is that you, Brother Simpkins? Is that you on the floor there?

Brother Simpkins [*Gasping*]. Help, mercy!

Walt. Bring a towel and some water quick, Lanie, there's something happened. [LANIE *runs into the kitchen and returns with a basin of water and a towel.*]

Lanie. Oh, me, look how his face is bleeding!

Walt. It's his nose, ain't it? Worse'n a butchered yearling. [*Bending over him and bathing his face.*] Who in the world done it, Brother?

Brother Simpkins. Lemme leave this place; lemme git away.

Walt [*Pushing him down and pouring water over him*]. Did I do it? I couldn't 'a' done it.

Lanie. Yes, you did, you sailed on him like a run-mad man, a-biting and a-scratching.

Walt [*Contritely*]. Good gracious me! A sort of spell come over me—I seen a vision. It wan't my fault, don't blame me. I can't help it. It was a power from above. The angel Michael stood out all of a suddent with a pile o' glory around him and he told me what to do. He give my arm power. He come in through that door there.

Brother Simpkins [*Sitting up*]. Git me some clothes. I'm going from here.

Lanie [*Coming up to him*]. I'll help you.

Brother Simpkins [*Snarling*]. You ain't gonna help me nothing. Get back from here, you sinful creature.

Lanie. Oh, Lord have mercy! [*She begins to sob again.*]

Brother Simpkins. May a curse come on this household for so persecuting a servant of the Lord! [WALT *runs into the kitchen and returns with a bottle.*]

Walt. Here's something that'll take the burn out'n them raw places. Put some on your face. [*He shoots the bottle to him.*]

Brother Simpkins [*Knocking it from him with a shout*]. That's liniment! You're trying to kill me!

Walt. Lord, I didn't mean any harm.

[*There is a stir on the porch at the right, and old man* SUT MAYNARD *creeps in on his all-fours, dressed in an old shirt and a torn pair of drawers. A mop of gray hair hangs down over his eyes. His face is swollen, and one eye is closed. He has a rope around his neck by which* JODIE *tries to pull him back.*]

Jodie. Pa, ain't you got no shame about ye? Gracious, what you all been doing to the preacher?

Walt. We all had a spell of unknown tongues a while back. Where'd you find Sut?

Jodie. Down there in the edge of the briar patch. The yellow jackets got after him down there and I heard him hollering. Make him come on home with me, Walt.

Lanie. Pa, what ails you?

Walt. Go on home, Sut. You and the preacher ain't fitten to be seen in public.

[BROTHER SIMPKINS *sits up nursing his head in his arms.*]

Sut [*Going up to* BROTHER SIMPKINS *and whining*]. Brother Simpkins, ain't I been humble enough?

Brother Simpkins [*Growling*]. I dunno—

Sut. You told me to go a day and night. I can't do it—

Brother Simpkins. Go on and do what you want to.

Sut. I'm a' old man and I can't stand much of the night air. [*He waits and the preacher makes no reply.*]

Jodie. No, he can't.

Sut. I done suffered my share. About a hundred of them yellow jackets stung me.

Brother Simpkins [*Angrily*]. I wisht a thousand of 'em had popped their tails into you.

Sut. Hanh?

Jodie. Now you see. [*Looking around the room.*] I couldn't do a thing with him till I'd put the rope around his neck. Then he made me drive him up the road here to see the preacher.

Sut. Brother Simpkins, I done been humbled in the dirt. Nebusadnezzar didn't suffer like me. Lemme quit now.

Brother Simpkins. Quit then. [*Flinging out his arms.*] Damn all of you, damn all of you!

Lanie. Lord 'a' mercy!

Jodie. He's gone to cussing.

Sut [*Rearing himself up on his haunches*]. Hanh? What you say?

Walt. Knowed he's a cussing man and a humbug. Sut, he's been trying to steal Lanie from me and get her to run off with him.

Brother Simpkins [*Staggering to his feet*]. Let me get some clothes. I'm going to the church.

Sut [*Jerking loose from* JODIE]. Are you that kind of man, are you, suh?

Walt. A vision come to us here in the

room and a' angel said he was a low suck-egg dog.

Sut [*Running around the room looking for a weapon*]. And they stung me till my eye's plumb closed. [*He trots into the kitchen.*]

Walt [*Going up to* LANIE *and snatching the locket from her neck*]. Here's your little purty, mister preacher. [*He throws it to him.*]

Sut [*Coming through the kitchen door with a hunk of wood in his hand and squealing*]. Lemme get to that there devil and I'll fix him.

Brother Simpkins [*Yelling*]. Keep that man off!

Walt. Go to him, Sut. [SUT *makes a dash for the preacher, who flees through the door at the right and into the darkness, trying to hold up the shreds of his trousers as he goes.*]

Sut. Come on, Jodie, come on. We'll catch him and beat hell out'n him. [*Old* SUT *dashes out after the preacher, the rope dangling behind.*]

Jodie. Run him down. [*He follows after, yelling in pursuit.*]

Walt [*Standing in the door*]. Sic him, boys! sic him! [*They are heard running and shouting down the road.* LANIE *rocks herself back and forth in a storm of grief. After a moment* WALT *returns to the table.*] They'll never catch that man. He'll be in Benson in twenty minutes.

Lanie. Oh Lordy, Lordy. . . .

Walt. You want some hot coffee. [*She makes no answer.*] All right then. [*He pours himself a cup and sips it from the saucer slowly.*] Don't you cry. I'll get you a locket a whole heap purtier'n that one— [*But* LANIE *rocks on.*]

V

BURIED TREASURE

Ever since wealth took the form of bullion or gold and silver coin, man has been fascinated by legends of buried money. Sometimes the burial was accidental, as when treasure ships foundered on some reef of the Spanish Main or when caravans of precious metals were dispersed by aborigines ignorant of their value. But in other instances pirates, freebooters, and highwaymen, suddenly burdened with more tangible wealth than they could comfortably use, saw fit to hide their stolen property in caves or forests. Even today, many years since the buccaneers themselves have disappeared, the names of Sir Henry Morgan, Captain Kidd, Blackbeard, and Jean Lafitte remain alive, and men still hope to stumble upon the hiding places where they cached their treasures. Hardly a year passes without at least one expedition being fitted out to explore the spot where, according to tradition, a galleon or frigate took its cargo of jewels and coin to Davy Jones's locker, and newspaper stories about deposits of money supposedly left by the highwaymen of the western and southern states are perennial. The more remote the place and the more unrewarding past efforts have been, the more durable seems to be the legend of buried treasure. Spanish America is particularly rich in these stories, probably because of the original Spanish intention to seek for gold and precious stones in the New World and also because of the very real treasures which the conquistadores brought back to Aragon and Castile. The storytellers of the Southwest, J. Frank Dobie conspicuous among them, have given ample space to the tales still linked with mountain and canyon and mesa. The Seven Cities of Cibola remain as fabulous today as they did when Cabeza de Vaca first heard of them, although generations of men have discovered that the real wealth of the Southwest lies in oil and cattle and citrus crops. But prospectors will continue to be deluded by mica and iron pyrites, and rumors of buried treasure will continue to tempt men into a more exciting life than everyday routine can afford.

THE GOLD-BUG

by Edgar Allan Poe

"The Gold-Bug," published originally in the Dollar Newspaper *in 1843, is probably the most celebrated of all stories dealing with buried treasure. Several elements combine to assure its success: Poe's mastery of suspense, his careful preparation of the climax, his literary style, and his skillful fusion of atmosphere and action. The hero, Legrand, erudite and intellectual, provides a sharp contrast to the naïve Negro servant, Jupiter. It is worth noting that Poe's interest in cryptograms led him to make the interpretation of the written clue more important than the finding of the treasure itself. Even though the wealth which is suddenly revealed is supposed to exceed a million dollars in value, it seems unimportant in comparison with the processes of deduction which led to its discovery. In Poe's tales of ratiocination it is always the analysis of the situation which holds the reader's attention. Poe increased the effect of this tale by throwing an air of mystery about the proceedings, by attributing the burying of the treasure to the notorious Captain Kidd, and by placing the most important part of the action at night in a desolate location.*

What ho! what ho! this fellow is dancing mad!
He hath been bitten by the Tarantula.
—*All in the Wrong*

Many years ago, I contracted an intimacy with a Mr. William Legrand. He was of an ancient Huguenot family, and had once been wealthy; but a series of misfortunes had reduced him to want. To avoid the mortification consequent upon his disasters, he left New Orleans, the city of his forefathers, and took up his residence at Sullivan's Island, near Charleston, South Carolina.

This island is a very singular one. It consists of little else than the sea sand, and is about three miles long. Its breadth at no point exceeds a quarter of a mile. It is separated from the mainland by a scarcely perceptible creek, oozing its way through a wilderness of reeds and slime, a favorite resort of the marsh-hen. The vegetation, as might be supposed, is scant, or at least dwarfish. No trees of any magnitude are to be seen. Near the western extremity, where Fort Moultrie stands, and where are some miserable frame buildings, tenanted, during summer, by the fugitives from Charleston dust and fever, may be found, indeed, the bristly palmetto; but the whole island, with the exception of this western point, and a line of hard, white beach on the sea-coast, is covered with a dense undergrowth of the sweet myrtle so much prized by the horticulturists of England. The shrub here often attains the height of fifteen or twenty feet, and forms an almost impenetrable coppice, burthening the air with its fragrance.

In the inmost recesses of this coppice, not far from the eastern or more remote end of the island, Legrand had built himself a small hut, which he occupied when I first, by mere accident, made his acquaintance. This soon ripened into friendship—for there was much in the recluse to excite interest and esteem. I found him well educated, with unusual powers of mind, but infected with misanthropy, and subject to perverse moods of alternate enthusiasm and melancholy. He had with him many books, but rarely employed them. His chief amusements were gunning and fishing, or sauntering along the beach and through the myrtles, in quest of shells or entomological specimens—his collection of the latter might have been envied by a Swammerdamm. In these excursions he was usually accompanied by an old Negro, called Jupiter, who had been manumitted before the reverses of the family, but who could be induced, neither by threats nor by promises, to abandon what he considered his right of attendance upon the footsteps of his young "Massa Will." It is not improbable that the relatives of Legrand, conceiving him to be somewhat unsettled in intellect, had contrived to instil this obstinacy into Jupiter, with a view to the supervision and guardianship of the wanderer.

The winters in the latitude of Sullivan's Island are seldom very severe, and in the fall of the year it is a rare event indeed when a fire is considered necessary. About the middle of October, 18—, there occurred, however, a day of remarkable chilliness. Just before sunset I scrambled my way through the evergreens to the hut of my friend, whom I had not visited for several weeks—my residence being, at that time, in Charleston, a distance of

nine miles from the island, while the facilities of passage and re-passage were very far behind those of the present day. Upon reaching the hut I rapped, as was my custom, and getting no reply, sought for the key where I knew it was secreted, unlocked the door, and went in. A fine fire was blazing upon the hearth. It was a novelty, and by no means an ungrateful one. I threw off an overcoat, took an arm-chair by the crackling logs, and awaited patiently the arrival of my hosts.

Soon after dark they arrived, and gave me a most cordial welcome. Jupiter, grinning from ear to ear, bustled about to prepare some marsh-hens for supper. Legrand was in one of his fits—how else shall I term them?—of enthusiasm. He had found an unknown bivalve, forming a new genus, and, more than this, he had hunted down and secured, with Jupiter's assistance, a *scarabaeus* which he believed to be totally new, but in respect to which he wished to have my opinion on the morrow.

"And why not to-night?" I asked, rubbing my hands over the blaze, and wishing the whole tribe of *scarabaei* at the devil.

"Ah, if I had only known you were here!" said Legrand, "but it's so long since I saw you; and how could I foresee that you would pay me a visit this very night of all others? As I was coming home I met Lieutenant G——, from the fort, and, very foolishly, I lent him the bug; so it will be impossible for you to see it until the morning. Stay here to-night, and I will send Jup down for it at sunrise. It is the loveliest thing in creation!"

"What?—sunrise?"

"Nonsense! no!—the bug. It is of a brilliant gold color—about the size of a large hickory-nut—with two jet black spots near one extremity of the back, and another, somewhat longer, at the other. The *antennae* are—"

"Dey aint *no* tin in him, Massa Will, I keep a tellin' on you," here interrupted

Jupiter; "de bug is a goole-bug, solid, ebery bit of him, inside and all, sep him wing—neber feel half so hebby a bug in my life."

"Well, suppose it is, Jup," replied Legrand, somewhat more earnestly, it seemed to me, than the case demanded; "is that any reason for your letting the birds burn? The color"—here he turned to me —"is really almost enough to warrant Jupiter's idea. You never saw a more brilliant metallic lustre than the scales emit— but of this you cannot judge till to-morrow. In the meantime I can give you some idea of the shape." Saying this, he seated himself at a small table, on which were a pen and ink, but no paper. He looked for some in a drawer, but found none.

"Never mind," he said at length, "this will answer"; and he drew from his waist-coat pocket a scrap of what I took to be very dirty foolscap, and made upon it a rough drawing with the pen. While he did this, I retained my seat by the fire, for I was still chilly. When the design was complete, he handed it to me without rising. As I received it, a loud growl was heard, succeeded by a scratching at the door. Jupiter opened it, and a large Newfoundland, belonging to Legrand, rushed in, leaped upon my shoulders, and loaded me with caresses; for I had shown him much attention during previous visits. When his gambols were over, I looked at the paper, and, to speak the truth, found myself not a little puzzled at what my friend had depicted.

"Well!" I said, after contemplating it for some minutes, "this *is* a strange *scarabaeus*, I must confess; new to me; never saw any thing like it before—unless it was a skull, or a death's-head, which it more nearly resembles than any thing else that has come under *my* observation."

"A death's-head!" echoed Legrand. "Oh —yes—well, it has something of that ap-pearance upon paper, no doubt. The two upper black spots look like eyes, eh? and the longer one at the bottom like a mouth —and then the shape of the whole is oval."

"Perhaps so," said I; "but, Legrand, I fear you are no artist. I must wait until I see the beetle itself, if I am to form any idea of its personal appearance."

"Well, I don't know," said he, a little nettled, "I draw tolerably—*should* do it at least—have had good masters, and flatter myself that I am not quite a blockhead."

"But, my dear fellow, you are joking then," said I, "this is a very passable *skull* —indeed, I may say that it is a very *excellent* skull, according to the vulgar notions about such specimens of physiology—and your *scarabaeus* must be the queerest *scarabaeus* in the world if it resembles it. Why, we may get up a very thrilling bit of superstition upon this hint. I presume you will call the bug *scarabaeus caput hominis,* or something of that kind—there are many similar titles in the Natural Histories. But where are the *antennae* you spoke of?"

"The *antennae!*" said Legrand, who seemed to be getting unaccountably warm upon the subject; "I am sure you must see the *antennae*. I made them as distinct as they are in the original insect, and I presume that is sufficient."

"Well, well," I said, "perhaps you have —still I don't see them"; and I handed him the paper without additional remark, not wishing to ruffle his temper; but I was much surprised at the turn affairs had taken; his ill humor puzzled me—and, as for the drawing of the beetle, there were positively *no antennae* visible, and the whole *did* bear a very close resemblance to the ordinary cuts of a death's-head.

He received the paper very peevishly, and was about to crumple it, apparently to throw it in the fire, when a casual glance at the design seemed suddenly to rivet his attention. In an instant his face grew violently red—in another as excessively pale.

For some minutes he continued to scrutinize the drawing minutely where he sat. At length he arose, took a candle from the table, and proceeded to seat himself upon a sea-chest in the farthest corner of the room. Here again he made an anxious examination of the paper; turning it in all directions. He said nothing, however, and his conduct greatly astonished me; yet I thought it prudent not to exacerbate the growing moodiness of his temper by any comment. Presently he took from his coat-pocket a wallet, placed the paper carefully in it, and deposited both in a writing-desk, which he locked. He now grew more composed in his demeanor; but his original air of enthusiasm had quite disappeared. Yet he seemed not so much sulky as abstracted. As the evening wore away he became more and more absorbed in revery, from which no sallies of mine could arouse him. It had been my intention to pass the night at the hut, as I had frequently done before, but, seeing my host in this mood, I deemed it proper to take leave. He did not press me to remain, but, as I departed, he shook my hand with even more than his usual cordiality.

It was about a month after this (and during the interval I had seen nothing of Legrand) when I received a visit, at Charleston, from his man, Jupiter. I had never seen the good old Negro look so dispirited, and I feared that some serious disaster had befallen my friend.

"Well, Jup," said I, "what is the matter now?—how is your master?"

"Why, to speak de troof, massa, him not so berry well as mought be."

"Not well! I am truly sorry to hear it. What does he complain of?"

"Dar! dat's it!—him neber 'plain of notin'—but him berry sick for all dat."

"*Very* sick, Jupiter!—why didn't you say so at once? Is he confined to bed?"

"No, dat he aint!—he aint 'fin'd nowhar —dat's just whar de shoe pinch—my mind is got to be berry hebby 'bout poor Massa Will."

"Jupiter, I should like to understand what it is you are talking about. You say your master is sick. Hasn't he told you what ails him?"

"Why, massa, 'taint worf while for to git mad about de matter—Massa Will say noffin at all aint de matter wid him—but den what make him go about looking dis here way, wid he head down and he soldiers up, and as white as a gose? And den he keep a syphon all de time—"

"Keeps a what, Jupiter?"

"Keeps a syphon wid de figgurs on de slate—de queerest figgurs I ebber did see. Ise gittin' to be skeered, I tell you. Hab for to keep mighty tight eye 'pon him 'noovers. Todder day he gib me slip 'fore de sun up and was gone de whole ob de blessed day. I had a big stick ready cut for to gib him deuced good beating when he did come—but Ise sich a fool dat I hadn't de heart arter all—he looked so berry poorly."

"Eh?—what?—ah yes!—upon the whole I think you had better not be too severe with the poor fellow—don't flog him, Jupiter—he can't very well stand it —but can you form no idea of what has occasioned this illness, or rather this change of conduct? Has any thing unpleasant happened since I saw you?"

"No, massa, dey aint bin noffin onpleasant *since* den—'twas *'fore* den I'm feared—'twas de berry day you was dare."

"How? what do you mean?"

"Why, massa, I mean de bug—dare now."

"The what?"

"De bug—I'm berry sartain dat Massa Will bin bit somewhere 'bout de head by dat goole-bug."

"And what cause have you, Jupiter, for such a supposition?"

"Claws enuff, massa, and mouff too. I nebber did see sich a deuced bug—he kick and he bite ebery ting what cum near him. Massa Will cotch him fuss, but had for to let him go 'gin mighty quick, I tell you—den was de time he must ha' got de bite. I didn't like de look ob de bug mouff, myself, nohow, so I wouldn't take hold ob him wid my finger, but I cotch him wid a piece ob paper dat I found. I wrap him up in de paper and stuff a piece of it in he mouff—dat was de way."

"And you think, then, that your master was really bitten by the beetle, and that the bite made him sick?"

"I don't think noffin' about it—I nose it. What make him dream 'bout de goole so much, if 'taint cause he bit by de goole-bug? Ise heerd 'bout dem goole-bugs 'fore dis."

"But how do you know he dreams about gold?"

"How I know? why, 'cause he talk about it in he sleep—dat's how I nose."

"Well, Jup, perhaps you are right; but to what fortunate circumstance am I to attribute the honor of a visit from you to-day?"

"What de matter, massa?"

"Did you bring any message from Mr. Legrand?"

"No, massa, I bring dis her pissel"; and here Jupiter handed me a note which ran thus:

MY DEAR ——

Why have I not seen you for so long a time? I hope you have not been so foolish as to take offence at any little *brusquerie* of mine; but no, that is improbable.

Since I saw you I have had great cause for anxiety. I have something to tell you, yet scarcely know how to tell it, or whether I should tell it at all.

I have not been quite well for some days past, and poor old Jup annoys me, almost beyond endurance, by his well-meant attentions. Would you believe it?—he had prepared a huge stick, the other day, with which to chastise me for giving him the slip, and spending the day, *solus*, among the hills on the main land. I verily believe that my ill looks alone saved me a flogging.

I have made no addition to my cabinet since we met.

If you can, in any way, make it convenient, come over with Jupiter. *Do* come. I wish to see you *to-night*, upon business of importance. I assure you that it is of the *highest* importance.

Ever yours,
WILLIAM LEGRAND

There was something in the tone of this note which gave me great uneasiness. Its whole style differed materially from that of Legrand. What could he be dreaming of? What new crotchet possessed his excitable brain? What "business of the highest importance" could *he* possibly have to transact? Jupiter's account of him boded no good. I dreaded lest the continued pressure of misfortune had, at length, fairly unsettled the reason of my friend. Without a moment's hesitation, therefore, I prepared to accompany the Negro.

Upon reaching the wharf, I noticed a scythe and three spades, all apparently new, lying in the bottom of the boat in which we were to embark.

"What is the meaning of all this, Jup?" I inquired.

"Him syfe, massa, and spade."

"Very true; but what are they doing here?"

"Him de syfe and de spade what Massa Will sis 'pon my buying for him in de town, and de debbil's own lot of money I had to gib for 'em."

"But what, in the name of all that is mysterious, is your 'Massa Will' going to do with scythes and spades?"

"Dat's more dan *I* know, and debbil take me if I don't b'lieve 'tis more dan he know too. But it's all cum ob de bug."

Finding that no satisfaction was to be obtained of Jupiter, whose whole intellect seemed to be absorbed by "de bug," I now stepped into the boat, and made sail. With a fair and strong breeze we soon ran into the little cove to the northward of Fort Moultrie, and a walk of some two miles brought us to the hut. It was about three in the afternoon when we arrived. Legrand had been waiting us in eager expectation. He grasped my hand with a nervous *em-*

pressement which alarmed me and strengthened the suspicions already entertained. His countenance was pale even to ghastliness, and his deep-set eyes glared with unnatural lustre. After some inquiries respecting his health, I asked him, not knowing what better to say, if he had yet obtained the *scarabaeus* from Lieutenant G———.

"Oh, yes," he replied, coloring violently, "I got it from him the next morning. Nothing should tempt me to part with that *scarabaeus*. Do you know that Jupiter is quite right about it?"

"In what way?" I asked, with a sad foreboding at heart.

"In supposing it to be a bug of *real gold*." He said this with an air of profound seriousness, and I felt inexpressibly shocked.

"This bug is to make my fortune," he continued, with a triumphant smile; "to reinstate me in my family possessions. Is it any wonder, then, that I prize it? Since Fortune has thought fit to bestow it upon me, I have only to use it properly, and I shall arrive at the gold of which it is the index. Jupiter, bring me that *scarabaeus!*"

"What! de bug, massa? I'd rudder not go fer trubble dat bug; you mus' git him for your own self." Hereupon Legrand arose, with a grave and stately air, and brought me the beetle from a glass case in which it was enclosed. It was a beautiful *scarabaeus,* and, at that time, unknown to naturalists—of course a great prize in a scientific point of view. There were two round black spots near one extremity of the back, and a long one near the other. The scales were exceedingly hard and glossy, with all the appearance of burnished gold. The weight of the insect was very remarkable, and, taking all things into consideration, I could hardly blame Jupiter for his opinion respecting it; but what to make of Legrand's concordance with that opinion, I could not, for the life of me, tell.

"I sent for you," said he, in a grandilo-

quent tone, when I had completed my examination of the beetle, "I sent for you that I might have your counsel and assistance in furthering the views of Fate and of the bug—"

"My dear Legrand," I cried, interrupting him, "you are certainly unwell, and had better use some little precautions. You shall go to bed, and I will remain with you a few days, until you get over this. You are feverish and—"

"Feel my pulse," said he.

I felt it, and, to say the truth, found not the slightest indication of fever.

"But you may be ill and yet have no fever. Allow me this once to prescribe for you. In the first place go to bed. In the next—"

"You are mistaken," he interposed, "I am as well as I can expect to be under the excitement which I suffer. If you really wish me well, you will relieve this excitement."

"And how is this to be done?"

"Very easily. Jupiter and myself are going upon an expedition into the hills, upon the main land, and, in this expedition, we shall need the aid of some person in whom we can confide. You are the only one we can trust. Whether we succeed or fail, the excitement which you now perceive in me will be equally allayed."

"I am anxious to oblige you in any way," I replied; "but do you mean to say that this infernal beetle has any connection with your expedition into the hills?"

"It has."

"Then, Legrand, I can become a party to no such absurd proceeding."

"I am sorry—very sorry—for we shall have to try it by ourselves."

"Try it by yourselves! The man is surely mad!—but stay!—how long do you propose to be absent?"

"Probably all night. We shall start immediately, and be back, at all events, by sunrise."

"And will you promise me, upon your honor, that when this freak of yours is over, and the bug business (good God!) settled to your satisfaction, you will then return home and follow my advice implicitly, as that of your physician?"

"Yes; I promise; and now let us be off, for we have no time to lose."

With a heavy heart I accompanied my friend. We started about four o'clock— Legrand, Jupiter, the dog, and myself. Jupiter had with him the scythe and spades —the whole of which he insisted upon carrying—more through fear, it seemed to me, of trusting either of the implements within reach of his master, than from any excess of industry or complaisance. His demeanor was dogged in the extreme, and "dat deuced bug" were the sole words which escaped his lips during the journey. For my own part, I had charge of a couple of dark lanterns, while Legrand contented himself with the *scarabaeus,* which he carried attached to the end of a bit of whipcord; twirling it to and fro, with the air of a conjuror, as he went. When I observed this last, plain evidence of my friend's aberration of mind, I could scarcely refrain from tears. I thought it best, however, to humor his fancy, at least for the present, or until I could adopt some more energetic measures with a chance of success. In the meantime, I endeavored, but all in vain, to sound him in regard to the object of the expedition. Having succeeded in inducing me to accompany him, he seemed unwilling to hold conversation upon any topic of minor importance, and to all my questions vouchsafed no other reply than "we shall see!"

We crossed the creek at the head of the island by means of a skiff, and, ascending the high grounds on the shore of the main land, proceeded in a northwesterly direction, through a tract of country excessively wild and desolate, where no trace of a human footstep was to be seen. Legrand led the way with decision; pausing only for an instant, here and there, to consult what appeared to be certain landmarks of his own contrivance upon a former occasion.

In this manner we journeyed for about two hours, and the sun was just setting when we entered a region infinitely more dreary than any yet seen. It was a species of table-land, near the summit of an almost inaccessible hill, densely wooded from base to pinnacle, and interspersed with huge crags that appeared to lie loosely upon the soil, and in many cases were prevented from precipitating themselves into the valleys below, merely by the support of the trees against which they reclined. Deep ravines, in various directions, gave an air of still sterner solemnity to the scene.

The natural platform to which we had clambered was thickly overgrown with brambles, through which we soon discovered that it would have been impossible to force our way but for the scythe; and Jupiter, by direction of his master, proceeded to clear for us a path to the foot of an enormously tall tulip-tree, which stood, with some eight or ten oaks, upon the level, and far surpassed them all, and all other trees which I had then ever seen, in the beauty of its foliage and form, in the wide spread of its branches, and in the general majesty of its appearance. When we reached this tree, Legrand turned to Jupiter, and asked him if he thought he could climb it. The old man seemed a little staggered by the question, and for some moments made no reply. At length he approached the huge trunk, walked slowly around it, and examined it with minute attention. When he had completed his scrutiny, he merely said:

"Yes, massa, Jup climb any tree he ebber see in he life."

"Then up with you as soon as possible, for it will soon be too dark to see what we are about."

"How far mus' go up, massa?" inquired Jupiter.

"Get up the main trunk first, and then I will tell you which way to go—and here —stop! take this beetle with you."

"De bug, Massa Will!—de goole-bug!" cried the Negro, drawing back in dismay— "what for mus' tote de bug way up de tree?—d——n if I do!"

"If you are afraid, Jup, a great big Negro like you, to take hold of a harmless little dead beetle, why you can carry it up by this string—but, if you do not take it up with you in some way, I shall be under the necessity of breaking your head with this shovel."

"What de matter now, massa?" said Jup, evidently shamed into compliance; "always want for to raise fuss wid old nigger. Was only funnin anyhow. *Me* feered de bug! what I keer for de bug?" Here he took cautiously hold of the extreme end of the string, and, maintaining the insect as far from his person as circumstances would permit, prepared to ascend the tree.

In youth, the tulip-tree, or *Liriodendron Tulipiferum*, the most magnificent of American foresters, has a trunk peculiarly smooth, and often rises to a great height without lateral branches; but, in its riper age, the bark becomes gnarled and uneven, while many short limbs make their appearance on the stem. Thus the difficulty of ascension, in the present case, lay more in semblance than in reality. Embracing the huge cylinder, as closely as possible, with his arms and knees, seizing with his hands some projections, and resting his naked toes upon others, Jupiter, after one or two narrow escapes from falling, at length wriggled himself into the first great fork, and seemed to consider the whole business as virtually accomplished. The *risk* of the achievement was, in fact, now over, although the climber was some

sixty or seventy feet from the ground.

"Which way mus' go now, Massa Will?" he asked.

"Keep up the largest branch—the one on this side," said Legrand. The Negro obeyed him promptly, and apparently with but little trouble; ascending higher and higher, until no glimpse of his squat figure could be obtained through the dense foliage which enveloped it. Presently his voice was heard in a sort of halloo.

"How much fudder is got for go?"

"How high up are you?" asked Legrand.

"Ebber so fur," replied the Negro; "can see de sky fru de top ob de tree."

"Never mind the sky, but attend to what I say. Look down the trunk and count the limbs below you on this side. How many limbs have you passed?"

"One, two, tree, four, fibe—I done pass fibe big limb, massa, 'pon dis side."

"Then go one limb higher."

In a few minutes the voice was heard again, announcing that the seventh limb was attained.

"Now, Jup," cried Legrand, evidently much excited, "I want you to work your way out upon that limb as far as you can. If you see any thing strange let me know."

By this time what little doubt I might have entertained of my poor friend's insanity was put finally at rest. I had no alternative but to conclude him stricken with lunacy, and I became seriously anxious about getting him home. While I was pondering upon what was best to be done, Jupiter's voice was again heard.

"Mos' feerd for to venture 'pon dis limb berry far—'tis dead limb putty much all de way."

"Did you say it was a *dead* limb, Jupiter?" cried Legrand in a quavering voice.

"Yes, massa, him dead as de door-nail —done up for sartain—done departed dis here life."

"What in the name of heaven shall I do?" asked Legrand, seemingly in the greatest distress.

"Do!" said I, glad of an opportunity to interpose a word, "why come home and go to bed. Come now!—that's a fine fellow. It's getting late, and, besides, you remember your promise."

"Jupiter," cried he, without heeding me in the least, "do you hear me?"

"Yes, Massa Will, hear you ebber so plain."

"Try the wood well, then, with your knife, and see if you think it *very* rotten."

"Him rotten, massa, sure nuff," replied the Negro in a few moments, "but not so berry rotten as mought be. Mought venture out leetle way 'pon de limb by myself, dat's true."

"By yourself!—what do you mean?"

"Why, I mean de bug. 'Tis *berry* hebby bug. Spose I drop him down fuss, and den de limb won't break wid just de weight ob one nigger."

"You infernal scoundrel!" cried Legrand, apparently much relieved, "what do you mean by telling me such nonsense as that? As sure as you drop that beetle I'll break your neck. Look here, Jupiter, do you hear me?"

"Yes, massa, needn't hollo at poor nigger dat style."

"Well! now listen!—if you will venture out on the limb as far as you think safe, and not let go the beetle, I'll make you a present of a silver dollar as soon as you get down."

"I'm gwine, Massa Will—deed I is," replied the Negro very promptly—"mos' out to de eend now."

"*Out to the end!*" here fairly screamed Legrand; "do you say you are out to the end of that limb?"

"Soon be to de eend, massa—o-o-o-o-oh! Lor-gol-a-marcy! what *is* dis here pon de tree?"

"Well!" cried Legrand, highly delighted, "what is it?"

"Why taint noffin but a skull—somebody bin lef' him head up de tree, and de crows done gobble ebery bit ob de meat off."

"A skull, you say!—very well,—how is it fastened to the limb?—what holds it on?"

"Sure nuff, massa; mus' look. Why dis berry curous sarcumstance, 'pon my word—dare's a great big nail in de skull, what fastens ob it on to de tree."

"Well now, Jupiter, do exactly as I tell you—do you hear?"

"Yes, massa."

"Pay attention, then—find the left eye of the skull."

"Hum! hoo! dat's good! why dey aint no eye lef' at all."

"Curse your stupidity! do you know your right hand from your left?"

"Yes, I knows dat—know all bout dat—'tis my lef' hand what I chops de wood wid."

"To be sure! you are left-handed; and your left eye is on the same side as your left hand. Now, I suppose, you can find the left eye of the skull, or the place where the left eye has been. Have you found it?"

Here was a long pause. At length the Negro asked:

"Is de lef' eye ob de skull 'pon de same side as de lef' hand ob de skull too?—cause de skull aint got not a bit ob a hand at all—nebber mind! I got de lef' eye now—here de lef' eye! what mus' do wid it?"

"Let the beetle drop through it, as far as the string will reach—but be careful and not let go your hold of the string."

"All dat done, Massa Will; mighty easy ting for to put the bug fru de hole—look out for him dar below!"

During this colloquy no portion of Jupiter's person could be seen; but the beetle, which he had suffered to descend, was now visible at the end of the string, and glistened, like a globe of burnished gold, in the last rays of the setting sun, some of which still faintly illumined the eminence upon which we stood. The *scarabaeus* hung quite clear of any branches; and, if allowed to fall, would have fallen at our feet. Legrand immediately took the scythe, and cleared with it a circular space, three or four yards in diameter, just beneath the insect, and, having accomplished this, ordered Jupiter to let go the string and come down from the tree.

Driving a peg, with great nicety, into the ground, at the precise spot where the beetle fell, my friend now produced from his pocket a tape measure. Fastening one end of this at that point of the trunk of the tree which was nearest the peg, he unrolled it till it reached the peg and thence further unrolled it, in the direction already established by the two points of the tree and the peg, for the distance of fifty feet— Jupiter clearing away the brambles with the scythe. At the spot thus attained a second peg was driven, and about this, as a centre, a rude circle, about four feet in diameter, described. Taking now a spade himself, and giving one to Jupiter and one to me, Legrand begged us to set about digging as quickly as possible.

To speak the truth, I had no especial relish for such amusement at any time, and, at that particular moment, would most willingly have declined it; for the night was coming on, and I felt much fatigued with the exercise already taken; but I saw no mode of escape, and was fearful of disturbing my poor friend's equanimity by a refusal. Could I have depended, indeed, upon Jupiter's aid, I would have had no hesitation in attempting to get the lunatic home by force; but I was too well assured of the old Negro's disposition, to hope that he would assist me, under any circumstances, in a personal contest with his master. I made no doubt that the latter had been infected with some of the innumerable Southern superstitions about money buried, and that his phantasy had received confirmation by the finding of the *scarabaeus*, or, perhaps, by Jupiter's obstinacy in maintaining it to be "a bug of real gold." A mind disposed to lunacy would readily be led away by such suggestions—especially if chiming in with favorite preconceived ideas—and then I called to mind the poor fellow's speech about the beetle's being "the index of his fortune." Upon the whole, I was sadly vexed and puzzled, but, at length, I concluded to make a virtue of necessity—to dig with a good will, and thus the sooner to convince the visionary, by ocular demonstration, of the fallacy of the opinions he entertained.

The lanterns having been lit, we all fell to work with a zeal worthy a more rational cause; and, as the glare fell upon our persons and implements, I could not help thinking how picturesque a group we composed, and how strange and suspicious our labors must have appeared to any interloper who, by chance, might have stumbled upon our whereabouts.

We dug very steadily for two hours. Little was said; and our chief embarrassment lay in the yelpings of the dog, who took exceeding interest in our proceedings. He, at length, became so obstreperous that we grew fearful of his giving the alarm to some stragglers in the vicinity,—or, rather, this was the apprehension of Legrand;—for myself, I should have rejoiced at any interruption which might have enabled me to get the wanderer home. The noise was, at length, very effectually silenced by Jupiter, who, getting out of the hole with a dogged air of deliberation, tied the brute's mouth up with one of his suspenders, and then returned, with a grave chuckle, to his task.

When the time mentioned had expired, we had reached a depth of five feet, and yet no signs of any treasure became manifest. A general pause ensued, and I began to hope that the farce was at an end. Legrand, however, although evidently much disconcerted, wiped his brow thoughtfully and recommenced. We had excavated the entire circle of four feet diameter, and now we slightly enlarged the limit, and went to the farther depth of two feet. Still nothing appeared. The gold-seeker, whom I sincerely pitied, at length clambered from the pit, with the bitterest disappointment imprinted upon every feature, and proceeded, slowly and reluctantly, to put on his coat, which he had thrown off at the beginning of his labor. In the meantime I made no remark. Jupiter, at a signal from his master, began to gather up his tools. This done, and the dog having been unmuzzled, we turned in profound silence toward home.

We had taken, perhaps, a dozen steps in this direction, when, with a loud oath, Legrand strode up to Jupiter, and seized him by the collar. The astonished Negro opened his eyes and mouth to the fullest extent, let fall the spades, and fell upon his knees.

"You scoundrel!" said Legrand, hissing out the syllables from between his clenched teeth—"you infernal black villain!—speak, I tell you!—answer me this instant, without prevarication!—which—which is your left eye?"

"Oh, my golly, Massa Will! aint dis here my lef' eye for sartain?" roared the terrified Jupiter, placing his hand upon his *right* organ of vision, and holding it there with a desperate pertinacity, as if in immediate dread of his master's attempt at a gouge.

"I thought so!—I knew it! hurrah!" vociferated Legrand, letting the Negro go and executing a series of curvets and caracols, much to the astonishment of his valet, who, arising from his knees, looked, mutely, from his master to myself, and then from myself to his master.

"Come! we must go back," said the latter, "the game's not up yet"; and he again led the way to the tulip-tree.

"Jupiter," said he, when we reached its foot, "come here! was the skull nailed to the limb with the face outward, or with the face to the limb?"

"De face was out, massa, so dat de crows could get at de eyes good, widout any trouble."

"Well, then, was it this eye or that through which you dropped the beetle?"—here Legrand touched each of Jupiter's eyes.

"'Twas dis eye,—massa—de lef' eye—jis as you tell me," and here it was his right eye that the Negro indicated.

"That will do—we must try it again."

Here my friend, about whose madness I now saw, or fancied that I saw, certain indications of method, removed the peg which marked the spot where the beetle fell, to a spot about three inches to the westward of its former position. Taking, now, the tape measure from the nearest point of the trunk to the peg, as before, and continuing the extension in a straight line to the distance of fifty feet, a spot was indicated, removed, by several yards, from the point at which we had been digging.

Around the new position a circle, somewhat larger than in the former instance, was now described, and we again set to work with the spade. I was dreadfully weary, but, scarcely understanding what had occasioned the change in my thoughts, I felt no longer any great aversion from the labor imposed. I had become most unaccountably interested—nay, even excited. Perhaps there was something, amid all the extravagant demeanor of Legrand—some air of forethought, or of deliberation, which impressed me. I dug eagerly, and now and then caught myself actually looking, with something that very much resembled expectation, for the fancied treasure, the vision of which had demented my unfortunate companion. At a period when such vagaries of thought most fully possessed me, and when we had been at work perhaps an hour and a half, we were again interrupted by the violent howlings of the dog. His uneasiness, in the first instance, had been, evidently, but the result of playfulness or caprice, but he now assumed a bitter and serious tone. Upon Jupiter's again attempting to muzzle him, he made furious resistance, and, leaping into the hole, tore up the mould frantically with his claws. In a few seconds he had uncovered a mass of human bones, forming two complete skeletons, intermingled with several buttons of metal, and what appeared to be the dust of decayed woollen. One or two strokes of a spade up-turned the blade of a large Spanish knife, and, as we dug farther, three or four loose pieces of gold and silver coin came to light.

At sight of these the joy of Jupiter could scarcely be restrained, but the countenance of his master wore an air of extreme disappointment. He urged us, however, to continue our exertions, and the words were hardly uttered when I stumbled and fell forward, having caught the toe of my boot in a large ring of iron that lay half buried in the loose earth.

We now worked in earnest, and never did I pass ten minutes of more intense excitement. During this interval we had fairly unearthed an oblong chest of wood, which, from its perfect preservation and wonderful hardness, had plainly been subjected to some mineralizing process—perhaps that of the bi-chloride of mercury. This box was three feet and a half long, three feet broad, and two and a half feet deep. It was firmly secured by bands of wrought iron, riveted, and forming a kind of open trellis-work over the whole. On each side of the chest, near the top, were three rings of iron —six in all—by means of which a firm hold could be obtained by six persons. Our utmost united endeavors served only

to disturb the coffer very slightly in its bed. We at once saw the impossibility of removing so great a weight. Luckily, the sole fastenings of the lid consisted of two sliding bolts. These we drew back—trembling and panting with anxiety. In an instant, a treasure of incalculable value lay gleaming before us. As the rays of the lanterns fell within the pit, there flashed upward a glow and a glare, from a confused heap of gold and of jewels, that absolutely dazzled our eyes.

I shall not pretend to describe the feelings with which I gazed. Amazement was, of course, predominant. Legrand appeared exhausted with excitement, and spoke very few words. Jupiter's countenance wore, for some minutes, as deadly a pallor as it is possible, in the nature of things, for any Negro's visage to assume. He seemed stupefied—thunderstricken. Presently he fell upon his knees in the pit, and burying his naked arms up to the elbows in gold, let them there remain, as if enjoying the luxury of a bath. At length, with a deep sigh, he exclaimed, as if in a soliloquy:

"And dis all cum ob de goole-bug! de putty goole-bug! the poor little goole-bug, what I boosed in dat sabage kind ob style! Aint you shamed ob yourself, nigger?— answer me dat!"

It became necessary, at last, that I should arouse both master and valet to the expediency of removing the treasure. It was growing late, and it behooved us to make exertion, that we might get every thing housed before daylight. It was difficult to say what should be done, and much time was spent in deliberation—so confused were the ideas of all. We, finally, lightened the box by removing two thirds of its contents, when we were enabled, with some trouble, to raise it from the hole. The articles taken out were deposited among the brambles, and the dog left to guard them, with strict orders from Jupiter neither, upon any pretence, to stir from the spot, nor to open his mouth until our return. We then hurriedly made for home with the chest; reaching the hut in safety, but after excessive toil, at one o'clock in the morning. Worn out as we were, it was not in human nature to do more immediately. We rested until two, and had supper; starting for the hills immediately afterward, armed with three stout sacks, which, by good luck, were upon the premises. A little before four we arrived at the pit, divided the remainder of the booty, as equally as might be, among us, and, leaving the holes unfilled, again set out for the hut, at which, for the second time, we deposited our golden burthens, just as the first faint streaks of the dawn gleamed from over the tree-tops in the east.

We were now thoroughly broken down; but the intense excitement of the time denied us repose. After an unquiet slumber of some three or four hours' duration, we arose, as if by preconcert, to make examination of our treasure.

The chest had been full to the brim, and we spent the whole day, and the greater part of the next night, in a scrutiny of its contents. There had been nothing like order or arrangement. Every thing had been heaped in promiscuously. Having assorted all with care, we found ourselves possessed of even vaster wealth than we had at first supposed. In coin there was rather more than four hundred and fifty thousand dollars—estimating the value of the pieces, as accurately as we could, by the tables of the period. There was not a particle of silver. All was gold of antique date and of great variety—French, Spanish, and German money, with a few English guineas, and some counters, of which we had never seen specimens before. There were several very large and heavy coins, so worn that we could make nothing of their inscriptions. There was no American money. The value of the jewels we found more difficulty in estimating. There were

diamonds—some of them exceedingly large and fine—a hundred and ten in all, and not one of them small; eighteen rubies of remarkable brilliancy;—three hundred and ten emeralds, all very beautiful; and twenty-one sapphires, with an opal. These stones had all been broken from their settings and thrown loose in the chest. The settings themselves, which we picked out from among the other gold, appeared to have been beaten up with hammers, as if to prevent identification. Besides all this, there was a vast quantity of solid gold ornaments: nearly two hundred massive finger- and ear-rings; rich chains—thirty of these, if I remember; eighty-three very large and heavy crucifixes; five gold censers of great value; a prodigious golden punch-bowl, ornamented with richly chased vine-leaves and Bacchanalian figures; with two sword-handles exquisitely embossed, and many other smaller articles which I cannot recollect. The weight of these valuables exceeded three hundred and fifty pounds avoirdupois; and in this estimate I have not included one hundred and ninety-seven superb gold watches; three of the number being worth each five hundred dollars, if one. Many of them were very old, and as timekeepers valueless; the works having suffered, more or less, from corrosion—but all were richly jewelled and in cases of great worth. We estimated the entire contents of the chest, that night, at a million and a half of dollars; and upon the subsequent disposal of the trinkets and jewels (a few being retained for our own use), it was found that we had greatly undervalued the treasure.

When, at length, we had concluded our examination, and the intense excitement of the time had, in some measure, subsided, Legrand, who saw that I was dying with impatience for a solution of this most extraordinary riddle, entered into a full detail of all the circumstances connected with it.

"You remember," said he, "the night when I handed you the rough sketch I had made of the *scarabaeus*. You recollect also, that I became quite vexed at you for insisting that my drawing resembled a death's-head. When you first made this assertion I thought you were jesting; but afterward I called to mind the peculiar spots on the back of the insect, and admitted to myself that your remark had some little foundation in fact. Still, the sneer at my graphic powers irritated me—for I am considered a good artist—and, therefore, when you handed me the scrap of parchment, I was about to crumple it up and throw it angrily into the fire."

"The scrap of paper, you mean," said I.

"No; it had much of the appearance of paper, and at first I supposed it to be such, but when I came to draw upon it, I discovered it at once to be a piece of very thin parchment. It was quite dirty, you remember. Well, as I was in the very act of crumpling it up, my glance fell upon the sketch at which you had been looking, and you may imagine my astonishment when I perceived, in fact, the figure of a death's-head just where, it seemed to me, I had made the drawing of the beetle. For a moment I was too much amazed to think with accuracy. I knew that my design was very different in detail from this—although there was a certain similarity in general outline. Presently I took a candle, and seating myself at the other end of the room, proceeded to scrutinize the parchment more closely. Upon turning it over, I saw my own sketch upon the reverse, just as I had made it. My first idea, now, was mere surprise at the really remarkable similarity of outline—at the singular coincidence involved in the fact that, unknown to me, there should have been a skull upon the other side of the parchment, immediately beneath my figure of the *scarabaeus*, and that this skull, not only in outline, but in size, should so closely resemble my

drawing. I say the singularity of this coincidence absolutely stupefied me for a time. This is the usual effect of such coincidences. The mind struggles to establish a connection—a sequence of cause and effect—and, being unable to do so, suffers a species of temporary paralysis. But, when I recovered from this stupor, there dawned upon me gradually a conviction which startled me even far more than the coincidence. I began distinctly, positively, to remember that there had been *no* drawing upon the parchment when I made my sketch of the *scarabaeus*. I became perfectly certain of this; for I recollected turning up first one side and then the other, in search of the cleanest spot. Had the skull been then there, of course I could not have failed to notice it. Here was indeed a mystery which I felt it impossible to explain; but, even at that early moment, there seemed to glimmer, faintly, within the most remote and secret chambers of my intellect, a glow-worm-like conception of that truth which last night's adventure brought to so magnificent a demonstration. I arose at once, and putting the parchment securely away, dismissed all further reflection until I should be alone.

"When you had gone, and when Jupiter was fast asleep, I betook myself to a more methodical investigation of the affair. In the first place I considered the manner in which the parchment had come into my possession. The spot where we discovered the *scarabaeus* was on the coast of the main-land, about a mile eastward of the island, and but a short distance above high-water mark. Upon my taking hold of it, it gave me a sharp bite, which caused me to let it drop. Jupiter, with his accustomed caution, before seizing the insect, which had flown toward him, looked about him for a leaf, or something of that nature, by which to take hold of it. It was at this moment that his eyes, and mine also, fell upon the scrap of parchment, which I then supposed to be paper. It was lying half buried in the sand, a corner sticking up. Near the spot where we found it, I observed the remnants of the hull of what appeared to have been a ship's long-boat. The wreck seemed to have been there for a very great while; for the resemblance to boat timbers could scarcely be traced.

"Well, Jupiter picked up the parchment, wrapped the beetle in it, and gave it to me. Soon afterward we turned to go home, and on the way met Lieutenant G——. I showed him the insect, and he begged me to let him take it to the fort. Upon my consenting, he thrust it forthwith into his waistcoat pocket, without the parchment in which it had been wrapped, and which I had continued to hold in my hand during his inspection. Perhaps he dreaded my changing my mind, and thought it best to make sure of the prize at once—you know how enthusiastic he is on all subjects connected with Natural History. At the same time, without being conscious of it, I must have deposited the parchment in my own pocket.

"You remember that when I went to the table, for the purpose of making a sketch of the beetle, I found no paper where it was usually kept. I looked in the drawer, and found none there. I searched my pockets, hoping to find an old letter, when my hand fell upon the parchment. I thus detail the precise mode in which it came into my possession; for the circumstances impressed me with peculiar force.

"No doubt you will think me fanciful—but I had already established a kind of connection. I had put together two links of a great chain. There was a boat lying upon the sea-coast, and not far from the boat was a parchment—not a paper—with a skull depicted upon it. You will, of course, ask 'where is the connection?' I reply that the skull, or death's-head, is the well-known emblem of the pirate. The flag of the death's-head is hoisted in all engagements.

"I have said that the scrap was parchment, and not paper. Parchment is durable—almost imperishable. Matters of little moment are rarely consigned to parchment; since, for the mere ordinary purposes of drawing or writing, it is not nearly so well adapted as paper. This reflection suggested some meaning—some relevancy—in the death's-head. I did not fail to observe, also, the form of the parchment. Although one of its corners had been, by some accident, destroyed, it could be seen that the original form was oblong. It was just such a slip, indeed, as might have been chosen for a memorandum—for a record of something to be long remembered and carefully preserved."

"But," I interposed, "you say that the skull was not upon the parchment when you made the drawing of the beetle. How then do you trace any connection between the boat and the skull—since this latter, according to your own admission, must have been designed (God only knows how or by whom) at some period subsequent to your sketching the scarabaeus?"

"Ah, hereupon turns the whole mystery; although the secret, at this point, I had comparatively little difficulty in solving. My steps were sure, and could afford a single result. I reasoned, for example, thus: When I drew the scarabaeus, there was no skull apparent upon the parchment. When I had completed the drawing I gave it to you, and observed you narrowly until you returned it. You, therefore, did not design the skull, and no one else was present to do it. Then it was not done by human agency. And nevertheless it was done.

"At this stage of my reflections I endeavored to remember, and did remember, with entire distinctness, every incident which occurred about the period in question. The weather was chilly (oh, rare and happy accident!), and a fire was blazing upon the hearth. I was heated with exercise and sat near the table. You, however, had drawn a chair close to the chimney. Just as I placed the parchment in your hand, and as you were in the act of inspecting it, Wolf, the Newfoundland, entered, and leaped upon your shoulders. With your left hand you caressed him and kept him off, while your right, holding the parchment, was permitted to fall listlessly between your knees, and in close proximity to the fire. At one moment I thought the blaze had caught it, and was about to caution you, but, before I could speak, you had withdrawn it, and were engaged in its examination. When I considered all these particulars, I doubted not for a moment that *heat* had been the agent in bringing to light, upon the parchment, the skull which I saw designed upon it. You are well aware that chemical preparations exist, and have existed time out of mind, by means of which it is possible to write upon either paper or vellum, so that the characters shall become visible only when subjected to the action of fire. Zaffre, digested in *aqua regia,* and diluted with four times its weight of water, is sometimes employed; a green tint results. The regulus of cobalt, dissolved in spirit of nitre, gives a red. These colors disappear at longer or shorter intervals after the material written upon cools, but again become apparent upon the re-application of heat.

"I now scrutinized the death's-head with care. Its outer edges—the edges of the drawing nearest the edge of the vellum— were far more *distinct* than the others. It was clear that the action of the caloric had been imperfect or unequal. I immediately kindled a fire, and subjected every portion of the parchment to a glowing heat. At first, the only effect was the strengthening of the faint lines in the skull; but, upon persevering in the experiment, there became visible, at the corner of the slip,

diagonally opposite to the spot in which the death's-head was delineated, the figure of what I at first supposed to be a goat. A closer scrutiny, however, satisfied me that it was intended for a kid."

"Ha! ha!" said I, "to be sure I have no right to laugh at you—a million and a half of money is too serious a matter for mirth—but you are not about to establish a third link in your chain—you will not find any especial connection between your pirates and a goat—pirates, you know, have nothing to do with goats; they appertain to the farming interest."

"But I have just said that the figure was *not* that of a goat."

"Well, a kid then—pretty much the same thing."

"Pretty much, but not altogether," said Legrand. "You may have heard of one *Captain* Kidd. I at once looked upon the figure of the animal as a kind of punning or hieroglyphical signature. I say signature; because its position upon the vellum suggested this idea. The death's-head at the corner diagonally opposite, had, in the same manner, the air of a stamp, or seal. But I was sorely put out by the absence of all else—of the body to my imagined instrument—of the text for my context."

"I presume you expected to find a letter between the stamp and the signature."

"Something of that kind. The fact is, I felt irresistibly impressed with a presentiment of some vast good fortune impending. I can scarcely say why. Perhaps, after all, it was rather a desire than an actual belief; —but do you know that Jupiter's silly words, about the bug being of solid gold, had a remarkable effect upon my fancy? And then the series of accidents and coincidences—these were so *very* extraordinary. Do you observe how mere an accident it was that these events should have occurred upon the *sole* day of all the year in which it has been, or may be sufficiently cool for fire, and that without the fire, or without the intervention of the dog at the precise moment in which he appeared, I should never have become aware of the death's-head, and so never the possessor of the treasure?"

"But proceed—I am all impatience."

"Well; you have heard, of course, the many stories current—the thousand vague rumors afloat about money buried, somewhere upon the Atlantic coast, by Kidd and his associates. These rumors must have had some foundation in fact. And that the rumors have existed so long and so continuous, could have resulted, it appeared to me, only from the circumstance of the buried treasure still *remaining* entombed. Had Kidd concealed his plunder for a time, and afterward reclaimed it, the rumors would scarcely have reached us in their present unvarying form. You will observe that the stories told are all about money-seekers, not about money-finders. Had the pirate recovered his money, there the affair would have dropped. It seemed to me that some accident—say the loss of a memorandum indicating its locality—had deprived him of the means of recovering it, and that this accident had become known to his followers, who otherwise might never have heard that treasure had been concealed at all, and who, busying themselves in vain, because unguided, attempts to regain it, had given first birth, and then universal currency, to the reports which are now so common. Have you ever heard of any important treasure being unearthed along the coast?"

"Never."

"But that Kidd's accumulations were immense, is well known. I took it for granted, therefore, that the earth still held them; and you will scarcely be surprised when I tell you that I felt a hope, nearly amounting to certainty, that the parchment so strangely found involved a lost record of the place of deposit."

"But how did you proceed?"

"I held the vellum again to the fire, after increasing the heat, but nothing appeared. I now thought it possible that the coating of dirt might have something to do with the failure: so I carefully rinsed the parchment by pouring warm water over it, and, having done this, I placed it in a tin pan, with the skull downward, and put the pan upon a furnace of lighted charcoal. In a few minutes, the pan having become thoroughly heated, I removed the slip, and, to my inexpressible joy, found it spotted, in several places, with what appeared to be figures arranged in lines. Again I placed it in the pan, and suffered it to remain another minute. Upon taking it off, the whole was just as you see it now."

Here Legrand, having re-heated the parchment, submitted it to my inspection. The following characters were rudely traced, in a red tint, between the death's-head and the goat:

53‡‡†305))6*;4826)4‡.)4‡);806*;48†8¶60))
85;1‡(;:‡*8†83(88)5*†;46(;88*96*?;8)*‡(;
485);5*†2:*‡(;4956*2(5*—4)8¶8*;4069285
);)6†8)4‡‡;1(‡9;48081;8:8‡1;48†85;4)485†5
28806*81(‡9;48;(88;4(‡?34;48)4‡;161;:188
;‡?;

"But," said I, returning him the slip, "I am as much in the dark as ever. Were all the jewels of Golconda awaiting me upon my solution of this enigma, I am quite sure that I should be unable to earn them."

"And yet," said Legrand, "the solution is by no means so difficult as you might be led to imagine from the first hasty inspection of the characters. These characters, as any one might readily guess, form a cipher—that is to say, they convey a meaning; but then from what is known of Kidd, I could not suppose him capable of constructing any of the more abstruse cryptographs. I made up my mind, at once, that this was of a simple species—such, however, as would appear, to the crude intellect of the sailor, absolutely insoluble without the key."

"And you really solved it?"

"Readily; I have solved others of an abstruseness ten thousand times greater. Circumstances, and a certain bias of mind, have led me to take interest in such riddles, and it may well be doubted whether human ingenuity can construct an enigma of the kind which human ingenuity may not, by proper application, resolve. In fact, having once established connected and legible characters, I scarcely gave a thought to the mere difficulty of developing their import.

"In the present case—indeed in all cases of secret writing—the first question regards the *language* of the cipher; for the principles of solution, so far, especially, as the more simple ciphers are concerned, depend upon, and are varied by, the genius of the particular idiom. In general, there is no alternative but experiment (directed by probabilities) of every tongue known to him who attempts the solution, until the true one be attained. But, with the cipher now before us, all difficulty is removed by the signature. The pun upon the word 'Kidd' is appreciable in no other language than the English. But for this consideration I should have begun my attempts with the Spanish and French, as the tongues in which a secret of this kind would most naturally have been written by a pirate of the Spanish main. As it was, I assumed the cryptograph to be English.

"You observe there are no divisions between the words. Had there been divisions the task would have been comparatively easy. In such cases I should have commenced with a collation and analysis of the shorter words, and, had a word of a single letter occurred, as is most likely (*a* or *I*, for example), I should have considered the solution as assured. But, there being no division, my first step was to ascertain the predominant letters, as well as the least frequent. Counting all,. I constructed a table thus:

Of the character 8 there are 33.
;	"	26.
4	"	19.
‡)	"	16.
*	"	13.
5	"	12.
6	"	11.
†1	"	8.
0	"	6.
92	"	5.
:3	"	4.
?	"	3.
¶	"	2.
—.	"	1.

"Now, in English, the letter which most frequently occurs is *e*. Afterward, the succession runs thus: *a o i d h n r s t u y c f g l m w b k p q x z*. *E* predominates so remarkably, that an individual sentence of any length is rarely seen in which it is not the prevailing character.

"Here, then, we have, in the very beginning, the groundwork for something more than a mere guess. The general use which may be made of the table is obvious—but, in this particular cipher, we shall only very partially require its aid. As our predominant character is 8, we will commence by assuming it as the *e* of the natural alphabet. To verify the supposition, let us observe if the 8 be seen often in couples—for *e* is doubled with great frequency in English —in such words, for example, as 'meet,' 'fleet,' 'speed,' 'seen,' 'been,' 'agree,' etc. In the present instance we see it doubled no less than five times, although the cryptograph is brief.

"Let us assume 8, then, as *e*. Now, of all *words* in the language, 'the' is most usual; let us see, therefore, whether there are not repetitions of any three characters, in the same order of collocation, the last of them being 8. If we discover repetitions of such letters, so arranged, they will most probably represent the word 'the.' Upon inspection, we find no less than seven such arrangements, the characters being ;48. We may, therefore, assume that ; represents *t*, 4 represents *h*, and 8 represents *e*—the last being now well confirmed. Thus a great step has been taken.

"But, having established a single word, we are enabled to establish a vastly important point; that is to say, several commencements and terminations of other words. Let us refer, for example, to the last instance but one, in which the combination ;48 occurs—not far from the end of the cipher. We know that the ; immediately ensuing is the commencement of a word, and, of the six characters succeeding this 'the,' we are cognizant of no less than five. Let us set these characters down, thus, by the letters we know them to represent, leaving a space for the unknown—

t eeth.

"Here we are enabled, at once, to discard the 'th,' as forming no portion of the word commencing with the first t; since, by experiment of the entire alphabet for a letter adapted to the vacancy, we perceive that no word can be formed of which this th can be a part. We are thus narrowed into

t ee,

and, going through the alphabet, if necessary, as before, we arrive at the word 'tree,' as the sole possible reading. We thus gain another letter, r, represented by (, with the words 'the tree' in juxtaposition.

"Looking beyond these words, for a short distance, we again see the combination ;48, and employ it by way of *termination* to what immediately precedes. We have thus this arrangement:

the tree ;4(‡?34 the,

or, substituting the natural letters, where known, it reads thus:

the tree thr‡?3h the.

"Now, if, in place of the unknown characters, we leave blank spaces, or substitute dots, we read thus:

the tree thr...h the,

when the word 'through' makes itself evident at once. But this discovery gives us

three new letters, o, u, and g, represented by ‡, ?, and 3.

"Looking now, narrowly, through the cipher for combinations of known characters, we find, not very far from the beginning, this arrangement,

83(88, or †egree,

which, plainly, is the conclusion of the word 'degree,' and gives us another letter, d, represented by †.

"Four letters beyond the word 'degree,' we perceive the combination

;46(;88

"Translating the known characters, and representing the unknown by dots, as before, we read thus:

th.rtee,

an arrangement immediately suggestive of the word 'thirteen,' and again furnishing us with two new characters, i and n, represented by 6 and *.

"Referring, now, to the beginning of the cryptograph, we find the combination,

53‡‡†

"Translating as before, we obtain

.good,

which assures us that the first letter is A, and that the first two words are 'A good.'

"It is now time that we arrange our key, as far as discovered, in a tabular form, to avoid confusion. It will stand thus:

5	represents	a
†	"	d
8	"	e
3	"	g
4	"	h
6	"	i
*	"	n
‡	"	o
(	"	r
;	"	t
?	"	u

"We have, therefore, no less than eleven of the most important letters represented, and it will be unnecessary to proceed with the details of the solution. I have said enough to convince you that ciphers of this nature are readily soluble, and to give you some insight into the *rationale* of their development. But be assured that the specimen before us appertains to the very simplest species of cryptograph. It now only remains to give you the full translation of the characters upon the parchment, as unriddled. Here it is:

A good glass in the bishop's hostel in the devil's seat forty-one degrees and thirteen minutes northeast and by north main branch seventh limb east side shoot from the left eye of the death's-head a bee-line from the tree through the shot fifty feet out.

"But," said I, "the enigma seems still in as bad a condition as ever. How is it possible to extort a meaning from all this jargon about 'devil's seats,' 'death's-heads,' and 'bishop's hostels'?"

"I confess," replied Legrand, "that the matter still wears a serious aspect, when regarded with a casual glance. My first endeavor was to divide the sentence into the natural division intended by the cryptographist."

"You mean, to punctuate it?"

"Something of that kind."

"But how was it possible to effect this?"

"I reflected that it had been a *point* with the writer to run his words together without division, so as to increase the difficulty of solution. Now, a not over-acute man, in pursuing such an object, would be nearly certain to overdo the matter. When, in the course of his composition, he arrived at a break in his subject which would naturally require a pause, or a point, he would be exceedingly apt to run his characters, at this place, more than usually close together. If you will observe the MS., in the present instance, you will easily detect five such cases of unusual crowding. Acting upon this hint, I made the division thus:

A good glass in the bishop's hostel in the devil's seat—forty-one degrees and thirteen minutes—northeast and by north—main branch seventh limb east side—shoot from the left eye of the death's-head—a bee-line from the tree through the shot fifty feet out.

"Even this division," said I, "leaves me still in the dark."

"It left me also in the dark," replied Legrand, "for a few days; during which I made diligent inquiry, in the neighborhood of Sullivan's Island, for any building which went by the name of the 'Bishop's Hotel'; for, of course, I dropped the obsolete word 'hostel.' Gaining no information on the subject, I was on the point of extending my sphere of search, and proceeding in a more systematic manner, when, one morning, it entered into my head, quite suddenly, that this 'Bishop's Hostel' might have some reference to an old family, of the name of Bessop, which, time out of mind, had held possession of an ancient manor-house, about four miles to the northward of the island. I accordingly went over to the plantation, and re-instituted my inquiries among the older Negroes of the place. At length one of the most aged of the women said that she had heard of such a place as *Bessop's Castle*, and thought that she could guide me to it, but that it was not a castle, nor a tavern, but a high rock.

"I offered to pay her well for her trouble, and, after some demur, she consented to accompany me to the spot. We found it without much difficulty, when, dismissing her, I proceeded to examine the place. The 'castle' consisted of an irregular assemblage of cliffs and rocks—one of the latter being quite remarkable for its height as well as for its insulated and artificial appearance. I clambered to its apex, and then felt much at a loss as to what should be next done.

"While I was busied in reflection, my eyes fell upon a narrow ledge in the eastern face of the rock, perhaps a yard below the summit upon which I stood. This ledge projected about eighteen inches, and was not more than a foot wide, while a niche in the cliff just above it gave it a rude resemblance to one of the hollow-backed chairs used by our ancestors. I made no doubt that here was the 'devil's-seat' alluded to in the MS., and now I seemed to grasp the full secret of the riddle.

"The 'good glass,' I knew, could have reference to nothing but a telescope; for the word 'glass' is rarely employed in any other sense by seamen. Now here, I at once saw, was a telescope to be used, and a definite point of view, *admitting no variation,* from which to use it. Nor did I hesitate to believe that the phrases, 'forty-one degrees and thirteen minutes,' and 'northeast and by north,' were intended as directions for the levelling of the glass. Greatly excited by these discoveries, I hurried home, procured a telescope, and returned to the rock.

"I let myself down to the ledge, and found that it was impossible to retain a seat upon it except in one particular position. This fact confirmed my preconceived idea. I proceeded to use the glass. Of course, the 'forty-one degrees and thirteen minutes' could allude to nothing but elevation above the visible horizon, since the horizontal direction was clearly indicated by the words, 'northeast and by north.' This latter direction I at once established by means of a pocket-compass; then, pointing the glass as nearly at an angle of forty-one degrees of elevation as I could do it by guess, I moved it cautiously up or down, until my attention was arrested by a circular rift or opening in the foliage of a large tree that overtopped its fellows in the distance. In the centre of this rift I perceived a white spot, but could not, at first, distinguish what it was. Adjusting the focus of the telescope, I again looked, and now made it out to be a human skull.

"Upon this discovery I was so sanguine as to consider the enigma solved; for the phrase 'main branch, seventh limb, east side,' could refer only to the position of the skull upon the tree, while 'shoot from the left eye of the death's-head' admitted, also, of but one interpretation, in regard to a search for buried treasure. I perceived that the design was to drop a bullet from the left eye of the skull, and that a bee-line, or, in other words, a straight line, drawn from the nearest point of the trunk through 'the shot' (or the spot where the bullet fell), and thence extended to a distance of fifty feet, would indicate a definite point— and beneath this point I thought it at least *possible* that a deposit of value lay concealed."

"All this," I said, "is exceedingly clear, and, although ingenious, still simple and explicit. When you left the 'Bishop's Hotel,' what then?"

"Why, having carefully taken the bearings of the tree, I turned homeward. The instant that I left 'the devil's-seat,' however, the circular rift vanished; nor could I get a glimpse of it afterward, turn as I would. What seems to me the chief ingenuity in this whole business, is the fact (for repeated experiment has convinced me it *is* a fact) that the circular opening in question is visible from no other attainable point of view than that afforded by the narrow ledge upon the face of the rock.

"In this expedition to the 'Bishop's Hotel I had been attended by Jupiter, who had, no doubt, observed, for some weeks past, the abstraction of my demeanor, and took especial care not to leave me alone. But, on the next day, getting up very early, I contrived to give him the slip, and went into the hills in search of the tree. After much toil I found it. When I came home at night my valet proposed to give me a flogging. With the rest of the adventure I believe you are as well acquainted as myself."

"I suppose," said I, "you missed the spot, in the first attempt at digging, through Jupiter's stupidity in letting the bug fall through the right instead of through the left eye of the skull."

"Precisely. This mistake made a difference of about two inches and a half in the 'shot'—that is to say, in the position of the peg nearest the tree; and had the treasure been *beneath* the 'shot,' the error would have been of little moment; but 'the shot,' together with the nearest point of the tree, were merely two points for the establishment of a line of direction; of course the error, however trivial in the beginning, increased as we proceeded with the line, and by the time we had gone fifty feet threw us quite off the scent. But for my deepseated impressions that treasure was here somewhere actually buried, we might have had all our labor in vain."

"But your grandiloquence, and your conduct in swinging the beetle—how excessively odd! I was sure you were mad. And why did you insist upon letting fall the bug, instead of a bullet, from the skull?"

"Why, to be frank, I felt somewhat annoyed by your evident suspicions touching my sanity, and so resolved to punish you quietly, in my own way, by a little bit of sober mystification. For this reason I swung the beetle, and for this reason I let it fall from the tree. An observation of yours about its great weight suggested the latter idea."

"Yes, I perceive; and now there is only one point which puzzles me. What are we to make of the skeletons found in the hole?"

"That is a question I am no more able to answer than yourself. There seems, however, only one plausible way of accounting for them—and yet it is dreadful to believe in such atrocity as my suggestion would imply. It is clear that Kidd—if Kidd indeed secreted this treasure, which I doubt not—it is clear that he must have had assistance in the labor. But this labor concluded, he may have thought it expedient to remove all participants in his secret. Perhaps a couple of blows with a mattock were sufficient, while his coadjutors were busy in the pit; perhaps it required a dozen —who shall tell?"

THE GREAT CARBUNCLE[1]

A MYSTERY OF THE WHITE MOUNTAINS

by Nathaniel Hawthorne

Hawthorne's original footnote to "The Great Carbuncle" calls it an Indian tradition. And certainly the quest for a gem of extraordinary brightness and power is not inharmonious with aboriginal desires. But Hawthorne carefully selected his seekers in order to contrast their purposes and point his moral. The alchemist, the merchant, the cynic, all impelled by ignoble motives, met only frustration or disaster. But the young couple with the fortitude to give up the quest and to be satisfied with the ordinary light of heaven found happiness. Like other buried treasure, the great carbuncle may still attract the greedy, but Hawthorne suggests with characteristic ambiguity that, according to legend, the stone lost its glamor when human beings rejected so dangerous a jewel. "The Great Carbuncle" is one of the stories in Twice-Told Tales *(1837).*

At nightfall, once in the olden time, on the rugged side of one of the Crystal Hills, a party of adventurers were refreshing themselves, after a toilsome and fruitless quest for the Great Carbuncle. They had come thither, not as friends nor partners in the enterprise, but each, save one youthful pair, impelled by his own selfish and solitary longing for this wondrous gem. Their feeling of brotherhood, however, was strong enough to induce them to contribute a mutual aid in building a rude hut of branches, and kindling a great fire of shattered pines, that had drifted down the headlong current of the Amonoosuck, on the lower bank of which they were to pass the night. There was but one of their number, perhaps, who had become so estranged from natural sympathies, by the absorbing spell of the pursuit, as to acknowledge no satisfaction at the sight of human faces, in the remote and solitary region whither they had ascended. A vast extent of wilderness lay between them and the nearest settlement, while a scant mile above their heads was that black verge where the hills throw off their shaggy mantle of forest trees, and either robe themselves in clouds or tower naked into the sky. The roar of the Amonoosuck would have been too awful for endurance if only a solitary man had listened, while the mountain stream talked with the wind.

The adventurers, therefore, exchanged

hospitable greetings, and welcomed one another to the hut, where each man was the host, and all were the guests of the whole company. They spread their individual supplies of food on the flat surface of a rock, and partook of a general repast; at the close of which, a sentiment of good fellowship was perceptible among the party, though repressed by the idea, that the renewed search for the Great Carbuncle must make them strangers again in the morning. Seven men and one young woman, they warmed themselves together at the fire, which extended its bright wall along the whole front of their wigwam. As they observed the various and contrasted figures that made up the assemblage, each man looking like a caricature of himself, in the unsteady light that flickered over him, they came mutually to the conclusion, that an odder society had never met, in city or wilderness, on mountain or plain.

The eldest of the group, a tall, lean, weather-beaten man, some sixty years of age, was clad in the skins of wild animals, whose fashion of dress he did well to imitate, since the deer, the wolf, and the bear, had long been his most intimate companions. He was one of those ill-fated mortals, such as the Indians told of, whom, in their early youth, the Great Carbuncle smote with a peculiar madness, and became the passionate dream of their existence. All who visited that region knew him as the Seeker, and by no other name. As none could remember when he first took up the search, there went a fable in the valley of the Saco, that for his inordinate lust after the Great Carbuncle, he had been con-

---

[1] The Indian tradition, on which this somewhat extravagant tale is founded, is both too wild and too beautiful to be adequately wrought up in prose. Sullivan, in his History of Maine, written since the Revolution, remarks, that even then the existence of the Great Carbuncle was not entirely discredited.

demned to wander among the mountains till the end of time, still with the same feverish hopes at sunrise—the same despair at eve. Near this miserable Seeker sat a little elderly personage, wearing a high-crowned hat, shaped somewhat like a crucible. He was from beyond the sea, a Doctor Cacaphodel, who had wilted and dried himself into a mummy by continually stooping over charcoal furnaces, and inhaling unwholesome fumes during his researches in chemistry and alchemy. It was told of him, whether truly or not, that, at the commencement of his studies, he had drained his body of all its richest blood, and wasted it, with other inestimable ingredients, in an unsuccessful experiment—and had never been a well man since. Another of the adventurers was Master Ichabod Pigsnort, a weighty merchant and selectman of Boston, and an elder of the famous Mr. Norton's church. His enemies had a ridiculous story that Master Pigsnort was accustomed to spend a whole hour after prayer time, every morning and evening, in wallowing naked among an immense quantity of pine-tree shillings, which were the earliest silver coinage of Massachusetts. The fourth whom we shall notice had no name that his companions knew of, and was chiefly distinguished by a sneer that always contorted his thin visage, and by a prodigious pair of spectacles, which were supposed to deform and discolor the whole face of nature, to this gentleman's perception. The fifth adventurer likewise lacked a name, which was the greater pity, as he appeared to be a poet. He was a bright-eyed man, but wofully pined away, which was no more than natural, if, as some people affirmed, his ordinary diet was fog, morning mist, and a slice of the densest cloud within his reach, sauced with moonshine whenever he could get it. Certain it is, that the poetry which flowed from him had a smack of all these dainties. The sixth of the party was a young man of haughty mien, and sat somewhat apart from the rest, wearing his plumed hat loftily among his elders, while the fire glittered on the rich embroidery of his dress, and gleamed intensely on the jewelled pommel of his sword. This was the Lord de Vere, who, when at home, was said to spend much of his time in the burial vault of his dead progenitors, rummaging their mouldy coffins in search of all the earthly pride and vainglory that was hidden among bones and dust; so that, besides his own share, he had the collected haughtiness of his whole line of ancestry.

Lastly, there was a handsome youth in rustic garb, and by his side a blooming little person, in whom a delicate shade of maiden reserve was just melting into the rich glow of a young wife's affection. Her name was Hannah, and her husband's Matthew; two homely names, yet well enough adapted to the simple pair, who seemed strangely out of place among the whimsical fraternity whose wits had been set agog by the Great Carbuncle.

Beneath the shelter of one hut, in the bright blaze of the same fire, sat this varied group of adventurers, all so intent upon a single object, that, of whatever else they began to speak, their closing words were sure to be illuminated with the Great Carbuncle. Several related the circumstances that brought them thither. One had listened to a traveller's tale of this marvellous stone in his own distant country, and had immediately been seized with such a thirst for beholding it as could only be quenched in its intensest lustre. Another, so long ago as when the famous Captain Smith visited these coasts, had seen it blazing far at sea, and had felt no rest in all the intervening years till now that he took up the search. A third, being encamped on a hunting expedition full forty miles south of the White Mountains, awoke at midnight, and beheld the Great Carbuncle gleaming like a meteor, so that the shadows of the trees fell backward from it. They spoke of the innumerable attempts which had been made to reach the spot, and of the singular fatality which had hitherto withheld success from all adventurers, though it might seem so easy to follow to its source a light that overpowered the moon, and almost matched the sun. It was observable that each smiled scornfully at the madness of every other in anticipating better fortune than the past, yet nourished a scarcely hidden conviction that he would himself be the favored one. As if to allay their too sanguine hopes, they recurred to the Indian traditions that a spirit kept watch about the gem, and bewildered those who sought it either by removing it from peak to peak of the higher hills, or by calling up a mist from the enchanted lake over which it hung. But these tales were deemed unworthy of credit, all professing to believe that the search had been baffled by want of sagacity or perseverance in the adventurers, or such other causes as might naturally obstruct the passage to any given point among the intricacies of forest, valley, and mountain.

In a pause of the conversation the wearer of the prodigious spectacles looked round upon the party, making each individual, in turn, the object of the sneer which invariably dwelt upon his countenance.

"So, fellow-pilgrims," said he, "here we are, seven wise men, and one fair damsel—who, doubtless, is as wise as any graybeard of the company: here we are, I say, all bound on the same goodly enterprise. Methinks, now, it were not amiss that each of us declare what he proposes to do with the Great Carbuncle, provided he have the good hap to clutch it. What says our friend in the bear skin? How mean you, good sir, to enjoy the prize which you have been seeking, the Lord knows how long, among the Crystal Hills?"

"How enjoy it!" exclaimed the aged Seeker, bitterly. "I hope for no enjoyment from it; that folly has passed long ago! I keep up the search for this accursed stone because the vain ambition of my youth has become a fate upon me in old age. The pursuit alone is my strength,—the energy of my soul,—the warmth of my blood,—and the pith and marrow of my bones! Were I to turn my back upon it I should fall down dead on the hither side of the Notch, which is the gateway of this mountain region. Yet not to have my wasted lifetime back again would I give up my hopes of the Great Carbuncle! Having found it, I shall bear it to a certain cavern that I wot of, and there, grasping it in my arms, lie down and die, and keep it buried with me forever."

"O wretch, regardless of the interests of science!" cried Doctor Cacaphodel, with philosophic indignation. "Thou art not worthy to behold, even from afar off, the lustre of this most precious gem that ever was concocted in the laboratory of Nature. Mine is the sole purpose for which a wise man may desire the possession of the Great Carbuncle. Immediately on obtaining it—for I have a presentiment, good people, that the prize is reserved to crown my scientific reputation—I shall return to Europe, and employ my remaining years in reducing it to its first elements. A portion of the stone will I grind to impalpable powder; other parts shall be dissolved in acids, or whatever solvents will act upon so admirable a composition; and the remainder I design to melt in the crucible, or set on fire with the blow-pipe. By these various methods I shall gain an accurate analysis, and finally bestow the result of my labors upon the world in a folio volume."

"Excellent!" quoth the man with the spectacles. "Nor need you hesitate, learned sir, on account of the necessary destruction of the gem; since the perusal of your folio may teach every mother's son of us to concoct a Great Carbuncle of his own."

"But, verily," said Master Ichabod Pigsnort, "for mine own part I object to the making of these counterfeits, as being calculated to reduce the marketable value of the true gem. I tell ye frankly, sirs, I have an interest in keeping up the price. Here have I quitted my regular traffic, leaving my warehouse in the care of my clerks, and putting my credit to great hazard, and, furthermore, have put myself in peril of death or captivity by the accursed heathen savages—and all this without daring to ask the prayers of the congregation, because the quest for the Great Carbuncle is deemed little better than a traffic with the Evil One. Now think ye that I would have done this grievous wrong to my soul, body, reputation, and estate, without a reasonable chance of profit?"

"Not I, pious Master Pigsnort," said the man with the spectacles. "I never laid such a great folly to thy charge."

"Truly, I hope not," said the merchant. "Now, as touching this Great Carbuncle, I am free to own that I have never had a glimpse of it; but be it only the hundredth part so bright as people tell, it will surely outvalue the Great Mogul's best diamond, which he holds at an incalculable sum. Wherefore, I am minded to put the Great Carbuncle on shipboard, and voyage with it to England, France, Spain, Italy, or into Heathendom, if Providence should send me thither, and, in a word, dispose of the gem to the best bidder among the potentates of the earth, that he may place it among his crown jewels. If any of ye have a wiser plan, let him expound it."

"That have I, thou sordid man!" exclaimed the poet. "Dost thou desire nothing brighter than gold that thou wouldst transmute all this ethereal lustre into such dross as thou wallowest in already? For myself, hiding the jewel under my cloak, I shall hie me back to my attic chamber, in one of the darksome alleys of London. There, night and day, will I gaze upon it; my soul shall drink its radiance; it shall be diffused throughout my intellectual powers, and gleam brightly in every line of poesy that I indite. Thus, long ages after I am gone, the splendor of the Great Carbuncle will blaze around my name!"

"Well said, Master Poet!" cried he of the spectacles. "Hide it under thy cloak, sayest thou? Why, it will gleam through the holes, and make thee look like a jack-o'-lantern!"

"To think!" ejaculated the Lord de Vere, rather to himself than his companions, the best of whom he held utterly unworthy of his intercourse—"to think that a fellow in a tattered cloak should talk of conveying the Great Carbuncle to a garret in Grub Street! Have not I resolved within myself that the whole earth contains no fitter ornament for the great hall of my ancestral castle? There shall it flame for ages, making a noonday of midnight, glittering on the suits of armor, the banners, and escutcheons, that hang around the wall, and keeping bright the memory of heroes. Wherefore have all other adventurers sought the prize in vain but that I might win it, make it a symbol of the glories of our lofty line? And never, on the diadem of the White Mountains, did the Great Carbuncle hold a place half so honored as is reserved for it in the hall of the De Veres!"

"It is a noble thought," said the Cynic, with an obsequious sneer. "Yet, might I presume to say so, the gem would make a rare sepulchral lamp, and would display the glories of your lordship's progenitors more truly in the ancestral vault than in the castle hall."

"Nay, forsooth," observed Matthew, the young rustic, who sat hand in hand with his bride, "the gentleman has bethought himself of a profitable use for this bright stone. Hannah here and I are seeking it for a like purpose."

"How, fellow!" exclaimed his lordship, in surprise. "What castle hall hast thou to hang it in?"

"No castle," replied Matthew, "but as neat a cottage as any within sight of the Crystal Hills. Ye must know, friends, that Hannah and I, being wedded the last week, have taken up the search of the Great Carbuncle, because we shall need its light in the long winter evenings; and it will be such a pretty thing to show the neighbors when they visit us. It will shine through the house so that we may pick up a pin in any corner, and will set all the windows aglowing as if there were a great fire of pine knots in the chimney. And then how pleasant, when we awake in the night to be able to see one another's faces!"

There was a general smile among the adventurers at the simplicity of the young couple's project in regard to this wondrous and invaluable stone, with which the greatest monarch on earth might have been proud to adorn his palace. Especially the man with spectacles, who had sneered at all the company in turn, now twisted his visage into such an expression of ill-natured mirth, that Matthew asked him, rather peevishly, what he himself meant to do with the Great Carbuncle.

"The Great Carbuncle!" answered the Cynic, with ineffable scorn. "Why, you blockhead, there is no such thing in *rerum natura*. I have come three thousand miles, and am resolved to set my foot on every peak of these mountains, and poke my head into every chasm, for the sole purpose of demonstrating to the satisfaction of any man one whit less an ass than thyself that the Great Carbuncle is all a humbug!"

Vain and foolish were the motives that had brought most of the adventurers to the Crystal Hills; but none so vain, so foolish, and so impious too, as that of the scoffer with the prodigious spectacles. He was one of those wretched and evil men whose yearnings are downward to the darkness, instead of heavenward, and who, could they but extinguish the lights which God hath kindled for us, would count the midnight gloom their chiefest glory. As the Cynic spoke, several of the party were startled by a gleam of red splendor, that showed the huge shapes of the surrounding mountains and the rock-bestrewn bed of the turbulent river with an illumination unlike that of their fire on the trunks and black boughs of the forest trees. They listened for the roll of thunder, but heard nothing, and were glad that the tempest came not near them. The stars, those dial-points of heaven, now warned the adventurers to close their eyes on the blazing logs, and open them, in dreams, to the glow of the Great Carbuncle.

The young married couple had taken their lodgings in the farthest corner of the wigwam, and were separated from the rest of the party by a curtain of curiously-woven twigs, such as might have hung, in deep festoons, around the bridal-bower of Eve. The modest little wife had wrought this piece of tapestry while the other guests were talking. She and her husband fell asleep with hands tenderly clasped, and awoke from visions of unearthly radiance to meet the more blessed light of one another's eyes. They awoke at the same instant, and with one happy smile beaming over their two faces, which grew brighter with their consciousness of the reality of life and love. But no sooner did she recollect where they were, than the bride peeped through the interstices of the leafy curtain, and saw that the outer room of the hut was deserted.

"Up, dear Matthew!" cried she, in haste. "The strange folk are all gone! Up, this very minute, or we shall lose the Great Carbuncle!"

In truth, so little did these poor young people deserve the mighty prize which had lured them thither, that they had slept peacefully all night, and till the summits of the hills were glittering with sunshine; while the other adventurers had tossed their limbs in feverish wakefulness, or dreamed of climbing precipices, and set off to realize their dreams with the earliest peep of dawn. But Matthew and Hannah, after their calm rest, were as light as two young deer, and merely stopped to say their prayers and wash themselves in a cold pool of the Amonoosuck, and then to taste a morsel of food, ere they turned their faces to the mountainside. It was a sweet emblem of conjugal affection, as they toiled up the difficult ascent, gathering strength from the mutual aid which they afforded. After several little accidents, such as a torn robe, a lost shoe, and the entanglement of Hannah's hair in a bough, they reached the upper verge of the forest, and were now to pursue a more adventurous course. The innumerable trunks and heavy foliage of the trees had hitherto shut in their thoughts, which now shrank affrighted from the region of wind and cloud and naked rocks and desolate sunshine, that rose immeasurably above them. They gazed back at the obscure wilderness which they had traversed, and longed to be buried again in its depths rather than trust themselves to so vast and visible a solitude.

"Shall we go on?" said Matthew, throwing his arm round Hannah's waist, both to protect her and to comfort his heart by drawing her close to it.

But the little bride, simple as she was, had a woman's love of jewels, and could not forego the hope of possessing the very brightest in the world, in spite of the perils with which it must be won.

"Let us climb a little higher," whispered she, yet tremulously, as she turned her face upward to the lonely sky.

"Come, then," said Matthew, mustering his manly courage and drawing her along with him, for she became timid again the moment that he grew bold.

And upward, accordingly, went the pilgrims of the Great Carbuncle, now treading upon the tops and thickly-interwoven branches of dwarf pines, which, by the growth of centuries, though mossy with age, had barely reached three feet in altitude. Next, they came to masses and fragments of naked rock heaped confusedly together, like a cairn reared by giants in memory of a giant chief. In this bleak realm of upper air nothing breathed, nothing grew; there was no life but what was concentrated in their two hearts; they had climbed so high that Nature herself seemed no longer to keep them company. She lingered beneath them, within the verge of the forest trees, and sent a farewell glance after her children as they strayed where her own green footprints had never been. But soon they were to be hidden from her eye. Densely and dark the mists began to gather below, casting black spots of shadow on the vast landscape, and sailing heavily to one centre, as if the loftiest mountain peak had summoned a council of its kindred clouds. Finally, the vapors welded themselves, as it were, into a mass, presenting the appearance of a pavement over which the wanderers might have trodden, but where they would vainly have sought an avenue to the blessed earth which they had lost. And the lovers yearned to behold that green earth again, more intensely, alas! than, beneath a clouded sky, they had ever desired a glimpse of heaven. They even felt it a relief to their desolation when the mists, creeping gradually up the mountain, concealed its lonely peak, and thus annihilated, at least for them, the whole region of visible space. But they drew closer together, with a fond and melancholy gaze, dreading lest the universal cloud should snatch them from each other's sight.

Still, perhaps, they would have been resolute to climb as far and as high, between earth and heaven, as they could find foothold, if Hannah's strength had not begun to fail, and with that, her courage also. Her breath grew short. She refused to burden her husband with her weight, but often tottered against his side, and recovered herself each time by a feebler effort.

At last, she sank down on one of the rocky steps of the acclivity.

"We are lost, dear Matthew," said she, mournfully. "We shall never find our way to the earth again. And oh how happy we might have been in our cottage!"

"Dear heart!—we will yet be happy there," answered Matthew. "Look! In this direction, the sunshine penetrates the dismal mist. By its aid, I can direct our course to the passage of the Notch. Let us go back, love, and dream no more of the Great Carbuncle!"

"The sun cannot be yonder," said Hannah, with despondence. "By this time it must be noon. If there could ever be any sunshine here, it would come from above our heads."

"But look!" repeated Matthew, in a somewhat altered tone. "It is brightening every moment. If not sunshine, what can it be?"

Nor could the young bride any longer deny that a radiance was breaking through the mist, and changing its dim hue to a dusky red, which continually grew more vivid, as if brilliant particles were interfused with the gloom. Now, also, the cloud began to roll away from the mountain, while, as it heavily withdrew, one object after another started out of its impenetrable obscurity into sight, with precisely the effect of a new creation, before the indistinctness of the old chaos had been completely swallowed up. As the process went on, they saw the gleaming of water close at their feet, and found themselves on the very border of a mountain lake, deep, bright, clear, and calmly beautiful, spreading from brim to brim of a basin that had been scooped out of the solid rock. A ray of glory flashed across its surface. The pilgrims looked whence it should proceed, but closed their eyes with a thrill of awful admiration, to exclude the fervid splendor that glowed from the brow of a cliff impending over the enchanted lake. For the simple pair had reached that lake of mystery, and found the long-sought shrine of the Great Carbuncle!

They threw their arms around each other, and trembled at their own success; for, as the legends of this wondrous gem rushed thick upon their memory, they felt themselves marked out by fate—and the consciousness was fearful. Often, from childhood upward, they had seen it shining like a distant star. And now that star was throwing its intensest lustre on their hearts. They seemed changed to one another's eyes, in the red brilliancy that flamed upon their cheeks, while it lent the same fire to the lake, the rocks, and sky, and to the mists which had rolled back before its power. But, with their next glance, they beheld an object that drew their attention even from the mighty stone. At the base of the cliff, directly beneath the Great Carbuncle, appeared the figure of a man, with his arms extended in the act of climbing, and his face turned upward, as if to drink the full gush of splendor. But he stirred not, no more than if changed to marble.

"It is the Seeker," whispered Hannah, convulsively grasping her husband's arm. "Matthew, he is dead."

"The joy of success has killed him," replied Matthew, trembling violently. "Or, perhaps, the very light of the Great Carbuncle was death!"

"The Great Carbuncle," cried a peevish voice behind them. "The Great Humbug! If you have found it, prithee point it out to me."

They turned their heads, and there was the Cynic, with his prodigious spectacles set carefully on his nose, staring now at the lake, now at the rocks, now at the distant masses of vapor, now right at the Great Carbuncle itself, yet seemingly as unconscious of its light as if all the scattered clouds were condensed about his person. Though its radiance actually threw the shadow of the unbeliever at his own feet, as he turned his back upon the glorious jewel, he would not be convinced that there was the least glimmer there.

"Where is your Great Humbug?" he repeated. "I challenge you to make me see it!"

"There," said Matthew, incensed at such perverse blindness, and turning the Cynic round towards the illuminated cliff. "Take off those abominable spectacles, and you cannot help seeing it!"

Now these colored spectacles probably darkened the Cynic's sight, in at least as great a degree as the smoked glasses through which people gaze at an eclipse. With resolute bravado, however, he snatched them from his nose, and fixed a bold stare full upon the ruddy blaze of the Great Carbuncle. But scarcely had he encountered it, when, with a deep, shuddering groan, he dropped his head, and pressed both hands across his miserable eyes. Thenceforth there was, in very truth, no light of the Great Carbuncle, nor any other light on earth, nor light of heaven itself, for the poor Cynic. So long accustomed to view all objects through a medium that deprived them of every glimpse of brightness, a single flash of so glorious a phenomenon, striking upon his naked vision, had blinded him forever.

"Matthew," said Hannah, clinging to him, "let us go hence!"

Matthew saw that she was faint, and kneeling down, supported her in his arms, while he threw some of the thrillingly cold water of the enchanted lake upon her face and bosom. It revived her, but could not renovate her courage.

"Yes, dearest!" cried Matthew, pressing her tremulous form to his breast,—"we will go hence, and return to our humble cottage. The blessed sunshine and the quiet moonlight shall come through our window. We will kindle the cheerful glow of our hearth, at eventide, and be happy in its light. But never again will we desire more light than all the world may share with us."

"No," said his bride, "for how could we live by day, or sleep by night, in this awful blaze of the Great Carbuncle!"

Out of the hollow of their hands, they drank each a draught from the lake, which presented them its waters uncontaminated by an earthly lip. Then, lending their guidance to the blinded Cynic, who uttered not a word, and even stifled his groans in his own most wretched heart, they began to descend the mountain. Yet, as they left the shore, till then untrodden, of the spirit's lake, they threw a farewell glance towards the cliff, and beheld the vapors gathering in dense volumes, through which the gem burned duskily.

As touching the other pilgrims of the Great Carbuncle, the legend goes on to tell, that the worshipful Master Ichabod Pigsnort soon gave up the quest as a desperate speculation, and wisely resolved to betake himself again to his warehouse, near the town dock, in Boston. But, as he passed through the Notch of the mountains, a war party of Indians captured our unlucky merchant, and carried him to Montreal, there holding him in bondage, till, by the payment of a heavy ransom, he had wofully subtracted from his hoard of pine-tree shillings. By his long absence, moreover, his affairs had become so disordered that for the rest of his life, instead of wallowing in silver, he had seldom a sixpence worth of copper. Doctor Cacaphodel, the alchemist, returned to his laboratory with a prodigious fragment of granite, which he ground to powder, dissolved in acids, melted in the crucible, and burned with the blow-pipe, and published the result of his experiments in one of the heaviest folios of the day. And, for all these purposes, the gem itself could not have answered better than the granite. The poet, by a somewhat similar mistake, made prize of a great piece of ice, which he found in a sunless chasm of the mountains, and swore that it corresponded, in all points, with his idea of the Great Carbuncle. The critics say, that, if his poetry lacked the splendor of the gem, it retained all the coldness of the ice. The Lord de Vere went back to his ancestral hall, where he contented himself with a wax-lighted chandelier, and filled, in due course of time, another coffin in the ancestral vault. As the funeral torches gleamed within that dark receptacle, there was no need of the Great Carbuncle to show the vanity of earthly pomp.

The Cynic, having cast aside his spectacles, wandered about the world, a miserable object, and was punished with an agonizing desire of light, for the wilful blindness of his former life. The whole night long, he would lift his splendor-blasted orbs to the moon and stars; he turned his face eastward, at sunrise, as duly as a Persian idolater; he made a pilgrimage to Rome, to witness the magnificent illumination of St. Peter's Church; and finally perished in the great fire of London, into the midst of which he had thrust himself, with the desperate idea of catching one feeble ray from the blaze that was kindling earth and heaven.

Matthew and his bride spent many peaceful years, and were fond of telling the legend of the Great Carbuncle. The tale, however, towards the close of their lengthened lives, did not meet with the full credence that had been accorded to it by those who remembered the ancient lustre of the gem. For it is affirmed that, from the hour when two mortals had shown themselves so simply wise as to reject a jewel which would have dimmed all earthly things, its splendor waned. When other pilgrims reached the cliff, they found only an opaque stone, with particles of mica glittering on its surface. There is also a tradition that, as the youthful pair departed, the gem was loosened from the forehead of the cliff, and fell into the enchanted lake, and that, at noontide, the Seeker's form may still be seen to bend over its quenchless gleam.

Some few believe that this inestimable stone is blazing as of old, and say that they have caught its radiance, like a flash of summer lightning, far down the valley of the Saco. And be it owned that, many a mile from the Crystal Hills, I saw a wondrous light around their summits, and was lured, by the faith of poesy, to be the latest pilgrim of the GREAT CARBUNCLE.

MIDAS ON A GOATSKIN

by J. Frank Dobie

Tales of lost mines and caches of silver have been current in the Southwest ever since the days of the Spanish conquistadores and the attempts of Coronado to find the Seven Cities of Cibola. History records that a substantial amount of silver was carried on muleback to Spanish galleons waiting at the Caribbean ports, and more recently old coins or perhaps even fragments of ingots have on rare occasions turned up. But generally the seekers after wealth discover that the map with the crucial route has been lost or that the trail markings have been obliterated by a spring freshet. Rumor, however, persists. Ranchers, sheepherders, and peons circulate legends about hidden bullion, and townspeople dream about expeditions to remote and inaccessible spots. Actually, few men are able to expend the time and money required by the vocation of treasure-hunting. Instead, like Dee Davis, they tell yarns about the fabulous wealth they some day intend to claim, and regale their willing audiences with legend and reminiscence. J. Frank Dobie has happily called these victims of their own imagination "the children of Coronado." "Midas on a Goatskin" is Chapter VII of Coronado's Children *(1930).*

High on a throne of royal state, which far
Outshone the wealth of Ormus and of Ind.
—*Paradise Lost.*

He's the second sorriest white man in Sabinal," my host said. "The sorriest white man keeps a Mexican woman without marrying her, but Dee Davis lawfully wedded his *pelada*. He's town scavenger, works at night, and sleeps most of the day. He'll probably be awake 'long about four o'clock this evening and more than ready to tell you the kind of yarns you want to hear."

We found Dee Davis just awaking from his siesta. He occupied a one-roomed shack and sat on a goatskin in the door, on the shady side of the house.

"I'm a great hand for goatskins," he said. "They make good settin' and they make good pallets."

I sat in a board-bottomed chair out on the hard, swept ground, shaded by an umbrella-China tree as well as by the wall. The shack was set back in a yard fenced with barbed wire. Within the same enclosure but farther towards the front was a little frame house occupied by Dee Davis's Mexican wife and their three or four half-breed children. The yard, or patio, was gay with red and orange zinnias and blue morning-glories. Out in a ramshackle picket corral to the rear a boy was playing with a burro.

"No, mister," went on Dee Davis, who

had got strung out in no time, "I don't reckon anything ever would have come of my dad's picking up those silver bars if it hadn't of been for a surveyor over in Del Rio.

"You see, Dad and Uncle Ben were frontiersmen of the old style and while they'd had a lot of experiences—yes, mister, a lot of experiences—they didn't know a thing about minerals. Well, along back in the eighties they took up some state land on Mud Creek and begun trying to farm a little. Mud Creek's east of Del Rio. The old Spanish crossing on Mud was worn deep and always washed, but it was still used a little. Well, one day not long after an awful rain, a reg'lar gully-washer and fence-lifter, Dad and Uncle Ben started to town. They were going down into the creek when, by heifers, what should show up right square in the old trail but the corner of some sort of metal bar. They got down out of their buggy and pried the bar out and then three other bars. The stuff was so heavy that after they put it in the buggy they had to walk and lead the horse. Instead of going on into town with it, they went back home. Well, they turned it over to Ma and then more or less forgot all about it, I guess—just went on struggling for a living.

"At that time I was still a kid and was away from home working for the San Antonio Land and Cattle Company, but I happened to ride in just a few days after the find. The Old Man and Uncle Ben never mentioned it, but Ma was so proud she was nearly busting, and as soon as I got inside the house she said she wanted to show me something. In one of the rooms was a bed with an old-timey covering on it that came down to the floor. She carried me to this bed, pulled up part of the cover that draped over to the floor, and told me to look. I looked, and, by heifers, there was bars as big as hogs. Yes, mister, as big as hogs.

"Nothing was done, however. We were a long ways from any kind of buying center and never saw anybody. As I said in the beginning, I don't know how long those bars might have stayed right there under that bed if it hadn't been for the surveyor. I won't call his name, because he's still alive and enjoying the fruits of his visit. My dad was a mighty interesting talker, and this surveyor used to come to see him just to hear him talk. Well, on one of these visits he stayed all night and slept on the bed that hid the bars. One of his shoes got under the bed, and next morning in stooping down to get it he saw the bars. At least that's the explanation he gave. Then, of course, he got the whole story as to how the bars came to be there and where they were dug up.

" 'What you going to do with 'em?' he asked Dad.

" 'Oh, I don't know,' Dad says to him. 'Nothing much, I guess. Ma here figgers the stuff might be silver, but I don't know what it is. More'n likely it's not anything worth having.'

" 'Well,' says the surveyor, 'you'd better let me get it assayed. I'm going down to Piedras Negras in my waggin next week and can take it along as well as not.'

"The upshot was that he took all the bars. Two or three months later when Dad saw him and asked him how the assay turned out, he kinder laughed and says, 'Aw pshaw, 'twan't nothing but babbitt-

ing.' Then he went on to explain how he'd left the whole caboodle down there to Piedras Negras because it wasn't worth hauling back.

"Well, it wasn't but a short time before we noticed this surveyor, who had been dog poor, was building a good house and buying land. He always seemed to have money and went right up. Also, he quit coming round to visit his old friend. Yes, mister, quit coming round.

"Some years went by and Dad died. The country had been consider'bly fenced up, though it's nothing but a ranch country yet, and the roads were changed. I was still follering cows, over in Old Mexico a good part of the time. Nobody was left out on Mud Creek. Uncle Ben had moved to Del Rio. One day when I was in there I asked him if he could go back to the old trail crossing on Mud. The idea of them bars and of there being more where they come from seemed to stick in my head.

" 'Sure, I can go to the crossing,' says Uncle Ben. 'It's right on the old Spanish Trail. Furthermore, it's plainly marked by the ruins of an old house on the east bank.'

" 'Well,' says I, 'we'll go over there sometime when we have a day to spare.'

"Finally, two or three years later, we got off. First we went up to the ruins of the house. About all left of it was a tumble-down stick-and-mud chimney.

"Uncle Ben and Dad, you understand, found the bars right down the bank from

this place. Just across the creek, on the side next to Del Rio, was a motte of *palo blanco* [hackberry] trees. The day was awfully hot and we crossed back over there to eat our dinner under the shade and rest up a little before we dug any. About the time we got our horses staked, I noticed a little cloud in the northwest. In less than an hour it was raining pitchforks and bob-tailed heifer yearlings, and Mud Creek was tearing down with enough water to swim a steamboat. There was nothing for us to do but go back to Del Rio.

"I've never been back to hunt those bars since. That was close to forty years ago. A good part of that time I've been raising a family, but my youngest boy—the one out there fooling with the burro—is nine years old now. As soon as he's twelve and able to shift for himself a little, I'm going back into that country and make several investigations."

Old Dee shifted his position on the goatskin.

"My eyes won't stand much light," he explained. "I have worked so long at night that I can see better in the darkness than in the daylight."

I noticed that his eyes were weak, but they had a strange light in them. It was very pleasant as we sat there in the shade, by the bright zinnias and the soft morning-glories. Pretty soon Dee Davis would have to milk his cow and then in the dark do his work as scavenger for the town. Still there was no hurry. Dee Davis's mind was far away from scavenger filth. He went on.

"You see, the old Spanish Trail crossed over into Texas from Mexico at the mouth of the Pecos River, came on east, circling Seminole Hill just west of Devil's River, on across Mud Creek, and then finally to San Antonio. From there it went to New Orleans. It was the route used by the *antiguas* for carrying their gold and silver out of Mexico to New Orleans. The country was full of Indians; it's still full of

dead Spaniards and of bullion and bags of money that the Indians captured and buried or caused the original owners to bury.

"Seminole Hill hides a lot of that treasure. They say that a big jag of Quantrill's loot is located about Seminole too, but I never took much stock in this guerrilla treasure. But listen, mister, and I'll tell you about something that I do take consider'ble stock in.

"Last winter an old Mexican *pastor* named Santiago was staying here in Sabinal with some of his *parientes*. He's a little bit kin to my wife. Now, about nine-tenths of the time a sheepherder don't have a thing to do but explore every cave and examine every rock his sheep get close to. Santiago had a dog that did most of the actual herding. Well, two years ago this fall he was herding sheep about Seminole Hill.

"According to his story—and I don't doubt his word—he went pirooting into a cave one day and stepped right on top of more money than he'd ever seen before all put together. It was just laying there on the floor, some of it stacked up and some of it scattered around every which way. He begun to gather some of it up and had put three pieces in his *hato*—a kind of wallet, you know, that *pastores* carry their provisions in—when he heard the terriblest noise behind him he had ever heard in all his born days. He said it was like the sounds of trace-chains rattling, and dried cowhides being drug at the end of a rope, and panther yells, and the groans of a dying man all mixed up. He was scared half out of his skin. He got out of the cave as fast as his legs would carry him.

"An hour or so later, when he'd kinder collected his wits, he discovered three of the coins still in his *hato*. They were old square 'dobe dollars like the Spanish used to make. As soon as he got a chance, he took them to Villa Acuna across the river from Del Rio, and there a barkeeper traded him three bottles of beer and three silver dollars, American, for them.

"Well, you know how superstitious Mexicans are. Wild horses couldn't drag old Santiago back inside that cave, but he promised to take me out there and show me the mouth of it. We were just waiting for milder weather when somebody sent in here and got him to herd sheep. Maybe he'll be back this winter. If he is, we'll go out to the cave. It won't take but a day."

Dee Davis rolled another cigarette from his supply of Black Horse leaf tobacco and corn shucks. His Mexican wife, plump and easy-going, came out into the yard and began watering the flowers from a tin can. He hardly noticed her, though as he glanced in her direction he seemed to inhale his smoke with a trifle more of deliberation. He was a spare man, and gray moustaches that drooped in Western sheriff style hid only partly a certain nervousness of the facial muscles; yet his few gestures and low voice were as deliberate—and as natural—as the flop of a burro's ears.

"What I'd rather get at than Santiago's cave," he resumed, "is that old smelter across the Rio Grande in Mexico just below the mouth of the Pecos. That smelter wasn't put there to grind corn on, or to boil frijoles in, or to roast goat ribs over, or anything like that. No, mister, not for anything like that.

"It's kinder under a bluff that fronts the river. I know one ranchman who had an expert mining engineer with him, and they spent a whole week exploring up and down the bluff and back in the mountains. I could of told them in a minute that the mine was not above the mouth of the Pecos. If it had of been above, the trails made by miners carrying *parihuelas* could still be seen. I've peered over every foot of that ground and not a *parihuela* trace is there. You don't know what a *parihuela*

is? Well, it's a kind of hod, shaped like a stretcher, with a pair of handles in front and a pair behind so two men can carry it. That's what the slave Indians carried ore on.

"No, sir, the mine that supplied that smelter—and it was a big mine—was below the mouth of the Pecos. It's covered up now by a bed of gravel that has probably washed in there during the last eighty or ninety years. All a man has to do to uncover the shaft is to take a few teams and scrapers and clear out the gravel. The mouth of the shaft will then be as plain as daylight. That will take a little capital. You ought to do this. I wish you would. All I want is a third for my information.

"Now, there is an old lost mine away back in the Santa Rosa Mountains that the Mexicans called El Lipano. The story goes that the Lipan Indians used to work it. It was gold and as rich as twenty-dollar gold pieces. El Lipano didn't have no smelter. The Lipans didn't need one.

"And I want to tell you that those Lipan Indians could smell gold as far as a hungry coyote can smell fresh liver. Yes, mister, they could smell it. One time out there in the Big Bend an old-timey Lipan came to D. C. Bourland's ranch and says to him, 'Show me the *tinaja* I'm looking for and I'll show you the gold.' He got down on his hands and knees and showed how his people used to pound out gold ornaments in the rock *tinajas* across the Rio Grande from Reagan Canyon.

"Now that long bluff overlooking the lost mine in the gravel I was just speaking about hides something worth while. I guess maybe you never met old Uncle Dick Sanders. I met him the first time while I was driving through the Indian Territory up the trail to Dodge. He was government interpreter for the Comanche Indians at Fort Sill and was a great hombre among them.

"Well, several years ago an old, old

Comanche who was dying sent for Uncle Dick.

" 'I'm dying,' the Comanche says. 'I want nothing more on this earth. You can do nothing for me. But you have been a true friend to me and my people. Before I leave, I want to do you a favor.'

"Then the old Indian, as Uncle Dick Sanders reported the facts to me, went on to tell how when he was a young buck he was with a party raiding horses below the Rio Grande. He said that while they were on a long bluff just south of the river they saw a Spanish cart train winding among the mountains. The soldiers to guard it were riding ahead, and while they were going down into a canyon out of sight, the Comanches made a dash, cut off three *carretas,* and killed the drivers.

"There wasn't a thing in the *carretas* but rawhide bags full of gold and silver coins. Well, this disgusted the Comanches mightily. Yes, mister, disgusted them. They might make an ornament out of a coin now and then, but they didn't know how to trade with money. They traded with buffalo robes and horses.

"So what they did now with the rawhide sacks was to cut them open and pour the gold and silver into some deep cracks they happened to notice in the long bluff. Two or three of the sacks, though, they brought over to this side of the Rio Grande and hid in a hole. Then they piled rocks over the hole. This place was between two forks, the old Comanche said, one a running river walled with rock and the other a deep, dry canyon. Not far below where the canyon emptied into the river, the river itself emptied into the Rio Grande.

"After the Comanche got through explaining all this to Uncle Dick Sanders, he asked for a lump of charcoal and a dressed deerskin. Then he drew on the skin a sketch of the Rio Grande, the bluffs to the south, a stream with a west prong coming in from the north, and the place of the buried coins. Of course he didn't put names on the map. The only name he knew was Rio Grande del Norte. When Sanders came down here looking for the Comanche stuff, of course he brought the map with him and he showed it to me. The charcoal lines had splotched until you could hardly trace them, but Sanders had got an Indian to trace them over with a kind of greenish paint.

"Uncle Dick had some sort of theory that the Comanche had mistook the Frio River for the Rio Grande. Naturally he hadn't got very far in locating the ground, much less the money. He was disgusted with the whole business. Told me I could use his information and have whatever I found. I'm satisfied that Devil's River and Painted Cave Canyon are the forks that the Indians hid the *maletas* of money between, and the long bluff on the south side of the Rio Grande where they poured coins into the chinks is the same bluff I've been talking about."

Dee Davis got up, reached for a stick, squatted on the ground, and outlined the deerskin map that Uncle Dick Sanders had shown him. Then he sat down again on the goatskin and contemplated the map in silence.

It was wonderfully pleasant sitting there in the shade, the shadows growing longer and the evening growing cooler, listening —whether to Dee Davis or to a hummingbird in the morning-glories. I did not want the tales to stop. I remarked that I had just been out in the Big Bend country and had camped on Reagan Canyon, famed for its relation to the Lost Nigger Mine. I expected that Dee Davis would know something about this. He did.

"Now listen," he interposed in his soft voice, "I don't expect you to tell me all you know about the Lost Nigger Mine, and I know some things I can't tell you. You'll understand that. You see I was *vaciero* for a string of *pastores* in that very country and got a good deal farther into the mountains, I guess, than any of the Reagans ever got. You may not believe me, but I'll swear on a stack of Bibles as high as your head that I can lead you straight to the nigger who found the mine. Of course I can't tell you where he is. You'll understand that. It was this away.

"One morning the Reagans sent Bill Kelley—that's the nigger's name—to hunt a horse that had got away with the saddle on. A few hours later Jim Reagan rode up on the nigger and asked him if he had found the horse.

" 'No, sah,' the nigger says, 'but jes' looky here, Mister Jim, I'se foun' a gold mine.'

" 'Damn your soul,' says Jim Reagan, 'we're not paying you to hunt gold mines. Pull your freight and bring in that horse.'

"Yes, mister, that's the way Jim Reagan took the news of the greatest gold mine that's ever been found in the Southwest— but he repented a million times afterwards.

"Well, as you've no doubt heard, the nigger got wind of how he was going to be pitched into the Rio Grande and so that night he lit a shuck on one of the Reagan horses. Then a good while afterwards when the Reagans found out how they'd played the wilds in running off, you might say, the goose that laid the golden egg, they started in to trail him down. No telling how many thousands of dollars they did spend trying to locate Nigger Bill— the only man who could put his hand on the gold.

"I've knowed a lot of the men who looked for the Lost Nigger Mine. Not one of them has gone to the right place. One other thing I'll tell you. Go to that round mountain down in the *vegas* on the Mexican side just opposite the old Reagan camp. They call this mountain El Diablo, also Niggerhead; some calls it El Capitan. Well, about half way up it is a kind of shelf, or mesa, maybe two acres wide. On this shelf close back against the mountain wall is a *chapote* bush. Look under that *chapote* and you'll see a hole about the size of an old-timey dug well. Look down this hole and you'll see an old ladder—the kind made without nails, rungs being tied on the poles with rawhide and the fibre of Spanish dagger. Well, right by that hole, back a little and sorter hid behind the *chapote,* I once upon a time found a *macapal.* I guess you want me to tell you what that is. It's a kind of basket in which Mexican miners used to carry up their ore. It's fastened on the head and shoulders.

"Now, I never heard of a *macapal* being used to haul water up in. And I didn't see any water in that hole. No, mister, I didn't see any water.

"As I said, as soon as my boy gets to be twelve years old—he's nine now—I'm going out in that country and use some of the knowledge I've been accumulating."

Dee Davis leaned over and began lacing the brogan shoes on his stockingless feet. It was about time for him to begin work. But I was loath to leave. How pleasant it was there! Maybe Dee Davis is "the second sorriest white man in Sabinal." I don't know, but it seemed to me then, and it seems to me still, that there are many ways of living worse than the way of this village scavenger with a soft goatskin to sit on, and aromatic Black Horse tobacco to inhale leisurely through a clean white shuck, and bright zinnias and blue morning-glories in the door-yard, and long siestas while the shadows of evening lengthen to soften the light of day, and an easy-going Mexican wife, and playing around a patient burro out in the corral an urchin that will be twelve *mañana,* as it were, and then—. Then silver bars out of Mud Creek as big as hogs—and heaps of old square 'dobe dollars in Santiago's cave on Seminole Hill—and Uncle Dick Sanders' gold in the chinks of the long bluff across the Rio Grande—and some-where in the gravel down under the bluff a rich mine that a few mules and scrapers might uncover in a day—and, maybe so, the golden Lipano out in the Santa Rosas beyond—and, certainly and above all, the great Lost Nigger Mine of free gold far up the Rio Bravo in the solitude of the Big Bend.

Dee Davis is just one of Coronado's children.

VI

FRONTIER HUMOR
and the
TALL TALE

The humor of the American frontier was crude and exaggerated. Life itself was raw, manners were coarse, and the comedy that developed was neither delicate nor subtle. Newspaper columnists like Josh Billings and Petroleum V. Nasby indulged in the deliberate illiteracy which is sometimes called "eye humor" because the atrocious misspellings must be seen to be believed. Subjects like putrefaction, the stench of unburied corpses, and funerals were given comic treatment; and deeds that seem today both cruel and pointless were considered extremely ludicrous. In similar vein, a premium was put on the grotesquely improbable; the boasts of the "half-horse, half-alligator" boatmen were as inflated as the currency issued by the wildcat banks. Exaggeration and overstatement marked the ranting of both Mike Fink and Davy Crockett. No early American book reflects the rawness of the frontier better than Longstreet's *Georgia Scenes*, and here the barbarism and lack of restraint are not minimized. But Faulkner's "Spotted Horses" tale a hundred years later is clear evidence that the red necks and crackers interested in a "horse swap" have not changed materially in that length of time. On the other hand, the indefensible meanness of a Simon Suggs or a Sut Lovingood has probably vanished with the society which bred them.

The tall tale, long a favorite brand of American humor, is nowhere better exemplified than in Thorpe's story of a bear hunt in Arkansas or Twain's celebrated account of a jumping frog. Both stories utilize the frame technique and introduce a conventional narrator who in turn can describe the real teller of the tale and make appropriate comment. The intrinsic value of the story is thus supplemented by the character contrast and by the two or three kinds of idiom employed. Both tales are effectively planned and build up to a strong climax, which is not marred by moral tag or by postscript.

THE HORSE·SWAP

by A. B. Longstreet

The Georgia backwoods is the scene of a number of Longstreet's tales of earthy and primitive life in the first half of the nineteenth century. Frontier. humor and cruelty are rich in his stories of a gander-pulling, a militia muster, and a horse trade, for the times did not permit sentimentality or even legal justice. The incident which forms the plot of "The Horse-Swap" is an old one in country life and reveals how each bargainer, by a combination of evasion and exaggeration, attempts to get the better of the other. Eventually, of course, a showdown develops, and the amused audience discovers that the trickster has himself been tricked. There is an interesting parallel between Longstreet's concise tale and William Faulkner's much longer story, "Spotted Horses." "The Horse-Swap" was published in Georgia Scenes *(1835). The text printed here is that of the new edition of 1897.*

During the session of the Supreme Court in the village of ——, about three weeks ago, when a number of people were collected in the principal street of the village, I observed a young man riding up and down the street, as I supposed, in a violent passion. He galloped this way, then that, and then the other; spurred his horse to one group of citizens, then to another; then dashed off at half-speed, as if fleeing from danger; and, suddenly checking his horse, returned first in a pace, then in a trot, and then in a canter. While he was performing these various evolutions he cursed, swore, whooped, screamed, and tossed himself in every attitude which man could assume on horseback. In short, he cavorted most magnanimously (a term which, in our tongue, expresses all that I have described, and a little more), and seemed to be setting all creation at defiance. As I like to see all that is passing, I determined to take a position a little nearer to him, and to ascertain, if possible, what it was that affected him so sensibly. Accordingly I approached a crowd before which he had stopped for a moment, and examined it with the strictest scrutiny. But I could see nothing in it that seemed to have anything to do with the cavorter. Every man appeared to be in good humor, and all minding their own business. Not one so much as noticed the principal figure. Still he went on. After a semicolon pause, which my appearance seemed to produce (for he eyed me closely as I approached), he fetched a whoop, and swore that "he could out-swap any live man, woman, or child that ever walked these hills, or that ever straddled horseflesh since the days of old daddy Adam. "Stranger," said he to me, "did you ever see the *Yellow* Blossom from Jasper?"

"No," said I, "but I have often heard of him."

"I'm the boy," continued he; "perhaps a *leetle*, jist a *leetle*, of the best man at a horse-swap that ever trod shoe-leather."

I began to feel my situation a little awkward, when I was relieved by a man somewhat advanced in years, who stepped up and began to survey the Yellow Blossom's horse with much apparent interest. This drew the rider's attention, and he turned the conversation from me to the stranger.

"Well, my old coon," said he, "do you want to swap *hosses?*"

"Why, I don't know," replied the stranger; "I believe I've got a beast I'd trade with you for that one, if you like him."

"Well, fetch up your nag, my old cock; you're jist the lark I wanted to get hold of. I am perhaps a *leetle*, jist a *leetle*, of the best man at a horse-swap that ever

stole *cracklins* out of his mammy's fat gourd. Where's your *hoss?*"

"I'll bring him presently; but I want to examine your horse a little."

"Oh, look at him," said the Blossom, alighting and hitting him a cut—"look at him! He's the best piece of *hossflesh* in the thirteen united univarsal worlds. There's no sort o' mistake in little Bullet. He can pick up miles on his feet, and fling 'em behind him as fast as the next man's *hoss*, I don't care where he comes from. And he can keep at it as long as the sun can shine without resting."

During this harangue little Bullet looked as if he understood it all, believed it, and was ready at any moment to verify it. He was a horse of goodly countenance, rather expressive of vigilance than fire; though an unnatural appearance of fierceness was thrown into it by the loss of his ears, which had been cropped pretty close to his head. Nature had done but little for Bullet's head and neck; but he managed, in a great measure, to hide their defects by bowing perpetually. He had obviously suffered severely for corn; but if his ribs and hipbones had not disclosed the fact, *he* never would have done it; for he was in all respects as cheerful and happy as if he commanded all the corn-cribs and fodder-stacks in Georgia. His height was about twelve hands; but as his shape partook somewhat of that of the giraffe, his haunches stood much lower. They were short, strait, peaked, and concave. Bullet's tail, however, made amends for all his defects. All that the artist could do to beautify it had been done; and all that horse could do to compliment the artist, Bullet did. His tail was nicked in superior style, and exhibited the line of beauty in so many directions that it could not fail to hit the most fastidious taste in some of them. From the root it dropped into a graceful festoon, then rose in a handsome curve, then resumed its first direction, and then mounted suddenly upward like a cypress knee to a perpendicular of about two and a half inches. The whole had a careless and bewitching inclination to the right. Bullet obviously knew where his beauty lay, and took all occasions to display it to the best advantage. If a stick cracked, or if any one moved suddenly about him, or coughed, or hawked, or spoke a little louder than common, up went Bullet's tail like lightning; and if the *going up* did not please, the *coming down* must of necessity, for it was as different from the other movement as was its direction. The first was a bold and rapid flight upward, usually to an angle of forty-five degrees. In this position he kept his interesting appendage until he satisfied himself that nothing in particular was to be done; when he commenced dropping it by half inches, in second beats, then in triple time, then faster and shorter, and faster and shorter still, until it finally died away imperceptibly into its natural position. If I might compare sights to sounds, I should say its *settling* was more like the note of a locust than anything else in nature.

Either from native sprightliness of disposition, from uncontrollable activity, or from an unconquerable habit of removing flies by the stamping of the feet, Bullet never stood still, but always kept up a gentle fly-scaring movement of his limbs, which was peculiarly interesting.

"I tell you, man," proceeded the Yellow Blossom, "he's the best live hoss that ever trod the grit of Georgia. Bob Smart knows the hoss. Come here, Bob, and mount this hoss, and show Bullet's motions." Here Bullet bristled up, and looked as if he had been hunting for Bob all day long, and had just found him. Bob sprang on his back. "Boo-oo-oo!" said Bob, with a fluttering noise of the lips, and away went Bullet as if in a quarter race, with all his beauties spread in handsome style.

"Now fetch him back," said Blossom. Bullet turned and came in pretty much as he went out.

"Now trot him by." Bullet reduced his tail to *customary,* sidled to the right and left airily, and exhibited at least three varieties of trot in the short space of fifty yards.

"Make him pace!" Bob commenced twitching the bridle and kicking at the same time. These inconsistent movements obviously (and most naturally) disconcerted Bullet; for it was impossible for him to learn from them whether he was to proceed or stand still. He started to trot, and was told that wouldn't do. He attempted a canter, and was checked again. He stopped, and was urged to go on. Bullet now rushed into the wide field of experiment, and struck out a gait of his own that completely turned the tables upon his rider, and certainly deserved a patent. It seemed to have derived its elements from the jig, the minuet, and the cotillon. If it was not a pace, it certainly had *pace* in it, and no man would venture to call it anything else; so it passed off to the satisfaction of the owner.

"Walk him!" Bullet was now at home again, and he walked as if money were staked on him.

The stranger, whose name I afterwards learned was Peter Ketch, having examined

Bullet to his heart's content, ordered his son Neddy to go and bring up Kit. Neddy soon appeared upon Kit, a well-formed sorrel of the middle size, and in good order. His *tout-ensemble* threw Bullet entirely in the shade, though a glance was sufficient to satisfy any one that Bullet had the decided advantage of him in point of intellect.

"Why, man," said Blossom, "do you bring such a hoss as that to trade for Bullet? Oh, I see, you've no notion of trading!"

"Ride him off, Neddy!" said Peter. Kit put off at a handsome lope.

"Trot him back!" Kit came in at a long, sweeping trot, and stopped suddenly at the crowd.

"Well," said Blossom, "let me look at him; maybe he'll do to plough."

"Examine him," said Peter, taking hold of the bridle close to the mouth; "he's nothing but a tacky. He ain't as *pretty* a horse as Bullet, I know, but he'll do. Start 'em together for a hundred and fifty *mile,* and if Kit ain't twenty mile ahead of him at the coming out, any man may take Kit for nothing. But he's a monstrous mean horse, gentlemen; any man may see that. He's the scariest horse, too, you ever saw. He won't do to hunt on, nohow. Stranger, will you let Neddy have your rifle to shoot off him? Lay the rifle between his ears, Neddy, and shoot at the blaze in that stump. Tell me when his head is high enough."

Ned fired and hit the blaze, and Kit did not move a hair's-breadth.

"Neddy, take a couple of sticks, and beat on that hogshead at Kit's tail."

Ned made a tremendous rattling, at which Bullet took fright, broke his bridle, and dashed off in grand style, and would have stopped all further negotiations by going home in disgust, had not a traveller arrested him and brought him back; but Kit did not move.

"I tell you, gentlemen," continued Peter,

"he's the scariest horse you ever saw. He ain't as gentle as Bullet, but he won't do any harm if you watch him. Shall I put him in a cart, gig, or wagon for you, stranger? He'll cut the same capers there he does here. He's a monstrous mean horse."

During all this time Blossom was examining him with the nicest scrutiny. Having examined his frame and limbs, he now looked at his eyes.

"He's got a curious look out of his eyes," said Blossom.

"Oh yes, sir," said Peter, "just as blind as a bat. Blind horses always have clear eyes. Make a motion at his eyes, if you please, sir."

Blossom did so, and Kit threw up his head rather as if something pricked him under the chin than as if fearing a blow. Blossom repeated the experiment, and Kit jerked back in considerable astonishment.

"Stone-blind, you see, gentlemen," proceeded Peter; "but he's just as good to travel of a dark night as if he had eyes."

"Blame my buttons," said Blossom, "if I like them eyes!"

"No," said Peter, "nor I neither. I'd rather have 'em made of diamonds; but they'll do—if they don't show as much white as Bullet's."

"Well," said Blossom, "make a pass at me."

"No," said Peter, "you made the banter, now make your pass."

"Well, I'm never afraid to price my hosses. You must give me twenty-five dollars boot."

"Oh, certainly; say fifty, and my saddle and bridle in. Here, Neddy, my son, take away daddy's horse."

"Well," said Blossom, "I've made my pass, now you make yours."

"I'm for short talk in a horse-swap, and therefore always tell a gentleman at once what I mean to do. You must give me ten dollars."

Blossom swore absolutely, roundly, and

profanely that he never would give boot.

"Well," said Peter, "I didn't care about trading; but you cut such high shines that I thought I'd like to back you out, and I've done it. Gentlemen, you see I've brought him to a hack."

"Come, old man," said Blossom, "I've been joking with you. I begin to think you do want to trade; therefore, give me five dollars and take Bullet. I'd rather lose ten dollars any time than not make a trade, though I hate to fling away a good hoss."

"Well," said Peter, "I'll be as clever as you are. Just put the five dollars on Bullet's back, and hand him over; it's a trade."

Blossom swore again, as roundly as before, that he would not give boot; and, said he, "Bullet wouldn't hold five dollars on his back, nohow. But, as I bantered you, if you say an even swap, here's at you."

"I told you," said Peter, "I'd be as clever as you; therefore, here goes two dollars more, just for trade sake. Give me three dollars, and it's a bargain."

Blossom repeated his former assertion; and here the parties stood for a long time, and the by-standers (for many were now collected) began to taunt both parties. After some time, however, it was pretty unanimously decided that the old man had backed Blossom out.

At length Blossom swore he "never would be backed out for three dollars after bantering a man"; and, accordingly, they closed the trade.

"Now," said Blossom, as he handed Peter the three dollars, "I'm a man that, when he makes a bad trade, makes the most of it until he can make a better. I'm for no rues and after-claps."

"That's just my way," said Peter; "I never goes to law to mend my bargains."

"Ah, you're the kind of boy I love to trade with. Here's your hoss, old man. Take the saddle and bridle off him, and I'll strip yours; but lift up the blanket easy from Bullet's back, for he's a mighty tender-backed hoss."

The old man removed the saddle, but the blanket stuck fast. He attempted to raise it, and Bullet bowed himself, switched his tail, danced a little, and gave signs of biting.

"Don't hurt him, old man," said Blossom, archly; "take it off easy. I am, perhaps, a leetle of the best man at a horse-swap that ever catched a coon."

Peter continued to pull at the blanket more and more roughly, and Bullet became more and more *cavortish,* insomuch that, when the blanket came off, he had reached the *kicking* point in good earnest.

The removal of the blanket disclosed a sore on Bullet's backbone that seemed to have defied all medical skill. It measured six full inches in length and four in breadth, and had as many features as Bullet had motions. My heart sickened at the sight; and I felt that the brute who had been riding him in that situation deserved the halter.

The prevailing feeling, however, was that of mirth. The laugh became loud and general at the old man's expense, and rustic witticisms were liberally bestowed upon him and his late purchase. These Blossom continued to provoke by various remarks. He asked the old man "if he thought Bullet would let five dollars lie on his back." He declared most seriously that he had owned that horse three months, and had never discovered before that he had a sore back, "or he never should have thought of trading him," etc., etc.

The old man bore it all with the most philosophic composure. He evinced no astonishment at his late discovery, and made no replies. But his son Neddy had not disciplined his feelings quite so well. His eyes opened wider and wider from the first to the last pull of the blanket, and when the whole sore burst upon his view, astonishment and fright seemed to contend for the mastery of his countenance. As the blanket disappeared, he stuck his hands in his breeches pockets, heaved a deep sigh, and lapsed into a profound reverie, from which he was only roused by the cuts at his father. He bore them as long as he could; and, when he could contain himself no longer, he began, with a certain wildness of expression which gave a peculiar interest to what he uttered: "His back's mighty bad off; but dod drot my soul if he's put it to daddy as bad as he thinks he has, for old Kit's both blind and *deef*, I'll be dod drot if he ein't!"

"The devil he is!" said Blossom.

"Yes, dod drot my soul if he *ein't!* You walk him, and see if he *ein't*. His eyes don't look like it; but he'd *jist as leve go*

agin the house with you, or in a ditch, as anyhow. Now you go try him." The laugh was now turned on Blossom, and many rushed to test the fidelity of the little boy's report. A few experiments established its truth beyond controversy.

"Neddy," said the old man. "you oughtn't to try and make people discontented with their things. Stranger, don't mind what the little boy says. If you can only get Kit rid of them little failings you'll find him all sorts of a horse. You are a *leetle* the best man at a horse-swap that ever I got hold of; but don't fool away Kit. Come, Neddy, my son, let's be moving; the stranger seems to be getting snappish."

FRESCOS FROM THE PAST

by Samuel Langhorne Clemens

Mark Twain's indebtedness to the school of southwestern humorists is as clearly apparent as is his superiority to all but the very best of them. Certainly he used similar material and employed similar methods. The celebrated account of raftmen's talk—which was designed originally as part of Huckleberry Finn *but actually appeared as Chapter III of* Life on the Mississippi *(1883)—is as full of ranting and boasting and absurd comparisons as anything by Thorpe or Crockett. Yet the sketch of the two bullies who were long on talk but short on action rings true. The account of the jumping frog is perhaps the best-known American tall tale. Here Twain contrasts sharply the eastern visitor, who is stiffly conventional, with Simon Wheeler, who is garrulous, colloquial, and prolix. It is open to question whether Twain is more interested in ridiculing Wheeler as a crude westerner who likes to tell interminable stories or in slyly satirizing the eastern visitor who is taken in before he realizes it.[1] At any rate, the reader becomes so delighted with Jim Smiley's gambling propensities and with his remarkable animals that he regrets being deprived of further details about the "yaller one-eyed cow."*

1. Cf. Paul Schmidt, "The Deadpan on Simon Wheeler," *Southwest Review* (Summer, 1956), XLI, 270–77.

By way of illustrating keelboat talk and manners, and that now departed and hardly-remembered raft-life, I will throw in, in this place, a chapter from a book which I have been working at, by fits and starts, during the past five or six years, and may possibly finish in the course of five or six more. The book is a story which details some passages in the life of an ignorant village boy, Huck Finn, son of the town drunkard of my time out West, there. He has run away from his persecuting father, and from a persecuting good widow who wishes to make a nice, truth-telling, respectable boy of him; and with him a slave of the widow's has also escaped. They have found a fragment of a lumber-raft (it is high water and dead summer time), and are floating down the river by night, and hiding in the willows by day—bound for Cairo, whence the negro will seek freedom in the heart of the free States. But, in a fog, they pass Cairo without knowing it. By and by they begin to suspect the truth, and Huck Finn is persuaded to end the dismal suspense by swimming down to a huge raft which they have seen in the distance ahead of them, creeping aboard under cover of the darkness, and gathering the needed information by eavesdropping:

But you know a young person can't wait very well when he is impatient to find a thing out. We talked it over, and by and by Jim said it was such a black night, now, that it wouldn't be no risk to swim down to the big raft and crawl aboard and listen—they would talk about Cairo, because they would be calculating to go ashore there for a spree, maybe; or any way they would send boats ashore to buy whiskey or fresh meat or something. Jim had a wonderful level head, for a nigger; he could most always start a good plan when you wanted one.

I stood up and shook my rags off and jumped into the river, and struck out for the raft's light. By and by, when I got down nearly to her, I eased up and went slow and cautious. But every thing was all right—nobody at the sweeps. So I swum down along the raft till I was most abreast the camp fire in the middle, then I crawled aboard and inched along and got in among some bundles of shingles on the weather side of the fire. There was thirteen men there—they was the watch on deck of course. And a mighty rough-looking lot, too. They had a jug, and tin cups, and they kept the jug moving. One man was singing—roaring, you may say; and it wasn't a nice song—for a parlor, any way. He roared through his nose, and strung out the last word of every line very long. When he was done they all fetched a kind of Injun war-whoop, and then another was sung. It begun:

> There was a woman in our towdn,
>   In our towdn did dwed'l [dwell],
> She loved her husband dear-i-lee,
>   But another man twyste as wed'l.
>
> Singing too, riloo, riloo, riloo,
>   Ri-too, riloo, rilay—e,
> She loved her husband dear-i-lee,
>   But another man twyste as wed'l.

And so on—fourteen verses. It was kind of poor, and when he was going to start on the next verse one of them said it was the tune the old cow died on; and another one said, "Oh, give us a rest!" And another told him to take a walk. They made fun of him till he got mad and jumped up and begun to cuss the crowd, and said he could lam any thief in the lot.

They was all about to make a break for him, but the biggest man there jumped up and says:

"Set whar you are gentlemen. Leave him to me; he's my meat."

Then he jumped up in the air three times and cracked his heels together every time. He flung off a buckskin coat that was all hung with fringes, and says, "You lay thar tell the chawin-up's done"; and flung his hat down, which was all over ribbons, and says, "You lay thar tell his sufferin's is over."

Then he jumped up in the air and cracked his heels together again and shouted out:

"Whoo-oop! I'm the old original iron-jawed, brass-mounted, copper-bellied corpse-maker from the wilds of Arkansaw! Look at me! I'm the man they call Sudden Death and General Desolation! Sired by a hurricane, dam'd by an earthquake, half-brother to the cholera, nearly related to the small-pox on the mother's side! Look at me! I take nineteen alligators and a bar'l of whiskey for breakfast when I'm in robust health, and a bushel of rattle-snakes and a dead body when I'm ailing! I split the everlasting rocks with my glance, and I squench the thunder when I speak! Whoo-oop! Stand back and give me room according to my strength! Blood's my natural drink, and the wails of the dying is music to my ear! Cast your eye on me, gentlemen! and lay low and hold your breath, for I'm 'bout to turn myself loose!"

All the time he was getting this off, he was shaking his head and looking fierce, and kind of swelling around in a little circle, tucking up his wrist-bands, and now and then straightening up and beating his breast with his fist, saying, "Look at me, gentlemen!" When he got through, he jumped up and cracked his heels together three times, and let off a roaring "Whoo-oop! I'm the bloodiest son of a wildcat that lives!"

Then the man that had started the row tilted his old slouch hat down over his right eye; then he bent stooping forward, with his back sagged and his south end sticking out far, and his fists a-shoving out and drawing in in front of him, and so went around in a little circle about three times, swelling himself up and breathing hard. Then he straightened, and jumped up and cracked his heels together three

times before he lit again (that made them cheer), and he began to shout like this:

"Whoo-oop! bow your neck and spread, for the kingdom of sorrow's a-coming! Hold me down to the earth, for I feel my powers a-working! whoo-oop! I'm a child of sin, *don't let me get a start!* Smoked glass, here, for all! Don't attempt to look at me with the naked eye, gentlemen! When I'm playful I use the meridians of longitude and parallels of latitude for a seine, and drag the Atlantic Ocean for whales! I scratch my head with the lightning and purr myself to sleep with the thunder! When I'm cold, I bile the Gulf of Mexico and bathe in it; when I'm hot I fan myself with an equinoctial storm; when I'm thirsty I reach up and suck a cloud dry like a sponge; when I range the earth hungry, famine follows in my tracks! Whoo-oop! Bow your neck and spread! I put my hand on the sun's face and make it night in the earth; I bite a piece out of the moon and hurry the seasons; I shake myself and crumble the mountains! Contemplate me through leather—*don't* use the naked eye! The massacre of isolated communities is the pastime of my idle moments, the destruction of nationalities the serious business of my life! The boundless vastness of the great American desert is my enclosed property, and I bury my dead on my own premises!" He jumped up and cracked his heels together three times before he lit (they cheered him again), and as he come down he shouted out: "Whoo-oop! bow your neck and spread, for the Pet Child of Calamity's a-coming!"

Then the other one went to swelling around and blowing again—the first one —the one they called Bob; next, the Child of Calamity chipped in again, swelling round and round each other and punching their fists most into each other's faces, and whooping and jawing like Injuns; then Bob called the Child names, and the Child called him names back again; next, Bob called him a heap rougher names; and the Child come back at him with the very worst kind of language; next, Bob knocked the Child's hat off, and the Child picked it up and kicked Bob's ribbony hat about six foot; Bob went and got it and said never mind, this warn't going to be the last of this thing, because he was a man that never forgot and never forgive, and so the Child better look out, for there was a time a-coming, just as sure as he was a living man, that he would have to answer to him with the best blood in his body. The Child said no man was willinger than he for that time to come, and he would give Bob fair warning, *now*, never to cross his path again, for he could never rest till he had waded in his blood, for such was his nature, though he was sparing him now on account of his family, if he had one.

Both of them was edging away in different directions, growling and shaking their heads and going on about what they was going to do; but a little black-whiskered chap skipped up and says:

"Come back here, you couple of chicken-livered cowards, and I'll thrash the two of ye!"

And he done it, too. He snatched them, he jerked them this way and that, he booted them around, he knocked them sprawling faster than they could get up. Why, it warn't two minutes till they begged like dogs—and how the other lot did yell and laugh and clap their hands all the way through, and shout, "Sail in, Corpse-Maker!" "Hi! at him again, Child of Calamity!" "Bully for you, little Davy!" Well, it was a perfect pow-wow for a while. Bob and the Child had red noses and black eyes when they got through. Little Davy made them own up that they was sneaks and cowards and not fit to eat with a dog or drink with a nigger; then Bob and the Child shook hands with each other, very solemn, and said they had always respected each other and was will-

ing to let bygones be bygones. So then they washed their faces in the river; and just then there was a loud order to stand by for a crossing, and some of them went forward to man the sweeps there, and the rest went aft to handle the after sweeps.

I lay still and waited for fifteen minutes, and had a smoke out of a pipe that one of them left in reach; then the crossing was finished, and they stumped back and had a drink around and went to talking and singing again. Next they got out an old fiddle, and one played, and another patted juba, and the rest turned themselves loose on a regular old-fashioned keelboat breakdown. They couldn't keep that up very long without getting winded, so by and by they settled around the jug again.

They sung "Jolly, Jolly Raftsman's the Life for Me," with a rousing chorus, and then they got to talking about differences betwixt hogs, and their different kind of habits; and next about women and their different ways; and next about the best ways to put out houses that was afire; and next about what ought to be done with the Injuns; and next about what a king had to do, and how much he got; and next about how to make cats fight; and next about what to do when a man has fits; and next about differences betwixt clear-water rivers and muddy-water ones. The man they called Ed said the muddy Mississippi water was wholesomer to drink than the clear water of the Ohio; he said if you let a pint of this yaller Mississippi water settle, you would have about a half to three-quarters of an inch of mud in the bottom, according to the stage of the river, and then it warn't no better than Ohio water—what you wanted to do was to keep it stirred up—and when the river was low, keep mud on hand to put in and thicken the water up the way it ought to be.

The Child of Calamity said that was so; he said there was nutritiousness in the mud, and a man that drunk Mississippi water could grow corn in his stomach if he wanted to. He says:

"You look at the graveyards; that tells the tale. Trees won't grow worth shucks in a Cincinnati graveyard, but in a Sent Louis graveyard they grow upwards of eight hundred foot high. It's all on account of the water the people drunk before they laid up. A Cincinnati corpse don't richen a soil any."

And they talked about how Ohio water didn't like to mix with Mississippi water. Ed said if you take the Mississippi on a rise when the Ohio is low, you'll find a wide bank of clear water all the way down the east side of the Mississippi for a hundred mile or more, and the minute you get out a quarter of a mile from shore and pass the line, it is all thick and yaller the rest of the way across. Then they talked about how to keep tobacco from getting mouldy, and from that they went into ghosts and told about a lot that other folks had seen; but Ed says:

"Why don't you tell something that you've seen yourselves? Now let me have a say. Five years ago I was on a raft as big as this, and right along here it was a bright moonshiny night, and I was on watch and boss of the stabboard oar forrard, and one of my pards was a man named Dick All-bright, and he come along to where I was sitting, forrard—gaping and stretching, he was—and stooped down on the edge of the raft and washed his face in the river, and come and set down by me and got out his pipe, and had just got it filled, when he looks up and says:

" 'Why looky-here,' he says, 'ain't that Buck Miller's place, over yander in the bend?'

" 'Yes,' says I, 'it is—why?' He laid his pipe down and leant his head on his hand, and says:

" 'I thought we'd be furder down.' I says:

" 'I thought it too, when I went off

watch'—we was standing six hours on and six off—'but the boys told me,' I says, 'that the raft didn't seem to hardly move, for the last hour,' says I, 'though she's a-slipping along all right, now,' says I. He give a kind of groan, and says:

" 'I've seed a raft act so before, along here,' he says, ' 'pears to me the current has most quit above the head of this bend durin' the last two years,' he says.

"Well, he raised up two or three times, and looked away off and around on the water. That started me at it too. A body is always doing what he sees somebody else doing, though there mayn't be no sense in it. Pretty soon I see a black something floating on the water away off to stabboard and quartering behind us. I see he was looking at it, too; I says:

" 'What's that?' He says, sort of pettish:

" 'Tain't nothing but an old empty bar'l.'

" 'An empty bar'l!' says I, 'why,' says I, 'a spy-glass is a fool to your eyes. How can you tell it's an empty bar'l?' He says:

" 'I don't know; I reckon it ain't a bar'l, but I thought it might be,' says he.

" 'Yes,' I says, 'so it might be, and it might be anything else, too; a body can't tell nothing about it, such a distance as that,' I says.

"We hadn't nothing else to do, so we kept on watching it. By and by I says,

" 'Why, looky-here, Dick Allbright, that thing's a-gaining on us, I believe.'

"He never said nothing. The thing gained and gained, and I judged it must be a dog that was about tired out. Well, we swung down into the crossing, and the thing floated across the bright streak of the moonshine, and by George, it *was* a bar'l. Says I:

" 'Dick Allbright, what made you think that thing was a bar'l, when it was half a mile off?' says I. Says he:

" 'I don't know.' Says I:

" 'You tell me, Dick Allbright.' Says he:

" 'Well, I knowed it was a bar'l; I've seen it before; lots has seen it; they says it's a ha'nted bar'l.'

"I called the rest of the watch, and they come and stood there, and I told them what Dick said. It floated right along abreast, now, and didn't gain any more. It was about twenty foot off. Some was for having it aboard, but the rest didn't want to. Dick Allbright said rafts that had fooled with it had got back luck by it. The captain of the watch said he didn't believe in it. He said he reckoned the bar'l gained on us because it was in a little better current than what we was. He said it would leave by and by.

"So then we went to talking about other things, and we had a song, and then a breakdown; and after that the captain of the watch called for another song; but it was clouding up now, and the bar'l stuck right thar in the same place, and the song didn't seem to have much warm-up to it, somehow, and so they didn't finish it, and there warn't any cheers, but it sort of dropped flat, and nobody said anything for a minute. Then everybody tried to talk at once, and one chap got off a joke, but it warn't no use, they didn't laugh, and even the chap that made the joke didn't laugh at it, which ain't usual. We all just settled down glum, and watched the bar'l, and was oneasy and oncomfortable. Well, sir, it shut down black and still, and then the wind began to moan around, and next the lightning began to play and the thunder to grumble. And pretty soon there was a regular storm, and in the middle of it a man that was running aft stumbled and fell and sprained his ankle so that he had to lay up. This made the boys shake their heads. And every time the lightning come, there was that bar'l, with the blue lights winking around it. We was always on the lookout for it. But by and by, toward dawn, she was gone. When the day come we couldn't see her anywhere, and we warn't sorry, either.

"But next night about half past nine, when there was songs and high jinks going on, here she comes again, and took her old roost on the stabboard side. There warn't no more high jinks. Everybody got solemn; nobody talked; you couldn't get anybody to do anything but set around moody and look at the bar'l. It begun to cloud up again. When the watch changed, the off watch stayed up, 'stead of turning in. The storm ripped and roared around all night, and in the middle of it another man tripped and sprained his ankle, and had to knock off. The bar'l left toward day, and nobody see it go.

"Everybody was sober and down in the mouth all day. I don't mean the kind of sober that comes of leaving liquor alone— not that. They was quiet, but they all drunk more than usual—not together, but each man sidled off and took it private, by himself.

"After dark the off watch didn't turn in; nobody sung, nobody talked; the boys didn't scatter around, neither; they sort of huddled together, forrard; and for two hours they set there, perfectly still, looking steady in the one direction, and heaving a sigh once in a while. And then, here comes the bar'l again. She took up her old place. She stayed there all night; nobody turned in. The storm come on again, after midnight. It got awful dark; and the rain poured down; hail, too; the thunder boomed and roared and bellowed; the wind blowed a hurricane; and the lightning spread over everything in big sheets of glare, and showed the whole raft as plain as day; and the river lashed up white as milk as far as you could see for miles, and there was that bar'l jiggering along, same as ever. The captain ordered the watch to man the after sweeps for a crossing, and nobody would go—no more sprained ankles for them, they said. They wouldn't even *walk* aft. Well then, just then the sky split wide open, with a crash, and the lightning killed two men of the after watch, and crippled two more. Crippled them how, say you? Why, *sprained their ankles!*

"The bar'l left in the dark betwixt lightnings, toward dawn. Well, not a body eat a bite at breakfast that morning. After that the men loafed around, in twos and threes, and talked low together. But none of them herded with Dick Allbright. They all give him the cold shake. If he come around where any of the men was, they split up and sidled away. They wouldn't man the sweeps with him. The captain had all the skiffs hauled up on the raft, alongside of his wigwam, and wouldn't let the dead men be took ashore to be planted; he didn't believe a man that got ashore would come back; and he was right.

"After night come, you could see pretty plain that there was going to be trouble if that bar'l come again; there was such a muttering going on. A good many wanted to kill Dick Allbright, because he'd seen the bar'l on other trips, and that had an ugly look. Some wanted to put him ashore. Some said, 'Let's all go ashore in a pile, if the bar'l comes again.'

"This kind of whispers was still going on, the men being bunched together forrard watching for the bar'l, when lo and behold you! here she comes again. Down she comes, slow and steady, and settles into her old tracks. You could 'a' heard a pin drop. Then up comes the captain, and says:

" 'Boys, don't be a pack of children and fools: I don't want the bar'l to be dogging us all the way to Orleans, and *you* don't; well, then, how's the best way to stop it? Burn it up—that's the way. I'm going to fetch it aboard,' he says. And before any body could say a word, in he went.

"He swum to it, and as he come pushing it to the raft, the men spread to one side.

But the old man got it aboard and busted in the head, and there was a baby in it! Yes, sir; a stark-naked baby. It was Dick Allbright's baby; he owned up and said so.

" 'Yes,' he says, a-leaning over it, 'yes, it is my own lamented darling, my poor lost Charles William Allbright deceased,' says he—for he could curl his tongue around the bulliest words in the language when he was a mind to, and lay them before you without a jint started, anywheres. Yes, he said, he used to live up at the head of this bend, and one night he choked his child, which was crying, not intending to kill it,—which was prob'ly a lie,—and then he was scared, and buried it in a bar'l, before his wife got home, and off he went, and struck the northern trail and went to rafting; and this was the third year that the bar'l had chased him. He said the bad luck always begun light, and lasted till four men was killed, and then the bar'l didn't come any more, after that. He said if the men would stand it one more night, —and was a-going on like that,—but the men had got enough. They started to get out a boat to take him ashore and lynch him, but he grabbed the little child all of a sudden and jumped overboard with it hugged up to his breast and shedding tears, and we never see him again in this life, poor old suffering soul, nor Charles William neither."

"*Who* was shedding tears?" says Bob; "was it Allbright or the baby?"

"Why, Allbright, of course; didn't I tell you the baby was dead? Been dead three years—how could it cry?"

"Well, never mind how it could cry— how could it *keep* all that time?" says Davy. "You answer me that."

"I don't know how it done it," says Ed. "It done it though—that's all I know about it."

"Say—what did they do with the bar'l?" says the Child of Calamity.

"Why, they hove it overboard, and it sunk like a chunk of lead."

"Edward, did the child look like it was choked?" says one.

"Did it have its hair parted?" says another.

"What was the brand on that bar'l, Eddy?" says a fellow they called Bill.

"Have you got the papers for them statistics, Edmund?" says Jimmy.

"Say, Edwin, was you one of the men that was killed by the lightning?" says Davy.

"Him? Oh, no! he was both of 'em," says Bob. Then they all haw-hawed.

"Say, Edward, don't you reckon you'd better take a pill? You look bad—don't you feel pale?" says the Child of Calamity.

"Oh, come, now, Eddy," says Jimmy, "show up; you must 'a' kept part of that bar'l to prove the thing by. Show us the bung-hole—do—and we'll all believe you."

"Say, boys," says Bill, "less divide it up. Thar's thirteen of us. I can swaller a thirteenth of the yarn, if you can worry down the rest."

Ed got up mad and said they could all go to some place which he ripped out pretty savage, and then walked off aft, cussing to himself, and they yelling and jeering at him, and roaring and laughing so you could hear them a mile.

"Boys, we'll split a watermelon on that," says the Child of Calamity; and he came rummaging around in the dark amongst the shingle bundles where I was, and put his hand on me. I was warm and soft and naked; so he says "Ouch!" and jumped back.

"Fetch a lantern or a chunk of fire here, boys—there's a snake here as big as a cow!"

So they run there with a lantern, and crowded up and looked in on me.

"Come out of that, you beggar!" says one.

"Who are you?" says another.

"What are you after here? Speak up prompt, or overboard you go."

"Snake him out, boys. Snatch him out by the heels."

I began to beg, and crept out amongst them trembling. They looked me over, wondering, and the Child of Calamity says:

"A cussed thief! Lend me a hand and less heave him overboard!"

"No," says Big Bob, "less get out the paint-pot and paint him a sky-blue all over from head to heel, and *then* heave him over."

"Good! that's it. Go for the paint, Jimmy."

When the paint come, and Bob took the brush and was just going to begin, the others laughing and rubbing their hands, I begun to cry, and that sort of worked on Davy, and he says:

" 'Vast there. He's nothing but a cub. I'll paint the man that teches him!"

So I looked around on them, and some of them grumbled and growled, and Bob put down the paint, and the others didn't take it up.

"Come here to the fire, and less see what you're up to here," says Davy. "Now set down there and give an account of yourself. How long have you been aboard here?"

"Not over a quarter of a minute, sir," says I.

"How did you get dry so quick?"

"I don't know, sir. I'm always that way, mostly."

"Oh, you are, are you? What's your name?"

I warn't going to tell my name. I didn't know what to say, so I just says:

"Charles William Allbright, sir."

Then they roared—the whole crowd; and I was mighty glad I said that, because, maybe, laughing would get them in a better humor.

When they got done laughing, Davy says:

"It won't hardly do, Charles William. You couldn't have growed this much in five year, and you was a baby, when you come out of the bar'l, you know, and dead at that. Come now, tell a straight story, and nobody'll hurt you, if you ain't up to anything wrong. What *is* your name?"

"Aleck Hopkins, sir. Aleck James Hopkins."

"Well, Aleck, where did you come from here?"

"From a trading-scow. She lays up the bend yonder. I was born on her. Pap has traded up and down here all his life; and he told me to swim off here, because when you went by he said he would like to get some of you to speak to a Mr. Jonas Turner, in Cairo, and tell him—"

"Oh, come!"

"Yes, sir, it's as true as the world. Pap he says—"

"Oh, your grandmother!"

They all laughed, and I tried again to talk, but they broke in on me and stopped me.

"Now, looky-here," says Davy; "you're scared, and so you talk wild. Honest, now, do you live in a scow, or is it a lie?"

"Yes, sir, in a trading-scow. She lays up at the head of the bend. But I warn't born in her. It's our first trip."

"Now you're talking! What did you come aboard here for? To steal?"

"No, sir, I didn't. It was only to get a ride on the raft. All boys does that."

"Well, I know that. But what did you hide for?"

"Sometimes they drive the boys off."

"So they do. They might steal. Looky-here; if we let you off this time, will you keep out of these kind of scrapes hereafter?"

" 'Deed I will, boss. You try me."

"All right, then. You ain't but little ways from shore. Overboard with you, and don't you make a fool of yourself another time this way. Blast it, boy, some raftsmen would rawhide you till you were black and blue!"

I didn't wait to kiss good-by, but went overboard and broke for shore. When Jim come along by and by, the big raft was far away out of sight around the point. I swum out and got aboard, and was mighty glad to see home again.

The boy did not get the information he was after, but his adventure has furnished the glimpse of the departed raftsman and keelboatman which I desire to offer in this place.

THE CELEBRATED JUMPING FROG OF CALAVERAS COUNTY

by Samuel Langhorne Clemens

In compliance with the request of a friend of mine, who wrote me from the East, I called on good-natured, garrulous old Simon Wheeler, and inquired after my friend's friend, *Leonidas W. Smiley,* as requested to do, and I hereunto append the result. I have a lurking suspicion that *Leonidas W.* Smiley is a myth; that my friend never knew such a personage; and that he only conjectured that, if I asked old Wheeler about him, it would remind him of his infamous *Jim* Smiley, and he would go to work and bore me nearly to death with some infernal reminiscence of him as long and tedious as it should be useless to me. If that was the design, it certainly succeeded.

I found Simon Wheeler dozing comfortably by the bar-room stove of the old, dilapidated tavern in the ancient mining camp of Angel's, and I noticed that he was fat and bald-headed, and had an expression of winning gentleness and simplicity upon his tranquil countenance. He roused up and gave me good-day. I told him a friend of mine had commissioned me to make some inquiries about a cherished companion of his boyhood named *Leonidas W.* Smiley—*Rev. Leonidas W.* Smiley—a young minister of the Gospel, who he had heard was at one time a resident of Angel's Camp. I added that, if Mr. Wheeler could tell me anything about this Rev. Leonidas W. Smiley, I would feel under many obligations to him.

Simon Wheeler backed me into a corner and blockaded me there with his chair, and then sat me down and reeled off the monotonous narrative which follows this paragraph. He never smiled, he never frowned, he never changed his voice from the gentle-flowing key to which he tuned the initial sentence, he never betrayed the slightest suspicion of enthusiasm; but all through the interminable narrative there ran a vein of impressive earnestness and sincerity, which showed me plainly that, so far from his imagining that there was anything ridiculous or funny about his story, he regarded it as a really important matter, and admired its two heroes as men of transcendent genius in *finesse.* To me, the spectacle of a man drifting serenely along through such a queer yarn without ever smiling, was exquisitely absurd. As I said before, I asked him to tell me what he knew of Rev. Leonidas W. Smiley, and he replied as follows. I let him go on in his own way, and never interrupted him once:

There was a feller here once by the name of *Jim* Smiley, in the winter of '49—or may be it was the spring of '50—I don't recollect exactly, somehow, though what makes me think it was one or the other is because I remember the big flume wasn't finished when he first came to the camp; but any way, he was the curiosest man about always betting on any thing that turned up you ever see, if he could get any body to bet on the other side; and if he couldn't, he'd change sides. Any way that suited the other man would suit him —any way just so's he got a bet, *he* was satisfied. But still he was lucky, uncommon lucky; he most always come out winner. He was always ready and laying for a chance; there couldn't be no solit'ry thing mentioned but that feller'd offer to bet on it, and take any side you please, as I was just telling you. If there was a horse-race, you'd find him flush, or you'd find him busted at the end of it; if there was a dog-fight, he'd bet on it; if there was a cat-fight, he'd bet on it; if there was a chicken-fight, he'd bet on it; why, if there was two birds setting on a fence, he would bet you which one would fly first; or if there was a camp-meeting, he would be there reg'lar, to bet on Parson Walker, which he judged to be the best exhorter about there, and so he was, too, and a good man. If he even seen a straddle-bug start to go anywheres, he would bet you how long it would take him to get wherever he was going to, and if you took him up, he would foller that straddle-bug to Mexico but what he would find out where he was bound for and how long he was on the road. Lots of the boys here has seen that Smiley, and can tell you about him. Why, it never made no differ-ence to *him*—he would bet on *any* thing— the dangdest feller. Parson Walker's wife laid very sick once, for a good while, and it seemed as if they warn't going to save her; but one morning he come in, and Smiley asked how she was, and he said

she was considerable better—thank the Lord for his inf'nite mercy—and coming on so smart that, with the blessing of Prov'dence, she'd get well yet; and Smiley, before he thought, says, "Well, I'll resk two-and-a-half that she don't, anyway."

Thish-yer Smiley had a mare—the boys called her the fifteen-minute nag, but that was only in fun, you know, because, of course, she was faster than that—and he used to win money on that horse, for all she was so slow and always had the asthma, or the distemper, or the consumption, or something of that kind. They used to give her two or three hundred yards start, and then pass her under way; but always at the fag-end of the race she'd get excited and desperate-like, and come ca-vorting and straddling up, and scattering her legs around limber, sometimes in the air, and sometimes out to one side amongst the fences, and kicking up m-o-r-e dust, and raising m-o-r-e racket with her cough-ing and sneezing and blowing her nose— and always fetch up at the stand just about a neck ahead, as near as you could cipher it down.

And he had a little small bull pup, that to look at him you'd think he wa'n't worth a cent, but to set around and look ornery, and lay for a chance to steal something. But as soon as money was up on him, he was a different dog; his underjaw'd begin to stick out like the fo'castle of a steamboat, and his teeth would uncover, and shine savage like the furnaces. And a dog might tackle him, and bully-rag him, and bite him, and throw him over his shoulder two or three times, and Andrew Jackson— which was the name of the pup—Andrew Jackson would never let on but what *he* was satisfied, and hadn't expected nothing else—and the bets being doubled and doubled on the other side all the time, till the money was all up; and then all of a sudden he would grab that other dog jest by the j'int of his hind leg and freeze to it

—not chaw, you understand, but only jest grip and hang on till they throwed up the sponge, if it was a year. Smiley always come out winner on that pup, till he harnessed a dog once that didn't have no hind legs, because they'd been sawed off by a circular saw, and when the thing had gone along far enough, and the money was all up, and he come to make a snatch for his pet holt, he saw in a minute how he'd been imposed on, and how the other dog had him in the door, so to speak, and he 'peared surprised, and then he looked sorter discouraged-like, and didn't try no more to win the fight, and so he got shucked out bad. He give Smiley a look, as much as to say his heart was broke, and it was *his* fault, for putting up a dog that hadn't no hind legs for him to take holt of, which was his main dependence in a fight, and then he limped off a piece and laid down and died. It was a good pup, was that Andrew Jackson, and would have made a name for hisself if he'd lived, for the stuff was in him, and he had genius—I know it, because he hadn't had no opportunities to speak of, and it don't stand to reason that a dog could make such a fight as he could under them circumstances, if he hadn't no talent. It always makes me feel sorry when I think of that last fight of his'n, and the way it turned out.

Well, thish-yer Smiley had rat-tarriers, and chicken cocks, and tom-cats, and all them kind of things, till you couldn't rest, and you couldn't fetch nothing for him to bet on but he'd match you. He ketched a frog one day, and took him home, and said he cal'klated to edercate him; and so he never done nothing for three months but set in his back yard and learn that frog to jump. And you bet he *did* learn him, too. He'd give him a little punch behind, and the next minute you'd see that frog whirling in the air like a doughnut—see him turn one summerset, or may be a couple, if he got a good start, and come

down flat-footed and all right, like a cat. He got him up so in the matter of catching flies, and kept him in practice so constant, that he'd nail a fly every time as far as he could see him. Smiley said all a frog wanted was education, and he could do most anything—and I believe him. Why, I've seen him set Dan'l Webster down here on this floor—Dan'l Webster was the name of the frog—and sing out, "Flies, Dan'l, flies!" and quicker'n you could wink, he'd spring straight up, and snake a fly off'n the counter there, and flop down on the floor again as solid as a gob of mud, and fall to scratching the side of his head with his hind foot as indifferent as if he hadn't no idea he'd been doin' any more'n any frog might do. You never see a frog so modest and straightfor'ard as he was, for all he was so gifted. And when it come to fair and square jumping on a dead level, he could get over more ground at one straddle than any animal of his breed you ever see. Jumping on a dead level was his strong suit, you understand; and when it come to that, Smiley would ante up money on him as long as he had a red. Smiley was monstrous proud of his frog, and well he might be, for fellers that had traveled and been everywheres, all said he laid over any frog that ever *they* see.

Well Smiley kept the beast in a little lattice box, and he used to fetch him down town sometimes and lay for a bet. One day a feller—a stranger in the camp, he was—come across him with his box, and says:

"What might it be that you've got in the box?"

And Smiley says, sorter indifferent like, "It might be a parrot, or it might be a canary, may be, but it ain't—it's only just a frog."

And the feller took it, and looked at it careful, and turned it round this way and that, and says, "H'm—so 'tis. Well, what's *he* good for?"

"Well," Smiley says, easy and careless,

"he's good enough for *one* thing, I should judge—he can outjump ary frog in Calaveras county."

The feller took the box again, and took another long, particular look, and give it back to Smiley, and says, very deliberate, "Well, I don't see no p'ints about that frog that's any better'n any other frog."

"May be you don't," Smiley says. "May be you understand frogs, and may be you don't understand 'em; may be you've had experience, and may be you an't only a amature, as it were. Anyways, I've got *my* opinion, and I'll risk forty dollars he can outjump any frog in Calaveras county."

And the feller studied a minute, and then says, kinder sad like, "Well, I'm only a stranger here, and I ain't got no frog, but if I had a frog, I'd bet you."

And then Smiley says, "That's all right —that's all right—if you'll hold my box a minute, I'll go and get you a frog." And so the feller took the box, and put up his forty dollars along with Smiley's, and set down to wait.

So he set there a good while thinking and thinking to hisself, and then he got the frog out and prized his mouth open and took a teaspoon and filled him full of quail shot—filled him pretty near up to his chin—and set him on the floor. Smiley he went to the swamp and slopped around in the mud for a long time, and finally he ketched a frog, and fetched him in, and give him to this feller, and says:

"Now, if you're ready, set him alongside of Dan'l, with his fore-paws just even with Dan'l, and I'll give the word." Then he says, "One—two—three—jump!" and him and the feller touched up the frogs from behind, and the new frog hopped off, but Dan'l give a heave, and hysted up his shoulders—so—like a Frenchman, but it wan't no use—he couldn't budge; he was planted as solid as an anvil, and he couldn't no more stir than if he was anchored out. Smiley was a good deal surprised, and he was disgusted too, but he didn't have no idea what the matter was, of course.

The feller took the money and started away; and when he was going out at the door, he sorter jerked his thumb over his shoulders—this way—at Dan'l, and says again, very deliberate, "Well, *I* don't see no p'ints about that frog that's any better'n any other frog."

Smiley he stood scratching his head and looking down at Dan'l a long time, and at last he says, "I do wonder what in the nation that frog throw'd off for—I wonder if there ain't something the matter with him—he 'pears to look mighty baggy, somehow." And he ketched Dan'l by the nap of the neck, and lifted him up and says, "Why, blame my cats, if he don't weigh five pound!" and turned him upside down, and he belched out a double handful of shot. And then he see how it was, and he was the maddest man—he set the frog down and took out after that feller, but he never ketched him. And—

[Here Simon Wheeler heard his name called from the front yard, and got up to see what was wanted.] And turning to me as he moved away, he said: "Just set where you are, stranger, and rest easy— I an't going to be gone a second."

But, by your leave, I did not think that a continuation of the history of the enterprising vagabond *Jim* Smiley would be likely to afford me much information concerning the *Rev. Leonidas W.* Smiley, and so I started away.

At the door I met the sociable Wheeler returning, and he buttonholed me and recommenced:

"Well, thish-yer Smiley had a yaller one-eyed cow that didn't have no tail, only jest a short stump like a bannanner, and—"

"Oh! hang Smiley and his afflicted cow!" I muttered, good-naturedly, and bidding the old gentleman good-day, I departed.

THE BIG BEAR OF ARKANSAS

by T. B. Thorpe

Thorpe's celebrated story about bear-hunting in Arkansas, which appeared originally in a New York sporting journal, The Spirit of the Times, *March 27, 1841, is built largely on contrast. By utilizing the frame technique, the author can introduce two narrators, one educated and dignified, the other crude and flamboyant. This method also permits the use of diction which is suitable to the hunter but would be inappropriate for the respectable traveler. It is interesting that Thorpe employs a series of marvels—the turkey, the mosquitoes, the sow—in order to discipline the audience into accepting the climactic incident, the killing of the "unhuntable bar." But even though Jim Doggett's primary aim is to impress on supposedly gullible strangers the wonders of the state of Arkansas, there is a mystery in the final event which even he cannot completely solve. The speed, the cunning, and the immunity of the bear suggest a fabulous creature which is of a quite different species from the ordinary exaggerated beasts of the tall tale. As James R. Masterson observed, the story contains a remarkable variety of humorous elements: "an eccentric character, a grotesque dialect, an encounter of wits, a sample of boasting, three or four tall tales, a pretended hint of the supernatural, and an ironical concession to prudery."* [1]

A steamboat on the Mississippi frequently, in making her regular trips, carries between places varying from one to two thousand miles apart; and as these boats advertise to land passengers and freight at "all intermediate landings," the heterogeneous character of the passengers of one of these up-country boats can scarcely be imagined by one who has never seen it with his own eyes. Starting from New Orleans in one of these boats, you will find yourself associated with men from every state in the Union, and from every portion of the globe; and a man of observation need not lack for amusement or instruction in such a crowd, if he will take the trouble to read the great book of character so favourably opened before him. Here may be seen jostling together the wealthy Southern planter, and the pedlar of tin-ware from New England—the Northern merchant, and the Southern jockey—a venerable bishop, and a desperate gambler—the land speculator, and the honest farmer—professional men of all creeds and characters—Wolvereens, Suckers, Hoosiers, Buckeyes,

1. James R. Masterson, *Tall Tales of Arkansaw* (Boston: Chapman & Grimes, 1942), p. 60.

and Corncrackers, beside a "plentiful sprinkling" of the half-horse and half-alligator species of men, who are peculiar to "old Mississippi," and who appear to gain a livelihood simply by going up and down the river. In the pursuit of pleasure or business, I have frequently found myself in such a crowd.

On one occasion, when in New Orleans, I had occasion to take a trip of a few miles up the Mississippi, and I hurried on board the well-known "high-pressure-and-beat-every-thing" steamboat "Invincible," just as the last note of the last bell was sounding; and when the confusion and bustle that is natural to a boat's getting under way had subsided, I discovered that I was associated in as heterogeneous a crowd as was ever got together. As my trip was to be of a few hours' duration only, I made no endeavours to become acquainted with my fellow passengers, most of whom would be together many days. Instead of this, I took out of my pocket the "latest paper," and more critically than usual examined its contents; my fellow passengers at the same time disposed themselves in little groups. While I was thus busily employed in reading, and my companions were more busily still employed in discussing such subjects as suited their humours best, we were startled most unexpectedly by a loud Indian whoop, uttered in the "social hall," that part of the cabin fitted off for a bar; then was to be heard a loud crowing, which would not have continued to have interested us—such sounds being quite common in that *place of spirits*—had not the hero of these windy accomplishments stuck his head into the cabin and hallooed out, "Hurra for the Big Bar of Arkansaw!" and then might be heard a confused hum of voices, unintelligible, save in such broken sentences as "horse," "screamer," "lightning is slow," &c. As might have been expected, this continued interruption attracted the attention of every one in the cabin; all conversation dropped, and in the midst of this surprise the "Big Bar" walked into the cabin, took a chair, put his feet on the stove, and looking back over his shoulder, passed the general and familiar salute of "Strangers, how are you?" He then expressed himself as much at home as if he had been at "the Forks of Cypress," and "perhaps a little more so." Some of the company at this familiarity looked a little angry, and some astonished; but in a moment every face was wreathed in a smile. There was something about the intruder that won the heart on sight. He appeared to be a man enjoying perfect health and contentment: his eyes were as sparkling as diamonds, and good-natured to simplicity. Then his perfect confidence in himself was irresistibly droll. "Perhaps," said he, "gentlemen," running on without a person speaking, "perhaps you have been to New Orleans often; I never made *the first visit before*, and I don't intend to make another in a crow's life. I am thrown away in that ar place, and useless, that ar a fact. Some of the gentlemen thar called me *green*— well, perhaps I am, said I, *but I arn't so at home*; and if I ain't off my trail much, the heads of them perlite chaps themselves weren't much the hardest; for according to my notion, they were *real know-nothings*, green as a pumpkin-vine— couldn't, in farming, I'll bet, raise a crop of turnips: and as for shooting, they'd miss a barn if the door was swinging, and that, too, with the best rifle in the country. And then they talked to me 'bout hunting, and laughed at my calling the principal game in Arkansaw poker, and high-low-jack. 'Perhaps,' said I, 'you prefer chickens and rolette'; at this they laughed harder than ever, and asked me if I lived in the woods, and didn't know what *game* was? At this I rather think I laughed. 'Yes,' I roared, and says, 'Strangers, if you'd asked me *how we got our meat* in

Arkansaw, I'd a told you at once, and given you a list of varmints that would make a caravan, beginning with the bar, and ending off with the cat; that's *meat* though, not game.' Game, indeed, that's what city folks call it; and with them it means chippen-birds and shite-pokes; maybe such trash live in my diggens, but I arn't noticed them yet; a bird any way is too trifling. I never did shoot at but one, and I'd never forgiven myself for that, had it weighed less than forty pounds. I wouldn't draw a rifle on any thing less than that; and when I meet with another wild turkey of the same weight I will drap him."

"A wild turkey weighing forty pounds!" exclaimed twenty voices in the cabin at once.

"Yes, strangers, and wasn't it a whopper? You see, the thing was so fat that it couldn't fly far; and when he fell out of the tree, after I shot him, on striking the ground he bust open behind, and the way the pound gobs of tallow rolled out of the opening was perfectly beautiful."

"Where did all that happen?" asked a cynical-looking Hoosier.

"Happen! happened in Arkansaw: where else could it have happened, but in the creation state, the finishing-up country—a state where the *sile* runs down to the centre of the 'arth, and government gives you a title to every inch of it? Then its airs—just breathe them, and they will make you snort like a horse. It's a state without a fault, it is."

"Excepting mosquitoes," cried the Hoosier.

"Well, stranger, except them; for it ar a fact that they are rather *enormous*, and do push themselves in somewhat troublesome. But, stranger, they never stick twice in the same place; and give them a fair chance for a few months, and you will get as much above noticing them as an alligator. They can't hurt my feelings, for they lay under the skin; and I never knew but one case of injury resulting from them, and that was to a Yankee; and they take worse to foreigners, anyhow, than they do to natives. But the way they used that fellow up! first they punched him until he swelled up and busted; then he su-per-a-ted, as the doctor called it, until he was as raw as beef; then he took the ager, owing to the warm weather, and finally he took a steamboat and left the country. He was the only man that ever took mosquitoes to heart that I know of. But mosquitoes is natur, and I never find fault with her. If they ar large, Arkansaw is large, her varmints ar large, her trees ar large, her rivers ar large, and a small mosquito would be of no more use in Arkansaw than preaching in a canebrake."

This knock-down argument in favour of big mosquitoes used the Hoosier up, and the logician started on a new track, to explain how numerous bear were in his "diggins," where he represented them to be "about as plenty as blackberries, and a little plentifuler."

Upon the utterance of this assertion, a timid little man near me inquired if the bear in Arkansaw ever attacked the settlers in numbers.

"No," said our hero, warming with the subject, "no, stranger, for you see it ain't the natur of bar to go in droves; but the way they squander about in pairs and single ones is edifying. And then the way I hunt them the old black rascals know the crack of my gun as well as they know a pig's squealing. They grow thin in our parts, it frightens them so, and they do take the noise dreadfully, poor things. That gun of mine is perfect *epidemic among bar*; if not watched closely, it will go off as quick on a warm scent as my dog Bowie-knife will: and then that dog—whew! why the fellow thinks that the world is full of bar, he find them so easy. It's lucky he don't talk as well as think; for with his natural modesty, if he should suddenly learn how much he is acknowledged to be ahead of all other dogs in the universe, he would be astonished to death in two minutes. Strangers, the dog knows a bar's way as well as a horse-jockey knows a woman's; he always barks at the right time, bites at the exact place, and whips without getting a scratch. I never could tell whether he was made expressly to hunt bar, or whether bar was made expressly for him to hunt; any way, I believe they were ordained to go together as naturally as Squire Jones says a man and woman is, when he moralizes in marrying a couple. In fact, Jones once said, said he, 'Marriage according to law is a civil contract of divine origin; it's common to all countries as well as Arkansaw, and people take to it as naturally as Jim Doggett's Bowie-knife takes to bar.' "

"What season of the year do your hunts take place?" inquired a gentlemanly foreigner, who, from some peculiarities of his baggage, I suspected to be an Englishman, on some hunting expedition, probably at the foot of the Rocky Mountains.

"The season for bar hunting, stranger," said the man of Arkansaw, "is generally all the year round, and the hunts take place about as regular. I read in history that varmints have their fat season, and their lean season. That is not the case in Arkansaw, feeding as they do upon the *spontenacious* productions of the sile, they have one continued fat season the year round; though in winter things in this way is rather more greasy than in summer, I must admit. For that reason bar with us run in warm weather, but in winter, they only waddle. Fat, fat! it's an enemy to speed; it tames everything that has plenty of it. I have seen wild turkeys, from its influence, as gentle as chickens. Run a bar in this fat condition, and the way it improves the critter for eating is amazing; it sort of mixes the ile up with the meat, until you can't tell t'other from which. I've done

this often. I recollect one perty morning in particular, of putting an old fellow on the stretch, and considering the weight he carried, he run well. But the dogs soon tired him down, and when I came up with him wasn't he in a beautiful sweat—I might say fever; and then to see his tongue sticking out of his mouth a feet, and his sides sinking and opening like bellows, and his cheeks so fat he couldn't look cross. In this fix I blazed at him, and pitch me naked into a briar patch if the steam didn't come out of the bullet-hole ten foot in a straight line. The fellow, I reckon, was made on the high-pressure system, and the lead sort of bust his biler."

"That column of steam was rather curious, or else the bear must have been *warm*," observed the foreigner, with a laugh.

"Stranger, as you observe, that bar was WARM, and the blowing off of the steam show'd it, and also how hard the varmint had been run. I have no doubt if he had kept on two miles farther his insides would have been stewed; and I expect to meet with a varmint yet of extra bottom, who will run himself into a skinful of bar's grease: it is possible, much onlikelier things have happened."

"Whereabouts are these bears so abundant?" inquired the foreigner, with increasing interest.

"Why, stranger, they inhabit the neighbourhood of my settlement, one of the prettiest places on old Mississippi—a perfect location, and no mistake; a place that had some defects until the river made the 'cut-off' at 'Shirt-tail bend,' and that remedied the evil, as it brought my cabin on the edge of the river—a great advantage in wet weather, I assure you, as you can now roll a barrel of whiskey into my yard in high water from a boat, as easy as falling off a log. It's a great improvement, as toting it by land in a jug, as I used to do, *evaporated* it too fast, and it became expensive. Just stop with me, stranger, a month or two, or a year if you like, and you will appreciate my place. I can give you plenty to eat; for beside hog and hominy, you can have bar-ham, and bar-sausages, and a mattrass of bar-skins to sleep on, and a wildcatskin, pulled off hull, stuffed with corn-shucks for a pillow. That bed would put you to sleep if you had the rheumatics in every joint in your body. I call that ar bed a *quietus*. Then look at my land—the government ain't got another such a piece to dispose of. Such timber, and such bottom land, why you can't preserve any thing natural you plant in it unless you pick it young, things thar will grow out of shape so quick. I once planted in those diggins a few potatoes and beets; they took a fine start, and after that an ox team couldn't have kept them from growing. About that time I went off to old Kentuck on bisiness, and did not hear from them things in three months, when I accidentally stumbled on a fellow who had stopped at my place, with an idea of buying me out. 'How did you like things?' said I. 'Pretty well,' said he; 'the cabin is convenient, and the timber land is good; but that bottom land ain't worth the first red cent.' 'Why?' said I. ' 'Cause,' said he. ' 'Cause what?' said I. ' 'Cause it's full of cedar stumps and Indian mounds,' said he, *'and it can't be cleared.'* 'Lord,' said I, 'them ar "cedar stumps" is beets, and them ar "Indian mounds" ar tater hills.' As I expected, the crop was overgrown and useless; the sile is too rich, *and planting in Arkansaw is dangerous.* I had a good-sized sow killed in that same bottom land. The old thief stole an ear of corn, and took it down where she slept at night to eat. Well, she left a grain or two on the ground, and lay down on them; before morning the corn shot up, and the percussion killed her dead. I don't plant any more; natur intended Arkansaw for a hunting ground, and I go according to natur."

The questioner who thus elicited the description of our hero's settlement, seemed to be perfectly satisfied and said no more; but the "Big Bar of Arkansaw" rambled on from one thing to another with a volubility perfectly astonishing, occasionally disputing with those around him, particularly with a "live Sucker" from Illinois, who had the daring to say that our Arkansaw friend's stories "smelt rather tall."

In this manner the evening was spent; but conscious that my own association with so singular a personage would probably end before morning, I asked him if he would not give me a description of some particular bear hunt; adding that I took great interest in such things, though I was no sportsman. The desire seemed to please him, and he squared himself round towards me, saying, that he could give me an idea of a bar hunt that was never beat in this world, or in any other. His manner was so singular, that half of his story consisted in his excellent way of telling it, the great peculiarity of which was the happy manner he had of emphasizing the prominent parts of his conversation. As near as I can recollect, I have italicized them, and given the story in his own words.

"Stranger," said he, "in bar hunts *I am numerous,* and which particular one, as you say, I shall tell, puzzles me. There was the old she devil I shot at the Hurricane last fall—then there was the old hog thief I popped over at the Bloody Crossing, and then—Yes, I have it! I will give you an idea of a hunt, in which the greatest bar was killed that ever lived, *none excepted;* about an old fellow that I hunted, more or less, for two or three years; and if that ain't a *particular bar hunt,* I ain't got one to tell. But in the first place, stranger, let me say, I am pleased with you, because you ain't ashamed to gain information by asking, and listening, and that's what I say to Countess's pups every day when I'm home;

and I have got great hopes of them ar pups, because they are continually *nosing* about; and though they stick it sometimes in the wrong place, they gain experience any how, and may learn something useful to boot. Well, as I was saying about this big bar, you see when I and some more first settled in our region, we were driven to hunting naturally; we soon liked it, and after that we found it an easy matter to make the thing our business. One old chap who had pioneered 'afore us, gave us to understand that we had settled in the right place. He dwelt upon its merits until it was affecting, and showed us, to prove his assertions, more marks on the sassafras trees than I ever saw on a tavern door 'lection time. 'Who keeps that ar reckoning?' said I. 'The bar,' said he. 'What for?' said I. 'Can't tell,' said he; 'but so it is; the bar bite the bark and wood too, at the highest point from the ground they can reach, and you can tell, by the marks,' said he, 'the length of the bar to an inch.' 'Enough,' said I; 'I've learned something here a'ready, and I'll put it in practice.'

"Well, stranger, just one month from that time I killed a bar, and told its exact length before I measured it, by those very marks; and when I did that, I swelled up considerable—I've been a prouder man ever since. So I went on, larning something every day, until I was reckoned a buster, and allowed to be decidedly the best bar hunter in my district; and that is a reputation as much harder to earn than to be reckoned first man in Congress, as an iron ramrod is harder than a toadstool. Did the varmints grow over-cunning by being fooled with by green-horn hunters, and by this means get troublesome, they send for me as a matter of course; and thus I do my own hunting, and most of my neighbours'. I walk into the varmints though, and it has become about as much the same to me as drinking. It is told in two sentences—a bar is started, and he is

killed. The thing is somewhat monotonous now—I know just how much they will run, where they will tire, how much they will growl, and what a thundering time I will have in getting them home. I could give you this history of the chase with all the particulars at the commencement, I know the signs so well—*Stranger, I'm certain.* Once I met with a match though, and I will tell you about it; for a common hunt would not be worth relating.

"On a fine fall day, long time ago, I was trailing about for bar, and what should I see but fresh marks on the sassafras trees, about eight inches above any in the forests that I knew of. Says I, 'them marks is a hoax, or it indicates the d——t bar that was ever grown.' In fact, stranger, I couldn't believe it was real, and I went on. Again I saw the same marks, at the same height, and I *knew the thing lived.* That conviction came home to my soul like an earthquake. Says I, 'here is something a-purpose for me: that bar is mine, or I give up the hunting business.' The very next morning what should I see but a number of buzzards hovering over my cornfield. 'The rascal has been there,' said I, 'for that sign is certain': and, sure enough, on examining, I found the bones of what had been as beautiful a hog the day before, as was ever raised by a Buckeye. Then I tracked the critter out of the field to the woods, and all the marks he left behind, showed me that he was *the bar.*

"Well, stranger, the first fair chase I ever had with that big critter, I saw him no less than three distinct times at a distance: the dogs run him over eighteen miles and broke down, my horse gave out, and I was as nearly used up as a man can be, made on *my* principle, *which is patent.* Before this adventure, such things were unknown to me as possible; but, strange as it was, that bar got me used to it before I was done with him; for he got so at last, that he would leave me on a long chase *quite easy.*

How he did it, I never could understand. That a bar runs at all, is puzzling; but how this one could tire down and bust up a pack of hounds and a horse, that were used to overhauling everything they started after in no time, was past my understanding. Well, stranger, that bar finally got so sassy, that he used to help himself to a hog off my premises whenever he wanted one; the buzzards followed after what he left, and so between *bar and buzzard*, I rather think I was *out of pork*.

"Well, missing that bar so often took hold of my vitals, and I wasted away. The thing had been carried too far, and it reduced me in flesh faster than an ager. I would see that bar in every thing I did; *he hunted me*, and that, too, like a devil, which I began to think he was. While in this fix, I made preparations to give him a last brush, and be done with it. Having completed every thing to my satisfaction, I started at sunrise, and to my great joy, I discovered from the way the dogs run, that they were near him; finding his trail was nothing, for that had become as plain to the pack as a turnpike road. On we went, and coming to an open country, what should I see but the bar very leisurely ascending a hill, and the dogs close at his heels, either a match for him this time in speed, or else he did not care to get out of their way—I don't know which. But wasn't he a beauty, though? I loved him like a brother.

"On he went, until he came to a tree, the limbs of which formed a crotch about six feet from the ground. Into this crotch he got and seated himself, the dogs yelling all around it; and there he sat eyeing them as quiet as a pond in low water. A greenhorn friend of mine, in company, reached shooting distance before me, and blazed away, hitting the critter in the centre of his forehead. The bar shook his head as the ball struck it, and then walked down from that tree as gently as a lady would from a car-

riage. 'Twas a beautiful sight to see him do that—he was in such a rage that he seemed to be as little afraid of the dogs as if they had been sucking pigs; and the dogs warn't slow in making a ring around him at a respectful distance, I tell you; even Bowie-knife, himself, stood off. Then the way his eyes flashed—why the fire of them would have singed a cat's hair; in fact that bar was in a *wrath all over*. Only one pup came near him, and he was brushed out so totally with the bar's left paw, that he entirely disappeared; and that made the old dogs more cautious still. In the mean time, I came up, and taking deliberate aim as a man should do, at his side, just back of his foreleg, *if my gun did not snap,* call me a coward, and I won't take it personal. Yes, stranger, *it snapped,* and I could not find a cap about my person. While in this predicament, I turned round to my fool friend—says I, 'Bill,' says I, 'you're an ass—you're a fool —you might as well have tried to kill that bar by barking the tree under his belly, as to have done it by hitting him in the head. Your shot has made a tiger of him, and blast me, if a dog gets killed or wounded when they come to blows, I will stick my knife into your liver, I will'—my wrath was up. I had lost my caps, my gun had snapped, the fellow with me had fired at the bar's head, and I expected every moment to see him close in with the dogs, and kill a dozen of them at least. In this thing I was mistaken, for the bar leaped over the ring formed by the dogs, and giving a fierce growl, was off—the pack, of course, in full cry after him. The run this time was short, for coming to the edge of a lake the varmint jumped in, and swam to a little island in the lake, which it reached just a moment before the dogs. 'I'll have him now,' said I, for I had found my caps in the *lining of my coat*—so, rolling a log into the lake, I paddled myself across to the island, just as the dogs had cornered the bar in a thicket. I rushed up and fired—at the same time the critter leaped over the dogs and came within three feet of me, running like mad; he jumped into the lake, and tried to mount the log I had just deserted, but every time he got half his body on it, it would roll over and send him under; the dogs, too, got around him, and pulled him about, and finally Bowie-knife clenched with him, and they sunk into the lake together. Stranger, about this time, I was excited, and I stripped off my coat, drew my knife, and intended to have taken a part with Bowie-knife myself, when the bar rose to the surface. But the varmint staid under—Bowie-knife came up alone, more dead than alive, and with the pack came ashore. 'Thank God,' said I, 'the old villain has got his deserts at last.' Determined to have the body, I cut a grape-vine for a rope, and dove down where I could see the bar in the water, fastened my queer rope to his leg, and fished him, with great difficulty, ashore. Stranger, may I be chawed to death by young alligators, if the thing I looked at wasn't a *she bar, and not the old critter after all.* The way matters got mixed on that island was onaccountably curious, and thinking of it made me more than ever convinced that I was hunting the devil himself. I went home that night and took to my bed—the thing was killing me. The entire team of Arkansaw in barhunting, acknowledged himself used up, and the fact sunk into my feelings like a snagged boat will in the Mississippi. I grew as cross as a bar with two cubs and a sore tail. The thing got out 'mong my neighbours, and I was asked how come on that individu-al that never lost a bar when once started? and if that same individ-u-al didn't wear telescopes when he turned a she bar, of ordinary size, into an old he one, a little larger than a horse? 'Perhaps,' said I, 'friends'—getting wrathy—'perhaps you want to call somebody a liar.' 'Oh, no,' said they, 'we only heard such things as being *rather common* of late, but we don't believe one word of it; oh, no,'—and then

they would ride off and laugh like so many hyenas over a dead nigger. It was too much, and I determined to catch that bar, go to Texas, or die,—and I made my preparations accordin'. I had the pack shut up and rested. I took my rifle to pieces and iled it. I put caps in every pocket about my person, *for fear of the lining.* I then told my neighbours, that on Monday morning— naming the day—I would start THAT BAR, and bring him home with me, or they might divide my settlement among them, the owner having disappeared. Well, stranger, on the morning previous to the great day of my hunting expedition, I went into the woods near my house, taking my gun and Bowie-knife along, just *from habit,* and there sitting down also from habit, what should I see, getting over my fence, but *the bar!* Yes, the old varmint was within a hundred yards of me, and the way he walked *over that fence*—stranger, he loomed up like a *black mist,* he seemed so large, and he walked right towards me. I raised myself, took deliberate aim, and fired. Instantly the varmint wheeled, gave a yell, and *walked through the fence* like a falling tree would through a cobweb. I started after, but was tripped up by my inexpressibles, which either from habit, or the excitement of the moment, were about my heels, and before I had really gathered myself up, I heard the old varmint groaning in a thicket near by, like a thousand sinners, and by the time I reached him he was a corpse. Stranger, it took five niggers and myself to put that carcase on a mule's back, and old long-ears waddled under the load, as if he was foundered in every leg of his body, and with a common whopper of a bar, he would have trotted off, and enjoyed himself. 'Twould astonish you to know how big he was: I made a *bedspread of his skin,* and the way it used to cover my bar mattress, and leave several feet on each side to tuck up, would have delighted you. It was in fact a creation bar, and if it had lived in Samson's time, and had met him, in a fair fight, it would have licked him in the twinkling of a dice-box. But, strangers, I never like the way I hunted, and *missed him.* There is something curious about it, I could never understand,—and I never was satisfied at his giving in so easy at last. Perhaps, he had heard of my preparations to hunt him the next day, so he jist come in, like Capt. Scott's coon, to save his wind to grunt with in dying; but that ain't likely. My private opinion is, that that bar was an *unhuntable bar, and died when his time come."*

When the story was ended, our hero sat some minutes with his auditors in a grave silence; I saw there was a mystery to him connected with the bear whose death he had just related, that had evidently made a strong impression on his mind. It was also evident that there was some superstitious awe connected with the affair,—a feeling common with all "children of the wood," when they meet with any thing out of their everyday experience. He was the first one, however, to break the silence, and jumping up, he asked all present to "liquor" before going to bed,—a thing which he did, with a number of companions, evidently to his heart's content.

Long before day, I was put ashore at my place of destination, and I can only follow with the reader, in imagination, our Arkansas friend, in his adventures at the "Forks of Cypress" on the Mississippi.

SICILY BURNS'S WEDDING

by George W. Harris

Sut Lovingood, as Franklin J. Meine has pointed out, is a unique character in American humor, "the genuine naïve roughneck mountaineer riotously bent on raising hell." [1] He is motivated neither by hatred nor by malice. He simply likes excitement, confusion, action, and the fact that his exploits are often cruel and reprehensible bothers him not at all. He glories in the role of a natural-born damned fool, sometimes abetted by whisky, and he is untroubled by a sense of morality or a conscience. Sut takes pleasure in telling about his prank of driving a maddened bull into a wedding party and of the ensuing carnage, but much of the humor of the selection depends on the salty language and the realistic details. Through Sut's picturesque description the whole disorganized scene comes alive. George W. Harris' tales of Sut Lovingood loose in the backwoods have few counterparts in early American writing. They were collected as Sut Lovingood's Yarns *in 1867.*

---

1. Franklin J. Meine, *Tall Tales of the Southwest* (New York: Alfred A. Knopf, 1930), p. xxiv.

Hey Ge-orge!" rang among the mountain slopes; and looking up to my left, I saw Sut tearing along down a steep point, heading me off, in a long kangaroo lope, holding his flask high above his head, and hat in hand. He brought up near me, banteringly shaking the half-full "tickler" within an inch of my face.

"Whar am yu gwine? Take a suck, hoss? This yere truck's *ole*. I kotch hit myse'f, hot this mornin from the still wum. Nara durn'd bit ove strike-nine in hit—I put that ar piece ove burnt dried peach in myse'f tu gin hit color—better nur old Bullen's plan: he puts in tan ooze, in what he sells, an' when that hain't handy, he uses the red warter outen a pon' jis' below his barn—makes a pow'ful natral color, but don't help the taste much. Then he correcks that wif red pepper; hits an orful mixtry, that whisky ole Bullen makes; no wonder he seed 'Hell-sarpints.' He's pisent ni ontu three quarters ove the b'levin parts ove his congregashun wif hit, an' tuther quarter he's sot intu ruff stealin an' cussin. Ef his still-'ous don't burn down, ur he peg out hisse'f, the neighborhood am ruinated a-pas salvashun. Hain't he the durndes sampil ove a passun yu ever seed enyhow?

"Say George, du yu see these yere wellpoles what I uses fur laigs? Yu sez yu sees em, dus yu?"

"Yes."

"Very well; I passed 'em a-pas' each uther tuther day, right peart. I put one out a-head jis' so, an' then tuther 'bout nine feet a-head ove hit agin jis' so, an' then kep on a-duin hit. I'll jis' gin yu leav tu go tu the devil ha'f hamon, ef I didn't make fewer tracks tu the mile, an' more tu the minit, than wer ever made by eny human man body since Bark Wilson beat the sawlog from the top ove the Frog Mountin intu the Oconee River, an' dove, an' dodged hit at las'. I hes allers look'd ontu that performince ove Bark's as onekel'd in his-

tery, allers givin way tu dad's ho'net race, however.

"George, every livin thing hes hits pint, a pint ove sum sort. Ole Bullen's pint is a durn'd fust rate, three bladed, dubbil barril'd, warter-proof, hypockracy, an' a niver-tirein appertite fur bal'face. Sicily Burns's pint am tu drive men folks plum crazy, an' then bring em too agin. Gin em a rale Orleans fever in five minits, an' then in five minits more, gin them a Floridy ager. Durn her, she's down on her heels flat-footed now. Dad's pint is tu be king ove all durn'd fools, ever since the day ove that feller what cribb'd up so much co'n down in Yegipt, long time ago (he run outen his coat yu minds). The Bibil tell us hu wer the stronges' man—hu wer the bes' man—hu wer the meekis' man, an' hu the wises' man, but leaves yu tu guess hu wer the bigges' fool.

"Well, any man what cudent guess arter readin that ar scrimmage wif an 'oman 'bout the coat, haint sense enuf to run intu the hous', ef hit wer rainin ded cats, that's all. Mam's pint am in kitchen insex, bakin hoecake, bilin greens, an' runnin bar laiged. My pint am in taking aboard big skeers, an' then beatin enybody's hoss, ur skared dorg, a-running frum onder em agin. I used tu think my pint an' dad's wer jis' the same, sulky, unmix'd king durn'd fool; but when he acted hoss, an' mistook hoss-flies fur ho'nets, I los' heart. Never mine, when I gits his 'sperence, I may be king fool, but yet great golly, he gets frum bad tu wus, monstrus fas'.

"Now ef a feller happens tu know what his pint am, he kin allers git along, sumhow, purvided he don't swar away his liberty tu a temprins s'ciety, live tu fur frum a still-'ous, an' too ni a chu'ch ur a jail. Them's my sentimints on 'pints'—an' yere's my sentimints ontu folks: Men wer made a-purpus jis' tu eat, drink, an' fur stayin awake in the yearly part ove the nites: an' wimen wer made tu cook the vittils, mix the sperits, an' help the men du the stayin awake. That's all, an' nuthin more, onless hits fur the wimen tu raise the devil atwix meals, an' knit socks atwix drams, an' the men to play short kerds, swap hosses wif fools, an' fite fur exercise, at odd spells.

"George, yu don't onderstan life yet scarcely at all; got a heap tu larn, a heap. But 'bout my swappin my laigs so fas'— these yere very par ove laigs. I hed got about a fox squirril skin full ove biled co'n juice packed onder my shut, an' onder my hide too, I mout es well add, an' wer aimin fur Bill Carr's on foot. When I got in sight ove ole man Burns's, I seed ni ontu fifty hosses an' muels hitch'd tu the fence. Durnashun! I jis' then tho't ove hit, 'twer Sicily's wedding day. She married old Clapshaw, the suckit rider. The very feller hu's faith gin out when he met me sendin sody all over creashun. Suckit-riders am surjestif things tu me. They preaches agin me, an' I hes no chance tu preach back at them. Ef I cud I'd make the institushun behave hitsef better nur hit dus. They hes sum wunderful pints, George. Thar am two things nobody never seed; wun am a dead muel, an' tuther is a suckit-rider's grave. Kaze why, the he muels all turn intu old field school-masters, an' the she ones intu strong minded wimen, an' then when thar time cums, they dies sorter like uther folks. An' the suckit-riders ride ontil they marry; ef they marrys money, they turns intu store-keepers, swaps hosses, an' stays away ove colleckshun Sundays. Them what marrys, an' by sum orful mistake *misses the money*, jis' turns intu polertishuns, sells 'ile well stock,' an' dies sorter in the human way too.

"But 'bout the wedding. Ole Burns hed a big black an' white bull, wif a ring in his snout, an' the rope tied up roun his ho'ns. They rid 'im tu mill, an' sich like vif a saddil made outen two dorgwood ɔrks, an' two clapboards, kivered wif a

ole piece ove carpet, rope girth, an' rope stirrups wif a loop in hit fur the foot. Ole 'Sock,' es they call'd the bull, hed jis' got back frum mill, an' wer turn'd intu the yard, saddil an' all, tu solace hissef a-pickin grass. I wer slungin roun the outside ove the hous', fur they hedn't hed the manners tu ax me in, when they sot down tu dinner. I wer pow'fully hurt 'bout hit, an' happen'd tu think—SODY. So I sot in a-watchin fur a chance tu du sumthin. I fus' tho't I'd shave ole Clapshaw's hoss's tail, go tu the stabil an' shave Sicily's mare's tail, an' ketch ole Burns out, an' shave his tail too. While I wer a-studyin 'bout this, ole Sock wer a-nosin 'roun, an' cum up ontu a big baskit what hilt a littil shattered co'n; he dipp'd in his head tu git hit, an' I slipp'd up an' jerked the handil over his ho'ns.

"Now, George, ef yu knows the nater ove a cow brute, they is the durndes fools amung all the beastes ('scept the Lovingoods) ; when they gits intu tribulashun, they knows nuffin but tu shot thar eyes, beller, an' back, an' keep a-backin. Well, when ole Sock raised his head an' foun hissef in darkness, he jis' twisted up his tail, snorted the shatter'd co'n outen the baskit, an' made a tremenjus lunge agin the hous'. I hearn the picters a-hangin agin the wall on the inside a-fallin. He fotch a deep loud rusty beller, mout been hearn a mile, an' then sot intu a onendin sistem ove backin. A big craw-fish wif a hungry coon a-reachin fur him, wer jis' nowhar. Fust agin one thing, then over anuther, an' at las' agin the bee-bainch, knockin hit an' a dozen stan ove bees heads over heels, an' then stompin back'ards thru the mess. Hit haint much wuf while tu tell what the bees did, ur how soon they sot intu duin hit. They am pow'ful quick-tempered littil critters, enyhow. The air wer dark wif 'em, an' Sock wer kivered all over, frum snout tu tail, so clost yu cudent a-sot down a grain ove wheat fur bees, an' they wer a-fitin one anuther in the air, fur a place on the bull. The hous' stood on sidelin groun, an' the back door wer even wif hit. So Sock happen tu hit hit plum, jis' backed intu the hous' onder 'bout two hundred an' fifty pouns ove steam, bawlin orful, an' every snort he fotch he snorted away a quart ove bees ofen his sweaty snout. He wer the leader ove the bigges' an' the madest army ove bees in the worild. Thar wer at leas' five solid bushels ove 'em. They hed filled the baskit, an' hed lodged ontu his tail, ten deep, ontil hit wer es thick es a waggin tung. He hed hit stuck strait up in the air, an' hit looked adzackly like a dead pine kivered wif ivey. I think he wer the hottes' and wus hurtin bull then livin; his temper, too, seemed tu be pow'-fully flustrated. Ove *all* the durn'd times an' kerryins on yu *ever* hearn tell on wer thar an' thar abouts.

"He cum tail fust agin the ole two story Dutch clock, an' fotch hit, bustin hits runnin geer outen hit, the littil wheels a-trundlin over the floor, an' the bees even chasin them. Nex pass, he fotch up agin the foot ove a big dubbil injine bedstead, rarin hit on aind, an' punchin one ove the posts thru a glass winder. The next tail fus' experdishun wer made aginst the cati-corner'd cupboard, outen which he made a perfeck momox. Fus' he upsot hit, smashin in the glass doors, an' then jis' sot in an' stomp'd everything on the shelves intu giblits, a-tryin tu back furder in that direckshun, an' tu git the bees ofen his laigs.

"Pickil crocks, perserves jars, vinegar jugs, seed bags, yarb bunches, paragorick bottils, aig baskits, an' delf war—all mix'd dam permiskusly, an' not worth the sortin, by a duller an' a 'alf. Nex he got a far back acrost the room agin the board pertishun; he went thru hit like hit hed been paper, takin wif him 'bout six foot squar ove hit in splinters, an' broken boards, intu the nex room, whar they wer eatin dinner,

an' rite yere the fitin becum gineral, an' the dancin, squawkin, cussin, an' dodgin begun.

"Clapshaw's ole mam wer es deaf es a dogiron, an sot at the aind ove the tabil, nex tu whar old Sock busted thru the wall; tail fus' he cum agin her cheer, a-histin her an' hit ontu the tabil. Now, the smashin ove delf, an' the mixin ove vittils begun. They hed sot severil tabils tugether tu make hit long enuf. So he jis' rolled 'em up a-top ove one anuther, an' thar sot ole Missis Clapshaw, a-straddil ove the top ove the pile, a-fitin bees like a mad windmill, wif her caliker cap in one han, fur a wepun, an' a cract frame in tuther, an' a-kickin, an' a-spurrin like she wer ridin a lazy hoss arter the doctor, an' a-screamin rape, fire, an' murder, es fas' es she cud name 'em over.

"Taters, cabbige, meat, soup, beans, sop, dumplins, an' the truck what you wallers 'em in; milk, plates, pies, puddins, an' every durn fixin yu cud think ove in a week, wer thar, mix'd an' mashed, like hit had been thru a thrashin-meesheen. Ole Sock still kep a-backin, an' backed the hole pile, ole 'oman an' all, also sum cheers, outen the frunt door, an' down seven steps intu the lane, an' then by golly, turn'd a fifteen hundred poun summerset hissef arter 'em, lit a-top ove the mix'd up mess, flat ove his back, an' then kicked hissef ontu his feet agin. About the time he ris, ole man Burns—yu know how fat, an' stumpy, an' cross-grained he is, enyhow—made a vigrus mad snatch at the baskit, an' got a savin holt ontu hit, but cudent *let go quick enuf;* fur ole Sock jis' snorted, bawled, an' histed the ole cuss heels fust up intu the air, an' he lit on the bull's back, an' hed the baskit in his han.

"Jis' es soon es ole Blackey got the use ove his eyes, he tore off down the lane tu out-run the bees, so durn'd fas' that ole Burns wer feard tu try tu git off. So he jis' socked his feet intu the rope loops, an' then cummenc'd the durndes' bull-ride ever mortal man ondertuck. Sock run atwix the hitched critters an' the rail-fence, ole Burns fust fitin him over the head wif the baskit tu stop him, an' then fitin the bees wif hit. I'll jis' be durn'd ef I didn't think he hed four ur five baskits, hit wer in so meny places at onst. Well, Burns, baskit, an' bull, an' bees, skared every durn'd hoss an' muel loose frum that fence—bees ontu all ove 'em, bees, by golly, everywhar. Mos' on 'em, too, tuck a fence-rail along, fas' tu the bridil reins. Now I'll jis gin yu leave tu kiss my sister Sall till she squalls, ef ever sich a sight wer seed ur sich nises hearn, es filled up that long lane. A heavy cloud ove dus', like a harycane hed been blowin, hid all the hosses, an' away abuv hit yu cud see tails, an' ainds ove fence-rails a-flyin about; now an' then a par ove bright hine shoes wud flash in the sun like two sparks, an' away ahead wer the baskit a-sirklin round an' about at randum. Brayin, nickerin, the bellerin ove the bull, clatterin ove runnin hoofs, an' a mons'ous rushin soun, made up the noise. Lively times in that lane jis' then, warn't thar?

"I swar ole Burns kin beat eny man on top ove the yeath a-fitin bees wif a baskit. Jis' set 'im a-straddil ove a mad bull, an' let thar be bees enuf tu exhite the ole man, an' the man what beats him kin break me. Hosses an' muels wer tuck up all over the county, an' sum wer forever los'. Yu cudent go eny course, in a cirkil ove a mile, an' not find buckils, stirrups, straps, saddil blankits, ur sumthin belongin tu a saddil hoss. Now don't forgit that about that hous' thar wer a good time bein had ginerally. Fellers an' gals loped outen windows, they rolled outen the doors in bunches, they clomb the chimleys, they darted onder the house jis' tu dart out agin, they tuck tu the thicket, they rolled in the wheat field, lay down in the krick, did everything but stan still. Sum made a straight run *fur* home, an' sum es strait a run *from* home; livelyest

folks I ever did see. Clapshaw crawled onder a straw pile in the barn, an' sot intu prayin—yu cud a-hearn him a mile—sumthin 'bout the plagues ove Yegipt, an' the pains ove the secon death. I tell yu now he lumbered.

"Sicily, she squatted in the cold spring, up tu her years, an' turn'd a milk crock over her head, while she wer a drownin a mess ove bees under her coats. I went to her, an' sez I, 'Yu hes got anuther new sensashun, haint yu?'

"Sez she, 'Shet yer mouth, yu cussed fool!'

"Sez I, 'Powerful sarchin feelin bees gins a body, don't they?'

" 'Oh, lordy, lordy, Sut, these yere 'bominabil insex is jis' burnin me up!'

" 'Gin 'em a mess OVE SODY,' sez I, 'that'll cool 'em off, an' skeer the las' durn'd one ofen the place.'

"She lifted the crock, so she cud flash her eyes at me, an' sed, 'Yu go tu hell!' *jis es plain.* I thought, takin all things tugether, that p'raps I mout es well put the mountin atwix me an' that plantashun; an' I did hit.

"Thar warnt an 'oman ur a gal at that weddin, but what thar frocks an' stockins wer too tite fur a week. Bees am wus on wimen than men, enyhow. They hev a farer chance at 'em. Nex day I passed ole Hawley's, an' his gal Betts wer sittin in the porch, wif a white handkerchef tied roun her jaws; her face wer es red as a beet, an' her eyebrows hung 'way over heavy. Sez I, 'Hed a fine time at the weddin, didn't yu?' 'Yu mus' be a durn'd fool,' wer every word she sed. I hadent gone a hundred yards, ontil I met Missis Brady, her hans fat, an' her ankils swelled ontil they shined.

"Sez she, 'Whar yu gwine, Sut?'

" 'Bee huntin,' sez I.

" 'Yu jis' say bees agin, yu infunel gallinipper, an' I'll scab yer head wif a rock.'

"Now haint hit strange how tetchus they am, on the subjick ove bees?

"Ove all the durn'd misfortinit weddins ever since ole Adam married that heifer what wer so fon' ove talkin tu snaix an' eatin appils, down ontil now, that one ove Sicily's an' Clapshaw's wer the worst one fur noise, disappintment, skeer, breakin things, hurtin, trubbil, vexashun ove spirrit, an' gineral swellin. Why, George, her an' him cudent sleep tugether fur ni ontu a week, on account ove the doins ove them ar hot-footed, 'vengeful, 'bominabil littil insex. They never will gee tugether, got tu bad a start, mine what I tell yu. Yu haint time now tu hear how ole Burns finished his bull-ride, an' how I cum tu du that lofty, topliftical speciment ove fas' runnin. I'll tell yu all that, sum other time. Ef eny ove 'em axes after me, tell 'em that I'm over in Fannin, on my way tu Dahlonega. They is huntin me tu kill me, I is fear'd.

"Hit am an orful thing, George, tu be a natral born durn'd fool. Yu'se never 'sperienced hit pussonally, hev yu? Hits made pow'fully agin our famerly, an all owin tu dad. I orter bust my head open agin a bluff ove rocks, an' jis' wud du it, ef I warn't a cussed coward. All my yeathly 'pendence is in these yere laigs—d'ye see 'em? Ef they don't fail, I may turn human sum day, that is sorter human, enuf tu be a Squire, ur school cummisiner. Ef I wer jis' es smart es I am mean an' ornary, I'd be President ove a Wild Cat Bank in less nor a week. Is sperrits plenty over wif yu?"

SIMON SUGGS ATTENDS A CAMP-MEETING

by Johnson J. Hooper

Manners were rough on the frontier, and chicanery and violence were common. The prankster, the demagogue, and the villain of darker colors had a field day at the expense of unsuspicious crowds. Simon Suggs, a notorious sharper and gambler, came to a camp-meeting with the frank purpose of making something out of it. By accident he found himself uncomfortably conspicuous; but, always an opportunist, he played the hypocrite to perfection, and having "sold" the audience completely, he rode off with the proceeds. Suggs is a good example of the trickster untroubled by qualms of conscience. His true character is kept before the reader by his tendency to drop into his habitual language of the gaming table. Hooper published his Adventures of Captain Simon Suggs *in 1845.*

Captain Suggs found himself as poor at the conclusion of the Creek war, as he had been at its commencement. Although no "arbitrary," "despotic," "corrupt," and "unprincipled" judge had fined him a thousand dollars for his proclamation of martial law at Fort Suggs, or the enforcement of its rules in the case of Mrs. Haycock; yet somehow—the thing is alike inexplicable to him and to us—the money which he had contrived, by various shifts, to obtain, melted away and was gone forever. To a man like the Captain, of intense domestic affections, this state of destitution was most distressing. "He could stand it himself—didn't care a d———n for it, no way," he observed, "but the old woman and the children; *that* bothered him!"

As he sat one day, ruminating upon the unpleasant condition of his "financial concerns," Mrs. Suggs informed him that "the sugar and coffee was nigh about out," and that there were not "a dozen j'ints and middlins, *all put together,* in the smokehouse." Suggs bounced up on the instant, exclaiming, "D———n it! *somebody* must suffer!" But whether this remark was intended to convey the idea that he and his family were about to experience the want of the necessaries of life; or that some other, and as yet unknown, individual should "suffer" to prevent that prospective exigency, must be left to the commentators, if perchance any of that ingenious class of persons should hereafter see proper to write notes for this history. It is enough for us that we give all the facts in this connection, so that ignorance of the subsequent conduct of Captain Suggs may not lead to an erroneous judgment in respect to his words.

Having uttered the exclamation we have repeated—and perhaps, hurriedly, walked once or twice across the room—Captain Suggs drew on his famous old green-blanket overcoat, and ordered his horse, and within five minutes was on his way to a camp-meeting, then in full blast on Sandy Creek, twenty miles distant, where he hoped to find amusement, at least. When he arrived there, he found the hollow square of the encampment filled with people, listening to the mid-day sermon, and its dozen accompanying "exhortations." A half-dozen preachers were dispensing the word; the one in the pulpit, a meek-faced old man, of great simplicity and benevolence. His voice was weak and cracked, notwithstanding which, however, he contrived to make himself heard occasionally, above the din of the exhorting, the singing, and the shouting which were going on around him. The rest were walking to and fro, (engaged in the other exercises we have indicated), among the "mourners"—a host of whom occupied the seat set apart for their especial use—or made personal appeals to the mere spectators. The excitement was intense. Men and women rolled about on the ground, or lay sobbing or shouting in promiscuous heaps. More than all, the negroes sang and screamed and prayed. Several, under the influence of what is technically called "the jerks," were plunging and pitching about with convulsive energy. The great object of all seemed to be, to see who could make the greatest noise—

> And each—for madness ruled the hour—
> Would try his own expressive power.

"Bless my poor old soul!" screamed the preacher in the pulpit; "ef yonder aint a squad in that corner that we aint got one outen yet! It'll never do"—raising his voice—"you must come outen that! Brother Fant, fetch up that youngster in the blue coat! I see the Lord's a-workin upon him! Fetch him along—glory—yes! —hold to him!"

"Keep the thing warm!" roared a sensual seeming man, of stout mould and florid countenance, who was exhorting among a bevy of young women, upon whom he was lavishing caresses. "Keep the thing warm, breethring!—come to the Lord, honey!" he added, as he vigorously hugged one of the damsels he sought to save.

"Oh, I've got him!" said another in exulting tones, as he led up a gawky youth among the mourners—"I've got him—he tried to git off, but—ha! Lord!"—shaking his head as much as to say, it took a smart fellow to escape him—"ha! Lord!"—and he wiped the perspiration from his face with one hand, and with the other, patted his neophyte on the shoulder—"he couldn't do it! No! Then he tried to argy wi' me—but bless the Lord!—he couldn't do that nother! Ha! Lord! I tuk him, fust in the Old Testament—bless the Lord!—and I argyed him all thro' Kings—then I throwed him into Proverbs,—and from that, here we had it up and down, kleer down to the New Testament, and then I begun to see it work him!—then we got into Matthy, and from Matthy right straight along to Acts; and *thar* I throwed him! Y-e-s—L-o-r-d!"—assuming the nasal twang and high pitch which are, in some parts, considered the perfection of rhetorical art—"Y-e-s L-o-r-d! and h-e-r-e he is! Now g-i-t down thar," addressing the subject, "and s-e-e ef the L-o-r-d won't do somethin' f-o-r you!" Having thus deposited his charge among the mourners, he started out, summarily to convert another soul!

"Gl-o-*ree!*" yelled a huge, greasy negro woman, as in a fit of the jerks, she threw herself convulsively from her feet, and fell "like a thousand of brick," across a diminutive old man in a little round hat, who was speaking consolation to one of the mourners.

"Good Lord, have mercy!" ejaculated the little man earnestly and unaffectedly, as he strove to crawl from under the sable mass which was crushing him.

In another part of the square a dozen old women were singing. They were in a state of absolute ecstasy, as their shrill pipes gave forth:

> I rode on the sky,
> Quite ondestified I,
> And the moon it was under my feet!

Near these last, stood a delicate woman in that hysterical condition in which the nerves are incontrollable, and which is vulgarly—and almost blasphemously—termed the "holy laugh." A hideous grin distorted her mouth, and was accompanied with a maniac's chuckle; while every muscle and nerve of her face twitched and jerked in horrible spasms.

Amid all this confusion and excitement Suggs stood unmoved. He viewed the whole affair as a grand deception—a sort of "opposition line" running against his own, and looked on with a sort of professional jealousy. Sometimes he would mutter running comments upon what passed before him.

"Well now," said he, as he observed the full-faced brother who was "officiating" among the women, "that ere feller takes *my* eye!—thar he's been this half-hour, a-figurin amongst them galls, and's never said the fust word to nobody else. Wonder what's the reason these here preachers never hugs up the old, ugly women? Never seed one do it in my life—the sperrit never moves 'em that way! It's nater tho'; and the women, *they* never flocks round one o' the old dried-up breethring—bet two to one old splinter-legs thar,"—nodding at one of the ministers—"won't git a chance to say turkey to a good-lookin gall today! Well! Who blames 'em? Nater will be nater, all the world over; and I judge ef I was a preacher, I should save the purtiest souls fust, myself!"

While the Captain was in the middle of this conversation with himself, he caught the attention of the preacher in the pulpit, who inferring from an indescribable something about his appearance that he was a person of some consequence, immediately determined to add him at once to the church if it could be done; and to that end began a vigorous, direct personal attack.

"Breethring," he exclaimed, "I see yonder a man that's a sinner; I *know* he's a sinner! Thar he stands," pointing at

Simon, "a missubble old crittur, with his head a-blossomin for the grave! A few more short years, and d-o-w-n he'll go to perdition, lessen the Lord have mercy on him! Come up here, you old hoary-headed sinner, a-n-d git down upon your knees, a-n-d put up your cry for the Lord to snatch you from the bottomless pit! You're ripe for the devil—you're b-o-u-n-d for hell, and the Lord only knows what'll become on you!"

"D——n it," thought Suggs, "ef I only had you down in the krick swamp for a minit or so, *I'd* show you who's *old!* *I'd* alter your tune *mighty* sudden, you sassy, 'saitful old rascal!" But he judiciously held his tongue and gave no utterance to the thought.

The attention of many having been directed to the Captain by the preacher's remarks, he was soon surrounded by numerous well-meaning, and doubtless very pious persons, each one of whom seemed bent on the application of his own particular recipe for the salvation of souls. For a long time the Captain stood silent, or answered the incessant stream of exhortations only with a sneer; but at length, his countenance began to give token of inward emotion. First his eye-lids twitched—then his upper lip quivered—next a transparent drop formed on one of his eye-lashes, and a similar one on the tip of his nose—and, at last, a sudden bursting of air from nose and mouth, told that Captain Suggs was overpowered by his emotions. At the moment of the explosion, he made a feint as if to rush from the crowd, but he was in experienced hands, who well knew that the battle was more than half won.

"Hold to him!" said one—"it's a-workin in him as strong as a Dick horse!"

"Pour it into him," said another, "it'll all come right directly!"

"That's the way I love to see 'em do," observed a third; "when you begin to draw the water from their eyes, taint gwine to be long afore you'll have 'em on their knees!"

And so they clung to the Captain manfully, and half dragged, half led him to the mourner's bench; by which he threw himself down, altogether unmanned, and bathed in tears. Great was the rejoicing of the brethren, as they sang, shouted, and prayed around him—for by this time it had come to be generally known that the "convicted" old man was Captain Suggs, the very "chief of sinners" in all that region.

The Captain remained grovelling in the dust during the usual time, and gave vent to even more than the requisite number of sobs, and groans, and heart-piercing cries. At length, when the proper time had arrived, he bounced up, and with a face radiant with joy, commenced a series of vaultings and tumblings, which "laid in the shade" all previous performances of the sort at that camp-meeting. The brethren were in ecstasies at this demonstrative evidence of completion of the work; and whenever Suggs shouted "Gloree!" at the top of his lungs, every one of them shouted it back, until the woods rang with echoes.

The effervescence having partially subsided, Suggs was put upon his pins to relate his experience, which he did somewhat in this style—first brushing the tear-drops from his eyes, and giving the end of his nose a preparatory wring with his fingers, to free it of the superabundant moisture:

"Friends," he said, "it don't take long to curry a short horse, accordin' to the old sayin', and I'll give you the perticklers of the way I was 'brought to a knowledge' "—here the Captain wiped his eyes, brushed the tip of his nose and snuffled a little—"in less'n no time."

"Praise the Lord!" ejaculated a by-stander.

"You see I come here full o' romancin' and devilment, and jist to make game of all the purceedins. Well, sure enough, I done so for some time, and was a-thinkin how I should play some trick—"

"Dear soul alive! *don't* he talk sweet!" cried an old lady in black silk—"Whar's John Dobbs? You Sukey!" screaming at a negro woman on the other side of the square—"ef you don't hunt up your mass John in a minute, and have him here to listen to this 'sperience, I'll tuck you up when I git home and give you a hundred and fifty lashes, madam!—see ef I don't! Blessed Lord!"—referring again to the Captain's relation—"ain't it a *precious* 'scource!"

"I was jist a-thinkin' how I should play some trick to turn it all into redecule when they began to come round me and talk. Long at fust I didn't mind it, but arter a little that brother"—pointing to the reverend gentleman who had so successfully carried the unbeliever through the Old and New Testaments, and who Simon was convinced was the "big dog of the tanyard"—"that brother spoke a word that struck me kleen to the heart, and run all over me, like fire in dry grass—"

"I—I—I can bring 'em!" cried the preacher alluded to, in a tone of exultation—"Lord thou knows ef thy servant can't stir 'em up, nobody else needn't try —but the glory aint mine! I'm a poor worrum of the dust," he added, with ill-managed affectation.

"And so from that I felt somethin' a-pullin' me inside—"

"Grace! grace! nothin' but grace!" exclaimed one; meaning that "grace" had been operating in the Captain's gastric region.

"And then," continued Suggs, "I wanted to git off, but they hilt me, and bimeby I felt so missuble, I had to go yonder"—pointing to the mourner's seat— "and when I lay down thar it got wuss and wuss, and 'peared like somethin' was a-mashin' down on my back—"

"That was his load o' sin," said one of the brethern—"never mind, it'll tumble off presently, see ef it don't!" and he shook his head professionally and knowingly.

"And it kept a-gittin heavier and heavier, ontwell it looked like it might be a four year old steer, or a big pine log, or somethin' of that sort—"

"Glory to my soul," shouted Mrs. Dobbs, "it's the sweetest talk I *ever* hearn! You Sukey! aint you got John yit? never mind, my lady, I'll settle wi' you!" Sukey quailed before the finger which her mistress shook at her.

"And arter awhile," Suggs went on, " 'peared like I fell into a trance, like, and I seed—"

"Now we'll git the good on it!" cried one of the sanctified.

"And I seed the biggest, longest, riproarenest, blackest, scaliest—" Captain Suggs paused, wiped his brow, and ejaculated "Ah, L-o-r-d!" so as to give full time for curiosity to become impatience to know what he saw.

"*Sarpent!* warn't it?" asked one of the preachers.

"No, not a sarpent," replied Suggs, blowing his nose.

"Do tell us *what* it war, soul alive!— whar *is* John?" said Mrs. Dobbs.

"Allegator!" said the Captain.

"Alligator!" repeated every woman present, and screamed for very life.

Mrs. Dobbs' nerves were so shaken by the announcement, that after repeating the horrible word, she screamed to Sukey, "You Sukey, I say, you S-u-u-k-e-ey! ef you let John come a-nigh this way, whar the dreadful alliga-shaw! what am I thinkin' 'bout? 'Twarn't nothin' but a vishin!"

"Well," said the Captain in continuation, "the allegator kept a-comin and a-comin' to'ards me, with his great long jaws a-gapin' open like a ten foot pair o' tailor's shears—"

"Oh! oh! oh! Lord! gracious above!" cried the women.

"Satan!" was the laconic ejaculation of the oldest preacher present, who thus informed the congregation that it was the devil which had attacked Suggs in the shape of an alligator.

"And then I concluded the jig was up, 'thout I could block his game some way; for I seed his idee was to snap off my head—"

The women screamed again.

"So I fixed myself jist like I was purfectly willin' for him to take my head, and rather he'd do it as not"—here the women shuddered perceptibly—"and so I hilt my head straight out"—the Captain illustrated by elongating his neck—"and when he come up and was a gwine to *shet down* on it, I jist pitched in a big rock which choked him to death, and that minit I felt the weight slide off, and I had the best feelins—sorter like you'll have from good sperrits—any body ever had!"

"Didn't I *tell* you so? Didn't I *tell* you so?" asked the brother who had predicted the off-tumbling of the load of sin. "Ha, Lord! fool *who*! I've been *all* along thar! —yes, *all along thar*! and I know every inch of the way jist as good as I do the road home!"—and then he turned round and round, and looked at all, to receive a silent tribute to his superior penetration.

Captain Suggs was now the "lion of the day." Nobody could pray so well, or exhort so movingly, as "brother Suggs." Nor did his natural modesty prevent the proper performance of appropriate exercises. With the reverend Bela Bugg (him to whom, under providence, he ascribed his conversion) he was a most especial favorite. They walked, sang, and prayed together for hours.

"Come, come up; thar's room for all!" cried brother Bugg, in his evening exhortation. "Come to the 'seat,' and ef you won't pray yourselves, let *me* pray for you!"

"Yes!" said Simon, by way of assisting his friend; "it's a game that all can win at! Ante up!, boys—friends I mean —don't back out!"

"Thar aint a sinner here," said Bugg, "no matter ef his soul's black as a nigger, but what thar's room for him!"

"No matter what sort of a hand you've got," added Simon in the fullness of his benevolence; "take stock! Here am *I*, the wickedest and blindest of sinners—has spent my whole life in the sarvice of the devil—has now come in on *narry pair* and won a *pile!*" and the Captain's face beamed with holy pleasure.

"D-o-n-'t be afeard!" cried the preacher; "come along! the meanest won't be turned away! humble yourselves and come!"

"No!" said Simon, still indulging in his favourite style of metaphor; "the bluff game aint played here! No runnin' of a body off! Every body holds four aces, and when you bet, you win!"

And thus the Captain continued, until the services were concluded, to assist in adding to the number at the mourner's seat; and up to the hour of retiring, he exhibited such enthusiasm in the cause, that he was unanimously voted to be the most efficient addition the church had made during that meeting.

The next morning, when the preacher of the day first entered the pulpit, he announced that "brother Simon Suggs," mourning over his past iniquities, and desirous of going to work in the cause as speedily as possible, would take up a collection to found a church in his own neighbourhood, at which he hoped to make himself useful as soon as he could prepare himself for the ministry, which the preacher didn't doubt, would be in a very few weeks, as brother Suggs was "a man of mighty good *judgment*, and of a great discorse." The funds were to be collected by "brother Suggs," and held in trust by brother Bela Bugg, who was the financial officer of the circuit, until some arrangement could be made to build a suitable house.

"Yes, breethring," said the Captain, rising to his feet; "I want to start a little 'sociation close to me, and I want you all to help. I'm mighty poor myself, as poor as any of you—don't leave, breethring"—observing that several of the well-to-do were about to go off—"don't leave; ef you aint able to afford any thing, jist give us your blessin' and it'll be all the same!"

This insinuation did the business, and the sensitive individuals reseated themselves.

"It's mighty little of this world's goods I've got," resumed Suggs, pulling off his hat and holding it before him; "but I'll bury *that* in the cause any how," and he deposited his last five-dollar bill in the hat.

There was a murmur of approbation at the Captain's liberality throughout the assembly.

Suggs now commenced collecting, and very prudently attacked first the gentlemen who had shown a disposition to escape. These, to exculpate themselves from anything like poverty, contributed handsomely.

"Look here, breethring," said the Captain, displaying the bank-notes thus received, "brother Snooks has drapt a five wi' me, and brother Snodgrass a ten! In course, 'taint expected that you *that aint as well off as them*, will give *as much*; let every one give *accordin'* to ther means."

This was another chain-shot that raked as it went! "Who so low" as not to be able to contribute as much as Snooks and Snodgrass?

"Here's all the *small* money I've got about me," said a burly old fellow, ostentatiously handing to Suggs, over the heads of a half dozen, a ten dollar bill.

"That's what I call maganimus!" exclaimed the Captain; "that's the way *every* rich man ought to do!"

These examples were followed, more or less closely, by almost all present, for Simon had excited the pride of purse of the congregation, and a very handsome sum was collected in a very short time.

The reverend Mr. Bugg, as soon as he observed that our hero had obtained all that was to be had at that time, went to him and inquired what amount had been collected. The Captain replied that it was still uncounted, but that it couldn't be much under a hundred.

"Well, brother Suggs, you'd better count it and turn it over to me now, I'm goin' to leave presently."

"No!" said Suggs—"can't do it!"

"Why?—what's the matter?" inquired Bugg.

"It's got to be *prayed over*, fust!" said Simon, a heavenly smile illuminating his whole face.

"Well," replied Bugg, "less go one side and do it!"

"No!" said Simon, solemnly.

Mr. Bugg gave a look of inquiry.

"You see that krick swamp?" asked Suggs—"I'm gwine down in *thar,* and I'm gwine to lay this money down *so*"—showing how he would place it on the ground—"and I'm gwine to git on these here knees"—slapping the right one—"and I'm n-e-v-e-r gwine to quit the grit ontwell I feel it's got the blessin'! And nobody aint got to be thar but me!"

Mr. Bugg greatly admired the Captain's fervent piety, and bidding him God-speed, turned off.

Captain Suggs "struck for" the swamp sure enough, where his horse was already hitched. "Ef them fellers aint done to a cracklin," he muttered to himself as he mounted, "*I'll* never bet on two pair agin! They're peart at the snap game, theyselves; but they're badly lewed this hitch! Well! Live and let live is a good old motter, and it's my sentiments adzactly!" And giving the spur to his horse, off he cantered.

SPOTTED HORSES

by William Faulkner

*Faulkner's fictional Yoknapatawpha County, located in northern Missis-
sippi, is a rural area populated by Negroes, small farmers, and townsfolk.
Here a waning aristocracy (the Sartoris, Compson, and Benbow families)
fights a losing battle in opposition to the avaricious, unscrupulous, uncouth
Snopes clan. A particularly dangerous adversary to the old order is Flem
Snopes, whose reticence and quietness seem disarming. It is only in later
segments of the Snopes saga—especially in* The Town *(1957)—that
Flem's passion for respectability drives him to do an occasional decent
thing. "Spotted Horses," part of the novel called* The Hamlet *(1940),
seems to relegate Flem Snopes to the background, yet the real conflict of the
story is represented by the opposition between him and the itinerant sewing-
machine salesman, V. K. Ratliff. The story is a highly comic picture of folk
life, and the horse auction and the stampede seem to owe something in both
theme and detail to the earlier backwoods fiction of Longstreet and Harris.
But the ambivalence visible in so much of Faulkner's fiction comes out in
the unfeeling treatment of Mrs. Armstid.*

A little while before sundown the men lounging about the gallery of the store saw, coming up the road from the south, a covered wagon drawn by mules and followed by a considerable string of obviously alive objects which in the levelling sun resembled vari-sized and -colored tatters torn at random from large billboards—circus posters, say—attached to the rear of the wagon and inherent with its own separate and collective motion, like the tail of a kite.

"What in the hell is that?" one said.

"It's a circus," Quick said. They began to rise, watching the wagon. Now they could see that the animals behind the wagon were horses. Two men rode in the wagon.

"Hell fire," the first man—his name was Freeman—said. "It's Flem Snopes." They were all standing when the wagon came up and stopped and Snopes got down and approached the steps. He might have departed only this morning. He wore the same cloth cap, the minute bow tie against the white shirt, the same gray trousers. He mounted the steps.

"Howdy, Flem," Quick said. The other looked briefly at all of them and none of them, mounting the steps. "Starting you a circus?"

"Gentlemen," he said. He crossed the gallery; they made way for him. Then they descended the steps and approached the wagon, at the tail of which the horses stood in a restive clump, larger than rabbits and gaudy as parrots and shackled to one another and to the wagon itself with sections of barbed wire. Calico-coated, small-bodied, with delicate legs and pink faces in which their mismatched eyes rolled wild and subdued, they huddled, gaudy, motionless, and alert, wild as deer, deadly as rattlesnakes, quiet as doves. The men stood at a respectful distance, looking at them. At that moment Jody Varner came through the group, shouldering himself to the front of it.

"Watch yourself, doc," a voice said from the rear. But it was already too late. The nearest animal rose on its hind legs with lightning rapidity and struck twice with its forefeet at Varner's face, faster than a boxer, the movement of its surge against the wire which held it travelling backward among the rest of the band in a wave of thuds and lunges. "Hup, you broom-tailed, hay-burning sidewinders," the same voice said. This was the second man who had arrived in the wagon. He was a stranger. He wore a heavy, densely black moustache, a wide pale hat. When he thrust himself through and turned to herd them back from the horses they saw, thrust into the hip pockets of his tight jeans pants, the butt of a heavy pearl-handled pistol and a florid carton such as small cakes come in. "Keep away from them, boys," he said. "They've got kind of skittish, they ain't been rode in so long."

"Since when have they been rode?" Quick said. The stranger looked at Quick. He had a broad, quite cold, wind-gnawed face and bleak, cold eyes. His belly fitted neat and smooth as a peg into the tight trousers.

"I reckon that was when they were rode on the ferry to get across the Mississippi River," Varner said. The stranger looked at him. "My name's Varner," Jody said.

"Hipps," the other said. "Call me Buck." Across the left side of his head, obliterating the tip of that ear, was a savage and recent gash gummed over with a blackish substance like axle-grease. They looked at the scar. Then they watched him remove the carton from his pocket and tilt a gingersnap into his hand and put the gingersnap into his mouth, beneath the moustache.

"You and Flem have some trouble back yonder?" Quick said. The stranger ceased chewing. When he looked directly at anyone, his eyes became like two pieces of flint turned suddenly up in dug earth.

"Back where?" he said.

"Your nigh ear," Quick said.

"Oh," the other said. "That." He touched his ear. "That was my mistake. I was absent-minded one night when I was staking them out. Studying about something else and forgot how long the wire was." He chewed. They looked at his ear. "Happen to any man careless around a horse. Put a little axle-dope on it and you won't notice it tomorrow though. They're pretty lively now, lazing along all day doing nothing. It'll work out of them in a couple of days." He put another gingersnap into his mouth, chewing, "Don't you believe they'll gentle?" No one answered. They looked at the ponies, grave and noncommittal. Jody turned and went back into the store. "Them's good, gentle ponies," the stranger said. "Watch now." He put the carton back into his pocket and approached the horses, his hand extended. The nearest one was standing on three legs now. It appeared to be asleep. Its eyelid drooped over the cerulean eye; its head was shaped like an ironing-board. Without even raising the eyelid it flicked its head, the yellow teeth cropped. For an instant it and the man appeared to be inextricable in one violence. Then they became motionless, the stranger's high heels dug into the earth, one hand gripping the animal's nostrils, holding the horse's head wrenched half around while it breathed in hoarse, smothered groans. "See?" the stranger said in a panting voice, the veins standing white and rigid in his neck and along his jaw. "See? All you got to do is handle them a little and work hell out of them for a couple of days. Now look out. Give me room back there." They gave back a little. The stranger gathered himself then sprang away. As he did so, a second horse slashed at his back, severing his vest from collar to hem down the back exactly as the trick swordsman severs a floating veil with one stroke.

"Sho now," Quick said. "But suppose a man don't happen to own a vest."

At that moment Jody Varner, followed by the blacksmith, thrust through them again. "All right, Buck," he said. "Better get them on into the lot. Eck here will help you." The stranger, the severed halves of the vest swinging from either shoulder, mounted to the wagon seat, the blacksmith following.

"Get up, you transmogrified hallucinations of Job and Jezebel," the stranger said. The wagon moved on, the tethered ponies coming gaudily into motion behind it, behind which in turn the men followed at a respectful distance, on up the road and into the lane and so to the lot gate behind Mrs. Littlejohn's. Eck got down and opened the gate. The wagon passed through but when the ponies saw the fence the herd surged backward against the wire which attached it to the wagon, standing on its collective hind legs and then trying to turn within itself, so that the wagon moved backward for a few feet until the Texan, cursing, managed to saw the mules about and so lock the wheels. The men following had already fallen rapidly back. "Here, Eck," the Texan said. "Get up here and take the reins." The blacksmith got back in the wagon and took the reins. Then they watched the Texan descend, carrying a looped-up blacksnake whip, and go around to the rear of the herd and drive it through the gate, the whip snaking about the harlequin rumps in methodical and pistol-like reports. Then the watchers hurried across Mrs. Littlejohn's yard and mounted to the veranda, one end of which overlooked the lot.

"How you reckon he ever got them tied together?" Freeman said.

"I'd a heap rather watch how he aims to turn them loose," Quick said. The Texan had climbed back into the halted wagon. Presently he and Eck both appeared at the rear end of the open hood. The Texan grasped the wire and began to draw the first horse up to the wagon, the animal plunging and surging back against the wire as though trying to hang itself, the contagion passing back through the herd from animal to animal until they were rearing and plunging again against the wire.

"Come on, grab a holt," the Texan said. Eck grasped the wire also. The horses laid back against it, the pink faces tossing above the back-surging mass. "Pull him up, pull him up," the Texan said sharply. "They couldn't get up here in the wagon even if they wanted to." The wagon moved gradually backward until the head of the first horse was snubbed up to the tail-gate. The Texan took a turn of the wire quickly about one of the wagon stakes. "Keep the slack out of it," he said. He vanished and reappeared, almost in the same second, with a pair of heavy wire-cutters. "Hold them like that," he said, and leaped. He vanished, broad hat, flapping vest, wire-cutters and all, into a kaleidoscopic maelstrom of long teeth and wild eyes and slashing feet, from which presently the horses began to burst one by one like partridges flushing, each wearing a necklace of barbed wire. The first one crossed the lot at top speed, on a straight line. It galloped into the fence without any diminution whatever. The wire gave, recovered, and slammed the horse to earth where it lay for a moment, glaring, its legs still galloping in air. It scrambled up without having ceased to gallop and crossed the lot and galloped into the opposite fence and was slammed again to earth. The others were now freed. They whipped and whirled about the lot like dizzy fish in a bowl. It had seemed like a big lot until now, but now the very idea that all that fury and motion should be transpiring inside any one fence was something to be repudiated with contempt, like a mirror trick. From the ultimate dust the stranger, carrying the wire-cutters and his vest completely gone now, emerged. He was not running, he merely moved with a light-poised and watchful celerity, weaving among the calico rushes of the animals, feinting and dodging like a boxer until he reached the gate and crossed the yard and mounted to the veranda. One sleeve of his shirt hung only at one point from his shoulder. He ripped it off and wiped his face with it and threw it away and took out the paper carton and shook a gingersnap into his hand. He was breathing only a little heavily. "Pretty lively now," he said. "But it'll work out of them in a couple of days." The ponies still streaked back and forth through the growing dusk like hysterical fish, but not so violently now.

"What'll you give a man to reduce them odds a little for you?" Quick said. The Texan looked at him, the eyes bleak, pleasant and hard above the chewing jaw, the heavy moustache. "To take one of them off your hands?" Quick said.

At that moment the little periwinkle-eyed boy came along the veranda, saying, "Papa, papa; where's papa?"

"Who you looking for, sonny?" one said.

"It's Eck's boy," Quick said. "He's still out yonder in the wagon. Helping Mr. Buck here." The boy went on to the end of the veranda, in diminutive overalls—a miniature replica of the men themselves.

"Papa," he said. "Papa." The blacksmith was still leaning from the rear of the wagon, still holding the end of the severed wire. The ponies, bunched for the moment, now slid past the wagon, flowing, stringing out again so that they ap-peared to have doubled in number, rushing on; the hard, rapid, light patter of unshod hooves came out of the dust. "Mamma says to come on to supper," the boy said.

The moon was almost full then. When supper was over and they had gathered again along the veranda, the alteration was hardly one of visibility even. It was merely a translation from the lapidary-dimensional of day to the treacherous and silver receptivity in which the horses huddled in mazy camouflage, or singly or in pairs rushed, fluid, phantom, and unceasing, to huddle again in mirage-like clumps from which came high, abrupt squeals and the vicious thudding of hooves.

Ratliff was among them now. He had returned just before supper. He had not dared to take his team into the lot at all. They were now in Bookwright's stable a half mile from the store. "So Flem has come home again," he said. "Well, well, well. Will Varner paid to get him to Texas, so I reckon it ain't no more than fair for you fellows to pay the freight on him back." From the lot there came a high, thin squeal. One of the animals emerged. It seemed not to gallop but to flow, bodiless, without dimension. Yet there was the rapid light beat of hard hooves on the packed earth.

"He ain't said they was his yet," Quick said.

"He ain't said they ain't neither," Freeman said.

"I see," Ratliff said. "That's what you are holding back on. Until he tells you whether they are his or not. Or maybe you can wait until the auction's over and split up and some can follow Flem and some can follow that Texas fellow and watch to see which one spends the money. But then, when a man's done got trimmed, I don't reckon he cares who's got the money."

"Maybe if Ratliff would leave here tonight, they wouldn't make him buy one of them ponies tomorrow," a third said.

"That's fact," Ratliff said. "A fellow can dodge a Snopes if he just starts lively enough. In fact, I don't believe he would have to pass more than two folks before he would have another victim intervened betwixt them. You folks ain't going to buy them things sho enough, are you?" Nobody answered. They sat on the steps, their backs against the veranda posts, or on the railing itself. Only Ratliff and Quick sat in chairs, so that to them the others were black silhouettes against the dreaming lambence of the moonlight beyond the veranda. The pear tree across the road opposite was now in full and frosty bloom, the twigs and branches springing not outward from the limbs but standing motionless and perpendicular above the horizontal boughs like the separate and upstreaming hair of a drowned woman sleeping upon the uttermost floor of the windless and tideless sea.

"Anse McCallum brought two of them horses back from Texas once," one of the men on the steps said. He did not move to speak. He was not speaking to anyone. "It was a good team. A little light. He worked it for ten years. Light work, it was."

"I mind it," another said. "Anse claimed he traded fourteen rifle cartridges for both of them, didn't he?"

"It was the rifle too, I heard," a third said.

"No, it was just the shells," the first said. "The fellow wanted to swap him four more for the rifle too, but Anse said he never needed them. Cost too much to get six of them back to Mississippi."

"Sho," the second said. "When a man don't have to invest so much into a horse or a team, he don't need to expect so much from it." The three of them were not talking any louder, they were merely talking among themselves, to one another, as if they sat there alone. Ratliff, invisible in

the shadow against the wall, made a sound, harsh, sardonic, not loud.

"Ratliff's laughing," a fourth said.

"Don't mind me," Ratliff said. The three speakers had not moved. They did not move now, yet there seemed to gather about the three silhouettes something stubborn, convinced, and passive, like children who have been chidden. A bird, a shadow, fleet and dark and swift, curved across the moonlight, upward into the pear tree and began to sing; a mockingbird.

"First one I've noticed this year," Freeman said.

"You can hear them along Whiteleaf every night," the first man said. "I heard one in February. In that snow. Singing in a gum."

"Gum is the first tree to put out," the third said. "That was why. It made it feel like singing, fixing to put out that way. That was why it taken a gum."

"Gum first to put out?" Quick said. "What about willow?"

"Willow ain't a tree," Freeman said. "It's a weed."

"Well, I don't know what it is," the fourth said. "But it ain't no weed. Because you can grub up a weed and you are done with it. I been grubbing up a clump of willows outen my spring pasture for fifteen years. They are the same size every year. Only difference is, it's just two or three more trees every time."

"And if I was you," Ratliff said, "that's just exactly where I would be come sunup tomorrow. Which of course you ain't going to do. I reckon there ain't nothing under the sun or in Frenchman's Bend neither that can keep you folks from giving Flem Snopes and that Texas man your money. But I'd sholy like to know just exactly who I was giving my money to. Seems like Eck here would tell you. Seems like he'd do that for his neighbors, don't it? Besides being Flem's cousin, him and that boy of his, Wallstreet, helped that

Texas man tote water for them tonight and Eck's going to help him feed them in the morning too. Why, maybe Eck will be the one that will catch them and lead them up one at a time for you folks to bid on them. Ain't that right, Eck?"

The other man sitting on the steps with his back against the post was the blacksmith. "I don't know," he said.

"Boys," Ratliff said, "Eck knows all about them horses. Flem's told him, how much they cost and how much him and that Texas man aim to get for them, make off of them. Come on, Eck. Tell us." The other did not move, sitting on the top step, not quite facing them, sitting there beneath the successive layers of their quiet and intent concentrated listening and waiting.

"I don't know," he said. Ratliff began to laugh. He sat in the chair, laughing while the others sat or lounged upon the steps and the railing, sitting beneath his laughing as Eck had sat beneath their listening and waiting. Ratliff ceased laughing. He rose. He yawned, quite loud.

"All right. You folks can buy them critters if you want to. But me, I'd just as soon buy a tiger or a rattlesnake. And if Flem Snopes offered me either one of them, I would be afraid to touch it for fear it would turn out to be a painted dog or a piece of garden hose when I went up to take possession of it. I bid you one and all goodnight." He entered the house. They did not look after him, though after a while they all shifted a little and looked down into the lot, upon the splotchy, sporadic surge and flow of the horses, from among which from time to time came an abrupt squeal, a thudding blow. In the pear tree the mockingbird's idiot reiteration pulsed and purled.

"Anse McCallum made a good team outen them two of hisn," the first man said. "They was a little light. That was all."

When the sun rose the next morning a wagon and three saddled mules stood in Mrs. Littlejohn's lane and six men and Eck Snopes' son were already leaning on the fence, looking at the horses which huddled in a quiet clump before the barn door, watching the men in their turn. A second wagon came up the road and into the lane and stopped, and then there were eight men beside the boy standing at the fence, beyond which the horses stood, their blue-and-brown eyeballs rolling alertly in their gaudy faces. "So this here is the Snopes circus, is it?" one of the newcomers said. He glanced at the faces, then he went to the end of the row and stood beside the blacksmith and the little boy. "Are them Flem's horses?" he said to the blacksmith.

"Eck don't know who them horses belong to any more than we do," one of the others said. "He knows that Flem come here on the same wagon with them, because he saw him. But that's all."

"And all he will know," a second said. "His own kin will be the last man in the world to find out anything about Flem Snopes' business."

"No," the first said. "He wouldn't even be that. The first man Flem would tell his business to would be the man that was left after the last man died. Flem Snopes don't even tell himself what he is up to. Not if he was laying in bed with himself in a empty house in the dark of the moon."

"That's a fact," a third said. "Flem would trim Eck or any other of his kin quick as he would us. Ain't that right, Eck?"

"I don't know," Eck said. They were watching the horses, which at that moment broke into a high-eared, stiff-kneed swirl and flowed in a patchwork wave across the lot and brought up again, facing the men along the fence, so they did not hear the Texan until he was among them. He wore a new shirt and another vest a little too small for him and he was just putting the paper carton back into his hip pocket.

"Morning, morning," he said. "Come to get an early pick, have you? Want to make me an offer for one or two before the bidding starts and runs the prices up?" They had not looked at the stranger long. They were not looking at him now, but at the horses in the lot, which had lowered their heads, snuffing into the dust.

"I reckon we'll look a while first," one said.

"You are in time to look at them eating breakfast, anyhow," the Texan said. "Which is more than they done without they staid up all night." He opened the gate and entered it. At once the horses jerked their heads up, watching him. "Here, Eck," the Texan said over his shoulder, "two or three of you boys help me drive them into the barn." After a moment Eck and two others approached the gate, the little boy at his father's heels, though the other did not see him until he turned to shut the gate.

"You stay out of here," Eck said. "One of them things will snap your head off same as a acorn before you even know it." He shut the gate and went on after the others, whom the Texan had now waved fanwise outward as he approached the horses which now drew into a restive huddle, beginning to mill slightly, watching the men. Mrs. Littlejohn came out of the kitchen and crossed the yard to the woodpile, watching the lot. She picked up two or three sticks of wood and paused, watching the lot again. Now there were two more men standing at the fence.

"Come on, come on," the Texan said. "They won't hurt you. They just ain't never been in under a roof before."

"I just as lief let them stay out here, if that's what they want to do," Eck said.

"Get yourself a stick—there's a bunch of wagon stakes against the fence yonder—and when one of them tries to rush you, bust him over the head so he will understand what you mean." One of the men went to the fence and got three of the stakes and returned and distributed them. Mrs. Littlejohn, her armful of wood complete now, paused again halfway back to the house, looking into the lot. The little boy was directly behind his father again, though this time the father had not discovered him yet. The men advanced toward the horses, the huddle of which began to break into gaudy units turning inward upon themselves. The Texan was cursing them in a loud steady cheerful voice. "Get in there, you banjo-faced jack rabbits. Don't hurry them, now. Let them take their time. Hi! Get in there. What do you think that barn is—a law court maybe? Or maybe a church and somebody is going to take up a collection on you?" The animals fell slowly back. Now and then one feinted to break from the huddle, the Texan driving it back each time with skillfully thrown bits of dirt. Then one at the rear saw the barn door just behind it but before the herd could break the Texan snatched the wagon stake from Eck and, followed by one of the other men, rushed at the horses and began to lay about the heads and shoulders, choosing by unerring instinct the point animal and striking it first square in the face then on the withers as it turned and then on the rump as it turned further, so that when the break came it was reversed and the entire herd rushed into the long open hallway and brought up against the further wall with a hollow, thunderous sound like that of a collapsing mine-shaft. "Seems to have held all right," the Texan said. He and the other man slammed the half-length doors and looked over them into the tunnel of the barn, at the far end of which the ponies were now a splotchy, phantom moiling punctuated by crackings of wooden partitions and the dry reports of hooves which gradually died away. "Yep, it held all right," the Texan said. The other two came to the doors and looked over them. The little boy came up beside his father now, trying to see through a crack, and Eck saw him.

"Didn't I tell you to stay out of here?" Eck said. "Don't you know them things will kill you quicker than you can say scat? You go and get outside of that fence and stay there."

"Why don't you get your paw to buy you one of them, Wall?" one of the men said.

"Me buy one of them things?" Eck said. "When I can go to the river anytime and catch me a snapping turtle or a moccasin for nothing? You go on, now. Get out of here and stay out." The Texan had entered the barn. One of the men closed the doors after him and put the bar up again and over the top of the doors they watched the Texan go on down the hallway, toward the ponies which now huddled like gaudy phantoms in the gloom, quiet now and already beginning to snuff experimentally into the long lipworn trough fastened against the rear wall. The little boy had merely gone around behind his father, to the other side, where he stood peering now through a knot-hole in a plank. The Texan opened a smaller door in the wall and entered it, though almost immediately he reappeared.

"I don't see nothing but shelled corn in here," he said. "Snopes said he would send some hay up here last night."

"Won't they eat corn either?" one of the men said.

"I don't know," the Texan said. "They ain't never seen any that I know of. We'll find out in a minute though." He disappeared, though they could still hear him in the crib. Then he emerged once more, carrying a big double-ended feed-basket, and retreated into the gloom where the parti-colored rumps of the horses were now ranged quietly along the feeding-trough. Mrs. Littlejohn appeared once more, on the veranda this time, carrying a big brass dinner bell. She raised it to make the first stroke. A small commotion set up among the ponies as the Texan approached but he began to speak to them at once, in a brisk loud unemphatic mixture of cursing and cajolery, disappearing among them. The men at the door heard the dry rattling of the corn-pellets into the trough, a sound broken by a single snort of amazed horror. A plank cracked with a loud report; before their eyes the depths of the hallway dissolved in loud fury, and while they stared over the doors, unable yet to begin to move, the entire interior exploded into mad tossing shapes like a downrush of flames.

"Hell fire," one of them said. "Jump!" he shouted. The three turned and ran frantically for the wagon, Eck last. Several voices from the fence were now shouting something but Eck did not even hear them until, in the act of scrambling madly at the tail-gate, he looked behind him and saw the little boy still leaning to the knot-hole in the door which in the next instant vanished into matchwood, the knot-hole itself exploding from his eye and leaving him, motionless in the diminutive overalls and still leaning forward a little until he vanished utterly beneath the towering parti-colored wave full of feet and glaring eyes and wild teeth which, overtopping, burst into scattering units, revealing at last the gaping orifice and the little boy still standing in it, unscratched, his eye still leaned to the vanished knot-hole.

"Wall!" Eck roared. The little boy turned and ran for the wagon. The horses were whipping back and forth across the lot, as if while in the barn they had once more doubled their number; two of them rushed up quattering and galloped all over the boy again without touching him as he ran, earnest and diminutive and seemingly without progress, though he reached the wagon at last, from which Eck, his sunburned skin now a sickly white, reached down and snatched the boy into the wagon by the straps of his overalls and slammed him face down across his knees and caught up a coiled hitching-rope from the bed of the wagon.

"Didn't I tell you to get out of here?" Eck said in a shaking voice. "Didn't I tell you?"

"If you're going to whip him, you better whip the rest of us too and then one of us can frail hell out of you," one of the others said.

"Or better still, take the rope and hang that durn fellow yonder," the second said. The Texan was now standing in the wrecked door of the barn, taking the gingersnap carton from his hip pocket. "Before he kills the rest of Frenchman's Bend too."

"You mean Flem Snopes," the first said. The Texan tilted the carton above his other open palm. The horses still rushed and swirled back and forth but they were beginning to slow now, trotting on high, stiff legs, although their eyes were still rolling whitely and various.

"I misdoubted that damn shell corn all along," the Texan said. "But at least they have seen what it looks like. They can't claim they ain't got nothing out of this trip." He shook the carton over his open hand. Nothing came out of it. Mrs. Littlejohn on the veranda made the first stroke with the dinner bell; at the sound the horses rushed again, the earth of the lot becoming vibrant with the light dry clatter of hooves. The Texan crumpled the carton and threw it aside. "Chuck wagon," he said. There were three more wagons in the lane now and there were twenty or more men at the fence when the Texan, followed by his three assistants and the little boy, passed through the gate. The bright cloudless early sun gleamed upon the pearl butt of the pistol in his hip pocket and upon the bell which Mrs. Littlejohn still rang, peremptory, strong, and loud.

When the Texan, picking his teeth with a splintered kitchen match, emerged from the house twenty minutes later, the tethered wagons and riding horses and mules extended from the lot gate to Varner's store, and there were more than fifty men now standing along the fence beside the gate, watching him quietly, a little covertly, as he approached, rolling a little, slightly bowlegged, the high heels of his carved boots printing neatly into the dust. "Morning, gents," he said. "Here, bud," he said to the little boy, who stood slightly behind him, looking at the protruding butt of the pistol. He took a coin from his pocket and gave it to the boy. "Run to the store and get me a box of gingersnaps." He looked about at the quiet faces, protuberant, sucking his teeth. He rolled the match from one side of his mouth to the other without touching it. "You boys done made your picks, have you? Ready to start her off, hah?" They did not answer. They were not looking at him now. That is, he began to have the feeling that each face had stopped looking at him the second before his gaze reached it. After a moment Freeman said:

"Ain't you going to wait for Flem?"

"Why?" the Texan said. Then Freeman stopped looking at him too. There was nothing in Freeman's face either. There was nothing, no alteration, in the Texan's voice. "Eck, you done already picked out yours. So we can start her off when you are ready."

"I reckon not," Eck said. "I wouldn't buy nothing I was afraid to walk up and touch."

"Them little ponies?" the Texan said. "You helped water and feed them. I bet that boy of yours could walk up to any one of them."

"He better not let me catch him," Eck said. The Texan looked about at the quiet faces, his gaze at once abstract and alert, with an impenetrable surface quality like flint, as though the surface were impervious or perhaps there was nothing behind it.

"Them ponies is gentle as a dove, boys. The man that buys them will get the best piece of horseflesh he ever forked or druv for the money. Naturally they got spirit; I ain't selling crowbait. Besides, who'd want Texas crowbait anyway, with Mississippi full of it?" His stare was still absent and unwinking; there was no mirth or humor in his voice and there was neither mirth nor humor in the single guffaw which came from the rear of the group. Two wagons were now drawing out of the road at the same time, up to the fence. The men got down from them and tied them to the fence and approached. "Come up, boys," the Texan said. "You're just in time to buy a good gentle horse cheap."

"How about that one that cut your vest off last night?" a voice said. This time three or four guffawed. The Texan looked toward the sound, bleak and unwinking.

"What about it?" he said. The laughter, if it had been laughter, ceased. The Texan turned to the nearest gatepost and climbed to the top of it, his alternate thighs deliberate and bulging in the tight trousers, the butt of the pistol catching and losing the sun in pearly gleams. Sitting on the post, he looked down at the faces along the fence which were attentive, grave, reserved and not looking at him. "All right," he said. "Who's going to start her off with a bid? Step right up; take your pick and make your bid, and when the last one is sold, walk in that lot and put your rope on the best piece of horseflesh you ever forked or druv for the money. There ain't a pony there that ain't worth fifteen dollars. Young, sound, good for saddle or work stock, guaranteed to outlast four ordinary horses; you couldn't kill one of

them with a axle-tree—" There was a small violent commotion at the rear of the group. The little boy appeared, burrowing among the motionless overalls. He approached the post, the new and unbroken paper carton lifted. The Texan leaned down and took it and tore the end from it and shook three or four of the cakes into the boy's hand, a hand as small and almost as black as that of a coon. He held the carton in his hand while he talked, pointing out the horses with it as he indicated them. "Look at that one with the three stocking-feet and the frost-bit ear; watch him now when they pass again. Look at that shoulder-action; that horse is worth twenty dollars of any man's money. Who'll make me a bid on him to start her off?" His voice was harsh, ready, forensic. Along the fence below him the men stood with, buttoned close in their overalls, the tobacco-sacks and worn purses the sparse silver and frayed bills hoarded a coin at a time in the cracks of chimneys or chinked into the logs of walls. From time to time the horses broke and rushed with purposeless violence and huddled again, watching the faces along the fence with wild mismatched eyes. The lane was full of wagons now. As the others arrived they would have to stop in the road beyond it and the occupants came up the lane on foot. Mrs. Littlejohn came out of her kitchen. She crossed the yard, looking toward the lot gate. There was a blackened wash pot set on four bricks in the corner of the yard. She built a fire beneath the pot and came to the fence and stood there for a time, her hands on her hips and the smoke from the fire drifting blue and slow behind her. Then she turned and went back into the house. "Come on, boys," the Texan said. "Who'll make me a bid?"

"Four bits," a voice said. The Texan did not even glance toward it.

"Or, if he don't suit you, how about that fiddle-head horse without no mane to speak of? For a saddle pony, I'd rather have him than that stocking-foot. I heard somebody say fifty cents just now. I reckon he meant five dollars, didn't he? Do I hear five dollars?"

"Four bits for the lot," the same voice said. This time there were no guffaws. It was the Texan who laughed, harshly, with only his lower face, as if he were reciting a multiplication table.

"Fifty cents for the dried mud offen them, he means," he said. "Who'll give a dollar more for the genuine Texas cockleburrs?" Mrs. Littlejohn came out of the kitchen, carrying the sawn half of a wooden hogshead which she set on a stump beside the smoking pot, and stood with her hands on her hips, looking into the lot for a while without coming to the fence this time. Then she went back into the house. "What's the matter with you boys?" the Texan said. "Here, Eck, you been helping me and you know them horses. How about making me a bid on that wall-eyed one you picked out last night? Here. Wait a minute." He thrust the paper carton into his other hip pocket and swung his feet inward and dropped, cat-light, into the lot. The ponies, huddled, watched him. Then they broke before him and slid stiffly along the fence. He turned them and they whirled and rushed back across the lot; whereupon, as though he had been waiting his chance when they should have turned their backs on him, the Texan began to run too, so that when they reached the opposite side of the lot and turned, slowing to huddle again, he was almost upon them. The earth became thunderous; dust arose, out of which the animals began to burst like flushed quail and into which, with that apparently unflagging faith in his own invulnerability, the Texan rushed. For an instant the watchers could see them in the dust—the pony backed into the angle of the fence and the stable, the man facing it, reaching toward

his hip. Then the beast rushed at him in a sort of fatal and hopeless desperation and he struck it between the eyes with the pistol-butt and felled it and leaped onto its prone head. The pony recovered almost at once and pawed itself to its knees and heaved at its prisoned head and fought itself up, dragging the man with it; for an instant in the dust the watchers saw the man free of the earth and in violent lateral motion like a rag attached to the horse's head. Then the Texan's feet came back to earth and the dust blew aside and revealed them, motionless, the Texan's sharp heels braced into the ground, one hand gripping the pony's forelock and the other its nostrils, the long evil muzzle wrung backward over its scarred shoulder while it breathed in labored and hollow groans. Mrs. Littlejohn was in the yard again. No one had seen her emerge this time. She carried an armful of clothing and a metal-ridged washboard and she was standing motionless at the kitchen steps, looking into the lot. Then she moved across the yard, still looking into the lot, and dumped the garments into the tub, still looking into the lot. "Look him over, boys," the Texan panted, turning his own suffused face and the protuberant glare of his eyes toward the fence. "Look him over quick. Them shoulders and—" He had relaxed for an instant apparently. The animal exploded again; again for an instant the Texan was free of the earth, though he was still talking: "—and legs you whoa I'll tear your face right look him over quick boys worth fifteen dollars of let me get a holt of who'll make me a bid whoa you blare-eyed jack rabbit, whoa!" They were moving now—a kaleidoscope of inextricable and incredible violence on the periphery of which the metal clasps of the Texan's suspenders sun-glinted in ceaseless orbit, with terrific slowness across the lot. Then the broad clay-colored hat soared deliberately outward; an instant later the Texan followed it, though still on his feet, and the pony shot free in mad, staglike bounds. The Texan picked up the hat and struck the dust from it against his leg, and returned to the fence and mounted the post again. He was breathing heavily. Still the faces did not look at him as he took the carton from his hip and shook a cake from it and put the cake into his mouth, chewing, breathing harshly. Mrs. Littlejohn turned away and began to bail water from the pot into the tub, though after each bucketful she turned her head and looked into the lot again. "Now, boys," the Texan said. "Who says that pony ain't worth fifteen dollars? You couldn't buy that much dynamite for just fifteen dollars. There ain't one of them can't do a mile in three minutes; turn them into pasture and they will board themselves; work them like hell all day and every time you think about it, lay them over the head with a singletree and after a couple of days every jack rabbit one of them will be so tame you will have to put them out of the house at night like a cat." He shook another cake from the carton and ate it. "Come on, Eck," he said. "Start her off. How about ten dollars for that horse, Eck?"

"What need I got for a horse I would need a bear-trap to catch?" Eck said.

"Didn't you just see me catch him?"

"I seen you," Eck said. "And I don't want nothing as big as a horse if I got to wrastle with it every time it finds me on the same side of a fence it's on."

"All right," the Texan said. He was still breathing harshly, but now there was nothing of fatigue or breathlessness in it. He shook another cake into his palm and inserted it beneath his moustache. "All right. I want to get this auction started. I ain't come here to live, no matter how good a country you folks claim you got. I'm going to give you that horse." For a moment there was no sound, not even that of breathing except the Texan's.

"You going to give it to me?" Eck said.

"Yes. Provided you will start the bidding on the next one." Again there was no sound save the Texan's breathing, and then the clash of Mrs. Littlejohn's pail against the rim of the pot.

"I just start the bidding," Eck said. "I don't have to buy it lessen I ain't overtopped." Another wagon had come up the lane. It was battered and paintless. One wheel had been repaired by crossed planks bound to the spokes with baling wire and the two underfed mules wore a battered harness patched with bits of cotton rope; the reins were ordinary cotton plowlines, not new. It contained a woman in a shapeless gray garment and a faded sunbonnet, and a man in faded and patched though clean overalls. There was not room for the wagon to draw out of the lane so the man left it standing where it was and got down and came forward—a thin man, not large, with something about his eyes, something strained and washed-out, at once vague and intense, who shoved into the crowd at the rear, saying,

"What? What's that? Did he give him that horse?"

"All right," the Texan said. "That wall-eyed horse with the scarred neck belong to you. Now. That one that looks like he's had his head in a flour barrel. What do you say? Ten dollars?"

"Did he give him that horse?" the newcomer said.

"A dollar," Eck said. The Texan's mouth was still open for speech; for an instant his face died so behind the hard eyes.

"A dollar?" he said. "One dollar? Did I actually hear that?"

"Durn it," Eck said. "Two dollars then. But I ain't—"

"Wait," the newcomer said. "You, up there on the post." The Texan looked at him. When the others turned, they saw that the woman had left the wagon too, though they had not known she was there since they had not seen the wagon drive up. She came among them behind the man, gaunt in the gray shapeless garment and the sunbonnet, wearing stained canvas gymnasium shoes. She overtook the man but she did not touch him, standing just behind him, her hands rolled before her into the gray dress.

"Henry," she said in a flat voice. The man looked over his shoulder.

"Get back to that wagon," he said.

"Here, missus," the Texan said. "Henry's going to get the bargain of his life in about a minute. Here, boys, let the missus come up close where she can see. Henry's going to pick out that saddle-horse the missus has been wanting. Who says ten—"

"Henry," the woman said. She did not raise her voice. She had not once looked at the Texan. She touched the man's arm. He turned and struck her hand down.

"Get back to that wagon like I told you." The woman stood behind him, her hands rolled again into her dress. She was not looking at anything, speaking to anyone.

"He ain't no more despair than to buy one of them things," she said. "And us not but five dollars away from the poorhouse, he ain't no more despair." The man turned upon her with that curious air of leashed, of dreamlike fury. The others lounged along the fence in attitudes gravely inattentive, almost oblivious. Mrs. Littlejohn had been washing for some time now, pumping rhythmically up and down above the washboard in the sud-foamed tub. She now stood erect again, her soap-raw hands on her hips, looking into the lot.

"Shut your mouth and get back in that wagon," the man said. "Do you want me to take a wagon stake to you?" He turned and looked up at the Texan. "Did you give him that horse?" he said. The Texan was looking at the woman. Then he looked at the man; still watching him, he

tilted the paper carton over his open palm. A single cake came out of it.

"Yes," he said.

"Is the fellow that bids in this next horse going to get that first one too?"

"No," the Texan said.

"All right," the other said. "Are you going to give a horse to the man that makes the first bid on the next one?"

"No," the Texan said.

"Then if you were just starting the auction off by giving away a horse, why didn't you wait till we were all here?" The Texan stopped looking at the other. He raised the empty carton and squinted carefully into it, as if it might contain a precious jewel or perhaps a deadly insect. Then he crumpled it and dropped it carefully beside the post on which he sat.

"Eck bids two dollars," he said. "I believe he still thinks he's bidding on them scraps of bob-wire they come here in instead of on one of the horses. But I got to accept it. But are you boys—"

"So Eck's going to get two horses at a dollar a head," the newcomer said. "Three dollars." The woman touched him again. He flung her hand off without turning and she stood again, her hands rolled into her dress across her flat stomach, not looking at anything.

"Misters," she said, "we got chaps in the house that never had shoes last winter. We ain't got corn to feed the stock. We got five dollars I earned weaving by firelight after dark. And he ain't no more despair."

"Henry bids three dollars," the Texan said. "Raise him a dollar, Eck, and the horse is yours." Beyond the fence the horses rushed suddenly and for no reason and as suddenly stopped, staring at the faces along the fence.

"Henry," the woman said. The man was watching Eck. His stained and broken teeth showed a little beneath his lip. His wrists dangled into fists below the faded sleeves of his shirt too short from many washings.

"Four dollars," Eck said.

"Five dollars!" the husband said, raising one clenched hand. He shouldered himself forward toward the gate-post. The woman did not follow him. She now looked at the Texan for the first time. Her eyes were a washed gray also, as though they had faded too like the dress and the sunbonnet.

"Mister," she said, "if you take that five dollars I earned my chaps a-weaving for one of them things, it'll be a curse on you and yours during all the time of man."

"Five dollars!" the husband shouted. He thrust himself up to the post, his clenched hand on a level with the Texan's knees. He opened it upon a wad of frayed banknotes and silver. "Five dollars! And the man that raises it will have to beat my head off or I'll beat hisn."

"All right," the Texan said. "Five dollars is bid. But don't you shake your hand at me."

At five o'clock that afternoon the Texan crumpled the third paper carton and dropped it to the earth beneath him. In the copper slant of the levelling sun which fell also upon the line of limp garments in Mrs. Littlejohn's backyard and which cast his shadow and that of the post on which he sat long across the lot where now and then the ponies still rushed in purposeless and tireless surges, the Texan straightened his leg and thrust his hand into his pocket and took out a coin and leaned down to the little boy. His voice was now hoarse, spent. "Here, bud," he said. "Run to the store and get me a box of gingersnaps." The men still stood along the fence, tireless, in their overalls and faded shirts. Flem Snopes was there now, appeared suddenly from nowhere, standing beside the fence with a space the width of three or four men on either side of him, standing there in his small yet definite isolation, chewing tobacco, in the same gray trousers and

minute bow tie in which he had departed last summer but in a new cap, gray too like the other, but new, and overlaid with a bright golfer's plaid, looking also at the horses in the lot. All of them save two had been sold for sums ranging from three dollars and a half to eleven and twelve dollars. The purchasers, as they had bid them in, had gathered as though by instinct into a separate group on the other side of the gate, where they stood with their hands lying upon the top strand of the fence, watching with a still more sober intensity the animals which some of them had owned for seven and eight hours now but had not yet laid hands upon. The husband, Henry, stood beside the post on which the Texan sat. The wife had gone back to the wagon, where she sat gray in the gray garment, motionless, looking at nothing, still, she might have been something inanimate which he had loaded into the wagon to move it somewhere, waiting now in the wagon until he should be ready to go on again, patient, insensate, timeless.

"I bought a horse and I paid cash for it," he said. His voice was harsh and spent too, the mad look in his eyes had a quality glazed now and even sightless. "And yet you expect me to stand around here till they are all sold before I can get my horse. Well, you can do all the expecting you want. I'm going to take my horse out of there and go home." The Texan looked down at him. The Texan's shirt was blotched with sweat. His big face was cold and still, his voice level.

"Take your horse then." After a moment Henry looked away. He stood with his head bent a little, swallowing from time to time.

"Ain't you going to catch him for me?"

"It ain't my horse," the Texan said in that flat still voice. After a while Henry raised his head. He did not look at the Texan.

"Who'll help me catch my horse?" he

said. Nobody answered. They stood along the fence, looking quietly into the lot where the ponies huddled, already beginning to fade a little where the long shadow of the house lay upon them, deepening. From Mrs. Littlejohn's kitchen the smell of frying ham came. A noisy cloud of sparrows swept across the lot and into a chinaberry tree beside the house, and in the high soft vague blue swallows stooped and whirled in erratic indecision, their cries like strings plucked at random. Without looking back, Henry raised his voice: "Bring that ere plow-line." After a time the wife moved. She got down from the wagon and took a coil of new cotton rope from it and approached. The husband took the rope from her and moved toward the gate. The Texan began to descend from the post, stiffly, as Henry put his hand on the latch. "Come on here," he said. The wife had stopped when he took the rope from her. She moved again, obediently, her hands rolled into the dress across her stomach, passing the Texan without looking at him.

"Don't go in there, missus," he said. She stopped, not looking at him, not looking at anything. The husband opened the gate and entered the lot and turned, holding the gate open but without raising his eyes.

"Come on here," he said.

"Don't you go in there, missus," the Texan said. The wife stood motionless between them, her face almost concealed by the sunbonnet, her hands folded across her stomach.

"I reckon I better," she said. The other men did not look at her at all, at her or Henry either. They stood along the fence, grave and quiet and inattentive, almost bemused. Then the wife passed through the gate; the husband shut it behind them and turned and began to move toward the huddled ponies, the wife following in the gray and shapeless garment within which she moved without inference of locomotion, like something on a moving platform, a float. The horses were watching them. They clotted and blended and shifted among themselves, on the point of breaking though not breaking yet. The husband shouted at them. He began to curse them, advancing, the wife following. Then the huddle broke, the animals moving with high, stiff knees, circling the two people who turned and followed again as the herd flowed and huddled again at the opposite side of the lot.

"There he is," the husband said. "Get him into that corner." The herd divided; the horse which the husband had bought jolted on stiff legs. The wife shouted at it; it spun and poised, plunging, then the husband struck it across the face with the coiled rope and it whirled and slammed into the corner of the fence. "Keep him there now," the husband said. He shook out the rope, advancing. The horse watched him with wild, glaring eyes; it rushed again, straight toward the wife. She shouted at it and waved her arms but it soared past her in a long bound and rushed again into the huddle of its fellows. They followed and hemmed it again into another corner; again the wife failed to stop its rush for freedom and the husband turned and struck her with the coiled rope. "Why didn't you head him?" he said. "Why didn't you?" He struck her again; she did not move, not even to fend the rope with a raised arm. The men along the fence stood quietly, their faces lowered as though brooding upon the earth at their feet. Only Flem Snopes was still watching —if he ever had been looking into the lot at all, standing in his little island of isolation, chewing with his characteristic faint sidewise thrust beneath the new plaid cap.

The Texan said something, not loud, harsh and short. He entered the lot and went to the husband and jerked the uplifted rope from his hand. The husband whirled as though he were about to spring at the Texan, crouched slightly, his knees bent and his arms held slightly away from his sides, though his gaze never mounted higher than the Texan's carved and dusty boots. Then the Texan took the husband by the arm and led him back toward the gate, the wife following, and through the gate which he held open for the woman and then closed. He took a wad of banknotes from his trousers and removed a bill from it and put it into the woman's hand. "Get him into the wagon and get him on home," he said.

"What's that for?" Flem Snopes said. He had approached. He now stood beside the post on which the Texan had been sitting. The Texan did not look at him.

"Thinks he bought one of them ponies," the Texan said. He spoke in a flat still voice, like that of a man after a sharp run. "Get him on away, missus."

"Give him back that money," the husband said, in his lifeless, spent tone. "I bought that horse and I aim to have him if I got to shoot him before I can put a rope on him." The Texan did not even look at him.

"Get him on away from here, missus," he said.

"You take your money and I take my horse," the husband said. He was shaking slowly and steadily now, as though he were cold. His hands opened and shut below the frayed cuffs of his shirt. "Give it back to him," he said.

"You don't own no horse of mine," the Texan said. "Get him on home, missus." The husband raised his spent face, his mad glazed eyes. He reached out his hand. The woman held the banknote in her folded hands across her stomach. For a while the husband's shaking hand merely fumbled at it. Then he drew the banknote free.

"It's my horse," he said. "I bought it. These fellows saw me. I paid for it. It's my horse. Here." He turned and extended the banknote toward Snopes. "You got something to do with these horses. I bought one. Here's the money for it. I bought one. Ask him." Snopes took the banknote. The others stood, gravely inattentive, in relaxed attitudes along the fence. The sun had gone now; there was nothing save violet shadow upon them and upon the lot where once more and for no reason the ponies rushed and flowed. At that moment the little boy came up, tireless and indefatigable still, with the new paper carton. The Texan took it, though he did not open it at once. He had dropped the rope and now the husband stooped for it, fumbling at it for some time before he lifted it from the ground. Then he stood with his head bent, his knuckles whitening on the rope. The woman had not moved. Twilight was coming fast now; there was a last mazy swirl of swallows against the high and changing azure. Then the Texan tore the end from the carton and tilted one of the cakes into his hand; he seemed to be watching the hand as it shut slowly upon the cake until a fine powder of snuff-colored dust began to rain from his fingers. He rubbed the hand carefully on his thigh and raised his head and glanced about until he saw the little boy and handed the carton back to him.

"Here, bud," he said. Then he looked at the woman, his voice flat, quiet again. "Mr. Snopes will have your money for you tomorrow. Better get him in the wagon and get him on home. He don't own no horse. You can get your money tomorrow from Mr. Snopes." The wife turned and went back to the wagon and got into it. No one watched her, nor the husband who still stood, his head bent, passing the rope from one hand to the other. They leaned along the fence, grave and quiet, as though the fence were in another land, another time.

"How many you got left?" Snopes said.

The Texan roused; they all seemed to rouse then, returning, listening again.

"Got three now," the Texan said. "Swap all three of them for a buggy or a—"

"It's out in the road," Snopes said, a little shortly, a little quickly, turning away. "Get your mules." He went on up the lane. They watched the Texan enter the lot and cross it, the horses flowing before him but without the old irrational violence, as if they too were spent, vitiated with the long day, and enter the barn and then emerge, leading the two harnessed mules. The wagon had been backed under the shed beside the barn. The Texan entered this and came out a moment later, carrying a bedding-roll and his coat, and led the mules back toward the gate, the ponies huddled again and watching him with their various unmatching eyes, quietly now, as if they too realized there was not only an armistice between them at last but that they would never look upon each other again in both their lives. Someone opened the gate. The Texan led the mules through it and they followed in a body, leaving the husband standing beside the closed gate, his head still bent and the coiled rope in his hand. They passed the wagon in which the wife sat, her gray garment fading into the dusk, almost the same color and as still, looking at nothing; they passed the clothesline with its limp and unwinded drying garments, walking through the hot vivid smell of ham from Mrs. Littlejohn's kitchen. When they reached the end of the lane they could see the moon, almost full, tremendous and pale and still lightless in the sky from which day had not quite gone. Snopes was standing at the end of the lane beside an empty buggy. It was the one with the glittering wheels and the fringed parasol top in which he and Will Varner had used to drive. The Texan was motionless too, looking at it.

"Well well well," he said. "So this is it."

"If it don't suit you, you can ride one of the mules back to Texas," Snopes said.

"You bet," the Texan said. "Only I ought to have a powder puff or at least a mandolin to ride it with." He backed the mules onto the tongue and lifted the breast-yoke. Two of them came forward and fastened the traces for him. Then they watched him get into the buggy and raise the reins.

"Where you heading for?" one said. "Back to Texas?"

"In this?" the Texan said. "I wouldn't get past the first Texas saloon without starting the vigilance committee. Besides, I ain't going to waste all this here lace-trimmed top and these spindle wheels just on Texas. Long as I am this far, I reckon I'll go on a day or two and look-see them Northern towns. Washington and New York and Baltimore. What's the short way to New York from here?" They didn't know. But they told him how to reach Jefferson.

"You're already headed right," Freeman said. "Just keep right on up the road past the schoolhouse."

"All right," the Texan said. "Well, remember about busting them ponies over the head now and then until they get used to you. You won't have any trouble with them then." He lifted the reins again. As he did so Snopes stepped forward and got into the buggy.

"I'll ride as far as Varner's with you," he said.

"I didn't know I was going past Varner's," the Texan said.

"You can go to town that way," Snopes said. "Drive on." The Texan shook the reins. Then he said,

"Whoa." He straightened his leg and put his hand into his pocket. "Here, bud," he said to the little boy, "run to the store and— Never mind. I'll stop and get it myself, long as I am going back that way. Well, boys," he said. "Take care of your-selves." He swung the team around. The buggy went on. They looked after it.

"I reckon he aims to kind of come up on Jefferson from behind," Quick said.

"He'll be lighter when he gets there," Freeman said. "He can come up to it easy from any side he wants."

"Yes," Bookwright said. "His pockets won't rattle." They went back to the lot; they passed on through the narrow way between the two lines of patient and mo-tionless wagons, which at the end was completely closed by the one in which the woman sat. The husband was still stand-ing beside the gate with his coiled rope, and now night had completely come. The light itself had not changed so much; if anything, it was brighter but with that other-worldly quality of moonlight, so that when they stood once more looking into the lot, the splotchy bodies of the ponies had a distinctness, almost a bril-liance, but without individual shape and without depth—no longer horses, no longer flesh and bone directed by a prin-ciple capable of calculated violence, no longer inherent with the capacity to hurt and harm.

"Well, what are we waiting for?" Free-man said. "For them to go to roost?"

"We better all get our ropes first," Quick said. "Get your ropes everybody." Some of them did not have ropes. When they left home that morning, they had not heard about the horses, the auction. They had merely happened through the village by chance and learned of it and stopped.

"Go to the store and get some then," Freeman said.

"The store will be closed now," Quick said.

"No it won't," Freeman said. "If it was closed, Lump Snopes would a been up here." So while the ones who had come prepared got their ropes from the wagons,

the others went down to the store. The clerk was just closing it.

"You all ain't started catching them yet, have you?" he said. "Good; I was afraid I wouldn't get there in time." He opened the door again and amid the old strong sunless smells of cheese and leather and molasses he measured and cut off sec-tions of plow-line for them and in a body and the clerk in the center and still talking, voluble and unlistened to, they re-turned up the road. The pear tree before Mrs. Littlejohn's was like drowned silver now in the moon. The mockingbird of last night, or another one, was already singing in it, and they now saw, tied to the fence, Ratliff's buckboard and team.

"I thought something was wrong all day," one said. "Ratliff wasn't there to give nobody advice." When they passed down the lane, Mrs. Littlejohn was in her back yard, gathering the garments from the clothesline; they could still smell the ham. The others were waiting at the gate, be-yond which the ponies, huddled again, were like phantom fish, suspended appar-ently without legs now in the brilliant treachery of the moon.

"I reckon the best way will be for us all to take and catch them one at a time," Freeman said.

"One at a time," the husband, Henry, said. Apparently he had not moved since the Texan had led his mules through the gate, save to lift his hands to the top of the gate, one of them still clutching the coiled rope. "One at a time," he said. He began to curse in a harsh, spent monotone. "After I've stood around here all day, waiting for that—" He cursed. He began to jerk at the gate, shaking it with spent violence until one of the others slid the latch back and it swung open and Henry entered it, the others following, the little boy pressing close behind his father until Eck became aware of him and turned.

"Here," he said. "Give me that rope. You stay out of here."

"Aw, paw," the boy said.

"No sir. Them things will kill you. They almost done it this morning. You stay out of here."

"But we got two to catch." For a moment Eck stood looking down at the boy. "That's right," he said. "We got two. But you stay close to me now. And when I holler run, you run. You hear me?"

"Spread out, boys," Freeman said. "Keep them in front of us." They began to advance across the lot in a ragged crescent-shaped line, each one with his rope. The ponies were now at the far side of the lot. One of them snorted; the mass shifted within itself but without breaking. Freeman, glancing back, saw the little boy. "Get that boy out of here," he said.

"I reckon you better," Eck said to the boy. "You go and get in the wagon yonder. You can see us catch them from there." The little boy turned and trotted toward the shed beneath which the wagon stood. The line of men advanced, Henry a little in front.

"Watch them close now," Freeman said. "Maybe we better try to get them into the barn first——" At that moment the huddle broke. It parted and flowed in both directions along the fence. The men at the ends of the line began to run, waving their arms and shouting. "Head them," Freeman said tensely. "Turn them back." They turned them, driving them back upon themselves again; the animals merged and spun in short, huddling rushes, phantom and inextricable. "Hold them now," Freeman said. "Don't let them get by us." The line advanced again. Eck turned; he did not know why—whether a sound, what. The little boy was just behind him again.

"Didn't I tell you to get in that wagon and stay there?" Eck said.

"Watch out, paw!" the boy said. "There he is! There's ourn!" It was the one the Texan had given Eck. "Catch him, paw!"

"Get out of my way," Eck said. "Get back to that wagon." The line was still advancing. The ponies milled, clotting, forced gradually backward toward the open door of the barn. Henry was still slightly in front, crouched slightly, his thin figure, even in the mazy moonlight, emanating something of that spent fury. The splotchy huddle of animals seemed to be moving before the advancing line of men like a snowball which they might have been pushing before them by some invisible means, gradually nearer and nearer to the black yawn of the barn door. Later it was obvious that the ponies were so intent upon the men that they did not realize the barn was even behind them until they backed into the shadow of it. Then an indescribable sound, a movement desperate and despairing, arose among them; for an instant of static horror men and animals faced one another, then the men whirled and ran before a gaudy vomit of long wild faces and splotched chests which overtook and scattered them and flung them sprawling aside and completely obliterated from sight Henry and the little boy, neither of whom had moved though Henry had flung up both arms, still holding his coiled rope, the herd sweeping on across the lot, to crash through the gate which the last man through it had neglected to close, leaving it slightly ajar, carrying all of the gate save the upright to which the hinges were nailed with them, and so among the teams and wagons which choked the lane, the teams springing and lunging too, snapping hitch-reins and tongues. Then the whole inextricable mass crashed among the wagons and eddied and divided about the one in which the woman sat, and rushed on down the lane and into the road, dividing, one half going one way and one half the other.

The men in the lot, except Henry, got

to their feet and ran toward the gate. The little boy once more had not been touched, not even thrown off his feet; for a while his father held him clear of the ground in one hand, shaking him like a rag doll. "Didn't I tell you to stay in that wagon?" Eck cried. "Didn't I tell you?"

"Look out, paw!" the boy chattered out of the violent shaking, "there's ourn! There he goes!" It was the horse the Texan had given them again. It was as if they owned no other, the other one did not exist; as if by some absolute and instantaneous rapport of blood they had relegated to oblivion the one for which they had paid money. They ran to the gate and down the lane where the other men had disappeared. They saw the horse the Texan had given them whirl and dash back and rush through the gate into Mrs. Littlejohn's yard and run up the front steps and crash once on the wooden veranda and vanish through the front door. Eck and the boy ran up onto the veranda. A lamp sat on a table just inside the door. In its mellow light they saw the horse fill the long hallway like a pinwheel, gaudy, furious and thunderous. A little further down the hall there was a varnished yellow melodeon. The horse crashed into it; it produced a single note, almost a chord, in bass, resonant and grave, of deep and sober astonishment; the horse with its monstrous and antic shadow whirled again and vanished through another door. It was a bedroom; Ratliff, in his underclothes and one sock and with the other sock in his hand and his back to the door, was leaning out the open window facing the lane, the lot. He looked back over his shoulder. For an instant he and the horse glared at one another. Then, he sprang through the window as the horse backed out of the room and into the hall again and whirled and saw Eck and the little boy just entering the front door, Eck still carrying his rope. It whirled again and

rushed on down the hall and onto the back porch just as Mrs. Littlejohn, carrying an armful of clothes from the line and the washboard, mounted the steps.

"Get out of here, you son of a bitch," she said. She struck with the washboard; it divided neatly on the long mad face and the horse whirled and rushed back up the hall, where Eck and the boy now stood.

"Get to hell out of here, Wall!" Eck roared. He dropped to the floor, covering his head with his arms. The boy did not move, and for the third time the horse soared above the unwinking eyes and the unbowed and untouched head and onto the front veranda again just as Ratliff, still carrying the sock, ran around the corner of the house and up the steps. The horse whirled without breaking or pausing. It galloped to the end of the veranda and took the railing and soared outward, hobgoblin and floating, in the moon. It landed in the lot still running and crossed the lot and galloped through the wrecked gate and among the overturned wagons and the still intact one in which Henry's wife still sat, and on down the lane and into the road.

A quarter of a mile further on, the road gashed pallid and moony between the moony shadows of the bordering trees, the horse still galloping, galloping its shadow into the dust, the road descending now toward the creek and the bridge. It was of wood, just wide enough for a single vehicle. When the horse reached it, it was occupied by a wagon coming from the opposite direction and drawn by two mules already asleep in the harness and the soporific motion. On the seat was Tull and his wife, in splint chairs in the wagon behind them sat their four daughters, all returning belated from an all-day visit with some of Mrs. Tull's kin. The horse neither checked nor swerved. It crashed once on the wooden bridge and rushed between the two mules which waked lunging in opposite directions in the traces, the horse now apparently scrambling along the wagon-tongue itself like a mad squirrel and scrabbling at the end-gate of the wagon with its forefeet as if it intended to climb into the wagon while Tull shouted at it and struck at its face with his whip. The mules were now trying to turn the wagon around in the middle of the bridge. It slewed and tilted, the bridge-rail cracked with a sharp report above the shrieks of the women; the horse scrambled at last across the back of one of the mules and Tull stood up in the wagon and kicked at its face. Then the front end of the wagon rose, flinging Tull, the reins now wrapped several times about his wrist, backward into the wagon bed among the overturned chairs and the exposed stockings and undergarments of his women. The pony scrambled free and crashed again on the wooden planking, galloping again. The wagon lurched again; the mules had finally turned it on the bridge where there was not room for it to turn and were now kicking themselves free of the traces. When they came free, they snatched Tull bodily out of the wagon. He struck the bridge on his face and was dragged for several feet before the wrist-wrapped reins broke. Far up the road now, distancing the frantic mules, the pony faded on. While the five women still shrieked above Tull's unconscious body, Eck and the little boy came up, trotting, Eck still carrying his rope. He was panting. "Which way'd he go?" he said.

In the now empty and moon-drenched lot, his wife and Mrs. Littlejohn and Ratliff and Lump Snopes, the clerk, and three other men raised Henry out of the trampled dust and carried him into Mrs. Littlejohn's back yard. His face was blanched and stony, his eyes were closed, the weight of his head tautened his throat across the protruding larynx; his teeth glinted dully beneath his lifted lip. They carried him on toward the house, through the dappled shade of the chinaberry trees. Across the dreaming and silver night a faint sound like remote thunder came and ceased. "There's one of them on the creek bridge," one of the men said.

"It's that one of Eck Snopes'," another said. "The one that was in the house." Mrs. Littlejohn had preceded them into the hall. When they entered with Henry, she had already taken the lamp from the table and she stood beside an open door, holding the lamp high.

"Bring him in here," she said. She entered the room first and set the lamp on the dresser. They followed with clumsy scufflings and pantings and laid Henry on the bed and Mrs. Littlejohn came to the bed and stood looking down at Henry's peaceful and bloodless face. "I'll declare," she said. "You men." They had drawn back a little, clumped, shifting from one foot to another, not looking at her nor at his wife either, who stood at the foot of the bed, motionless, her hands folded into her dress. "You all get out of here, V. K.," she said to Ratliff. "Go outside. See if you can't find something else to play with that will kill some more of you."

"All right," Ratliff said. "Come on, boys. Ain't no more horses to catch in here." They followed him toward the door, on tiptoe, their shoes scuffling, their shadows monstrous on the wall.

"Go get Will Varner," Mrs. Littlejohn said. "I reckon you can tell him it's still a mule." They went out; they didn't look back. They tiptoed up the hall and crossed the veranda and descended into the moonlight. Now that they could pay attention to it, the silver air seemed to be filled with faint and sourceless sounds—shouts, thin and distant, again a brief thunder of hooves on a wooden bridge, more shouts faint and thin and earnest and clear as bells; once they even distinguished the words: "Whooey. Head him."

"He went through that house quick,"

Ratliff said. "He must have found another woman at home." Then Henry screamed in the house behind them. They looked back into the dark hall where a square of light fell through the bedroom door, listening while the scream sank into a harsh respiration. "Ah. Ah. Ah" on a rising note about to become screaming again. "Come on," Ratliff said. "We better get Varner." They went up the road in a body, treading the moon-blanched dust in the tremulous April night murmurous with the moving of sap and the wet bursting of burgeoning leaf and bud and constant with the thin and urgent cries and the brief and fading bursts of galloping hooves. Varner's house was dark, blank and without depth in the moonlight. They stood, clumped darkly in the silver yard and called up at the blank windows until suddenly someone was standing in one of them. It was Flem Snopes' wife. She was in a white garment; the heavy braided club of her hair looked almost black against it. She did not lean out, she merely stood there, full in the moon, apparently blank-eyed or certainly not looking downward at them— the heavy gold hair, the mask not tragic and perhaps not even doomed: just damned, the strong faint lift of breasts beneath marblelike fall of the garment; to those below what Brunhilde, what Rhine-maiden on what spurious river-rock of papier-mache, what Helen returned to what topless and shoddy Argos, waiting for no one. "Evening, Mrs. Snopes," Ratliff said. "We want Uncle Will. Henry Armstid is hurt at Mrs. Littlejohn's." She vanished from the window. They waited in the moonlight, listening to the faint remote shouts and cries, until Varner emerged, sooner than they had actually expected, hunching into his coat and buttoning his trousers over the tail of his nightshirt, his suspenders still dangling in twin loops below the coat. He was carrying the battered bag which contained the plumber-

like tools with which he drenched and wormed and blistered and floated or drew the teeth of horses and mules; he came down the steps, lean and loosejointed, his shrewd ruthless head cocked a little as he listened also to the faint bell-like cries and shouts with which the silver air was full.

"Are they still trying to catch them rabbits?" he said.

"All of them except Henry Armstid," Ratliff said. "He caught his."

"Hah," Varner said. "That you, V. K.? How many did you buy?"

"I was too late," Ratliff said. "I never got back in time."

"Hah," Varner said. They moved on to the gate and into the road again. "Well, it's a good bright cool night for running them." The moon was now high overhead, a pearled and mazy yawn in the soft sky, the ultimate ends of which rolled onward, whorl on whorl, beyond the pale stars and by pale stars surrounded. They walked in a close clump, tramping their shadows into the road's mild dust, blotting the shadows of the burgeoning trees which soared, trunk branch and twig against the pale sky, delicate and finely thinned. They passed the dark store. Then the pear tree came in sight. It rose in mazed and silver immobility like exploding snow; the mockingbird still sang in it. "Look at that tree," Varner said. "It ought to make this year, sho."

"Corn'll make this year too," one said.

"A moon like this is good for every growing thing outen earth," Varner said. "I mind when me and Mrs. Varner was expecting Eula. Already had a mess of children and maybe we ought to quit then. But I wanted some more gals. Others had done married and moved away, and a passel of boys, soon as they get big enough to be worth anything, they ain't got time to work. Got to set around the store and talk. But a gal will stay home and work until she does get married. So there was a old woman told my mammy once that if a woman showed her belly to the full moon after she had done caught, it would be a gal. So Mrs. Varner taken and laid every night with the moon on her nekid belly, until it fulled and after. I could lay my ear to her belly and hear Eula kicking and scrouging like all get-out, feeling the moon.''

"You mean it actually worked sho enough, Uncle Will?'' the other said.

"Hah,'' Varner said. "You might try it. You get enough women showing their nekid bellies to the moon or the sun either or even just to your hand fumbling around often enough and more than likely after a while there will be something in it you can lay your ear and listen to, provided something come up and you ain't got away by that time. Hah, V. K.?'' Someone guffawed.

"Don't ask me,'' Ratliff said. "I can't even get nowhere in time to buy a cheap horse.'' Two or three guffawed this time. Then they began to hear Henry's respirations from the house: "Ah. Ah. Ah.'' and they ceased abruptly, as if they had not been aware of their closeness to it. Varner walked on in front, lean, shambling, yet moving quite rapidly, though his head was still slanted with listening as the faint, urgent, indomitable cries murmured in the silver lambence, sourceless, at times almost musical, like fading bell-notes; again there was a brief rapid thunder of hooves on wooden planking.

"There's another one on the creek bridge,'' one said.

"They are going to come out even on them things, after all,'' Varner said. "They'll get the money back in exercise and relaxation. You take a man that ain't got no other relaxation all year long except dodging mule-dung up and down a field furrow. And a night like this one, when a man ain't old enough yet to lay still and sleep, and yet he ain't young enough

anymore to be tomcatting in and out of other folks' back windows, something like this is good for him. It'll make him sleep tomorrow night anyhow, provided he gets back home by then. If we had just knowed about this in time, we could have trained up a pack of horse-dogs. Then we could have held one of these field trials.''

"That's one way to look at it, I reckon,'' Ratliff said. "In fact, it might be a considerable comfort to Bookwright and Quick and Freeman and Eck Snopes and them other new horse-owners if that side of it could be brought to their attention, because the chances are ain't none of them thought to look at it in that light yet. Probably there ain't a one of them that believes now there's any cure a tall for that Texas disease Flem Snopes and that Dead-eye Dick brought here.''

"Hah,'' Varner said. He opened Mrs. Littlejohn's gate. The dim light still fell outward across the hall from the bedroom door; beyond it, Armstid was saying "Ah. Ah. Ah'' steadily. "There's a pill for every ill but the last one.''

"Even if there was always time to take it,'' Ratliff said.

"Hah,'' Varner said again. He glanced back at Ratliff for an instant, pausing. But the little hard bright eyes were invisible now; it was only the bushy overhang of the brows which seemed to concentrate downward toward him in writhen immobility, not frowning but with a sort of fierce risibility. "Even if there was time to take it. Breathing is a sight-draft dated yesterday.''

At nine o'clock on the second morning after that, five men were sitting or squatting along the gallery of the store. The sixth was Ratliff. He was standing up, and talking: "Maybe there wasn't but one of them things in Mrs. Littlejohn's house that night, like Eck says. But it was the biggest drove of just one horse I ever seen. It was in my rooms and it was on the front porch and I could hear Mrs. Littlejohn hitting it over the head with that washboard in the back yard all at the same time. And still it was missing everybody everytime. I reckon that's what that Texas man meant by calling them bargains: that a man would need to be powerful unlucky to ever get close enough to one of them to get hurt." They laughed, all except Eck himself. He and the little boy were eating. When they mounted the steps, Eck had gone on into the store and emerged with a paper sack, from which he took a segment of cheese and with his pocket knife divided it carefully into two exact halves and gave one to the boy and took a handful of crackers from the sack and gave them to the boy, and now they squatted against the wall side by side and, save for the difference in size, identical, eating.

"I wonder what that horse thought Ratliff was," one said. He held a spray of peach bloom between his teeth. It bore four blossoms like miniature ballet skirts of pink tulle. "Jumping out windows and running indoors in his shirt-tail? I wonder how many Ratliffs that horse thought he saw?"

"I don't know," Ratliff said. "But if he saw just half as many of me as I saw of him, he was sholy surrounded. Everytime I turned my head, that thing was just running over me or just swirling to run back over that boy again. And that boy there, he stayed right under it one time to my certain knowledge for a full one-and-one-half minutes without ducking his head or even batting his eyes. Yes sir, when I looked around and seen that varmint in the door behind me blaring its eyes at me, I'd a made sho Flem Snopes had brought a tiger back from Texas except I knowed that couldn't no just one tiger completely fill a entire room." They laughed again, quietly. Lump Snopes, the clerk, sitting in the only chair tilted back against the door-facing and partly blocking the entrance, cackled suddenly.

"If Flem had knowed how quick you fellows was going to snap them horses up, he'd a probably brought some tigers," he said. "Monkeys too."

"So they was Flem's horses," Ratliff said. The laughter stopped. The other three had open knives in their hands, with which they had been trimming idly at chips and slivers of wood. Now they sat apparently absorbed in the delicate and almost tedious movements of the knife-blades. The clerk had looked quickly up and found Ratliff watching him. His constant expression of incorrigible and mirthful disbelief had left him now; only the empty wrinkles of it remained about his mouth and eyes.

"Has Flem ever said they was?" he said. "But you town fellows are smarter than us country folks. Likely you done already read Flem's mind." But Ratliff was not looking at him now.

"And I reckon we'd a bought them," he said. He stood above them again, easy, intelligent, perhaps a little sombre but still perfectly impenetrable. "Eck here, for instance. With a wife and family to support. He owns two of them, though to be sho he never had to pay money for but one. I heard folks chasing them things up until midnight last night, but Eck and that boy ain't been home at all in two days." They laughed again, except Eck. He pared off a bit of cheese and speared it on the knife-point and put it into his mouth.

"Eck caught one of hisn," the second man said.

"That so?" Ratliff said. "Which one was it, Eck? The one he give you or the one you bought?"

"The one he give me," Eck said, chewing.

"Well, well," Ratliff said. "I hadn't heard about that. But Eck's still one horse short. And the one he had to pay money for. Which is pure proof enough that them horses wasn't Flem's because wouldn't no man even give his own blood kin something he couldn't even catch." They laughed again, but they stopped when the clerk spoke. There was no mirth in his voice at all.

"Listen," he said. "All right. We done all admitted you are too smart for anybody to get ahead of. You never bought no horse from Flem or nobody else, so maybe it ain't none of your business and maybe you better just leave it at that."

"Sholy," Ratliff said. "It's done already been left at that two nights ago. The fellow that forgot to shut that lot gate done that. With the exception of Eck's horse. And we know that wasn't Flem's, because that horse was give to Eck for nothing."

"There's others besides Eck that ain't got back home yet," the man with the peach spray said. "Bookwright and Quick are still chasing theirs. They was reported three miles west of Burtsboro Old Town at eight o'clock last night. They ain't got close enough to it yet to tell which one it belongs to."

"Sholy," Ratliff said. "The only new horse-owner in this country that could a been found without bloodhounds since whoever it was left that gate open two nights ago, is Henry Armstid. He's laying right there in Mrs. Littlejohn's bedroom where he can watch the lot so that any time the one he bought happens to run back into it, all he's got to do is to holler at his wife to run out with the rope and catch it—" He ceased, though he said, "Morning, Flem," so immediately afterward and with no change whatever in tone, that the pause was not even discernible. With the exception of the clerk, who sprang up, vacated the chair with a sort of servile alacrity, and Eck and the little boy who continued to eat, they watched above their stilled hands as Snopes in the gray trousers and the minute tie and the new cap with its bright overplaid mounted the steps. He was chewing; he already carried a piece of white pine board; he jerked his head at them, looking at nobody, and took the vacated chair and opened his knife and began to whittle. The clerk now leaned in the opposite side of the door, rubbing his back against the facing. The expression of merry and invincible disbelief had returned to his face, with a quality watchful and secret.

"You're just in time," he said. "Ratliff here seems to be in a considerable sweat about who actually owned them horses." Snopes drew his knife-blade neatly along the board, the neat, surgeon-like sliver curling before it. The others were whittling again, looking carefully at nothing, except Eck and the boy, who were still eating, and the clerk rubbing his back against the door-facing and watching Snopes with that secret and alert intensity. "Maybe you could put his mind at rest." Snopes turned his head slightly and spat, across the gallery and the steps and into the dust beyond them. He drew the knife back and began another curling sliver.

"He was there too," Snopes said. "He knows as much as anybody else." This time the clerk guffawed, chortling, his features gathering toward the center of his face as though plucked there by a hand. He slapped his leg, cackling.

"You might as well to quit," he said. "You can't beat him."

"I reckon not," Ratliff said. He stood above them, not looking at any of them, his gaze fixed apparently on the empty road beyond Mrs. Littlejohn's house, impenetrable, brooding even. A hulking, half-grown boy in overalls too small for him, appeared suddenly from nowhere in particular. He stood for a while in the road, just beyond spitting-range of the gallery, with the air of having come from nowhere in particular and of not knowing where he would go next when he should move again and of not being troubled by that fact. He was looking at nothing, certainly not toward the gallery, and no one on the gallery so much as looked at him except the little boy, who now watched the boy in the road, his periwinkle eyes grave and steady above the bitten cracker in his halted hand. The boy in the road moved on, thickly undulant in the tight overalls, and vanished beyond the corner of the store, the round head and the unwinking eyes of the little boy on the gallery turning steadily to watch him out of sight. Then the little boy bit the cracker again, chewing. "Of course there's Mrs. Tull," Ratliff said. "But that's Eck she's going to sue for damaging Tull against that bridge. And as for Henry Armstid——"

"If a man ain't got gumption enough to protect himself, it's his own look-out," the clerk said.

"Sholy," Ratliff said, still in that dreamy, abstracted tone, actually speaking over his shoulder even. "And Henry Armstid, that's all right because from what I hear of the conversation that taken place, Henry had already stopped owning that horse he thought was his before that Texas man left. And as for that broke leg, that won't put him out none because his wife can make his crop." The clerk had ceased to rub his back against the door. He watched the back of Ratliff's head, unwinking too, sober and intent; he glanced at Snopes who, chewing, was watching another sliver curl away from the advancing knife-blade, then he watched the back of Ratliff's head again.

"It won't be the first time she has made their crop," the man with the peach spray said. Ratliff glanced at him.

"You ought to know. This won't be the first time I ever saw you in their field, doing plowing Henry never got around to. How many days have you already given them this year?" The man with the peach spray removed it and spat carefully and put the spray back between his teeth.

"She can run a furrow straight as I can," the second said.

"They're unlucky," the third said. "When you are unlucky, it don't matter much what you do."

"Sholy," Ratliff said. "I've heard laziness called bad luck so much that maybe it is."

"He ain't lazy," the third said. "When their mule died three or four years ago, him and her broke their land working time about in the traces with the other mule. They ain't lazy."

"So that's all right," Ratliff said, gazing up the empty road again. "Likely she will begin right away to finish the plowing; that oldest gal is pretty near big enough to work with a mule, ain't she? or at least to hold the plow steady while Mrs. Armstid helps the mule?" He glanced again toward the man with the peach spray as though for an answer, but he was not looking at the other and he went on talking without any pause. The clerk stood with his rump and back pressed against the door-facing as if he had paused in the act of scratching, watching Ratliff quite hard now, unwinking. If Ratliff had looked at Flem Snopes, he would have seen nothing below the down-slanted peak of the cap save the steady motion of his jaws. Another sliver was curling with neat deliberation before the moving knife. "Plenty of time now because all she's got to do after she finishes washing Mrs. Littlejohn's dishes and sweeping out the house to pay hers and Henry's board, is to go out home and milk and cook up enough vittles to last the children until tomorrow and feed them and get the littlest ones to sleep and wait outside the door until that biggest gal gets the bar up and gets into bed herself with the axe——"

"The axe?" the man with the peach spray said.

"She takes it to bed with her. She's just twelve, and what with this country still more or less full of them uncaught horses that never belonged to Flem Snopes, likely she feels maybe she can't swing a mere washboard like Mrs. Littlejohn can —and then come back and wash up the supper dishes. And after that, not nothing to do until morning except to stay close enough where Henry can call her until it's light enough to chop the wood to cook breakfast and then help Mrs. Littlejohn wash the dishes and make the beds and sweep while watching the road. Because likely any time now Flem Snopes will get back from wherever he has been since the auction, which of course is to town naturally to see about his cousin that's got into a little legal trouble, and so get that five dollars. 'Only maybe he won't give it back to me,' she says, and maybe that's what Mrs. Littlejohn thought too, because she never said nothing. I could hear her—"

"And where did you happen to be during all this?" the clerk said.

"Listening," Ratliff said. He glanced back at the clerk, then he was looking away again, almost standing with his back to them. "—could hear her dumping the dishes into the pan like she was throwing them at it. 'Do you reckon he will give it back to me?' Mrs. Armstid says. 'That Texas man give it to him and said he would. All the folks there saw him give Mr. Snopes the money and heard him say I could get it from Mr. Snopes tomorrow.' Mrs. Littlejohn was washing the dishes now, washing them like a man would, like they was made out of iron. 'No,' she says. 'But asking him won't do no hurt.'—'If he wouldn't give it back, it ain't no use to ask,' Mrs. Armstid says.—'Suit yourself,' Mrs. Littlejohn says. 'It's your money.' Then I couldn't hear nothing but the dishes for a while. 'Do you reckon he might give it back to me?' Mrs. Armstid says. 'That Texas man said he would. They all heard him say it.'—'Then go and ask him for it,' Mrs. Littlejohn says. Then I couldn't hear nothing but the dishes again. 'He won't give it back to me,' Mrs. Armstid says.—'All right,' Mrs. Littlejohn says. 'Don't ask him, then.' Then I just heard the dishes. They would have two

pans, both washing. 'You don't reckon he would, do you?' Mrs. Armstid says. Mrs. Littlejohn never said nothing. It sounded like she was throwing the dishes at one another. 'Maybe I better go and talk to Henry,' Mrs. Armstid says.—'I would,' Mrs. Littlejohn says. And I be dog if it didn't sound exactly like she had two plates in her hands, beating them together like these here brass bucket-lids in a band. 'Then Henry can buy another five-dollar horse with it. Maybe he'll buy one next time that will out and out kill him. If I just thought he would, I'd give him back that money, myself.'—'I reckon I better talk to him first,' Mrs. Armstid says. And then it sounded just like Mrs. Littlejohn taken up the dishes and pans and all and throwed the whole business at the cook-stove—" Ratliff ceased. Behind him the clerk was hissing "Psst! Psst! Flem. Flem!" Then he stopped, and all of them watched Mrs. Armstid approach and mount the steps, gaunt in the shapeless gray garment, the stained tennis shoes hissing faintly on the boards. She came among them and stood, facing Snopes but not looking at anyone, her hands rolled into her apron.

"He said that day he wouldn't sell Henry that horse," she said in a flat toneless voice. "He said you had the money and I could get it from you." Snopes raised his head and turned it slightly again and spat neatly past the woman, across the gallery and into the road.

"He took all the money with him when he left," he said. Motionless, the gray garment hanging in rigid, almost formal folds like drapery in bronze, Mrs. Armstid appeared to be watching something near Snopes' feet, as though she had not heard him, or as if she had quitted her body as soon as she finished speaking and although her body, hearing, had received the words, they would have no life nor meaning until she returned. The clerk was rubbing his back steadily against the door-facing again, watching her. The little boy was watching her too with his unwinking ineffable gaze, but nobody else was. The man with the peach spray removed it and spat and put the twig back into his mouth.

"He said Henry hadn't bought no horse," she said. "He said I could get the money from you."

"I reckon he forgot it," Snopes said. "He took all the money away with him when he left." He watched her a moment longer, then he trimmed again at the stick. The clerk rubbed his back gently against the door, watching her. After a time Mrs. Armstid raised her head and looked up the road where it went on, mild with spring dust, past Mrs. Littlejohn's, beginning to rise, on past the not-yet-bloomed (that would be in June) locust grove across the way, on past the schoolhouse, the weathered roof of which, rising beyond an orchard of peach and pear trees, resembled a hive swarmed about by a cloud of pink-and-white bees, ascending, mounting toward the crest of the hill where the church stood among its sparse gleam of marble head-stones in the sombre cedar grove where during the long afternoons of summer the constant mourning doves called back and forth. She moved; once more the rubber soles hissed on the gnawed boards.

"I reckon it's about time to get dinner started," she said.

"How's Henry this morning, Mrs. Armstid?" Ratliff said. She looked at him, pausing, the blank eyes waking for an instant.

"He's resting, I thank you kindly," she said. Then the eyes died again and she moved again. Snopes rose from the chair, closing his knife with his thumb and brushing a litter of minute shavings from his lap.

"Wait a minute," he said. Mrs. Armstid paused again, half-turning, though still not looking at Snopes nor at any of them.

Because she can't possibly actually believe it, Ratliff told himself, any more than I do. Snopes entered the store, the clerk, motionless again, his back and rump pressed against the door-facing as though waiting to start rubbing again, watched him enter, his head turning as the other passed him like the head of an owl, the little eyes blinking rapidly now. Jody Varner came up the road on his horse. He did not pass but instead turned in beside the store, toward the mulberry tree behind it where he was in the habit of hitching his horse. A wagon came up the road, creaking past. The man driving it lifted his hand; one or two of the men on the gallery lifted theirs in response. The wagon went on. Mrs. Armstid looked after it. Snopes came out of the door, carrying a small striped paper bag and approached Mrs. Armstid. "Here," he said. Her hand turned just enough to receive it. "A little sweetening for the chaps," he said. His other hand was already in his pocket, and as he turned back to the chair, he drew something from his pocket and handed it to the clerk, who took it. It was a five-cent piece. He sat down in the chair and tilted it back against the door again. He now had the knife in his hand again, already open. He turned his head slightly and spat again, neatly past the gray garment, into the road. The little boy was watching the sack in Mrs. Armstid's hand. Then she seemed to discover it also, rousing.

"Your're right kind," she said. She rolled the sack into the apron, the little boy's unwinking gaze fixed upon the lump her hands made beneath the cloth. She moved again. "I reckon I better get on and help with dinner," she said. She descended the steps, though as soon as she reached the level earth and began to retreat, the gray folds of the garment once more lost all inference and intimation of locomotion, so that she seemed to progress without motion like a figure on a retreating and diminishing float; a gray and blasted tree-trunk moving, somehow intact and upright, upon an unhurried flood. The clerk in the doorway cackled suddenly, explosively, chortling. He slapped his thigh.

"By God," he said. "You can't beat him."

Jody Varner, entering the store from the rear, paused in midstride like a pointing bird-dog. Then, on tiptoe, in complete silence and with astonishing speed, he darted behind the counter and sped up the gloomy tunnel, at the end of which a hulking, bear-shaped figure stooped, its entire head and shoulders wedged into the glass case which contained the needles and thread and snuff and tobacco and the stale gaudy candy. He snatched the boy savagely and viciously out; the boy gave a choked cry and struggled flabbily, cramming a final handful of something into his mouth, chewing. But he ceased to struggle almost at once and became slack and inert save for his jaws. Varner dragged him around the counter as the clerk entered, seemed to bounce suddenly into the store with a sort of alert concern. "You, Saint Elmo!" he said.

"Ain't I told you and told you to keep him out of here?" Varner demanded, shaking the boy. "He's damn near eaten that candy-case clean. Stand up!" The boy hung like a half-filled sack from Varner's hand, chewing with a kind of fatalistic desperation, the eyes shut tight in the vast flaccid colorless face, the ears moving steadily and faintly to the chewing. Save for the jaw and the ears, he appeared to have gone to sleep chewing.

"You, Saint Elmo!" the clerk said. "Stand up!" The boy assumed his own weight, though he did not open his eyes yet nor cease to chew. Varner released him. "Git on home," the clerk said. The boy turned obediently to re-enter the store. Varner jerked him about again.

"Not that way," he said. The boy crossed the gallery and descended the steps, the tight overalls undulant and reluctant across his flabby thighs. Before he reached the ground, his hand rose from his pocket to his mouth; again his ears moved faintly to the motion of chewing.

"He's worse than a rat, ain't he?" the clerk said.

"Rat, hell," Varner said, breathing harshly. "He's worse than a goat. First thing I know, he'll graze on back and work through that lace leather and them hame-strings and lap-links and ring-bolts and eat me and you and him all three clean out the back door. And then be damned if I wouldn't be afraid to turn my back for fear he would cross the road and start in on the gin and the blacksmith shop. Now you mind what I say. If I catch him hanging around here one more time, I'm going to set a bear-trap for him."

He went out onto the gallery, the clerk following. "Well, Eck," he said, "I hear you caught one of your horses."

"That's right," Eck said. He and the little boy had finished the crackers and cheese and he had sat for some time now, holding the empty bag.

"It was the one he give you, wasn't it?" Varner said.

"That's right," Eck said.

"Give the other one to me, paw," the little boy said.

"What happened?" Varner said.

"He broke his neck," Eck said.

"I know," Varner said. "But how?" Eck did not move. Watching him, they could almost see him visibly gathering and arranging words, speech. Varner, looking down at him, began to laugh steadily and harshly, sucking his teeth. "I'll tell you what happened. Eck and that boy finally run it into that blind lane of Freeman's, after a chase of about twenty-four hours. They figured it couldn't possibly climb them eight-foot fences of Freeman's so him and the boy tied their rope across the end of the lane, about three feet off the ground. And sho enough, soon as the horse come to the end of the lane and seen Freeman's barn, it whirled just like Eck figured it would and come helling back up that lane like a scared hen-hawk. It probably never even seen the rope at all. Mrs. Freeman was watching from where she had run up onto the porch. She said that when it hit that rope, it looked just like one of these here great big Christmas pinwheels. But the one you bought got clean away, didn't it?"

"That's right," Eck said. "I never had time to see which way the other one went."

"Give him to me, paw," the little boy said.

"You wait till we catch him," Eck said. "We'll see about it then."

THE CATS THAT CLAWED TO HEAVEN

by Percy MacKaye

During his wanderings in the Kentucky mountains Percy MacKaye picked up many tall tales which the narrators usually ascribed to an ancient fabulist· of the hills named Solomon Shell. This mountain Münchhausen, as MacKaye called him, had died some time before, but his stories lived after him and took on forms which even their original narrator might have found strange. For the sake of consistency and also for the convenience of characterizing a living storyteller, MacKaye used Solomon Shell as the medium for his tales. Stories such as that about the fighting cats gain impact because of the picturesque diction in which they are told and at the same time seem genuine mountain fantasies. "The Cats That Clawed to Heaven" appears in Tall Tales of the Kentucky Mountains *(1926).*

Come here'n, Hanky and Henny! Quit your scratch-fightin'! Ef you leetle twin fellers starts a clawin'-match, you maht end up like the twin painter-cats done.

Where-all did *they* end? They ended plumb up in heaven, that's whar! My

Gub! Air ye aimin' to haul me into court fer testimony? You'll shore raise to be jedge and sheriff yit!

Well, yere's the evidence, then.—

Yis, painters is kindly overgrowed wild-cats. Some calls 'em mount'in-lions. Git-tin' sca'cer nowadays, but I's shot a sight in my time.

Me and Chunk Farley used to paar off and go trackin' 'em. Chunk hisself was a crack shot and 'lowed he could outaim me shootin'. But I disputed him his record. Anyways, one evenin' us come to a show-down.

Preachin' Charlie Boggs had aimed to jine us huntin' that time, but me and Chunk skun off in the middle of his sar-mon. Us had ben huntin' all daylight, and no luck yit. The corn-shuckin' moon were jist uppin' her over the ridge, but she hadn't tipped to us in the shadder bottom. We was fordin' a branch. Both to onct, us stopped still, shin-deep in the tide.

Right thar on the crick bank laid a painter big's a cow-heifer. Two leetle cub-kittens was cuddlin' betwixt her paws. Tongue-lickin' 'em, she was, and never seen us.

Click! went our triggers to onct.

She lipt to her laigs, nosin' us, a-swarp-in' her gret tail.

Bang! she rolled in the tide!

"I fotched her!" hollered Chunk.

"Me, you mean!" says I.

We had her up the bank in two jiffies, daid as a dollar.

"Right purty a hide for my ole wo-man," I says.

"The cat's mine," says Chunk. "Th'ain't but one bullet-hole in her."

"So there ain't," says I, "but I reckon we don't start no feud, Chunk. Let's we divvy the kittens."

Well, so us done hit. Yan two leetle yaller kits was curled up thar on the moss-bank, as like as two buttons, and purty as

twin peas in a pod. Chunk picks up one cub-kit, and me t'other; but yit we stands starin' at the ole daid painter.

"Tell ye what, Chunk," says I. "We'll match for her."

"How?" he axes.

"With these-yere kittens. We'll keep 'em a six-month. You raise yourn, leetle Catcher, thar; and I'll raise mine, here, leetle Scratcher. Come next spring, we'll match 'em in a fightin'-bout: and which-ever feller's cat licks t'other's, the owner of the champeen wins the ole painter's hide. Meanwhiles we'll salt the hide."

"Done!" says Chunk. So us skun the painter and went home.

Soon as hit was salted, us handed hit over to Preachin' Charlie to trustee hit as ompire.

Lorsy, the rinktums I had raisin' that cub-kitten, Scratcher!

Mice and rats—he'd set up midnights on the bed-quilt and eat 'em in alive! In three days there warn't a varmint on the place left. My ole woman got moughty peeved 'cause I had to restock our rat-fam-ine with groundhogs to keep my tom-kit fed up for the prize match. My ole sow, Chinkapin, suspicioned him and sulked she wouldn't raise no shoat-babies that fall to feed cat-flesh. So she packed off. I's tell ye later whar I found her.

Meanwhiles little kit Scratcher was big-gin' and biggin' to a half-grown'd painter-cat.

Well, at last come round the six-month mornin', and here come Chunk Farley lead-in' Catcher, his twin half-grown'der, in a toggle-chain. Along with him was Preach-in' Charlie, totin' the ole painter's hide. Redbuds was purty abloom, and us met up to my ole smoke-house, me with my Scratcher on a hitch-rope.

Jericho! Those cats shied like they was furreigners 'stid o' twin brothers. Bubbled up their backs like milk bilin', and spit fire and steam.

"Hold your fightin' partners!" hollers Preachin' Charlie. "Ef be I'm ompirin' this-yere cat-bout, hit's goin' to be fit out with eethical and matheematical keerectitude. First-offly we settles the handicap."

Well, sirs, us up and weighted those cats on the balancers: tipped jist even, they did; not the ace of an ounce betwixt 'em.

Nextly we measured 'em, up, down, through, and acrosst, top to toe: not the haar of an inch between Catcher and Scratcher! Twins they was to a dot.

"Pint-blank even! Thar won't be no handicap," says Charlie; and then he laid down the law on our proceedin's.

Up he clumb on the smoke-house, lays hisself along the ridge-comb, retchin' out his hand with a hunk o' raw meat, which he steadies hit plump halfly on the tip-notch of the beam-saddle.

Meanwhiles, at the right-hand eaves-drip, Chunk raises his cat on the roof-slide, nose-up towards the meat, and holds on by the tail, keepin' the rump prezactly even with the eaves' aidge.

Likewisely, on the left hand, I does the very selfsame with *my* cat.

"Right smart aimed, fellers," says Preachin' Charlie, lookin' down, each side, moughty judeecious. "The twin nozzles is p'inted plumb straight at the target. Now, then, arter I says grace on this-yer meat, when you hears me holler, 'Haids on!' you let go tails."

So us shet our eyes whiles the preacher spoke him a few graceful words, beseechin' a heavenly guidance fer the twins. Then we hears him holler out, "Haids on!"

Bing flew the tails, and me and Chunk was seein' day-stars on our backs.

"Catcher!" Chunk yells.

"Scratcher!" I hollers.

Next thing we see was them cat-cubs top o' the ridge-comb, haids on, with their jaws lock-jammed in the middle o' that raw meat, clawin' fer heaven.

"Topple him down, Catcher! Tumble him, Scratcher!"

We scritched all dad-blazes!

But hit were jist vanity of vanities, callin' 'em back. Them twins was balanced plumb even and bound fer paradise.

For, ye see, Catcher was prezactly the same twin-strongness as Scratcher; and Scratcher was excisely the same twin-cleverness as Catcher. Neither one could outeven t'other. *Both* was champeens.

Nary cat couldn't down his twin, so the only way they could travel was *up*. And the more they nacherly clawed, the more they jist nacherly riz.

So thar they went clapper-clawin' in a yaller cloud, scratch-fightin' to glory, fur flyin' like goose-feathers, on up, neck and neck, nail and toe, crop and crupper, away on, spout-up'ards, like a razzle o' dead leaves in a whirl-storm.

Last thing us seen was a little fog-skiff, fadin' out, like the old moon by daytime, the fur feathers snowin' down.

"Dad-fetch ye, Preachin' Charlie!" says I. "What made ye so plumb matheemati-cal?"

"What-all in tarnation did ye speak that heavenly grace fer?" axes Chunk, moughty sulkin'.

Preachin' Charlie slid down off the roof.

"I reckon, fellers," says he, "you won't be needin' me for ompire agin till the next jedgment risin'. Meanwhiles I'll jist trustee this-here salted hide."

So he went on home, packin' the ole painter's skin with him.

Poor Chunk he never come back to that smoke-house till six months arter then. Hit were corn-shuckin' time, our huntin' day come round agin.

I met him thar, and we stood neck and neck, starin' uply.—

The fur was fallin' thar yit.

VII

LITERARY BALLADS

The folk tale and the ballad are probably the oldest forms of popular literature, and even in a sophisticated age they remain very close to the people. Francis J. Child's admirable collection of English and Scottish popular ballads reveals that for centuries these songs have been treasured and preserved by the oral tradition of Great Britain.[1] But many have also crossed the Atlantic and have been found by collectors, often in corrupt or debased versions, from Virginia and Georgia to Tennessee and Arkansas. Recently MacEdward Leach, in *The Ballad Book*, has demonstrated that numerous American variants of the traditional British ballads exist and has even attempted to add original American ballads to the corpus of three hundred and five titles established by Child.[2] But the popular ballad is usually anonymous, repetitive, and metrically rough. A story told in song, it is of folk origin and lacks the polish provided by literary craftsmen. The literary ballad, on the other hand, though it undeniably loses some of the freshness, drama, and charm of the popular ballad, gains in clearness, smoothness, and euphony. In the hands of Sir Walter Scott it remains a stirring tale but it also appeals to a sensitive ear. Excellent literary ballads came from the pens of such American poets as Longfellow and Whittier and at the same time preserved such famous native traditions as Paul Revere's warning ride or Barbara Frietchie's patriotic gesture. But the literary ballad as a poetic form has also appealed to twentieth-century poets like Stephen Vincent Benét, Robert Penn Warren, and John Crowe Ransom, and they have successfully brought a sophisticated and often ironic technique to frontier or legendary material. "Lily-white hands" and "red gold" are stereotypes appropriate to the older popular ballads. Instead of weeping over the grave of the romantic lovers where a briar and a rose intertwined symbolize eternal devotion, the American reader can remember pioneers like William Sycamore, whose bones, picked clean as a whistle, lie unburied on a western prairie.

1. Francis J. Child, *English and Scottish Popular Ballads* (5 vols.; 1882–98). Child's work is out of print; a convenient, one-volume abridgment of it was published in 1904; see Helen Child Sargent and George Lyman Kittredge (eds.), *English and Scottish Popular Ballads* (Boston: Houghton Mifflin Co., 1904).
2. MacEdward Leach, *The Ballad Book* (New York: Harper & Bros., 1955).

The Wreck of the Hesperus

by Henry Wadsworth Longfellow

As a balladist, Longfellow was particularly effective, since he not only had a command of singing, musical lines but could tell a story succinctly and with dramatic emphasis. In contrast to the popular ballads, Long-fellow's narrative poems are smooth and polished verse. On the other hand, they are also sentimentalized. Longfellow found it difficult to resist adding a terminal moral which is often inharmonious with the narrative structure. The closing lines of his familiar "The Wreck of the Hesperus" are a case in point. The ballad of Paul Revere has had the effect of making a folk hero out of the New England patriot.

It was the schooner *Hesperus,*
    That sailed the wintry sea;
And the skipper had taken his little daughtèr,
    To bear him company.

Blue were her eyes as the fairy-flax,
    Her cheeks like the dawn of day,
And her bosom white as the hawthorn buds,
    That ope in the month of May.

The skipper he stood beside the helm,
    His pipe was in his mouth,
And he watched how the veering flaw did blow
    The smoke now West, now South.

Then up and spake an old Sailòr,
    Had sailed to the Spanish Main,
"I pray thee, put into yonder port,
    For I fear a hurricane.

"Last night, the moon had a golden ring,
    And to-night no moon we see!"
The skipper, he blew a whiff from his pipe,
    And a scornful laugh laughed he.

Colder and louder blew the wind,
    A gale from the Northeast,
The snow fell hissing in the brine,
    And the billows frothed like yeast.

Down came the storm, and smote amain
    The vessel in its strength;
She shuddered and paused, like a frighted steed,
    Then leaped her cable's length.

"Come hither! come hither! my little daughtèr,
    And do not tremble so;
For I can weather the roughest gale
    That ever wind did blow."

He wrapped her warm in his seaman's coat
    Against the stinging blast;
He cut a rope from a broken spar,
    And bound her to the mast.

"O father! I hear the church-bells ring,
    Oh say, what may it be?"
" 'Tis a fog-bell on a rock-bound coast!"—
    And he steered for the open sea.

"O father! I hear the sound of guns,
    Oh say, what may it be?"
"Some ship in distress, that cannot live
    In such an angry sea!"

"O father! I see a gleaming light,
    Oh say, what may it be?"
But the father answered never a word,
    A frozen corpse was he.

Lashed to the helm, all stiff and stark,
    With his face turned to the skies,

The lantern gleamed through the gleaming snow
　　On his fixed and glassy eyes.

Then the maiden clasped her hands and prayed
　　That savèd she might be;
And she thought of Christ, who stilled the wave,
　　On the Lake of Galilee.

And fast through the midnight dark and drear,
　　Through the whistling sleet and snow,
Like a sheeted ghost, the vessel swept
　　Towards the reef of Norman's Woe.

And ever the fitful gusts between
　　A sound came from the land;
It was the sound of the trampling surf
　　On the rocks and the hard sea-sand.

The breakers were right beneath her bows,
　　She drifted a dreary wreck,
And a whooping billow swept the crew
　　Like icicles from her deck.

She struck where the white and fleecy waves
　　Looked soft as carded wool,
But the cruel rocks, they gored her side
　　Like the horns of an angry bull.

Her rattling shrouds, all sheathed in ice,
　　With the masts went by the board;
Like a vessel of glass, she stove and sank,
　　Ho! ho! the breakers roared!

At daybreak, on the bleak sea-beach,
　　A fisherman stood aghast,
To see the form of a maiden fair,
　　Lashed close to a drifting mast.

The salt sea was frozen on her breast,
　　The salt tears in her eyes;
And he saw her hair, like the brown seaweed,
　　On the billows fall and rise.

Such was the wreck of the *Hesperus*,
　　In the midnight and the snow!
Christ save us all from a death like this,
　　On the reef of Norman's Woe!

Paul Revere's Ride

by Henry Wadsworth Longfellow

Listen, my children, and you shall hear
Of the midnight ride of Paul Revere,
On the eighteenth of April, in Seventy-five;
Hardly a man is now alive
Who remembers that famous day and year.

He said to his friend, "If the British march
By land or sea from the town tonight,
Hang a lantern aloft in the belfry arch
Of the North Church tower as a signal light,—
One, if by land, and two, if by sea;
And I on the opposite shore will be,
Ready to ride and spread the alarm
Through every Middlesex village and farm,
For the country folk to be up and to arm."

Then he said, "Good night!" and with muffled oar
Silently rowed to the Charlestown shore,
Just as the moon rose over the bay,
Where swinging wide at her moorings lay
The *Somerset*, British man-of-war;
A phantom ship, with each mast and spar
Across the moon like a prison bar,
And a huge black hulk that was magnified
By its own reflection in the tide.

Meanwhile, his friend, through alley and street,
Wanders and watches with eager ears,
Till in the silence around him he hears
The muster of men at the barrack door,
The sound of arms, and the tramp of feet,
And the measured tread of the grenadiers,
Marching down to their boats on the shore.

Then he climbed the tower of the Old North Church,
By the wooden stairs, with stealthy tread,
To the belfry chamber overhead,
And startled the pigeons from their perch

On the somber rafters, that round him made
Masses and moving shapes of shade,—
By the trembling ladder, steep and tall,
To the highest window in the wall,
Where he paused to listen and look down
A moment on the roofs of the town,
And the moonlight flowing over all.

Beneath, in the churchyard, lay the dead,
In their night-encampment on the hill,
Wrapped in silence so deep and still
That he could hear, like a sentinel's tread,
The watchful night-wind, as it went
Creeping along from tent to tent,
And seeming to whisper, "All is well!"
A moment only he feels the spell
Of the place and the hour, and the secret dread
Of the lonely belfry and the dead;
For suddenly all his thoughts are bent
On a shadowy something far away,
Where the river widens to meet the bay,—
A line of black that bends and floats
On the rising tide, like a bridge of boats.

Meanwhile, impatient to mount and ride,
Booted and spurred, with a heavy stride
On the opposite shore walked Paul Revere.
Now he patted his horse's side,
Now gazed at the landscape far and near,
Then, impetuous stamped the earth,
And turned and tightened his saddle-girth;
But mostly he watched with eager search
The belfry-tower of the Old North Church,
As it rose above the graves on the hill,
Lonely and spectral and somber and still.
And lo! as he looks, on the belfry's height
A glimmer, and then a gleam of light!
He springs to the saddle, the bridle he turns,
But lingers and gazes, till full on his sight
A second lamp in the belfry burns!

A hurry of hoofs in a village street,
A shape in the moonlight, a bulk in the dark,
And beneath, from the pebbles, in passing, a spark
Struck out by a steed flying fearless and fleet:

That was all! And yet, through the gloom and the light,
The fate of a nation was riding that night;
And the spark struck out by that steed, in his flight,
Kindled the land into flame with its heat.

He has left the village and mounted the steep,
And beneath him, tranquil and broad and deep,
Is the Mystic, meeting the ocean tides;
And under the alders that skirt its edge,
Now soft on the sand, now loud on the ledge,
Is heard the tramp of his steed as he rides.

It was twelve by the village clock
When he crossed the bridge into Medford town.
He heard the crowing of the cock,
And the barking of the farmer's dog,
And felt the damp of the river fog,
That rises after the sun goes down.

It was one by the village clock
When he galloped into Lexington.
He saw the gilded weathercock
Swim in the moonlight as he passed,
And the meetinghouse windows, blank and bare,
Gaze at him with a spectral glare,
As if they already stood aghast
At the bloody work they would look upon.

It was two by the village clock
When he came to the bridge in Concord town.
He heard the bleating of the flock,
And the twitter of birds among the trees,
And felt the breath of the morning breeze
Blowing over the meadows brown.
And one was safe and asleep in his bed
Who at the bridge would be first to fall,
Who that day would be lying dead,
Pierced by a British musket-ball.

You know the rest. In the books you have read,
How the British Regulars fired and fled,—
How the farmers gave them ball for ball,
From behind each fence and farmyard wall,
Chasing the red-coats down the lane,
Then crossing the fields to emerge again
Under the trees at the turn of the road,
And only pausing to fire and load.

So through the night rode Paul Revere;
And so through the night went his cry of alarm
To every Middlesex village and farm,—
A cry of defiance and not of fear,
A voice in the darkness, a knock at the door,
And a word that shall echo forevermore!
For, borne on the night-wind of the Past,
Through all our history, to the last,
In the hour of darkness and peril and need,
The people will waken and listen to hear
The hurrying hoof-beats of that steed,
And the midnight message of Paul Revere.

Telling The Bees

by John Greenleaf Whittier

Whittier was at his best in depicting traditional Yankee customs and rural scenes. In "Telling the Bees" he used an old folk belief that it is necessary to inform the bees of a death in the house to prevent them from swarming and disappearing. The ballad about Floyd Ireson tells a dramatic story tersely and employs both incremental repetition and a refrain. Barbara Frietchie's altercation with Stonewall Jackson may or may not have a historical basis, but the heroine of the incident has become, through the hands of the poet, one of the more viable American traditions.

Here is the place; right over the hill
  Runs the path I took;
You can see the gap in the old wall still,
  And the stepping-stones in the shallow brook.

There is the house, with the gate red-barred,
  And the poplars tall;
And the barn's brown length, and the cattle-yard,
  And the white horns tossing above the wall.

There are the beehives ranged in the sun;
  And down by the brink
Of the brook are her poor flowers, weed-o'errun,
  Pansy and daffodil, rose and pink.

A year has gone, as the tortoise goes,
  Heavy and slow;
And the same rose blows, and the same sun glows,
  And the same brook sings of a year ago.

There's the same sweet clover-smell in the breeze;
  And the June sun warm
Tangles his wings of fire in the trees,
  Setting, as then, over Fernside farm.

I mind me how with a lover's care
  From my Sunday coat
I brushed off the burrs, and smoothed my hair,
  And cooled at the brookside my brow and throat.

Since we parted, a month had passed,—
  To love, a year;
Down through the beeches I looked at last
  On the little red gate and the well-sweep near.

I can see it all now,—the slantwise rain
  Of light through the leaves,
The sundown's blaze on her window-pane,
  The bloom of her roses under the eaves.

Just the same as a month before,—
  The house and the trees,
The barn's brown gable, the vine by the door,—
  Nothing changed but the hives of bees.

Before them, under the garden wall,
  Forward and back,
Went drearily singing the chore-girl small,
  Draping each hive with a shred of black.

Trembling, I listened: the summer sun
  Had the chill of snow;
For I knew she was telling the bees of one
  Gone on the journey we all must go!

Then I said to myself, "My Mary weeps
  For the dead to-day:
Haply her blind old grandsire sleeps
  The fret and the pain of his age away."

But her dog whined low; on the doorway sill,
  With his cane to his chin,
The old man sat; and the chore-girl still
  Sung to the bees stealing out and in.

And the song she was singing ever since
  In my ear sounds on:—
"Stay at home, pretty bees, fly not hence!
  Mistress Mary is dead and gone!"

Skipper Ireson's Ride

by John Greenleaf Whittier

Of all the rides since the birth of time,
Told in story or sung in rhyme,—
On Apuleius's Golden Ass,
Or one-eyed Calender's horse of brass,
Witch astride of a human back,
Islam's prophet on Al-Borák,—
The strangest ride that ever was sped
Was Ireson's, out from Marblehead!
  Old Floyd Ireson, for his hard heart,
   Tarred and feathered and carried in a cart
    By the women of Marblehead!

Body of turkey, head of owl,
Wings a-droop like a rained-on fowl,
Feathered and ruffled in every part,
Skipper Ireson stood in the cart.
Scores of women, old and young,
Strong of muscle, and glib of tongue,
Pushed and pulled up the rocky lane,
Shouting and singing the shrill refrain:
   "Here's Flud Oirson, fur his horrd horrt,
    Torr'd an' futherr'd an' corr'd in a corrt
     By the women o' Morble'ead!"

Wrinkled scolds with hands on hips,
Girls in bloom of cheek and lips,
Wild-eyed, free-limbed, such as chase
Bacchus round some antique vase,
Brief of skirt, with ankles bare,
Loose of kerchief and loose of hair,
With conch-shells blowing and fish-horns' twang,
Over and over the Maenads sang:
   "Here's Flud Oirson, fur his horrd horrt,
    Torr'd an' futherr'd an' corr'd in a corrt
     By the women o' Morble'ead!"

Small pity for him!—He sailed away
From a leaking ship in Chaleur Bay,—
Sailed away from a sinking wreck,
With his own town's-people on her deck!
"Lay by! lay by!" they called to him.
Back he answered, "Sink or swim!
Brag of your catch of fish again!"
And off he sailed through the fog and rain!
   Old Floyd Ireson, for his hard heart,
    Tarred and feathered and carried in a cart
     By the women of Marblehead!

Fathoms deep in dark Chaleur
That wreck shall lie forevermore.
Mother and sister, wife and maid,
Looked from the rocks of Marblehead
Over the moaning and rainy sea,—
Looked for the coming that might not be!
What did the winds and the sea-birds say
Of the cruel captain who sailed away—?
   Old Floyd Ireson, for his hard heart,
    Tarred and feathered and carried in a cart
     By the women of Marblehead!

Through the street, on either side,
Up flew windows, doors swung wide;
Sharp-tongued spinsters, old wives gray,
Treble lent the fish-horn's bray.
Sea-worn grandsires, cripple-bound,
Hulks of old sailors run aground,
Shook head, and fist, and hat, and cane,
And cracked with curses the hoarse refrain:
   "Here's Flud Oirson, fur his horrd horrt,
   Torr'd an' futherr'd an' corr'd in a corrt
      By the women o' Morble'ead!"

Sweetly along the Salem road
Bloom of orchard and lilac showed.
Little the wicked skipper knew
Of the fields so green and the sky so blue.
Riding there in his sorry trim,
Like an Indian idol glum and grim,
Scarcely he seemed the sound to hear
Of voices shouting, far and near:
   "Here's Flud Oirson, fur his horrd horrt,
   Torr'd an' futherr'd an' corr'd in a corrt
      By the women o' Morble'ead!"

"Hear me, neighbors!" at last he cried,—
"What to me is this noisy ride?
What is the shame that clothes the skin
To the nameless horror that lives within?
Waking or sleeping, I see a wreck,
And hear a cry from a reeling deck!
Hate me and curse me,—I only dread
The hand of God and the face of the dead!"
   Said old Floyd Ireson, for his hard heart,
   Tarred and feathered and carried in a cart
      By the women of Marblehead!

Then the wife of the skipper lost at sea
Said, "God has touched him! why should we!"
Said an old wife mourning her only son,
"Cut the rogue's tether and let him run!"
So with soft relentings and rude excuse,
Half scorn, half pity, they cut him loose,
And gave him a cloak to hide him in,
And left him alone with his shame and sin.
   Poor Floyd Ireson, for his hard heart,
   Tarred and feathered and carried in a cart
      By the women of Marblehead!

Barbara Frietchie

by John Greenleaf Whittier

Up from the meadows rich with corn,
Clear in the cool September morn,

The clustered spires of Frederick stand
Green-walled by the hills of Maryland.

Round about them orchards sweep,
Apple and peach tree fruited deep,

Fair as the garden of the Lord
To the eyes of the famished rebel horde,

On that pleasant morn of the early fall
When Lee marched over the mountain-wall;

Over the mountains winding down,
Horse and foot, into Frederick town.

Forty flags with their silver stars,
Forty flags with their crimson bars,

Flapped in the morning wind: the sun
Of noon looked down, and saw not one.

Up rose old Barbara Frietchie then,
Bowed with her fourscore years and ten;

Bravest of all in Frederick town,
She took up the flag the men hauled down;

In her attic window the staff she set,
To show that one heart was loyal yet.

Up the street came the rebel tread,
Stonewall Jackson riding ahead.

Under his slouched hat left and right
He glanced; the old flag met his sight.

"Halt!"—the dust-brown ranks stood fast,
"Fire!"—out blazed the rifle-blast.

It shivered the window, pane and sash;
It rent the banner with seam and gash.

Quick, as it fell, from the broken staff
Dame Barbara snatched the silken scarf.

She leaned far out on the window-sill,
And shook it forth with a royal will.

"Shoot, if you must, this old gray head,
But spare your country's flag," she said.

A shade of sadness, a blush of shame,
Over the face of the leader came;

The nobler nature within him stirred
To life at that woman's deed and word;

"Who touches a hair on yon gray head
Dies like a dog! March on!" he said.

All day long through Frederick street
Sounded the tread of marching feet:

All day long that free flag tost
Over the heads of the rebel host.

Ever its torn folds rose and fell
On the loyal winds that loved it well;

And through the hill-gaps sunset light
Shone over it with a warm good-night.

Barbara Frietchie's work is o'er,
And the Rebel rides on his raids no more.

Honor to her! and let a tear
Fall, for her sake, on Stonewall's bier.

Over Barbara Frietchie's grave,
Flag of Freedom and Union, wave!

Peace and order and beauty draw
Round thy symbol of light and law;

And ever the stars above look down
On thy stars below in Frederick town!

The Revenge of Hamish

by Sidney Lanier

Sidney Lanier is usually remembered for his wonderfully evocative pictures of the southern landscape and for his sensuous descriptions of southern nature. But he was a versatile craftsman who could do many things well. The inspiration for the ballad "The Revenge of Hamish" was bookish, but despite a literary source and a foreign scene Lanier makes the story vivid. The hexameter lines with frequent anapaestic feet, the wealth of descriptive details, and the deliberate use of alliteration distinguish the poem from the popular ballad, yet it has some of the ballad's dramatic impact. "The Revenge of Hamish" had magazine publication in 1878. Poems of Sidney Lanier first appeared in 1884.

It was three slim does and a ten-tined buck in the bracken lay;
 And all of a sudden the sinister smell of a man,
 Awaft on a wind-shift, wavered and ran
Down the hillside and sifted along through the bracken and passed that way.

Then Nan got a-tremble at nostril; she was the daintiest doe;
    In the print of her velvet flank on the velvet fern
    She reared, and rounded her ears in turn.
Then the buck leapt up, and his head as a king's to a crown did go

Full high in the breeze, and he stood as if Death had the form of a deer;
    And the two slim does long lazily stretching arose,
    For their day-dream slowlier came to a close,
Till they woke and were still, breath-bound with waiting and wonder and fear.

Then Alan the huntsman sprang over the hillock, the hounds shot by,
    The does and the ten-tined buck made a marvellous bound,
    The hounds swept after with never a sound,
But Alan loud winded his horn in sign that the quarry was nigh.

For at dawn of that day proud Maclean of Lochbuy to the hunt had waxed wild,
    And he cursed at old Alan till Alan fared off with the hounds
    For to drive him the deer to the lower glen-grounds:
"I will kill a red deer," quoth Maclean, "in the sight of the wife and the child."

So gayly he paced with the wife and the child to his chosen stand;
    But he hurried tall Hamish the henchman ahead: "Go turn,"—
    Cried Maclean,—"if the deer seek to cross to the burn,
Do thou turn them to me: nor fail, lest thy back be red as thy hand."

Now hard-fortuned Hamish, half blown of his breath with the height of the hill,
    Was white in the face when the ten-tined buck and the does
    Drew leaping to burn-ward; huskily rose
His shouts, and his nether lip twitched, and his legs were o'er-weak for his will.

So the deer darted lightly by Hamish and bounded away to the burn.
    But Maclean never bating his watch tarried waiting below;
    Still Hamish hung heavy with fear for to go
All the space of an hour; then he went, and his face was greenish and stern,

And his eye sat back in the socket, and shrunken the eye-balls shone,
    As withdrawn from a vision of deeds it were shame to see.
    "Now, now, grim henchman, what is't with thee?"
Brake Maclean, and his wrath rose red as a beacon the wind hath upblown.

"Three does and a ten-tined buck made out," spoke Hamish, full mild,
    "And I ran for to turn, but my breath it was blown, and they passed;
    I was weak, for ye called ere I broke me my fast."
Cried Maclean: "Now a ten-tined buck in the sight of the wife and the child

"I had killed if the gluttonous kern had not wrought me a snail's own wrong!"
    Then he sounded, and down came kinsmen and clansmen all:

"Ten blows, for ten tine, on his back let fall,
And reckon no stroke if the blood follow not at the bite of thong!"

So Hamish made bare, and took him his strokes; at the last he smiled.
  "Now I'll to the burn," quoth Maclean, "for it still may be,
  If a slimmer-paunched henchman will hurry with me,
I shall kill me the ten-tined buck for a gift to the wife and the child!"

Then the clansmen departed, by this path and that; and over the hill
  Sped Maclean with an outward wrath for an inward shame;
  And that place of the lashing full quiet became;
And the wife and the child stood sad; and bloody-backed Hamish sat still.

But look! red Hamish has risen; quick about and about turns he.
  "There is none betwixt me and the crag-top!" he screams under breath.
  Then, livid as Lazarus lately from death,
He snatches the child from the mother, and clambers the crag toward the sea.

Now the mother drops breath; she is dumb, and her heart goes dead for a space,
  Till the motherhood, mistress of death, shrieks, shrieks through the glen,
  And that place of the lashing is live with men,
And Maclean, and the gillie that told him, dash up in a desperate race.

Not a breath's time for asking; an eye-glance reveals all the tale untold.
  They follow mad Hamish afar up the crag toward the sea,
  And the lady cries: "Clansmen, run for a fee!—
Yon castle and lands to the two first hands that shall hook him and hold

"Fast Hamish back from the brink!"—and ever she flies up the steep,
  And the clansmen pant, and they sweat, and they jostle and strain.
  But, mother, 'tis vain; but, father, 'tis vain;
Stern Hamish stands bold on the brink, and dangles the child o'er the deep.

Now a faintness falls on the men that run, and they all stand still.
  And the wife prays Hamish as if he were God, on her knees,
  Crying: "Hamish! O Hamish! but please, but please
For to spare him!" and Hamish still dangles the child, with a wavering will.

On a sudden he turns; with a sea-hawk scream, and a gibe, and a song,
  Cries: "So; I will spare ye the child if, in sight of ye all,
  Ten blows on Maclean's bare back shall fall,
And ye reckon no stroke if the blood follow not at the bite of the thong!"

Then Maclean he set hardly his tooth to his lip that his tooth was red,
  Breathed short for a space, said: "Nay, but it never shall be!
  Let me hurl off the damnable hound in the sea!"
But the wife: "Can Hamish go fish us the child from the sea, if dead?

"Say yea!—Let them lash *me*, Hamish?"—"Nay!"—"Husband, the lashing will heal;
 But, oh, who will heal me the bonny sweet bairn in his grave?
 Could ye cure me my heart with the death of a knave?
Quick! Love! I will bare thee—so—kneel!" Then Maclean 'gan slowly to kneel

With never a word, till presently downward he jerked to the earth.
 Then the henchman—he that smote Hamish—would tremble and lag;
 "Strike, hard!" quoth Hamish, full stern, from the crag;
Then he struck him, and "One!" sang Hamish, and danced with the child in his mirth.

And no man spake beside Hamish; he counted each stroke with a song.
 When the last stroke fell, then he moved him a pace down the height,
 And he held forth the child in the heart-aching sight,
Of the mother, and looked all pitiful grave, as repenting a wrong.

And there as the motherly arms stretched out with the thanksgiving prayer—
 And there as the mother crept up with a fearful swift pace,
 Till her finger nigh felt of the bairnie's face—
In a flash fierce Hamish turned round and lifted the child in the air,

And sprang with the child in his arms from the horrible height in the sea,
 Shrill screeching, "Revenge!" in the wind-rush; and pallid Maclean,
 Age-feeble with anger and impotent pain,
Crawled up on the crag, and lay flat, and locked hold of dead roots of a tree,

And gazed hungrily o'er, and the blood from his back drip-dripped in the brine,
 And a sea-hawk flung down a skeleton fish as he flew,
 And the mother stared white on the waste of blue,
And the wind drove a cloud to seaward, and the sun began to shine.

Kit Carson's Ride

by Joaquin Miller

Although buffalo no longer "come like a cloud on the plain," the West as region and concept still looms important on the American horizon, and radio and horse-opera have kept the Indian menace alive. Joaquin Miller's stirring ballad of a wild pursuit across the prairies by Comanches, perhaps the fiercest of the mounted Indians, becomes even more exciting when the fugitives have to face not just savages but a prairie fire. The poem has some of the qualities of the traditional popular ballad: concision, few apparent connectives, a dramatic story, and a conclusion which is not spoiled by anticlimax. "Kit Carson's Ride" was published in Songs of the Sierras *(1871).*

Room! room to turn round in, to breathe and be free,
To grow to be giant, to sail as to sea
With the speed of the wind on a steed with his mane
To the wind, without pathway or route or a rein.
Room! room to be free where the white-border'd sea
Blows a kiss to a brother as boundless as he;
Where the buffalo come like a cloud on the plain,
Pouring on like the tide of a storm-driven main,
And the lodge of the hunter to friend or to foe
Offers rest; and unquestion'd you come or you go.
My plains of America! Seas of wild lands!
From a land in the seas in a raiment of foam,
That has reached to a stranger the welcome of home,
I turn to you, lean to you, lift you my hands!

Run? Run? See this flank, sir, and I do love him so!
But he's blind, badger blind. Whoa, Pache, boy, whoa.
No, you wouldn't believe it to look at his eyes,
But he's blind, badger blind, and it happen'd this wise.

"We lay in the grass and the sunburnt clover
That spread on the ground like a great brown cover
Northward and southward, and west and away
To the Brazos, where our lodges lay,
One broad and unbroken level of brown.
We were waiting the curtains of night to come down

326

To cover us trio and conceal our flight
With my brown bride, won from an Indian town
That lay to the rear the full ride of a night.

"We lounged in the grass—her eyes were in mine,
And her hands on my knee, and her hair was as wine
In its wealth and its flood, pouring on and all over
Her bosom wine red, and press'd never by one.
Her touch was as warm as the tinge of the clover
Burnt brown as it reach'd to the kiss of the sun.
Her words they were low as the lute-throated dove,
And as laden with love as the heart when it beats
In its hot, eager answer to earliest love,
Or the bee hurried home by its burthen of sweets.

"We lay low in the grass on the broad plain levels,
Old Revels and I, and my stolen brown bride;
'Forty full miles if a foot to ride!
Forty full miles if a foot, and the devils
Of red Comanches are hot on the track
When once they strike it. Let the sun go down
Soon, very soon,' muttered bearded old Revels
As he peer'd at the sun, lying low on his back,
Holding fast to his lasso. Then he jerk'd at his steed
And he sprang to his feet, and glanced swiftly around,
And then dropp'd, as if shot, with an ear to the ground;
Then again to his feet, and to me, to my bride,
While his eyes were like flame, his face like a shroud,
His form like a king, and his beard like a cloud,
And his voice loud and shrill, as both trumpet and reed,—
'Pull, pull in your lassoes, and bridle to steed,
And speed you if ever for life you would speed.
Aye, ride for your lives, for your lives you must ride!
For the plain is aflame, the prairie on fire,
And feet of wild horses hard flying before
I heard like a sea breaking high on the shore,
While the buffalo come like a surge of the sea,
Driven far by the flame, driving fast on us three
As a hurricane comes, crushing palms in his ire.'

"We drew in the lassoes, seized saddle and rein,
Threw them on, cinched them on, cinched them over again,
And again drew the girth; and spring we to horse,
With head to the Brazos, with a sound in the air
Like the surge of a sea, with a flash in the eye,
From that red wall of flame reaching up to the sky,

A red wall of flame and a black rolling sea
Rushing fast upon us, as the wind sweeping free
And afar from the desert blown hollow and hoarse.

"Not a word, not a wail from a lip was let fall,
We broke not a whisper, we breathed not a prayer,
There was work to be done, there was death in the air,
And the chance was as one to a thousand for all.

"Twenty miles! . . . thirty miles! . . . a dim distant speck . . .
Then a long reaching line, and the Brazos in sight!
And I rose in my seat with a shout of delight.
I stood in my stirrup and look'd to my right—
But Revels was gone; I glanced by my shoulder
And saw his horse stagger; I saw his head drooping
Hard down on his breast, and his naked breast stooping
Low down to the mane, as so swifter and bolder
Ran reaching out for us the red-footed fire.
He rode neck to neck with a buffalo bull,
That made the earth shake where he came in his course,
The monarch of millions, with shaggy mane full
Of smoke and of dust, and it shook with desire
Of battle, with rage and with bellowings hoarse.
His keen, crooked horns, through the storm of his mane,
Like black lances lifted and lifted again;
And I looked but this once, for the fire licked through
And Revels was gone, as we rode two and two.

"I look'd to my left then—and nose, neck, and shoulder
Sank slowly, sank surely, till back to my thighs,
And up through the black blowing veil of her hair
Did beam full in mine her two marvelous eyes,
With a longing and love yet a look of despair
And of pity for me, as she felt the smoke fold her,
And flames reaching far for her glorious hair,
Her sinking horse falter'd, plunged, fell and was gone
As I reached through the flame and I bore her still on.
On! into the Brazos, she, Pache and I—
Poor, burnt, blinded Pache. I love him . . . That's why."

Captain Carpenter

by John Crowe Ransom

Although John Crowe Ransom has not been a prolific poet, he is the author of a small body of artistic and highly polished verse. In particular, his imagery is original and meticulous. In his story of Captain Carpenter, the doughty champion who lost his nose, arms, ears, eyes, and finally his heart in bloody conflict, Ransom utilized the ballad form for satirical purposes and ridiculed his hero somewhat as Cervantes did Don Quixote. Archaic words suggest a remote scene, and the final curse of hell directed at the villain is a touch borrowed from older popular narrative. The familiar form and subject reinforce the paradoxes of Ransom's highly sophisticated art. The ballad appears in Selected Poems *(1945).*

Captain Carpenter rose up in his prime
Put on his pistols and went riding out
But had got wellnigh nowhere at that time
Till he fell in with ladies in a rout.

It was a pretty lady and all her train
That played with him so sweetly but before
An hour she'd taken a sword with all her main
And twined him of his nose for evermore.

Captain Carpenter mounted up one day
And rode straightway into a stranger rogue
That looked unchristian but be that as may
The Captain did not wait upon prologue.

But drew upon him out of his great heart
The other swung against him with a club

And cracked his two legs at the shinny part
And let him roll and stick like any tub.

Captain Carpenter rode many a time
From male and female took he sundry harms
He met the wife of Satan crying "I'm
The she-wolf bids you shall bear no more arms."

Their strokes and counters whistled in the wind
I wish he had delivered half his blows
But where she should have made off like a hind
The bitch bit off his arms at the elbows.

And Captain Carpenter parted with his ears
To a black devil that used him in this wise
O Jesus ere his threescore and ten years
Another had plucked out his sweet blue eyes.

Captain Carpenter got up on his roan
And sallied from the gate in hell's despite
I heard him asking in the grimmest tone
If any enemy yet there was to fight?

"To any adversary it is fame
If he risk to be wounded by my tongue
Or burnt in two beneath my red heart's flame
Such are the perils he is cast among.

"But if he can he has a pretty choice
From an anatomy with little to lose
Whether he cut my tongue and take my voice
Or whether it be my round red heart he choose."

It was the neatest knave that ever was seen
Stepping in perfume from his lady's bower
Who at this word put in his merry mien
And fell on Captain Carpenter like a tower.

I would not knock old fellows in the dust
But there lay Captain Carpenter on his back
His weapons were the old heart in his bust
And a blade shook between rotten teeth alack.

The rogue in scarlet and grey soon knew his mind
He wished to get his trophy and depart
With gentle apology and touch refined
He pierced him and produced the Captain's heart.

God's mercy rest on Captain Carpenter now
I thought him Sirs an honest gentleman
Citizen husband soldier and scholar enow
Let jangling kites eat of him if they can.

But God's deep curses follow after those
That shore him of his goodly nose and ears
His legs and strong arms at the two elbows
And eyes that had not watered seventy years.

The curse of hell upon the sleek upstart
That got the Captain finally on his back
And took the red red vitals of his heart
And made the kites to whet their beaks clack clack.

The Ballad of William Sycamore

(1790–1871)

by Stephen Vincent Benét

Stephen Vincent Benét was particularly successful in evoking the American past in terms of individuals. In John Brown's Body he gave a succinct history of the Civil War through folk spokesmen carefully chosen to represent both sides and various social strata. In his musical ballad about a frontiersman he compressed generations of western expansion into the span of one human life. William Sycamore is the composite scout and Indian fighter who is constantly lured westward until his steps falter and civilization catches up with him. The terseness of the ballad form is particularly appropriate to this miniature saga of frontier life.

y father, he was a mountaineer,
His fist was a knotty hammer;
He was quick on his feet as a running deer,
And he spoke with a Yankee stammer.

My mother, she was merry and brave,
And so she came to her labor,

With a tall green fir for her doctor grave
And a stream for her comforting neighbor.

And some are wrapped in the linen fine,
And some like a godling's scion;
But I was cradled on twigs of pine
In the skin of a mountain lion.

And some remember a white, starched lap
And a ewer with silver handles;
But I remember a coonskin cap
And the smell of bayberry candles.

The cabin logs, with the bark still rough,
And my mother who laughed at trifles,
And the tall, lank visitors, brown as snuff,
With their long, straight squirrel-rifles.

I can hear them dance, like a foggy song,
Through the deepest one of my slumbers,
The fiddle squeaking the boots along
And my father calling the numbers.

The quick feet shaking the puncheon-floor,
And the fiddle squealing and squealing,
Till the dried herbs rattled above the door
And the dust went up to the ceiling.

There are children lucky from dawn till dusk,
But never a child so lucky!
For I cut my teeth on "Money Musk"
In the Bloody Ground of Kentucky!

When I grew tall as the Indian corn,
My father had little to lend me,
But he gave me his great, old powder-horn
And his woodsman's skill to befriend me.

With a leather shirt to cover my back,
And a redskin nose to unravel
Each forest sign, I carried my pack
As far as a scout could travel.

Till I lost my boyhood and found my wife,
A girl like a Salem clipper!
A woman straight as a hunting-knife
With eyes as bright as the Dipper!

We cleared our camp where the buffalo feed,
Unheard-of streams were our flagons;
And I sowed my sons like the apple-seed
On the trail of the Western wagons.

They were right, tight boys, never sulky or slow,
A fruitful, a goodly muster.
The eldest died at the Alamo.
The youngest fell with Custer.

The letter that told it burned my hand.
Yet we smiled and said, "So be it!"
But I could not live when they fenced the land,
For it broke my heart to see it.

I saddled a red, unbroken colt
And rode him into the day there;
And he threw me down like a thunderbolt
And rolled on me as I lay there.

The hunter's whistle hummed in my ear
As the city-men tried to move me,
And I died in my boots like a pioneer
With the whole wide sky above me.

Now I lie in the heart of the fat, black soil,
Like the seed of a prairie-thistle;
It has washed my bones with honey and oil
And picked them clean as a whistle.

And my youth returns, like the rains of Spring,
And my sons, like the wild-geese flying;
And I lie and hear the meadow-lark sing
And have much content in my dying.

Go play with the towns you have built of blocks,
The towns where you would have bound me!
I sleep in my earth like a tired fox,
And my buffalo have found me.

The Lady of the Tomahawk

by Robert P. Tristram Coffin

In a stream of essays, stories, and poems Coffin sought to interpret his native Maine. Among the themes that attracted his attention were Indian fighting, the Colonial period, shipping, and life on the rocky, coastal farms. In "The Lady of the Tomahawk," Coffin told the story of Hannah Dustin, the heroine of one of the most famous captivity narratives, and described not only her fortitude on the forest trails but also her dexterity in using an Indian weapon so that at a crucial time she could make good her escape. Coffin's ballad about a historical figure shows the poet's customary facility and ease in versification.

Hannah was a lady,
　　She had a feather-bed,
And she'd worked Jonah and the whale
　　Upon the linen spread.
She did her honest household part
To give our land a godly start.

Red Injuns broke the china
　　Her use had never flawed,
They ripped her goose-tick up with knives
　　And shook the down abroad.
They took her up the Merrimac
With only one shirt to her back.

Hannah Dustin pondered
　　On her cupboard's wrongs,
Hannah Dustin duly mastered
　　The red-hot Injun sons.
She lay beside her brown new mates
Remembering the Derby plates.

She got the chief to show her
　　How he aimed his blow
And cut the white man's crop of hair
　　And left the brains to show.
The Lord had made her quick to learn
The way to carve or chop or churn.

The moon was on the hilltop,
    Sleep was on the waves,
Hannah took the tomahawk
    And scalped all twenty braves.
She left her master last of all,
And at the ears she shaved his poll.

Homeward down the river
    She paddled her canoe.
She went to her old cellar-place
    To see what she could do.
She found some bits of plates that matched,
What plates she could she went and patched.

She built her chimney higher
    Than it had been before,
She hung her twenty sable scalps
    Above her modest door.
She sat a-plucking new gray geese
For new mattresses in peace.

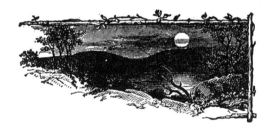

VIII

HEROES
and
DEMIGODS

Many avenues lead to the American Pantheon—politics, invention, exploration, sports, science, soldiering, business. In a land devoid of hereditary nobility we confer honorary degrees and titles suggestive of popular acclaim. We consistently laud achievement and daring and bigness, and yet we respect the rebel and the critic. If most of the public attention centers on Fords and Carnegies and Roosevelts, there has always been a place for a Thoreau, with time for his own business at Walden Pond. The great folk heroes of American life, however, can easily be divided into two categories: those who are the product of the imagination and those who actually lived. On one side of the center line between myth and reality belong Paul Bunyan, John Henry, Pecos Bill, Febold Feboldson, Stormalong, Rip Van Winkle, Uncle Remus, and Leatherstocking; on the other stand Johnny Appleseed, Mike Fink, Davy Crockett, Daniel Boone, John Brown, Andrew Jackson, and Lincoln. But in the popular mind many of the traits of these heroes, if not the heroes themselves, have merged. The blurring often produces inflated images; and the figures, historic or fictitious, become foci for the accreting legends and tales. Davy Crockett and, to some extent, Mike Fink are the protagonists of episodes almost as fabulous as those related about Paul Bunyan or John Henry. Andrew Jackson in Lindsay's poem becomes a hero eight feet tall. The wealth of anecdotal material about Lincoln defies a library to hold it; and Lincoln himself for many years has enjoyed in the American mind a stature far superior even to his elongated frame. As historical figures recede into the past, the imagination either forgets them or inflates them. And, if the latter process holds, the folk hero becomes truly fabulous in size, in endurance, in speed and strength, in wisdom and cunning, in superhuman achievement. Our American gods are not always comic, as has been contended, but they are invariably gigantic and restless.

Sunrise in His Pocket

by [Davy Crockett]

Whether or not Davy Crockett wrote the accounts of these fantastic exploits, there is no doubt that he was the comic, demigod protagonist. He was the western superman who terrified the animals into abject surrender by merely appearing on the scene; he could outbargain, outdrink, and outfight any antagonist; and he was naturally the person called upon when something happened to disturb the orderly functioning of the universe. In fact—and particularly in myth—Crockett was notable for bold talk and extravagant deeds. His famous motto, "Be sure you're right, and then go ahead," typifies the spirit of frontier individualism. Crockett is an excellent example of a folk hero whose deeds the popular imagination has magnified a hundredfold.

One January morning it was so all-screwen-up cold that the forest trees war so stiff that they couldn't shake, and the very day-break froze fast as it war tryin' to dawn. The tinder-box in my cabin would no more ketch fire than a sunk raft at the bottom o' the sea. Seein' that daylight war so far behind time, I thought creation war in a fair way for freezin' fast.

"So," thinks I, "I must strike a leetle fire from my fingers, light my pipe, travel out a few leagues, and see about it."

Then I brought my knuckles together like two thunder clouds, but the sparks froze up afore I could begin to collect 'em —so out I walked, and endeavored to keep myself unfriz by goin' at a hop, step and jump gait, and whistlin' the tune of "fire in the mountains!" as I went along in three double quick time. Well, arter I had walked about twenty-five miles up the peak o' Daybreak Hill, I soon discovered what war the matter. The airth had actually friz fast in her axis, and couldn't turn round; the sun had got jammed between two cakes o' ice under the wheels, an' thar he had bin shinin' and workin' to get loose, till he friz fast in his cold sweat.

"C-r-e-a-t-i-o-n!" thought I, "this are the toughest sort o' suspension, and it mustn't be endured—somethin' must be done, or human creation is done for."

It war then so antedeluvian and premature cold that my upper and lower teeth an' tongue war all collapsed together as tight as a friz oyster. I took a fresh twenty pound bear off o' my back that I'd picked up on the road, an' beat the animal agin the ice till the hot ile began to walk out on him at all sides. I then took an' held

339

him over the airth's axes, an' squeezed him till I thaw'd 'em loose, poured about a ton on it over the sun's face, give the airth's cog-wheel one kick backward, till I got the sun loose—whistled "Push along, keep movin'!" an' in about fifteen seconds the airth gin a grunt, and begun movin'— the sun walked up beautiful, salutin' me with sich a wind o' gratitude that it made me sneeze. I lit my pipe by the blaze o' his top-knot, shouldered my bear, an' walked home, introducin' the people to fresh daylight with a piece of sunrise in my pocket, with which I cooked my bear steaks, an' enjoyed one o' the best breakfasts I had tasted for some time. If I didn't, jist wake some mornin' and go with me to the office o' sunrise!

Grinning the Bark Off a Tree

by [*Davy Crockett*]

That Colonel Crockett could avail himself, in electioneering, of the advantages which well applied satire ensues, the following anecdote will sufficiently prove:

In the canvass of the Congressional election of 18——, Mr. ****** was the Colonel's opponent—a gentleman of the most pleasing and conciliating manners—who seldom addressed a person or a company without wearing upon his countenance a peculiarly good humoured smile. The Colonel, to counteract the influence of this winning attribute, thus alluded to it in a stump speech:

"Yes, gentlemen, he may get some votes by *grinning*, for he can *outgrin me*—and you know I ain't slow—and to prove to you that I am not, I will tell you an anecdote. I was concerned myself—and I was fooled a little of the wickedest. You all know I love hunting. Well, I discovered a long time ago that a 'coon couldn't stand my grin. I could bring one tumbling down from the highest tree. I never wasted powder and lead, when I wanted one of the creatures. Well, as I was walking out one night, a few hundred yards from my house, looking carelessly about me, I saw a 'coon planted upon one of the highest limbs of an old tree. The night was very *moony* and clear, and old Ratler was with me; but Ratler won't bark at a 'coon—he's a queer dog in that way. So, I thought I'd bring the lark down in the usual way, *by a grin.* I set myself—and, after grinning at the 'coon a reasonable time, found that he didn't come down. I wondered what was the reason—and I took another steady grin at him. Still he was *there.* It made me a little mad; so I felt round and got an old limb about five feet long, and, planting one end upon the ground, I placed my chin upon the other, and took *a rest.* I then grinned my best for about five minutes; but the cursed 'coon hung on. So, finding I could not bring him down by grinning, I determined to have him—for I thought he must be a droll chap. I went over to the house, got my axe, returned to the tree, saw the 'coon still there, and began to cut away. Down it come, and I ran forward; but d——n the 'coon was there to be seen. I found that what I had taken for one, was a large knot upon the branch of the tree and, upon looking at it closely, I saw that *I had grinned all the bark off, and left the knot perfectly smooth.*

"Now, fellow-citizens," continued the Colonel, "you must be convinced that, in the *grinning line,* I myself am not slow—yet, when I look upon my opponent's countenance, I must admit that he is my superior. You must all admit it. Therefore, be wide awake—look sharp—and do not let him grin you out of your votes."

The Winter of the Blue Snow

by James Stevens

Unlike such historical figures as Mike Fink, Johnny Appleseed, and Davy Crockett, around whom a mass of anecdotes and stories accreted, Paul Bunyan seems to be a deliberate invention of gifted storytellers. Despite his synthetic origin, he has become firmly established in the mind of the American people—not only in the northern tier of states, where his lumbering activities supposedly had focus, but elsewhere as well. Areas as far apart as West Virginia and the Texas oilfields provide a locale for Paul Bunyan stories. Although his exact origin is in dispute, a French Canadian nativity is often suggested. In Stevens' version, Paul evinces many of the attributes which have fixed the popular conception of him. He is physically a giant, he is basically a man of action, his one function in life is destructive, and he is an isolated figure almost completely lacking in human companionship. It is interesting to note that the sense of humor and the loquacity implied in this story are not normally characteristic of Paul Bunyan in other tales. The colorful and carefully detailed garb in which the giant logger sets out in quest of Niagara would seem to be the fancy of an inventive novelist rather than the authentic product of the folk imagination. On the other hand, the exaggeration of deed and size is characteristic of the whole Paul Bunyan cycle.

Paul Bunyan was the one historian of the useful and the beautiful; other writers of history tell only of terrible and dramatic events. Therefore the chronicles of Paul Bunyan, the mighty logger, the inventor of the lumber industry, the leader-hero of the best band of bullies, the finest bunch of savages, that ever tramped the continent, the master orator of a land that has since grown forests of orators—his chronicles alone tell of the Winter of the Blue Snow.

The blue snow fell first in the North. It fell scantily in its earlier hours, its sapphire flakes floating down on the waves of a mild winter wind, and glittering in an ashen gold light, a sober pale radiance which shimmered through silver mists. There was poetry in the spectacle of these hours. And then the hard gray ground of a peopleless land was hidden under a blanket of dark blue. And the nameless frozen lakes and rivers, the silent valleys and the windy hills of the country were all spread over with a sky-dyed snow. When the last light of this day went out, the boughs of the great pines were creaking under heavy wet masses of snow like torn bales of blue cotton. There was a rush in the snowfall now, as a fiercer wind whipped it on; its heavy flakes were driven down in thick, whirling clusters, in streaming veils, leaping lines and dashing columns; and there were cloudlike swarms of the blue flakes, which settled slowly, floating easily in the hard wind. This wind got so strong that it shivered the timber, and the piles of blue snow which had gathered on the pine boughs were shaken down. Most of this snow fell into blue mounds around the trees, but some of it fell on the fauna of the forest, adding to their troublement.

At the time of the Winter of the Blue Snow, the forest creatures of this land lived a free and easy life. Man was not there to embarrass them with accusations of trespass and to slay them for their ignorance of the crime. Their main problem was the overcrowding of the forests. The vast moose herds, who populated the woods so densely that traffic through their favorite timber was dangerous, made the matter of getting food a simple one for the carnivorous animals. There were many moose to spare, and the elders of the herds, like most prolific parents, never became frantically resentful over the loss of an offspring. The moose themselves, of course, lived easily on the crisp, juicy moose grass which grew so plenteously in these regions before the blue snow. So the carnivorous creatures of the forests lived a fast and furious life; and it is certain that if they were capable of praise, they had good praises for the moose meat which they got with such little difficulty. The coal-black bruins of the North were an especially happy crowd. Theirs was a gay, frolicsome life in the summer time, when the big bruins danced and galloped through sunny valleys and the small ones had rolling races on shady hillsides. In the fall, all fat and drowsy from moose meat, the bruins would go to sleep in their warm caves and dream pleasantly all winter.

They were all dreaming now; and the blue snow would no doubt have fallen and melted away without their knowledge had it not been for the moose herds which crowded the forest aisles. Moose at that time did not have it in them to enjoy wonder, and they had not learned to combat fear, for they were never afraid. Still, they had some imagination, and the moose trembled when the first blue snowflakes fell among them. They kept up an appearance of unconcern at first, eating moose moss as usual; but they sniffed gingerly at the blue streaks in it, and they stole furtive glances at each other as they bravely ate. This strange snowfall was certainly breeding fear of it in the hearts of all the moose, but each one seemed determined to be the last one to show it. However, as the day-end got near, and the wind grew more boisterous, shaking snow masses from the trees, some of the moose had fits of trembling and eye-rolling which they could not conceal. When a heap of snow dropped on the back of some timid moose, he would twist his head sharply and stare with bulging eyes at the mysteriously fearsome color, then he would prance wildly until the unwelcome snow was bucked from his shivering back. When the early shadows of evening came among the trees, the moose all had a heavy darkness of fear in their hearts. Little was needed to put them in a panic.

It was a great bull moose, a herd king, who forgot the example he owed to his weaker kindred and unloosed a thunderous bellow of terror which started the moose flight, the first memorable incident of the Winter of the Blue Snow. An overladen bough cracked above him; it fell and straddled him from quivering tail to flailing horns, burying him under its wet blue load. He reared out roaring, and his own herd echoed the cry; then a storm of moose bellows crashed through the forest. The tumult died, but there followed the earthshaking thunder of a stampede.

The bruins, awakened from their pleasant dreams, came out from their caves and blinked at the hosts of terrified moose which were galloping past. The earthshaking uproar of the flight at last thoroughly aroused the bruins, and they began to sniff the air uneasily. Then they noticed the blue snow; and now in front of every cave crowds of bruins were staring down at the snow; and each bruin was swaying heavily, lifting his left front foot as he swayed to the right, and lifting his right front foot as he swayed to the left. The bruins had no courage either, and, once they had got sleep out of their heads, nearly all of them took out after the moose herds. The wind roared louder with every passing minute this night. And the flakes of the blue snow were as dense as the particles

of a fog. At dawn a blue blizzard was raging. But the fauna of the forest plunged tirelessly on, seeking a refuge of white snow.

And Niagara, made faithless by the Blue Terror, galloped behind them— Niagara, the great moose hound, breadwinner for the student of history, Paul Bunyon (his real name), and his companion also.

Paul Bunyon lived at Tonnere Bay. He dwelt in a cave that was as large as ten Mammoth Caves and which had a roof loftier than any tower or spire. But this cave was none too vast for Paul Bunyon, the one man of this region, but one man as great as a city of ordinary men. His tarpaulins and blankets covered one-fourth of the cave floor; his hunting clothes, traps and seines filled another quarter; and the rest of the space was occupied by a fireplace and his papers and books.

For Paul Bunyon was a student now. There had been a time when he had gone forth in the hunting and fishing season to gather the huge supplies of provender which he required, but now his days and nights were all spent with his books. Paul Bunyon's favorite food was raw moose meat, and after he found Niagara in the Tall Wolf country he no longer needed to hunt. Each night Niagara trotted out in the darkness and satisfied his own hunger, then he carried mouthfuls of moose to the cave until he had a day's supply of meat for his master. Niagara was ever careful not to frighten the moose herds; he hunted stealthily and with quiet. The moose at night were only conscious of a dark cloud looming over them, then numbers of the herds would disappear without painful sound. The moose, if they had thought about it, would have been only thankful to Niagara for lessening the congestion of the forests.

So Paul Bunyon fared well on the moose meat which Niagara brought him, and he lived contentedly as a student in his cave at Tonnere Bay. Each day he studied, and far into the night he figured. Taking a trimmed pine tree for a pencil, he would char its end in the fire and use the cave floor for a slate. He was not long in learning all the history worth knowing, and he became as good a figurer as any man could be.

Vague ambitions began to stir in his soul after this and he often deserted his studies to dream about them. He knew he would not spend his days forever in the cave at Tonnere Bay. Somewhere in the future a great Work was waiting to be done by him. Now it was only a dream; but he was sure that it would be a reality; and he came to think more and more about it. The books were opened less and less; the pine tree pencil was seldom brought from its corner. Paul Bunyon now used another pine tree which still had its boughs; it was a young one, and he brushed his curly black beard with it as he dreamed. But he was still a contented man at the time of the Winter of the Blue Snow, for his dreams had not yet blazed up in a desire for any certain attainment.

On the first day of the blue snow, Paul Bunyon was in a particularly contented mood. He sat all that day before his fire; so charmed with drowsy thoughts was he that he did not once look out. It had been dark a long time before he rolled into his blankets. He awoke at the dawn of a day that had scarcely more light than the night. He was cold, and he got up to throw an armful of trees on the fire. Then he saw the blue drifts which had piled up before the cave, and he saw the fog of the blue blizzard. He heard the roar of a terrific wind, too, and he knew that the storm was perilous as well as strange. But Paul Bunyon thought gladly of the blue snow, for it was a beautiful event, and the historians he liked most would write wonderful books about it.

He kicked the drifts away from the cave entrance, but the usual pile of slain moose was not under them. Paul Bunyon was a little worried, as he thought that Niagara might have lost himself in the blue blizzard. The possibility that the unnatural color of the storm might send the fauna of the forest, and Niagara as well, into panicky flight did not occur to him. He was sure that Niagara would return with a grand supply of moose meat when the blue blizzard had passed.

But the moose herds were now far to the North, fleeing blindly from the blue snow. The bruins galloped after them. Before the day was over, Niagara had overtaken the bruins and was gaining on the moose. At nightfall his lunging strides had carried him far ahead of all the fauna of the forest. He galloped yet faster as he reached the blacker darkness of the Arctic winter. Now the darkness was so heavy that even his powerful eyes could not see in it. . . . Niagara at last ran head-on into the North Pole; the terrific speed at which he was traveling threw his body whirling high in the air; when Niagara fell he crashed through ninety feet of ice, and the polar fields cracked explosively as his struggles convulsed the waters under them. . . . Then only mournful blasts of wind sounded in the night of the Farthest North.

The moose were wearied out before they reached the white Arctic, and hordes of them fell and perished in the blizzard; many others died from fright, and only a tiny remnant of the great herds survived. Some of the bruins reached the polar fields, and they have lived there since. Their hair had turned white from fright, and their descendants still wear that mark of fear. Others were not frightened so much, and their hair only turned gray. They did not run out of the timber, and their descendants, the silver-tip grizzlies, still live in the Northern woods. The baby bruins were only scared out of their growth, and their black descendants now grow no larger than the cubs of Paul Bunyon's time.

Being ignorant of this disaster, Paul Bunyon was comfortable enough while the blizzard lasted. He had a good store of trees on hand and his cave was warm in the storm. He got hungry in the last days; but this emotion, or any emotion, for that matter, could have but little power over him when he was dreaming. And he dreamed deeply now of great enterprises; his dreams were formless, without any substance of reality; but they had brilliant colors, and they made him very hopeful.

The sun shone at last from a whitish blue sky, and the strange snow fell no more. A snapping cold was in the land; and pine boughs were bangled and brocaded with glittering blue crystals, and crusty blue snow crackled underfoot.

Paul Bunyon strapped on his snow shoes and started out through the Border forests in search of Niagara. His was a kingly figure as he mushed through the pine trees, looming above all but the very tallest of them. He wore a wine-red hunting cap, and his glossy hair and beard shone under it with a blackness that blended with the cap's color perfectly. His unique eyebrows were black also; covering a fourth of his forehead above the eyes, they narrowed where they arched down under his temples, and they ended in thin curls just in front of his ears. His mustache had natural twirls and he never disturbed it. He wore a yellow muffler this morning under his virile curly beard. His mackinaw coat was of huge orange and purple checks. His mackinaw pants were sober-seeming, having tan and light gray checks, but some small crimson dots and crosses brightened them. Green wool socks showed above his black boots, which had buckskin laces and big brass eyelets and hooks. And he wore striped mittens of white and plum color. Paul Bunyon was a gorgeous picture this morning in the frozen fields and forests, all covered with blue snow which sparkled in a pale gold light.

That day and the next, and for five more days, he searched in vain for Niagara; and neither did he see any moose herds in the woods. Only the frost crackles broke the silences of the deserted blue forests. And at last Paul Bunyon returned to his cave, feeling depressed and lonely. He had not thought that the companionship of Niagara could mean so much to him. In his mood of depression he forgot his hunger and made no further effort to find food.

Lonely Paul Bunyon lay sleepless in his blankets this night, his eyes gleaming through hedgelike eyelashes as their gaze restlessly followed the red flares that shot from the fire and streaked the walls and roof of the cave. He did not realize that his first creative idea was now struggling for birth. He could yet feel no shape of it. He was only conscious of an unaccustomed turmoil of mind. Wearied with fruitless thought, he at last fell into a doze. But Paul Bunyon was not fated to sleep this night. A sustained crashing roar, as of the splintering of millions of timbers, brought him up suddenly; it was hushed for a short second; then a thudding boom sounded from Tonnere Bay. Paul Bunyon leaped to the cave door, and in the moonlight he saw a white wave of water rolling over the blue beach. It came near to the cave before it stopped and receded. He pulled on his boots, and two strides brought him down to the bay. It had been covered with ice seven feet thick, and the cakes of this broken ice were now tossing on heaving waters. Now Paul Bunyon saw two ears show sometimes above the billows; they were of the shape of moose ears, but enormous as his two forefingers. Paul Bunyon waded out into the waters, and he reached these ears a mile from shore. He seized them without fear and he lifted . . . now a head with closed eyes appeared . . . shoulders and forelegs . . . body and hips . . . rear legs and curled tail. It was a calf, newborn apparently, though it was of such a size that Paul Bunyon had to use both arms to carry it.

"*Nom d'un nom!*" exclaimed Paul Bunyon. "*Pauvre petite bleue bête!*"

For this great baby calf was of a bright blue hue which was neither darker nor lighter than the color of the beautiful strange snow. A blue baby ox calf. For such was its sex. Its ears drooped pitifully, and its scrawny, big-jointed legs hung limply below Paul Bunyon's arms. A spasmodic shiver ran from its head to its tail, and its savior was glad to feel this shiver, for it showed that life remained. Paul Bunyon was touched with a tenderness that drove out his loneliness. "*Ma bête,*" he said. "*Mon cher bleu bébé ausha.*"

He turned back through the waters, and the ice cakes pounded each other into bits as they rolled together in his wake. In thirty seconds Paul Bunyon was back in his cave. He spread out his blankets in front of the fire, and he laid Bébé upon them.

Through the night Paul Bunyon worked over the blue ox calf, nursing him back to warm life; and in the morning Bébé was breathing regularly and seemed to rest. Paul Bunyon leaned over to hear his exhalations, and the blue ox calf suddenly opened his mouth and caressed Paul Bunyon's neck with his tongue. Paul Bunyon then discovered that he was ticklish in this region, for the caress impelled him to roll and laugh. The serious student Paul Bunyon had never laughed before; and he now enjoyed the new pleasure to the utmost.

"*Eh, Bébé!*" he chuckled. "*Eh, Bébé! Sacré bleu! Bon bleu, mon cher!*" Bébé raised his eyelids with astonishment upon hearing this cave-shaking chuckle, revealing large, bulging orbs which were of even a heavenlier blue than his silken hair. Such affection and intelligence shone in his eyes that Paul Bunyon wished he would keep

his eyes opened. But Bébé was weary and weak, and he closed them again.

He is hungry, thought Paul Bunyon; and he went out to find him food. None of the animals he knew about could supply milk for such a calf as this blue Bébé. But he was newborn and his parents should be somewhere in the neighborhood. Paul Bunyon stepped up on the cliff over which Bébé had bounced when he fell into Tonnere Bay. From here a wide swath of smashed timber ran straight up the side of the tallest Northern mountain. It was here that Bébé had made his thunderous roll of the night before.

Six strides brought Paul Bunyon to the mountain-top. One of its jagged peaks was broken off, showing where Bébé had stumbled over it and fallen. Then Paul Bunyon followed the calf tracks down the land side of the mountain. For two hours he trailed them, but they grew fainter as he went on, and in the Big Bay country the last fall of the blue snow had covered them. Paul Bunyon now had no doubt that Bébé's mother had been frightened by the strange color of the snow and that his blueness was a birthmark. Like Niagara and the fauna of the forest, the parents had stampeded, forgetting the little one. It was no use to search for them.

Paul Bunyon circled back through the forest and gathered a great load of moose moss before he returned to the cave. This rich food would meet the lack of milk. Bébé was asleep before the fireplace when Paul Bunyon returned, and he still slumbered while his friend prepared him some moose moss soup. But when a kettle full of steaming odorous food was set before him, he opened his eyes with amazing energy and sat up. It was then that Bébé first showed the depth and circumference of his natural appetite, an appetite which was to have its effect on history. He drank most of the moose moss soup at three gulps, he seized the rim of the kettle in his teeth and tilted it up until even the last ten gallons were drained out of it; then, looking roguishly at Paul Bunyon the while, he bit off a large section of the kettle rim and chewed it down, switching his pretty tail to show his enjoyment.

"Eh, Bébé!" roared Paul Bunyon, doubling up with laughter for the second time in his life. And he praised the blue snow for giving him such a creature, and did not mourn Niagara, who had never been amusing. But now, as Paul Bunyon doubled over for another rare roar of laughter, he got one more surprise. He was struck with terrific force from the rear and knocked flat. Paul Bunyon hit the cave floor so hard that its walls were shaken, and a cloud of stones dropped from the roof, covering him from his hips to his thighs. Paul Bunyon dug himself out with no displeasure. He was marveling too much to be wrathful.

There is strength in this baby animal, he thought; surely he has the muscle and energy for great deeds; for that was such a tremendous butting he gave me that I am more comfortable standing than sitting. So he stood and admired this strong and energetic ox calf, who was calmly seated on his haunches before the fireplace, now throwing his head to the right as he licked his right shoulder, now throwing his head to the left as he licked his left shoulder. While Paul Bunyon admired, he pondered; then, even as Bébé had given him his first laugh, the ox calf now showed him the outline of his first real idea. The thought struck him that his student's life was finally over; there was nothing more for him to learn; there was everything for him to do. The hour for action was at hand.

Indeed, if he was to keep this blue ox calf, action was truly necessary. Bébé had shown that his superabundance of vitality made him dangerous as well as delightful and amusing. This inexhaustible energy of his must be put to work; this vast store of

power in an ox-hide should be developed and harnessed to give reality to some one of Paul Bunyon's vague dreams.

Soon the well-fed blue ox calf lay down and slept contentedly. But Paul Bunyon did not sleep. One after another, occupations, enterprises and industries which would be worthy of his knowledge and his extraordinary mental and physical powers, and which would also offer labor great enough for Bébé when he was grown, were considered by Paul Bunyon; but nothing that he thought about satisfied him in the least. Certainly he would have to invent something new; and as he thought of invention, his imagination blazed up like a fire in a dry forest. He was so unused to it that it got out of control, and its smoky flames hid his idea rather than illuminating it.

Wearied at last, he lay on his side, for he remembered his bruises, and he fell into a troubled doze. Now he dreamed and saw great blazing letters which formed the words REAL AMERICA. He sat up, and his bruises gave him such sudden pain that the dream vanished utterly. But he dreamed again before morning. In this second dream he saw no words, but a forest. A flame like a scythe blade sheared through the trees and they fell. Then Paul Bunyon saw in his dream a forest of stumps, and trees were fallen among them.

For many days Paul Bunyon thought about these dreams as he gathered moose moss for Bébé and seined fish from the bay for himself. And for many nights he tried to dream again, but his sleep was the untroubled sleep of the weary.

Bébé grew wonderfully as the weeks went by, and the moose moss made him saucy as well as fat. His bulging blue eyes got a jovial look that was never to leave them. His bellow already had bass tones in it. He would paw and snort and lift his tail as vigorously as any ordinary ox ten times his age. His chest deepened, his back widened, muscle-masses began to swell and quiver under the fat of his shoulders and haunches. The drifts of the beautiful unnatural snow melted away in streams of blue water, and the marvelous color of this historical winter vanished, but the glittering blue of Bébé's silken hair remained. His tail brush was of a darker blue; it looked like a heavily foliaged cypress bough in purple twilight; and Bébé was proud of this wonderful tail brush that belonged to him, for he would twist it from behind him and turn his head and stare at it by the hour.

Now spring came and Paul Bunyon determined to start out with his blue ox calf and try to find the meanings of his dreams. The bright warm hours of these days gave him a tormenting physical restlessness; and his imagination ranged through a thousand lands, playing over a thousand activities. It was certainly the time to begin a Life Work.

Each day Paul Bunyon pondered his two dreams without finding substantial meaning in them. The first one indicated that he should go to Real America; and this Paul Bunyon finally resolved to do, hoping that he would discover the Work that was meant for him and the blue ox calf. He knew that he could not fare worse in that land, for few of the fauna of his native country had returned with the spring, and Paul Bunyon could not live well on a fish diet. Bébé's growing appetite, too, made some move a necessity, for the blue snow had killed the moose grass, and moose moss was a dry food without nourishment in the summer. The more Paul Bunyon thought about Real America, the better he liked the idea of going there. Moose and grass, at least, were to be found across the Border. And no doubt Real America was his Land of Opportunity.

So one fine day Paul Bunyon and Bébé came down to the Border. The blue ox calf frolicked with his master and bellowed happily when he saw the green grass and clover on the hills of Real America. He was for rushing over at once, but Paul Bunyon, the student, was not unmindful of his duty to his new country; he would not enter it without fitting ceremonies and pledges, though Bébé butted him soundly in resenting the delay.

Now Paul Bunyon lifted his hands solemnly and spoke in the rightful language of Real America.

"In becoming a Real American, I became Paul *Bunyan*," he declared. "I am Paul *Bunyon* no more. Even so shall my blue ox calf be called Babe, and Bébé no longer. We are now Real Americans both, hearts, souls and hides."

After uttering these words with feeling and solemnity, an emotion more expansive, more uplifting and more inspiring than any he had ever known possessed Paul Bunyan and transfigured him. His chest swelled, his eyes danced and glittered, and his cheeks shone rosily through the black curls of his beard.

"And I'm glad of it!" he roared. "By the holy old mackinaw, and by the hell-jumping, high-tailed, fuzzy-eared, whistling old jeem cris and seventeen slippery saints, I'm *proud* of it, too! Gloriously proud!"

Then he felt amazed beyond words that the simple fact of entering Real America and becoming a Real American could make him feel so exalted, so pure, so noble, so good. And an indomitable conquering spirit had come to him also. He now felt that he could whip his weight in wildcats, that he could pull the clouds out of the sky, or chew up stones, or tell the whole world anything.

"Since becoming a Real American," roared Paul Bunyon, "I can look any man straight in the eye and tell him to go to hell! If I could meet a man of my own size, I'd prove this instantly. We may find such a man and celebrate our naturalization in a Real American manner. We shall see. Yay, Babe!"

Then the two great Real Americans leaped over the Border. Freedom and Inspiration and Uplift were in the very air of this country, and Babe and Paul Bunyan got more noble feelings in every breath. They were greatly exhilarated physically at first; and they galloped over valleys and hills without looking about them, but only breathing this soul-flushing air and roaring and bellowing their delight in it.

But before the day was over, Paul Bunyan discovered that Real America had its sober, matter-of-fact side also. A whisper stirred in his heart: "To work! Take advantage of your opportunity!" The whisper got louder and more insistent every moment; and at last the idea it spoke possessed Paul Bunyan, and he sat down to ponder it, letting Babe graze and roll on the clover-covered hills.

Now the whisper became an insistent cry: "Work! Work! Work!" Paul Bunyan looked up, and he seemed to see the word shining among the clouds; he looked down then into the vast valley, and he seemed to see—by the holy old mackinaw! he did see—the forest of his second dream! And now he knew it: his Life Work was to begin here.

For many days and nights Paul Bunyan pondered on the hillside before the Great Idea came to him. Like all Great Ideas, it was simple enough, once he had thought of it. Real America was covered with forests. A forest was composed of trees. A felled and trimmed tree was a log. Paul Bunyan threw aside his pine tree beard brush and jumped to his feet with a great shout.

"What greater work could be done in Real America than to make logs from trees?" he cried. "Logging! I shall invent this industry and make it the greatest

one of all time! I shall become a figure as admired in history as any of the great ones I have read about."

Paul Bunyan then delivered his first oration. The blue ox calf was his only listener; and this was a pity, for Paul Bunyan's first oratorical effort, inspired as it was, surely was one of his noblest ones. But we know the outline of this oration, if not the words. It dealt mainly with the logging method which he had devised in the moment, the one which he used in his first work. So he told of his plan to uproot the trees by hand, and to transport the logs overland, binding a bundle of them on one side of Babe, and hanging a sack of rocks from the other side for ballast. It was months after this that he made his first improvement, the using of a second bundle of logs, instead of rocks, for ballast. And at this moment Paul Bunyan, for all his foresight and imagination, could not have dreamed of the superb tools and marvelous logging methods that he was to originate, or of the countless crews of little loggers that he was to import from France, Ireland, Scotland and Scandinavia, or of the tremendous river drives and the mammoth camp life he was to create. He would have been bewildered then by the fact that he would some day need a foreman as grand as himself for his Life Work; and the notion that he would some day need help in his figuring would have seemed like a far-fetched jest.

No; in this first oration, imaginative and eloquent as it must have been, Paul Bunyan only spoke of simple work for himself and Babe. But he only tells us that the oration was not a long one, for the call to Work came more insistently as he ended each period. At last he had to answer this powerful call. He commanded, "Yay, Babe!" and the baby blue ox and Paul Bunyan descended into the valley to begin the first logging in the Real American woods.

Paul's Wife

by Robert Frost

Very few of the Paul Bunyan stories even suggest that the giant lumber-jack had a domestic life. Life in the woods was strongly masculine, and the average logger enjoyed the society of women only when he came to town after the spring drives were over. Thus the unique feature of Frost's tale is that the poet introduced a bit of romance into Paul Bunyan's life. But he preserved the flavor of the saga by having the hero saw his wife out of a white-pine log.

To drive Paul out of any lumber camp
All that was needed was to say to him,
'How is the wife, Paul?'—and he'd disappear.
Some said it was because he had no wife,
And hated to be twitted on the subject.
Others because he'd come within a day
Or so of having one, and then been jilted.
Others because he'd had one once, a good one,
Who'd run away with some one else and left him.
And others still because he had one now
He only had to be reminded of,—
He was all duty to her in a minute:
He had to run right off to look her up,
As if to say, 'That's so, how is my wife?
I hope she isn't getting into mischief.'
No one was anxious to get rid of Paul.
He'd been the hero of the mountain camps
Ever since, just to show them, he had slipped
The bark of a whole tamarack off whole,
As clean as boys do off a willow twig
To make a willow whistle on a Sunday
In April by subsiding meadow brooks.
They seemed to ask him just to see him go,
'How is the wife, Paul?' and he always went.
He never stopped to murder anyone
Who asked the question. He just disappeared—
Nobody knew in what direction,
Although it wasn't usually long
Before they heard of him in some new camp,
The same Paul at the same old feats of logging.

The question everywhere was why should Paul
Object to being asked a civil question—
A man you could say almost anything to
Short of a fighting word. You have the answers.
And there was one more not so fair to Paul:
That Paul had married a wife not his equal.
Paul was ashamed of her. To match a hero,
She would have had to be a heroine;
Instead of which she was some half-breed squaw.
But if the story Murphy told was true,
She wasn't anything to be ashamed of.

You know Paul could do wonders. Everyone's
Heard how he thrashed the horses on a load
That wouldn't budge until they simply stretched
Their rawhide harness from the load to camp.
Paul told the boss the load would be all right,
'The sun will bring your load in'—and it did—
By shrinking the rawhide to natural length.
That's what is called a stretcher. But I guess
The one about his jumping so's to land
With both his feet at once against the ceiling,
And then land safely right side up again,
Back on the floor, is fact or pretty near fact.
Well this is such a yarn. Paul sawed his wife
Out of a white-pine log. Murphy was there,
And, as you might say, saw the lady born.
Paul worked at anything in lumbering.
He'd been hard at it taking boards away
For—I forget—the last ambitious sawyer
To want to find out if he couldn't pile
The lumber on Paul till Paul begged for mercy.
They'd sliced the first slab off a big butt log,
And the sawyer had slammed the carriage back
To slam end on again against the saw teeth.
To judge them by the way they caught themselves
When they saw what had happened to the log,
They must have had a guilty expectation
Something was going to go with their slambanging.
Something had left a broad black streak of grease
On the new wood the whole length of the log
Except, perhaps, a foot at either end.
But when Paul put his finger in the grease,
It wasn't grease at all, but a long slot.
The log was hollow. They were sawing pine.
'First time I ever saw a hollow pine.
That comes of having Paul around the place.

Take it to hell for me,' the sawyer said.
Everyone had to have a look at it,
And tell Paul what he ought to do about it.
(They treated it as his.) 'You take a jack-knife,
And spread the opening, and you've got a dug-out
All dug to go a-fishing in.' To Paul
The hollow looked too sound and clean and empty
Ever to have housed birds or beasts or bees.
There was no entrance for them to get in by.
It looked to him like some new kind of hollow
He thought he'd *better* take his jack-knife to.
So after work that evening he came back
And let enough light into it by cutting
To see if it was empty. He made out in there
A slender length of pith, or was it pith?
It might have been the skin a snake had cast
And left stood up on end inside the tree
The hundred years the tree must have been growing.
More cutting and he had this in both hands,
And, looking from it to the pond near by,
Paul wondered how it would respond to water.
Not a breeze stirred, but just the breath of air
He made in walking slowly to the beach
Blew it once off his hands and almost broke it.
He laid it at the edge where it could drink.
At the first drink it rustled and grew limp.
At the next drink it grew invisible.
Paul dragged the shallows for it with his fingers,
And thought it must have melted. It was gone.
And then beyond the open water, dim with midges,
Where the log drive lay pressed against the boom,
It slowly rose a person, rose a girl,
Her wet hair heavy on her like a helmet,
Who, leaning on a log looked back at Paul.
And that made Paul in turn look back
To see if it was anyone behind him
That she was looking at instead of him.
Murphy had been there watching all the time,
But from a shed where neither of them could see him
There was a moment of suspense in birth
When the girl seemed too water-logged to live,
Before she caught her first breath with a gasp
And laughed. Then she climbed slowly to her feet,
And walked off talking to herself or Paul
Across the logs like backs of alligators,
Paul taking after her around the pond,

Next evening Murphy and some other fellows
Got drunk, and tracked the pair up Catamount,
From the bare top of which there is a view
To other hills across a kettle valley.
And there, well after dark, let Murphy tell it,
They saw Paul and his creature keeping house.
It was the only glimpse that anyone
Has had of Paul and her since Murphy saw them
Falling in love across the twilight mill-pond.
More than a mile across the wilderness
They sat together half-way up a cliff
In a small niche let into it, the girl
Brightly, as if a star played on the place,
Paul darkly, like her shadow. All the light
Was from the girl herself, though, not from a star,
As was apparent from what happened next.
All those great ruffians put their throats together,
And let out a loud yell, and threw a bottle,
As a brute tribute of respect to beauty.
Of course the bottle fell short by a mile,
But the shout reached the girl and put her light out,
She went out like a firefly, and that was all.

So there were witnesses that Paul was married,
And not to anyone to be ashamed of.
Everyone had been wrong in judging Paul.
Murphy told me Paul put on all those airs
About his wife to keep her to himself.
Paul was what's called a terrible possessor.
Owning a wife with him meant owning her.
She wasn't anybody else's business,
Either to praise her, or so much as name her,
And he'd thank people not to think of her.
Murphy's idea was that a man like Paul
Wouldn't be spoken to about a wife
In any way the world knew how to speak.

The Birth of John Henry

by Roark Bradford

The natal day of all heroes, both historical and imaginary, is usually one of miracles. The skies and elements combine to make the event memorable, animals do marvelous things, and human beings suddenly become clairvoyant. In his account of the birth of John Henry, the "natchal man" who became a phenomenal steel-driver, Bradford skillfully used this atmosphere and at the same time emphasized the abnormal size and appetite of his gargantuan baby. John Henry, of course, does not need to go through the usual experiences of infancy. After his hunger has been heartily appeased, he is ready for his lifework. This tale is the opening chapter of John Henry *(1931).*

Now John Henry was a man, but he's long dead.

The night John Henry was born the moon was copper-colored and the sky was black. The stars wouldn't shine and the rain fell hard. Forked lightning cleaved the air and the earth trembled like a leaf. The panthers squalled in the brake like a baby and the Mississippi River ran upstream a thousand miles. John Henry weighed forty-four pounds.

John Henry was born on the banks of the Black River, where all good rousterbouts come from. He came into the world with a cotton-hook for a right hand and a river song on his tongue:

Looked up and down de river,
    Twice as far as I could see.
Seed befo' I gits to be twenty-one,
    De Anchor Line gonter b'long to
        me, Lawd, Lawd,
    Anchor Line gonter b'long to me.

They didn't know what to make of John Henry when he was born. They looked at him and then went and looked at the river.

"He got a bass voice like a preacher," his mamma said.

"He got shoulders like a cotton-rollin' rousterbout," his papa said.

"He got blue gums like a conjure man," the nurse woman said.

"I might preach some," said John

Henry, "but I ain't gonter be no preacher. I might roll cotton on de boats, but I ain't gonter be no cotton-rollin' rousterbout. I might got blue gums like a conjure man, but I ain't gonter git familiar wid de sperits. 'Cause my name is John Henry, and when fo'ks call me by my name, dey'll know I'm a natchal man."

"His name is John Henry," said his mamma. "Hit's a fack."

"And when you calls him by his name," said his papa, "he's a natchal man."

So about that time John Henry raised up and stretched. "Well," he said, "ain't hit about supper-time?"

"Sho hit's about supper-time," said his mamma.

"And after," said his papa.

"And long after," said the nurse woman.

"Well," said John Henry, "did de dogs had they supper?"

"They did," said his mamma.

"All de dogs," said his papa.

"Long since," said the nurse woman.

"Well, den," said John Henry, "ain't I as good as de dogs?"

And when John Henry said that he got mad. He reared back in his bed and broke out the slats. He opened his mouth and yowled, and it put out the lamp. He cleaved his tongue and spat, and it put out the fire. "Don't make me mad!" said John Henry, and the thunder rumbled and rolled. "Don't let me git mad on de day I'm bawn, 'cause I'm skeered of my own-se'f when I gits mad."

And John Henry stood up in the middle of the floor and he told them what he wanted to eat. "Bring me four ham bones and a pot full of cabbages," he said. "Bring me a bait of turnip greens tree-top tall, and season hit down wid a side er middlin'. Bring me a pone er cold cawn bread and some hot potlicker to wash hit down. Bring me two hog jowls and a kittleful er whippowill peas. Bring me a skilletful er red-hot biscuits and a big jugful er cane molasses. 'Cause my name is John Henry, and I'll see you soon."

So John Henry walked out of the house and away from the Black River country where all good rousterbouts are born.

Ossawatomie

by Carl Sandburg

John Brown has not only appealed to the folk imagination but has attracted writers and artists. One remembers the grandiose figure, holding a Bible in one hand and a rifle in the other, in the mural by John Steuart Curry. In "Ossawatomie," Sandburg in a few terse lines has suggested the vitality and the strength of the Brown legend.

I don't know how he came,
Shambling, dark, and strong.

He stood in the city and told men:
My people are fools, my people are young and strong,
    my people must learn, my people are terrible
    workers and fighters.
Always he kept on asking: Where did that blood come from?

They said: You for the fool killer,
        you for the booby hatch
        and a necktie party.

They hauled him into jail.
They sneered at him and spit on him,
And he wrecked their jails,
Singing, "God damn your jails,"
And when he was most in jail
Crummy among the crazy in the dark
Then he was most of all out of jail
Shambling, dark, and strong,
Always asking: Where did that blood come from?

They laid hands on him
And the fool killers had a laugh
And the necktie party was a go, by God.
They laid hands on him and he was a goner.
    They hammered him to pieces and he stood up.
They buried him and he walked out of the grave, by God,
    Asking again: Where did that blood come from?

The Statue of Old Andrew Jackson

by Vachel Lindsay

Few American poets have been more sensitive to the literary possibilities of folklore than Lindsay. His lineage included no New England strains, and he was proud of his claim to Indian and possibly Spanish forebears. He constantly found subjects for his verse in the heroes of the American scene, just as he introduced cakewalks, chanteys, revival hymns, and jazz effects into his prosody. A member of the Disciples of Christ Church himself, he praised its founder, Alexander Campbell, and he found in John Chapman (Johnny Appleseed) a genuine apostle to the wilderness. In his work he celebrated John L. Sullivan and General William Booth, Pocahontas and Mark Twain, Governor John P. Altgeld of Illinois, Jackson and Lincoln and William Jennings Bryan. His tributes to these heroes seldom picture them as historical figures alone. Instead they take on the stature of mythical champions whose real fame is inextricably mixed with accreted legend. Thus, Lincoln is the ghost of a prairie lawyer walking the streets at midnight; Jackson steps away from his equestrian statue as a demonic warrior; and Bryan comes charging from a remote West inhabited by fabulous animals. Lindsay found support for these interpretations in the folk reputations of his heroes. But he also contributed to the extension of the fame of these figures, and his art benefited by the inclusion of their unhistorical attributes.

Andrew Jackson was eight feet tall.
His arm was a hickory limb and a maul.
His sword was so long he dragged it on the ground.
Every friend was an equal. Every foe was a hound.

Andrew Jackson was a Democrat,
Defying kings in his old cocked hat.
His vast steed rocked like a hobby-horse.
But he sat straight up. He held his course.

He licked the British at Noo Orleans;
Beat them out of their elegant jeans.
He piled the cotton-bales twenty feet high,
And he snorted "freedom," and it flashed from his eye.

And the American Eagle swooped through the air,
And cheered when he heard the Jackson swear:—
"By the Eternal, let them come.
Sound Yankee Doodle. Let the bullets hum."

And his wild men, straight from the woods, fought on
Till the British fops were dead and gone.

And now old Andrew Jackson fights
To set the sad big world to rights.
He joins the British and the French.
He cheers up the Italian trench.
He's making Democrats of these,
And freedom's sons of Japanese.
His hobby horse will gallop on
Till all the infernal Huns are gone.

Yes,
Yes,
Yes!
By the Eternal!
Old Andrew Jackson!

The Apple-Barrel of Johnny Appleseed

by Vachel Lindsay

On the mountain peak, called 'Going-To-The-Sun,'
I saw gray Johnny Appleseed at prayer
Just as the sunset made the old earth fair.
Then darkness came; in an instant, like great smoke,
The sun fell down as though its great hoops broke
And dark rich apples, poured from the dim flame
Where the sun set, came rolling toward the peak,
A storm of fruit, a mighty cider-reek,
The perfume of the orchards of the world,
From apple-shadows: red and russet domes
That turned to clouds of glory and strange homes
Above the mountain tops for cloud-born souls:—
Reproofs for men who build the world like moles,
Models for men, if they would build the world
As Johnny Appleseed would have it done—
Praying, and reading the books of Swedenborg
On the mountain top called 'Going-To-The-Sun.

Bryan, Bryan, Bryan, Bryan

by Vachel Lindsay

I

In a nation of one hundred fine, mob-hearted, lynching, relenting,
repenting millions,
There are plenty of sweeping, swinging, stinging, gorgeous things to shout
about,
And knock your old blue devils out.

I brag and chant of Bryan, Bryan, Bryan,
Candidate for president who sketched a silver Zion,
The one American Poet who could sing outdoors,
He brought in tides of wonder, of unprecedented splendor,
Wild roses from the plains, that made hearts tender,
All the funny circus silks
Of politics unfurled,
Bartlett pears of romance that were honey at the cores,
And torchlights down the street, to the end of the world.

There were truths eternal in the gab and tittle-tattle.
There were real heads broken in the fustian and the rattle.
There were real lines drawn:
Not the silver and the gold,

But Nebraska's cry went eastward against the dour and old,
The mean and cold.

It was eighteen ninety-six, and I was just sixteen
And Altgeld ruled in Springfield, Illinois,
When there came from the sunset Nebraska's shout of joy:
In a coat like a deacon, in a black Stetson hat
He scourged the elephant plutocrats
With barbed wire from the Platte.
The scales dropped from their mighty eyes.
They saw that summer's noon
A tribe of wonders coming
To a marching tune.

Oh, the longhorns from Texas,
The jay hawks from Kansas,
The plop-eyed bungaroo and giant giassicus,
The varmint, chipmunk, bugaboo,
The horned-toad, prairie-dog and ballyhoo,
From all the newborn states arow,
Bidding the eagles of the west fly on,
Bidding the eagles of the west fly on.
The fawn, prodactyl and thing-a-ma-jig,
The rakaboor, the hellangone,
The whangdoodle, batfowl and pig,
The coyote, wild-cat and grizzly in a glow,
In a miracle of health and speed, the whole breed abreast,
They leaped the Mississippi, blue border of the West,
From the Gulf to Canada, two thousand miles long:—
Against the towns of Tubal Cain,
Ah,—sharp was their song.
Against the towns of Tubal Cain, too cunning for the young,
The longhorn calf, the buffalo and wampus gave tongue.

These creatures were defending things Mark Hanna never dreamed:
The moods of airy childhood that in desert dews gleamed,
The gossamers and whimsies,
The monkeyshines and didoes
Rank and strange
Of the canyons and the range,
The ultimate fantastics
Of the far western slope,
And of prairie schooner children
Born beneath the stars,
Beneath falling snows,
Of the babies born at midnight
In the sod huts of lost hope,

With no physician there,
Except a Kansas prayer,
With the Indian raid a howling through the air.

And all these in their helpless days
By the dour East oppressed,
Mean paternalism
Making their mistakes for them,
Crucifying half the West,
Till the whole Atlantic coast
Seemed a giant spiders' nest.

And these children and their sons
At last rode through the cactus,
A cliff of mighty cowboys
On the lope,
With gun and rope.
And all the way to frightened Maine the old East heard them call,
And saw our Bryan by a mile lead the wall
Of men and whirling flowers and beasts,
The bard and the prophet of them all.
Prairie avenger, mountain lion,
Bryan, Bryan, Bryan, Bryan,
Gigantic troubadour, speaking like a siege gun,
Smashing Plymouth Rock with his boulders from the West,
And just a hundred miles behind, tornadoes piled across the sky,
Blotting out sun and moon,
A sign on high.

Headlong, dazed and blinking in the weird green light,
The scalawags made moan,
Afraid to fight.

II

When Bryan came to Springfield, and Altgeld gave him greeting,
Rochester was deserted, Divernon was deserted,
Mechanicsburg, Riverton, Chickenbristle, Cotton Hill,
Empty: for all Sangamon drove to the meeting—
In silver-decked racing cart,
Buggy, buckboard, carryall,
Carriage, phaeton, whatever would haul,
And silver-decked farm-wagons gritted, banged and rolled,
With the new tale of Bryan by the iron tires told.

The State House loomed afar,
A speck, a hive, a football,

A captive balloon!
And the town was all one spreading wing of bunting, plumes, and sun-
    shine,
Every rag and flag, and Bryan picture sold,
When the rigs in many a dusty line
Jammed our streets at noon,
And joined the wild parade against the power of gold.

We roamed, we boys from High School,
With mankind,
While Springfield gleamed,
Silk-lined.
Oh, Tom Dines, and Art Fitzgerald,
And the gangs that they could get!
I can hear them yelling yet.
Helping the incantation,
Defying aristocracy,
With every bridle gone,
Ridding the world of the low down mean,
Bidding the eagles of the West fly on,
Bidding the eagles of the West fly on,
We were bully, wild and woolly,
Never yet curried below the knees.
We saw flowers in the air,
Fair as the Pleiades, bright as Orion,
—Hopes of all mankind,
Made rare, resistless, thrice refined.
Oh, we bucks from every Springfield ward!
Colts of democracy—
Yet time-winds out of Chaos from the star-fields of the Lord.

The long parade rolled on. I stood by my best girl.
She was a cool young citizen, with wise and laughing eyes.
With my necktie by my ear, I was stepping on my dear,
But she kept like a pattern, without a shaken curl.
She wore in her hair a brave prairie rose.
Her gold chums cut her, for that was not the pose.
No Gibson Girl would wear it in that fresh way.
But we were fairy Democrats, and this was our day.

The earth rocked like the ocean, the sidewalk was a deck.
The houses for the moment were lost in the wide wreck.
And the bands played strange and stranger music as they trailed along.
Against the ways of Tubal Cain,
Ah, sharp was their song!
The demons in the bricks, the demons in the grass,
The demons in the bank-vaults peered out to see us pass,

And the angels in the trees, the angels in the grass,
The angels in the flags, peered out to see us pass.
And the sidewalk was our chariot, and the flowers bloomed higher,
And the street turned to silver and the grass turned to fire,
And then it was but grass, and the town was there again,
A place for women and men.

III

Then we stood where we could see
Every band,
And the speaker's stand.
And Bryan took the platform.
And he was introduced.
And he lifted his hand
And cast a new spell.
Progressive silence fell
In Springfield,
In Illinois,
Around the world.
Then we heard these glacial boulders across the prairie rolled:
"The people have a right to make their own mistakes . . .
You shall not crucify mankind
Upon a cross of gold."

And everybody heard him—
In the streets and State House yard.
And everybody heard him
In Springfield,
In Illinois,
Around and around and around the world,
That danced upon its axis
And like a darling broncho whirled.

IV

July, August, suspense.
Wall Street lost to sense.
August, September, October,
More suspense,
And the whole East down like a wind-smashed fence.

Then Hanna to the rescue,
Hanna of Ohio,
Rallying the roller-tops,
Rallying the bucket-shops.
Threatening drouth and death,

Promising manna,
Rallying the trusts against the bawling flannelmouth;
Invading misers' cellars,
Tin-cans, socks,
Melting down the rocks,
Pouring out the long green to a million workers,
Spondulix by the mountain-load, to stop each new tornado,
And beat the cheapskate, blatherskite,
Populistic, anarchistic,
Deacon—desperado.

V

Election night at midnight:
Boy Bryan's defeat.
Defeat of western silver.
Defeat of the wheat.
Victory of letterfiles
And plutocrats in miles
With dollar signs upon their coats,
Diamond watchchains on their vests
And spats on their feet.
Victory of custodians,
Plymouth Rock,
And all that inbred landlord stock.
Victory of the neat.
Defeat of the aspen groves of Colorado valleys,
The blue bells of the Rockies,
And blue bonnets of old Texas,
By the Pittsburg alleys.
Defeat of alfalfa and the Mariposa lily.
Defeat of the Pacific and the long Mississippi.
Defeat of the young by the old and silly.
Defeat of tornadoes by the poison vats supreme.
Defeat of my boyhood, defeat of my dream.

VI

Where is McKinley, that respectable McKinley,
The man without an angle or a tangle,
Who soothed down the city man and soothed down the farmer,
The German, the Irish, the Southerner, the Northerner,
Who climbed every greasy pole, and slipped through every crack;
Who soothed down the gambling hall, the bar-room, the church,
The devil vote, the angel vote, the neutral vote,
The desperately wicked, and their victims on the rack,

The gold vote, the silver vote, the brass vote, the lead vote,
Every vote? . . .

Where is McKinley, Mark Hanna's McKinley,
His slave, his echo, his suit of clothes?
Gone to join the shadows, with the pomps of that time,
And the flame of that summer's prairie rose.

Where is Cleveland whom the Democratic platform
Read from the party in a glorious hour,
Gone to join the shadows with pitchfork Tillman,
And sledge-hammer Altgeld who wrecked his power.

Where is Hanna, bulldog Hanna.
Low-browed Hanna, who said: "Stand pat"?
Gone to his place with old Pierpont Morgan.
Gone somewhere . . . with lean rat Platt.

Where is Roosevelt, the young dude cowboy,
Who hated Bryan, then aped his way?
Gone to join the shadows with mighty Cromwell
And tall King Saul, till the Judgment day.

Where is Altgeld, brave as the truth,
Whose name the few still say with tears?
Gone to join the ironies with Old John Brown,
Whose fame rings loud for a thousand years.

Where is that boy, that Heaven-born Bryan,
That Homer Bryan, who sang from the West?
Gone to join the shadows with Altgeld the Eagle,
Where the kings and the slaves and the troubadours rest.

IX

YANKEES

The Yankee is the oldest character type in American drama. Ever since 1787, when Royall Tyler introduced a servant named Jonathan into his comedy *The Contrast*, the Yankee has been a familiar figure on the American stage. Numerous audiences recognized and enjoyed the salty countryman, coarsely dressed, crude in manners, naïve and uncultivated, but shrewd in practical matters and a hard bargainer. Interpreted by actors like Hill and Marble he was distinctly original. As Constance Rourke observed, "No character precisely like him had appeared before in the realm of the imagination." But the Yankee also existed in real life— plain, honest, freshly idiomatic in speech, usually reticent but occasionally garrulous and even oracular. This was the figure who was soon to be reflected in other forms of literature. Seba Smith's famous Jack Downing not only caught the popular favor but stimulated many imitations. Lowell captured Yankee idiom and thought in *The Biglow Papers*. Sketches of Yankee husbandmen appear in the pages of Emerson and Thoreau and flavor the New England local-color sketches of the later nineteenth century. Mrs. Stowe's Sam Lawson is in the main tradition, as are the storytellers created by Rowland E. Robinson and George Wasson. But the Yankee of these folk tales is a more fully rounded character than his stage cousin, and he no longer occupies a subordinate position. He is often both protagonist and narrator. He remains shrewd and blunt, but he is also humorous, whimsical, imaginative. He is full of weather lore, local superstitions, regional traditions, and he relishes tall tales. Probably he even half believes the ghost stories and supernatural incidents which his reason teaches him to reject. The Yankee is indeed an American original and probably has contributed the most important lineaments to our national type-symbol, Uncle Sam.

The Courtin'

by James Russell Lowell

Few writers have used dialect more skillfully and more successfully than Lowell. Whether he was expressing the New England aversion to the Mexican War through the mouth of a Yankee rustic or simply telling a folk idyl, he transcribed carefully the illiteracies, the nasal pronunciation, and the country idioms. Particularly effective is the account of a rural courtship in which a shy maiden and a bashful suitor have difficulty in reaching an understanding. Here country manners and folk speech are genuinely complementary.

God makes sech nights, all white an'
    still
  Fur'z you can look or listen,
Moonshine an' snow on field an' hill,
  All silence an' all glisten.

Zekle crep' up quite unbeknown
  An' peeked in thru' the winder,
An' there sot Huldy all alone,
  'ith no one nigh to hender.

A fireplace filled the room's one side
  With half a cord o' wood in—
There warn't no stoves (tell comfort died)
  To bake ye to a puddin'.

The wa'nut logs shot sparkles out
  Towards the pootiest, bless her,
An' leetle flames danced all about
  The chiny on the dresser.

Agin the chimbley crook-necks hung,
  An' in amongst 'em rusted
The ole queen's-arm thet gran'ther Young
  Fetched back f'om Concord busted.

The very room, coz sne was in,
  Seemed warm f'om floor to ceilin',
An' she looked full ez rosy agin
  Ez the apples she was peelin'.

'Twas kin' o' kingdom-come to look
  On sech a blessed cretur,
A dogrose blushin' to a brook
  Ain't modester nor sweeter.

He was six foot o' man, A 1,
  Clear grit an' human natur';
None couldn't quicker pitch a ton
  Nor dror a furrer straighter.

He'd sparked it with full twenty gals,
  Hed squired 'em, danced 'em, druv 'em,
Fust this one, an' then thet, by spells—
  All is, he couldn't love 'em.

But long o' her his veins 'ould run
  All crinkly like curled maple,
The side she breshed felt full o' sun
  Ez a south slope in Ap'il.

She thought no v'ice hed sech a swing
  Ez hisn in the choir;
My! when he made Ole Hunderd ring,
  She *knowed* the Lord was nigher.

An' she'd blush scarlit, right in prayer,
  When her new meetin'-bunnet
Felt somehow thru' its crown a pair
  O' blue eyes sot upun it.

Thet night, I tell ye, she looked *some!*
  She seemed to 've gut a new soul,
For she felt sartin-sure he'd come,
  Down to her very shoe-sole.

She heered a foot, an' knowed it tu,
  A-raspin' on the scraper,—
All ways to once her feelin's flew
  Like sparks in burnt-up paper.

He kin' o' l'itered on the mat,
  Some doubtfle o' the sekle,

His heart kep' goin' pity-pat,
But hern went pity Zekle.

An' yit she gin her cheer a jerk
Ez though she wished him furder,
An' on her apples kep' to work,
Parin' away like murder.

"You want to see my Pa, I s'pose?"
"Wal . . . no. . . . I come dasignin' "—
"To see my Ma? She's sprinklin' clo'es
Agin to-morrer's i'nin'."

To say why gals acts so or so,
Or don't, 'ould be persumin';
Mebby to mean *yes* an' say *no*
Comes nateral to women.

He stood a spell on one foot fust,
Then stood a spell on t'other,
An' on which one he felt the wust
He couldn't ha' told ye nuther.

Says he, "I'd better call agin";
Says she, "Think likely, Mister":
Thet last word pricked him like a pin,
An' . . . Wal, he up an' kist her.

When Ma bimeby upon 'em slips,
Huldy sot pale ez ashes,
All kin' o' smily roun' the lips
An' teary roun' the lashes.

For she was jes' the quiet kind
Whose naturs never vary,
Like streams that keep a summer mind
Snowhid in Jenooary.

The blood clost roun' her heart felt glued
Too tight for all expressin',
Tell mother see how metters stood,
An' gin 'em both her blessin'.

Then her red come back like the tide
Down to the Bay o' Fundy,
An' all I know is they was cried
In meetin' come nex' Sunday.

Sunthin' In the Pastoral Line

by James Russell Lowell

Once git a smell o' musk into a draw,
An' it clings hold like precerdents in law:
Your gra'ma'am put it there,—when, goodness knows,—
To jes' this-worldify her Sunday-clo'es;
But the old chist wun't sarve her gran'son's wife
(For, 'thout new funnitoor, wut good in life?),
An' so ole clawfoot, from the precinks dread
O' the spare chamber, slinks into the shed,
Where, dim with dust, it fust or last subsides
To holdin' seeds an' fifty things besides;
But better days stick fast in heart an' husk,
An' all you keep in't gits a scent o' musk.

Jes' so with poets: wut they've airly read
Gits kind o' worked into their heart an' head,
So's 't they can't seem to write but jest on sheers
With furrin countries or played-out ideers
Nor hev a feelin', ef it doosn't smack
O' wut some critter chose to feel 'way back:
This makes 'em talk o' daisies, larks, an' things,
Ez though we'd nothin' here that blows an' sings
(Why, I'd give more for one live bobolink
Than a square mile o' larks in printer's ink),—
This makes 'em think our fust o' May is May,
Which 'tain't, for all the almanicks can say.

O little city-gals, don't never go it
Blind on the word o' noospaper or poet!
They're apt to puff, an' May-day seldom looks
Up in the country ez 't doos in books;
They're no more like than hornets'-nests an' hives,
Or printed sarmons be to holy lives.
I, with my trouses perched on cowhide boots,
Tuggin' my foundered feet out by the roots,
Hev seen ye come to fling on April's hearse
Your muslin nosegays from the milliner's,
Puzzlin' to find dry ground your queen to choose,
An' dance your throats sore in morocker shoes:
I've seen ye an' felt proud, thet, come wut would,

Our Pilgrim stock wuz pethed with hardihood.
Pleasure doos make us Yankees kind o' winch,
Ez though 'twuz sunthin' paid for by the inch;
But yit we du contrive to worry thru,
Ef Dooty tells us thet the thing's to du,
An' kerry a hollerday, ef we set out,
Ez stiddily ez though 'twuz a redoubt.

I, country-born an' bred, know where to find
Some blooms thet make the season suit the mind,
An' seem to metch the doubtin' bluebird's notes,—
Half-vent'rin' liverworts in furry coats,
Bloodroots, whose rolled-up leaves ef you oncurl,
Each on 'em's cradle to a baby-pearl,—
But these are jes' Spring's pickets; sure ez sin,
The rebble frosts'll try to drive 'em in;
For half our May's so awfully like Mayn't,
'twould rile a Shaker or an evrige saint;
Though I own up I like our back'ard springs
Thet kind o' haggle with their greens an' things,
An' when you 'most give up, 'uthout more words
Toss the fields full o' blossoms, leaves, an' birds;
Thet's Northun natur', slow an' apt to doubt,
But when it *doos* git stirred, ther' 's no gin-out!

Fust come the blackbirds clatt'rin' in tall trees,
An' settlin' things in windy Congresses,—
Queer politicians, though, for I'll be skinned
Ef all on 'em don't head aginst the wind.
'fore long the trees begin to show belief,—
The maple crimsons to a coral-reef,
Then saffern swarms swing off from all the willers
So plump they look like yaller caterpillars,
Then gray hossches'nuts lettle hands unfold
Softer'n a baby's be at three days old:
Thet's robin-redbreast's almanick; he knows
Thet arter this ther' 's only blossom-snows;
So, choosin' out a handy crotch an' spouse,
He goes to plast'rin' his adobë house.

Then seems to come a hitch,—things lag behind,
Till some fine mornin' Spring makes up her mind,
An' ez, when snow-swelled rivers cresh their dams
Heaped-up with ice thet dovetails in an' jams
A leak comes spirtin' thru some pin-hole cleft,
Grows stronger, fercer, tears out right an' left,
Then all the waters bow themselves an' come,

Suddin, in one gret slope o' shedderin' foam,
Jes' so our Spring gits everythin' in tune
An' gives one leap from Aperl into June:
Then all comes crowdin' in; afore you think
Young oak-leaves mist the side-hill woods with pink;
The catbird in the laylock-bush is loud;
The orchards turn to heaps o' rosy cloud;
Red-cedars blossom tu, though few folks know it,
An' look all dipt in sunshine like a poet;
The lime-trees pile their solid stacks o' shade
An' drows'ly simmer with the bees' sweet trade;
In ellum-shrouds the flashin' hangbird clings
An' for the summer vy'ge his hammock slings;
All down the loose-walled lanes in archin' bowers
The barb'ry droops its strings o' golden flowers,
Whose shrinkin' hearts the school-gals love to try
With pins,—they'll worry yourn so, boys, bimeby!
But I don't love your cat'logue style,—do you?—
Ez ef to sell off Natur' by vendoo;
One word with blood in't 's twice ez good ez two:
'nuff sed, June's bridesman, poet o' the year,
Gladness on wings, the bobolink, is here;
Half-hid in tip-top apple-blooms he swings,
Or climbs aginst the breeze with quiverin' wings,
Or, givin' way to 't in a mock despair,
Runs down, a brook o' laughter, thru the air.

I ollus feel the sap start in my veins
In Spring, with curus heats an' prickly pains,
Thet drive me, when I git a chance, to walk
Off by myself to hev a privit talk
With a queer critter thet can't seem to 'gree
Along o' me like most folks,—Mister Me.
Ther' 's times when I'm unsoshle ez a stone,
An' sort o' suffercate to be alone,—
I'm crowded jes' to think thet folks are nigh,
An' can't bear nothin' closer than the sky;
Now the wind's full ez shifty in the mind
Ez wut it is ou'-doors, ef I ain't blind,
An' sometimes, in the fairest sou'west weather,
My innard vane points east for weeks together,
My natur' gits all goose-flesh, an' my sins
Come drizzlin' on my conscience sharp ez pins:
Wal, et sech times I jes' slip out o' sight
An' take it out in a fair stan'-up fight
With the one cuss I can't lay on the shelf,
The crook'dest stick in all the heap,—Myself.

'Twuz so las' Sabbath arter meetin'-time:
Findin' my feelin's wouldn't noways rhyme
With nobody's, but off the hendle flew
An' took things from an east-wind pint o' view,
I started off to lose me in the hills
Where the pines be, up back o' 'Siah's Mills:
Pines, ef you're blue, are the best friends I know,
They mope an' sigh an' sheer your feelin's so,—
They hesh the ground beneath so, tu, I swan,
You half-forgit you've gut a body on.
Ther' 's a small school'us' there where four roads meet,
The door-steps hollered out by little feet,
An' side-posts carved with names whose owners grew
To gret men, some on 'em, an' deacons, tu;
'taint used no longer, coz the town hez gut
A high-school, where they teach the Lord knows wut:
Three-story larnin' 's pop'lar now; I guess
We thriv' ez wal on jes' two stories less,
For it strikes me ther' 's sech a thing ez sinnin'
By overloadin' children's underpinnin':
Wal, here it wuz I larned my A B C,
An' it's a kind o' favorite spot with me.

We're curus critters: Now ain't jes' the minute
Thet ever fits us easy while we're in it;
Long ez 'twuz futur', 'twould be perfect bliss,—
Soon ez it's past, *thet* time's wuth ten o' this;
An' yet there ain't a man thet need be told
Thet Now's the only bird lays eggs o' gold.
A knee-high lad, I used to plot an' plan
An' think 'twuz life's cap-sheaf to be a man;
Now, gittin' gray, there's nothin' I enjoy
Like dreamin' back along into a boy:
So the ole school'us' is a place I choose
Afore all others, ef I want to muse;
I set down where I used to set, an' git
My boyhood back, an' better things with it,—
Faith, Hope, an' sunthin', ef it isn't Cherrity,
It's want o' guile, an' thet's ez gret a rerrity,
While Fancy's cushin', free to Prince and Clown,
Makes the hard bench ez soft ez milk-weed-down.

Now, 'fore I knowed, thet Sabbath arternoon
When I sot out to tramp myself in tune,
I found me in the school'us' on my seat,
Drummin' the march to No-where's with my feet.
Thinkin' o' nothin', I've heerd ole folks say

Is a hard kind o' dooty in its way:
It's thinkin' everythin' you ever knew,
Or ever hearn, to make your feelin's blue.
I sot there tryin' thet on for a spell:
I thought o' the Rebellion, then o' Hell,
Which some folks tell ye now is jest a metterfor
(A the'ry, p'raps, it wun't *feel* none the better for);
I thought o' Reconstruction, wut we'd win
Patchin' our patent self-blow-up agin:
I thought ef this 'ere milkin' o' the wits,
So much a month, warn't givin' Natur' fits,—
Ef folks warn't druv, findin' their own milk fail,
To work the cow thet hez an iron tail,
An' ef idees 'thout ripenin' in the pan
Would send up cream to humor ary man:
From this to thet I let my worryin' creep,
Till finally I must ha' fell asleep.

Our lives in sleep are some like streams thet glide
'twixt flesh an' sperrit boundin' on each side,
Where both shores' shadders kind o' mix an' mingle
In sunthin' thet ain't jes' like either single;
An' when you cast off moorin's from To-day,
An' down towards To-morrer drift away,
The imiges thet tengle on the stream
Make a new upside-down'ard world o' dream:
Sometimes they seem like sunrise-streaks an' warnin's
O' wut'll be in Heaven on Sabbath-mornin's,
An', mixed right in ez ef jest out o' spite,
Sunthin' thet says your supper ain't gone right.
I'm gret on dreams, an' often when I wake,
I've lived so much it makes my mem'ry ache,
An' can't skurce take a cat-nap in my cheer
'thout hevin' 'em, some good, some bad, all queer.

Now I wuz settin' where I'd ben, it seemed,
An' ain't sure yit whether I r'ally dreamed,
Nor, ef I did, how long I might ha' slep,
When I hearn some un stompin' up the step,
An' lookin' round, ef two an' two make four,
I see a Pilgrim Father in the door.
He wore a steeple-hat, tall boots, an' spurs
With rowels to 'em big ez ches'nut-burrs,
An' his gret sword behind him sloped away
Long 'z a man's speech thet dunno wut to say.—
"Ef your name's Biglow, an' your given-name
Hosee," sez he, "it's arter you I came;

I'm your gret-gran'ther multiplied by three."—
"My *wut?*" sez I.—"Your gret-gret-gret," sez he:
"You wouldn't ha never ben here but for me.
Two hundred an' three year ago this May
The ship I come in sailed up Boston Bay;
I'd been a cunnle in our Civil War,—
But wut on airth hev *you* gut up one for?
Coz we du things in England, 'tain't for you
To git a notion you can du 'em tu:
I'm told you write in public prints: ef true,
It's nateral you should know a thing or two."—
"Thet air's an argymunt I can't endorse,—
'twould prove, coz you wear spurs, you kep' a horse:
For brains," sez I, "wutever you may think,
Ain't boun' to cash the drafs o' pen-an'-ink,—
Though mos' folks write ez ef they hoped jes' quickenin'
The churn would argoo skim-milk into thickenin';
But skim-milk ain't a thing to change its view
O' wut it's meant for more'n a smoky flue.
But du pray tell me, 'fore we furder go,
How in all Natur' did you come to know
'bout our affairs," sez I, "in Kingdom-Come?"—
"Wal, I worked round at sperrit-rappin' some,
An' danced the tables till their legs wuz gone,
In hopes o' larnin' wut wuz goin' on,"
Sez he, "but mejums lie so like all-split
Thet I concluded it wuz best to quit.
But, come now, ef you wun't confess to knowin',
You've some conjectures how the thing's a-goin'."—
"Gran'ther," sez I, "a vane warn't never known
Nor asked to hev a jedgment of its own;
An' yit, ef 'tain't gut rusty in the jints,
It's safe to trust its say on certin pints:
It knows the wind's opinions to a T,
An' the wind settles wut the weather'll be."
"I never thought a scion of our stock
Could grow the wood to make a weathercock;
When I wuz younger'n you, skurce more'n a shaver,
No airthly wind," sez he, "could make me waver!"
(Ez he said this, he clinched his jaw an' forehead,
Hitchin' his belt to bring his sword-hilt forrard.)—
"Jes' so it wuz with me," sez I, "I swow,
When *I* wuz younger'n wut you see me now,—
Nothin' from Adam's fall to Huldy's bonnet
Thet I warn't full-cocked with my jedgment on it;
But now I'm gettin' on in life, I find
It's a sight harder to make up my mind,—

Nor I don't often try tu, when events
Will du it for me free of all expense.
The moral question's ollus plain enough,—
It's jes' the human-natur' side thet's tough;
Wut's best to think mayn't puzzle me nor you,—
The pinch comes in decidin' wut to *du;*
Ef you *read* History, all runs smooth ez grease,
Coz there the men ain't nothin' more'n idees,—
But come to *make* it, ez we must to-day,
Th' idees hev arms an' legs an' stop the way:
It's easy fixin' things in facts an' figgers,—
They can't resist, nor warn't brought up with niggers;
But come to try your the'ry on,—why, then
Your facts an' figgers change to ign'ant men
Actin' ez ugly—'' —"Smite 'em hip an' thigh!"
Sez gran'ther, "and let every man-child die!
Oh for three weeks o' Crommle an' the Lord!
Up, Isr'el, to your tents an' grind the sword!"—
"Thet kind o' thing worked wal in ole Judee,
But you forgit how long it's ben A.D.;
You think thet's ellerkence,—I call it shoddy,
A thing," sez I, "wun't cover soul nor body;
I like the plain all-wool o' common-sense,
Thet warms ye now, an' will a twelvemonth hence.
You took to follerin' where the Prophets beckoned,
An', fust you knowed on, back come Charles the Second;
Now wut I want's to hev all *we* gain stick,
An' not to start Millennium too quick;
We hain't to punish only, but to keep,
An' the cure's gut to go a cent'ry deep."
"Wall, milk-an'-water ain't the best o' glue,"
Sez he, "an' so you'll find afore you're thru;
Ef reshness venters sunthin', shilly-shally
Loses ez often wut's ten times the vally.
Thet exe of ourn, when Charles's neck gut split,
Opened a gap thet ain't bridged over yit:
Slav'ry's your Charles, the Lord hez gin the exe"—
"Our Charles," sez I, "hez gut eight million necks.
The hardest question ain't the black man's right,
The trouble is to 'mancipate the white;
One's chained in body an' can be sot free,
But t'other's chained in soul to an idee:
It's a long job, but we shall worry thru it;
Ef bagnets fail, the spellin'-book must du it."
"Hosee," sez he, "I think you're goin' to fail:
The rettlesnake ain't dangerous in the tail;
This 'ere rebellion's nothing but the rettle,—

You'll stomp on thet an' think you've won the bettle;
It's Slavery thet's the fangs an' thinkin' head,
An' ef you want selvation, cresh it dead,—
An' cresh it suddin, or you'll larn by waitin'
Thet Chance wun't stop to listen to debatin'!"—
"God's truth!" sez I,—"an' ef I held the club,
An' knowed jes' where to strike,—but there's the rub!"—
"Strike soon," sez he, "or you'll be deadly ailin',—
Folks thet's afeared to fail are sure o' failin';
God hates your sneakin' creturs thet believe
He'll settle things they run away an' leave!"
He brought his foot down fercely, ez he spoke,
An' give me sech a startle thet I woke.

The Paring-Bee

by Rowland E. Robinson

In the older country districts any event which gathered the neighbors from miles around for the purpose of communal activity and frolic was pleasantly anticipated. Hence there were spelling-bees, quilting-bees, raising-bees, each usually terminated by refreshments and some kind of dance. The Vermont paring-bee so vividly described by Robinson may have begun with confusion similar to "a hoorah's nest" but it was sure to offer pleasure to all who attended, plenty of food and drink, courting games for the adolescents, fiddle playing, and a square dance. Robinson's Vermont tales are particularly attractive because of his knowledge of rural life and his command of country idiom. The old cobbler, Uncle Lisha, who is often the narrator, combines Yankee dialect with a wealth of homely illustration and reference. "The Paring-Bee" is as much a genre picture as Whittier's "Snow-Bound," and it shows a folk close to the soil and sensitive to changes in weather, seasons, and people. The tale was published in Danvis Folks *(1894).*

Next morning Uncle Lisha laid aside his holiday attire with a sense of great relief from the constraint and care which their wearing had imposed upon him, and put on his ordinary garb with the comfortable feeling of being rehabilitated in his

real self. Making such haste with his breakfast that Aunt Jerusha said he was "in a
bigger hurry 'n. a boy a-goin' a-fishin',"
he put on his leather apron and set about
the odd jobs of mending for the family.

Sam and his father went out to their
husking, and the door between the kitchen
and the shop being opened, that the old
man might have the companionship of the
women folks, the house presently rang
with the merry thud of the hammer on
his lapstone.

Huldah was paring apples with a worn-
out shoe knife discarded from Uncle
Lisha's kit, and Aunt Jerusha quartered
and cored them with frugal care that the
least possible share should go to the pigs,
while the baby made frequent excursions
on all fours between the two great objects
of interest presented by the two industries.

Now he brought a chubby fistful of
stolen shoe pegs to his mother's knee, then
made restitution to the owner with a slice
of apple, begrimed by repeated contact
with the floor during its transportation.

"Why, yes, bub," said the old man,
beaming down a kindly glance through his
round glasses upon the upturned baby face
as he took the proffered gift and laid it on
the bench beside him, "it's turrible nice,
but Uncle Lisher don't 'pear tu feel like
eatin' on't jest naow. He hain't apple hungry; guess he eat tew much breakfus' er
suthin'. Ta' keer. Don't put his leetle
hanny ont' the lapstun. Git it smashed
finer 'n a barn. No, bubby, couldn't hev
the wax. Gaum him all up so 't mammy 'd
hafter nigh abaout skin him tu git him
clean ag'in; an' haow she would scold
both on us, an' haow we would cry, would
n't we? Here, take a pooty paig to Aunt
Jerushy an' ask her 'f she ever see sech a
cur'osity. Clipper, naow."

"Thank ye, a thaousan' times, you
darlin' creetur," cried Aunt Jerusha, when
the child had scrambled to her with his

gift. "I never see a neater paig an' I'm
a-goin' tu keep it tu hev me a shoe made.
These 'ere apples seems ef they was gittin'
turrible meller, Huldy, an' wa'n't a-goin'
tu keep no gret spell."

"I know it," said Huldah, putting a
thin slice between her lips and meditatively
munching it. "There's lots an' sacks on
'em that's all squ'sh, an' ef we save many
of 'em we've got tu hev a parin'-bee ef
you an' Uncle Lisher could stan' the rumpus."

"Stan' it! Law sakes. I could stan' a
lettle o' the young folkses catousin, an'
he'd enj'y it jest as much as any on 'em,
furzino. But apple cuts is turrible wasteful
an' mussin' an' gin'ally cost more 'n they
come tu."

"But we'd get the apples worked off an'
the young folks'd have a good time. I wonder if father Lovel would care?"

"Law sakes alive," said Aunt Jerusha,
"if he c'd stan' S'manthy twenty year,
I guess he c'n stan' one evenin's catousin.
But hear me talk, an' she an ol' neighbor
an' your mother-in-law ef she was a-livin'.
Lisher!" she called, "du you s'pose you
an' Timerthy could stan' it, ef we had a
apple cut?" and she shook her knife at
Huldah while they paused in their work
to hear his answer.

"A apple cut? A parin'-bee? Good airth
an' seas! You jest try it an' see. I bate ye,
me an' him'll shake our hommels wi' the
spryest on em."

"What'd I tell ye?" Aunt Jerusha whispered triumphantly.

When the subject was broached to them
at dinner, Sam and his father made no objections, and it was settled that the entertainment should be given as soon as the
necessary preparations could be made.

A whole day was spent in bountiful if
not elaborate cooking; the frying of at
least a bushel of doughnuts and the making and baking of pumpkin pies, whose
crowded ranks filled half the pantry

shelves. Then the rooms were put in cleanly order, which Aunt Jerusha declared, while giving her best efforts to it, "A useless work, a-scrubbin' an' puttin' tu rights jest tu hev 'em mussed an' cluttered intu jest a hoorah's nest."

Meantime invitations were issued, not on perfumed paper, but by hearty word of mouth, and given pretty generally yet discreetly.

"Don't ye gin no invite tu none o' them Forge fellers," said Huldah as Sam lingered on the threshold in indecision between the various routes. "They're such a rantankerous passel o' critters, allers fer raisin' a rumpus. An' don't ye forgit tu gin Tom Hamlin a bid, an' his parin'-machine, both on 'em, for one hain't no good withaout t' other. An' come raound by Joel Bartlett's an' git ten paound o' his best cheese, but don't let him know what ye want on 't. He would n't knowingly let his cheese git mixed up wi' no sech worl' people's fryvolity."

"Sho, I guess his screuples hain't wuth more 'n seven cents a paound," said Sam irreverently.

"An' I hope you'll make it a pint tu give Peltier a bid tu the apple cut," Uncle Lisha called from the shop; "he needs chirkin' up wust of any on us, the poor love-cracked creetur. Ef Danvis gals is pooty 's they was when aour womern was gals, Samwill, the' 'll be some here pooty enough tu take his mind off 'm that lake shore gill flirt, maremaid, I d' know but she is. Did he find her in the lake, Samwill? An' ef ye can scare up a fiddler, git him. What's come o' that leetle hump-backed feller 'at, when he sot in the corner a-fiddlin', you couldn't see nothin' on, behind his fiddle. But good airth an' seas, he 'd saw that fiddle all up into tunes. He'd be ekernomical for a kitchen tunk, gitten' intu a corner so, aout'n the way."

Sam hurried away before he should be burdened with further instructions, lamenting as he went the loss of so fine a hunting morning.

On the evening appointed for the entertainment the full moon was seen, but as a pale and dimly defined blotch behind the gray veil of cloud that overspread the sky and blended with the vague rim of the horizon.

There was a dull, sullen chill in the air, which was motionless in the expectancy wherewith nature so often awaits her changes. The night was jarred by the rumble of wagons jolting over the frozen roads and pierced by the merry voices of coming guests.

Some of these were occupants of the wagons, above whose rumble and clatter they strove to make one another hear between abrupt breaks of the thread of conversation when a wheel struck a stone or dropped into a rut. Some were coming across the fields on foot in couples and squads, but it was noticeable that the couples emerged from the half gloom before their voices were heard, while the gabble and laughter of the groups ran far before them to herald their coming.

Beams of light shone hospitably forth from every window of the kitchen and square room, and the heavy latch clanked and the door slammed announcement of the frequent arrivals.

The women folks came from the bedrooms, where they had bestowed their hoods and shawls and cloaks on Huldah's bed, each with an apron shielding the front of her tidy calico or homespun woolen gown. The men hung their coats on the pegs of the kitchen wall and became comfortable in their accustomed indoor shirtsleeves.

Soon pans and knives were brought forth, bushel baskets of apples lugged in, chairs drawn into convenient groups, and the business of the evening began.

Tom Hamlin and another almost as famous an apple parer bestrode their machines, placed on the seats of high-backed chairs, and entered upon such a strife for the championship that the clattering din of their clumsily geared machines was almost incessant, and the parings spurting from their knives in curved jets were scarcely broken in the quick shifting of the apples on the forks. Presently a dozen pairs of hands were busy quartering the peeled apples, as many more were coring them, while others strung them with wire needles on long strings of pack thread, for drying.

Every one except Tom Hamlin and his rival was talking, and almost every voice strove to make itself heard above every other and the deafening clatter of the machines. Some couples with heads close together utilized the uproar to say things meant for no other ears.

In the centre of an interested group, Uncle Lisha, splitting apples with his shoe knife, roared like a lion concerning the wonders of the West, and to as interested a feminine audience, Aunt Jerusha quavered shrilly of the discomforts of Western life while she industriously strung the quarters of apples in her pan.

"Fifty an' a hundred acres in one field o' wheat an' the hull on 't as level as the Forge Pawnd," Uncle Lisha shouted.

"Ten mile tu the nighest store," shrieked his wife to her group of listeners, "an' when you got to 't, the tea an' snuff they kept wa'nt wuth a-kerryin' hum, though goodness knows they ast enough for 'em. Land sakes! how be I goin' to git a pinch o' snuff, wi' both my han's in these 'ere apples?"

"Jest look o' Mandy Varney," cried a buxom damsel to those around her. "She hain't done nothin' only chank every identicle quarter she's cored, an' listen to that Jim Putnam, sence she soddaown. Wonder ef she thinks it's a-sparkin' bee steaddy a parin'-bee?"

"What s'pose the reason is, the' hain't none o' Cap'n Peck's folks come?" inquired another high-keyed voice; to which a middle-aged matron answered, with a backward toss of the head, while she kept her eyes rigidly fixed upon her apple and knife, "Proberbly they're 'bove goin' to such common duins, naow 't he's sot in the Leegislatur. Ef 't was 'fore 'lection the' 'd all ha' come fast 'nough."

"They du say 'at on the stren'th on 't she's ben tu V'gennes an' bought a hull set o' flowin' blue dishes. Clapham had n't nothin' quite good enough for a member o' the Leegislatur's wife," cried another.

"Highty tighty," said the elder matron, "an' there be them 'at hain't so turrible old that remember when the hull fam'ly eat the' puddin' an' milk aouten braown airthenware bowls, an' glad 'nough to get 'em." Even Danvis was not without its social jealousies.

"Suthin' ben a ketchin' Joel Bartlett's sheep," announced one of a knot of married men, who, assembled apart from their wives, were not laboring very assiduously. "Some thinks it's dawgs an' some thinks it's a animil."

" 'Tain't no ways likely it's a bear," another remarked; "the time o' the year's ag'in that. But it might be a painter."

"Wal, no, I don't favor the idee, 'cause the' was ten or a dozen sheep 't was killed aout an' aout; jest the' thrut cut. A painter would n't ha' killed more 'n one or tew, an' sati'fied hisself a-eatin' the meat. Hain't that so, Samwill?" appealing to their host, who had come within call as he moved from group to group to see that each was properly provided for.

"I cal'late it's a wolf," he said, "from what I've hearn tell o' their duins. More'n all that, I've consaited all the fall 'at the' was one a-hangin' raound, fer I've seen signs 'at I could n't lay to no other critter. But ef he don't make himself scace 'fore many hours, I reckon we'll have a chance to find aout what he is, fer ef it don't snow before mornin' I miss my guess.''

"I'm a-goin' aout tu take a look o' the weather jest fer greens," said one of the party, rising with a sigh of relief and dropping his pan in his chair. After an absence which must have enabled him to make a thorough study of the weather, he reentered the kitchen so powdered with snow that he did not need to proclaim that "it was snowin' like fun."

Many of the company needed further ocular proof of his report, and hastened forth to obtain it, while others were content to cool their noses against the window panes and stare out upon the landscape grown more obscure behind the veil of falling snow, all dull and lifeless, but for the candles' weird reflections—unreal lights by which, perhaps, witches were holding carnival. Perhaps it was the hope of beholding them that so long kept some fair cheeks in close proximity to bearded ones.

"If it holds up by mornin' I'll take a rantomscoot up back o' Joel's and see what tracks I c'n find," Sam said, and hurried away as Tom Hamlin, tossing away the last apple and kicking over the empty basket, shouted, "Fetch on your apples ef you want 'em skinned."

So with unflagging zeal and unabated clamor of voices, and clatter of implements and machines, the work went on till half a dozen bushels of apples were on the strings and ready to festoon the kitchen walls and poles that hung from hooks in the ceiling, and the welcome announcement was made that the labor of the evening was over.

"Naow, then," said Sam, making his way with careful steps across the floor, slippery with scattered skins and cores, "we'll clear up the thickest o' this mess and then we'll see ef aour womern folks

has saved any cold victuals fer us. I believe I saw some cold 'taters in the buttry an' I do' know but the' 's some o' Drive's johnny-cake left."

But before the floor was cleaned, a dozen girls must try for their lover's initials with apple parings whirled thrice above their heads and cast over the right shoulder to the floor behind them.

"Wal! fer all the world," cried Amanda Varney, blushing as red as the apple peeling she had just cast behind her, and was now regarding with surprised delight, "ef it hain't a perfect P."

"It might be most anything," said Mary Ann Jones, who in the early evening had called attention to Amanda's flirtation.

"'T would be good enough ef you'd ha' made it," said Amanda; "I'll leave it tu Uncle Lisher ef 't ain't a good P," as the old man drew near the circle widening to admit him.

"Yes," he said, after adjusting his spectacles and critically examining the initial. "It's julluk handwritin'. But it don't stan' fer Putnam ner fer Peggs. It's tew long and lank. Guess it stands fer Peltier. Come here, Peltier."

The young man, who was moping in a corner, made his way toward them. "It 'pears tu be p'inted by fortin 'at you've got tu dance 'long wi' Mandy. Naow, you be ready tu take your place wi' her soon's we get suthin' tu eat." Then whispering into his ear like a blast of north-east wind, "Naow du try tu shake some o' the sorrow aout o' your heart when th' dancin' begins."

"Gosh, Uncle Lisher," said Pelatiah, aghast at the plan, and casting a hopeless glance upon his big boots. "I can't dance no more 'n a thirty-foot ladder."

"Wal, 'f you hain't got the tools, I do' know who hes, an' you've got tu use 'em if I hafter yard ye top o' the hot stove. Come, gals, le' 's git things sot tu rights so 't we c'n eat an' git tu the rale business o' the evenin'."

Then the guests, ranged along the walls of the kitchen and spare room, were amply served with Huldah's doughnuts, pies, and cheese, and Sam's cider received its usual compliments.

Then the young people engaged in romping games, the Needle's Eye, wherein every one who could sing and every one who could not, sang, or tried to sing, at the top of their voices:—

The needle's eye, that doth soffy the thread that
  runs so treue,
It has caught many a smiling lass and naow it has
  caught yeou!

or with a volume and zest that would have pleased Gran'ther Hill more than the melody, "We're marching onward tow-ard Quebec." In every game the forfeits were invariably kisses, given and paid in the simplest and most direct manner, or when so decreed, in the contortions of a "double and twisted Loddy massy." The movements of another popular game were timed to the words of "Come, Philander, le' 's be a-marchin'." The elders looked on in amused toleration, while a few joined the young folks' games only to be reminded, by grudgingly paid forfeits, that the freshness of youth had departed from their wrinkled cheeks.

"Come," at last cried Uncle Lisha, who by tacit consent assumed the office of master of ceremonies, "you young folks orter be abaout cl'yed wi' bussin' an' we ol' folks has eat saour grapes long 'nough, so le' 's all turn tu an' hev a leetle sensible enj'yment a-dancin'. Where's thet aire leetle fiddler?"

"He hain't come anigh," Sam answered. "He promised he'd come sartin sure, but I'm most afeerd he's run ag'in a snag tu Hamner's 'at he won't git clear on, 'fore mornin'. It's tew tarnal bad."

"Well, that's a pretty haow de du," said the old man, "but we won't be cheated aout'n aour dancin' by one drunken fiddler. Tom Hamlin, 'd ye fetch yer jewsharp in your pocket? er can you dig one up, Samwill?" Tom "hed n't never thought on 't," nor could Sam find the only instrument upon which he ever played.

"Wal, then, I've got tu sing, which I'll make you hear me, ef I don't charm none. Chuse your pardners naow or never an' form ont' the floor. Come, Peltier, git Mandy and stan' up tu the dough dish."

Pelatiah hung back bashfully till Amanda, seeing her rival, Mary Ann, led out by Putnam, blushing with vexation, met him more than halfway, and he found his unwilling feet taking him to his place in the waiting ranks.

"All ready. Naow I'm goin' tu sing," shouted Uncle Lisha, and began to roar in stentorian tones:—

Lum tiddle, lum tiddle, t'l law day,
  Lum tiddle—

"Good airth an' seas! Why don't ye start yer hommels? D' ye s'pose I'm goin' tu set an' holler all night for you tu stan' an' gawp julluk tew rows o' stancheled calves?"

Thus adjured the first couple paddled and sailed down the middle, when he again took up his wordless song, and twenty-four pairs of feet, impatient for their turn, began to stamp and shuffle to its rhythm:—

Lum tid-dle, lum tid-dle, t'l law day,
  lum tid-dle, lum tid-dle, t'l law day,
  do day hum, do day hum, do day
    hum, t'l law day.

Antoine, sitting by Uncle Lisha, and attempting to catch the tune in snatches of undertone, played an imaginary fiddle and pranced time with both feet after the Canadian fashion, evidently considering himself the chief performer.

The dancers quickly caught the inspiration of well-meant, if unmelodious, strains, and whirled and capered in perfect abandonment to their influence. Even Pelatiah's bashfulness melted away in the excitement, and he made wild rushes at wrong moments and in wrong directions, which involved him and his partner in bewildering entanglement with other couples.

> Turn yer pardener half way raound,
> Lum tiddle, lum tiddle, t'l law day,
> Half way raound, half way raound,
> do day hum, t'l law day.

Uncle Lisha sang at him vociferously, and Antoine chimed in with, "Turn yo' pahdny wrong side aout," to Pelatiah's complete bewilderment. Then young Putnam, striving to outdo his own agile steps, as he pranced down the middle with Mary Ann Jones, slipped on a fragment of apple peel and fell headlong, plowing his way along a rank of dancers and turning a furrow of them on top of himself. Uncle Lisha still sang on, his voice rising above the din of shrieks and laughter, till it dawned upon him that no one was dancing and his music was being poured forth to no purpose.

In the lull that presently succeeded the confusion the company became aware of the notes of a fiddle, whence coming no one could conjecture, faintly yet distinctly playing the familiar air of "Money Musk." While all listened, some puzzled and some breathless, and some superstitiously alarmed, Solon Briggs oracularly voiced the prevailing feeling, in a solemn, awe-stricken tone:—

"That fiddle hain't performed by no livin' han's. Watson Parmer has pairished, mis'rable, in the element of the snow, and his speerit has come to fulfill his 'pintment made to Samule. It's Watson Parmer's indivisible apperagotion."

"Beeswax," cried John Dart, listening at the open door. "Go to thunder wi' yer speerits! It's someb'dy in the woodshed. Gimme a light an' I'll see who 't is."

Taking a candle and protecting it with his hollowed hand, he made his way to the woodshed, followed by the bolder of the company, close at his heels, the more timid crowding one another in the rear, where the light of the open door mistily illumined the falling snow. Under cover of the shed, and held high above Dart's head, the candle struggled with the gloom, till it disclosed a dismally comic little figure crouched in a limp heap, with its back against a barrel, its disproportionately long legs looped over the bar of a sawhorse on which it had attempted to seat itself. The snow-laden hat had fallen over the face, and the short body was hidden by the fiddle which the owner was playing with a skill that had survived inebriation, while in a thin and drunken voice he prompted the movements of a country dance.

"Firsh cou'le. Daow' er mi'le. Balansh. Daow a rou' shide."

"Wal, I swan," Dart ejaculated, " 'f 't ain't speerits, arter all. Hamner's, inside o' Wat Parmer. Hamner 'd ortu be kicked tu death by cripples for a-lettin' on him git so. Wat," taking the hat from the fiddler's face, shaking the snow from it, and adjusting it in its proper place, "don't be a-wastin' your music on the wood pile. You can't git no dancin' aout on 't. Come int' the haouse."

But the hunchback's face, vacant of everything save its habitual expression of pain, only stared blindly into space and the merry tune went on.

"You might as well talk tu a post. Take a holt o' the light, some on ye"; and giving the candle into other hands, he got behind the little man, and, placing his arms under the limp legs, lifted him as easily as one might a child, and in such a position the playing of the violin was not interrupted, and so, preceded by the candle-bearer, carried him into the house. As they entered, Palmer's drunken fancy moved him to strike up, "The Campbells are Coming."

"The camels is comin'?" cried Beau Putnam. "Don't ye see the hump?"

"Shut yer head, you blasted monkey," Dart growled so savagely that the grin faded out of Putnam's face, and the laugh that his coarse jest created died out in a suppressed titter.

"Here's your music, Lovel," Dart announced, as he deposited his light burden on a chair, "the best fiddler in Charlotte county. He's a leetle mite tired jest naow, but when he gits rested he 'll set all yer feet flyin' in spite of ye. Mis' Lovel, won't ye give him a cup o' tea, hot an' strong?"

When the little man had been somewhat restored to his proper self, he tuned his violin and then drew from it such blithe and melodious strains that all forgot his deformity. Even he, with loving eyes fixed upon his instrument, his worn face alight with a tender emotion that softened the lines which pain and dissipation had drawn upon it, seemed for the time also to have forgotten it.

Uncle Lisha, relieved of his musical labors, abandoned himself to the pleasures of the dance with a grace and agility that filled Aunt Jerusha's heart with pride, albeit they were such as a sportive bear exhibits. Antoine was given the floor for a while, as, to a tune of his own choosing, he danced a Canadian jig. Every one was a wide-awake and active participant in the gayety except the baby and the old hound, the one sleeping, undisturbed by the noise and commotion, whereof the other was a resigned but unhappy spectator under the circumscribed shelter of the stove.

When the dance ended, and the guests, even now acknowledging no fatigue, began to depart, the morning star was shining through the breaking clouds and the day was faintly dawning upon a world whose new whiteness looked strange to eyes that last beheld it, dun and gray with the dreariness of late autumn.

"Naow fetch on that leetle fiddler," John Dart commanded when he had tucked his Sarah Ann snugly in the buffalo-skins. "I'm a-goin' tu git him safte past Hamner's ef I hafter lock him up in his fiddle box. We wanter keep him for another apple cut. Here, Wat, cuddle in there 'twixt me an' Sary Ann, we're both on us small. Here ye be. Good-night, Lovel, ef 't ain't tew airly. I'll be on hand ef the' 's a wolf hunt. G'lang, Bob."

"It's complete trackin' snow," said Sam to a group of hunters who lingered last at his threshold, and he stooped to imprint the snowy banking with his finger. "I'll see what it's got tu tell us an' let you know. Good-mornin'."

The wagons moving over the muffled roads, and the quiet of the sleepy junketers, marked their departure with silence as noticeable as the noise of their coming.

John Wadleigh's Trial

by Seba Smith

Although Seba Smith is better known for his Jack Downing letters and for his portrait of the shrewd countryman from the state of Maine who becomes a self-appointed political adviser to Andrew Jackson, he also delineated other aspects of the Yankee character. In 'Way Down East; or, Portraitures of Yankee Life *(1854), in which "John Wadleigh's Trial" is the initial story, Smith dealt with digging for treasure, festivals, and courtships. He was also interested in manners under a theocratic government, when sleeping in church was considered a cardinal sin even though complete somnolence did not come until the preacher had reached "tenthly" in his sermon. The trial of John Wadleigh for desecration of the Sabbath is peculiarly a folk performance, since it takes place in a private home and is conducted by lawyers more familiar with homely diction than with legal finesse. Moreover, the attempt of a blind man to define a state of sleep by the sounds of breathing seems the very essence of folk humor.*

The pilgrim fathers of New England, and their children of the first and second generations, are justly renowned for their grave character, their moral uprightness, which sometimes was rather more than perpendicular, and the vigilant circumspection which each one exercised over his neighbor as well as himself. It is true that Connecticut, from an industrious promulgation of her "Blue Laws," has acquired more fame on this score than other portions of the "universal Yankee nation," but this negative testimony against the rest of New England ought not to be allowed too much weight, for wherever the light of history does gleam upon portions further "Down East," it shows a people not a whit behind Connecticut in their resolute enforcement of all the decencies of life, and their stern and watchful regard for the well-being of society. The justice of this remark will sufficiently appear by a few brief quotations from their judicial records.

In the early court records of New Hampshire, in the year 1655, may be found the following entry:

"The Grand Jury do present the wife of Mathew Giles, for swearing and reviling the constable when he came for the rates, and likewise railing on the prudenshall men and their wives. Sentenced to be whipped seven stripes, or to be redeemed with forty shillings, and to be bound to her good behavior."

Another entry upon the records the same year is as follows:

"The Grand Jury do present Jane Canny, the wife of Thomas Canny, for beating her son-in-law, Jeremy Tibbetts, and his wife; and likewise for striking her husband in a canoe, and giving him reviling speeches. Admonished by the court, and to pay two shillings and sixpence."

If it is consistent with rational philosophy to draw an inference from two facts, we might here consider it proved, that the pilgrim ladies of 1655 had considerable human nature in them. And from the following record the same year, it would appear also that there were some of the male gender among them at that day, who still exhibited a little of the old Adam.

"Philip Edgerly, for giving out reproachful speeches against the worshipful Captain Weggen, is sentenced by the court to make a public acknowledgement three several days; the first day in the head of the train band; the other two days are to be the most public meeting days in Dover, when Oyster River people shall be there present; which is to be done within four months after this present day. And in case he doth not perform as aforesaid, he is to be whipped, not exceeding ten stripes, and to be fined five pounds to the county."

The reader cannot but notice in this case, last cited, with what stern purpose and judicial acumen the severity of the penalty is made to correspond with the enormity of the offence. The crime, it will be seen, was an aggravated one. The gentleman against whom the reproachful speeches were uttered was a Captain; and not only a Captain, but a worshipful Captain. Whether Captain Weggen was the commanding officer of the train band, or not, does not appear; but there was an

appropriate fitness in requiring, that the crime of uttering reproachful speeches against *any Captain,* should be publicly acknowledged at the head of the *train band.* There the culprit would have to face all the officers, from the captain down to the corporal, and all the soldiers, from the top to the bottom of the company, could point the finger of scorn at him.

But as the injured party in this case was a *worshipful* captain, it was very proper that a penalty of a higher grade should be affixed to the sentence. Hence the withering exposure of the offender to make public acknowledgments on two several occasions, "to be the most public meeting days in Dover, *when Oyster River people shall be there present."*

Whatever may be said at the present day, as to the temperance reformation being of modern origin, it may be affirmed without hazard that the good people of New England two hundred years ago, were decided and strenuous advocates of temperance. They were not tee-totallers; they did not prohibit the use of those "creature comforts" altogether; but if any one among them proved to be a wine-bibber, or abused his privilege of drinking, woe be to him, he had to feel the force of the law and good government. Witness the following court record in New Hampshire, in 1657:

"Thomas Crawlie and Mathew Layn, presented for drinking fourteen pints of wine at one time. Fined three shillings and fourpence, and two fees and sixpence."

The good people of the province of Maine in those early days have also left proof, that they were on the side of industrious and good habits and wholesome instruction. Their Grand Juries present as follows:

"We present Charles Potum, for living an idle, lazy life, following no settled employment. Major Bryant Pembleton joined with the Selectmen of Cape Porpus to dispose of Potum according to law, and to put him under family government."

So it seems there were some men, even in the early days of the Pilgrims, who enjoyed that more prevalent luxury of modern times, living *under family government*.

Again say the Grand Jury, "We present the Selectmen of the town of Kittery, for not taking care that their children and youth be taught their catechism and education according to law."

They took good care in those good old times, that the dealings between man and man should be on equitable and fair principles, and without extortion. In 1640, the Grand Jury say—

"Imprimis, we do present Mr. John Winter, of Richmond's Island, for extortion; for that Thomas Wise, of Casco, hath declared upon his oath that he paid unto Mr. John Winter a noble (six shillings and eightpence), for a gallon of aqua vitae, about two months since; and further, he declareth that the said Winter bought of Mr. George Luxton, when he was last in Casco Bay, a hogshead of aqua vitae for seven pounds sterling."

The punishment inflicted on Mr. John Winter, for extorting from his customer two hundred per cent. profit on his merchandise, is not stated; but if one Thomas Warnerton, who flourished in the neighborhood at that time, had any agency in fixing the penalty, it probably went rather hard with him; for this latter gentleman must have had a special interest in keeping the price of the article down, inasmuch as it is related of him, that in taking leave of a friend, who was departing for England, "he drank to him a pint of *kill-devil*, alias rum, at a draught."

Juliana Cloyse, wife of John Cloyse, was "presented for a talebearer from house to house, setting differences between neighbors." It was the misfortune of Juliana Cloyse that she lived at too early an age of the world. Had her lot been cast in this day and generation, she would probably have met with no such trouble.

Thomas Tailor was presented "for abusing Captain R. Raynes, being in authority, for *thee-ing* and *thou-ing* of him, and many other abusive speeches."

At a town meeting in Portsmouth, March 12, 1672, "voted, that if any shall smoke tobacco in the meeting-house at any public meeting, he shall pay a fine of five shillings, for the benefit of the town."

In a previous year, September 25th, at a town meeting, it was "ordered that a cage be made, or some other means be invented by the Selectmen, *to punish such as sleep* or *take tobacco* on the Lord's day, at meeting, in the time of the public exercise."

It appears from this record that the town reposed unlimited confidence in the *inventive* powers of the Selectmen; and it appears also that the energetic order of the town, passed on this occasion, was a few years afterwards successfully carried into practical operation. The following is preserved on the town records, July 24, 1771.

"The Selectmen agree with John Pickering *to build a cage twelve feet square, with stocks within it, and a pillory on the top, a convenient space from the west end of the meeting-house.*"

Thus far we have confined ourselves to official records; but some of the unofficial and unwritten records of those days are of equal importance to be transmitted to posterity, one of which it is our present purpose to endeavor to rescue from oblivion.

The affair of the cage, with stocks inside, and a pillory on the top, served to wake up the congregation for a while, so that no one was caught napping or chewing tobacco in the meeting-house during the public exercises for several Sabbaths after this invention of the Selectmen became a "fixed fact" at the west end of the meeting-house. As the novelty of the thing wore off, however, the terror in some degree seemed to depart with it. There was a visible carelessness on the part of several old offenders, who were observed to relax their attention to the services, wearing very sleepy looks, sometimes yawning, and occasionally putting themselves into unseemly positions, concealing their faces, so that the searching scrutiny of old Deacon Winslow himself could not decide for certainty whether they were asleep or not.

Among these delinquents, John Wadleigh seemed to be the most conspicuous, often leaning his head so as to hide his eyes during half sermon time. He was also gruff and stubborn when questioned on the subject. So marked was the periodical reeling of his head, that Deacon Winslow began to watch him as narrowly as a cat would a mouse. Not that the Deacon neglected the sermon; he always took care of that matter, and for his own edification, as well as an example to the congregation, he steadily kept one eye on the minister, while the other was on John Wadleigh. There began to be sundry shrugs of the shoulders among the knowing ones of the congregation, and remarks were occasionally dropt, such as "Don't you believe John Wadleigh was asleep during half the sermon yesterday?" with the reply, "Why yes, I know he was; but he must look out, or he'll buy the rabbit, for Deacon Winslow keeps his eye upon him, and if he don't make an example of him before long, I won't guess again."

It was whispered by some, who were out of the pale of the church, that the Deacon's watchful powers with regard to Wadleigh were a little more acute in consequence of Wadleigh's having over-reached him somewhat in the sale of a cow, at which the Deacon, who prided himself on his sound judgment, it was alleged, always felt a little mortified. The Deacon however was a very upright specimen of the old

puritan race, and it is not probable his sense of justice and right was much warped. True, he manifested considerable zeal in looking after the delinquencies of John Wadleigh, but his "zeal was according to knowledge"; he knew Wadleigh to be a disregarder of the Sabbath, sleepy-headed and profane, and he did therefore feel a zealous and charitable desire to administer to him a little wholesome reproof, provided it could be done in a just, lawful, and Christian manner.

He even felt it excusable, to accomplish so good a purpose, to enter into a pious fraud with Parson Moody. He had observed that though Wadleigh generally appeared to be asleep at the close of the sermon, yet when the congregation immediately rose up to prayers, he always managed some how or other to be up with them, but with a flushed face and guilty countenance. The Deacon believed, and it was the general opinion, that Wadleigh was asleep on these occasions, and that when the congregation began to rise, it always awoke him. He therefore suggested to Parson Moody, that on the next Sabbath, at the close of the sermon, instead of immediately commencing his prayers, he should sit quietly down three or four minutes, as though he were a little fatigued, or had some notes to look over, and see whether Wadleigh would not continue to sleep on, while the attention of every one awake would of course be attracted to the Parson. This little plan was tried, but without any very satisfactory result. It added something to the presumptive testimony in the case, but nothing clear and positive. Wadleigh held his head down about half a minute after the monotonous tones of the preacher's voice had ceased to fall upon his ear, when he started suddenly, rose to his feet, looked round a moment confusedly, and sat down again.

At last, however, repeated complaints having been made to the Grand Jury, they saw fit to "present John Wadleigh for a common sleeper on the Lord's day, at the publique meeting," a thing which Deacon Winslow earnestly declared they ought to have done weeks before they did.

The Deacon was in fact the most important personage in town, being not only the first officer in the church, but also a civil magistrate, before whom most of the important causes in the place were tried. Of course the offender Wadleigh, when the Grand Jury had once caught him in their net, had a pretty fair chance of having justice meted out to him. The jury met early on Monday morning, and the first business before them was the case of Wadleigh, against whom a fresh lot of complaints had come in. They were not long in finding a bill against him as above-mentioned, and a warrant was put into the hands of Bill Cleaves, the constable, to hunt Wadleigh up, and take him before Deacon 'Squire Winslow, and summon in the witnesses for his trial.

Bill Cleaves tipped his hat to the 'Squire as he went by upon his official duties, and gave him to understand what was going on. Whereupon 'Squire Winslow proceeded to put his house in court-order, having the floor of his large open hall, where he generally held his courts, swept and newly sanded, and things all put to rights. One o'clock was the hour appointed for the trial, for as the neighborhood all dined at twelve, the 'Squire said that would give them an opportunity to go to the work with a full stomach and at their leisure.

Accordingly, at one o'clock the parties began to assemble in the hall. 'Squire Winslow, who believed that a pipe after dinner was a good settler to the stomach, and always practised accordingly, came in with a pipe in his mouth, his spectacles resting on the top of his forehead, and taking a comfortable position in his chair, placed his feet, where he had a perfect right to place them, being in a land of Liberty,

and in his own house, *upon the top of the table*. The prisoner, who had been found asleep in his chair at his own dinner table, was taken away suddenly, like Cincinnatus or Putnam from the plough, and brought into court, *just as he was*, in his shirt sleeves, and placed at the other end of the table, opposite the feet of Gamaliel. Lawyer Chandler, who was always on hand to help the 'Squire along in all knotty cases, appeared with book in hand ready to lay down the law and testimony. Lawyer Stebbins was allowed by the courtesy of the court to take his seat by the side of the prisoner to see that he had fair play shown him. Bill Cleaves, the constable, took his seat a little behind the 'Squire, crossed his legs, and fell to smoking a cigar with great composure.

'Squire Winslow's faithful bull dog, Jowler, whose duty it was to keep order in the house, took his watchful station under the table, directly under his master's feet, ready for any emergency. While the constable's dog, Trip, who had done his part in running down the game and getting it housed, felt that his duties were over, and caring but little for the court scene, he had stretched himself upon the floor, and was as sound asleep as ever John Wadleigh was in church. The other witnesses and spectators present were too numerous to mention.

The indictment was read, and the prisoner called upon to answer, who, at the suggestion of Lawyer Stebbins, replied, "Not guilty"; at which Deacon 'Squire Winslow shook his head, and remarked in a low tone, "We shall see about that."

The first point made by Lawyer Chandler, was, that *the prisoner should prove his innocence;* and he argued the point with much force and eloquence. It was no easy matter to prove that a man was actually asleep, but it was easy enough for a man to prove that he was awake. Therefore, from the nature of the case, the burden of the proof ought to lay upon the prisoner. "Now, we charge that on sundry occasions, Wadleigh was asleep in church, against the laws of the town and the well-being of society. Now, if he was not so asleep, let him prove his *alibi*. A criminal always has a right to an *alibi* if he can prove it. May it please your honor, I take that ground," said Chandler, "and there I stick; I call upon the prisoner to prove his *alibi*."

Lawyer Stebbins stoutly contended that the *alibi* could not apply in this case. He had never heard nor read of its being used in any case except murder. And the wisdom of the court finally overruled that it belonged to the prosecutors to prove the sleep.

"Well, if that be the case," said Chandler, "I move, your honor, that Solomon Young be sworn. I had no idea the burden of proof was going to lay on us, but still I've come prepared for it."

Solomon Young was sworn, and took the stand.

Question by Chandler.—Do you know that John Wadleigh sleeps in meeting?

Witness.—I guess taint no secret; I don't know anybody but what does know it.

Chandler.—Well, do *you* know it? That's the question.

Stebbins objected to the question. It was a leading question, and they had no right to put leading questions to the witness.

Chandler.—Well, then, let the court put the questions.

Justice Winslow.—*What* do you know about John Wadleigh's sleeping in meeting?

Witness.—I know *all* about it, taint no secret, I guess.

Justice.—Then tell us all about it; that's just what we want to know.

Witness (scratching his head).—Well, the long and short of it is, John Wadleigh is a hard worken man. That is, he works mighty hard doing nothing; and that's the hardest work there is done. It'll make a feller sleepy quicker than poppy leaves. So it stands to reason that Wadleigh would naterally be a very sleepy sort of person. Well, Parson Moody's sarmons are sometimes naterally pretty long, and the weather is sometimes naterally considerable warm, and the sarmons is sometimes rather heavy-like.

"Stop, stop," said 'Squire Winslow, "no reflections upon Parson Moody; that is not what you were called here for."

Witness.—I don't cast no reflections on Parson Moody. I was only telling what I know about John Wadleigh's sleeping in meeting; and it's my opinion, especially in warm weather, that sarmons that are heavy-like and an hour long naterally have a tendency—

"Stop, stop, I say," said 'Squire Winslow, "if you repeat any of these reflections on Parson Moody again, I'll commit you to the cage for contempt of court."

Witness.—I don't cast no reflections on Parson Moody. I was only telling what I know about John Wadleigh's sleeping in meeting.

'Squire Winslow.—Well, go on, and tell us all about that; you want called here to testify about Parson Moody.

Witness.—That's what I'm trying to do, if you wouldn't keep putting me out. And it's my opinion in warm weather, folks is considerable apt to sleep in meeting; especially when the sarmon—I mean especially when they get pretty tired. I know I find it pretty hard work to get by seventhly and eighthly in the sarmon myself; but if I once get by there, I generally get into a kind of waking train again, and make out to weather it. But it isn't so with Wadleigh; I've generally noticed if he begins to gape at seventhly and eighthly, it's a gone goose with him before he gets through tenthly, and he has to look out for another prop to his head somewhere, for his neck isn't stiff enough to hold it up. And from tenthly up to sixteenthly he's dead as a door nail; till the Amen brings the people up to prayers, and then Wadleigh comes up with a jerk, jest like opening a jack-knife.

Stebbins, cross-examining the witness. —Mr. Young, how do you *know* that Wadleigh is asleep on these occasions you speak of?

Witness.—Cause he is; everybody says he is.

Stebbins.—That won't do; we don't want you to tell us what everybody says. You must tell *how* you know he is asleep?

Witness.—Well, cause he begins to gape at seventhly and eighthly, and props his head up at tenthly, and don't stir again till the Amen.

Stebbins.—Well how do you *know* he is asleep at that time?

Witness.—Cause when I see him settle down in that kind of way, and cover his face up so I can't see his eyes, I know he's asleep.

Stebbins.—That's no proof at all; the witness only knows he was asleep because he couldn't see his eyes.

Chandler.—Well, this witness has proved that the prisoner exhibited all the outward signs of sleep; now I will introduce one to show that he also exhibited internal evidence of being asleep. Your honor must know that it is a law in physics and metaphysics, and the universal science of medicine, that being deprived of one sense sharpens the other senses in a most wonderful degree. Now I move your honor that my blind friend here behind me, Jonathan Staples, be sworn.

Jonathan Staples was sworn accordingly.

Chandler.—Now, Staples, do you know that John Wadleigh sleeps in meeting?

Staples.—Yes, I du.

Chandler.—Do you *know* it?

Staples.—Yes, I know it.

'Squire Winslow.—*How* do you know it?

Staples.—Why, don't I hear him sleep every Sabbath?

Chandler.—What is the state of your hearing?

Staples.—It is as sharp as a needle with two pints.

Chandler.—Can you always tell by a person's breathing, whether he is asleep or awake?

Staples.—Jest as easy as I can tell whether I'm asleep or awake myself.

Chandler.—Tell us where you sit in meeting, and how you know Wadleigh is asleep.

Staples.—Well, I goes to meeting of a Sabbath, and commonly takes my seat in the seventh seat at the west end of the meeting-house. And John Wadleigh he sets in the sixth seat, and that brings him almost right afore me. All the first part of the exercises he has a waking breath, till it gets along into the sarmon, say about seventhly or eighthly, and then he begins to have a sleepy breath; and when it gets along into tenthly, he commonly goes it like a porpus.

'Squire Winslow.—Do you know him to be asleep at these times?

Staples.—I guess I du; I don't see how I could help it. I know him to be asleep jest as well as I know I'm awake.

'Squire Winslow.—Well, that's sufficient, unless Mr. Stebbins wishes to ask any questions.

Stebbins.—Now, Staples, do you pretend to say that you can tell John Wadleigh's breath from the breath of any other person in meeting?

Staples.—Sartinly I do. Aint everybody's breath pitched on a different key? There's as much difference in breathing as there is in speaking.

Chandler.—I'm willing, your honor, to rest the cause here. I have a plenty more witnesses as good as these, but I consider the case so clearly proved that it is hardly necessary to bring on any more unless my friend Stebbins should offer anything on the other side which may need to be answered.

Stebbins.—I don't consider it necessary, may it please your honor, for me to say a single word. I don't consider that there has been the least particle of evidence offered here yet, to prove that John Wadleigh ever slept a wink in meeting in all his life. And surely your honor won't convict this man without any proof at all against him. Look at the evidence, sir; what does it amount to? One man has seen him lean his head, and another has heard him breathe; and that is the sum total. Why, sir, if you convict a man on such evidence as this, no man is safe. Every man is liable to lean his head and to breathe in meeting. And if that is to be considered evidence of sleep, I repeat, who is safe? No, sir; as I said before, I don't consider it necessary for me to say one word on the subject, for there has been no evidence offered to prove the offence charged.

Here Lawyer Chandler rose with fire in his eyes and thunder on his tongue.

"May it please your honor," said he, "I am astonished, I am amazed at the hardihood and effrontery of my learned friend, the counsel on the opposite side of this cause. Why, sir, if there ever was a case made out in any court under heaven, by clear, positive, and irresistible evidence, it is this. Sir, I say, sir, evidence as clear as sunshine and irresistible as thunder. Yes, sir, an unimpeachable witness swears to you, that he sees the culprit Wadleigh, the prisoner at the bar, gaping in meeting and exhibiting all the signs of going to sleep; then he sees him flatting away and muzzling about to find a prop for his head. Now, sir, men don't want a prop for their heads when they are awake. It's only when they are asleep they want a prop for their heads, sir. Well, now sir, follow the prisoner along a little further, and what do we find, sir? Do we find him wide awake, sir, and attending to the services as a Christian and as a man ought to do? No, sir. We find him from tenthly up to sixteenthly, as dead as a door nail. Them's the witnesses' words, sir, as dead as a door nail. What next, sir? Why, then the witness swears to you, that when the congregation rise up to prayers, Wadleigh comes up with a jerk, jest like opening a jack-knife. Them's the witnesses' very words, sir. Now, sir, persons that's awake don't get up in meeting in that kind of style. It's only them that's waked up out of a sudden sleep, that comes up with a jerk, like the opening of a jack-knife, sir. What stronger proof do we need, or rather what stronger proof could we have, of all the outward signs of sleep, than we have from this witness? With regard to the internal evidence of sleep, another witness swears to you that he hears Wadleigh asleep every Sabbath; that he can tell when a person is asleep or awake by his breathing, as easily as he can tell whether he's asleep or awake himself. This witness swears to you that during the first part of the exercises Wadleigh has a waking breath, and when the minister gets along to seventhly and eighthly he begins to have a very sleepy breath. Well, sir, when the minister gets to tenthly, the witness swears to you that Wadleigh commonly goes it like a porpus. Yes, sir, so sound asleep, that's the inference, so sound asleep, that he goes it like a porpus.

"Sir, I will not say another word. I will not waste words upon a case so strong, so clear, and so perfectly made out. If this evidence doesn't prove the culprit Wadleigh to be a common sleeper in meeting on the Lord's day, then there is no dependence to place in human testimony. Sir, I have done. Whether this man is to be convicted or not, I clear my skirts; and when posterity shall see the account of this trial, should the culprit go clear, they may cry out 'judgment has fled to brutish beasts and men have lost their reason'; but they shall not say Chandler did not do his duty."

The effect of this speech on the court and audience was tremendous. It was some min-

utes before a word was spoken, or any person moved. All eyes still seemed to be rivetted upon 'Squire Chandler. At last 'Squire Winslow spoke.

"This is a very clear case," said he; "there can be no question of the prisoner's guilt; and he is sentenced to be confined in the cage four hours, and in the stocks one hour. Constable Cleaves will take charge of the prisoner, and see the sentence properly executed."

Evenings at Simeon's Store

by George S. Wasson

Stories of witchcraft or satanic interference die hard, especially when retired Yankee sea captains meet for a "yarn session" at a quiet country store. The old salts whom Wasson pictures in their reunion at Simeon's store somewhere on the Maine coast are full of marvels and legends, and storytellers like Captain Job Gaskett don't need much encouragement. Nights when the surf breaks a clean torch on every reef provide just the right atmosphere for these tales. Then recollections of hags who could interfere with domestic or agricultural life come to mind, and serious discussions develop about the proper season in which to kill hogs or how to cure rheumatism. The more familiar these stories are, the more convincing they become, at least to the assembled audience. They are also reinforced by the down-east dialect and the homely idioms of the Yankee speakers. "Evenings at Simeon's Store" originally appeared in the Atlantic Monthly *(November, 1902).*

After several days of strong easterly wind with rain and sleet, it had fallen nearly calm, and a dense, dripping fog settled over Killick Cove as night came on early with dungeon-like blackness. Across the rain-soaked pastures sounded loudly

the hollow rote of the sea, broken periodically by the foghorn's sepulchral note and the mournful clang of the bell buoy on the Hue and Cry.

Clad in oilskins and rubber boots, certain faithful pilgrims to the store, who had

• From *Cap'n Simeon's Store,* by George S. Wasson, published, 1903, by Houghton Mifflin Company. Reprinted by permission of Houghton Mifflin Company.

wallowed up through the mud and darkness from the Lower Neck, reported it as "breakin' a clean torch" on every ledge outside, and bewailed the probable loss of lobster traps and trawls.

Surely a more fitting night on which to consider witchcraft, forerunners, and like subjects could not have been chosen, and Cap'n Job Gaskett's black eyes snapped excitedly as he once more declared his firm belief that witches still practiced their art in the vicinity, though possibly in a less open manner than in the old days when Sarah Kentall and Hetty Moye "hove" their dreaded bridles at will, or in the much more recent times when Aunt Polly Belknap exacted tribute from mariners about to sail.

As the most recent occurrence upholding him in his well-known belief, Cap'n Job related the following singular experience of his wife:—

"My woman," said he, "she sot out one time las' fall to drive way up back here a-visitin' of her cousin to Lyndon Corners. 'T was some consid'ble time sence she 'd been over the ro'd, you un'stan', an' bimeby she come to a place where she kind o' got off'n her course altogether; she lost her reck'nin' you might say, an' could n't see ary 'marks,' nor git ary soundin's, nary one o' the two.

"Wal, fin'lly she see a woman out waterin' plants down by the gate in front of a little, small ole red house there was, so she let the mare come to, passed the time o' day 'long o' the woman, an' asked her 'bout which was the right ways to take. Wal, this here woman she made off 's ef she was ter'ble perlite an' 'commodatin' like, an' went to work right away an' pricked off a new course for my woman to run, plain 's could be, but she kep' up a stiddy clatter o' talk same 's ef she had n't seen nary soul for a fortni't, an' fin'lly nothin' would n't do but my woman should turn to an' have a dish o' tea 'long o' her, seein'

how it was hard on to noontime a'ready. Wal, when my woman come to leave, she follered her chock down to the gate ag'in, a-makin' off to be ter'ble anxious for fear 't would storm 'fore ever my woman got to the Corners.

"Oh, she done her little act up in complete shape, I tell ye, but what I'm comin' at 's, when my woman took holt o' them reins to start, that 'ere mare could n't make out to raise a huff off'n the groun', no ways she could fix it. My woman 'lows she done her dingdes' a-tryin' to git a move on to that hoss ag'in, but 't wa'nt a part'cle o' use, an' fin'lly it come acrosst her all of a sudden jes' what was to pay.

"She jes' took an' unhitched a blame' great shawl-pin she had on to her by good luck, an' 'fore ever this here set-fired ole witch knowed what she was up to, my woman reached out'n that wagon an' fetched a kind o' rakin' jab like with that pin, chock down the length o' the creetur's bare arm, so 's to start the blood a-squirtin' in good shape, I tell ye, an' jes' the very minute she done so, the mare started off down the ro'd same 's a bullet out'n a gun, an' left that air ole witch a-hoppin' roun' there, screechin' fit to stund ye.

"She 'd went to work an' teched that 'ere mare, ye see; she 'd jes' up an' hove a spell acrosst the whole d——n bus'niss, an' nothin' only blood would n't break it."

After some few remarks in commendation of Mrs. Gaskett's sagacity on this occasion, Simeon inquired from his high perch behind the desk whether Cap'n Job had heard anything from his oil-can recently, and as it proved there were several present unfamiliar with the facts in this strange case, Cap'n Gaskett obligingly furnished them again as follows:—

"When I painted my house an' outbuildin's eight year ago come springtime, there was a four-gallon oil-can lef' kickin' 'bout the yard, and fin'lly I took an' I hove her into the barn to be red on her.

Wal, she laid there up in one corner all quiet 'nough for a spell; month or more I guess 't was she laid there into that krawm-heap, till one time I was out there grindin' up my ax, an' all to once I heerd a set-fired funny thumpin' soun'—ker-chunk! ker-plunk! Sup'n that ways she 'peared to soun', but six on 'em to a lick, allus.

"There wa'n't nary soul into that barn but me, I knowed that all right, but to make a dead sure thing, I up an' ransacked that buildin' high an' low, but it did n't 'mount to nothin' 't all, for I foun' them thumps come direc' out'n that ole oil-can, an' nowheres else. 'S I say, at the fus' send-off, there was allus jes' six on 'em to a time, an' I knowed they was a forerunner, fas' 'nough, but 't was some few days 'fore ever I ketched on to jes' what 't was they meant, till one af'noon I was a-settin' out there kind o' studyin' of it over, an' I see all to once that them six thumps was a sign that Sister Jane was goin' to stop roun' here 'long on us jes' six months, an' no longer. She 'd jes' barely commenced to be sickly 'bout that time, you rec'lec'.

"Wal sir, that ole can kep' right on thumpin' out six clips to a time for jes' one month, an' then she let up on one thump, an' slacked down to five. I use' to git so aggravated 'long o' the dodblasted ole thing, I 'd up an' kick her all round the barn floor chock out into the henyard, but 't wa'n't no manner o' use, an' never made a mite o' diff'rence, not a mite.

"Soon 's ever I 'd come to git through kickin' of her, she 'd jes' up an' give out them same ole thumps same 's she 'd been doin' of, so fin'lly I never paid no more 'tention to her, an' she kep' right on thumpin' whenever she got good an' ready, but I took pertik'ler notice ev'ry month she let up on one thump, an' Sister Jane she kep' right on failin' stiddy all the time. Wal sir, them thumps fin'lly come down to one, an' that one kep' on dwindlin' away

fainter an' fainter, till bimeby Jane she died. The ole can sets up there into the barn yit, but nary yip has come out'n her sence."

A pause followed this narrative of Cap'n Job's, during which his listeners chewed their quids reflectively, while the clucking of Cap'n Roundturn's false teeth became painfully noticeable.

"Them kind o' things is sing'lar, an' there 's no rubbin' of it out, neither," continued Job in a few minutes. "I cal'late there won't never be no def'nition to 'em. Now there was one o' them drummer fellers put up to my house over night one time, an' I was tellin' him 'bout that air scrape o' my woman's when the ole witch teched the mare, same 's I was jes' now speakin' of. Wal sir, this here drummer he was an extry smart 'pearin' sort o' chap, an' I 'lowed he was posted on mos' ev'ry-thing chock to the handle. Why, he had a head on to him same 's a wooden god; bigger 'n what Dan'l Webster's ever dared to be, so 's 't I cal'lated you could n't stick him on nothin' in reason, but be dinged ef he did n't own up that three or four o' them yarns I give him that night was reg'lar ole chinchers, an' no mistake!

"Said they jes' knocked him silly, they did, so 's 't he would n't preten' to give no why an' wherefore to 'em, but he 'lowed how he see in his paper one time where a lot o' them rich college fellers up to the west'ard there had turned to an' j'ined a sort o' club like, or some sich thing, to hol' reg'lar meetin's an' overhaul jes' sich works as I was tellin' 'bout, so 's to see ef they could n't git the true bearin's on 'em some ways or 'nother.

"I tol' him, 's I, they can't never tell nothin' 'bout 'em, for the reason it wa'n't never cal'lated we *should* git holt on't. It'll be jes' time an' money hove clean away, 's I, an' that's all it'll 'mount to."

"That 's true 's preachin'!" assented Cap'n Roundturn. "What ever them pore

half fools kin make out'n it won't 'mount
to a row o' pins, but Godfrey mighty!
Them fellers' time don't come very high,
by no manner o' means, an' somebody
may git a dollar out'n 'em, some ways!
I sh'd say bes' give 'em plenty o' slack
line, an' tell 'em to go it, full tilt."

"Wal, yas," said Cap'n Gaskett, "I
s'pose they might 's well mull the thing
over amongst 'em. 'T won't do no great
hurt, ef it don't do no good, as the feller
said when he went to work an' leggo his
anchor without no cable bent on to it! But
ef them fellers lacks mateeril for to try
their headpieces on to, I'll bate a hat I kin
deal out 'nough on 't so 's to keep 'em
guessin' for the nex' twelvemonth, an' resk
it.

"Now you take the time they fetched
Cap'n Thaddy Kentall ashore from his
vess'l here to this Cove. You rec'lect it,
Cap'n Roundturn? 'T was the time I re-
topped the ole Fair Wind up there to your
shore, much 's thirty-five year sence, I
guess. That air ole crooked apple tree that
stan's cluss to the eastern end o' the Kentall
place was all chock-a-block with blossoms
when they fetched Cap'n Thaddy up there
that spring, but soon 's ever he was to bed
in good shape, be jiggered ef them blossoms
did n't commence a-fallin' off'n her!

"They pretended to say 'long the fus'
send-off how Cap'n Thaddy had ketched
a fever, but it turned out sup'n ailed his
liver; that's what it was the matter on him,
—his liver kep' shrinkin' away stiddy, an'
them set-fired blossoms kep' on droppin'
an' droppin' jes' so stiddy. Bimeby, when
they 'd ev'ry dod-blasted one fell off'n that
tree, be dinged ef the leaves did n't commence a-dreepin' off'n her too!

"That's a fac'! I'm givin' of it to ye
straight 's a gun bar'l. I was right to home
here through the hull on 't, repairin' up
my vess'l, an' was knowin' to all the pertik'lers jes' like a book. The way 't was,
Cap'n Thaddy's liver fin'lly come to git

completely eat up, or else she dried up, or
run out, I can't rightly say fer certain now
jes' what it was ailed her, but any ways, I
know Cap'n Thaddy lost his liver clip an'
clean an' time *she* was all gone, that air
apple tree was stripped chock down to bare
poles; yes sir, jes' naked 's ever she was in
winter time!

"Wal, ole Doctor Windseye he started
in to grow a bran'-noo liver into Cap'n
Thaddy, but it 'peared 's though he could
n't make out to git no great headway on
'long the fus' on 't, an' I know 't was kind
o' hinted roun' on the sly that ole Doc
had went to work an' bit off more 'n what
he could chaw.

"Any ways, Cap'n Thaddy he jes' laid
there to bed for weeks so blame sick he did
n't give a tinker's d———n ef school kep'
or not, but bimeby, though, ole Doc he
fin'lly made out to git a noo liver sprouted
in good shape, an' jes' soon 's ever he done
so, set-fire ef them apple-tree leaves did n't
commence to bud out ag'in, an' time the
Cap'n's noo liver had got a real good holt
on to him, that air tree was all bloomed
out ag'in solid full o' blossoms, same 's
she was when they fetched him ashore.
Yas sir, she was, an' now let them club
fellers up there to the west'ard jes' shove
that air into their pipes an' smoke it a
spell!

"Way 't was in them days, folks round
here kind o' 'lowed how ole Doc done a
big job for Cap'n Thaddy, but gracious
evers! You take it this day o' the world,
an' them hospittle fellers grows noo livers
right 'long; 't ain't the fus' bit o' put-out
to 'em now'days, they tell me."

Although this striking story was perfectly well known throughout the village,
Cap'n Job's hearers listened attentively to
the end, partly because he was recognized
as high authority upon the subject in hand,
and partly because repetition of stories was
a privilege shared by all frequenters of the
store. At this point in the proceedings

Sheriff Windseye said to a man reclining upon a pile of meal bags:—

"Le' 's see, John Ed, wa'n't it you that run acrosst ole Skipper Nate Perkins out here in the Bay, one time?"

"Yas sir!" promptly answered this individual. "I see him, an' passed the time o' day 'long on him, sure's ever you 'er settin' where you be. 'T was more 'n a dozen years after he was los', but he let on jes' who he was, though I should hev knowed his v'ice all right ef he had n't hev tol' me."

"He'd took the shape of a hagdon, had n't he, John Ed?" interrupted Cap'n Gaskett. "The mos' o' them ole fellers doos, I've allus took notice."

"Yas," replied John Ed, as he straightened up, and tapped the ashes from his cob pipe. "Yas sir, that's jes' the very shape he showed hisself to me in—jes' one o' these common hagdons, or mack'rel gulls, I b'lieve some folks calls 'em.

"The way 't was that time was like this. When I sot out that mornin', 't was thick o' fog, an' pooty nigh stark calm, too. I had to row my hooker more 'n two mile outside 'fore ever I struck ary breeze at all. Then I took jes' an air o' win' out here to the south'ard, an' made out to fan 'long for a spell, but 't was dretful mod'rit, an' part the time there wa'n't scursely steerage-way on to her. My gear was all sot out on Betty Moody's Ten Acre Lot that time, but 't was so master thick I could n't see nary marks, an' I mus' have fooled away 'nother hour 'fore ever I sighted my gear.

"Wal, I commenced under-runnin' the fus' trawl, an' pooty quick I see this here hagdon a-roostin' right a-top o' my weather trawl buoy. 'T was gittin' on 'long toewards noontime then, an' there fin'lly come quite a scale, so 's 't the sun pooty nigh come out, an' I see this here feller settin' there cockin' of his blame head at me, plain 's could be, a-top o' that kag.

"Wal, thinks I to myself, dinged ef you don't make out to be some tame, you! Wonder how nigh I kin git to ye, 'fore ever ye 'll up an' skip! Wal, I kep' on under-runnin' that trawl sort o' easy like, an' gainin' up on to him all the time, till I'll bate I wa'n't two bo't's lengths off'n him, when he up an' says jes' nat'ral 's life, 'Good-mornin', John Ed,' 's he. Wal, now, it gimme a master start, that did, there 's no rubbin' that out, though 's a gin'ral thing sich works don't jar me not for a cent, but this here come on to me so dod-blowed suddin, ye see!

"I knowed right away jes' who 't was, though, soon 's ever he yipped, an' 's I, 'This here 's Skipper Nate Perkins, ain't it?'

"'That's jes' who 't is!' 's he. 'How's all the folks there to the Cove?' 's he.

"Wal sir, by that time I was all tanto ag'in, an' cool 's a cowcumber, so I turned to an' give him a kind o' gin'ral av'rage how things was workin' ashore here, an' sot out to try an' pump him a grain 'bout hisself, but he would n't gimme no more chance.

"'Give 'em all my bes' respec's to hum there,' 's he, an' off he went 'bout eas'-suth'eas', I jedged, jes' though the devil kicked him on end.

"Course, I'd allus hearn the ole folks tell 'bout hagdons bein' them that 's dead, an' 'specially them that 's been los' to sea, but I never give the thing no great thought till I come to see it proved this way."

"Oh, wal, there now!" put in Cap'n Job. "For the matter o' that, it don't need no provin', not at this day o' the world, it don't. It 's gospel truth, an' I've knowed it ever sence I was the bigness of a b'layin' pin. Skipper Nate Perkins, the one you was talkin' 'long on, was los' into the ole Harvester, in the fall o' '71. I know ole Enoch Windseye over to the Neck here, he was shipped to go cook 'long o' him, an' come down to the w'arft where the vess'l was layin' the night afore they was to sail, cal'latin' to stow his dunnage aboard, but he see a rat run ashore on a line from the vess'l, an' he jes' shifted his mind on the spot, an' 'lowed he would n't go no how, so Skipper Nate he shipped one o' them Kunkett Blakeleys to go cook in the room on him, an' in jes' two weeks' time to a day they was ev'ry soul on 'em drownded. You kin bate high rats ain't cal'latin' to skin out'n a vess'l that way for nothin', an' never was!

"But talkin' 'bout losin' vess'ls puts me in mind o' the time father was los' in the ole Good Intent, there. I wa'n't but 'bout ten year ole then, an' there was six on us young uns to home 'long o' mother. 'T was a ter'ble ole breeze o' win', that one was, an' you take it down to the Bay She-lore, where father was to, an' nineteen sail on our 'Merican fishermen was los'. It blowed here right out endways, an' for the matter o' that, it swep' the whole coast clip an' clean, but what I'm comin' at 's this.

"Up to our house there, 'long toewards midnight, they commenced poundin' an' bangin' of her fit to stave her sides an' ruf in chock to the cellar! Of all the hell-fired rackers ever I hearn yit, that was the wusst one! It skeered us young uns mos' to con-niptions, but mother she bunched us all together downstairs into the settin'-room an' tol' me an' brother Sam jes' what the matter was. You could n't learn her nothin' 'bout them kind o' things, 'cause she'd been there afore, mother had, an' she knowed blame well father's vess'l was a goner, soon 's ever them hellish works commenced.

"Wal sir, they kep' up that air bangin' an' whangin' o' that ole house pooty nigh all night long, without no let-up. Why, them clips they give it sounded for all the world jes' like somebody was standin' off an' givin' of it to her with thund'rin' great mallets an' top-mauls, so 's 't you 'd cal-'lated for sure they 'd stove off half the shingles, an' shook the plasterin' down 'fore they slacked up! But come nex' mornin', an' there wa'n't so much 's a scratch to be seen on to that air house from cellar to garret!"

"Be dod-blowed ef that ain't 'bout the sing'lares' thing ever I heerd tell on!" ex-claimed Simeon, removing his spectacles, and gazing earnestly at Job over the desk. "An' you preten' to say the ole Good In-tent was los' that same night?"

"Yas siree, I do!" replied Cap'n Job decidedly. "She made out to turn turtle on 'em 'bout two o'clock in the mornin', nigh 's ever we could make out. There wa'n't but half a dozen sail o' the whole fleet that clawed out'n the Bay in that breeze o' win', an' four o' them was 'pinks.' Course you know how 't is down there into that set-fired guzzle-trap; ef you git ketched, you got to crack on sail an' sock it to a vess'l scan'lous to git sea-room, but this time the fleet was doin' well fishin', an' they hung on too long. I been there times 'nough sence so 's to know jes' how it worked. Ef a craf' won't lug sail, your name's mud, that's the whole story.

"Ole Skipper Lish Perkins he was to the Bay this time in the ole Paytriot, an' come out'n it jes' by the skin o' his teeth, too, an' I tell ye when the Paytriot would n't wear a cluss-reefed mains'l an' the bunnet out'n her jib, it wa'n't no sense for any the res' part o' the fleet to try it on, not a d——n mite, but this time Skip' Lish 'lowed she would n't so much's look at it under them sails; allst the creetur 'd do was to lay ri' down chock to her hatches an' waller! They blowed away mos' ev'rythin' they had aboard in the shape o' muslin, but fin'lly some ways or 'nother they come out'n it. Skip' Lish he allus stuck to it he was in comp'ny that night long o' father into the Good Intent, an' 'lowed how he see her hove down by a master great holler sea, a reg'lar ole he one, 't was, so 's 't she never got on her legs ag'in. This was somewhere 's nigh two in the mornin', an' they never see no sign on her sence, nor her crowd, neither!"

"But that there bastin' they give the house that night, Job, that's what jes' gits me!" said Simeon. "Puts me in mind o' the works the ole folks allus an' forever use' to be gossipin' 'bout when we was youngsters.

"Sich works ain't nigh so common roun' here o' late years as they was them times. Now you take it 'fore Hetty Moye an' Aunt Polly lit out, an' them two jes' fairly kep' things a-hummin' here to this Cove with their set-fired pranks an' works! Blame ef 't wa'n't downright horrid the works them two ole critters was into in them days!"

"Oh, them was jes' rank pizen, them two was," observed Cap'n Job, tilting back in his chair against the counter. "You jes' take an' let a pore feller once git on the wrong side o' Aunt Polly, an' 't was all day with him, be jiggered ef it wa'n't, now! She'd d——n quick figger out some ways to git her come-uppance 'long on him, an' don't you think for a minute she would n't!"

"Lord sakes! I guess she would some quick!" cried Simeon. "An' you come to take Hetty Moye there, you take an' let her jes' git that dod-blasted ole bridle o' hern roun' a feller's neck good an' taut, an' it's a chance ef he did n't wish mos' damnly he had n't never been borned 'fore ever she got through 'long on him!

"They allus 'lowed how she driv Cap'n Zachy Condon chock down to Kunkett ole harbor an' back ag'in the same night on one o' them hell-fired exhibitions o' hern, an' the pore old creetur was so tuckered an' beat out he never sot foot out o' bed for three weeks. I tell ye, it doos jes' knock tar-water the doin's an' goin's on there was here to this Cove in them days!

Blame ef 't ain't some sing'lar! Why, I don't cal'late there was ary skipper to this place but what dassen't turn to an' git his vess'l under way without he'd been up an' fixed things all straight 'long o' Aunt Polly fus'. Lord Harry! What slathers o' terbacker I've seed backed up to her place there in my time!"

"That 's a fac', Simeon!" exclaimed Sheriff Windseye. "An' snuff, too! Any God's quantity o' tea an' snuff she use' to git, right 'long stiddy. Why, 't was allus counted a reg'lar temptation o' Prov'dence to make a start for the Cape Shore in the spring o' the year without you 'd been up an' bought your luck there to Aunt Polly's in good shape. I take notice I allus done so myself, an' I guess them that hain't 's plaguy scatt'rin' here to the Cove, ef they 've got any age at all on to 'em. It's some sing'lar, though, how them ole witch-women has died out roun' this part o' the country."

"Died out be jiggered!" cried Cap'n Job Gaskett indignantly. "Them style o' folks ain't died out by a jugful; not yit awhile, they ain't! Don't you go runnin' 'way 'long o' no sich idee 's that air, Cap'n, 'cause ef ye do, 'tween you an' me an' the win'lass-bitt, you'll git everlastin'ly lef'. I'm tellin' ye there 's folks right here to this Cove today that 's jes' as well fittin' to heave the bridle, an' tech cream, an' blas' crops, an' upset loads o' hay, an' raise gin'ral ructions as ary one o' them ole style folks was, an' nothin' only the sod won't take it out'n 'em, neither, but the thing on 't is, they 're more slyer an' cunninger 'bout gittin' in their work, now'days, that's allst there is to it."

"Wal, I dunno 'bout that, Cap'n Job," replied the Sheriff doubtfully. "Folks roun' here 's gittin' mos' too posted at this day o' the worl' for to take a great sight o' stock into sich works."

"'T ain't a question o' bein' posted at all," Cap'n Job persisted, warming up in defense of his favorite theory. "Forty year ago folks roun' here was better posted 'n they be now, an' a d——n sight smarter in ev'ry way, shape, an' manner. Look a' the Wes' Injy bus'niss there was carried on to this Cove; look a' the master fleet o' fishermen there was fitted out here ev'ry springtime; thirty odd sail o' vess'ls owned right here to this one place; look a' the fish there was made here, an' the coop'rin' shops there was here, an' now look a' what is there here?

"Nothin'. Jes' plain nothin'. Ev'ry dod-blasted thing jes' deado! Vess'ls all gone, w'arfts all gone, an' all our smart men gone too, up back o' the meetin'-house here, but I take pertik'ler notice that when they was livin', an' doin' more bus'niss in a week 'n what you fellers see in a year's time, they did n't begredge a dollar for the sake o' keepin' on the right side o' Polly Belknap! You kin claim folks roun' here is a ter'ble sight better posted now'days, but ef there 's ary man 'live here to this Cove to-day could learn them ole sirs how to git a livin', I'll thank ye to jes' up an' p'int him out to me. That 's ev'ry cussed thing I'll ask on ye; jes' up an' p'int him right out." And Cap'n Job looked about him at the assemblage defiantly.

"Yas sir," Cap'n Roundturn replied at length. "There was cert'nly a tremendius smart set o' men doin' bus'niss here to this Cove them days, an' 'twa'n't no habit o' our'n to take much chances, neither. I'll presume to say there ain't no case on record where a vess'l ever lef' this Cove on her fus' trip in the spring o' the year without she'd made a short hitch to the nor'rard fus' for luck. Mebbe there wa'n't nothin' into sich a pro-cess, an' then ag'in mebbe there was a set-fired heap into it, an' I allus felt consid'ble easier for doin' of it, to the las' o' my goin' on the water."

"So did I, Cap'n!" cried Job Gaskett; "I allus done so, reg'lar, an' so I would now ef I wa'n't lookin' for trouble, but I cal'late Cap'n Windseye here 'lows how 't wa'n't nothin' but witchery into it."

"No sich a thing!" the Sheriff shouted, at once resenting this slur upon his seamanship. "I allus made a hitch to the nor'rard quick's ever my anchor was broke out! I ain't claimin' there 's witch-works into no sich custom as that air. We all on us done it, an' I kin show you them that doos so to-day, but my p'int is that folks roun' here ain't so skeered o' witch-doin's as they was form'ly."

"Wal," retorted Cap'n Job, "ef they hain't, it's their own lookout. Them that knows nothin' fears nothin', an' I ain't s'posed to allus keep an eye to wind'ard for 'em. But bein' 's we're on this tack this evenin', I kin tell ye another kind o' sing'lar thing father see one time when he was into the ole Mirandy, boun' home here with a trip o' fish from Canso, 'long o' ole Skip' Adam Whitten.

"They 'd took a fresh eas'ly breeze, an' hooped her right 'long in good shape, till father he cal'lated he was well to the west-'ard o' Cape 'Lizbeth, but it had been thick o' fog all the time comin' 'long, so 's 't they had n't sighted nothin' 't all. 'Long in the evenin' she shet in thicker 'n ever; one o' them reg'lar ole black, dreepin' fogs same 's to-night, so 's 't ye could n't even see the win'lass from jes' beaft the foremas', an' father he commenced bimeby to git kind o' fidgety like at not makin' nothin', so fin'lly he goes chock for'rard so 's t' listen an' see ef he could n't git holt o' the rote on Boon Islant. This was 'bout nine in the evenin', 'cordin' to his tell, an' the win' had kind o' petered out on 'em, but there was a devil of an ole sea heavin' in, so 's 't ev'rything 'long shore was breakin' a clean torch. Wal, father he was stannin' there for'rard listenin' away for allst he was wuth, an' hopin' every minute to git holt o' sup'n, when all of a suddin there come a bust o' music right alof', pooty nigh overhead, an' bang up ole music she was too, jes' like one o' these here ban's, only there was a singin' o' women's v'ices mixed up into it some ways, so 's 't all han's aboard 'lowed they never heerd the beat of it.

"Wal sir, while they was all han's on 'em stannin' roun' on deck there takin' of it in, wha' 'd that air ole fogbank do but scale in a big hole right direc' over the vess'l, an' the stars come out jes' bright 's ever you see 'em the pooties' night ever growed, but all roun' ev'rywheres else, without 't was right in this hole, the fog was thick as ma'sh mud, so 's 't you could slice it up in chunks with a knife.

"Course, it give 'em all han's a consid-'ble start, an' they all 'lowed 't was a sign, but father he could n't 'pear to git over it all the way home, no how. He kep' cal-'latin' to find somebody dead for cert'n, soon 's ever he got ashore, but nothin' ever come out'n it without 't was at jes' twenty minutes pas' nine o'clock that same evenin' me an' brother Sam was borned!"

"Sho!" exclaimed Sheriff Windseye. "I don't doubt but that the ole man was glad to find it wa'n't no wuss. Wal, I mus' be gittin' 'long up the ro'd. Goin' up my way, Eph?"

"Hold on a minute 'fore you fill away, Cap'n," said Job. "There 's jes' one thing I sh'd like to ask ye 'bout 'fore this settin' 's closed. P'raps you'll preten' to say it don't make no diff'rence with the pork ef you stick a hog on the flood tide or on the ebb?"

"Wal," said the Sheriff after a moment's reflection, "I ain't prepared to give no 'pinion on that 'ere jes' yit. I've allus heerd tell how it done so, o' course, but I ain't never made no pertik'ler test on myself."

"Oh, you hain't!" cried Job. "Wal, now, I jes' hev! I've took an' tested of it right chock to the handle, an' you'll find pork that 's killed on the ebb 'll shrink away one quarter part ev'ry dog-gone time! Now there was ole Skip' Ben Kentall up on the milldam ro'd there, he was called a master han' to stick pigs, an' done 'bout the whole o' sich jobs up round there after he come to quit goin'. Them folks up there use' to 'low Skip' Ben knowed jes' the bearin's o' the creetur's jug'lar so 's 't he could allus fetch it the very fust swipe o' the knife, an' you take him, an' he was allus jes' so keerful to make dead sure the tide had n't pinched off a grain 'fore ever he commenced. He knowed blame well jes' how the thing worked, an' so doos mos' the whole o' them ole farmers up back here, now'days.

"You turn to an' frog it up on the Kun-kett ro'd there an' ask ole Jeff Blakeley how 't is 'bout. You take an' go up to his place there, an' tell him to his face you got your doubts 'bout it, an' see how quick he'll go into the air! I cal'late he'd up an' take a stick o' cord-wood to a feller ef he sh'd go up there an' hang it out there wa'n't nothin' into it. But there! what 's the good talkin'? It's the truth all right, an' soon 's ever you come to look at it, there ain't a thing onraytionable 'bout it, not a thing. You can't deny but that the ebb tide's ter'ble drawrin', kin you? How many sick folks kin you make out to reckon up here to this Cove, that's died without 's on the ebb? Guess you'll find them that hain't 's consid'ble few an' fur between, now. The ebb tide makes out to jes' dreen the life right out'n 'em slick 's a whistle!

"Then ag'in, you take an' go down to the shore here anywheres to fill a bucket o' salt water to wash anybody with that's rheumaticky, an' you've allus got to fill it on the ebb, so's 't it'll be good an' draw-rin', you know, or ef you don't, you'll be apt to wisht mos' damnly ye had, for water that's filled on the flood 'll drive them gripes an' rheumatics chock to the vitils, sure 's ever the sun rises an' sets!"

X

NEGRO TALES

No population group has made a more important and substantial contribution to the civilization of the United States than the Negroes. In their spirituals, their work and blues songs, their folk tales, and their jazz they have supplied an original element without which the national culture would be the poorer. But like American civilization in general the Negro contribution is a synthesis of many elements and hence difficult to analyze. To a certain residue of African lore and chant the Negroes resident in the United States have added borrowings from the Indians and from the southern white people, particularly of a mythological and religious nature. The primitive assimilation of some of this material is illustrated in the stories of Roark Bradford, which provided Marc Connelly with the theme and substance of his notable drama *Green Pastures*. In the last decades of the nineteenth century Joel Chandler Harris drew a vast amount of folk material—songs, tales, proverbs—from the Georgia plantations and imposed an artistic form upon them. His creation of Uncle Remus provided unity and focus for his tales but sometimes shifted the interest from the story to the narrator, since the character of the old Negro is often the most vital element in the tales. In this way the artistic appeal of the narratives is augmented while their value as pure folklore diminishes. It is interesting to compare in this connection the work of Harris with the carefully recorded tales of Zora Neale Hurston, a trained anthropologist, who collected her material in the field and who was meticulous in transcribing what she heard without attempting to impose an artificial framework on the stories. In Miss Hurston's *Mules and Men* it is always the substance which holds our attention, never the informant or the narrator. But the perennial appeal of Uncle Remus is ample proof of the literary genius of Joel Chandler Harris.

UNCLE REMUS INITIATES THE LITTLE BOY

by Joel Chandler Harris

The fable in which animals speak and act like human beings has a long and distinguished history. The earliest animal narratives were purely factual, but in the hands of Aesop and later fabulists the fable became a vehicle for a moral. In the plantation stories of Joel Chandler Harris there is occasionally a moral, but it is seldom obtrusive. Harris also established a narrative device which he consistently adhered to—that of Uncle Remus telling stories in response to the questions of a little boy. The setting is a plantation and the characters and atmosphere suggest southern life. Harris usually chose the rabbit, the most inoffensive of animals, as the hero-prankster of his tales, although occasionally the terrapin is given that role. Although there is no need to read allegory into the stories, there is often the implication that the rabbit represents the Negro and that the Negro can best advance his own aims by pitting cunning and strategy against the superior strength of his antagonists. It is an interesting point whether the character of Uncle Remus weakens or strengthens the stories as folk tales, but there can be no doubt that in creating the old Negro storyteller Harris has added an imperishable figure to the American portrait gallery.

One evening recently, the lady whom Uncle Remus calls "Miss Sally" missed her little seven-year-old. Making search for him through the house and through the yard, she heard the sound of voices in the old man's cabin, and, looking through the window, saw the child sitting by Uncle Remus. His head rested against the old man's arm, and he was gazing with an expression of the most intense interest into the rough, weather-beaten face, that beamed so kindly upon him. This is what "Miss Sally" heard:

"Bimeby, one day, arter Brer Fox bin doin' all dat he could fer ter ketch Brer Rabbit, en Brer Rabbit bin doin' all he could fer ter keep 'im fum it, Brer Fox say to hisse'f dat he'd put up a game on Brer Rabbit, en he ain't mo'n got de wuds out'n his mouf twel Brer Rabbit come a

407

lopin' up de big road, lookin' des ez plump, en ez fat, en ez sassy ez a Moggin hoss in a barley-patch.

" 'Hol' on dar, Brer Rabbit,' sez Brer Fox, sezee.

" 'I ain't got time, Brer Fox,' sez Brer Rabbit, sezee, sorter mendin' his licks.

" 'I wanter have some confab wid you, Brer Rabbit,' sez Brer Fox, sezee.

" 'All right, Brer Fox, but you better holler fum whar you stan'. I'm monstus full er fleas dis mawnin',' sez Brer Rabbit, sezee.

" 'I seed Brer B'ar yistiddy,' sez Brer Fox, sezee, 'en he sorter rake me over de coals kaze you en me ain't make frens en live naberly, en I tole 'im dat I'd see you.'

"Den Brer Rabbit scratch one year wid his off hinefoot sorter jub'usly, en den he ups en sez, sezee:

" 'All a settin', Brer Fox. Spose'n you drap roun' termorrer en take dinner wid me. We ain't got no great doin's at our house, but I speck de ole 'oman en de chilluns kin sorter scramble roun' en git up sump'n fer ter stay yo' stummuck.'

" 'I'm 'gree'ble, Brer Rabbit,' sez Brer Fox, sezee.

" 'Den I'll 'pen' on you,' sez Brer Rabbit, sezee.

"Nex' day, Mr. Rabbit an' Miss Rabbit got up soon, 'fo' day, en raided on a gyarden like Miss Sally's out dar, en got some cabbiges, en some roas'n years, en some sparrer-grass, en dey fix up a smashin' dinner. Bimeby one er de little Rabbits, playin' out in de back-yard, come runnin' in hollerin', 'Oh, ma! oh, ma! I seed Mr. Fox a comin'!' En den Brer Rabbit he tuck de chilluns by der years en make um set down, en den him en Miss Rabbit sorter dally roun' waitin' for Brer Fox. En dey keep on waitin', but no Brer Fox ain't come. Atter'while Brer Rabbit goes to de do', easy like, en peep out, en dar, stickin' out fum behime de cornder, wuz de tip-een'

er Brer Fox tail. Den Brer Rabbit shut de do' en sot down, en put his paws behime his years en begin fer ter sing:

De place wharbouts you spill de grease,
  Right dar youer boun' ter slide,
An' whar you fine a bunch er ha'r,
  You'll sholy fine de hide.

"Nex' day, Brer Fox sont word by Mr. Mink, en skuze hisse'f kaze he wuz too sick fer ter come, en he ax Brer Rabbit fer ter come en take dinner wid him, en Brer Rabbit say he wuz 'gree'ble.

"Bimeby, w'en de shadders wuz at der shortes', Brer Rabbit he sorter brush up en santer down ter Brer Fox's house, en w'en he got dar, he yer somebody groanin', en he look in de do' en dar he see Brer Fox settin' up in a rockin' cheer all wrop up wid flannil, en he look mighty weak. Brer Rabbit look all 'roun', he did, but he ain't see no dinner. De dishpan wuz settin' on de table, en close by wuz a kyarvin' knife.

" 'Look like you gwineter have chicken fer dinner, Brer Fox,' sez Brer Rabbit, sezee.

" 'Yes, Brer Rabbit, deyer nice, en fresh, en tender,' sez Brer Fox, sezee.

"Den Brer Rabbit sorter pull his mustarsh, en say: 'You ain't got no calamus root, is you, Brer Fox? I done got so now dat I can't eat no chicken 'ceppin she's seasoned up wid calamus root.' En wid dat Brer Rabbit lipt out er de do' and dodge 'mong de bushes, en sot dar watchin' fer Brer Fox; en he ain't watch long, nudder, kaze Brer Fox flung off de flannil en crope out er de house en got whar he could close in on Brer Rabbit, en bimeby Brer Rabbit holler out: 'Oh, Brer Fox! I'll des put yo' calamus root out yer on dish yer stump. Better come git it while hit's fresh,' and wid dat Brer Rabbit gallop off home. En Brer Fox ain't never kotch 'im yit, en w'at's mo', honey, he ain't gwineter."

THE WONDERFUL TAR-BABY STORY

by Joel Chandler Harris

idn't the fox *never* catch the rabbit, Uncle Remus?" asked the little boy the next evening.

"He come mighty nigh it, honey, sho's you born—Brer Fox did. One day atter Brer Rabbit fool 'im wid dat calamus root, Brer Fox went ter wuk en got 'im some tar, en mix it wid some turkentine, en fix up a contrapshun w'at he call a Tar-Baby, en he tuck dish yer Tar-Baby en he sot 'er in de big road, en den he lay off in de bushes fer to see w'at de news wuz gwineter be. En he didn't hatter wait long, nudder, kaze bimeby here come Brer Rabbit pacin' down de road—lippity-clippity, clippity-lippity—des ez sassy ez a jay-bird. Brer Fox, he lay low. Brer Rabbit come prancin' 'long twel he spy de Tar-Baby, en den he fotch up on his behime legs like he wuz 'stonished. De Tar-Baby, she sot dar, she did, en Brer Fox, he lay low.

" 'Mawnin'!' sez Brer Rabbit, sezee— 'nice wedder dis mawnin',' sezee.

"Tar-Baby ain't sayin' nothin', en Brer Fox, he lay low.

" 'How duz yo' symtums seem ter segashuate?' sez Brer Rabbit, sezee.

"Brer Fox, he wink his eye slow, en lay low, en de Tar-Baby, she ain't sayin' nothin'.

" 'How you come on, den? Is you deaf?' sez Brer Rabbit, sezee. 'Kaze if you is, I kin holler louder,' sezee.

"Tar-Baby stay still, en Brer Fox, he lay low.

" 'Youer stuck up, dat's w'at you is,' says Brer Rabbit, sezee, 'en I'm gwineter kyore you, dat's w'at I'm a gwineter do,' sezee.

"Brer Fox, he sorter chuckle in his stummuck, he did, but Tar-Baby ain't sayin' nothin'.

" 'I'm gwineter larn you how ter talk ter 'specttubble fokes ef hit's de las' ack,' sez Brer Rabbit, sezee. 'Ef you don't take off dat hat en tell me howdy, I'm gwineter bus' you wide open,' sezee.

"Tar-Baby stay still, en Brer Fox, he lay low.

"Brer Rabbit keep on axin' 'im, en de Tar-Baby, she keep on sayin' nothin', twel present'y Brer Rabbit draw back wid his fis', he did, en blip he tuck 'er side de head. His fis' stuck, en he can't pull loose. De tar hilt 'im. But Tar-Baby, she stay still, en Brer Fox, he lay low.

" 'Ef you don't lemme loose, I'll knock you agin,' sez Brer Rabbit, sezee, en wid dat he fotch 'er a wipe wid de udder han', en dat stuck. Tar-Baby, she ain't sayin' nothin', en Brer Fox, he lay low.

" 'Tu'n me loose, fo' I kick de natal stuffin' outen you,' sez Brer Rabbit, sezee, but de Tar-Baby, she ain't sayin' nothin'. She des hilt on, en den Brer Rabbit lose de use er his feet in de same way. Brer Fox, he lay low. Den Brer Rabbit squall out dat ef de Tar-Baby don't tu'n 'im loose he butt 'er cranksided. En den he butted, en his head got stuck. Den Brer Fox, he sa'ntered fort', lookin' des ez innercent ez one er yo' mammy's mockin'-birds.

" 'Howdy, Brer Rabbit,' sez Brer Fox, sezee. 'You look sorter stuck up dis mawnin',' sezee, en den he rolled on de groun', en laft en laft twel he couldn't laff no mo'. 'I speck you'll take dinner wid me dis time, Brer Rabbit. I done laid in some calamus root, en I ain't gwineter take no skuse,' sez Brer Fox, sezee."

Here Uncle Remus paused, and drew a two-pound yam out of the ashes.

"Did the fox eat the rabbit?" asked the little boy to whom the story had been told.

"Dat's all de fur de tale goes," replied the old man. "He mout, en den agin he moutent. Some say Jedge B'ar come 'long en loosed 'im—some say he didn't. I hear Miss Sally callin'. You better run 'long."

HOW MR. RABBIT WAS TOO SHARP FOR MR. FOX

by Joel Chandler Harris

Uncle Remus," said the little boy one evening, when he had found the old man with little or nothing to do, "did the fox kill and eat the rabbit when he caught him with the Tar-Baby?"

"Law, honey, ain't I tell you 'bout dat?" replied the old darkey, chuckling slyly. "I 'clar ter grashus I ought er tole you dat, but old man Nod was ridin' on my eyeleds 'twel a leetle mo'n I'd a dis'-member'd my own name, en den on to dat here come yo' mammy hollerin' atter you.

"W'at I tell you w'en I fus' begin? I tole you Brer Rabbit wuz a monstus soon creetur; leas'ways dat's w'at I laid out fer ter tell you. Well, den, honey, don't you go en make no udder calkala-shuns, kaze in dem days Brer Rabbit en his fambly wuz at de head er de gang w'en enny racket wuz on han', en dar dey stayed. 'Fo' you begins fer ter wipe yo' eyes 'bout Brer Rabbit, you wait en see whar'bouts Brer Rabbit gwineter fetch up at. But dat's needer yer ner dar.

"W'en Brer Fox fine Brer Rabbit mixt up wid de Tar-Baby, he feel mighty good, en he roll on de groun' en laff. Bimeby he up'n say, sezee:

"'Well, I speck I got you dis time, Brer Rabbit,' sezee; 'maybe I ain't, but I speck I is. You been runnin' round here sassin' atter me a mighty long time, but I speck you done come ter de een' er de row. You bin cuttin' up yo' capers en bouncin' roun' in dis neighberhood ontwel you come ter b'leeve yo'se'f de boss er de whole gang. En den youer allers some'rs whar you got no bizness,' sez Brer Fox, sezee. 'Who ax you fer ter come en strike up a'quaintance wid dish yer Tar-Baby? En who stuck you up dar whar you iz? Nobody in de roun' worril. You des tuck en jam yo'se'f on dat Tar-Baby widout waitin' fer enny invite,' sez Brer Fox, sezee, 'en dar you is, en dar you'll stay twel I fixes up a bresh-pile and fires her up, kaze I'm gwineter bobbycue you dis day, sho,' sez Brer Fox, sezee.

"Den Brer Rabbit talk mighty 'umble.

" 'I don't keer w'at you do wid me, Brer Fox,' sezee, 'so you don't fling me in dat brier-patch. Roas' me, Brer Fox,' sezee, 'but don't fling me in dat brier-patch,' sezee.

" 'Hit's so much trouble fer ter kindle a fier,' sez Brer Fox, sezee, 'dat I speck I'll hatter hang you,' sezee.

" 'Hang me des ez high as you please, Brer Fox,' sez Brer Rabbit, sezee, 'but do fer de Lord's sake don't fling me in dat brier-patch,' sezee.

" 'I ain't got no string,' sez Brer Fox, sezee, 'en now I speck I'll hatter drown you,' sezee.

" 'Drown me des ez deep ez you please, Brer Fox,' sez Brer Rabbit, sezee, 'but do don't fling me in dat brier-patch,' sezee.

" 'Dey ain't no water nigh,' sez Brer Fox, sezee, 'en now I speck I'll hatter skin you,' sezee.

" 'Skin me, Brer Fox,' sez Brer Rabbit, sezee, 'snatch out my eyeballs. t'ar out my years by de roots, en cut off my legs,' sezee, 'but do please, Brer Fox, don't fling me in dat brier-patch,' sezee.

"Co'se Brer Fox wanter hurt Brer Rabbit bad ez he kin, so he cotch 'im by de behime legs en slung 'im right in de middle er de brier-patch. Dar wuz a considerbul flutter whar Brer Rabbit struck de bushes, en Brer Fox sorter hang roun' fer ter see w'at wuz gwineter happen. Bimeby he hear somebody call 'im, en way up de hill he see Brer Rabbit settin' cross-legged on a chinkapin log koamin' de pitch outen his har wid a chip. Den Brer Fox know dat he bin swop off mighty bad. Brer Rabbit wuz bleedzed fer ter fling back some er his sass, en he holler out:

" 'Bred en bawn in a brier-patch, Brer Fox—bred en bawn in a brier-patch!' en wid dat he skip out des ez lively ez a cricket in de embers.''

MR. BENJAMIN RAM
AND HIS WONDERFUL FIDDLE

by Joel Chandler Harris

I 'speck you done year tell er ole man Benjermun Ram," said Uncle Remus, with a great affectation of indifference, after a pause.

"Old man who?" asked the little boy.

"Old man Benjermun Ram. I 'speck you done year tell er him too long 'go ter talk 'bout."

"Why, no, I haven't, Uncle Remus!" exclaimed the little boy, protesting and laughing. "He must have been a mighty funny old man."

"Dat's ez may be," responded Uncle Remus, sententiously. "Fun deze days wouldn't er counted fer fun in dem days; en many's de time w'at I see folks laughin'," continued the old man, with such withering sarcasm that the little boy immediately became serious,—"many's de time w'at I sees um laughin' en laughin', w'en I lay dey ain't kin tell w'at deyer laughin' at deyse'f. En 'tain't der laughin' w'at pesters me, nudder,"—relenting a little,—"hit's dish yer ev'lastin' snickle en giggle, giggle en snickle."

Having thus mapped out, in a dim and uncertain way, what older people than the little boy might have been excused for accepting as a sort of moral basis, Uncle Remus proceeded:

"Dish yer Mr. Benjermun Ram, w'ich he done come up inter my min', was one er deze yer ole-timers. Dey tells me dat he 'uz a fiddler fum away back yander—one er dem ar kinder fiddlers w'at can't git de chune down fine 'less dey pats der foot. He stay all by he own-alone se'f 'way out in de middle un a big new-groun', en he sech a handy man fer ter have at a frolic dat de yuther creeturs like 'im mighty well, en w'en dey tuck a notion fer ter shake der foot, w'ich de notion tuck 'n' struck um eve'y once in a w'ile, nuthin' 'ud do but dey mus' sen' fer ole man Benjermun Ram en he fiddle; en dey do say," continued Uncle Remus, closing his eyes in a sort of ecstasy, "dat w'en he squar' hisse'f back in a cheer, en git in a weavin' way, he kin des snatch dem old-time chunes fum who lay de rail. En den,

412

w'en de frolic wuz done, dey'd all fling in, dem yuther creeturs would, en fill up a bag er peas fer ole Mr. Benjermun Ram fer ter kyar home wid 'im.

"One time, des 'bout Christmas, Miss Meadows en Miss Motts en de gals, dey up 'n' say dat dey'd sorter gin a blow-out, en dey got wud ter ole man Benjermun Ram w'ich dey 'speckted 'im fer ter be on han'. W'en de time come fer Mr. Benjermun Ram fer ter start, de win' blow cole en de cloud 'gun ter spread out 'cross de elements —but no marter fer dat; ole man Benjermun Ram tuck down he walkin'-cane, he did, en tie up de fiddle in a bag, en sot out fer Miss Meadows. He thunk he know de way, but hit keep on gittin' col'er, en col'er, en mo' cloudy, twel bimeby, fus' news you know, ole Mr. Benjermun Ram done lose de way. Ef he'd er kep' on down de big road fum de start, it moughter bin diffunt, but he tuck a nigh-cut, en he ain't git fur 'fo' he done los' sho' 'nuff. He go dis away, en he go dat away, en he go de yuther way, yit all de same he wus done los'. Some folks would er sot right flat down whar dey wus en study out de way, but ole man Benjermun Ram ain't got wrinkle on he hawn fer nothin', kaze he done got de name er ole Billy Hardhead long 'fo' dat. Den ag'in, some folks would er stop right still in der tracks en holler en bawl fer ter see ef dey can't roust up some er de neighbors, but ole Mr. Benjermun Ram, he des stick he jowl in de win', he did, en he march right on des 'zackly like he know he ain't gwine de wrong way. He keep on, but 'twan't long 'fo' he 'gun ter feel right lonesome, mo' speshually w'en hit come up in he min' how Miss Meadows en de gals en all de comp'ny be bleedz ter do de bes' dey kin widout any fiddlin'; en hit kinder make he marrer git cole w'en he study 'bout how he gotter sleep out dar in de woods by hisse'f.

"Yit, all de same, he keep on twel de dark 'gun ter drap down, en den he keep on still, en bimeby he come ter a little rise whar dey wuz a clay-gall. W'en he git dar he stop en look 'roun', he did, en 'way off down in de holler, dar he see a light shinin', en w'en he see dis, ole man Benjermun Ram tuck he foot in he han', en make he way todes it des lak it de ve'y place w'at he bin huntin'. 'Twan't long 'fo' he come ter de house whar de light is, en, bless you soul, he don't make no bones er knockin'. Den somebody holler out:

" 'Who dat?'

" 'I'm Mr. Benjermun Ram, en I done lose de way, en I come fer ter ax you ef you can't take me in fer de night,' sezee.

"In common," continued Uncle Remus, "ole Mr. Benjermun Ram wuz a mighty rough-en-spoken somebody, but you better b'leeve he talk monst'us perlite dis time.

"Den some un on t'er side er de do' ax Mr. Benjermun Ram fer ter walk right in, en wid dat he open de do' en walk in, en make a bow like fiddlin' folks does w'en dey goes in comp'ny; but he ain't no sooner made he bow en look 'roun' twel he 'gun ter shake en shiver lak he done bin stricken wid de swamp ager, kaze, settin' right dar 'fo' de fier wuz ole Brer Wolf, wid his toofies showin' up all w'ite en shiny like dey wuz bran new. Ef ole Mr. Benjermun Ram ain't bin so ole en stiff I boun' you he'd er broke en run, but 'mos' 'fo' he had time fer ter study 'bout gittin' 'way, ole Brer Wolf done bin jump up en shet de do' en fassen' 'er wid a great big chain. Ole Mr. Benjermun Ram he know he in fer't, en he tuck'n put on a bol' face ez he kin, but he des nat'ally hone fer ter be los' in de woods some mo'. Den he make 'n'er low bow, en he hope Brer Wolf and all his folks is well, en den he say, sezee, dat he des drap in fer ter wom hisse'f, en 'quire uv de way ter Miss Meadows', en ef Brer Wolf be so good ez ter set 'im in de road ag'in, he be off putty soon en be much 'blige in de bargains.

" 'Tooby sho', Mr. Ram,' sez Brer Wolf, sezee, w'iles he lick he chops en

grin; 'des put yo' walkin'-cane in de cor-
der over dar, en set yo' bag down on de
flo', en make yo'se'f at home,' sezee. 'We
ain't got much,' sezee, 'but w'at we is got
is yone w'iles you stays, en I boun' we'll
take good keer un you,' sezee; en wid dat
Brer Wolf laugh en show his toofies so bad
dat ole man Benjermun Ram come mighty
nigh havin' 'n'er ager.

"Den Brer Wolf tuck'n' flung 'n'er
lighter'd-knot on de fier, en den he slip
inter de back room, en present'y, w'iles ole
Mr. Benjermun Ram wuz settin' dar
shakin' in he shoes, he year Brer Wolf
whispun' ter he ole 'oman:

" 'Ole 'oman! ole 'oman! Fling 'way yo'
smoke meat—fresh meat fer supper! Fling
'way yo' smoke meat—fresh meat fer supper!'

"Den ole Miss Wolf, she talk out loud,
so Mr. Benjermun Ram kin year:

" 'Tooby sho' I'll fix 'im some supper.
We er 'way off yer in de woods, so fur
fum comp'ny dat goodness knows I'm
mighty glad ter see Mr. Benjermun Ram.'

"Den Mr. Benjermun Ram year ole
Miss Wolf whettin' 'er knife on a rock—
shirrah! shirrah! shirrah!—en ev'y time
he year de knife say shirrah! he know he
dat much nigher de dinner-pot. He know
he can't git 'way, en w'iles he settin' dar
studyin', hit 'come 'cross he min' dat he
des mought ez well play one mo' chune on
he fiddle 'fo' de wuss come ter de wuss.
Wid dat he ontie de bag en take out de
fiddle, en 'gun ter chune 'er up—plink,
plank, plunk, plink! plunk, plank, plink,
plunk!"

Uncle Remus's imitation of the tuning
of a fiddle was marvellous enough to produce a startling effect upon a much less enthusiastic listener than the little boy. It
was given in perfect good faith, but the
serious expression on the old man's face
was so irresistibly comic that the child
laughed until the tears ran down his face.
Uncle Remus very properly accepted this as

a tribute to his wonderful resources as a
story-teller, and continued, in great good-
humor:

"W'en ole Miss Wolf year dat kinder
fuss, co'se she dunner w'at is it, en she drap
'er knife en lissen. Ole Mr. Benjermun Ram
ain't know dis, en he keep on chunin' up—
plank, plink, plunk, plank! Den ole Miss
Wolf, she tuck'n' hunch Brer Wolf wid'er
elbow, en she say, sez she:

" 'Hey, ole man! w'at dat?'

"Den bofe un um cock up der years
en lissen, en des 'bout dat time, ole Mr.
Benjermun Ram he sling de butt er de
fiddle up und' he chin, en struck up one er
dem ole-time chunes."

"Well, what tune was it, Uncle Remus?" the little boy asked, with some display of impatience.

"Ef I ain't done gone en fergit dat chune
off'n my min'," continued Uncle Remus;
"hit sorter went like dat ar song 'bout
'Sheep shell co'n wid de rattle er his ho'n';
en yit hit mout er been dat ar yuther one
'bout 'Roll de key, ladies, roll dem keys.'
Brer Wolf en ole Miss Wolf, dey lissen en
lissen, en de mo' w'at dey lissen de skeerder
dey git, twel bimeby dey tuck ter der heels
en make a break fer de swamp at de back
er de house, des lak de patter-rollers wuz
atter um.

"W'en ole man Benjermun Ram sorter
let up wid he fiddlin', he don't see no
Brer Wolf, en he don't year no ole Miss
Wolf. Den he look in de back room; no
Wolf dar. Den he look in de back po'ch;
no Wolf dar. Den he look in de closet en
de cubberd; no Wolf aint dar yit. Den
ole Mr. Benjermun Ram, he tuck 'n' shot
all de do's, en lock um, en he s'arch 'roun',
en he fine some peas en fodder in de lof',
w'ich he et um fer he supper, en den he lie
down front er de fier en sleep soun' ez
a log.

"Nex' mawnin' he 'uz up en stirrin'
monst'us soon, en he put out fum dar, en
he fine de way ter Miss Meadows' time

'nuff fer ter play at de frolic. W'en he git dar, Miss Meadows en de gals, dey run ter de gate fer ter meet 'im, en dis un tuck he hat, en dat un tuck he cane, en t'er 'n tuck he fiddle, en den dey up 'n' say:

" 'Law, Mr. Ram! whar de name er goodness is you bin? We so glad you come. Stir 'roun' yer, folks, en git Mr. Ram a cup er hot coffee.'

"Dey make a mighty big ter-do 'bout Mr. Benjermun Ram, Miss Meadows en Miss Motts en de gals did, but 'twix' you en me en de bedpos', honey, dey'd er had der frolic wh'er de ole chap 'uz dar er not, kaze de gals done make 'rangerments wid Brer Rabbit fer ter pat fer um, en in dem days Brer Rabbit wuz a patter, mon. He mos' sho'ly wuz."

REV. MIZRAIM HAM'S DISCOURSE

by Baynard Rush Hall

The camp meeting was one of the most interesting phenomena of the American frontier. Edward Eggleston has called the Methodist circuit rider the most important civilizing influence in the early Middle West; and certainly the camp meeting, at which itinerant Methodist and Baptist preachers exhorted large audiences, did much to advance religion and morality. Unfortunately, the speakers were often ignorant and untrained men whose chief goal was to provoke a mass hysteria. Hall's sketch of a Negro preacher in the Indiana backwoods emphasizes the crudeness of the appeal and the theatricality of the method. It is also interesting as an example of an effort to employ biblical names and events and to give them a local application. This same combination of familiar scriptural imagery and primitive anthropomorphic religion appears in one of the most successful plays of the modern American theater, Marc Connelly's Green Pastures. Hall, of course, had a satiric purpose in mind in recording the Reverend Mizraim Ham's discourse, since he wished to underscore the crudity of life in a region where he, an educated minister of the gospel, happened to be residing. But the strong folk quality of the preacher's language is obvious. The sketch appears in The New Purchase, originally published in 1843.

ᴮruthurn and sisturn, tention, if you please, while I want you for to understand this here battul most purtiklur 'zact or may be you moughtn't comprend 'um. Furst place, I'm gwyin to undevur to sarcumscribe fust the 'cashin of this here battul: second place, the 'comdashins of the armies: third place, the folkses as was gwyin for to fite and didn't want to, and some did: and last and fourth place, I'm gwyin for to show purtiklur 'zact them as fit juul, and git victry and git kily'd.

"Tention, if you pleases, while I fustly sarcumscribe the 'casion of this here battul. Bruthurn and sisturn, you see them thar hethun Fillystines, what warnt circumcised, they wants to ketch King Sol and his 'ar folks for to make um slave: and so they cums down to pick a quorl, and begins a totin off all their cawn, and wouldn't 'low um to make no hoes to hoe um, nor no homnee. And that 'ar, you ses, stick in King Solsis gizurd; and he ups and says, says he, 'I'm not gwying to be used up that 'ar way by them uncircumcis'd hethun Fillystines, and let um tote off our folkses cawn to chuck to thar hogs, and take away our hoes so we can't hoe um—and so, Jonathum, we'll drum up and list soljurs and try um a battul.' And then King Sol and his 'ar folks they goes up, and the hethun and theirn comes down and makes war. And this is the 'cashin why they fit.

"Tention 'gin, if you pleases, I'm gwyin in the next place secondly, to show the 'comdashins of this here battul which was so fashin like. The Filystines they had thar army up thar on a mounting, and King Sol he had hissin over thar, like across a branch, amoss like that a one thar—(pointing)—and it was chuck full of sling rock all along on the bottom. And so they was both on um camp'd out; this a one on this 'ar side, and tother a one on tother, and the lilly branch tween um—and them's the comdashins.

"Tention once more agin, as 'caze next place thirdly I'm a gwyin to give purtiklur 'zact 'count of sum folkeses what fit and sum didn't want to. And, lubly sinnahs, maybe you minds um, as how King Sol, and his soljurs was pepper hot for fite when he fust liss um; but now, lubly sinnahs, when they gits up to the Fillystines, they cool off mighty quick, I tell you! 'Caze why? I tell you; why, 'caze a grate, big, ugly ole jiunt, with grate big eyes, so fashin—(Mr. Ham made giant's eyes here)—he kums a rampin out afrunt o' them 'ar rigiments, like the ole devul a gwyin about like a half-starv'd lion a seeking to devour poor lubly sinnahs! And he cum a jumpin and a tearin out so fashin—(actions to suit)—to git sum of King Solsis soljurs to fite um juul: and King Sol, lubly bruthurn and sisturn, he gits sker'd mighty quick, and he says to Jonathun and tother big officers, says he—'I ain't a gwyin for to fite that grate big fellah.' And arter that they ups and says—'We ain't a gwyin for to fite um nuthur, 'caze he's all kiver'd with sheetirun, and his head's up so high we muss stand a hoss back to reach um!' the jiunt he was so *big!!*

"And then King Sol he quite down in the jaw, and he turn and ax if somebody wouldn't hunt up a soljur as would fite juul with um; and he'd give um his dawtah, the prinsuss, for wife, and make um king's son-in-law. And then one ole koretur, they call him Abnah, he comes up and say to Sol so: 'Please your majuste, sir, I kin git a young fellah to fite um,' says he. And Abnah tells how Davy had jist rid up in his carruge and left um with the man what tend the hossis—and how he heern Davy a quorl'n with his bruthurs and a wantum to fite the jiunt. Then King Sol, he feel mighty glad, I tell you, sinnahs, and he make um bring um up, and King Sol he begins a talkin so, and Davy he answers so:—

" 'What's your name, lilly fellah?'

" 'I was crissen'd Davy.'

" 'Whose your farder?'

" 'They call um Jesse.'

" 'What you follur for livin?'

" 'I tend my farder's-sheep.'

" 'What you kum arter? Ain't you af-feerd of that 'ar grate ugly ole jiunt up thar, lilly Davy?'

" 'I kum to see arter my udder brudurs, and bring um in our carrruge some cheese and muttun, and some clene shirt and trowsur, and have tother ones wash'd. And when I kum I hear ole Goliawh a hollerin out for somebody to cum and fite juul with um: and all the soljurs round thar they begins for to make traks mighty quick, I tell you, please your majuste, sir, for thar tents; but, says I, what you run for? I'm not a gwyin for to run away—if King Sol wants some body for to fite the juul, I'll fit um for um.'

" 'I mighty feerd, lilly Davy, you too leetul for um—'

" 'No! King Sol, I kin lick um. One day I git asleep ahind a rock, and out kums a lion and a bawr, and begins a totin off a lilly lam; and when I heern um roarin and pawin 'bout, I rubs my eyes and sees um gwyin to the mountings—and I arter and ketch'd up and kill um both without no gun nor sword—and I bring back poor lilly lam. I kin lick ole Goliawh, I tell you, please your majuste, sir.'

"Then King Sol he wery glad, and pat um on the head, and calls um 'lilly Davy,' and wants to put on um his own armur made of brass and sheetirun, and to take his sword, but Davy didn't like um, but said he'd trust to his sling. And then out he goes to fite the ole jiunt; and this 'ar brings me to the fourth and last diwishin of our surmun.

"Tention once more agin' for lass time, as I'm gwyin to give most purtikuurlust 'zactest 'count of the juul atween lilly Davy and ole Goliawh the jiunt, to show, lubly sinnah! how the Lord's peepul with-out no carnul gun nor a sword, can fite ole Bellzybub and knock um over with the sling rock of prayer, as lilly Davy knock over Goliawh with hissin out of the Branch.

"And to 'lusterut the juul and make um spikus, I'll show 'zactly how they talk'd, and jawd, and fit it all out: and so ole Goliawh when he see Davy a kumun, he hollurs out so, and lilly Davy he say back so:—

" 'What you kum for, lilly Jew?—'

" 'What I kum for! you'll find out mighty quick, I tell you—I kum for fite juul—'

" 'Huhh! huhh! haw!—'tink I'm gwyin to fite puttee lilly baby? I want King Sol or Abnah, or a big soljur man—'

" 'Hole your jaw—I'll make you laugh tother side, ole grizzle-gruzzle, 'rectly,—I'm man enough for biggest jiunt Fillys-tine."

" 'Go way, poor lilly boy! go home, lilly baby, to your mudder, and git sugar plum—I no want kill puttee lilly boy—'

" 'Kum on!—dont be afeerd!—dont go for to run away!—I'll ketch you and lick you—'

" 'You d——n leetul raskul—I'll kuss you by all our gods—I'll cut out your sassy tung—I'll break your blackguard jaw,—I'll rip you up and give um to the dogs and crows—'

" 'Don't kuss so, ole Golly! I 'sposed you wanted to fite juul—so kum on with your old irun-pot hat on—you'll git belly full mighty quick—'

" 'You nasty leetul raskul, I'll kum and kill you dead as chopped sassudge.' "

Here the preacher represented the ad-vance of the parties; and gave a florid and wonderfully effective description of the clos-ing act partly by words and partly by pan-tomime; exhibiting innumerable marches and counter-marches to get to wind-ward, and all the postures, and gestures, and defiances, till at last he personated David putting his hand into a bag for a stone:—and then making his cotton handkerchief into a sling, he whirled it with fury half a dozen times around his head, and then let fly with much skill at Goliath; and at the same instant halloing with the phrenzy of a madman—"Hurraw! for lilly Davy!" At that cry he, with his left hand, struck himself a violent slap on the forehead, to represent the blow of the sling stone hitting the giant; and then in person of Goliath he dropped *quasi* dead upon the platform amid the deafening plaudits of the congregation; all of whom, some spiritually, some sympathetically, and some carnally, took up the preacher's triumph shout—

"Hurraw! for lilly Davy."

How the Rev. Mizraim Ham made his exit from the boards I could not see—perhaps he rolled or crawled off. But he did not suffer decapitation, like "ole Golly": since, in ten minutes, his woolly pate suddenly popped up among the other sacred heads that were visible over the front railing of the rostrum, as all kept moving to and fro in the wild tossings of religious phrenzy.

CHRISTMAS-NIGHT IN THE QUARTERS

by Irwin Russell

Russell wrote very little but remains well known as the author of one of the earliest sketches of Negro life in dialect, "Christmas-Night in the Quarters." On Christmas night Negroes traditionally "hold high carnival," and Russell's poem suggests that teamsters, fiddlers, and even the preacher join the festivity. At the conclusion there is an amusing tall tale which adapts biblical tradition to local geography. Noah's ark floats down a river which floods over the levees, and Ham, the first banjoist, takes hair from a possum for the instrument's strings and thus leaves the animal's tail permanently denuded.

● From *Christmas-Night in the Quarters and Other Poems*, by Irwin Russell, with an Introduction by Joel Chandler Harris and a Historical Sketch by Maurice Garland Fulton (New York: The Century Co., 1917), pp. 3–24. Reprinted by permission of Appleton-Century-Crofts, Inc., New York.

When merry Christmas-day is done
And Christmas-night is just begun;
While clouds in slow procession drift,
To wish the moon-man "Christmas gift,"
Yet linger overhead, to know
What causes all the stir below;
At Uncle Johnny Booker's ball
The darkies hold high carnival.
From all the country-side they throng,
With laughter, shouts, and scraps of song,—
Their whole deportment plainly showing
That to the Frolic they are going.
Some take the path with shoes in hand,
To traverse muddy bottom-land;
Aristocrats their steeds bestride—
Four on a mule, behold them ride!
And ten great oxen draw apace
The wagon from "de odder place,"
With forty guests, whose conversation
Betokens glad anticipation.
Not so with him who drives: old Jim
Is sagely solemn, hard, and grim,
And frolics have no joys for him.
He seldom speaks but to condemn—
Or utter some wise apothegm—
Or else, some crabbed thought pursuing,
Talk to his team, as now he's doing.

Come up heah, Star! Yee-bawee!
    You alluz is a-laggin'—
Mus' be you think I's dead,
    An' dis de huss you's draggin'—
You's 'mos' too lazy to draw yo' bref'
    Let 'lone drawin' de waggin.

Dis team—quit bel'rin, sah!
    De ladies don't submit 'at—
Dis team—you ol' fool ox,
    You heah me tell you quit 'at?
Dis team's des like de 'Nited States;
    Dat's what I's tryin' to git at!

De people rides behin',
    De pollytishners haulin'—
Sh'u'd be a well-bruk ox,
    To foller dat ar callin'—

An' sometimes nuffin won't do dem steers,
   But what dey mus' be stallin'!

Woo bahgh! Buck-kannon! Yes sar,
   Sometimes dey will be stickin';
An' den, fus thing dey knows,
   Dey takes a rale good lickin'.
De folks gits down: an' den watch out
   For hommerin' an' kickin'.

Dey blows upon dey hands,
   Den flings 'em wid de nails up,
Jumps up an' cracks dey heels,
   An' pruzently dey sails up,
An' makes dem oxen hump deysef,
   By twistin' all dey tails up!

In this our age of printer's ink
'Tis books that show us how to think—
The rule reversed, and set at naught,
That held that books were born of thought.
We form our minds by pedants' rules,
And all we know is from the schools;
And when we work, or when we play,
We do it in an ordered way—
And Nature's self pronounce a ban on,
Whene'er she dares transgress a canon.
Untrammeled thus the simple race is
That "wuks the craps" on cotton places.
Original in act and thought,
Because unlearned and untaught.
Observe them at their Christmas party:
How unrestrained their mirth—how hearty!
How many things they say and do
That never would occur to you!
See Brudder Brown—whose saving grace
Would sanctify a quarter-race—
Out on the crowded floor advance,
To "beg a blessin' on dis dance."

O Mahsr! let dis gath'rin fin' a blessin in yo' sight!
Don't jedge us hard fur what we does—you know it's Chrismus-night;
An' all de balunce ob de yeah we does as right's we kin.
Ef dancin's wrong, O Mahsr! let de time excuse de sin!

We labors in de vineya'd, wukin' hard an' true;
Now, shorely you won't notus, ef we eats a grape or two,
An' takes a leetle holiday,—a leetle restin'-spell,—
Bekase, nex' week, we'll start in fresh, an' labor twicet as well.

Remember, Mahsr,—min' dis now,—de sinfullness ob sin
Is 'pendin' 'pon de sperrit what we goes an' does it in:
An' in a righchis frame ob min' we's gwine to dance an' sing,
A-feelin' like King David, when he cut de pigeon-wing.

It seems to me—indeed it do—I mebbe mout be wrong—
That people raly *ought* to dance, when Chrismus comes along;
Des dance bekase dey's happy—like de birds hops in de trees,
De pine-top fiddle soundin' to de bowin' ob de breeze.

We has no ark to dance afore, like Isrul's prophet king;
We has no harp to soun' de chords, to holp us out to sing;
But 'cordin' to de gif's we has we does de bes' we knows,
An' folks don't 'spise the vi'let-flower bekase it ain't de rose.

You bless us, please, sah, eben ef we's doin' wrong to-night;
Kase den we'll need de blessin' more'n ef we's doin' right;
An' let de blessin' stay wid us, untel we comes to die,
An' goes to keep our Chrismus wid dem sheriffs in de sky!

Yes, tell dem preshis anguls we's a-gwine to jine 'em soon:
Our voices we's a-trainin' fur to sing de glory tune;
We's ready when you wants us, an' it ain' no matter when—
O Mahsr! call yo' chillen soon, an' take 'em home! Amen.

> The rev'rend man is scarcely through,
> When all the noise begins anew,
> And with such force assaults the ears,
> That through the din one hardly hears
> Old fiddling Josey "sound his A,"
> Correct the pitch, begin to play,
> Stop, satisfied, then, with the bow,
> Rap out the signal dancers know:

> *Git yo' pardners, fust kwattilion!*
> Stomp yo' feet, an' raise 'em high;
> Tune is: "Oh! dat water-million!
> Gwine to git to home bime-by."
> *S'lute yo' pardners!*—scrape perlitely—

Don't be bumpin' 'gin de res'—
Balance all!—now, step out rightly;
Alluz dance yo' lebbel bes'.
Fo'wa'd foah!—whoop up, niggers!
Back ag'in!—don't be so slow!—
Swing cornahs!—min' de figgers!
When I hollers, den yo' go.
Top ladies cross ober!
Hol' on, till I takes a dram—
Gemmen solo!—yes, I's sober—
Cain't say how de fiddle am.
Hands around!—hol' up yo' faces,
Don't be lookin' at yo' feet!
Swing yo' pardners to yo' places!
Dat's de way—dat's hard to beat.
Sides for'w'd!—when you's ready—
Make a bow as low's you kin!
Swing acrost wid opp'site lady!
Now we'll let you swap ag'in:
Ladies change!—shet up dat talkin';
Do yo' talkin' arter while!
Right and lef'!—don't want no walkin'—
Make yo' steps, an' show yo' style!

And so the "set" proceeds—its length
Determined by the dancers' strength:
And all agree to yield the palm
For grace and skill to "Georgy Sam,"
Who stamps so hard, and leaps so high,
"Des watch him!" is the wond'ring cry—
"De nigger mus' be, for a fac',
Own cousin to a jumpin'-jack!"
On, on, the restless fiddle sounds,
Still chorused by the curs and hounds;
Dance after dance succeeding fast,
Till supper is announced at last.
That scene—but why attempt to show it?
The most inventive modern poet,
In fine new words whose hope and trust is,
Could form no phrase to do it justice!
When supper ends—that is not so soon—
The fiddle strikes the same old tune;
The dancers pound the floor again,
With all they have of might and main;
Old gossips, *almost* turning pale,
Attend Aunt Cassy's gruesome tale

Of conjurors, and ghosts, and devils,
That in the smoke-house hold their revels;
Each drowsy baby droops his head,
Yet scorns the very thought of bed:——
So wears the night, and wears so fast,
All wonder when they find it past,
And hear the signal sound to go
From what few cocks are left to crow.
Then, one and all, you hear them shout:
"Hi! Booker! fotch de banjo out,
An' gib us *one* song 'fore we goes—
One ob de berry bes' you knows!"
Responding to the welcome call,
He takes the banjo from the wall,
And tunes the strings with skill and care,
Then strikes them with a master's air,
And tells, in melody and rime,
This legend of the olden time:

Go 'way, fiddle! folks is tired o' hearin' you a-squakin'!
Keep silence fur yo' betters!—don't you heah de banjo talkin'?
About de 'possum's tail she's gwine to lecter—ladies, listen!—
About de ha'r whut isn't da, an' why de ha'r is missin':

"Dar's gwine to be a' oberflow," said Noah, lookin' solemn—
Fur Noah tuk the "Herald," an' he read de ribber column—
An' so he sot his hands to wuk a-cl'arin' timber-patches,
And 'lowed he's gwine to build a boat to beat the steamah *Natchez*.

Ol' Noah kep' a-nailin' an' a-chippin' an' a-sawin';
An' all de wicked neighbors kep' a-laughin' an' a-pshawin';
But Noah didn't min' 'em, knowin' whut wuz gwine to happen:
An' forty days an' forty nights de rain it kep' a-drappin'.

Now, Noah had done cotched a lot ob ebry sort o' beas'es—
Ob all de shows a-trabbelin', it beat 'em all to pieces!
He had a Morgan colt an' sebral head o' Jarsey cattle—
An' druv 'em 'board de Ark as soon's he heered de thunder rattle.

Den sech anoder fall ob rain!—it come so awful hebby,
De ribber riz immetjitly, an' busted troo de lebbee;
De people all wuz drownded out—'cep' Noah an' de critters,
An' men he'd hired to work de boat—an' one to mix de bitters.

De Ark she kep' a-sailin' an' a-sailin' *an'* a-sailin';
De lion got his dander up, an' like to bruk de palin';

De sarpents hissed; de painters yelled; tell, whut wid all de fussin',
You c'u'dn't hardly heah de mate a-bossin' roun' an' cussin'.

Now, Ham, de only nigger whut wuz runnin' on de packet,
Got lonesome in de barber-shop, an' c'u'dn't stan' de racket;
An' so, fur to amuse he-se'f, he steamed some wood an' bent it,
An' soon he had a banjo made—de fust dat wuz invented.

He wet de ledder, stretched it on; made bridge an' screws an' aprin;
An' fitted in a proper neck—'twuz berry long an' tap'rin';
He tuk some tin, an' twisted him a thimble fur to ring it;
An' den de mighty question riz: how wuz he gwine to string it?

De 'possum had as fine a tail as dis dat I's a-singin';
De ha'r's so long an' thick an' strong,—des fit fur banjo-stringin';
Dat nigger shaved 'em off as short as wash-day-dinner graces;
An' sorted ob 'em by de size, f'om little E's to basses.

He strung her, tuned her, struck a jig,—'t wuz "Nebber min' de wedder,"—
She soun' like forty-lebben bands a-playin' all togedder;
Some went to pattin'; some to dancin': Noah called de figgers;
An' Ham he sot an' knocked de tune, de happiest ob niggers!

Now, sence dat time—it's mighty strange—dere's not de slightes' showin'
Ob any h'ar at all upon de 'possum's tail a-growin';
And curi's, too, dat nigger's ways: his people nebber los' 'em—
Fur whar you finds de nigger—dar's de banjo an' de 'possum.

The night is spent; and as the day
Throws up the first faint flash of gray,
The guests pursue their homeward way;
And through the field beyond the gin,
Just as the stars are going in,
See Santa Claus departing—grieving—
His own dear Land of Cotton leaving.
His work is done; he fain would rest
Where people know and love him best.
He pauses, listens, looks about;
But go he must: his pass is out.
So, coughing down the rising tears,
He climbs the fence and disappears.
And thus observes a colored youth
(The common sentiment, in sooth):
"Oh! what a blessin' 't wud ha' been,
Ef Santy had been born a twin!
We'd hab two Chrismuses a yeah—
Or p'r'aps one brudder'd settle heah!"

A VISIT TO DADDY CUDJOE

by Julia Peterkin

Julia Peterkin's novels of Negro life in South Carolina are rich in the details of plantation activities and manners. Her intimate knowledge of the desires and foibles, the fears and superstitions, of her characters gives her fiction a special authority, and she is peculiarly sensitive to the difficult Gullah dialect. Love potions and charms are still efficacious to the isolated rural Negro, and the conjurer's magic is commonly accepted. When Mary had strong doubts about the fidelity of her lover, July, it was natural for her to seek help to hold him. The account of her visit to Old Daddy Cudjoe, which forms Chapter XII of Scarlet Sister Mary *(1928), reveals her faith in amulets and spells as well as the fearsome combination of objects which the old conjurer assures her will toll back her errant lover. But Daddy Cudjoe seems to have less confidence in his concoction than his petitioner shows; at least his advice, "as much good fish is in de river as ever was caught out," is, in the circumstances, hardly consoling.*

The road leaving the Quarters ran straight to the river which was the plantation's main highway out into the world, the faithful carrier which took away its bales of cotton and brought back all its luxuries. The road's deep ruts cut by slow-moving wagon-wheels ran side by side past cotton-fields, through woods where last year's fallen leaves and brown pine-needles made them dim and where every grass-blade or leaf budding up above the ground was crushed back into the earth by the cloven feet of patient oxen or small, round, quicker-stepping mule hoofs.

As the road reached the brow of the hill, it slackened its gait and sent a small fork off to one side. Mary followed this as it crept cautiously and with painstaking curves through thickets, under low-hanging trees whose roots clutched the earth, until the cabin where Old Daddy Cudjoe lived came in sight. Small, dilapidated, paintless, lonely, it squatted low on the ground in the midst of a confusion of little rickety outbuildings. A crape-myrtle tree beside it was gorgeous with leaves that the heat had dyed in every shade of crimson and yellow. Frosty blueberries filled the tall cedar that rose behind it and a giant hickory scattered golden leaves over the cabin's sagging roof every time a breeze came up from the river and stirred the air.

Daddy Cudjoe's cabin sat on a hill just above the river bank, its weathered roof green with moss, its old cracked sides the color of the deep shadows cast around it by

425

the twisted live-oak trees. Chickens scratched around the door. A mother hog lying under a tree fed her babies and, when Mary passed, she blinked and grunted but did not move. An old horse munched eagerly at a dry grass patch, and one of his eyes was white with blindness.

Daddy Cudjoe, a shriveled, old, crooked-legged, white-bearded man, came hobbling up from the spring with a bucket of water, and his face beamed as he spied Mary. His stumbling old feet hurried faster until he reached her, then putting his bucket on the ground, he took off his tattered old hat, and plucking at a white forelock with his crumpled fingers, he pulled a foot back and made a fine bow.

His words were broken into bits by stammering, but Mary understood them; he was glad to see her; she looked as sweet and pretty as a flower garden in the springtime; she must come in and sit down and have a cup of newly steeped life-elastic tea that he had just finished brewing; it would do her good. Nothing is better in the fall than life-elastic tea.

Daddy Cudjoe was used to having people come to him for advice, and he knew how to make them feel at home. Mary had never been here before, but when she was a child, whenever she saw the old, white-haired, bent man passing the house, or in the woods digging roots, she always ran from him, and he would stop and laugh and shake his fist and cackle out, "You better run! If I catch you, I'll conjure you!" and he looked so strange, with his black eyes shining under thick, white, bushy brows, she believed he would.

His cabin's two rooms ran the length of the house with a low board wall between them, one for Daddy Cudjoe to sleep in and the other for him to work in. Mary sat down by the fireplace, whose hearth was filled with steaming pots. Strange smells rose. Medicine, charms, love- and hate-potions all mixed their breaths together as they brewed side by side on the red coals.

"De sight o you face makes my eyeballs feel pure rich," Daddy Cudjoe greeted Mary.

He poured her the drink, then he rubbed his knotted hands together, and with a kind smile asked, "What you want, daughter?"

There was no use to hesitate, she might as well talk right out.

"I want a charm for July, Daddy Cudjoe. July's got a side-gal."

Daddy looked grave.

"How long you been married, honey?"

"Me an' him ain' been married a year yet."

"Who is de side-gal, daughter?"

"Cinder."

At this answer he puckered up his lips and puffed out his cheeks. "Cinder? Why, Cinder's de very one what come here last month and got a love-charm to catch em a beau. You don' mean dat gal is used em on you husband? Jedus have mercy. You womens is someting else." He threw back his head and cackled long and loud.

"Now, de beau's lawful lady is come for someting to get e husband back. Well, I declare. I got to make a charm to fight a charm. Black hand is got to squeeze black hand. Dat ain' no easy ting, gal. I got to study a minute."

Then Mary told him July was not the only thing giving her trouble. Cinder had put a hand on everything in her house. The fire was conjured so it muttered and popped red coals out on the bare floor scorching black spots in the clean boards around the hearth. Food stuck to the pots. Water would hardly boil in the kettle. Wind flew down the chimney in hard gusts driving smoke into the room and fanning up the ashes, scattering them in the victuals. Her baby was in mortal danger too, for he cried out in his sleep, frightened by evil things he saw in his dreams.

"I'd like to kill Cinder, Daddy—kill em dead. If you'll gi me a pizen I'll feed it to em till e is stone dead."

Daddy shook his head kindly. "No, honey, you wrong. Pizen ain' to be trusted. Sometimes, it works backwards as well as forwards, you might be de one to dead. Hatin ain' good for you, neither. It'll pizen you breast milk an' make you baby sick. It's better to go easy wid conjure. You must stop frettin an' bein scared. Keep you belly full o victuals, make you mouth smile, laugh an' be merry if you can. Don' never let people see you down-hearted, or a-hangin you head, an' lookin sorrowful. Dat ain' de way. No. Mens don' crave a sorrowful, sad-lookin 'oman. Don' never let a man feel sorry for you if you want em to stick to you."

He got up and went out of the door into the yard and Mary could hear him puttering around, scratching in the earth as if he were digging up something. Presently he came back smiling and poured her out a cup of tea from another one of the several pots boiling on the hearth.

"Drink dis, honey. It'll do you all de good whilst I fix you someting to try. If July ain' conjured too bad already e won' never get shet o' de spell we'll work on em. I ain' never seen no man get loose from a 'oman what wears dis mixtry. It's de powerful-est one I knows."

Daddy took a needle and stuck the little finger on her right hand and took a drop of her blood on a wisp of cotton. "You right hand is de strong hand, honey," he said. "It's de hand what catches an' holds."

Then he took a bit of skin from her left heel. "Dis is de foot what walks fastest, honey."

A bit of toe-nail from a toe on her left foot was added to one hair plucked from her left armpit as near to her heart as she could get it. These were all mixed with some sort of conjure root and tied into a tiny scrap of white cloth with a string long enough to go around her neck. Daddy Cudjoe was excited. His eyes shone and sweat ran down off his forehead as he handed the bag to her with a high crackling laugh.

"Put em on, gal. Wear em day an' night. If e don' work, den I'll quit makin love-charms for de rest o my life. Dat charm is a man. Great Gawd, yes. E's a mans o monkeys, honey."

As Mary took it her heart began beating violently. Lord, yes, she could feel it was strong! Now she'd hurry home with it for July might by some chance come back on the regular boat this afternoon instead of waiting for the excursion boat tonight.

"How much I owe you, Daddy?"

"Honey, you don' owe me a Gawd's ting but a sweet smile. An' I wish you all de luck in dis world. I hope you will get you husband back an' keep em de rest o you life."

The old man seemed really grateful to her for coming to him. Perhaps he was lonely, living so far off by himself.

"Come see me sometimes, Daddy."

"Gawd bless you, chile, I'll do it. But befo you go let me get you some fresh eggs to take home. When you eat em, hang de shells side de mantelpiece so de fire'll keep em warm. Dey'll make you hens lay good. Come look at some fine new layin stock shut up in a pen."

He hobbled ahead of her toward the back of the cabin where a rickety hand-split clapboard fence enclosed a small yard. Taking down the props of the hingeless gate, he showed Mary six straw-necked pullets and a young cockerel.

"Dey's fine, Daddy," Mary praised.

"Is you like em?" he asked with pride. "I sent all de way 'cross de river an' got em. Le me know when you got a hen settin an' I'll gi you a clutch o eggs for seed."

A tall black rooster on the outside

walked up close to the open gate, and stretching up his neck gave a long shrill crow. The smile left Daddy Cudjoe's face.

He picked out a stick and threw it violently, stammering and spluttering and shaking his fist threateningly at the offending fowl, declaring that any rooster old as that ought to know how to settle down and behave himself. He had ten grown hens running loose outside with him in the open yard; all he could say grace over, to save his life; yet, instead of attending to his own business and helping those hens scratch and find worms for themselves and for the children they had for him, there he was, running up and down by that fence, peeping through the cracks at those pullets, calling them and making a big to-do, telling them to come see what a fine thing he had found for them to eat, talking all kinds of sweet-mouthed talk to them, until the fools had their combs all bloody from reaching their heads through the fence. They believed every word the scoundrel said. They had no sense at all.

The rooster stood eyeing Daddy Cudjoe from a safe distance. When he flopped his wings and stretched his neck and gave a bold crow, Daddy laughed, "I hear you, son. I hear how you sass me. But you better mind, or you'll be a-stewin in a pot befo you know it." His words were threatening but his eyes were twinkling; he said people and fowls were much alike. That same rooster was just like a man.

A man may have the finest wife in the world, but just let a strange woman come around and smile at him a little, and he turns to a fool right away. He will start lying and doing everything he can to fool the strange woman into loving him, but as soon as she does he will leave her and go trying to find some other new woman to fool. It is a hard thing to keep a man satisfied. A hard thing. If it wasn't for love-charms and conjures to help women keep their lawful husbands at home and

out of devilment, only God knows what would become of the world.

"Whe is you husband, to-day, daughter?"

Mary shook her head. July was gone on the excursion and Cinder was with him.

Daddy Cudjoe turned away and gazed at the rice-fields that lay sunlit and still under a circle of soft blue sky. "Po lil gal," he pitied. "I'm too sorry to see you a-frettin. But remember dis: as much good fish is in de river as ever was caught out. July ain' de onliest man in de world. No. Gawd made plenty just as good as him. Just as good. Don' forget dat."

A wild plum thicket full of reddening leaves stood close at the old man's elbow, and when he put out a hand to pat Mary's shoulder and emphasize what he was telling her, one of the slim thorny switches reached out and caught his sleeve. He jerked quickly away from it. "What you mean by pickin at me?" he asked it gruffly. "I know what I'm a-tellin dis gal." Then he snapped the branch off with his short knotted fingers and twisted it between them until all its red leaves were gone, and its sharp thorns were left stark naked.

"I'm a-tellin you what Gawd loves, daughter; de truth, de pure truth. Gawd made plenty o' men besides July. If dat charm don' fetch you husband back to you, you use it on somebody else."

"But I don' want nobody else, Daddy. Not nobody but July."

Then Daddy cackled out merrily again. "You's young, honey. You ain' got much sense, but you'll learn better. Sho. I got good hopes o you. Good hopes. Some o dese days you'll learn better." Daddy Cudjoe laughed, then wiped the tears out of his eyes. "You can' nebber blongst to nobody, honey, an' nobody can' blongst to you. But Ki! Dat ain' reason fo cry! You breath come an' go mighty sweet when e free, but you strive fo hold em. Den e bitter!"

AT CANDLE-LIGHTIN' TIME

by Paul Laurence Dunbar

The two poems by Dunbar reveal a Negro writer's sympathetic view of Negro life on a southern plantation. Both picture relaxation rather than toil: a tenant farmer returning to his cabin and enjoying an evening with his family after long hours of tilling corn, and a community feast and hoedown in which all the neighbors participate. The farmer makes use of the simplest devices to entertain his children, who feign surprise even though frequent repetition has brought familiarity. Surely the forming of animal heads on the wall by means of finger gestures and firelight from the hearth fire must be one of the most primitive kinds of folk art. The cabin party, on the other hand, starts at a more sophisticated level when the guests appear in all their finery and imitate the manners of their superiors. But soon natural high spirits break out, the dancing grows tumultuous, and bits of familiar tunes or ballads excite the crowd. Even the colored preacher has difficulty restraining his feet, while he can barely finish the blessing before he wishes to start the feast. Although Dunbar is not oblivious to the comic aspects of the scene, he is not writing satirically about these plantation folk. After all, as his narrator puts it, the guests "jes' had one scrumptious time."

When I come in f'om de co'n-fiel' aftah wo'kin' ha'd all day,
It's amazin' nice to fin' my suppah all erpon de way;
An' it's nice to smell de coffee bubblin' ovah in de pot,
An' it's fine to see de meat a-sizzlin' teasin'-lak an' hot.

But when suppah-time is ovah, an' de t'ings is cleahed away;
Den de happy hours dat foller are de sweetes' of de day.
When my co'ncob pipe is sta'ted, an' de smoke is drawin' prime,
My ole 'ooman says, "I reckon, Ike, it's candle-lightin' time."

Den de chillun snuggle up to me, an' all commence to call,
"Oh, say, daddy, now it's time to mek de shadders on de wall."
So I puts my han's togethah—evah daddy knows de way,—
An' de chillun snuggle closer roun' ez I begin to say:—

"Fus' thin' hyeah come Mistah Rabbit; don' you see him wo'k his eahs?
Huh, uh! dis mus' be a donkey,—look, how innercent he 'pears!
Dah's de ole black swan a-swimmin'—ain't she got a' awful neck?
Who's dis feller dat's a-comin'? Why, dat's ole dog Tray, I 'spec!"

Dat's de way I run on, tryin' fu' to please 'em all I can;
Den I hollahs, "Now be keerful—dis hyeah las' 's de buga-man!"

429

An' dey runs an' hides dey faces; dey ain't skeered—dey's lettin' on:
But de play ain't raaly ovah twell dat buga-man is gone.

So I jes' teks up my banjo, an' I plays a little chune,
An' you see dem haids come peepin' out to listen mighty soon.
Den my wife says, "Sich a pappy fu' to give you sich a fright!
Jes' you go. to baid, an' leave him: say yo' prayers an' say good-night."

THE PARTY

by Paul Laurence Dunbar

Dey had a gread big pahty down to Tom's de othah night;
Was I dah? You bet! I nevah in my life see sich a sight;
All de folks f'om fou' plantations was invited, an' dey come,
Dey come troopin' thick ez chillun when dey hyeahs a fife an' drum.
Evahbody dressed deir fines'—Heish yo' mouf an' git away,
Ain't seen no sich fancy dressin' sence las' quah'tly meetin' day;
Gals all dressed in silks an' satins, not a wrinkle ner a crease,
Eyes a-battin', teeth a-shinin', haih breshed back ez slick ez grease;
Sku'ts all tucked an' puffed an' ruffled, evah blessed seam an' stitch;
Ef you'd seen 'em wif deir mistus, couldn't swahed to which was which.
Men all dressed up in Prince Alberts, swallertails 'u'd tek you' bref!
I cain't tell you nothin' 'bout it, yo' ought to seen it fu' yo'se'f.
Who was dah? Now who you askin'? How you 'spect I gwine to know?
You mus' think I stood an' counted evahbody at de do'.
Ole man Babah's house boy Isaac, brung dat gal, Malindy Jane,

Huh a-hangin' to his elbow, him a struttin' wif a cane;
My, but Hahvey Jones was jealous! seemed to stick him lak a tho'n;
But he laughed with Viney Cahteh, tryin' ha'd to not let on,
But a pusson would 'a' noticed f'om de d'rection of his look,
Dat he was watchin' ev'ry step dat Ike an' Lindy took.
Ike he foun' a cheer an' asked huh: "Won't you set down?" wif a smile,
An' she answe'd up a-bowin', "Oh, I reckon 'tain't wuth while."
Dat was jes' fu' style, I reckon, 'cause she sot down jes' de same,
An' she stayed dah 'twell he fetched huh fu' to jine some so't o' game;
Den I hyeahed huh sayin' propah, ez she riz to go away,
"Oh, you raly mus' excuse me, fu' I hardly keers to play."
But I seen huh in a minute wif de othahs on de flo',
An' dah wasn't any one o' dem a-playin' any mo';
Comin' down de flo' a-bowin' an' a-swayin' an' a-swingin',
Puttin' on huh high-toned mannahs all de time dat she was singin':
"Oh, swing Johnny up an' down, swing him all aroun',
Swing Johnny up an' down, swing him all aroun',
Oh, swing Johnny up an' down, swing him all aroun',
Fa' you well, my dahlin'."
Had to laff at ole man Johnson, he's a caution now, you bet—
Hittin' clost onto a hunderd, but he's spry an' nimble yet;
He 'lowed how a-so't o' gigglin', "I ain't ole, I'll let you see,
D'ain't no use in gittin' feeble, now you youngstahs jes' watch me,"
An', he grabbed ole Aunt Marier—weighs th'ee hunderd mo'er less,
An' he spun huh 'round de cabin swingin' Johnny lak de res'.
Evahbody laffed an' hollahed: "Go it, swing huh, Uncle Jim!"
An' he swung huh too, I reckon, lak a youngstah, who but him.
Dat was bettah'n young Scott Thomas, tryin' to be so awful smaht.
You know when dey gits to singin' an' dey comes to dat ere paht:
                "In some lady's new brick house
            In some lady's gyahden.
                Ef you don't let me out, I will jump out,
            So fa' you well, my dahlin'."
Den dey's got a circle 'roun' you, an' you's got to break de line;
Well, dat dahky was so anxious, lak to bust hisse'f a-tryin';
Kep' on blund'rin' 'roun' an' foolin' 'twell he giv' one gread big jump,
Broke de line, an' lit head-fo'most in de fiahplace right plump;
Hit 'ad fiah in it, mind you; well, I thought my soul I'd bust,
Tried my best to keep f'om laffin', but hit seemed like die I must!
Y'ought to seen dat man a-scramblin' f'om de ashes an' de grime.
Did it bu'n him? Sich a question, why he didn't give it time;
Th'ow'd dem ashes and dem cindahs evah which-a-way I guess,
An' you nevah did, I reckon, clap yo' eyes on sich a mess;
Fu' he sholy made a picter an' a funny one to boot,
Wif his clothes all full o' ashes an' his face all full o' soot.
Well, hit laked to stopped de pahty, an' I reckon lak ez not
Dat it would ef Tom's wife, Mandy, hadn't happened on de spot,

To invite us out to suppah—well, we scrambled to de table,
An' I'd lak to tell you 'bout it—what we had—but I ain't able,
Mention jes' a few things, dough I know I hadn't orter,
Fu' I know 'twill staht a hank'rin' an' yo' mouf'll 'mence to worter.
We had wheat bread white ez cotton an' a egg pone jes' like gol',
Hog jole, bilin' hot an' steamin', roasted shoat an' ham sliced cold—
Look out! What's de mattah wif you? Don't be fallin' on de flo';
Ef it's go'n to 'fect you dat way, I won't tell you nothin' mo'.
Dah now—well, we had hot chittlin's—now you's tryin' ag'in to fall,
Cain't you stan' to hyeah about it? S'pose you'd been an' seed it all;
Seed dem gread big sweet pertaters, layin' by de possum's side,
Seed dat coon in all his gravy, reckon den you'd up and died!
Mandy 'lowed "you all mus' 'scuse me, d' wa'n't much upon my she'ves,
But I's done my bes' to suit you, so set down an' he'p yo'se'ves."
Tom, he 'lowed: "I don't b'lieve in 'pologizin' an' perfessin',
Let 'em tek it lak dey ketch it. Eldah Thompson, ask de blessin'."
Wish you'd seed dat colo'ed preachah cleah his th'oat an' bow his head;
One eye shet an' one eye open,—dis is evah wud he said:
"Lawd, look down in tendah mussy on sich generous hea'ts ez dese;
Makes us truly thankful, amen. Pass dat possum, ef you please!"
Well, we eat and drunk ouah po'tion, 'twell dah wasn't nothin' lef',
An' we felt jes' like new sausage, we was mos' nigh stuffed to def!
Tom, he knowed how we'd be feelin', so he had de fiddlah 'roun',
An' he made us cleah de cabin fu' to dance dat suppah down.
Jim, de fiddlah, chuned his fiddle, put some rosum on his bow,
Set a pine box on de table, mounted it an' let huh go!
He's a fiddlah, now I tell you, an' he made dat fiddle ring,
'Twell de ol'est an' de lamest had to give deir feet a fling.
Jigs, cotillions, reels an' break-downs, cordrills an' a waltz er two;
Bless yo' soul, dat music winged 'em an' dem people lak to flew.
Cripple Joe, de ole rheumatic, danced dat flo' f'om side to middle,
Th'owed away his crutch an' hopped it, what's rheumatics 'ginst a fiddle?
Eldah Thompson got so tickled dat he lak to lo' his grace,
Had to tek bofe feet an' hol' dem so's to keep 'em in deir place.
An' de Christuns an' de sinnahs got so mixed up on dat flo',
Dat I don't see how dey'd pahted ef de trump had chanced to blow.
Well, we danced dat way an' capahed in de mos' redic'lous way,
'Twell de roostahs in de bahnyard cleahed deir th'oats an' crowed fu' day.
Y'ought to been dah, fu' I tell you evahthing was rich an' prime,
An' dey ain't no use in talkin', we jes' had one scrumptious time!

OLE MASSA AND JOHN WHO WANTED TO GO TO HEAVEN

by Zora Neale Hurston

This anecdote of slavery times reveals a very human relationship between the Negro and his plantation master and suggests that all the trickery was not on one side. There is an interesting contrast between John, who hides his sloth behind a primitive scriptural imagery, and his wife, who is suspicious of John's piety and rather relishes his unceremonious flight across the cornfield. The story appears in Mules and Men *(1935).*

You know befo' surrender Ole Massa had a nigger name John and John always prayed every night befo' he went to bed and his prayer was for God to come git him and take him to Heaven right away. He didn't even want to take time to die. He wanted de Lawd to come git him just like he was—boot, sock and all. He'd git down on his knees and say: "O Lawd, it's once more and again yo' humble servant is knee-bent and body-bowed—my heart beneath my knees and my knees in some lonesome valley, crying for mercy while mercy kin be found. O Lawd, Ah'm astin' you in de humblest way I know how to be *so* pleased as to come in yo' fiery chariot and take me to yo' Heben and its immortal glory. Come Lawd, you know Ah have such a hard time. Ole Massa works me so hard, and don't gimme no time to rest. So come, Lawd, wid peace in one hand and pardon in de other and take me away from this sin-sorrowing world. Ah'm tired and Ah want to go home."

So one night Ole Massa passed by John's shack and heard him beggin' de Lawd to come git him in his fiery chariot and take him away; so he made up his mind to find out if John meant dat thing. So he goes on up to de big house and got hisself a bed sheet and come on back. He throwed de sheet over his head and knocked on de door.

John quit prayin' and ast: "Who dat?"

Ole Massa say: "It's me, John, de Lawd, done come wid my fiery chariot to take you away from this sin-sick world."

Right under de bed John had business. He told his wife: "Tell Him Ah ain't here, Liza."

At first Liza didn't say nothin' at all, but de Lawd kept right on callin' John: "Come on, John, and go to Heben wid me where you won't have to plough no mo' furrows and hoe no mo' corn. Come on, John."

Liza says: "John ain't here, Lawd, you hafta come back another time."

Lawd says: "Well, then Liza, you'll do."

Liza whispers and says: "John, come out from underneath dat bed and g'wan wid de Lawd. You been beggin' him to come git you. Now g'wan wid him."

John back under de bed not saying a mumblin' word. De Lawd out on de door step kept on callin'.

Liza says: "John, Ah thought you was

433

so anxious to get to Heben. Come out and go on wid God."

John says: "Don't you hear him say 'You'll do'? Why don't you go wid him?"

"Ah ain't a goin' nowhere. Youse de one been whoopin' and hollerin' for him to come git you and if you don't come out from under dat bed Ah'm gointer tell God youse here."

Ole Massa makin' out he's God, says: "Come on, Liza, you'll do."

Liza says: "O, Lawd, John is right here underneath de bed."

"Come on, John, and go to Heben wid me and its immortal glory."

John crept out from under de bed and went to de door and cracked it and when he seen all dat white standin' on de doorsteps he jumped back. He says: "O, Lawd, Ah can't go to Heben wid you in yo' fiery chariot in dese ole dirty britches; gimme time to put on my Sunday pants."

"All right, John, put on yo' Sunday pants."

John fooled around just as long as he could, changing them pants, but when he went back to de door, de big white glory was still standin' there. So he says agin: "O, Lawd, de Good Book says in Heben no filth is found and I got on dis dirty sweaty shirt. Ah can't go wid you in dis old nasty shirt. Gimme time to put on my Sunday shirt!"

"All right, John, go put on yo' Sunday shirt."

John took and fumbled around a long time changing his shirt, and den he went back to de door, but Ole Massa was still on de door step. John didn't had nothin' else to change so he opened de door a little piece and says:

"O, Lawd, Ah'm ready to go to Heben wid you in yo' fiery chariot, but de radiance of yo' countenance is so bright, Ah can't come out by you. Stand back jus' a li'l way please."

Ole Massa stepped back a li'l bit.

John looked out agin and says: "O, Lawd, you know dat po' humble me is less than de dust beneath yo' shoe soles. And de radiance of yo' countenance is so bright Ah can't come out by you. Please, please, Lawd in yo' tender mercy, stand back a li'l bit further."

Ole Massa stepped back a li'l bit mo'.

John looked out agin and he says: "O, Lawd, Heben is so high and wese so low; youse so great and Ah'm so weak and yo' strength is too much for us poor sufferin' sinners. So once mo' and agin yo' humber servant is knee-bent and body-bowed askin' you one mo' favor befo' Ah step into yo' fiery chariot to go to Heben wid you and wash in yo' glory—be so pleased in yo' tender mercy as to stand back jus' a li'l bit further."

Ole Massa stepped back a step or two mo' and out dat door John come like a streak of lightning. All across de punkin patch, thru de cotton over de pasture— John wid Ole Massa right behind him. By de time dey hit de cornfield John was way ahead of Ole Massa.

Back in de shack one of de children was cryin' and she ast Liza: "Mama, you reckon God's gointer ketch papa and carry him to Heben wid him?"

"Shet yo' mouf, talkin' foolishness!" Liza clashed at de chile. "You know de Lawd can't outrun yo' pappy—specially when he's barefooted at dat."

XI

FOLK SONGS
and
BALLADS

American colonials long continued to enjoy the literary herit-age of their homelands before they essayed a literature of their own. They continued to solace and amuse themselves with the folk songs they brought with them before they made new ones out of their American experience. And in folk song, as in litera-ture, the processes of fresh composition were imitative and adap-tive rather than originally creative. Accordingly, most of the folk songs, that is, those of unknown or forgotten authorship that have been preserved by memory and oral transmission rather than by print and that exist only in variants rather than in standard texts, are importations. The best American folk songs are those modeled upon Old World pieces, but even so there is a large body of native American pieces which bear the stamp of the American scene and experience. Of these, the ballads—folk songs that tell a story—are perhaps the most distinctive.

Well over one-third of the three hundred and five ballads contained in *The English and Scottish Popular Ballads,* edited by Francis J. Child, have enjoyed oral circulation in America. Many of these, such as "Barbara Allen," "Lord Randal," "Lord Lovel," and "The Devil's Nine Questions," have been so adapted to the American setting that, in the words of one scholar, they are "as American as anything not Red Indian can be." This British component of American folk song has been made familiar by numerous collections, by studies of the use made of it in artistic literature, by innumerable phonograph recordings, and by the radio and television presentations of such singers as Jean Ritchie, John Jacob Niles, and Andrew Rowan Summers.

Besides these "classic" examples of British balladry, a much larger number of other ballads, most of them of the "broadside" type, have made their way into American tradition. Many of the old ballads of the Child type were also printed as broadsides. But the broadside of the type here meant is a journalistic compo-sition, usually on some memorable or sensational event, in ballad form and generally in pedestrian style, printed on one side of a sheet of paper, often with a crude woodcut and an indication of some older tune to which the ballad is to be sung. Such pieces were printed to be sold in the stalls or hawked about in the streets or at country fairs, and for a long time they served as the news-papers of their day. Examples of such are "The Wexford (*or* Oxford, *or* Knoxville, *or* Shreveport) Girl," "The Little Mohee," "The Nightingale," and "A Pretty Fair Maid." These, particularly the murder and disaster broadsides, have been the models for American ballads rather than the ballads of the Child type.

SPRINGFIELD MOUNTAIN

*Reputed to be the oldest native American ballad still in oral circulation,
"Springfield Mountain" is based upon the death by snakebite of Timothy
Myrick, son of Lieutenant Thomas Myrick, at Wilberham (then Springfield Mountain), Massachusetts, August 7, 1761. Who composed it and
when is uncertain, and the date of the earliest known text is a matter of
conjecture. The original crude and doleful little ballad was taken up and
burlesqued by minstrel and vaudeville singers. The result of oral transmission has been at least four types of variants. The following two, "The
Myrick" and "The Molly," exemplify the range.*

[The Myrick]

On Springfield Mountain there did dwell,
a likely youth 'twas known full well,
Left't Merrick's only Son,
A likely youth near twenty-one.

One Friday morning he did go
down to the Meadow for to mow;
He mowed around and he did feel
a poisoning Serpent at his heel.

When he received this deadly wound
He dropped his Scythe upon the ground
and straight for home was his intent,
calling aloud Still as he went.

't was all around his voice was heard
but unto him no friend appeared;

● *Bulletin of the Folksong Society of the Northeast*, Vols. VII and XI. Reprinted by permission of Mac-
Edward Leach. See, also, for a brief discussion of the history of the ballad and two additional texts
MacEdward Leach, *The Ballad Book* (New York: Harper & Bros., 1955), pp. 719–23.

They thought he did Some workman call
but Timothy alone must fall.

At length his careful Father went
to seek his Son in discontent
and there his only Son he found
Dead as a Stone lay on the ground.

't was the seventh of August year 61
this fatal accident was done.
May this a warning be to all
to be prepared when God shall call.

Who knows but that his blessed feet
are treading the Celestial Street,
the brightest Angels bowing round
Jehovah and his golden crown.

[The Molly]

On Springfield Mountain there did dwell
A comely youth I knew full well,
  Ri tu ri nu, ri tu di na,
  Ri tu di nu, ri tu di na.

One Monday morning he did go
Down in the meadow for to mow.

He scarce had mow-ed half the field,
When a Pesky Sarpent bit his heel.

He took his scythe and with a blow
He laid the pesky Sarpent low.

He took the Sarpent in his hand,
And straightway went to Molly Bland.

Oh Molly, Molly, here you see
The Pesky Sarpent what bit me.

Now Molly had a ruby lip
With which the pizen she did sip.

But Molly had a rotten tooth,
Which the Pizen struck and killed 'em both.

The neighbors found that they were dead,
So laid them both upon one bed.

And all their friends both far and near
Did cry and howl they were so dear.

Now all you maids a warning take,
From Molly Bland and Tommy Blake.

And mind when you're in love, don't pass
Too near to patches of high grass.

PAUL JONES

This is a North Carolina traditional version of a broadside celebrating the victory of Commodore Paul Jones, with the Bonhomme Richard *and the* Pallas, *over the British ships* Serapis *and* Countess of Scarborough, *off the coast of England in 1778.*

A forty-gun frigate from Baltimore came,
Her guns mounted forty, and *Richard* by name,
Went cruising the channel of old England,
With a noble commander, Paul Jones was the man.

● From *The Frank C. Brown Collection of North Carolina Folklore*, Vol. II, *Ballads*, edited by Henry M. Belden and Arthur Palmer Hudson (Durham, N.C.: Duke University Press, 1952), p. 524. Reprinted by permission of Duke University Press.

We had not sailed long before we did spy
A large forty-four and a twenty close by,
All these warlike vessels full laden with store;
Our captain pursued them on the bold York shore.

At the hour of twelve Pierce came alongside
With a large speaking trumpet: "Whence came you?" he cried.
"Quick give me an answer, I've hailed you before,
Or at this moment a broadside I'll pour."

We fought them five glasses, five glasses so hot,
Till sixty bright seamen lay dead on the spot,
Full seventy wounded lay bleeding in gore.
How fierce our loud cannons on the *Richard* did roar.

Our gunner got frightened, to Paul Jones he came.
"Our ship she is sinking, likewise in a flame."
Paul Jones he smiled in the height of his pride,
Saying, "This day I'll conquer or sink alongside."

Here's a health to those widows who shortly must weep,
For the loss of their husbands who sunk in the deep.
Here's a health to those young girls who shortly must mourn
For the loss of their sweethearts that's overboard thrown.

Here's a health to Paul Jones with sword in hand—
He was foremost in action, in giving command.
Here's a health to Paul Jones and all his crew—
If we hadn't a French captain, boys, what could we do?

YOUNG CHARLOTTE

Based upon a local incident, composed by Seba Smith, and published in his newspaper in the 1840's, the ballad "Young Charlotte" was carried west by the Mormons and has achieved wide diffusion, retaining in popular tradition the main features of narrative and diction.

● From *Folksongs of Mississippi and Their Background*, by Arthur Palmer Hudson (Chapel Hill: University of North Carolina Press, 1936), pp. 182–84. Reprinted by permission of the University of North Carolina Press.

Young Charlotte lived on a mountain-
side
  In a wild and lonely spot;
There was no dwelling in five miles around
  Except her father's cot.

'Twas Christmas Eve, the sun was low;
  Young friends had gathered there.
Her father kept a social cot,
  And she was very fair.

'Twas Christmas Eve, the sun was low;
  She seemed a wandering eye.
And away to the frozen window [she]
    went
  To see the sleighs go by.

At length she spied a well-known sleigh
  Come dashing to the door.
Next was heard young Charlotte's voice,
  Though loud the wind did roar.

"At a village fifteen miles away
  There is a merry ball tonight."
"The air is freezing, desperate cold."
  "But our hearts are warm and light."

"Daughter dear," the mother said,
  "Put this blanket around you,
For there's a desperate storm abroad to-
    night,
  And you'll catch your death of cold."

"Oh no, oh no," the daughter said, and
    laughed.
  "Like a Gypsy queen
To ride with a blanket muffled up
  I never could be seen.

"My silken coat it is enough,
  It is lined throughout and out;
Besides, I have a silken scarf
  To tie my neck about."

Her cloak and bonnet soon were on.
  She stepped into the sleigh,

And away over hills and mountains went,
  And over hills and away.

"Such a night," said Charlotte, "I never
    knew;
  These lines I can scarcely hold."
Then Charlotte uttered these few words:
  "I'm growing very cold."

"This ice," says Charlotte, "is freezing fast;
  It is gathering on my brow."
Then Charlotte uttered these few words:
  "I'm growing warmer now."

He drove up to the tavern door,
  Then jumped out and said,
"Why sit you there like a monument?
  Surely you are not dead?"

He asked her once, he asked her twice,
  He asked her three times o'er.
He took her by her hands—
  "Oh, God, they are cold, to warm no
    more."

He twined his arms around her neck,
  He kissed her marble brow.
His thoughts flew back to where she said,
  "I'm growing warmer now."

'Twas there he knelt down by her side,
  And the bitter tears did flow,
Saying, "Oh, behold my blooming bride
  That I shall never, never know!"

NAOMI WISE

The murder of a girl by her lover is a favorite theme of balladry, for which there are many British models. "Naomi (or Little Omie) Wise" seems to be a North Carolina product, growing out of the murder of Naomi Wise by Jonathan Lewis in 1808. It has achieved wide diffusion throughout the United States, with a considerable number of variations and with additional stanzas.

Come all you good people, I'd have you draw near,
A sorrowful story you quickly shall hear;
A story I'll tell you about N'omi Wise,
How she was deluded by Lewis's lies.

He promised to marry and use me quite well;
But conduct contrary I sadly must tell.
He promised to meet me at Adams's spring:
He promised me marriage and many fine things.

Still nothing he gave, but yet flattered the case.
He says we'll be married and have no disgrace,
Come get up behind me, we'll go up to town,
And there we'll be married, in union be bound.

I got up behind him and straightway did go
To the bank of Deep River where the water did flow;
He says now Naomi, I'll tell you my mind,
I intend here to drown you and leave you behind.

O pity your infant and spare me my life;
Let me go rejected and be not your wife.
No pity, no pity, this monster did cry;
In Deep River's bottom your body shall lie.

The wretch then did choke her, as we understand,
And threw her in the river below the milldam.
Be it murder or treason, O! what a great crime,
To drown poor Naomi and leave her behind.

Naomi was missing they all did well know,
And hunting for her to the river did go;

● From *The Frank C. Brown Collection of North Carolina Folklore*, Vol. II, *Ballads*, edited by Henry M. Belden and Arthur Palmer Hudson (Durham, N.C.: Duke University Press, 1952), pp. 692–93. Reprinted by permission of Duke University Press.

And there found her floating on the water so deep,
Which caused all the people to sigh and to weep.

The neighbors were sent for to see the great sight,
While she lay floating all that long night;
So early next morning the inquest was held;
The jury correctly the murder did tell.

JESSE JAMES

As Jesse James is, after Mark Twain and possibly Harry Truman, the most famous son of Missouri, he is also, next to Robin Hood, the favorite hero of outlaw ballads, of which there is a cycle. Where, when, and by whom the following ballad about him was made up is still a matter of uncertainty. The following is what Professor Belden called "the vulgate version." "Mr. Howard" was the alias of Jesse at the time of his death.

Jesse James was a lad that killed many a man.
He robbed the Danville train.
But that dirty little coward that shot Mr. Howard
Has laid poor Jesse in his grave.

It was Robert Ford, that dirty little coward,
I wonder how he does feel;
For he ate of Jesse's bread and slept in Jesse's bed
And laid poor Jesse in the grave.

(*Chorus*)
Poor Jesse had a wife to mourn for his life,
His children they were brave;

● From *Ballads and Songs, Collected by the Missouri Folk-Lore Society,* edited by H. M. Belden (Columbia, Mo.: University of Missouri Studies, Vol. XV, No. 1, 1940), pp. 401–4. Reprinted by permission of the University of Missouri.

But that dirty little coward that shot Mr. Howard
Has laid poor Jesse in the grave.

It was his brother Frank who robbed the Gallatin bank
And carried the money from the town.
It was at this very place they had a little chase,
For they shot Capt. Sheets to the ground.

They went to the crossing not very far from here,
And there they did the same;
With the agent on his knees he delivered up the keys
To the outlaws Frank and Jesse James.

It was on Wednesday night, the moon was shining bright,
They robbed the Glenville train.
The people they did say, for many miles away,
It was robbed by Frank and Jesse James.

It was on Saturday night, Jesse was at home,
Talking with his family brave.
Robert Ford came along like a thief in the night
And laid poor Jesse in the grave.

The people held their breath when they heard of Jesse's death
And wondered how he ever came to die.
It was one of the gang called little Robert Ford,
He shot poor Jesse on the sly.

This song was made by Billy Gashade
As soon as the news did arrive.
He said there is no man with the law in his hand
Can take Jesse James when alive.

JOE BOWERS

"Joe Bowers" came out of the California gold rush in 1849 and the early 1850's, telling the story of a Missourian who went to California with the Argonauts. One romantic account of the origin of this ballad is to be found in H. C. Merwin's Life of Bret Harte (1911). It is more likely of minstrel origin. It is interesting as affording a model for the "Pike County Ballads" by John Hay, Bret Harte, and others. It was popular among Confederates during the Civil War.

● From *Folksongs of Mississippi and Their Background*, by Arthur Palmer Hudson (Chapel Hill: University of North Carolina Press, 1936), pp. 197–98. Reprinted by permission of the University of North Carolina Press.

My name it is Joe Bowers.
  I got a brother Ike.
I come from Missouri—
  Yes, all the way from Pike.

I'll tell you how I came here,
  And how I came to roam
And leave my dear old mammy
  So far away from home.

I used to love a girl there;
  Her name was Sally Black.
I asked her for to marry me;
  She said it was a fact.

She said to me, "Joe Bowers,
  Before we hitch for life
You ought to have a little hut
  To take your little wife."

Said I to her, "O Sally,
  O Sally, for your sake
I'll go to California
  And try to raise a stake."

When I got to that country
  I didn't have a red.
I had such wolfish feelings
  Till I almost wished I was dead.

But when I thought of Sally,
  It made my feelings git,
And whispered hopes to Bowers
  (I wisht I had 'em yit).

And I went to mining,
  Put in my heaviest licks,
Came down upon the gold dust
  Just like ten thousand bricks.

I worked both late and early
  Through battle, smoke, and snow.
I'm working for my Sally,
  And all the same for Joe.

One day I got a letter
  From my dear brother Ike;
It came from old Missouri,
  Yes, all the way from Pike.

And when I read that letter
  It almost made me swear:
That Sally had married a butcher,
  And the butcher had red hair.

And what was worse than that—
  I almost wisht I was dead—
That Sally had a baby,
  And the baby's hair was red.

THE BUFFALO SKINNERS

In the Bulletin of the Folk-Song Society of the Northeast *(Cambridge, Mass., 1930–37), No. 6 (1933), pp. 12–13, Mrs. Fanny Eckstorm pointed out that this ballad is an adaptation of an older ballad, "Canaday-I-O." It has appeared in many collections, notably those of the Lomaxes and Carl Sandburg. It has been noted that the date "seventy-three" is correct as marking the year in which professional buffalo-hunters from Dodge City first entered the northern part of the Texas panhandle. George Lyman Kittredge is reported to have pronounced this the best western ballad.*

Come all you jolly fellows and listen to my song,
There are not many verses, it will not detain you long;
It's concerning some young fellows who did agree to go
And spend one summer pleasantly on the range of the buffalo.

It happened in Jacksboro in the spring of seventy-three,
A man by the name of Crego came stepping up to me,
Saying, "How do you do, young fellow, and how would you like to go
And spend one summer pleasantly on the range of the buffalo?"

"It's me being out of employment," this to Crego I did say,
"This going out on the buffalo range depends upon the pay.
But if you will pay good wages and transportation too,
I think, sir, I will go with you to the range of the buffalo."

"Yes, I will pay good wages, give transportation too,
Provided you will go with me and stay the summer through;
But if you should grow homesick, come back to Jacksboro,
I won't pay transportation from the range of the buffalo."

It's now our outfit was complete—seven able-bodied men,
With navy six and needle gun—our troubles did begin;
Our way it was a pleasant one, the route we had to go,
Until we crossed Pease River on the range of the buffalo.

It's now we've crossed Pease River, our troubles have begun.
The first damned tail I went to rip, Christ! how I cut my thumb!
While skinning the damned old stinkers our lives wasn't a show,
For the Indians watched to pick us off while skinning the buffalo.

He fed us on such sorry chuck I wished myself most dead,
It was old jerked beef, croton coffee, and sour bread.

● From *Cowboy Songs and Other Frontier Ballads*, collected by John A. Lomax (New York: Sturgis & Walton, 1917), pp. 158–61. Reprinted by permission of Duell, Sloan & Pearce, Inc., New York.

Pease River's as salty as hell fire, the water I could never go,—
O God! I wished I had never come to the range of the buffalo.

Our meat it was buffalo hump and iron wedge bread,
And all we had to sleep on was a buffalo robe for a bed;
The fleas and gray-backs worked on us, O boys, it was not slow,
I'll tell you there's no worse hell on earth than the range of the buffalo.

Our hearts were cased with buffalo hocks, our souls were cased with steel,
And the hardships of that summer would nearly make us reel.
While skinning the damned old stinkers our lives they had no show,
For the Indians waited to pick us off on the hills of Mexico.

The season being near over, old Crego he did say
The crowd had been extravagant, was in debt to him that day,—
We coaxed him and we begged him and still it was no go, —
We left old Crego's bones to bleach on the range of the buffalo.

Oh, it's now we've crossed Pease River and homeward we are bound,
No more in that hell-fired country shall ever we be found.
Go home to our wives and sweethearts, tell others not to go,
For God's forsaken the buffalo range and the damned old buffalo.

THE OLD CHISHOLM TRAIL

"The Chisholm Trail . . . strung across a thousand miles of prairie, has enriched American folk music in the dozens of ballads composed about it. Actually, the Chisholm Trail exists as a myth in the American imagination."—Joe B. Frantz and Julian Ernest Choate, Jr., The American Cowboy: The Myth and the Reality *(Norman: University of Oklahoma Press, 1955), p. 33.*

● From *Cowboy Songs and Other Frontier Ballads*, collected by John A. Lomax (New York: Sturgis & Walton, 1917), pp. 58–61. Reprinted by permission of Duell, Sloan & Pearce, Inc., New York.

Come along, boys, and listen to my tale,
I'll tell you of my troubles on the old Chisholm trail.

> Coma ti yi youpy, youpy ya, youpy ya,
> Coma ti yi, youpy, youpy ya.

I started up the trail October twenty-third,
I started up the trail with the 2-U herd.

Oh, a ten dollar hoss and a forty dollar saddle,—
And I'm goin' to punchin' Texas cattle.

I woke up one morning on the old Chisholm trail,
Rope in my hand and a cow by the tail.

I'm up in the mornin' afore daylight
And afore I sleep the moon shines bright.

Old Ben Bolt was a blamed good boss
But he'd go to see the girls on a sore-backed hoss.

Old Ben Bolt was a fine old man
And you'd know there was whiskey wherever he'd land.

My hoss throwed me off at the creek called Mud,
My hoss throwed me off round the 2-U herd.

Last time I saw him he was going cross the level
A-kicking up his heels and a-running like the devil.

It's cloudy in the West, a-looking like rain,
And my damned old slicker's in the wagon again.

Crippled my hoss, I don't know how,
Ropin' at the horns of a 2-U cow.

We hit Caldwell and we hit her on the fly,
We bedded down the cattle on the hill close by.

No chaps, no slicker, and it's pouring down rain,
And I swear, by God, I'll never night-herd again.

Feet in the stirrups and a seat in the saddle,
I hung and I rattled with them long-horn cattle.

Last night I was on guard and the leader broke the ranks,
I hit my horse down the shoulders and I spurred him in the flanks.

The wind commenced to blow, and the rain began to fall,
Hit looked, by grab, like we was goin' to lose 'em all.

I jumped in the saddle and grabbed holt the horn,
Best blamed cow-puncher ever was born.

I popped my foot in the stirrup and gave a little yell,
The tail cattle broke and the leaders went to hell.

I don't give a damn if they never do stop;
I'll ride as long as an eight-day clock.

Foot in the stirrup and hand on the horn,
Best damned cowboy ever was born.

I herded and I hollered and I done very well,
Till the boss said, "Boys, just let 'em go to hell."

Stray in the herd and the boss said kill it,
So I shot him in the rump with the handle of the skillet.

We rounded 'em up and put 'em on the cars,
And that was the last of the old Two Bars.

Oh, it's bacon and beans most every day,—
I'd as soon be a-eatin' prairie hay.

I'm on my best horse and I'm goin' at a run,
I'm the quickest shootin' cowboy that ever pulled a gun.

I went to the wagon to get my roll,
To come back to Texas, dad-burn my soul.

I went to the boss to draw my roll,
He had it figgered out I was nine dollars in the hole.

I'll sell my outfit just as soon as I can,
I won't punch cattle for no damned man.

Goin' back home to draw my money,
Goin' back home to see my honey.

With my knees in the saddle and my seat in the sky,
I'll quit punchin' cows in the sweet by and by.

    Coma ti yi youpy, youpy ya, youpy ya,
    Coma ti yi youpy, youpy ya.

THE JAM ON GERRY'S ROCK

*According to Fannie Hardy Eckstorm and Mary Winslow Smyth,
Minstrelsy of Maine (Boston, 1927), pp. 176–98, this ballad was com-
posed in Maine, on an incident that occurred on the West Branch of the
Penobscot River.*

Come all of you bold shanty boys, and list while I relate
Concerning a young shanty boy and his untimely fate,
Concerning a young river-man, so manly, true and brave;
'Twas on the jam at Gerry's Rock he met a watery grave.

It was on Sunday morning as you will quickly hear,
Our logs were piled up mountains high, we could not keep them clear.
Our foreman said, "Turn out brave boys, with heart devoid of fear;
We'll break the jam on Gerry's Rock and for Eganstown we'll steer."

Now some of them were willing while others they were not,
For to work on jams on Sunday they did not think we ought;
But six of our Canadian boys did volunteer to go
And break the jam on Gerry's Rock with the foreman, young Monroe.

They had not rolled off many logs when they heard his clear voice say:
"I'd have you boys be on your guard for the jam will soon give way."
These words were scarcely spoken when the mass did break and go,
And it carried off those six brave youths and their foreman, Jack Monroe.

When the rest of our brave shanty boys the sad news came to hear
In search of their dead comrades to the river they did steer;
Some of the mangled bodies a-floating down did go,
While crushed and bleeding near the bank was that of young Monroe.

They took him from his watery grave, brushed back his raven hair;
There was one fair girl among them whose sad cries rent the air—
There was one fair form among them, a maid from Saginaw town,
Whose moans and cries rose to the skies for her true love who'd gone down.

Fair Clara was a noble girl, the river-man's true friend;
She lived with her widowed mother dear, down at the river's bend;
The wages of her own true love the 'boss' to her did pay,
And the shanty boys for her made up a generous purse next day.

● From *Minstrelsy of Maine*, collected by Fannie Hardy Eckstorm and Mary Winslow Smyth (Boston and
New York: Houghton Mifflin Company, 1927), pp. 82–84. Reprinted by permission of Charlotte W.
Hardy, executrix of Fannie Hardy Eckstorm Estate.

They buried him with sorrow deep, 'twas on the first of May;
"Come all of you, bold shanty boys, and for your comrade pray!"
Engraved upon a hemlock-tree that by the grave did grow,
Was the name and date of the sad, sad fate of the shanty boy, Monroe.

Fair Clara did not long survive, her heart broke with her grief,
And scarcely two months afterward death came to her relief.
And when the time had passed away and she was called to go,
Her last request was granted, to be laid by young Monroe.

Come all of you bold shanty boys, I would have you call and see
Those green mounds by the riverside, where grows the hemlock-tree.
The shanty boys cleared off the wood by the lovers there laid low—
'Twas the handsome Clara Vernon and her true love, Jack Monroe.

PO' LAZ'US

Sung in Alabama, Louisiana, Mississippi, Texas, and other southern states, often by convicts and chain-gangs, "Po' Laz'us," in the opinion of the late John A. Lomax, is the best Negro ballad. The starkness of its tragedy is greatly heightened by the melody. With the addition of exclamatory "Hanhs!" at phrasal intervals, it is used as a work song; otherwise, it is sung straight as a ballad. The editors explain that "commissary county" means "counter of the commissary store."

High Sheriff tol' de deputy, "Go out an' bring me Laz'us."
High Sheriff tol' de deputy, "Go out an' bring me Laz'us.
Bring him back dead or alive, Lawd, Lawd, bring him dead or alive."

O de deputy 'gin to wonder, where in de worl' he could fin' him?
O de deputy 'gin to wonder, where in de worl' he could fin' him?
"Well, I don' know, Lawd, Lawd, I jes' don' know."

• From *The 111 Best American Ballads: FOLK SONG U.S.A.*, collected, adapted, and arranged by John A. Lomax and Alan Lomax (Duell, Sloan & Pearce, 1949), pp. 308–9. Reprinted by permission of Duell, Sloan & Pearce, Inc., New York.

O dey found po' Laz'us way out between two mountains,
O dey found po' Laz'us way out between two mountains,
An' dey blowed him down, Lawd, Lawd, an' dey blowed him down.

Ol' Laz'us tol' de deputy he had never been arrested,
Ol' Laz'us tol' de deputy he had never been arrested,
By no one man, Lawd, Lawd, by no one man.

So dey shot po' Laz'us, shot him wid a great big number,
Dey shot po' Laz'us, shot him wid a great big number,
Number *Forty-Five*, Lawd, Lawd, number *Forty-Five*.

An' dey taken po' Laz'us an' dey laid him on de commissary county,
Dey taken po' Laz'us an' dey laid him on de commissary county,
An' dey walked away, Lawd, Lawd, an' dey walked away.

Laz'us tol' de deputy, "Please gimme a cool drink o' water,
Laz'us tol' de deputy, "Please gimme a cool drink o' water,
Jes' befo' I die, Lawd, Lawd, jes' befo' I die."

Laz'us' sister run an' tol' her mother,
Laz'us' sister run an' tol' her mother,
"Po' Laz'us dead, Lawd, Lawd, po' Laz'us dead."

Laz'us' mother, she laid down her sewin',
Laz'us' mother, she laid down her sewin',
She begin to cry, Lawd, Lawd, she begin to cry.

Laz'us' mother, she come a-screamin' an' a-cryin',
Laz'us' mother, she come a-screamin' an' a-cryin',
"Dat's my only son, Lawd, Lawd, dat's my only son!"

Laz'us' father, he sho' was hard-hearted,
Laz'us' father, he sho' was hard-hearted,
Didn't say a word, Lawd, Lawd, didn't say a word.

Laz'us' sister, she couldn't go to de funeral,
Laz'us' sister, she couldn't go to de funeral,
Didn't have no shoes, Lawd, Lawd, didn't have no shoes.

[A pause—then the gang sings:]

Cap'n did you hear about—all yo' men gonna leave you?
Cap'n did you hear about—all yo' men gonna leave you?
Nex' pay-day, Lawd, Lawd, nex' pay-day.

MISTER BOLL WEEVIL

The "ballet" of the boll weevil is an ironically humorous account of the plight of Southern cotton farmers after the appearance of the pest from Mexico in the early 1900's. It has been variously reported from popular tradition, mainly in the South. It was a favorite number of the Negro singer Leadbelly.

First time I saw little Weevil he was on the western plain,
Next time I saw him he was riding a Memphis train.
    He was seeking him a home, a happy home.

Next time I saw him he was settin' on a cotton square.
The next time I saw him he had a family there.
    He was seeking him a home, a happy home.

Next time I saw him he was runnin' a spinnin' wheel;
The next time I saw him he was ridin' in an automobile.
    He was seeking him a home, a happy home.

Mr. Merchant said to the farmer: "Well, what do you think of that?
If you'll get rid of little Weevil, I'll give you a Stetson hat."
    He's seeking him a home, a happy home.

Mr. Farmer took little Weevil and put him in paris green.
"Thank you, Mr. Farmer; it's the best I ever seen.
    I'm going to have a home, a happy home."

Then he took little Weevil, put him in a block of ice.
"Thank you, Mr. Farmer; it is so cool and nice.
    I'm going to have a home, a happy home."

Mr. Farmer then got angry and sent him up in a balloon.
"Good-by, Mr. Farmer; I'll see you again next June.
    I'll be seeking a home, a happy home."

Little Weevil took Mr. Farmer, throwed him in the sand,
Put on Mr. Farmer's overcoat, stood up like a natural man.
    "I'm going to have a home, a happy home."

● From *Folksongs of Mississippi and Their Background*, by Arthur Palmer Hudson (Chapel Hill: University of North Carolina Press, 1936), pp. 199–200. Reprinted by permission of the University of North Carolina Press.

Little Weevil said to the sharpshooter: "Better get up on your feet.
Look down across the Delta at the cotton we'll have to reap.
   We've got us a home, a happy home."

Mr. Merchant said to the farmer: "I can not see your route.
Got a mortgage on old Beck and Kate; just as well be taking them out,
   And bring them home, and bring them home."

"Come on, old woman, and we will travel out West.
The weevils et up everything we've got but your old cotton dress,
   And it's full of holes, it's full of holes."

THE GOOD OLD REBEL

The original of this ballad was composed by Innes Randolph (1837–87), a member of General J. E. B. Stuart's staff in the Confederate Army who settled in Baltimore and wrote for the Baltimore American. It was published in that newspaper and was included in Poems by Innes Randolph *(Baltimore, 1898), pp. 30–31. Becoming immensely popular in the South as an expression of resentment against Reconstruction, it was set to music and has become a genuine folk song, with many variants and with numerous claims and attributions of authorship. The following text is a composite of two variants from oral tradition. It may be compared with the original, which has been reprinted in* The Oxford Book of Light Verse, *pp. 228–29.*

● The first three stanzas from *The Frank C. Brown Collection of North Carolina Folklore,* Vol. III, *Folk Songs,* edited by Henry M. Belden and Arthur Palmer Hudson (Durham, N.C.: Duke University Press, 1952), pp. 464–65; the last two from Arthur Palmer Hudson, *Folksongs of Mississippi and Their Background* (Chapel Hill: University of North Carolina Press, 1936), p. 260.

Oh, I'm a good ole Rebel, an' that's jes' what I am,
An' fer this "Land of Freedom" I do not care a damn.
I'm glad I fit against it, I only wisht we'd won,
An' I don't want no pardon fer anything I done.

I followed Ole Marse Robert fer fo' years nigh about,
Got wounded in three places, an' starved at P'int Lookout.
I cotch the rheumatism a-campin' in the snow,
But I killed a chance of Yankees, an' I'd lak to kill some mo'.

Three hundred thousand Yankees lie stiff in Southern dust;
We killed three hundred thousand befo' they conquered us.
They died of Southern fever, an' Southern shell an' shot;
I wisht it was three million instid of what we got.

I hate the Constitution, the Great Republic too;
I hate the mighty eagle and the uniform of blue.
I hate the Glorious Banner and all their flags and fuss;
Them lyin', thievin' Yankees, I hate 'em wuss and wuss.

I won't be reconstructed, I'm better now than them;
For those dirty carpet-baggers I don't give a damn.
So I'm off to the Border as soon as I can go;
I'll git me a gun and leave fer Mexico.

KENTUCKY PARTY

by Elizabeth Madox Roberts

Modern Kentucky is the scene of most of Miss Roberts' novels of share-croppers and tenant farmers. Her hill people are impoverished, uneducated, and rather shiftless, but they preserve many bits of traditional custom and speech in their daily life. Crops are planted or harvested according to agricul-tural folklore, weather tokens are carefully watched for, old social practices are observed, and proverbs creep into daily language. Ellen Chesser, the heroine of The Time of Man *(1926), goes to a neighborhood party and, in response to the demand that each guest contribute part of the entertain-ment, sings fragments of old ballads. Her rendition of "Lord Lovel," although it differs from the versions preserved by Francis James Child in his famous collection, reveals that ancient English and Scottish popular ballads still linger in the Kentucky hill country.*

Too eager to wait for supper, Ellen brushed back her hair before the kitchen mirror, put on her cloak, and ran away toward Dorine Wheatley's home where there was to be a party. Her head was bare in the frosty night and her hair caught the vigor of the air and crisped richly over her forehead. Her dark skirt had been brushed that afternoon and her waist inspected for holes and loose buttons. Her shoes had been viewed in several moods, critically, hopelessly, hopefully, carelessly, mournfully, but in all moods they were old and worn. When she drew near the small white house that stood close beside the road, half a mile from her home, noises were bursting from its walls, voices and footfalls. A thin flat music came merrily over the other sounds, over the quick feet pursuing other quick feet, a slow foot settling back upon itself leisurely, little steps of women and long heavy steps of men. Ellen did not think to knock at the door. She lifted the latch with her thumb and went headlong into the room where many people were standing about or sitting, strange people. She closed the door behind her back and stood leaning against the doorframe, her body trembling. A voice was saying, "Did the prize come?"

"Came yesterday evening," Dorine's voice called out from some other room.

It had seemed a little house when Ellen had come to bring the apple. Now it seemed large to be holding many people. All were laughing and talking very loud but Dorine's voice came again out of the jargon of words and laughter and shuffling feet.

"It's Ellen Chesser. Here's a chair."

The other people seemed to have come much earlier and all the first awkwardness was worn away. The party was congratulatory, for Dorine had won a three-piece combing set in a satin-lined box, had won it by selling eight boxes of some salve. Now that all the guests had arrived the prize was brought to the table and displayed. It was a brush and a comb and a hand mirror, all of a hard white stuff. The articles were fastened by little clasps onto a ground of pink satin.

"Ain't that something pretty now!" voices cried out.

"Eight boxes! That was a heap to sell!"

"It wasn't so easy to do, either," Dorine said. She wore a pink dress and her cheeks were pink and warm.

"Name who bought," her mother said.

"Eli bought one and Elmer Ware, and then Ras O'Shay and Mammy. That's four. And then Sallie Lou and Mrs. Al Wakefield and Jonas Prather and Mr. Jim. Eight boxes of Lily-bud salve I sold." Ellen wished that she had bought one. But then she had not known about it and besides she had no money.

"I bought it to grease my old buggy with," a young man said.

"I bought mine to see if hit might cure my hens outen their roup." A half-dozen unflattering reasons were offered.

Dorine made faces at the speakers. The combing set was passed around and dark rough hands took out the white pieces and passed them to other dark hands. Splintered fingers caught on the soft spines of the satin. Someone discovered that the lining would come out of the box, for it was a crust of cloth glued onto wooden pegs. The three pieces of the set, the two linings of the box, and the box, six articles, were passed through the room. The prize was put together and taken apart several times for joy in the wonder of its mechanism. Ellen sat in her chair, out from the wall, conspicuous, miserable, her feet crossed under her dress, her eyes looking everywhere. She did not want to be sitting on the best chair out in the middle of the room, the chair nobody else would take because it was the best. Scarcely anyone knew her and she longed to be in a corner, but she dared not move. At the same time she longed to be known and to be liked. If the boy with the little beady eyes had said something to her she should have been most happy, or if the girl with the white stockings had, although that last was far too much to hope for. Effie Turpin stood over by the fireplace and presently Ellen knew that the girl called Maggie was a Turpin also although she was prettier than Effie. She wished that someone would ask her to move back into a corner, or she wished that she could say something pleasing and quick and that one or two would look at her and know what she meant. She wanted everyone to like her, to take her into the dance, into the game, into the jokes, or even into the crowd that went into the other room to be out of the way of the dancers.

"Maybe this lady would be good enough to move back." Someone had said it and she was sitting in a corner. She sat, eager, ashamed, embarrassed, the joy of people near making her breath flutter. She heard names called and soon she had a flow of names confused in her mind, blended with running currents of action, looks and words. The fat girl was always slapping at the boy with the beady eyes and these two were always coming back to Tim MacNeal and the girl with the white stockings. The graphophone was wound for the dance and then the music came from a large blue and pink metal morning-glory. In another room Mr. Jim Townley strummed a guitar and now and then he sang a line. Once his voice jerked into the middle of his tonk tonk a-tonk of guitar strings with

> Oh . . .
> Say darlin' say
> When I'm far away. . . .

The dance ended and there was a romp. Ellen rose from her chair and went into the other room where she stopped at the door to look about her. Mr. Jim finished a stave with a tender arpeggio on the instrument and then muted the strings with a gesture and a little upward flash of his eyes which was directed toward her as she stood just before him. Suddenly she went out of her regret for her torn shoes, out of her memory of herself, out of her lonely nights, out of her presence sitting strangely in the corner at a party.

"I can sing a song," she said.

The people close around grew still. Ellen was standing by the door, terrified at what her lips were saying, her body leaning a little forward from the hips.

"Well, sing it," Mr. Townley said. "Hush, everybody, hush you-all. Ellen Chesser is a-goen to sing a song."

"I can sing 'Lady Nancy Belle'—that's a story one Mammy taught me a long time ago, one she learned offen her grannie, or I can sing 'Lucy Is a Mighty Generous Lady,' whichever you'd rather."

"Sing both."

"Sing the story one."

"Aw, let her sing the Lucy one."

"Sing both."

Nervous movements came over her mouth and strained at her eyes and her throat, but she took a deep breath, caught her breath twice, and began in a shy voice, smiling a little, looking at Mr. Townley, or casting down her eyes. After she was well started Mr. Townley caught her tune and began to touch the chords on his instrument, and this pleased her very much. She sang:

> Lord Lovel he stood by his castle wall
> A-comben his milk-white steed;
> Down came the Lady Nancy Belle
> A-wishen her lover good-speed.
> A-wishen her lover good-speed.
>
> "Oh, where are you goen, Lord Lovel?"
> she cried,
> "Oh, where are you goen?" cried she;
> "I'm a-goen, my dear Lady Nancy Belle,
> Strange countries for to see. . . ."

She sang of the departing lover and of his promise to return in a year or two or at most in three. But when he had been gone but a year and a day a languishing thought of Nancy Belle came over his mind and he returned only to find the bells of St. Pancras tolling and all the people mourning for Nancy Belle who was dead.

> He ordered the grave to be opened wide,
> The shroud to be turned down;
> He kissed and kissed those clay cold lips,
> And the tears came a-trinklen down.

Ellen sang with bright eyes, her low voice going to the end of the room, settling down over the hushed feet and the listening faces. She had forgotten herself in her pleasure. All had crowded into this room from the other rooms and the guitar was beating a-tonk-a a-tonk-a a-tonk a-tonk, true to every measure.

> Lady Nancy died like it might be today;
> Lord Lovel like it might be tomorrow;
> Lady Nancy died for pure pure grief;
> Lord Lovel he died for sorrow.

> Lady Nancy was laid in St. Pancras church,
> Lord Lovel was laid in the choir;
> And out of her breast there grew a red rose,
> And out of his a briar.

> They grew and they grew to the old
>   church top,
> And when they could grow no higher;
> There they tied in a true lovers' knot
> For all true lovers to admire.

There was a great laugh and a clapping of hands and a stamping of feet when she had finished. Mr. Townley made a great bow for her.

"Hit's a story about a couple of sweethearts, that's what hit is," one said.

"Hit's like a book to read."

"Miss Nancy, she died like it would be one day, and this man, her sweetheart, like it might be the next."

"Yes, but all he could grow outen his grave was a briar, and that's something to chop down and grub out."

"Hit means a briar rose, you durn fool you."

"It's like a story book to read. Get her to sing it again."

"Let her sing 'Lucy a Generous Lady.' "

Ellen said she would not sing again. "Lady Nancy" was a long song, long enough, she said. She felt confused, wrecked, when her voice ran off the song, ran off the last word of the song. She had moved a long way from herself sitting neglected in the corner and she could not know where her place would now be. She thought the party would break in two, but Dorine came forward proudly and took her by the arm and introduced her to everybody present.

"Let me make you acquainted with Jonas Prather," she said.

"Howdy do. I'm right glad to know you."

"Let me make you acquainted with Eli Prather."

They shook her hand. After she had been introduced to everyone Jonas asked her to dance and then she stood in the long line with the others singing,

> Susie says she loves him
> A long summer day. . . .

When their turn came with Jonas she went down the lines, she turning all the men while he turned the girls. After a while names became permanently attached to figures and faces. The boy with the little beady eyes was Eli Prather, cousin to Jonas, and the fat girl was Rosie O'Shay.

"Eli *talks* to Rosie," Jonas said to her in a low tone. *Talks* to Rosie, *talks*—she knew what he meant.

The lovers would slap each other on the back, going out onto the porch in a romp every little while. "Say, you can stay in here and kiss. You don't have to be a-goen out in the cold. Might as well," some voice called out.

The girl with the white stockings was Sallie Lou Brown and her fellow was Tim MacNeal. Sallie Lou was very quick with her white stockings that twinkled in and out of her dress as she danced, and her green flowered dress made her look very slim up and down. Rosie's dress was dark and her shoes were old and scabbed, but she had a good time, and Ellen minded her own broken shoes much less. The Turpin girls had on dim cotton dresses of no color at all, and some of the young men had no neckties. A feeling of intimacy with the place had come to Ellen and this helped her to move lightly in the dance-games. She knew the fireplace with the broken dogiron and she knew the knot-holes in the floor by the door and the window where the water bucket stood. Mr. Wheatley, Dorine's father, took off his shoes and walked about the house in his stockings. They were of gray wool and they wrinkled about the ankles just as Ellen knew. Voices grew familiar as recognized from the other room, and gestures and looks came back again and again to this one and that. All were weary of dancing, and they gathered about the fire in the larger room, jostling one another on the wide stone hearth, their voices flowing fast, running out from the high warmth of their blood.

"Durned if here ain't a louse," one said.

"Oh, shut up!"

"Keep hit to yourself, hit's your'n."

"Well it is one, now."

"Well kill hit, then."

"Hit's a tater bug."

"Hit's a gnat or a flea, maybe."

"Flea your hind leg! Hit's a body louse."

"Step on it with your foot."

"What was it, Dorine?"

"It was a spider, Mammy."

"Call hit a spider for manners!"

They were sitting on chairs and benches and on the floor, drinking a hot drink made of eggs and milk, a custard, from cups and mugs. There were small round cakes. "There's plenty of spoons for everybody to have one," Mrs. Wheatley said. She was eager for everyone to like the custard. They romped over the food, pulling at arms and legs, pinching flesh. They did like the custard and each one tried to say how much he liked it until Eli outspoke all the rest.

"Gee durn! I wish I had a stream of this-here stuff a-runnen through me all the time."

Eli closed his eyes to feel the stream he had pictured and everybody laughed, feeling it likewise. Elmer slapped Ellen on the back in his happiness and she was glad again that she was there. Mr. Wheatley sang a bit of a verse:

The Mammoth Cave, oh, what a spot!
In summer cold, in winter hot!

"Eli and Rosie, now that's a match," Erastus said. "I seen the minute they commenced to spark each other."

"Eli and Rosie, they already promised to name their first after me," Tim said.

"You go on!" Rosie said. She was taking her cup for more custard.

"Already promised. Sure. Tim T. Prather. I can see him now."

"A lousy brat, hit'll be. No help to hit. Tim T. Prather! God knows!"

"A-squallen and a-puken. I can see hit myself. Timothy T. Prather. Look at Rosie blush."

"You go on!" Rosie said.

Mr. Wheatley sang again, his refrain "Black cat kicked out the yellow cat's eye...."

"That-there yeller cat was a tom cat. I see two cats once out behind the barn," Ras said.

"Shut up, Ras," Elmer said. "Where you been brought up?"

"Well, I know cats, now. That-there black cat, she was a puss cat and that-there yeller he was a tom. Black, he lost an eye."

Tim MacNeal held a mug of custard over Eli Prather's head, spilling a little.

"I baptize you in the name of the Father, Son, and Holy Ghost."

"Quit, I already been bapsoused, soused, I say."

"I saw you when you was pulled up outen the water. You looked like a drowned rat."

"Washed your sins away, didn't you, Eli? The creek was muddied all that next day. I went by and I seen what was left back in Dover Creek."

"Preacher said baptizen wouldn't do me e'er bit of good. Said they'd have to take a scrub brush."

"Saw old Sallie Lou a-cryen the night she joined."

> Whoop law, Lizie poor gal,
> Whoop law, Lizie Jane,
> Whoop law, Lizie poor li'l gal,
> She died carryen that ball and chain.

"Saw old Sallie Lou a-cryen."

"Old Sallie Lou was a-mournen for her sins. I see her on the mourners' bench that night."

"Home! Who said home? Home's a fool beside this-here place. Strike her up again with a tune, Mr. Jim, and let's dance another round."

They were going home, everyone leaving at one time, with loud goodbyes for Dorine and her mother and father flung back from the road. There were many goodbyes and parting messages.

"Go through Wakefield's, Jim, you and Maggie and Ras, and take Ellen home," Mrs. Wheatley called from the house door.

Tim MacNeal and Sallie Lou rode away together, driving a wild little half-broken horse that went jumping off in the crisp air. Mr. Jim had a lantern to peer out the ruts of the road, and near him walked Erastus and Maggie and Jonas. Effie Turpin walked behind him to borrow of his light, and Ellen moved along among them but she thought nothing of herself. They were five shapes lying beyond herself, herself forgotten, five shapes, one of them carrying a light, a deep voice, a high voice, and muffled words, now reached up and now bent down in sweet arcs, in high

bridges suddenly flung across chasms of thought, in little down-drooping sayings, low and final. All of them were beautiful to her in their closeness, their offered friendship. She walked home in silence, forgetting to speak. They were tired after the long merry evening, and their weariness made them speak gently.

"Hit's a mild winter for sure," a voice said.

"It sure is."

"I look for a heap of sickness along February."

"And the old a-dyen off."

"Oh, that's what I'm a-thinken."

"I tell you what I've seen in my time. I've seen a winter so mild the grass was a-growen and the birds a-singen right along from sunup to sundown."

"It's a dove though really tells when spring's come."

They walked quietly on, their feet making uneven rhythms on the road. "It's a dove though really tells when spring's come" lingered on as tone refalling on Ellen's ears, "It's a dove though really tells," a phrase from some playing instrument. They passed under low trees for a space and then came onto an open stretch of road.

"I vow there's a heap of stars out tonight."

"And them that's out is a long way off."

"How far is it to a star? How far now do you reckon it is to that yon one in the row off north there?"

"Hit's a far piece, a right far piece."

"It's a million times as far as from here to the North Pole and back, they say."

"Now, no!"

"You can't think hit. You can't get your mind on hit, someways you can't."

"You can't get your mind to think on it."

"Ah, gee! ain't there a heap of 'em!"

"There's more every way you look.

There might maybe be a million and I'd never know hit."

"And they're up there night in and night out, year in and year out, and how many times do we take notice to it?"

"I heared tell about a man once that followed studyen the stars all his life."

"That's something to do now, if a man had time."

"That's hit, if a man had time."

Five shapes were thumping the dry road with their feet, stumbling a little, five abreast now and now drifting into forms like those the stars made in the sky. It was here that she felt them become six, herself making part of the forms, herself merged richly with the design.

"I studied a heap about the stars, since you named it, in my own mind I have. Now I wonder what they're made outen."

"And what they're for, nohow."

"Ah, God-almighty, ain't we little things a-goen around."

"Ah, God-almighty, we are now and that's a fact."

"But of a morning, when you go out to feed and water, how often do you ever remember the stars you saw last night?"

"I studied about that once before in my time. I was watchen a fish trap all night down on the river."

"And once I got to looken at the moon. That's something worth studyen now."

"God knows!"

"It is and that's a fact!"

"I heard about a man once that followed nothing else but to study the stars his whole enduren life."

They stopped at a small white gate beyond a leafless cherry thicket.

"Goodnight, Ellen."

"Goodnight, Jonas."

"Goodnight, Mr. Jim."

"Goodnight."

"Goodnight."

"Goodnight."

I HEAR AMERICA SINGING

by Walt Whitman

Although Whitman did not use folklore in the obvious connotation of the term, his poetry is full of folk concepts and allusions. His verse catalogues are a complete list of the occupations of the people, his idiom is that of the folk, and his vignettes of ordinary life are particularly vivid and clear. Even when he projects himself into the past, as, for example, in his accounts of a Texas battlefield or the famous sea victory of John Paul Jones, the stories achieve the tone of legend. The poems that follow are taken from Leaves of Grass, the first edition of which appeared in 1855. Whitman subsequently enlarged and revised his first book of poetry but retained the original title. "Song of Myself" appeared in the 1855 volume. "I Hear America Singing" was first published in 1860.

I hear America singing, the varied carols I hear,
Those of mechanics, each one singing his as it should be, blithe and strong,
The carpenter singing his as he measures his plank or beam,
The mason singing his as he makes ready for work, or leaves off work,
The boatman singing what belongs to him in his boat, the deckhand singing on the steamboat deck,
The shoemaker singing as he sits on his bench, the hatter singing as he stands,
The wood-cutter's song, the ploughboy's on his way in the morning, or at noon intermission or at sundown,
The delicious singing of the mother, or of the young wife at work, or of the girl sewing or washing,
Each singing what belongs to him or her and to none else,
The day what belongs to the day—at night the party of young fellows, robust, friendly,
Singing with open mouths their strong melodious songs.

SELECTIONS FROM SONG OF MYSELF

by Walt Whitman

1. OCCUPATIONS

The quadroon girl is sold at the auction-stand, the drunkard nods by
the bar-room stove,

The machinist rolls up his sleeves, the policeman travels his beat, the gate-
keeper marks who pass,

The young fellow drives the express-wagon, (I love him, though I do
not know him;)

The half-breed straps on his light boots to compete in the race,

The western turkey-shooting draws old and young, some lean on their
rifles, some sit on logs,

Out from the crowd steps the marksman, takes his position, levels his piece;

The groups of newly-come immigrants cover the wharf or levee,

As the woolly-pates hoe in the sugar-field, the overseer views them from his
saddle,

The bugle calls in the ball-room, the gentlemen run for their partners, the
dancers bow to each other,

The youth lies awake in the cedar-roof'd garret and harks to the musical
rain, . . .

Upon the race-course, or enjoying picnics or jigs or a good game of
base-ball,

At he-festivals, with blackguard gibes, ironical license, bull-dances, drinking, laughter,

At the cider-mill tasting the sweets of the brown mash, sucking the juice
through a straw,

At apple-peelings wanting kisses for all the red fruit I find,

At musters, beach-parties, friendly bees, huskings, house-raisings; . . .

2. THE MURDER OF FOUR HUNDRED AND TWELVE

Now I tell what I knew in Texas in my early youth,

(I tell not the fall of Alamo,

No one escaped to tell the fall of Alamo,

The hundred and fifty are dumb yet at Alamo,)

'Tis the tale of the murder in cold blood of four hundred and twelve
young men.

Retreating they had form'd in a hollow square with their baggage for
breastworks,

Nine hundred lives out of the surrounding enemy's, nine times their
      number, was the price they took in advance,
Their colonel was wounded and their ammunition gone,
They treated for an honorable capitulation, receiv'd writing and seal, gave
      up their arms and march'd back prisoners of war.

They were the glory of the race of rangers,
Matchless with horse, rifle, song, supper, courtship,
Large, turbulent, generous, handsome, proud, and affectionate,
Bearded, sunburnt, drest in the free costume of hunters,
Not a single one over thirty years of age.

The second First-day morning they were brought out in squads and
      massacred, it was beautiful early summer,
The work commenced about five o'clock and was over by eight.
None obey'd the command to kneel,
Some made a mad and helpless rush, some stood stark and straight,
A few fell at once, shot in the temple or heart, the living and dead lay
      together,
The maim'd and mangled dug in the dirt, the new-comers saw them there,
Some half-kill'd attempted to crawl away,
These were despatch'd with bayonets or batter'd with the blunts of muskets,
A youth not seventeen years old seiz'd his assassin till two more came to
      release him,
The three were all torn and cover'd with the boy's blood.

At eleven o'clock began the burning of the bodies;
That is the tale of the murder of the four hundred and twelve young men.

3. AN OLD-TIME SEA-FIGHT

Would you hear of an old-time sea-fight?
Would you learn who won by the light of the moon and stars?
List to the yarn, as my grandmother's father the sailor told it to me.

Our foe was no skulk in his ship I tell you, (said he,)
His was the surly English pluck, and there is no tougher or truer, and never
      was, and never will be;
Along the lower'd eve he came horribly raking us.

We closed with him, the yards entangled, the cannon touch'd,
My captain lash'd fast with his own hands.

We had receiv'd some eighteen pound shots under the water,
On our lower-gun-deck two large pieces had burst at the first fire, killing all
    around and blowing up overhead.

Fighting at sun-down, fighting at dark,
Ten o'clock at night, the full moon well up, our leaks on the gain, and five
    feet of water reported,
The master-at-arms loosing the prisoners confined in the afterhold to give
    them a chance for themselves.

The transit to and from the magazine is now stopt by the sentinels,
They see so many strange faces they do not know whom to trust.

Our frigate takes fire,
The other asks if we demand quarter?
If our colors are struck and the fighting done?

Now I laugh content, for I hear the voice of my little captain,
We have not struck, he composedly cries, *we have just begun our part of
    the fighting.*

Only three guns are in use,
One is directed by the captain himself against the enemy's mainmast,
Two well serv'd with grape and canister silence his musketry and clear
    his decks.

The tops alone second the fire of this little battery, especially the main-top,
They hold out bravely during the whole of the action.

Not a moment's cease,
The leaks gain fast on the pumps, the fire eats toward the powder-magazine.

One of the pumps has been shot away, it is generally thought we are
    sinking.
Serene stands the little captain,
He is not hurried, his voice is neither high nor low,
His eyes give more light to us than our battle-lanterns.

Toward twelve there in the beams of the moon they surrender to us.

Stretch'd and still lies the midnight,
Two great hulls motionless on the breast of the darkness,

Our vessel riddled and slowly sinking, preparations to pass to the one we
  have conquer'd,
The captain on the quarter-deck coldly giving his orders through a counte-
  nance white as a sheet,
Near by the corpse of the child that serv'd in the cabin,
The dead face of an old salt with long white hair and carefully curl'd
  whiskers,
The flames spite of all that can be done flickering aloft and below,
The husky voices of the two or three officers yet fit for duty,
Formless stacks of bodies and bodies by themselves, dabs of flesh upon
  the masts and spars,
Cut of cordage, dangle of rigging, slight shock of the soothe of waves,
Black and impassive guns, litter of powder-parcels, strong scent,
A few large stars overhead, silent and mournful shining,
Delicate sniffs of sea-breeze, smells of sedgy grass and fields by the shore,
  death-messages given in charge to survivors,
The hiss of the surgeon's knife, the gnawing teeth of his saw,
Wheeze, cluck, swash of falling blood, short wild scream, and long, dull,
  tapering groan,
These so, these irretrievable.

XII

FOLK WISDOM

Proverbs, apothegms, and just plain wisecracks have always been part of the American vocabulary, for in them is to be found the voice of the folk. Benjamin Franklin searched the literatures of Europe for proverbs, many of which he sharpened or altered, to be included in his various almanacs. Occasionally he even contributed proverbs of his own. Since his time the crackerbox tradition has not languished. The Yankee humorists of the early nineteenth century, the journalists and professional comedians of the Civil War period, the rustic commentators of the last fifty years provide a multitude of examples. Aphorisms in illiterate English poured from the pen of Josh Billings. Bill Nye and Artemus Ward used the same medium. Caustic maxims came from Ambrose Bierce and even from Mark Twain's Pudd'nhead Wilson. The terse encomiums on thrift and temperance uttered by E. W. Howe, the Sage of Potato Hill, sound like a Franklin removed to Kansas and suddenly become dour. Finley Peter Dunne draped the Irish brogue of Mr. Dooley around many a pointed statement on domestic and political life, and Kin Hubbard's Abe Martin of Brown County became the agent for keen and acerb comment on Hoosier society. Damon Runyon and Ring Lardner used modern slang as their means of communication, and Will Rogers typified to a large audience the man of the street, simple, plain, forthright, speaking directly from the horse's mouth. The decades between Franklin's almanacs and Carl Sandburg's *The People, Yes* embrace the rise to power of the modern United States, the most powerful nation in the world's history. Yet the character of the folk in the course of two hundred years seems to have changed but little. Many of the proverbs familiar to Franklin reappear in Sandburg; the modern poet kept his ear as close to the ground as the eighteenth-century rationalist. Both attempted to record and to represent the wisdom of the folk. And if Franklin was guided by a wise skepticism, the burden of Sandburg's book seems to be an abiding faith in the American people.

The Way to Wealth

by Benjamin Franklin

After having published Poor Richard's Almanack *for twenty-five years, Franklin terminated his venture, but not before he had extracted from his annual volumes enough maxims to make a sermon on thrift. The result is a memorable collection of prudential advice enriched by many homely examples and concrete experiences. Few of the saws quoted here were original with Franklin. Indeed, Carl Van Doren in his admirable biography has pointed out Franklin's indebtedness to a number of sages in foreign countries and has also remarked that not all of the proverbs were designed to encourage frugality;[1] some of the more famous sayings would seem to condone quite another kind of conduct. But it is also true that Franklin rarely left a proverb as he found it. He polished it, sharpened it, and sometimes made it terser and more specific, so that today we think of Franklin as a master of proverbial wisdom. At any rate, Father Abraham's speech at a vendue is a mosaic of good counsel, aimed at an ordinary audience that would relish the singular combination of homely advice, philosophy, skepticism, and sophistication. Franklin wrote nothing which has proved more durable than this fugue on the theme of thrift.*

Courteous Reader,

I have heard that nothing gives an Author so great Pleasure, as to find his Works respectfully quoted by other learned Authors. This Pleasure I have seldom enjoyed; for tho' I have been, if I may say it without Vanity, an *eminent Author* of Almanacks annually now a full Quarter of a Century, my Brother Authors in the same Way, for what Reason I know not, have ever been very sparing in their Applauses, and no other Author has taken the least Notice of me, so that did not my Writings produce me some solid *Pudding*, the great Deficiency of *Praise* would have quite discouraged me.

I concluded at length, that the People were the best Judges of my Merit; for they buy my Works; and besides, in my Rambles, where I am not personally known, I have frequently heard one or other of my Adages repeated, with, *as Poor Richard says,* at the End on 't; this gave me some Satisfaction, as it showed not only that my Instructions were regarded, but discovered likewise some Respect for my Authority; and I own, that to encourage the Practice of remembering and repeating those wise Sentences, I have sometimes *quoted myself* with great Gravity.

Judge then how much I must have been gratified by an Incident I am going to relate to you. I stopt my Horse lately where a great Number of People were collected at a Vendue of Merchant Goods. The Hour of Sale not being come, they were conversing on the Badness of the Times and one of the Company call'd to a plain

1. Carl Van Doren, *Benjamin Franklin* (New York: Viking Press, 1938), Chapter IV.

clean old Man, with white Locks, "Pray, Father Abraham, what think you of the Times? Won't these heavy Taxes quite ruin the Country? How shall we be ever able to pay them? What would you advise us to?" Father *Abraham* stood up, and reply'd, "If you'd have my Advice, I'll give it you in short, for *A Word to the Wise is enough,* and *many Words won't fill a Bushel,* as *Poor Richard* says." They join'd in desiring him to speak his Mind, and gathering round him, he proceeded as follows:

"Friends," says he, "and Neighbours, the Taxes are indeed very heavy, and if those laid on by the Government were the only Ones we had to pay, we might more easily discharge them; but we have many others, and much more grievous to some of us. We are taxed twice as much by our *Idleness,* three times as much by our *Pride,* and four times as much by our *Folly;* and from these Taxes the Commissioners cannot ease or deliver us by allowing an Abatement. However let us hearken to good Advice, and something may be done for us; *God helps them that help themselves,* as *Poor Richard* says, in his Almanack of 1733.

It would be thought a hard Government that should tax its People one-tenth Part of their *Time,* to be employed in its Service. But *Idleness* taxes many of us much more, if we reckon all that is spent in absolute *Sloth,* or doing of nothing, with that which is spent in idle Employments or Amusements, that amount to nothing. *Sloth,* by bringing on Diseases, absolutely shortens Life. *Sloth, like Rust, consumes faster than Labour wears; while the used Key is always bright,* as *Poor Richard* says. *But dost thou love Life, then do not squander Time; for that's the stuff Life is made of,* as *Poor Richard* says. How much more than is necessary do we spend in sleep, forgetting that *The Sleeping Fox*

catches no Poultry, and that *There will be sleeping enough in the Grave,* as *Poor Richard* says.

If Time be of all Things the most precious, wasting Time must be, as *Poor Richard* says, *the greatest Prodigality;* since, as he elsewhere tells us, *Lost Time is never found again; and what we call Time enough, always proves little enough:* Let us then up and be doing, and doing to the Purpose; so by Diligence shall we do more with less Perplexity. *Sloth makes all Things difficult, but Industry all easy,* as *Poor Richard* says; and *He that riseth late, must trot all Day, and shall scarce overtake his Business at Night.* While *Laziness travels so slowly, that Poverty soon overtakes him,* as we read in *Poor Richard,* who adds, *Drive thy Business, let not that drive thee;* and *Early to Bed, and early to rise, makes a Man healthy, wealthy, and wise.*

So what signifies *wishing* and *hoping* for better Times. We may make these Times better, if we bestir ourselves. *Industry need not wish,* as *Poor Richard* says, and *He that lives upon Hope will die fasting.* There are *no Gains, without Pains;* then *Help Hands, for I have no Lands,* or if I have, they are smartly taxed. And, as *Poor Richard* likewise observes, *He that hath a Trade hath an Estate;* and *He that hath a Calling, hath an Office of Profit and Honour;* but then the *Trade* must be worked at, and the *Calling* well followed, or neither the *Estate*, nor the *Office*, will enable us to pay our Taxes. If we are industrious, we shall never starve; for, as *Poor Richard* says, *At the working Man's House* Hunger *looks in, but dares not enter.* Nor will the Bailiff or the Constable enter, for *Industry pays Debts, while Despair encreaseth them*, says *Poor Richard.* What though you have found no Treasure, nor has any rich Relation left you a Legacy, *Diligence is the Mother of Good luck*, as *Poor Richard* says, *and God gives all Things to Industry. Then plough deep, while Sluggards sleep, and you shall have Corn to sell and to keep*, says *Poor Dick.* Work while it is called To-day, for you know not how much you may be hindered To-morrow, which makes *Poor Richard* say, *One To-day is worth two To-morrows*, and farther, *Have you somewhat to do To-morrow, do it To-day.* If you were a Servant, would you not be ashamed that a good Master should catch you idle? Are you then your own Master, *be ashamed to catch yourself idle*, as *Poor Dick* says. When there is so much to be done for yourself, your Family, your Country, and your gracious King, be up by Peep of Day; *Let not the Sun look down and say, Inglorious here he lies.* Handle your Tools without Mittens; remember that *the Cat in Gloves catches no Mice*, as *Poor Richard* says. 'Tis true there is much to be done, and perhaps you are weakhanded, but stick to it steadily; and you will see great Effects, for *constant Dropping wears away Stones*, and by *Diligence and Patience the Mouse ate in two the Cable*; and *little Strokes fell great Oaks*, as *Poor Richard* says in his Almanack, the Year I cannot just now remember.

Methinks I hear some of you say, *Must a Man afford himself no Leisure?* I will tell thee, my Friend, what *Poor Richard* says, *Employ thy Time well, if thou meanest to gain Leisure; and, since thou art not sure of a Minute, throw not away an Hour.* Leisure, is Time for doing something useful; this Leisure the diligent Man will obtain, but the lazy Man never; so that, as *Poor Richard* says, *A Life of Leisure and a Life of Laziness are two Things.* Do you imagine that Sloth will afford you more Comfort than Labour? No, for as *Poor Richard* says, *Trouble springs from Idleness, and grievous Toil from needless Ease. Many without Labour, would live by their Wits only, but they break for want of Stock.* Whereas Industry gives Comfort, and Plenty, and Respect: *Fly Pleasures, and they'll follow you.* The diligent Spinner has a large Shift; and *now I have a Sheep and a Cow, every Body bids me Good morrow*; all which is well said by *Poor Richard.*

But with our Industry, we must likewise be *steady, settled* and *careful*, and oversee our own Affairs *with our own Eyes*, and not trust too much to others; for, as *Poor Richard* says,

> I never saw an oft removed Tree,
> Nor yet an oft removed Family,
> That throve so well as those that settled be.

And again, *Three Removes is as bad as a Fire*; and again, *Keep thy Shop, and thy Shop will keep thee*; and again, *If you would have your Business done, go; If not, send.* And again,

> He that by the Plough would thrive,
> Himself must either hold or drive.

And again, *The Eye of a Master will do more Work than both his Hands*; and again, *Want of Care does us more Damage than Want of Knowledge*; and again, *Not to oversee Workmen, is to leave them your Purse open.* Trusting too much to others Care is the Ruin of many; for, as the *Almanack* says, *In the Affairs of this World, Men are saved, not by Faith, but by the Want of it*; but a Man's own Care is profitable; for, saith *Poor Dick, Learning is to the Studious,* and *Riches to the Careful,* as well as *Power to the Bold,* and *Heaven to the Virtuous.* And farther, *If you would have a faithful Servant, and one that you like, serve yourself.* And again, he adviseth to Circumspection and Care, even in the smallest Matters, because sometimes *a little Neglect may breed great Mischief;* adding, *For want of a Nail the Shoe was lost; for want of a Shoe the Horse was lost; and for want of a Horse the Rider was lost,* being overtaken and slain by the Enemy, all for want of Care about a Horse shoe Nail.

So much for Industry, my Friends, and Attention to one's own Business; but to these we must add *Frugality,* if we would make our *Industry* more certainly successful. A Man may, if he knows not how to save as he gets, *keep his Nose all his Life to the Grindstone,* and die not worth a *Groat* at last. *A fat Kitchen makes a Lean Will,* as *Poor Richard* says; and,

> Many Estates are spent in the Getting,
> Since Women for Tea forsook Spinning
>   and Knitting,
> And Men for Punch forsook Hewing and
>   Splitting.

If you would be wealthy, says he, in another Almanack, *think of Saving as well as Getting: The Indies have not made Spain rich, because her Outgoes are greater than her Incomes.* Away then with your expensive Follies, and you will not have so much Cause to complain of hard Times, heavy Taxes, and chargeable Families; for, as *Poor Dick* says,

> Women and Wine, Game and Deceit,
> Make the Wealth small, and the Wants great.

And farther, *What maintains one Vice, would bring up two Children.* You may think perhaps, That a *little* Tea, or a *little* Punch now and then, Diet a *little* more costly, Clothes a *little* finer, and a *little* Entertainment now and then, can be

no *great* Matter; but remember what *Poor Richard* says, *Many a Little makes a Mickle;* and farther, *Beware of little Expences; a small Leak will sink a great Ship;* and again, *Who Dainties love, shall Beggars prove;* and moreover, *Fools make Feasts, and wise Men eat them.*

Here you are all got together at this Vendue of *Fineries* and *Knicknacks.* You call them *Goods,* but if you do not take Care, they will prove *Evils* to some of you. You expect they will be sold *cheap,* and perhaps they may for less than they cost; but if you have no Occasion for them, they must be *dear* to you. Remember what *Poor Richard* says, *Buy what thou hast no Need of, and ere long thou shalt sell thy Necessaries.* And again, *At a great Pennyworth pause a while:* He means, that perhaps the Cheapness is *apparent* only, and not *Real;* or the bargain, by straitening thee in thy Business, may do thee more Harm than Good. For in another Place he says, *Many have been ruined by buying good Pennyworths.* Again, *Poor Richard* says, 'tis *foolish to lay out Money in a Purchase of Repentance;* and yet this Folly is practised every Day at Vendues, for want of minding the Almanack. *Wise Men,* as *Poor Dick* says, *learn by others Harms, Fools scarcely by their own;* but *Felix quem faciunt aliena pericula cautum.* Many a one, for the Sake of Finery on the Back, have gone with a hungry Belly, and half-starved their Families. *Silks and Sattins, Scarlet and Velvets,* as *Poor Richard* says, *put out the Kitchen Fire.*

These are not the *Necessaries* of Life; they can scarcely be called the *Conveniences;* and yet only because they look pretty, how many *want* to *have* them! The *artificial* Wants of Mankind thus become more numerous than the *Natural;* and, as *Poor Dick* says, *for one poor Person, there are an hundred indigent.* By these, and other Extravagancies, the Genteel are reduced to Poverty, and forced to borrow of those whom they formerly despised, but who through *Industry* and *Frugality* have maintained their Standing; in which Case it appears plainly, that a *Ploughman on his Legs is higher than a Gentleman on his Knees*, as *Poor Richard* says. Perhaps they have had a small Estate left them, which they knew not the Getting of; they think, *'tis Day, and will never be Night;* that a little to be spent out of *so much,* is not worth minding; *A Child and a Fool,* as *Poor Richard* says, *imagine Twenty shillings and Twenty Years can never be spent* but, *always taking out of the Meal-tub, and never putting in, soon comes to the Bottom;* then, as *Poor Dick* says, *When the Well's dry, they know the Worth of Water.* But this they might have known before, if they had taken his Advice; *If you would know the Value of Money, go and try to borrow some;* for, *he that goes a borrowing goes a sorrowing;* and indeed so does he that lends to such People, when he goes *to get it in again.* *Poor Dick* farther advises, and says,

> *Fond Pride of Dress is sure a very Curse;*
> *E'er Fancy you consult, consult your Purse.*

And again, *Pride is as loud a Beggar as Want and a great deal more saucy.* When you have bought one fine Thing, you must buy ten more, that your Appearance may be all of a Piece; but *Poor Dick* says, *'Tis easier to suppress the first Desire, than to satisfy all that follows it.* And 'tis as truly Folly for the Poor to ape the Rich, as for the Frog to swell, in order to equal the ox.

> *Great Estates may venture more,*
> *But little Boats should keep near Shore.*

'Tis, however, a Folly soon punished; for *Pride that dines on Vanity, sups on Contempt,* as *Poor Richard* says. And in another Place, *Pride breakfasted with Plenty, dined with Poverty, and supped with In-*

famy. And after all, of what Use is this *Pride of Appearance,* for which so much is risked, so much is suffered? It cannot promote Health, or ease Pain; it makes no Increase of Merit in the Person, it creates Envy, it hastens Misfortune.

> *What is a Butterfly? At best*
> *He's but a Caterpillar drest*
> *The gaudy Fop's his Picture just,*

as *Poor Richard* says.

But what Madness must it be to *run in Debt* for these Superfluities! We are offered, by the Terms of this Vendue, *Six Months' Credit;* and that perhaps has induced some of us to attend it, because we cannot spare the ready Money, and hope now to be fine without it. But, ah, think what you do when you run in Debt; *you give to another Power over your Liberty.* If you cannot pay at the Time, you will be ashamed to see your Creditor; you will be in Fear when you speak to him; you will make poor pitiful sneaking Excuses, and by Degrees come to lose your Veracity, and sink into base downright lying; for, as *Poor Richard* says, *The second Vice is Lying, the first is running in Debt.* And again, to the same Purpose, *Lying rides upon Debt's Back.* Whereas a free-born *Englishman* ought not to be ashamed or afraid to see or speak to any Man living. But Poverty often deprives a Man of all Spirit and Virtue: *'Tis hard for an empty Bag to stand upright,* as *Poor Richard* truly says.

What would you think of that Prince, or that Government, who should issue an Edict forbidding you to dress like a Gentleman or a Gentlewoman, on Pain of Imprisonment or Servitude? Would you not say, that you were free, have a Right to dress as you please, and that such an Edict would be a Breach of your Privileges, and such a Government tyrannical? And yet you are about to put yourself under that tyranny, when you run in Debt for such Dress! Your Creditor has Authority, at his

Pleasure to deprive you of your Liberty, by confining you in Gaol for Life, or to sell you for a Servant, if you should not be able to pay him! When you have got your Bargain, you may, perhaps, think little of Payment; but *Creditors, Poor Richard tells us, have better Memories than Debtors;* and in another Place says, *Creditors are a superstitious Sect, great Observers of set Days and Times.* The Day comes round before you are aware, and the Demand is made before you are prepared to satisfy it; or if you bear your Debt in Mind, the Term which at first seemed so long, will, as it lessens, appear extremely short. *Time* will seem to have added Wings to his Heels as well as Shoulders. *Those have a short Lent,* saith *Poor Richard, who owe Money to be paid at Easter.* Then since, as he says, *The Borrower is a Slave to the Lender, and the Debtor to the Creditor,* disdain the Chain, preserve your Freedom; and maintain your Independency: Be *Industrious* and *free;* be *frugal* and *free.* At present, perhaps, you may think yourself in thriving Circumstances, and that you can bear a little Extravagance without Injury; but,

> *For Age and Want, save while you may;*
> *No Morning Sun lasts a whole Day,*

as *Poor Richard* says. Gain may be temporary and uncertain, but ever while you live, Expence is constant and certain; and *'tis easier to build two Chimnies, than to keep one in Fuel,* as *Poor Richard* says. So, *Rather go to Bed supperless than rise in Debt.*

> *Get what you can, and what you get hold;*
> *'Tis the Stone that will turn all your lead*
>   *into Gold,*

as *Poor Richard* says. And when you have got the Philosopher's Stone, sure you will no longer complain of bad Times, or the Difficulty of paying Taxes.

This Doctrine, my Friends, is *Reason* and *Wisdom;* but after all, do not depend too much upon your own *Industry,* and *Frugality,* and *Prudence,* though excellent Things, for they may all be blasted without the Blessing of Heaven; and therefore, ask that Blessing humbly, and be not uncharitable to those that at present seem to want it, but comfort and help them. Remember, *Job* suffered, and was afterwards prosperous.

And now to conclude, *Experience keeps a dear School, but Fools will learn in no other, and scarce in that;* for it is true, *we may give Advice, but we cannot give Conduct,* as *Poor Richard* says: However, remember this, *They that won't be counselled, can't be helped,* as *Poor Richard* says: And farther, That, *if you will not hear Reason, she'll surely rap your knuckles."*

Thus the old Gentleman ended his Harangue. The People heard it, and approved the Doctrine, and immediately practised the contrary, just as if it had been a common Sermon; for the Vendue opened, and they began to buy extravagantly, notwithstanding his Cautions and their own Fear of Taxes. I found the good Man had thoroughly studied my Almanacks, and digested all I had dropt on those Topicks during the Course of Five-and-twenty Years. The frequent Mention he made of me must have tired any one else, but my Vanity was wonderfully delighted with it, though I was conscious that not a tenth Part of the Wisdom was my own which he ascribed to me, but rather the *Gleanings* I had made of the Sense of all Ages and Nations. However, I resolved to be the better for the Echo of it; and though I had at first determined to buy Stuff for a new Coat, I went away resolved to wear my old One a little longer. *Reader,* if thou wilt do the same, thy Profit will be as great as mine. I *am, as ever, Thine to serve thee.*

RICHARD SAUNDERS.

July 7, 1757

PLANTATION PROVERBS

by Joel Chandler Harris

Uncle Remus frequently introduced proverbial sayings into his narratives of animals and people. Most of them were derived from rural life and had some application to the story being told. But Harris also inserted into his collections of Uncle Remus tales entire passages of proverbs which reflect close observation of Negro life and a quiet and amusing skepticism. This particular batch of maxims comes from Uncle Remus: His Songs and His Sayings *(1881).*

Big 'possum clime little tree.

Dem w'at eats kin say grace.

Ole man Know-All died las' year.

Better de gravy dan no grease 'tall.

Dram ain't good twel you git it.

Lazy fokes' stummucks don't git tired.

Rheumatiz don't he'p at de log-rollin'.

Mole don't see w'at his naber doin'.

Save de pacin' mar' fer Sunday.

Don't rain eve'y time de pig squeal.

Crow en corn can't grow in de same fiel'.

Tattlin' 'oman can't make de bread rise.

Rails split 'fo' bre'kfus' 'll season de dinner.

Dem w'at knows too much sleeps under de ash-hopper.

Ef you wanter see yo' own sins, clean up a new groun'.

Hog dunner w'ich part un 'im 'll season de turnip salad.

Hit's a blessin' de w'ite sow don't shake de plum-tree.

Winter grape sour, whedder you kin reach 'im or not.

Mighty po' bee dat don't make mo' honey dan he want.

Kwishins on mule's foots done gone out er fashun.

Pigs dunno w'at a pen's fer.

Possum's tail good as a paw.

Dogs don't bite at de front gate.

Colt in de barley-patch kick high.

Jay-bird don't rob his own nes'.

Pullet can't roost too high for de owl.

Meat fried 'fo' day won't las' twel night.

Stump water won't kyo de gripes.

De howlin' dog know w'at he sees.

Bline hoss don't fall w'en he follers de bit.

Hongry nigger won't w'ar his maul out.

475

Don't fling away de empty wallet.

Black-snake know de way ter de hin nes'.

Looks won't do ter split rails wid.

Settin' hens don't hanker arter fresh aigs.

Tater-vine growin' w'ile you sleep.

Hit take two birds fer to make a nes'.

Ef you bleedzd ter eat dirt, eat clean dirt.

Tarrypin walk fast 'nuff fer to go visitin'.

Empty smoke-house makes de pullet holler.

W'en coon take water he fixin' fer ter fight.

Corn makes mo' at de mill dan it does in de crib.

Good luck say: "Op'n yo' mouf en shet yo' eyes."

Nigger dat gets hurt wukkin oughter show de skyars.

Fiddlin' nigger say hit's long ways ter de dance.

Rooster makes mo' racket dan de hin w'at lay de aig.

Meller mush-million hollers at you fum over de fence.

Nigger wid a pocket-han'kcher better be looked atter.

Rain-crow don't sing no chune, but youk'n 'pen' on 'im.

One-eyed mule can't be handled on de bline side.

Moon may shine, but a lightered knot's mighty handy.

Licker talks mighty loud w'en it git loose fum de jug.

De proudness un a man don't count w'en his head's cold.

Hongry rooster don't cackle w'en he fine a wum.

Some niggers mighty smart, but dey can't drive de pidgins ter roos'.

You may know de way, but better keep yo' eyes on de seven stairs.

All de buzzards in de settlement 'll come to de gray mule's funer'l.

Youk'n hide de fier, but w'at you gwine do wid de smoke?

Ter-morrow may be de carridge-driver's day for ploughin'.

Hit's a mighty deaf nigger dat don't year de dinner-ho'n.

Hit takes a bee fer ter git de sweetness out'n de hoar-houn' blossom.

Ha'nts don't bodder longer hones' folks, but you better go 'roun' de grave-yard.

De pig dat runs off wid de year er corn gits little mo' dan de cob.

Sleepin' in de fence-cornder don't fetch Christmus in de kitchen.

De spring-house may freeze, but de niggers 'll keep de shuck-pen warm.

'Twix' de bug en de bee-martin 'tain't hard ter tell w'ich gwineter git kotch.

Don't 'spute wid de squinch-owl. Jam de shovel in de fier.

You'd see mo' er de mink ef he know'd whar de yard dog sleeps.

Troubles is seasonin'. 'Simmons ain't good twel dey 'er fros'-bit.

Watch out w'en you'er gittin' all you want. Fattenin' hogs ain't in luck.

Abe Martin of Brown County

by Kin Hubbard

The tradition of the crackerbox philosopher has always been strong in American life and has not lacked exemplars, from Josh Billings to Will Rogers. The observer poses as being uneducated and often illiterate but reveals himself to be shrewd and candid in his remarks. Frank McKinney Hubbard's Abe Martin is a rural spectator who is amused by the life around him and who is impelled to speculate and dissect. Abe's sayings delighted audiences when they first appeared in newspapers and almanacs, and they still survive in the contemporary press. They have the concision and impact of proverbs, but they also reflect the sharp eyes of a salty observer. Thus, to Abe's practical mind the old maxim of wealth being the cause of all sin takes on a more modern dress: "Not havin' money is th' root o' most evil." These remarks of Abe Martin come chiefly from Back Country Folks *and* New Sayings.

A loafer allus has th' correct time.

Ther's generally a false bottom in a bushel o' fun.

Kindness goes a long way lots o' times when it ought t' stay at home.

One good thing about a little town—you kin git in th' band.

A newspaper picture makes anybuddy look guilty.

Fun is like life insurance, th' older you git th' more it costs.

A loafer must feel funny when a holiday comes along.

Some girls git all ther is out o' life in one summer.

Folks that rush in allus crawl out.

A rhubarb pie wouldn't be so bad if it didn't overflow its banks.

If at first you do succeed don't take any more chances.

You'd never know some folks had been on a vacation if they didn't come back.

• The first ten maxims are from *Abe Martin's Almanack*, by Kin Hubbard. Copyright, 1911, by Doubleday & Co., Inc. The last forty maxims are from *Back Country Folks* and *New Sayings*, by Kin Hubbard. Published by the Abe Martin Company, Indianapolis, Ind., n.d. Reprinted by permission of Mrs. Josephine J. Hubbard.

Hardly anybuddy would work fer what they're worth.

Th' wild oats crop is allus a failure.

Nobuddy kin eat as much meat as th' feller that don't earn his salt.

Hush money often makes more noise than any other kind.

Now an' then an innocent man is sent t' th' legislature.

Th' pedestrian that refused t' waive his rights yisterday is still in a critical condition.

Some folks jist read th' headlines an' others know what they're talkin' about.

Some fellers don't care what they say an' neither does anybuddy else.

A girl should allus dance with one arm free.

A friend is like a umbreller. He's never there when you want him, an' if he is he's broke.

Few o' us kin stand prosperity—especially if it's our neighbors.

Th' best way out of it is not t' be in it.

Some folks kin live out o' office but they don't thrive.

Nothin' retards digestion like hatin' somebuddy.

Any fool kin git in th' limelight, but it takes a general t' stay there.

Some folks are too shiftless t' collect ther own thoughts.

We're never so positive about anything as we are about somethin' we're wrong about.

It's the good loser that finally loses out.

Th' only way t' entertain some folks is t' listen t' 'em.

Give some folks enough rope an' they'll rope you in.

A woman allus smiles when she says she's awfully sorry.

An amateur show is good if it's bad an' awful if it's good.

A rabbit is too proud t' fight, hence so many fur topped shoes.

A word t' th' wise is superfluous.

It seems like th' folks that are 'all right when you git t' know 'em' never have very long funerals.

It's sweet t' be remembered, but it's often cheaper t' be overlooked.

Not havin' money is th' root o' most evil.

Politicians an' actors never quit in time.

Th' short-sighted feller is th' first t' see his finish.

Some women don't only make good wives, but purty fair husbands too.

You kin allus tell a feller who lives in a rented house by th' place he strikes matches.

Opportunity rarely shows up, but temptation has a reg'lar route.

Nobuddy is as full of advice as a failure.

A warnin' is all th' average American needs t' make him take a chance.

You'd think some o' th' candidates wuz after th' woodpecker vote by th' way they tack ther cards on th' telephone poles.

Never put anything in th' laundry t'day that you kin wear t'morrow.

Truth is stranger than fiction, but not near as plentiful.

Nothin's as bad as it's printed.

The People, Yes

by Carl Sandburg

Carl Sandburg's literary career has had three chief aspects. In his early creative years he was known as a lyric poet who employed free verse to describe urban and prairie scenes and whose Chicago Poems (1916) attracted wide attention. Later he devoted many years to a biography of Abraham Lincoln and became one of the best-known Lincoln scholars. But he also was interested in balladry and folk song, combining a collector's zeal with a performer's skill. In the process of collecting the songs of a people he also collected their sayings and proverbs, and he gave freely of his treasures to audiences throughout the land. In such a volume as The People, Yes (1936), Section forty-nine of which is reprinted below, he did not always attempt to provide either a framework or continuity. Rather he recorded maxim, anecdote, and wisecrack very much as he heard them, in the conviction that the only way to suggest the voice of the people was to let the people speak—vulgarly, naïvely, or shrewdly as the case might be. As with Franklin's proverbs, few of Sandburg's remarks are original, but in their diction and juxtaposition they indicate some of the personality of the writer while they still reflect the popular mind.

He was a king or a shah, an ahkoond or rajah,
the head man of the country,
and he commanded the learned men of the books
they must put all their books in one,
which they did,
and this one book into a single page,
which they did.
"Suppose next," said the head man, who was
either a king or shah, an ahkoond or rajah,
"Suppose now you give my people
the history of the world and its peoples
in three words—come, go to work!"
And the learned men sat long into the night
and confabulated over their ponderings
and brought back three words:
   "Born,
    troubled,
    died."

This was their history of Everyman.
"Give me next for my people," spoke the head man,
"in one word the inside kernel of all you know,
the knowledge of your ten thousand books
with a forecast of what will happen next—
this for my people in one word."
And again they sat into the peep of dawn
and the arguments raged
and the glass prisms of the chandeliers shook
and at last they came to a unanimous verdict
and brought the head man one word:
      "Maybe."

And in that country and in other countries
over mountain ranges where white clouds rested
and beyond the blue sea and its endless tumblers
the people by sunlight, by candlelight, by lanterns
by the new white bulbs spoken to with buttons,
the people had sayings touching the phrase
      "Born, troubled, died,"
carrying farther the one word: "maybe,"
spacing values between serenity and anguish,
from daily humdrum and the kitchen stove
to the inevitable rainbow or evening star,
sayings:

What should I say when it is better to say nothing?
What is said is said and no sponge can wipe it out.
    Ask the young people—they know everything.
    They say—what say they? Let them say.
Have you noticed painted flowers give no smell?
A woman and a melon are not to be known by their outsides.
The handsomest woman can give only what she has.
The miser and the pig are no use till dead.
An old man in love is a flower in winter.
    Bean by bean we fill the sack.
    Step by step one goes far.
No matter how important you are, you may get the measles.
    Wash a dog, comb a dog, still a dog.
    Fresh milk is not to be had from a statue.
    Apes may put on finery but they are still apes.
Every man must eat his peck of dirt before he dies.
    God knows well who are the best pilgrims.
    The ache for glory sends free people into slavery.
He who is made of honey will be eaten to death by flies.
No matter how cheap you make shoes geese will go barefoot.
He drives the wind from his house with his hat.

Wedlock is a padlock.
Take a good look at the mother before
getting tied up with the daughter.
Let a mother be ever so bad she wishes
her daughter to be good.
The man hardly ever marries the woman
he jokes about: she often marries the
man she laughs at.
Keep your eyes open before marriage,
half-shut afterward.

In heaven an angel is nobody in particular.
Even if your stomach be strong, eat as few
    cockroaches as possible.
The curse of the Spanish gypsy: May you be
    a mail carrier and have sore feet.
Well lathered is half shaved.
A wife is not a guitar you hang on the wall after playing it.
The liar forgets.
A redheaded man in the orchestra is a sure sign
    of trouble.
The shabby genteel would better be in rags.
As sure as God made little apples he was busy
    as a cranberry merchant.
It will last about as long as a snowball in hell.
I wouldn't take a million dollars for this baby and
    I wouldn't give ten cents for another.

Blue eyes say love me or I die.
Black eyes say love me or I kill you.
The sun rises and sets in her eyes.
    Wishes won't wash dishes.
May all your children be acrobats.
    Leave something to wish for.
    Lips however rosy must be fed.
    Some kill with a feather.
    By night all cats are gray.
Life goes before we know what it is.
    One fool is enough in a house.
Even God gets tired of too much hallelujah.
Take it easy and live long as brothers.
    The baby's smile pays the bill.

Yesterday is gone, tomorrow may never come,
    today is here.
The sins of omission are those we should have
    committed and didn't.

May you live to pick flowers off your enemies' graves.
Some of them are so lazy they get up early in the morning
     so as to have more time to lay around and do nothing.
Some of them are dirty as a slut that's too lazy to lick herself.
Let the guts be full for they carry the legs.

The hypocrite talks like a saint and hides his cat claws.
The half-wit was asked how he found the lost horse no others
     could locate and explained, "I thought to myself where I
     would go if I was a horse and went there and he had."
He who has one foot in a brothel has another in a hospital.
When the boy is growing he has a wolf in his belly.
Handsome women generally fall into the hands of men not worth
     a second look.
When someone hits you with a rock hit him with a piece of
     cotton.
Love your neighbor as yourself but don't take down your fence.
A fence should be horse-high, pig-tight, bull-strong.
               Except in fairy stories the bashful get less.
               A beggar's hand has no bottom.
               Polite words open iron gates.
               Be polite but not too polite.

BIOGRAPHICAL NOTES

BIOGRAPHICAL NOTES

AUSTIN, WILLIAM (1778–1841), a Harvard graduate and Massachusetts lawyer, wrote an early travel book, *Letters from London* (1804), and a volume of essays explaining Unitarianism. He was also a fairly frequent contributor to magazines. His famous short story, "Peter Rugg, the Missing Man," appeared originally in Joseph Buckingham's *New England Galaxy* (1824).

BENÉT, STEPHEN VINCENT (1898–1943), a graduate of Yale, was a versatile writer who did distinguished work in the fields of fiction and verse. His novels, such as *Jean Huguenot* (1923) and *Spanish Bayonet* (1926), were less successful than his short stories, in the best of which he combined humor, folklore, a creative fancy, and a firm sense of the American scene. His untimely death cut short a promising career as a radio script writer. Benét was awarded the Pulitzer Prize for his *John Brown's Body* (1928), a folk epic of the Civil War which presents the crucial years of the American republic with extraordinary perceptiveness and charm. Of an ambitious narrative poem which was to trace American history in general, only *Western Star* (1945) was completed.

BRADFORD, ROARK (1896–1948), born in Tennessee, worked as a newspaper reporter on several southern newspapers and was Sunday editor of the *New Orleans Times-Picayune* from 1924 to 1926. Subsequently he was a free-lance writer who was most successful in dealing with Negro characters and southern locales. He wrote a number of short stories, collected in such volumes as *Ol' Man Adam an' His Chillun* (1928) and *Let the Band Play Dixie* (1934), and a biography of the Negro folk hero John Henry (1931), which Bradford himself later dramatized.

CARMER, CARL (1893–   ), a native of Cortland, New York, took degrees at Hamilton College and Harvard and for a number of years taught English (he was a member of the faculty at the University of Alabama from 1921 to 1927). A prolific writer of fiction and legends drawn largely from folklore, he is the author of *Stars Fell on Alabama* (1934), *Listen for a Lonesome Drum* (1936), *Genesee Fever* (1941), and *Dark Trees to the Wind* (1949). He is also the editor of the "Rivers of America" series, to which he contributed the book on the Hudson River.

CHESNUTT, CHARLES WADDELL (1858–1932), born in Cleveland, was a schoolteacher in North Carolina and later a lawyer in Ohio. He was one of the first Negroes to make serious use of the short story as a literary medium. The best of his stories appear in *The Conjure Woman* and *The Wife of His Youth,* both published in 1899. Later novels, such as *The Marrow of Tradition* (1901), attracted less attention although they intelligently explored racial friction in the South at the turn of the century.

CLEMENS, SAMUEL LANGHORNE (1835–1910), better known under his pseudonym, Mark Twain, was born at Florida, Missouri, of southern parentage. During his youth his home was Hannibal, where Twain had a scanty schooling, observed the color and excitement of river life, and served his apprenticeship as a typesetter and printer. From 1857 to 1861 he was a pilot on Mississippi River steamboats; but when the Civil War closed the river to commercial navigation, Twain accompanied his brother, Orion Clemens, to Nevada. In the next few years he was a prospector in the western mining camps, a reporter at Virginia City, and a feature writer and critic in San Francisco. After a trip to the Hawaiian Islands, Twain left the Pacific Coast to join an excursion to the Mediterranean and the Holy Land. His first major book, *Innocents Abroad* (1869), was based on the reports written during his travels in Europe and the Near East. Twain's later life was spent mostly in Hartford, but he was an inveterate traveler and lived abroad for substantial periods. His most important books were based on his youthful days in Hannibal and on his western experiences: *Roughing It* (1872), *The Adventures of Tom Sawyer* (1876), *Life on the Mississippi* (1883), and *The Adventures of Huckleberry Finn* (1885). In his later years Twain suffered business reverses and domestic losses which explain in part the bitter pessimism of books like *The Mysterious Stranger* (1916). His other work includes volumes of travel impressions, a biography of Joan of Arc, and satires like *A Connecticut Yankee in King Arthur's Court* (1889). Twain was a great success on the lecture platform, where his drawling presentation and skill as a raconteur gave particular point to the yarns and tall tales in which he so often indulged. He was also a master of ordinary American idiom, and his colloquial, natural style has been extremely influential in twentieth-century writing.

COFFIN, ROBERT P. TRISTRAM (1892–1955), born in Brunswick, Maine, was graduated from Bowdoin College and was also a Rhodes Scholar at Oxford. For many years he was a professor of English at Bowdoin. A prolific writer of verse and prose, mostly with Maine subjects, he produced narrative poems, fiction, biography, history, and essays. He is best known for his New England ballads and portraits and for his vivid sketches of farmers and sailors, in all of which he showed an intimate knowledge of his chosen locale. Among his books are an account of the Kennebec River (1937); novels, such as *Red Sky in the Morning* (1935); biographies, such as *Captain Abby and Captain John* (1939); and verse narratives, such as *Ballads of Square-Toed Americans* (1933). His *Collected Poems* appeared originally in 1939.

CROCKETT, DAVID (1786–1836), frontiersman and politician, was born in Tennessee. After various experiences as soldier, hunter, and borderer, he represented a Tennessee district in the House of Representatives. Later he joined the Texas forces fighting against Mexican imperialism and died at the Alamo in San Antonio. Although his literacy was questionable, Crockett's name is attached to various books, notably the autobiography published in 1834. Other volumes purporting to be truthful chronicles of his life were either burlesque biographies or hastily compiled campaign documents. With the famous Crockett almanacs issued in Nashville from 1835 to 1838 and subsequently in other cities, Davy Crockett had nothing to do. Crockett, in typical folk-hero fashion, has become the symbol of the half-horse, half-alligator, ring-tailed-roarer frontiersman.

DOBIE, J. FRANK (1888–   ), born on a Texas ranch, for many years a member of the English faculty of the University of Texas, is probably the best-known interpreter of southwestern life and lore. His *Guide to Life and Literature of the Southwest* first appeared in 1943. Among his many books are *Coronado's Children* (1931), *Apache Gold and Yaqui Silver* (1939), *The Longhorns* (1941), and *The Mustangs* (1952).

DUNBAR, PAUL LAURENCE (1872–1906), was born in Dayton, Ohio, and attended high school there. Lacking funds to go to college, he worked as an elevator operator but began to write verse at an early age and to contribute to newspapers. His first book, *Oak and Ivy*, appeared in 1893 and was followed two years later by *Majors and Minors*; in 1896 he published *Lyrics of Lowly Life*, with a preface by William Dean Howells. The accolade given him by Howells advanced his reputation, and his poetry quickly found a wide audience through magazine and book publication. The *Complete Poems of Paul Laurence Dunbar* appeared first in 1913. He was also the author of four novels. Dunbar was the first Negro poet to achieve general recognition, the result of his skillful handling of Negro idiom and his genuine lyrical gifts. Although he did not confine himself to dialect, his best work appears in that medium.

EASTMAN, MARY (1818–80), was born in Virginia, the daughter of an army surgeon. In 1835 she married Seth Eastman, an army topographical engineer, whom she accompanied on various western tours of duty. Until 1848 Captain Eastman was stationed at Fort Snelling, Minnesota, where he had ample opportunity to observe the life, manners, and customs of the Sioux. Mrs. Eastman shared these interests and in 1849 published *Dahcotah; or, Life and Legends of the Sioux*, a volume illustrated with paintings by her husband. Subsequently the Eastmans collaborated on a valuable *American Aboriginal Portfolio* (1853). "Oeche-Monesa; the Wanderer," reprinted from *Dahcotah*, reveals Mrs. Eastman's familiarity with Indian legend and mythology.

FAULKNER, WILLIAM (1897–   ), a native of Mississippi, is one of the most distinguished novelists of the twentieth century. Much of his life has been spent in Oxford, Lafayette County, Mississippi (in his fiction the town becomes "Jefferson" and the county "Yoknapatawpha"), and this region has provided him with the setting and the characters for such books as *Sartoris* and *The Sound and the Fury*, both published in 1926, *Sanctuary* (1931), *Absalom, Absalom!* (1936), *The Hamlet* (1940), and *Intruder in the Dust* (1948). *A Fable*, published in 1954, is localized chiefly in France. Faulkner is frequently criticized for the sordidness and sinisterness of his subjects, yet few novelists are so universally admired today for their technical virtuosity and their creative imagination. His reputation reached its climax when he was awarded the Nobel Prize for literature in 1950.

FRANKLIN, BENJAMIN (1706–90), one of the notable Americans of the eighteenth century, was born in Boston but spent much of his life in Philadelphia. Largely self-educated, he became famous as a publisher, editor, philosopher, scientist, and statesman. After useful activity in Philadelphia and Pennsylvania, he represented his country abroad and was instrumental in negotiating for French help for the youthful United States. His scientific experiments are too familiar to need chronicling. Franklin was a skillful pamphleteer and a memorable writer of expository prose. Although most famous as the author of the autobiography, which was not published in accurate and complete form until 1868, he wrote essays, bagatelles, satirical sketches, and, for twenty-five years (1732–56), edited *Poor Richard's Almanack*. "The Way to Wealth" is a kind of anthology of Franklin's prudential maxims.

FROST, ROBERT (1875–   ), although born in San Francisco, is usually considered the chief spokesman for rural New England. At the same time he is a poet of stature whose genius has brought universal truth and meaning to his poems of field and wood and farm. For many years he has combined writing, farming, and teaching, and he has lectured at Dartmouth, Harvard, Michigan, and Amherst. Since *A Boy's Will* appeared in 1913 and *North of Boston* the following year, Frost has published many volumes of verse and has won the Pulitzer Prize several times. His *Collected Poems* appeared in 1930, with revisions and additions in 1939 and 1949. At mid-century Frost was undoubtedly the most important living American poet. No one else could match the vigorous colloquial style and the quiet authenticity of his interpretations.

GREEN, PAUL (1894–   ), born in rural North Carolina, was graduated from the University of North Carolina and later did graduate study at Cornell. For a number of years he taught philosophy at his alma mater, but his chief interest has been in writing. His early plays were usually in one act and dealt with Negro and tenant-farmer life. But longer dramas like *The Field God, In Abraham's Bosom*, and *Johnny Johnson* established him as one of the important playwrights of our time. He has written short stories, verse, and novels, but his major work in recent years has taken the form of symphonic dramas or civic pageants, such as *The Lost Colony, The Common Glory*, and *Faith of Our Fathers*. In all his writing he has drawn clearly and strongly from the folkways of his native state.

HALL, BAYNARD RUSH (1793–1863), born in Philadelphia, was educated at Union College and Princeton Theological Seminary and eventually became a Presbyterian clergyman in the Indiana backwoods. Here for a number of years he was both minister and teacher. Disappointed in his ambition to become president of the newly formed state university, he left Indiana and in 1843, under the pseudonym of Robert Carlton, published *The New Purchase,* a volume of reminiscences and history. Hall was a shrewd observer of crude society, but he could never forget his own superiority in training and intelligence. His descriptions of Indiana rural life in the 1820's, consequently, are unusually bitter and derisive.

HALL, JAMES (1793–1868), a notable spokesman of the early Ohio Valley, was a soldier, lawyer, judge, editor, and banker as well as a writer. A Philadelphian by birth, he fought in the War of 1812, then studied law at Pittsburgh and migrated to Illinois in 1820. His later life he spent in the banking business at Cincinnati. Hall wrote a number of historical and statistical volumes about the Middle West, and his *Romance of Western History* (1857) is still a useful survey. But he is best known for his sketches and tales of frontier life. *Letters from the West,* published in London in 1828, recounts vividly a spring trip down the Ohio River on a keelboat. Hall's short stories have been collected in such volumes as *Legends of the West* (1832) and *Tales of the Border* (1835). His one novel, *The Harpe's Head,* appeared in 1833.

HARRIS, GEORGE WASHINGTON (1814–69), although born in Pennsylvania, spent much of his life in Knoxville, Tennessee. He was a steamboat captain on the Tennessee River and later became a locomotive engineer. He is best known for the yarns and tall tales, sometimes bawdy as well as coarse, which he collected in his *Sut Lovingood* (1867). His tales were widely enjoyed and imitated, and Harris is generally recognized today as the most gifted southwestern humorist before Mark Twain.

HARRIS, JOEL CHANDLER (1848–1908), born on a Georgia plantation, got most of his education in newspaper offices. For about twenty-five years he was a member of the staff of the *Atlanta Constitution,* and to that paper he contributed many of his Uncle Remus tales. His plantation experiences and his close observation of rural life enabled him to create (he himself preferred the word "transcribe") the Negro folk tales which brought him an international reputation. *Uncle Remus: His Songs and His Sayings* (1881) was his first Uncle Remus volume; *Nights with Uncle Remus* appeared in 1883, and several other collections followed. Harris also wrote other fiction about the South, in which Reconstruction problems, poor whites, and tenant farmers all figured. But nothing quite matched his creation of the old Negro storyteller, with his garrulousness, his supposed knowledge of birds and beasts, his superstitions and legends, and his sly humor. Harris disclaimed any scientific knowledge of his field, but neither his command of dialect nor his understanding of folklore has been successfully challenged.

HAWTHORNE, NATHANIEL (1804–64), a native and long a resident of Salem, Massachusetts, was graduated from Bowdoin College and experienced a long period of obscurity before *Twice-Told Tales* (1837) brought him recognition and *The Scarlet Letter* (1850) fame. While working on *The House of the Seven Gables* (1851), he made the acquaintance of Herman Melville and may have had something to do with the ultimate shaping of *Moby-Dick*. In later years Hawthorne was the American consul at Liverpool, and his last complete novel, *The Marble Faun* (1860), was written abroad. Hawthorne made good use of his Puritan heritage in his fiction, although he did not always subscribe to Puritan ethics and morality. His stories are rich in New England traditions and legends, but he normally subordinated his folk material to his concern with problems of guilt and conscience. Moreover, his ambiguous supernaturalism freed his readers from the obligation to accept literally the occasional Gothic touches in his stories. His fiction reveals how great genius can transmute folk material without debasing it.

HEARN, LAFCADIO (1850–1904), one of the most extraordinary figures in American literature, was born on the island of Santa Maura (formerly Leucadia) of a Greek mother and an Anglo-Irish father. He was educated sporadically in Ireland, England, and France and was brought up chiefly by a distant relative, Mrs. Brenane. At the age of nineteen he came to the United States and made a precarious living as a newspaper reporter in Cincinnati and New Orleans, overcoming such obstacles as egregious poverty, poor health, and limited sight (an accident made him blind in one eye at the age of thirteen). During his eleven years in North America he contributed to various newspapers and magazines and developed a strong interest in Creole life and mores. Among his earlier works are the highly colored romance, *Chita* (1889), and *Two Years in the French West Indies* (1890), a memorable account of his experiences in Martinique. In 1890 he went to Japan on a vague commission from the Harper publishing firm to report the Orient to the American public. But Hearn fell in love with Japan and remained there for the rest of his life, becoming a Japanese citizen, marrying a Japanese wife, and becoming a convert to Buddhism. Among his brilliant studies of Japanese life are *Out of the East* (1895), *Kokoro* (1896), *Exotics and Retrospectives* (1898), *Kwaidan* (1904), and *Japan: An Attempt at Interpretation* (1904). Hearn never interested himself in economic or political affairs but was fascinated by the art, legends, superstitions, and folklore of his adopted country. As a consequence, his books retain much of their original validity as an interpretation of the Japanese mind. An inveterate romantic, he frequently allowed his love of color and the bizarre to get the best of him, but he also combined careful workmanship with sensitive observation and a brilliant style.

HOOPER, JOHNSON J. (1815–62), was born in Wilmington, North Carolina, and though irregularly educated was both a lawyer and a newspaperman in later years, He contributed many sketches of frontier life to the New York *Spirit of the Times* in the 1840's and in 1845 collected the best of them in *Some Adventures of Captain Simon Suggs, Late of the Tallapoosa Volunteers*. In creating Simon Suggs he added a picaresque hero to the humor of the Southwest and the backwoods.

HUBBARD, FRANK MCKINNEY (KIN) (1868–1930), was born at Bellefontaine, Ohio, and found most of his education in printing offices. For many years he was on the staff of the *Indianapolis News*, producing caricatures and comic drawings and writing satiric prose. In 1904 he created the character of Abe Martin, supposedly a rural philosopher from Brown County, who observed life somewhat wryly and uttered caustic comments on people and fads. *Abe Martin's Almanac* appeared in 1905 and had many sequels. Hubbard published *Abe Martin, Hoss Sense and Nonsense* in 1926. Throughout many volumes Hubbard retained his single point of view. Although some of Abe Martin's humor seems topical and moribund today, many of his observations are still fresh and pertinent.

HURSTON, ZORA NEALE (1903–   ), born in Florida, was educated at Howard University and Barnard College, where she studied anthropology with Franz Boas. For a time she was the private secretary of the novelist Fannie Hurst. Her professional training and her natural interest in her own people led her to observe Negro life in the deep South, and out of this experience came several stimulating volumes: *Jonah's Gourd Vine* (1934), *Mules and Men* (1935), and *Their Eyes Were Watching God* (1937). She published an autobiography, *Dust Tracks on a Road,* in 1942.

IRVING, WASHINGTON (1783–1859), was the first American writer to attract substantial attention abroad. He spent his youth in New York City and in rambling around the lower Hudson Valley, where he undoubtedly found many of the traditions he afterward used to good purpose. From 1815 to 1832 he lived in Europe, and he was subsequently United States minister to Spain. His extensive literary work includes many types of writing: sketches, essays, plays, travel narratives. Best known perhaps are the *History of New York* (1809), supposedly the work of Diedrich Knickerbocker, *The Sketch Book* (1819), *The Alhambra* (1832), *A Tour on the Prairies* (1835), and biographies of Columbus, Mahomet, and Washington. Irving began his writing career as a humorist, quickly turned to a sentimentalist, and ended as a historian. He was always interested in legend and myth, and his best-known tales are either appropriations of themes from other lands or are adaptations of foreign folklore.

LANIER, SIDNEY (1842–81), combined in unusual degree high gifts as poet, musician, and critic. Born at Macon, he grew up in Georgia and was graduated from Oglethorpe University. Here a teacher stimulated his interest in the relations of science, poetry, and religion. He served in the Confederate Army until he was captured and imprisoned at Point Lookout, where he wrote poetry and solaced his fellow-prisoners with his flute music. After the war, with impaired health, he practiced law and clerked in a hotel at Macon. While on a visit to New York, he heard an orchestra play Wagner and determined to devote the rest of his life to an artistic career. For a while he was a flautist in Peabody's Orchestra in Baltimore. Established as a musician and man of letters, he was appointed lecturer in English literature at Johns Hopkins University. His lectures were incorporated in two books, *The Science of English Verse* (1880) and *The English Novel* (1883). He wrote one novel, *Tiger-Lilies* (1867), and contributed verse to the major magazines. His best poetry, such as "Corn," "The Symphony," "The Marshes of Glynn," and "The Revenge of Hamish" (one of the best American literary ballads), appears in *Poems of Sidney Lanier* (1884). Lanier's verse exemplifies an extraordinarily felicitous union of poetry and music devoted to the expression of noble and moving themes.

LINDSAY, NICHOLAS VACHEL (1879–1931), was born and died in the same house in Springfield, Illinois. He attended Hiram College and subsequently had instruction in painting and drawing at the Chicago Art Institute. For a time his attention was divided between art and verse; he once remarked that he always conceived his poetry visually before he wrote it. In his youth he was a kind of evangelist for culture and civic improvement, and he tramped hundreds of miles trading his rhymes for food and shelter. After the publication of "The Congo" in Harriet Monroe's *Poetry: A Magazine of Verse* in 1914, he became famous for his platform recitations, and he brought spoken verse to many schools, lecture halls, and auditoriums throughout the country. Lindsay became notable for a "jazz" style of poetry which emphasized staccato rhythms, alliteration, and resonant cadences, although much of his verse was phrased in quieter language. His *Collected Poems* appeared first in 1923; a revised edition was published two years later.

LONGFELLOW, HENRY WADSWORTH (1807–82), born in Portland, Maine, was graduated from Bowdoin College. After extensive travel and study in Europe he returned to Bowdoin to teach foreign languages and subsequently was professor of Romance languages at Harvard for almost twenty years. His poetic work was voluminous and varied, including ballads, long narrative poems, sonnets, lyrics, closet dramas, and translations. A polished craftsman, he won readers more by his meticulous skill and his moral sentiment than by his originality. He drew his subjects from the myths and legendry of many countries, but he probably won his most instant success with the publication of *The Song of Hiawatha* in 1855. Generations of American children have become familiar with his lyrics of home and fireside, but his most admirable poetic achievement appears in his sonnets. His literary ballads are also among the best of their kind.

LONGSTREET, AUGUSTUS BALDWIN (1790–1870), one of the earliest American regional writers, was born in Augusta, Georgia, became a Methodist Episcopal clergyman, and served as president of both the University of Mississippi and the University of South Carolina. In 1835 he published his *Georgia Scenes, Characters, Incidents, etc., in the First Half Century of the Republic,* a volume which, because of its sharp, specific observation of backwoods life, became a landmark in American realistic writing. The book was published anonymously and went through a number of editions despite Longstreet's reluctance to claim authorship. It has had considerable effect on later humorous and realistic fiction dealing with the deep South.

LOWELL, JAMES RUSSELL (1819–91), had a distinguished career as poet, teacher, journalist, and diplomat. Born in Cambridge, he was graduated from Harvard and eventually succeeded Longfellow in the chair of Romance languages there. He was also the first editor of the *Atlantic Monthly* (1857–61) and served as the American minister to both Spain and Great Britain. His reputation as a poet has declined considerably since the nineteenth century, and today he is remembered more for his *Biglow Papers* (two series, 1848, 1867), which reveal his mastery of dialect and the Yankee character, than for his more pretentious verse. Lowell was also a widely read literary critic; the best of his appreciations of writers appear in *Among My Books* (1870 and 1876) and *My Study Windows* (1871). Some of his political essays were collected in *Democracy and Other Addresses* (1887).

MACKAYE, PERCY (1875–1956), the son of the dramatist and producer, Steele MacKaye, was born in New York City and was graduated from Harvard. In a long career devoted to writing, he produced poetic plays, verse, pageants, fiction, and comedies, revealing in everything he wrote a strong literary sense and technical virtuosity. Among his early works were plays inspired by Chaucer, Hawthorne, and the Joan of Arc story. Many of these were collected in *Poems and Plays* (1916). In later years he was attracted by the Kentucky hill people, about whom he wrote plays and short stories; *Tall Tales of the Kentucky Mountains* appeared in 1926. In the spring of 1949 the Pasadena Play House produced his most ambitious dramatic work, a tetralogy based on the Hamlet theme but preceding the events of Shakespeare's tragedy. His two-volume biography of his father, *Epoch, the Life of Steele MacKaye,* was published in 1927.

MILLER, JOAQUIN (1839–1913); Cincinnatus Heine Miller, better known as Joaquin Miller, was born in Indiana while his parents were en route to Oregon in a covered wagon. His youth was unsettled and adventurous. He frequented the California mining camps and lived for a time with the Digger Indians, then studied law and was admitted to the bar, edited a newspaper in Oregon, visited England in 1871, and wrote plays and verse. Miller took no pains to hide a flamboyant personality and oftentimes affected roles and garb for publicity purposes. But he had a genuine poetic gift, and his ability in both lyric and narrative verse is evident in *Songs of the Sierras* (1871) and in his *Complete Poetical Works* (1897; revised in 1902). He also wrote *Life amongst the Modocs* (1873) and a play about the Mormons in the Far West, *The Danites in the Sierras* (1882).

PETERKIN, JULIA MOOD (1880–   ), born in Laurens County, South Carolina, married William George Peterkin in 1903 and has lived much of her life on a Carolina plantation. She made excellent use of her intimate knowledge of Negro life and folklore, and in various novels she described the Gullah Negroes of the South Carolina coastal region. *Green Thursday* appeared in 1924, *Black April* in 1927, and *Scarlet Sister Mary* in 1928. The last novel was awarded a Pulitzer Prize and was subsequently dramatized. *Roll, Jordan, Roll* was published in 1933.

POE, EDGAR ALLAN (1809–49), was born in Boston, where his parents were professional actors. After his mother's death he was adopted by a Richmond merchant, John Allan, in whose house he grew up. Poe attended the University of Virginia briefly and subsequently West Point; but his gambling and intemperance brought on a cleavage between him and his foster father, and his academic education was quickly terminated. Resorting to journalism, Poe became associated with literary periodicals in

Richmond, Philadelphia, and New York and usually proved himself to be a competent and astute editor. But irregularity of habit and occasional indulgence in drink and drugs made it impossible for him to retain editorial positions. He quickly won distinction for his verse, his short fiction, and his criticism, but his personal belligerence and his scorn for the literary coteries of his time prevented him from occupying the place to which his genius entitled him. While still a student he published *Tamerlane* in 1827, and *Al Aaraaf, Tamerlane, and Minor Poems* in 1829. *Poems* appeared in 1831, and his *Tales of the Grotesque and Arabesque* in 1840. His high technical ability is particularly apparent in the rhythm and euphony of his lyrics and in his tales of ratiocination. By emphasizing totality and single effect in his fiction, Poe was a major influence in the development of the short story.

RANDOLPH, VANCE (1892–   ), Kansas-born, was graduated from the Kansas State Teachers College and subsequently did graduate work at the University of Kansas. He has been a teacher, a scenario writer, and a collector and transcriber of folklore. He edited the four-volume collection of *Ozark Folksongs* (1946–50) and has published several folk-tale miscellanies: *Ozark Mountain Folks* (1932), *We Always Lie to Strangers* (1951), and *The Devil's Pretty Daughter and Other Ozark Folk Tales* (1955).

RANSOM, JOHN CROWE (1888–   ), born at Pulaski, Tennessee, was educated at Vanderbilt University and at Oxford, where he was a Rhodes scholar. For twenty-three years he was a member of the department of English at Vanderbilt; since 1937 he has served as professor of English at Kenyon College, where he also has edited the *Kenyon Review*. He has lectured widely in other American colleges and universities and has won a reputation as a writer of distinguished criticism and poetry. *Selected Poems*, published in 1945, includes the verse which he would most like to see preserved.

ROBERTS, ELIZABETH MADOX (1886–1941), was born in Kentucky and used her native state as a setting for a series of sensitive and artistic novels. In *The Great Meadow* (1930), she ventured into historical fiction, whereas *The Time of Man* (1926), *He Sent Forth a Raven* (1935), and *Black Is My Truelove's Hair* (1938) reflect the rural Kentucky of her own day.

ROBINSON, ROWLAND E. (1833–1900), a Vermont Quaker, was well known in his day for his faithful transcriptions of rural life. His rustic storytellers spin their yarns in colloquial idiom and reflect both vividly and humorously the traditions and rustic mores of the Vermont hinterland. Perhaps the best of his dozen books are *Uncle Lisha's Shop* (1887), *Danvis Folks* (1894), and *Sam Lovel's Camp* (1899).

RUSSELL, IRWIN (1853–79), was recognized by Joel Chandler Harris and Thomas Nelson Page as a pioneer in the treatment of Negro life in dialect poetry. Born at Port Gibson, Mississippi, he spent a number of years in St. Louis and was graduated from St. Louis University. Later he returned to Port Gibson, studied law, and was admitted to the bar. On various adventurous trips to New Orleans and Texas he acquired a knowledge of men and manners as well as a taste for strong drink. His literary work appeared first in local newspapers and subsequently in national magazines like *Scribner's* and *St. Nicholas*. In 1878 he experienced the hardships and perils of a yellow-fever epidemic at Port Gibson, losing his father and his sweetheart. Later that year he was welcomed by the literati of New York; but instead of remaining in the city, he worked his passage to New Orleans as a fireman on a steamer. He died in a cheap boardinghouse in New Orleans on December 27, 1879. His reputation rests largely upon *Poems by Irwin Russell*, with a preface by Joel Chandler Harris (1888), and *Christmas-Night in the Quarters*, with a biographical-critical sketch by M. G. Fulton (1917). The title poem of the latter book is a pleasing little idyl, treating in authentic language the character, customs, mythology, and religious ideas of the plantation Negro.

SANDBURG, CARL (1878–   ), born in Galesburg, Illinois, served in the Spanish-American War, attended Lombard College in his native city, and then devoted himself to journalism. For many years he was on the staff of the *Chicago Daily News*. He published *Chicago Poems* in 1916, *Cornhuskers* in 1918, and *Smoke and Steel* in 1920. These collections, largely written in free verse, revealed Sandburg as a sympathetic poet of the city and the factory as well as of the prairie landscape. *The People, Yes* (1936) is an interesting collection of original verse sandwiched in between maxims, anecdotes, tall tales, slang, and popular traditions. For many years Sandburg devoted himself to a biography of Abraham Lincoln, which eventually was published in six volumes. *The Prairie Years* (1926), in which he dealt with Lincoln's Illinois background and his rise to political importance, is probably the most valuable portion. In recent years Sandburg has published a novel, *Remembrance Rock* (1948), and *Always the Young Strangers* (1953), the first portion of his autobiography. He is also widely known for his interest in American balladry and for his rendition of American folk songs on the concert stage.

SCHOOLCRAFT, HENRY ROWE (1793–1864), born in New York state, was a geologist, ethnologist, and explorer. He came west as a young man and traveled widely in the Lake Superior region. For many years he was an Indian agent at Sault Ste. Marie in Michigan, in which position he familiarized himself with the history and cultural traditions of the Ojibwas. His exploring expedition in 1832 led to his discovery of the source of the Mississippi River in Lake Itasca in northern Minnesota. Schoolcraft published a valuable collection of Ojibwa tales and legends entitled *Algic Researches* in 1839. With some additional material it was republished as *The Myth of Hiawatha* in 1856. In its original form it provided the chief source for Longfellow's famous poem. Schoolcraft's most ambitious work appeared in six parts at Philadelphia from 1851 to 1857 and was entitled *Historical and Statistical Information Respecting the History, Condition, and Prospects of the Indian Tribes of the United States*. Recent scholars have rejected some of Schoolcraft's data and modified some of his conclusions, but his importance as a pioneer student of the American Indian remains unchallenged.

SIGOURNEY, LYDIA HUNTLEY (1791–1865), was born in Norwich, Connecticut. She was a precocious child and early wrote verse. After a short period of teaching school she married Charles Sigourney, a Hartford merchant. She was a prolific poet and produced many volumes of sentimental and moralistic verse. *Moral Pieces in Prose and Verse* (1815), *Traits of the Aborigines* (1822), and an autobiography, *Letters of Life* (1866), are representative books.

SMITH, SEBA (1792–1868), born in Buckfield, Maine, was a journalist who, in 1829, founded the first daily newspaper in his state, the *Portland Courier*. In order to stimulate local interest, he contributed to his paper a series of articles supposedly written by Jack Downing, a shrewd but uncultivated rustic. Downing's letters became extremely popular, were widely imitated, and eventually became a useful satirical device. Smith collected the early letters in 1833 as *The Life and Writings of Major Jack Downing of Downingville*. Somewhat later he published some local-color stories under the title *'Way Down East; or, Portraitures of Yankee Life* (1854). Jack Downing was the prototype of many later adaptations of the Yankee character.

STEVENS, JAMES (1892–   ), born in Iowa, has been associated most of his life with the lumber industry. As a boy he worked in the logging camps of the Northwest; later he was associated with the West Coast Lumbermen's Association and became a public relations counsel for the industry. He was one of the first writers to synthesize the tales about a fabulous lumberjack and fix them around the person of Paul Bunyan. Several of his stories which appeared originally in the *American Mercury* were collected in *Paul Bunyan* (1925). Other books include *Brawnyman* (1926), *Homer in the Sagebrush* (1928), *The Saginaw Paul Bunyan* (1932), *Timber!* (1942), and *Washington: The Enterprise State* (1953). In all of his stories about the logging camps Stevens deftly combines authentic atmosphere and a lively imagination.

STOWE, HARRIET BEECHER (1811–96), the daughter of Lyman Beecher and the wife of Calvin Stowe, was born in Litchfield, Connecticut. For seventeen years she lived in Cincinnati, where she became an ardent abolitionist and observed characters and incidents which she later successfully employed in her famous novel, *Uncle Tom's Cabin* (1852). After she returned to New England to live, she wrote several perceptive and finely executed novels of regional life, notably *The Minister's Wooing* (1859), *Oldtown Folks* (1869), and *Poganuc People* (1878), as well as a number of stories in which Sam Lawson was narrator or protagonist. Mrs. Stowe's later work is far superior in insight and artistry to *Uncle Tom's Cabin*, though it never enjoyed the vogue of her early success. She remains, however, an important novelist of rural New England.

THORPE, THOMAS BANGS (1815–78), born in Massachusetts, migrated to Louisiana, edited a newspaper in New Orleans, served as a soldier in the Mexican War, and wrote a number of memorable local-color sketches. He was a contributor to Porter's *Spirit of the Times*, a New York humorous periodical devoted to backwoods and frontier material. Thorpe's best stories were collected in *The Mysteries of the Backwoods* (1846), and *The Hive of the Bee Hunter* (1854). "The Big Bear of Arkansas" is one of the most famous American tall tales and may have influenced William Faulkner's "The Bear."

WASSON, GEORGE SAVARY (1855–1932), although born in Massachusetts, lived much of his life at Kittery Point, Maine, and devoted his fiction to the characters and talk of the Maine seacoast. He contributed a number of stories to the *Atlantic Monthly* and other magazines, and he collected the best of these tales in *Cap'n Simeon's Store* (1903). Wasson was particularly skillful in catching the superstitions, the traditions, the weather lore, and the nautical idiom of the old salts whom he characterized so successfully in his stories.

WHITMAN, WALT (1819–92), born on Long Island, moved to Brooklyn as a child and was variously typesetter, carpenter, schoolteacher, and newspaperman. For several years he was on the staff of the *Brooklyn Eagle*. In 1855 he published the first edition of *Leaves of Grass*—the most famous single volume of verse published in the United States—and in the next thirty-five years he revised and enlarged the original book. During the Civil War, Whitman served as a hospital nurse and later was given a minor post in a department of the federal government. A paralytic stroke suffered in 1873 partially immobilized him, and he lived the remainder of his life as a semi-invalid in Camden, New Jersey. Whitman published various poems stimulated by the Civil War in *Drum-Taps* (1865) and wrote a bitter arraignment of the corruption and degradation observable in national life in *Democratic Vistas* (1871). *Specimen Days and Collect*, a random gathering of reminiscences and portraits, appeared in 1883. Whitman early devoted himself to the common man as subject and reader. But his poetry never found the enthusiastic acceptance by the masses that he thought a great poet ought to have. Nevertheless, his fame has grown gradually, until today he is recognized as the greatest American poet. With his revolt against formal style and his championing of democracy, individualism, and nationalism, he has been extremely influential among twentieth-century poets.

WHITTIER, JOHN GREENLEAF (1807–92), born of Quaker parentage in Haverhill, Massachusetts, was largely self-educated and was a man of limited culture. He became a violent abolitionist and, of all the New England writers, was perhaps the most outspoken opponent of slavery. He wrote poetry in various forms—ballads and narratives, sentimental and descriptive lyrics, hymns and occasional verse. Much of his topical writing has been justly forgotten, but his simple sincerity still imparts value to his celebration of landscape or domestic scene. He also excelled in short, terse narratives like "Skipper Ireson's Ride." Probably his best-known poem is *Snow-Bound*, originally published in 1866. His picture here of a farm family temporarily isolated by a winter storm is a memorable feat in genre painting.

BIBLIOGRAPHY

BIBLIOGRAPHY

I. Periodicals:

Journal of American Folklore. 1888————.
Publications of the Texas Folklore Society. 1916————.
Southern Folklore Quarterly. 1937————.
New York Folklore Quarterly. 1945————.
California Folklore Quarterly. 1942————. (Now *Western Folklore.*)
Midwest Folklore. 1951————.

II. Collections of Songs and Ballads:

ASTROV, MARGOT. *The Winged Serpent.* New York: John Day Co., 1946.

BECK, EARL C. *Songs of the Michigan Lumberjacks.* Ann Arbor: University of Michigan Press, 1941.

————. *They Knew Paul Bunyan.* Ann Arbor: University of Michigan Press, 1956.

BELDEN, H. M. *Ballads and Songs Collected by the Missouri Folklore Society.* Columbia, Mo., 1940.

BELDEN, H. M., and HUDSON, A. P. "Folk Ballads" (Vol. II) and "Folk Songs" (Vol. III) in the *Frank C. Brown Collection of North Carolina Folklore.* Chapel Hill: University of North Carolina Press, 1952.

BLEGEN, THEODORE C., and RUUD, MARTIN B. *Norwegian Emigrant Songs and Ballads.* Minneapolis: University of Minnesota Press, 1936.

BREWSTER, PAUL G. *Ballads and Songs of Indiana.* Bloomington: Indiana University Press, 1940.

COX, JOHN H. *Folk-Songs of the South.* Cambridge: Harvard University Press, 1925.

CRONYN, GEORGE W. *The Path on the Rainbow.* New York: Boni & Liveright, 1918.

ECKSTORM, FANNIE H., and SMYTH, MARY W. *Minstrelsy of Maine.* Boston and New York: Houghton Mifflin Co., 1927.

EDDY, MARY O. *Ballads and Songs from Ohio.* New York: J. J. Augustin, 1939.

501

FRIEDMAN, ALBERT B. *The Viking Book of Folk Ballads*. New York: Viking Press, 1956.

GRAY, ROLAND P. *Songs and Ballads of the Maine Lumberjacks*. Cambridge: Harvard University Press, 1924.

HUDSON, ARTHUR PALMER. *Folksongs of Mississippi and Their Background*. Chapel Hill: University of North Carolina Press, 1936.

KORSON, G. G. *Minstrels of the Mine Patch*. Philadelphia: University of Pennsylvania Press, 1938.

————. *Coal Dust on the Fiddle*. Philadelphia: University of Pennsylvania Press, 1943.

LEACH, MACEDWARD. *The Ballad Book*. New York and London: Harper & Bros., 1955.

LOMAX, JOHN A. *Cowboy Songs and Other Frontier Ballads*. New York: Sturgis & Walton, 1917.

LOMAX, JOHN A., and LOMAX, ALAN. *American Ballads and Folk Songs*. New York: The Macmillan Co., 1934.

———— and ————. *Folk Song U.S.A.* New York: Duell, Sloan & Pearce, 1947.

POUND, LOUISE. *American Ballads and Songs*. New York: Charles Scribner's Sons, 1922.

RANDOLPH, VANCE. *Ozark Folksongs*. 4 vols. Columbia, Mo.: State Historical Society of Missouri, 1946–50.

RICKABY, FRANZ. *Ballads and Songs of the Shanty-Boy*. Cambridge: Harvard University Press, 1926.

SANDBURG, CARL. *The American Songbag*. New York: Harcourt, Brace & Co., 1927.

SARGENT, HELEN CHILD, and KITTREDGE, GEORGE LYMAN. *English and Scottish Popular Ballads*. Boston: Houghton Mifflin Co., 1904.

SHARP, CECIL J. *English Folk Songs from the Southern Appalachians*. 2 vols. London: Oxford University Press, 1932.

SMITH, REED. *South Carolina Ballads*. Cambridge: Harvard University Press, 1928.

WHITE, NEWMAN I. *American Negro Folk-Songs*. Cambridge: Harvard University Press, 1928.

III. Collections of Tales and Stories:

BOATRIGHT, MODY C. *Tall Tales from Texas*. Dallas: Southwest Press, 1934.

BOTKIN, BENJAMIN A. *A Treasury of American Folklore*. New York: Crown Publishers, Inc., 1944.

————. *A Treasury of Western Folklore*. New York: Crown Publishers, Inc., 1951.

————. *A Treasury of Southern Folklore*. New York: Crown Publishers, Inc., 1949.

————. *A Treasury of New England Folklore*.   New York: Crown Publishers, Inc., 1947.

————. *Sidewalks of America*.   Indianapolis and New York: Bobbs-Merrill Co., Inc., 1954.

————. *A Treasury of Mississippi River Folklore*.   New York: Crown Publishers, Inc., 1955.

BOTKIN, BENJAMIN A., and HARLOW, ALVIN F.   *A Treasury of Railroad Folklore*.   New York: Crown Publishers, Inc., 1953.

BRADFORD, ROARK.   *Ol' Man Adam an' His Chillun*.   New York and London: Harper & Bros., 1928.

————. *John Henry*.   New York and London: Harper & Bros., 1931.

CHASE, RICHARD.   *Grandfather Tales*.   Boston: Houghton Mifflin Co., 1948.

————. *The Jack Tales*.   Boston: Houghton Mifflin Co., 1953.

————. *American Folk Tales and Songs*.   New York: New American Library, 1956.

DOBIE, J. FRANK.   *Coronado's Children*.   Dallas: Southwest Press, 1930.

DORSON, RICHARD M.   *Jonathan Draws the Long Bow*.   Cambridge: Harvard University Press, 1946.

————. *Davy Crockett, American Comic Legend*.   New York: Rockland Editions, 1939.

————. *Bloodstoppers and Bearwalkers*.   Cambridge: Harvard University Press, 1952.

————. *Negro Folktales in Michigan*.   Cambridge: Harvard University Press, 1956.

FELTON, HAROLD W.   *Legends of Paul Bunyan*.   New York: Alfred A. Knopf, Inc., 1947.

GONZALES, AMBROSE E.   *The Black Border*.   Columbia, S.C.: The State Co., 1922.

————. *The Captain*.   Columbia, S.C.: The State Co., 1924.

HUDSON, ARTHUR PALMER.   *Humor of the Old Deep South*.   New York: The Macmillan Co., 1936.

HURSTON, ZORA NEALE.   *Mules and Men*.   Philadelphia and London: J. B. Lippincott Co., 1935.

JONES, JAMES ATHEARN.   *Tales of an Indian Camp*.   3 vols.   London: Henry Colburn & Richard Bentley, 1829.

LINDERMAN, FRANK B.   *Old Man Coyote*.   New York: Junior Literary Guild, 1932.

MACKAYE, PERCY.   *Tall Tales of the Kentucky Mountains*.   New York: George H. Doran, 1926.

MASTERSON, JAMES R.   *Tall Tales of Arkansaw*.   Boston: Chapman & Grimes, 1943.

MEINE, FRANKLIN J.   *Tall Tales of the Southwest*.   New York: Alfred A. Knopf, Inc., 1930.

MONTAGUE, MARGARET PRESCOTT. *Up Eel River*. New York: The Macmillan Co., 1928.

PARSONS, ELSIE CLEWS. *Folk-Lore of the Sea Islands, South Carolina*. Cambridge and New York: American Folk-Lore Society, 1923.

RANDOLPH, VANCE. *Ozark Mountain Folks*. New York: Vanguard Press, 1932.

———. *We Always Lie to Strangers*. New York: Columbia University Press, 1951.

———. *Who Blowed Up the Church House? and Other Ozark Folk Tales*. New York: Columbia University Press, 1952.

———. *The Devil's Pretty Daughter*. New York: Columbia University Press, 1955.

ROBERTS, LEONARD W. *South from Hell-fer-Sartin*. Lexington: University of Kentucky Press, 1955.

SALE, JOHN B. *The Tree Named John*. Chapel Hill: University of North Carolina Press, 1929.

SCHOOLCRAFT, HENRY ROWE. *Algic Researches*. New York: Harper & Bros., 1839.

———. *The Myth of Hiawatha*. Philadelphia: J. B. Lippincott & Co., 1856.

———. *The Indian Fairy Book*. New York: Mason Bros., 1856.

SHAY, FRANK. *Here's Audacity!* New York: The Macaulay Co., 1930.

SHEPHARD, ESTHER. *Paul Bunyan*. New York: Harcourt, Brace & Co., 1941.

SKINNER, CHARLES M. *Myths and Legends of Our Own Land*. Philadelphia and London: J. B. Lippincott Co., 1896.

———. *American Myths and Legends*. Philadelphia and London: J. B. Lippincott Co., 1903.

STEVENS, JAMES. *Paul Bunyan*. Garden City, L.I.: Garden City Publishing Co., 1925.

THOMPSON, HAROLD W. *Body, Boots and Britches*. Philadelphia: J. B. Lippincott Co., 1940.

THOMPSON, STITH. *Tales of the North American Indians*. Cambridge: Harvard University Press, 1929.

WILLIAMS, MENTOR L. *Schoolcraft's Indian Legends*. East Lansing, Mich.: Michigan State University Press, 1956.

IV. Criticism and Analysis:

BLAIR, WALTER. *Native American Humor*. New York and Cincinnati: American Book Co., 1937.

BLAIR, WALTER, and MEINE, FRANKLIN J. *Mike Fink, King of Mississippi Keelboatmen*. New York: Henry Holt & Co., 1933.

———— and ————. *Half Horse, Half Alligator: The Growth of the Mike Fink Legend.* Chicago: University of Chicago Press, 1956.

BOATRIGHT, MODY C. *Folk Laughter on the American Frontier.* New York: The Macmillan Co., 1949.

BRINTON, DANIEL G. *The Myths of the New World.* New York: Henry Holt & Co., 1876.

BROOKES, STELLA B. *Joel Chandler Harris, Folklorist.* Athens: University of Georgia Press, 1950.

COFFIN, TRISTRAM P. *The British Traditional Ballad in North America.* Philadelphia: American Folklore Society, 1950.

DAVIDSON, LEVETTE J. *A Guide to American Folklore.* Denver: University of Denver Press, 1951.

DE VOTO, BERNARD. *Mark Twain's America.* Boston: Little, Brown & Co., 1932.

FISKE, JOHN. *Myths and Myth-Makers.* Boston: J. R. Osgood & Co., 1872.

FRANTZ, JOE B., and CHOATE, J. E., JR. *The American Cowboy.* Norman: University of Oklahoma Press, 1955.

FRAZER, JAMES G. *The Golden Bough.* Abridged ed. London: The Macmillan Co., 1950.

GEROULD, GORDON HALL. *The Ballad of Tradition.* Oxford: Oxford University Press, 1932.

HOFFMAN, DANIEL G. *Paul Bunyan, Last of the Frontier Demigods.* Philadelphia: University of Pennsylvania Press, 1952.

HOOLE, W. S. *Alias Simon Suggs.* Tuscaloosa: University of Alabama Press, 1952.

JOHNSON, GUY B. *John Henry: Tracking Down a Negro Legend.* Chapel Hill: University of North Carolina Press, 1929.

KITTREDGE, GEORGE LYMAN. *The Old Farmer and His Almanack.* Boston: W. Ware & Co., 1904.

LAWS, GEORGE MALCOLM. *Native American Balladry.* Philadelphia: American Folklore Society, 1950.

PRICE, ROBERT. *Johnny Appleseed, Man and Myth.* Bloomington: Indiana University Press, 1954.

PUCKETT, NEWBELL NILES. *Folk Beliefs of the Southern Negro.* Chapel Hill: University of North Carolina Press, 1926.

ROURKE, CONSTANCE. *American Humor.* New York: Harcourt, Brace & Co., 1931.

————. *The Roots of American Culture and Other Essays.* New York: Harcourt, Brace & Co., 1942.

————. *Davy Crockett.* New York: Harcourt, Brace & Co., 1934.

SMITH, HENRY NASH. *Virgin Land.* Cambridge: Harvard University Press, 1950.

THOMPSON, STITH. *Motif Index of Folk Literature.* 6 vols. Bloomington: Indiana University Press, 1932–36. Revised and enlarged edition, Bloomington: Indiana University Press, 1955–57.

————. *The Folktale.* New York: Dryden Press, 1946.

WEST, VICTOR ROYCE.   *Folklore in the Works of Mark Twain.*   Lincoln: University of Nebraska Press, 1930.

WIMBERLY, LOWRY C.   *Folklore in the English and Scottish Ballads.* Chicago: University of Chicago Press, 1928.

INDEX
of
AUTHORS and TITLES

INDEX OF AUTHORS AND TITLES